INFORMATION SYSTEMS CONCEPTS

INFORMATION SYSTEMS CONCEPTS

Raymond McLeod, Jr.
Texas A & M University

MACMILLAN PUBLISHING COMPANY
New York

MAXWELL MACMILLAN CANADA
Toronto

Editor: Charles Stewart
Production Manager: Paul Smolenski
Cover Designer: Robert Vega
Cover Illustration: Pablo Picasso, *The Bird Cage*, Bridgeman/Art Resource, NY
©1993, ARS New York/SPADEM, Paris

This book was set by GTS Graphics, and was printed and bound by R.R. Donnelley & Sons Company - Crawfordsville.
The cover was printed by New England Book Components, Inc.

Macmillan Publishing Company
866 Third Avenue, New York, New York 10022

Library of Congress Cataloging-in-Publication Data

McLeod, Raymond.
    Information systems concepts / Raymond McLeod, Jr.
        p. cm.
    "The bulk of this book is reprinted from Information systems,
  ©1990 by Macmillan Publishing Company"—T.p. verso.
    Includes index.
    ISBN 0-02-379473-9
    1. Management information systems. I. McLeod, Raymond.
Information systems/ II. Title.
T58.6.M25   1994
658.4′038—dc20   93-25603
                                                              CIP

ISBN 0-02-379473-9
Printing: 1 2 3 4 5 6 7 8 9 10   Year: 4 5 6 7 8 9

Dedication

To Martha, Shar Bear, and Glenn

The author and publisher extend their gratitude to the many corporate and private sources that provided artwork and other materials for this text. Their contributions are invaluable to both the text and its readers.

CONTENTS

CHAPTER 3: Using Prewritten Software 65

PART III BUSINESS PROBLEMS AND PROBLEM SOLVERS 91

CHAPTER 4: Business Organizations and Systems 92

CHAPTER 7:   Problem-Solving Processes and Tools 158

PART IV THE COMPUTER AS A PROBLEM-SOLVING TOOL 191

CHAPTER 8: Fundamentals of Computer Processing 193

CHAPTER 9: Secondary Storage and the Database 226

PART V PROBLEM-SOLVING SYSTEMS 291

CHAPTER 11: Data Processing Systems 292

CHAPTER 12: Management Information Systems 315

CHAPTER 13: Decision Support Systems 338

PREFACE

It has been over thirty years since the first computer was installed for business use. Although that is only one tick of the clock in the history of mankind, much has happened in terms of computers, computer users, and computer applications in those few years. The first computers occupied entire rooms and were so expensive that only the largest organizations could afford them. You know how dramatically that situation has changed.

While only a handful of computer scientists knew about computers during the early years, almost everyone today not only knows about them but takes them for granted. We are aware that they are being used when we purchase airline tickets and shop at supermarkets and department stores, but give them no special thought.

Computer use has changed as well. At first they only processed data, but today they perform a wide variety of tasks that include controlling robots, vending money from automatic teller machines, and helping the hearing impaired.

Computer education also has undergone change. The first courses were offered by computer manufacturers for their employees and customers. As computer use became more widespread, colleges got into the act and it became possible to major in computer science or some aspect of computer use in business.

The introductory college computer course historically has emphasized computer technology, called *hardware*, and programming. However, this is changing due primarily to the popularity of prewritten computer *software*, or programs, such as Lotus, dBASE, and WordPerfect. Many colleges are recognizing that you do not necessarily need to know how to program to use the computer and are substituting prewritten software for the programming requirement.

The prewritten software can be learned quickly and is often referred to as *user friendly*. The user-friendly software, combined with low-priced small computers, is making it possible to use the computer without relying on computer specialists—a situation called *end-user computing*.

College educators have been kept busy keeping up with the trends—revising curricula, adding new courses, and acquiring the needed hardware and software. Indications are that the period of change is not over. There is more to come.

Computer Education for Future Managers

Most of the students who major in business intend to become managers someday. Managers are involved in many diverse activities, but an important one is problem solving. Each day, managers solve problems relating to their employees, to the financial and material resources for which they are responsible, and to persons and groups outside the firm such as customers, bankers, stockholders, and so on.

It has become increasingly obvious that the computer can help a manager solve problems. The computer can provide information that notifies the manager of a problem or impending problem, provide information so that the problem can be understood, compare alternate solutions, and provide information so that the manager will know how well the solution is working.

Strangely enough, the content of the introductory computer course has not followed this trend. Most of the textbooks that are used in the first course do not prepare future managers specifically to use the computer as a problem-solving tool. This text responds to that need.

The main objective of *Information Systems Concepts* is to provide future managers with an understanding of the computer that will enable its use in solving management problems. All of the topics and their organization have been selected with this objective in mind. After studying this text, you should not only appreciate the potential of the computer as a problem-solving tool, but also be able to use the computer for that purpose.

Computer Education for Future Computer Specialists

Although users will be doing more and more of their own computing, computer specialists will still be needed. The specialists will implement the difficult systems that are beyond the skills of the users, and for this reason the specialists need a greater depth of technical knowledge. Some schools, recognizing the unique demands of the two career paths, are offering two sets of computer courses.

While this approach is fine, there are still many schools that believe both future users and computer specialists can, and should, take the same introductory course. After all, the users and specialists will be working together after graduation, so they might as well have a common foundation.

Although this text is written with future managers in mind, it can also provide a valuable introduction to future computer specialists. The text will enable the specialists to better appreciate the users' needs and how those needs can be met with computer-based solutions.

Modular Format

The text is organized in a modular format that allows the instructor almost complete flexibility in the selection of both the topics and their sequence. There are fifteen chapters that are organized into five parts.

Part 1 of the text consists of the first chapter and provides an overview of the computer as a problem-solving tool. Part 2, which consists of Chapters 2 and 3, addresses the use of programming languages and prewritten software. These first three chapters should be presented as a unit at the beginning of the course as shown in Figure P.1. After that has been accomplished, *any of four textbook modules* can be covered. The modules include Part 3 of the text (Chapters 4–7), Part 4 of the text (Chapters 8–10), and Part 5 of the text (Chapters 11–16). All four modules, or any combination, can be covered in any sequence.

Modular Format of the Chapters In addition, complete flexibility exists within Parts 3, 4, and 5 of the text. Any combination of chapters can be included, and they can be covered in any sequence. For example, if traditional data processing is to be emphasized, Chapter 6 of Part 3 can be included to describe the work performed by managers and information specialists in designing computer-based systems; the other chapters in Part 3 can be omitted.

Although this flexibility in chapter selection and sequence exists, the chapters are presented in the text in a *logical order.* Unless there is some reason to do otherwise, it is recommended that they be presented in the same order as they appear in the text.

A Complete Package

A complete set of materials is available to instructors and students to facilitate use of the text.

```
                    ┌─────────────────────┐
                    │ Parts 1 and 2       │
                    │ ┌─────────────────┐ │
                    │ │ 1               │ │
                    │ │   Introduction  │ │
                    │ └─────────────────┘ │
                    │ ┌─────────────────┐ │
                    │ │ 2 and 3         │ │
                    │ │   Computer      │ │
                    │ │   software      │ │
                    │ └─────────────────┘ │
                    └─────────────────────┘
```

Part 3	Part 4	Part 5
4 Organizations and systems	8 Computer fundamentals	11 Data processing systems
5 Business problems	9 Database	12 Management information systems
6 Business problem solvers	10 Data communications	13 Decision support systems
7 Problem-solving processes		14 Office automation
		15 Expert systems and beyond
		16 Emerging trends informatoin systems
Textbook module	Textbook module	Textbook module

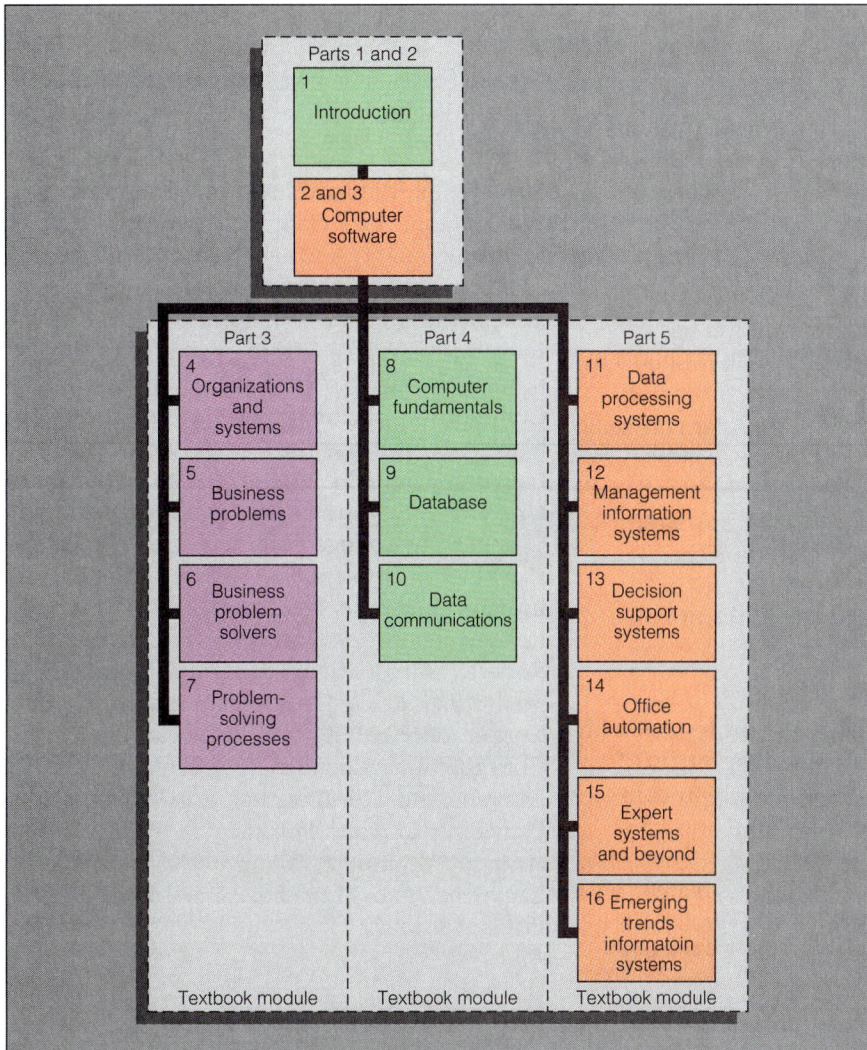

- *Transparency Masters* are available to instructors to facilitate the classroom display of the more important diagrams and illustrations from the text.

- The *Instructor's Manual/Lecture Notes/Transparency Masters* includes suggestions for designing the course and for presenting each chapter. It also includes sample syllabi and special lectures.

- The *Test Bank* consists of true-false and multiple-choice questions plus a 10-point "pop" quiz for each chapter.

Diskette-based materials include the following:

- The Macmillan Test Generation System, which automatically assembles true-false, fill-in-the-blank, and multiple choice exams from the test bank. It also allows instructors to add their own questions to the test bank.

This complete set of materials is intended to support both the instructors and the students as the textbook is used as a basis for the introduction to computing course.

Acknowledgments

Throughout the text I use the term *we.* Although there is only one author, it has been a group effort. Our efforts have been influenced by suggestions offered by college professors who teach the introductory computer course. First there was a mail survey that defined course trends and needs. Some 186 responses were received, and this information was supplemented by a focus group session that included leading computer educators from schools of various sizes. The input from the focus group served to fine tune the approach, and writing began.

The chapters were reviewed by professors with expertise in the various areas. I especially thank the following reviewers for their comments throughout the process of manuscript development: Gary R. Armstrong, Shippensburg University of Pennsylvania; David R. Bryant, Pepperdine University; Eli Boyd Cohen, Bradley University; Meg Kletke, Oklahoma State University; Guy L. Langsford, California State University, Northridge; J. A. Parsons, Northern Michigan University; Marian Sackson, Pace University; and Kathy Brittain White, University of North Carolina Greensboro.

I also thank: William Burrows, University of Washington; Terry Campbell, Pennsylvania State University; Andrew J. Ciulla, University of Maryland, Baltimore County Campus; James W. Cox, Lane Community College; Caroline N. Curtis, Lorain County Community College; Robert L. Gray, Virginia Commonwealth University; Arthur B. Kahn, University of Baltimore; Thom Luce, Ohio University; Jane M. Mackay, Texas Christian University; Edward G. Martin, Kingsborough Community College; Robert C. Meier, Western Washington University; Marilyn Moore, Indiana University Northwest; Thomas A. Pollack, Duquesne University; Robert S. Roberts, University of Oklahoma, Norman; Stanford H. Rowe II, Dow Corning Corporation; Nita Hewitt Rutkosky, Pierce College; Linda Salchenberger, Loyola University of Chicago; Hamilton W. Stirling, University of South Florida at St. Petersburg; Anthony Verstraete, Pennsylvania State University, and Ahmed S. Zaki, College of William & Mary.

Since it is impossible for one person to be expert in all phases of computer use, I have relied on many computer professionals for help. One of the advantages of teaching at a school with a large MIS staff is the benefit of being able to walk down the hall and find someone with just the type of expert knowledge that you need. I made that trip many times and received help from Joobin Choobineh, Jim Courtney, George Fowler, Bill Fuerst, Joe L. Poitevent, and Marietta J. Tretter.

Help was also provided by persons in industry—Donald H. Bender of GPM Life (San Antonio), John Berry of J. T. Berry Company (Midland), Dwain R. Boelter of Personnel Decisions, Inc. (Minneapolis), Jon Bullock of Arthur Andersen & Co., David Dietzel of Federal Express, Ric Guenther of Sikes Jennings Kelly & Brewer (Houston), and P. R. Jeanneret of Jeanneret & Associates (Houston).

Even though I have received much help along the way, I alone am responsible for the manner in which the material is presented. In some cases I was advised to do one thing and elected to do otherwise. Therefore, any shortcomings are my own doing.

When we embarked on this project, we had only a general idea of what we wanted to accomplish. No one had ever traveled this particular path before. The specifications came together over time and we are satisfied that we met our objective. We hope that you are satisfied as well that *Information Systems Concepts* enables you to use the computer as a problem-solving tool.

Raymond McLeod, Jr.
Department of Business Analysis and Research
College of Business Administration
Texas A & M University
College Station, Texas 77843

INFORMATION SYSTEMS CONCEPTS

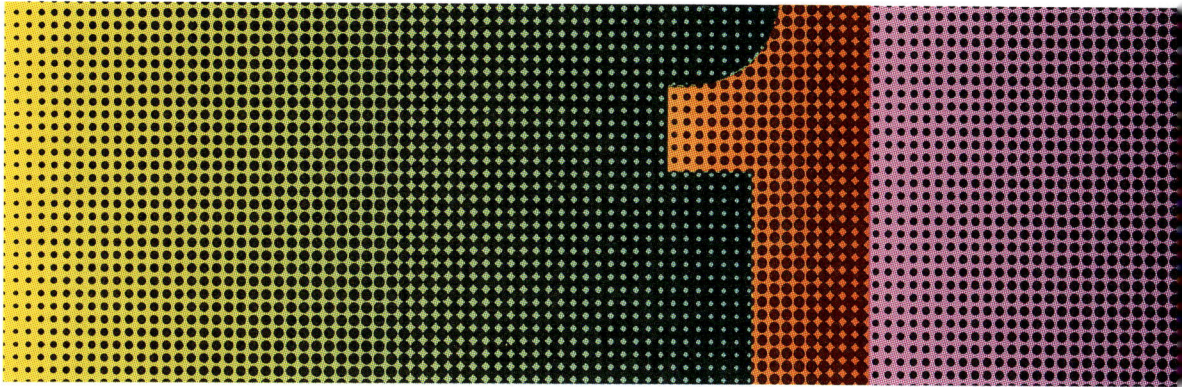

Introduction to Problem Solving and Information Systems

The text is organized into five parts, and each part deals with a basic topic relating to solving business problems using the computer. The parts provide an introduction to information systems, an introduction to computer software, a description of business problems and problem solvers, an explanation of how the computer can be used as a problem-solving tool, examples of problem-solving systems, and a look at emerging trends.

This first part consists of a single chapter that introduces you to the subject of problem solving and the importance of information in that process. The information is provided by an information system, and the computer plays an important role in that system.

Do not become discouraged as you begin to learn about the computer. Computing has its own vocabulary, but it will not take long for you to become acquainted with the basic terms and concepts. Then, you will realize that computing is really very logical and understandable and not such a mystery after all.

This first part of the text is a very important introduction that presents basic concepts and terminology. Take advantage of this opportunity to lay a strong foundation upon which to build your computer knowledge.

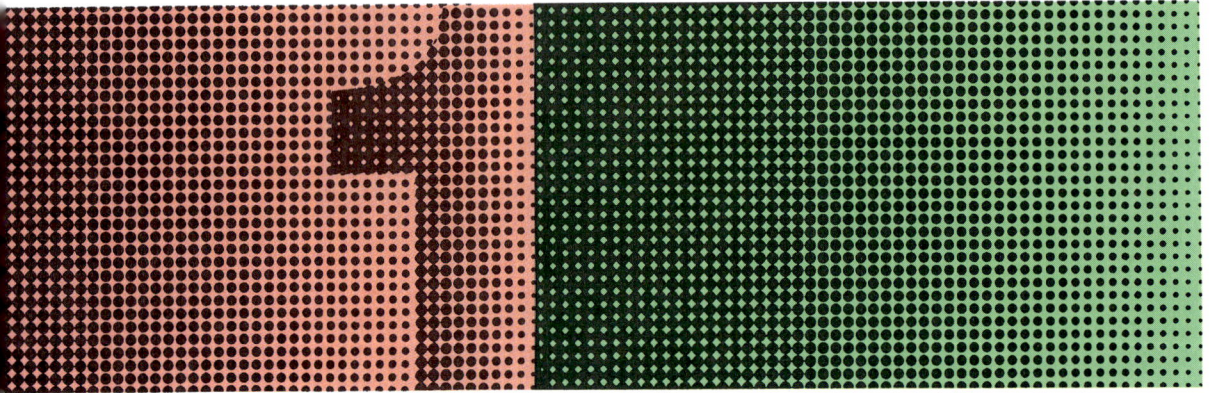

Problem Solving and Information Systems

LEARNING OBJECTIVES   After studying this chapter, you should:

- Recognize that a wide variety of organizations fall into the business category
- Appreciate that a problem can be good as well as bad
- Understand that problems are caused by influences both inside and outside the organization
- Know who the problem solvers are and the general approach that they take
- Appreciate the role that information plays in problem solution
- Have a fundamental understanding of the computer as an information system
- Recognize the distinction between computer literacy and information literacy

OVERVIEW

In this first chapter, we set the stage for the entire book by focusing on problem solving in business. We explain what a problem is, what causes it, who solves it, and how it is solved. We recognize the role of information in the problem-solving process, and identify the characteristics of a complete information system.

The computer is only one element in that information system, but it is an important element. We explain how computer technology has evolved in a relatively short time, and how the computer maintains data in a database and makes information available to users. Five major computer application areas are identified and explained.

Traditionally only information specialists used the computer, but today more and more people throughout the organization are using the computer for problem solving. These users are also working jointly with information specialists to develop systems that require the skills of both groups.

The term computer literacy has been used a great deal during the past few years. Everyone in our modern society should have computer literacy. In other words, everyone should understand the computer and be able to use it effectively.

For business professionals who will be using the computer in problem solving, however, an additional literacy is needed—information literacy. This is a new term, and we explain what it includes and why it is critical to careers in both management and information systems.

OBJECTIVE OF THE TEXT

This text is written for college students who plan to become managers. If you fit into this category, you have a need to develop your problem-solving skills. Managers do things other than solve problems, but the ability to react successfully to problem situations is a skill that does not go unrewarded. If a manager can solve problems, there will always be career opportunities available.

The Text Is for Computer Specialists as Well as Managers

If you do not plan to become a manager, but plan to become a computer specialist, you also can benefit from this text. As a computer specialist you must work with the user in developing problem-solving systems. This text gives you the view of those systems and their uses, which is the key to doing an effective job.

The Text Offers a New Approach

The computer has been used in business for approximately forty years, and that use has included problem solving. Strange as it may seem, however, the introductory computer texts generally have ignored this fact. Rather, emphasis has been on accounting applications—using the computer to process payroll, maintain inventory, and send out bills. The rationale has been that college students with little or no business background cannot appreciate how the computer can be used in solving business problems.

While this argument appears sound, the penalty for taking this position is severe. It means that the most valuable use of the computer in business is ignored in the introductory course. The computer is much more valuable in solving problems than in performing accounting applications. When used in accounting, the computer benefits the firm by reducing clerical costs.

FIGURE 1.1

Business Problem Solvers

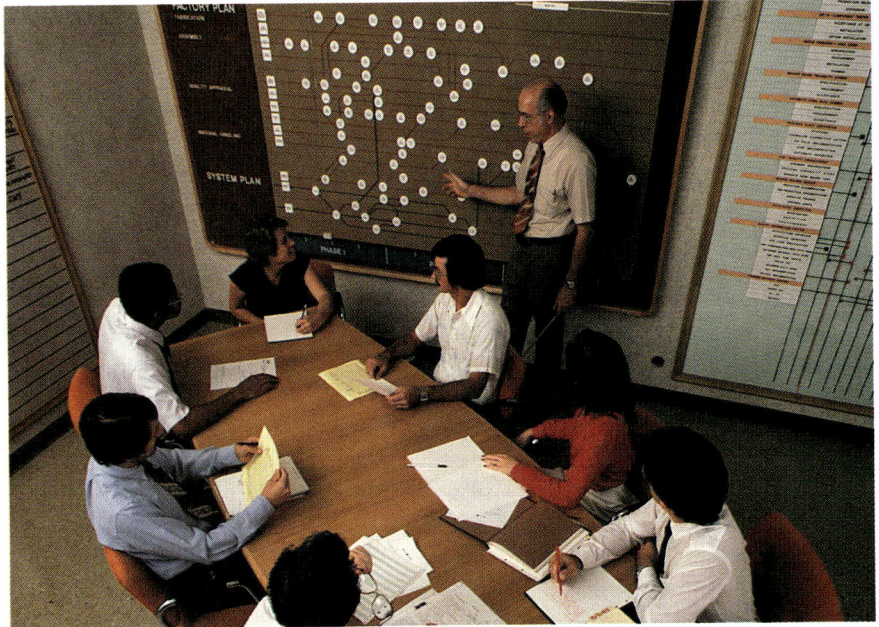

When used for problem solving, the computer *has the potential* for increasing revenues many times greater than the reduced clerical costs. The computer therefore can influence profits much more dramatically in solving problems than in processing accounting data.

Our belief is that a problem-solving approach is feasible as long as the necessary background material is provided along with the computer material. We assume no previous business experience, and explain fundamental concepts and define key terms as they are introduced. As you learn about computers, you will also learn about business—about the organizations, the managers, and the processes. We will not attempt to give you everything that you will need to become an expert in business problem solving, but we will give you the foundation. You can build upon this foundation in other courses and in the pursuit of your career.

Business Is Defined Broadly

Before we begin, a word of explanation is in order to the nonbusiness major. You may be saying: "This book isn't for me because I'm not going into business." We define business, and management, very broadly. For example, we regard a symphony orchestra as a business, and the conductor as a manager. We regard a church as a business, and the pastor or priest as a manager. Both the symphony and the church make available a product or service. Both consist of a combination of people, facilities, equipment, and funds that must be controlled so that the product or service lives up to

expectations. In the case of the symphony, the product is good music and the pleasure that it brings. In the case of the church, the product is spiritual peace of mind, social interaction, and other benefits. By the same reasoning, educational TV stations, United Way campaigns, and the Girl Scouts are viewed as business organizations, and their leaders are viewed as managers. So, regardless of your career plans, you will be faced with problems, and the computer can be used to help you solve them.

WHAT IS A PROBLEM?

The word *problem* sounds like something bad. "The next exam will have six *problems*." "She's a *problem* child." "What's his *problem*?" Many problems that occur in business fit this image—they are bad. For example, too many employees lack the necessary skills, customer orders cannot be processed fast enough during peak sales periods, and the plant equipment breaks down. When managers are faced with these bad situations, their challenge is to make them good, or, at least, make them not so bad.

If managers were always faced with such bad situations, the work would be very depressing. Thankfully, good things also come along, and these good things are considered to be a form of problem as well.

When a manager is faced with a good situation, such as sales of a product that exceed the plan, the task is to capitalize on this turn of events. Perhaps the sales can be increased even more, or an increase can be achieved for other products as well.

When we use the word **problem**, we include conditions or events that damage, or threaten to damage, the organization in some negative way and also conditions or events that improve, or offer the opportunity to improve, the organization in some positive way. **Problem solving** is the activity of responding successfully to indications of both weakness and opportunity. Strange as it may seem, the problem solver follows the same procedure in reacting to the good situations as to the bad. Also, the computer can be applied equally well in both cases.

WHAT CAUSES PROBLEMS IN BUSINESS?

Many problems are caused by persons or organizations outside of the manager's firm. We will use the term **firm** throughout the text. Keep in mind that it applies to all types of organizations. The manager generally has more control over the internal causes than the external ones, but not as much as you might think.

Environmental Influences

The term **environment** is used to mean everything outside of the firm. That includes the local community, competition, the economy, and so on. Some of the most serious problems originate in the environment, and some of the problems that appear to be internal actually are caused by the environment.

The World and National Economy

You know that during recent years both the United States and the world economies have been under considerable strain. First, there was the energy shortage of the mid-1970s, and then the oil glut of the mid-1980s. These fluctuations affected all of the industrial nations of the world. Unemployment and inflation existed worldwide. Companies faced shrinking markets for their products and services. Many organizations, large as well as small, did not survive. The situation is much improved today, but managers in every country are aware that their organizations are part of a world environment, not just a national, regional, or local one.

Government Actions

Our own government exerts a strong influence on the operations of United States business. A good example of government influence is the Federal Reserve System, or Fed. When federal policy makers determine that there is too much money in circulation, the Fed raises the interest rate that it charges banks for money they borrow from the Fed. The banks must, in turn, raise the interest rates for their customers—firms and individuals alike. Such actions have severe impacts on certain industries. Automobile manufacturing and real estate sales are prime examples.

Competitor Actions

Whereas the agencies pulling the strings of the economy and the government do not have anything against our firm, our competitors do. Most often, they would like to put us out of business. For this reason the threat of competition is always present, and managers must remain alert to what competition is doing. When competition takes some action, the potential

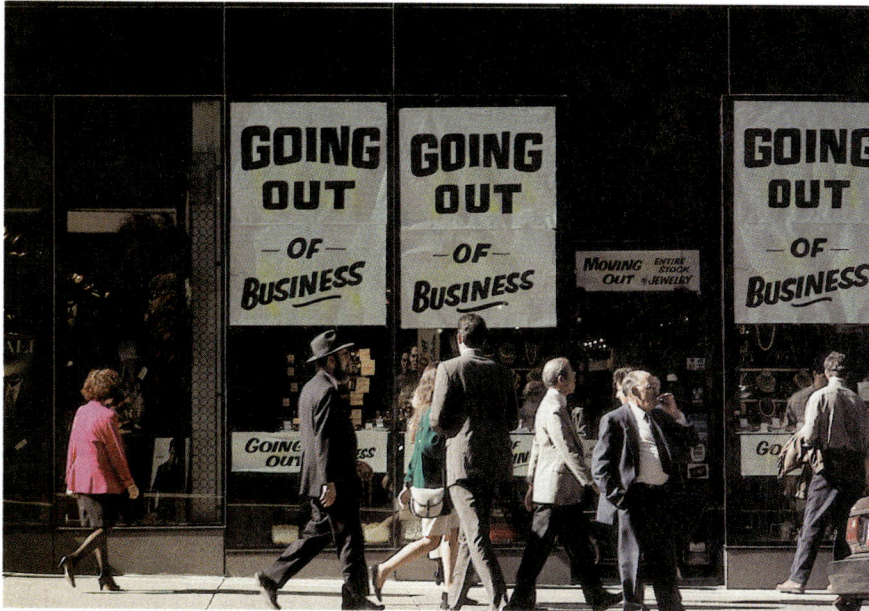

FIGURE 1.3
Even Small Firms
Are a Part of the
World Economy

impact on our firm must be gauged. We may have to react by taking a counter action.

All organizations use supplies of some sort. Home builders use lumber, nails, bricks, and shingles. Insurance firms use typewriter ribbons, computer tapes, paper clips, and ballpoint pens. What happens when one of a firm's suppliers goes out of business, or its workers go on strike? It could put the firm out of business. A firm and its suppliers comprise a network of mutually dependent organizations. They can benefit each other, and they can cause each other problems.

Supplier Actions

Firms attempt to meet the needs of their customers by supplying the necessary products and services. Firms use various means to identify these needs—customer service departments that listen to customer complaints, toll-free customer hotlines, and mail and telephone surveys. The information gathered identifies activities of the firm that are not measuring up to expectations, as well as opportunities for new products and services.

Information Provided by Customers

Internal Influences

While most of a firm's problems are likely to originate in the environment, there are times when the firm itself is to blame. Perhaps the firm would like to follow a certain course of action, but the necessary resources are not available. In some cases, problems are caused by the personalities of persons within the firm or a conflict of personal goals.

The main resources of a firm are its personnel, facilities, equipment, and supplies. These resources are purchased with money—money obtained from sales of the firm's products and services, obtained from the sale of

Inadequate Resources

stock, or borrowed from lending institutions. A manager must work with what is available. Perhaps the firm would like to announce a revolutionary new product, but does not have a sales force to market it. Or, the firm does not have enough money to replace the aging plant equipment. In each case, the manager must address the issue and devise a solution strategy that fits within the available resources.

Human Behavior

Even if there were no pressures from the environment and the firm had unlimited resources there still would be problems. The reason is that a business organization consists of people. Everyone is different and has different goals and value systems. Sometimes personalities clash, and people cannot get along with one another. Sometimes the behavior of the manager causes the friction. The good manager is aware of the human element and keeps behavioral problems from getting out of hand.

WHO SOLVES PROBLEMS?

We have been using the word *manager,* implying that he or she is the problem solver. It is true that the manager must solve problems. The manager is the captain of the ship, so to speak, and he or she must keep things running smoothly.

Actually, there are three classifications of employees in the firm who engage in problem solving—managers, nonmanagers, and specialists.

Managers

A **manager** is someone who directs the activity of others. Managers usually are arranged in a hierarchy as shown in the **organization chart** in Figure 1.4. The president has responsibility for everyone in the company, the vice presidents are responsible for persons in their areas, and so on down the line. Managers also are responsible for nonpersonnel resources—the facilities, equipment, supplies, and money in their areas. Each of the resources must be managed.

Managers are expected to solve problems that arise in their areas, but they do not have to solve them alone. In most cases, several people—nonmanagers and specialists as well as managers—become involved.

Nonmanagers

A **nonmanager** is someone who does not direct the activity of others. Examples are secretaries, plant workers, and salesclerks. If the problem is a small one, a nonmanager can solve it without notifying a manager. For example, a plant worker can rearrange his or her work area to make the work flow more smoothly.

Specialists

A number of people in a firm specialize in problem solving. Some managers have special assistants who help in identifying and solving problems of particular types. A top manager may have an **administrative assistant** who solves administrative (or paperwork) problems. Larger firms also have **internal auditors** who examine administrative procedures to ensure that they are proper. Very often, the internal auditor will call problems to the attention of management and will recommend solutions. Manufacturing firms usually have **industrial engineers** who design production pro-

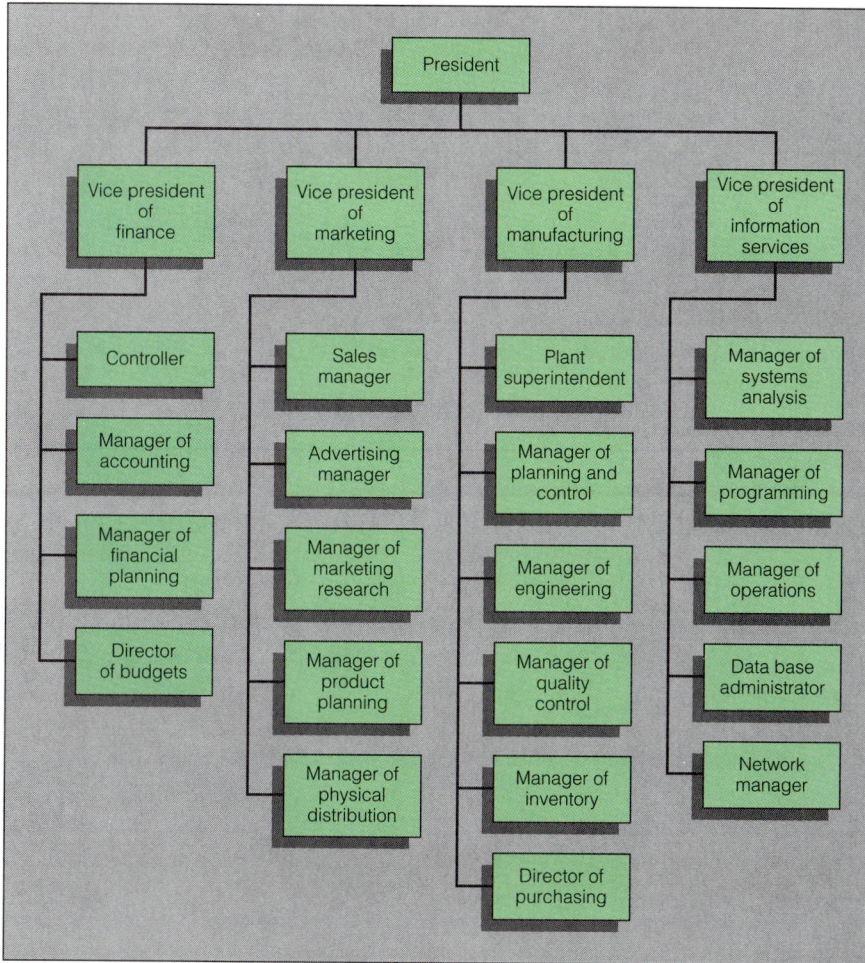

FIGURE 1.4

An Organization
Chart

cesses to achieve maximum efficiency. Another group of internal problem solvers are the **information specialists**—the persons who are the computer professionals. When the computer is a part of a problem—either as the cause or the solution—the information specialists very often are involved.

In addition to the specialists who are on the company's payroll, there are outsiders who help. **Consultants** may be called in to address a particular class of problem. Consultants are available from such general consulting firms as McKinsey & Company and from such accounting firms as Arthur Andersen & Co. Sometimes the **external auditors** working for the accounting firms uncover problems during their annual inspection of the firm's accounting records and help in the solution. Finally, persons representing the firm's suppliers can be a part of the problem-solving team. **Vendor representatives** are especially valuable when they work for such computer manufacturers as Hewlett-Packard, Unisys, or Cray.

So, you can see that there are a lot of problem solvers. Problem solving is more of a group activity than an individual one. A good manager will use all of the help that is available in an effort to achieve the best solution.

HOW ARE PROBLEMS SOLVED?

Elizabeth Barrett Browning probably would have said "How do I solve problems? Let me count the ways." There are almost as many procedures for solution as there are problems. Each problem tends to be unique in some way. That is the feature that makes problem solving both interesting and challenging.

We will devote considerable space to the process of problem solving in this text and will not attempt a complete coverage here. But, if we were to look at problem solving in general, we would find that the problem solvers take four basic steps:

1. Understand the problem to be solved
2. Evaluate alternate solutions
3. Implement the best solution
4. Follow up to make certain that the solution is working

Much time is spent in studying the problem so that it is understood. This first step is key to the others. If a problem is not understood, then it is unlikely to be solved.

The second step of considering alternate solutions is where experience pays off. The experienced manager, nonmanager, or specialist will think of many more possible solutions than will the inexperienced person. Experience also helps the problem solvers evaluate the different alternatives so that the one with the best chance of success is selected.

Finally, a manager soon learns that identification of the solution is not the end. The manager will remain involved until she or he is certain that the problem is solved. Some solutions take months or years to take effect.

The Role of Decision Making in Problem Solving

The terms problem solving and decision making do not have the same meaning. A **decision** is the selection of a course of action. A manager will make many decisions during the process of solving a single problem. The manager will make decisions to understand the problem (Where is it? What is the cause?), to evaluate alternate solutions (What are the alternatives? Which is best?), to implement the solution (When should it be implemented? How?), and to follow up on the solution (Who should make the evaluation? What criteria should be used?).

A good problem solution requires a series of good decisions. In a way, solving a problem is like building a brick wall. Just as you build the wall one brick at a time, you produce the solution one decision at a time.

The Role of Information in Problem Solving

The problem solver must have information to make each decision. The information reduces the uncertainty surrounding both the problem defini-

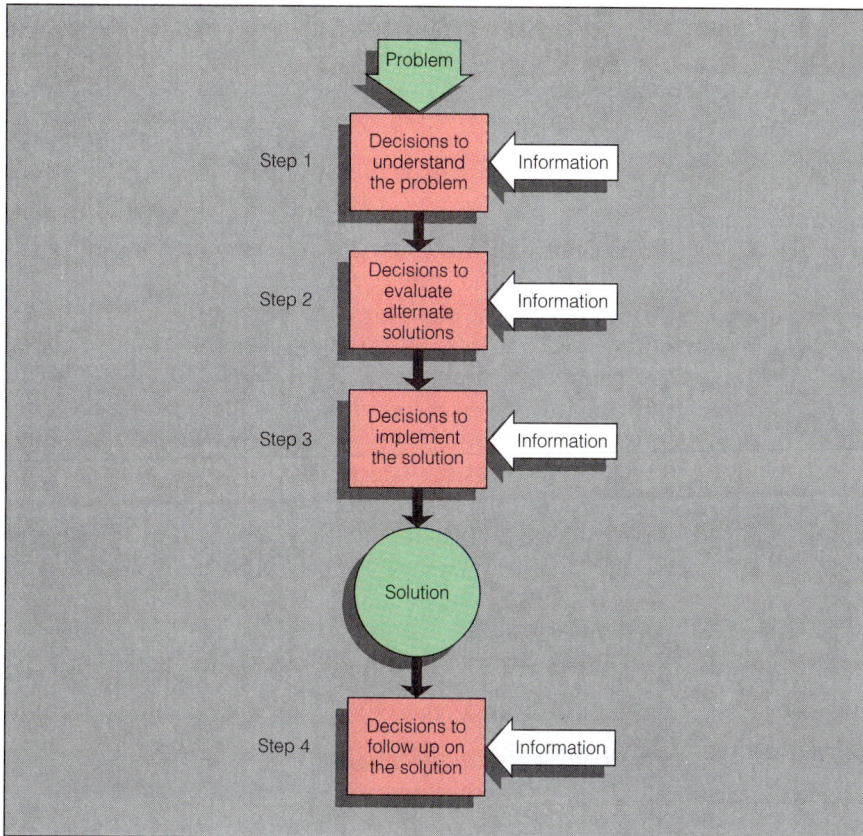

FIGURE 1.5

Information Helps Managers Make Decisions to Solve Problems

tion and the potential effectiveness of the solution. Sometimes the information comes from the problem solver's brain—a result of past learning and experience. At other times the problem solver augments this knowledge with new information. It might be necessary to retrieve information that is stored in file cabinets or in the computer. It might even be necessary to gather new data, such as that obtained in a market survey.

Figure 1.5 shows how information is used in making each of the groups of decisions that contribute to problem solution.

THE NEED FOR A COMPLETE INFORMATION SYSTEM

During the early years of the computer, some firms attempted to implement what they called **total information systems.** The computer-based systems were supposed to contain *all* of the information that a problem solver might need. These efforts generally met with failure. Both the managers and the information specialists realized that problem solvers need more information than can be stored in a computer. When we use the term **complete information system,** we do not mean a system that contains everything.

Rather, we mean a system that has the ability to gather information from all sources and use all media to present the information. The system consists of both formal and informal components and enables the manager to understand what happened in the past, what is happening now, and what might happen in the future.

Internal and Environmental Sources

A firm generates most of its information internally. The accounting system captures data that describes the firm's activities. A large volume of information, however, comes from the outside. Some of this environmental information is free—government statistics, material found in libraries, knowledge gained by word of mouth, and so forth. The rest of the environmental information has a cost attached. A firm often will build special systems to gather information from the environment. Salespersons are expected to learn about competitive activity from their customers, design engineers contract with product-testing labs to tear apart competitive products to see how they are built, financial officers subscribe to governmental and banking bulletins, and the president and other personnel attend special seminars offered by the American Management Association or the National Association of Manufacturers. In each of these examples, the firm obtains information from sources in the environment.

The information system should include both internal and environmental sources.

Written and Verbal Media

Much information exists in a written form. The computer is excellent for providing such information, as are other systems consisting of typewriters, copying machines, printing presses, and manual recording.

Even so, many people believe that more information flows through a business firm in a verbal than a written form. To appreciate this opinion you only have to observe the employees during coffee-break time. The same type of verbal interaction enables the employees to perform their various duties. Managers usually discuss their problems with other persons. The discussions center on the problem and the possible solutions. This verbal information is used in conjunction with written information so that the entire picture may be seen. Firms often establish problem-solving committees that meet regularly to share verbal and written information. Figure 1.6 presents a "Star Trek" version of the group problem-solving scene. Here, each manager has a computer for displaying information during the discussion. Rooms containing such equipment and used for such purposes are often called decision rooms.

It is important to include both written and verbal information in the information system.

Formal and Informal Systems

All companies have formal procedures that everyone is expected to follow. The procedures are in writing and constitute the **policy manual** and the

FIGURE 1.6

A Decision Room
Equipped with
Computer Screens

procedure manual. When a policy or procedure is spelled out in writing, it is a formal system.

Managers go to great lengths to specify policies and procedures, but they know that the formal systems will not cover everything. The systems cover only the most important, recurring activities. The formal systems are supplemented by systems devised "on the spot" to handle unexpected or relatively minor problems. These systems that are not documented in writing are called informal systems.

Information provided by the computer is the output of a formal system, as is information provided by weekly conferences and typed monthly reports. Examples of informal systems are telephone calls, letters, memos, and special meetings.

The information system should include informal as well as formal components.

Past, Present, and Projection Information

The information system should provide the manager with a picture of what has happened in the past so that the present and the future can be viewed in the proper perspective. Information on present activity must be reported quickly, allowing the manager the opportunity to act upon it. In addition, the information system should enable the manager to project the impact of decisions on the future performance of the firm.

A Model of a Complete Information System

Figure 1.7 shows a complete information system. The internal and environmental sources are at the top, the written and verbal media are in the center, and the manager and problem-solving activity are at the bottom.

FIGURE 1.7

A Complete
Information System

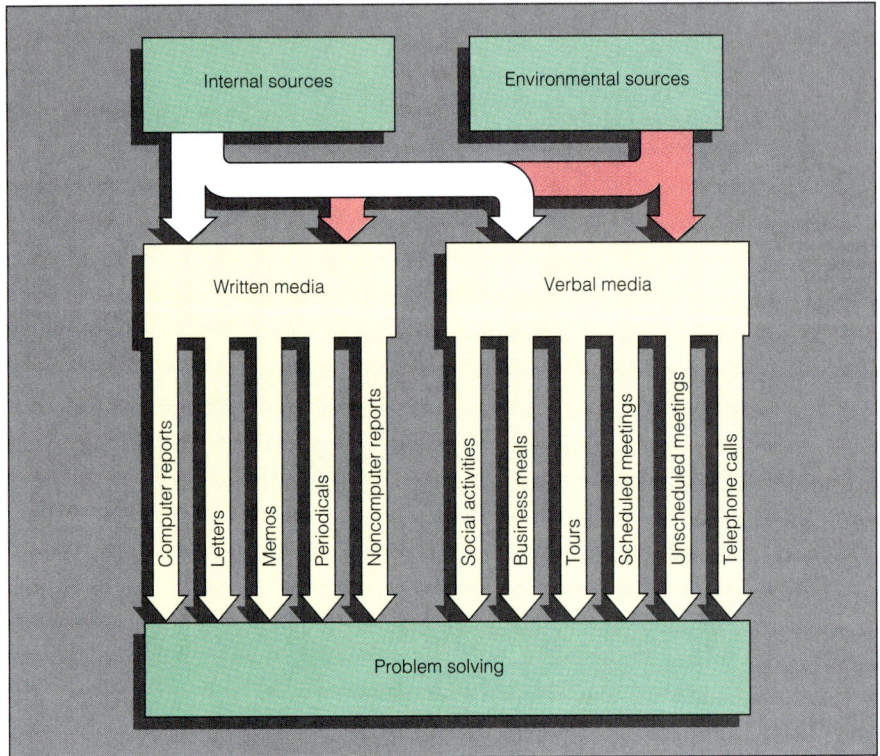

You can see that each source provides both written and verbal media. The written media include computer reports, letters, memos, periodicals (magazines, newspapers, and the like), and noncomputer reports (reports prepared manually, with a typewriter, and so on). Verbal media include social activities (the golf course or cocktail party), business meals, tours (where the managers leave their offices to see what is going on), scheduled and unscheduled meetings, and telephone calls.

All of the arrows connecting the two sources to the media are of the same size, as are all of the media arrows. This implies that all of the flows carry the same amount of information. This is not always true since each manager usually has a few pet sources and media. In spite of this fact, a good manager is unlikely to pass up any opportunity to obtain good information. All of the sources and media are included in a complete information system.

THE COMPUTER AS AN ELEMENT IN AN INFORMATION SYSTEM

When a firm decides to incorporate a computer into its information system, a long-term project is begun that includes many important decisions. Since

FIGURE 1.8

Computers Come in
All Sizes

there are so many types of computers on the market and they can be used
in so many ways, the firm's managers are faced with many choices.
Information specialists help the managers make the right decisions.

Evolution in Size

Computers come in all sizes, as pictured in Figure 1.8. Large ones are called
mainframes. The mainframes have been around the longest, and there are
a lot of them, especially in larger organizations.

The most powerful computers, however, are called **supercomputers.** The
supercomputers are so powerful that they are found in only a few of the
larger business organizations. Supercomputers most often are used for scientific calculations.

The recent trend has not been to larger computers, but to smaller ones.
In the 1970s, this trend got its start with **minicomputers,** or **minis.** These
computers were smaller than the mainframes but, in many cases, outper-
formed the larger units.

The minis were received so well that computer manufacturers produced
even smaller units—called **microcomputers** or **micros.** Most of the microcomputer's main circuitry is in the form of a small silicon chip, smaller
than your fingernail. The chip, shown in Figure 1.9, is called a **microprocessor.**

FIGURE 1.9

A Microprocessor

You also hear terms like small business computer and personal computer. A **small business computer** is a mini or micro that is usually found in smaller firms, and provides the computational support for the entire organization. A **personal computer** is a micro that is used by only a single person, or perhaps by a few people working in the same area. You find personal computers everywhere—in large organizations, in small ones, and even in homes.

The trend to smaller size has been accompanied by reduced costs, but not by reduced performance. The desktop microcomputer of today carries a much more powerful processing punch than did the first giant units that occupied entire rooms.

Basic Computer Components

Although computers come in all sizes, certain component units are common to all. Figure 1.10 illustrates the basic units of a computer. The units, usually packaged in separate cabinets, are interconnected with electrical cables. The flow of data through the system is represented by the arrows.

The most important unit is the **central processing unit** or **CPU.** This unit includes a storage unit called **primary storage,** often called **main memory.** Primary storage contains both the data being processed and the instructions for processing that data.

One or more **input units** enter data into primary storage. Keyboard terminals such as the one pictured in Figure 1.11 are very popular. Also used

FIGURE 1.10

Basic Computer
Components

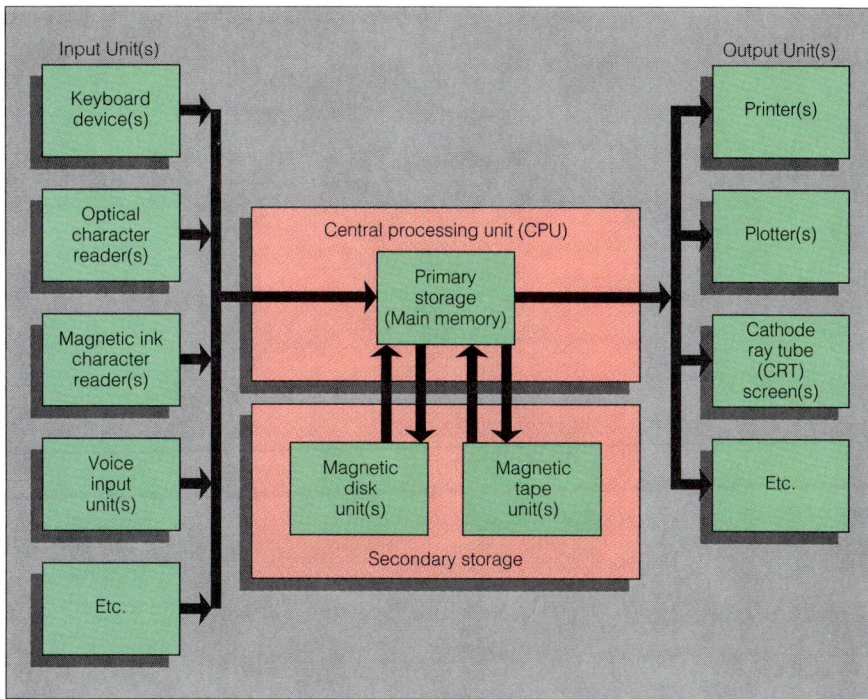

are optical character recognition units such as those found at supermarket checkout counters. Banks use magnetic ink character recognition units to read the specially shaped characters on the bottom of checks. It is even possible to enter data and instructions using the human voice, and other ways as well.

Since primary storage is limited in its capacity, an additional storage area, called **secondary storage** or **auxiliary storage,** is needed. Secondary storage most often takes the form of magnetic disk and magnetic tape units. Secondary storage contains both programs and data that are not being used currently.

The results of the processing are recorded by the **output units.** Output can be printed on a printer, printed in the form of graphs on a plotter, or displayed on a television-like screen called a **cathode-ray tube** or **CRT.** Other output units are less popular.

We explain each of these units in detail in Part 4 of the text.

HOW THE COMPUTER PRODUCES INFORMATION

The computer produces information from data. **Data** takes the form of facts and figures that are relatively meaningless to the user. **Information** is processed data; it is meaningful to the user.

FIGURE 1.11

A User Commu-
nicating with a
Computer Using a
Keyboard Terminal

The data is entered into the computer by the input units or secondary storage. In some cases the data is transformed into information immediately and transmitted to the output units. In other cases the data is held in secondary storage until it is needed. When the information is produced, it is made available to the user in different forms.

Data Storage

The term **database** describes all of the firm's data that is held in computer storage. The data exists in a hierarchy within this database as illustrated in Figure 1.12. On the lowest level are **data elements** that consist of single values such as employee name, employee number, date of birth, and hourly rate of pay. Data elements for a particular subject are combined into a **record.** All of the data elements that we just identified would be included in an employee record. All records of a single type are contained in a **file.** The employee file contains all of the firm's employee records, for example. All of the files make up the database.

Information Output

There are four basic ways that a computer provides information to a problem solver—periodic reports, special reports, the output from mathematical models, and the output from knowledge-based systems.

Periodic Reports

A **periodic report** is one that is prepared according to some schedule, perhaps monthly, quarterly, or annually. The report is prepared automatically for each period regardless of the activities of the firm or any special needs

FIGURE 1.12   The Hierarchy of Data

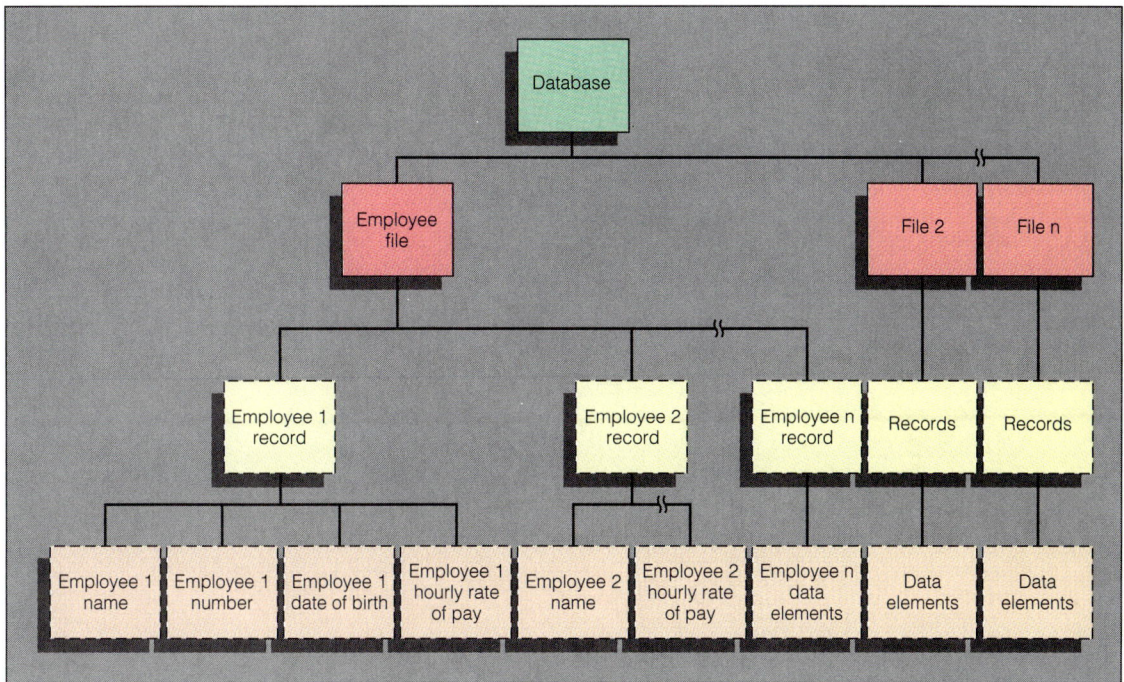

of the managers. The income statement pictured in Figure 1.13 is an example. Periodic reports convey much important information, but tend to describe what happened in the past.

A **special report** is one that is not prepared according to a schedule, but because of a need. Perhaps a manager asks for a report in order to understand a new problem, or the firm has a policy of preparing a report when an accident occurs.

Special Reports

A special report that shows the status of a production job appears in Figure 1.14.

A **mathematical model** is a formula that is used for **simulation,** or representation, of conditions and actions that exist within the firm and between the firm and its environment. Computers are ideally suited to performing the mathematical computations.

Output from Mathematical Models

Managers use mathematical models to project how certain decisions might influence the firm's operations. This is called playing the **What-If game.** As an example, a manager can use a model to evaluate the possible consequences of a price change. The manager says, in effect, "What if I change the price? What will be the likely result?" The result is printed or displayed as shown in Figure 1.15.

FIGURE 1.13

An Income Statement Reflects Revenues, Expenses, and Profits for a Prior Period

GREAT LAKES BOAT AND MARINE

Income Statement

For the Period January 1 through December 31

Gross sales		$54,000
Less: Returns and allowances		$ 4,000
Net sales		$50,000
Cost of goods sold		
Beginning inventory at cost	$ 8,000	
Purchases	$29,000	
Less: Ending inventory at cost	$ 7,000	
Cost of goods sold		$30,000
Gross margin (gross profit)		$20,000
Expenses		
Selling expenses	$10,000	
Administrative expenses	$ 4,500	
General expenses	$ 1,500	
Total expenses		$16,000
Net profit		$ 4,000

FIGURE 1.14

A Special Report Displayed on a Manager's Screen

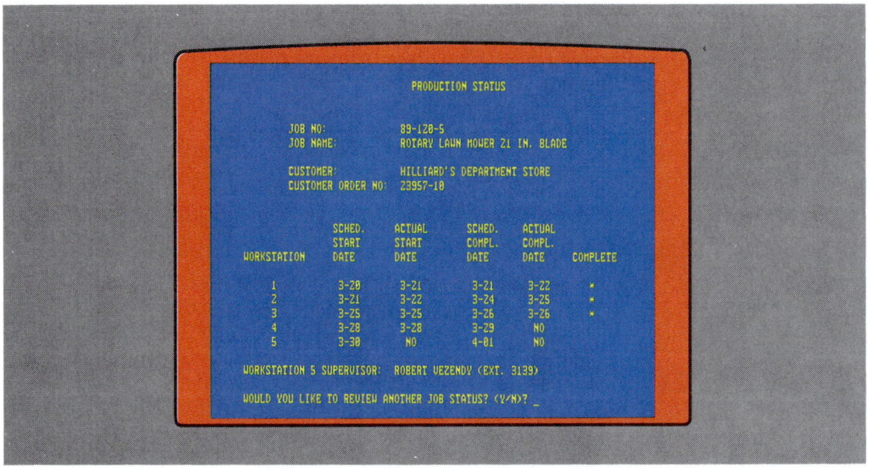

PRODUCTION STATUS

JOB NO: 89-128-5
JOB NAME: ROTARY LAWN MOWER 21 IN. BLADE

CUSTOMER: HILLIARD'S DEPARTMENT STORE
CUSTOMER ORDER NO: 23957-18

WORKSTATION	SCHED. START DATE	ACTUAL START DATE	SCHED. COMPL. DATE	ACTUAL COMPL. DATE	COMPLETE
1	3-28	3-21	3-21	3-22	*
2	3-21	3-22	3-24	3-25	*
3	3-25	3-25	3-26	3-26	*
4	3-28	3-28	3-29	NO	
5	3-38	NO	4-81	NO	

WORKSTATION 5 SUPERVISOR: ROBERT VEZENDV (EXT. 3139)

WOULD YOU LIKE TO REVIEW ANOTHER JOB STATUS? (Y/N)? _

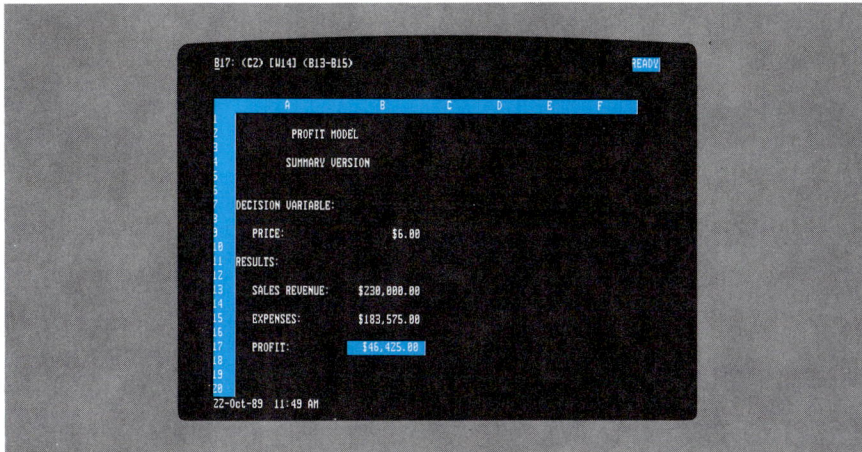

FIGURE 1.15
The Output from a
Mathematical
Model

A **knowledge-based system** is one that incorporates some degree of
human reasoning so that it can perform part of the problem solving for the
user. Knowledge-based systems are examples of **artificial intelligence,** the
activity of providing computers with capabilities, which, if observed in
humans, would be considered intelligent. Whereas mathematical models
emphasize the use of mathematical formulas, knowledge-based systems
emphasize the use of logic. We address knowledge-based systems in
Chapter 15.

*Output from
knowledge-based
systems*

COMPUTER APPLICATION AREAS

The jobs that computers perform are called **applications.** There are five
major application areas in business—data processing, management information systems, decision support systems, office automation, and expert
systems.

The first computers were used only to process accounting data. Originally,
this use was called **electronic data processing,** or **EDP,** but it was shortened to **data processing.** For the first ten or so years of the computer era,
from about 1954 to 1964, the larger organizations (both government and
business) used their computers mainly for data processing.

Data Processing

After a while the big organizations had put most of their accounting work
on the computer and looked around for the next application. Their attention fell upon the managers, who had not benefitted a great deal from data
processing. It was recognized that the computer could also produce information for the managers to use in solving problems, and the idea of the
management information system was born. The term **MIS** became the
buzzword in the computer industry. MIS held great promise.

*Management
Information
Systems*

Firms quickly learned, however, that MIS was difficult to implement.
The managers often could not specify what information was needed, either
because they did not know or could not put their thoughts into words. In
many cases the information specialists attempted to provide the informa-

FIGURE 1.16

A Video Conference

tion that *they thought* the managers might need. The results usually were disappointing. Many firms scrapped their MIS efforts completely or settled for less ambitious accomplishments.

Decision Support Systems

Things looked pretty bleak in the early 1970s when two Massachusetts Institute of Technology (MIT) professors named G. Anthony Gorry and Michael S. Scott Morton originated the concept of the computer as a **decision support system,** or **DSS.** At first the concept seemed to be the same as MIS. After all, the MIS had been intended to help managers make decisions so that they could solve problems. The DSS, however, was more modest in scope. The idea was that a DSS would assist a manager or group of managers in making a *single decision.* Whereas a firm would have only a single MIS, it would have many DSSs.

Another key ingredient to the DSS concept was the notion that it would only *assist* in decision making. The concept recognized that there are features of problems that are impossible to enter into the computer. So, the DSS represented a way for the manager and the computer to work together in problem solution.

Since a DSS attempted to accomplish less than did the MIS, the DSS concept met with much better results.

During the same period that the MIS and DSS concepts evolved, efforts were initiated to increase the productivity of office workers. The application area called **office automation,** or **OA,** was the result. Some of the OA applications, such as word processing, electronic mail, and computer conferencing, involve the use of computers. Others, such as audio conferencing, video conferencing, and facsimile transmission, do not. A photograph of problem solvers engaged in a video conference appears in Figure 1.16. The participants can view and hear each other, even though they are in separate locations—often far apart.

 The feature that ties together all of the OA applications is their objective of improving communications. The communications convey the information that is used in problem solving.

Office Automation

Today, much attention is being focused on the application of computers to functions that normally are performed by humans, such as perception and learning. The application is called **artificial intelligence**. Artificial intelligence consists of several subsidiary areas, and the one of prime interest in business is expert systems.

 An **expert system** is a knowledge-based system that permits the computer to serve as a consultant to the problem solver. The consultant's knowledge exists in the form of rules and other knowledge representation that have been provided by experts who are the acknowledged leaders in their particular fields. The expert system expands the manager's problem-solving ability to include the expert's knowledge, thereby enabling the manager to perform at a higher level than ordinarily would be possible. Thus far, the accomplishments of expert systems in business have been modest, but the potential impact is great.

Expert Systems

A COMPUTER-BASED INFORMATION SYSTEM

We have recognized that managers make decisions to solve problems and that information is used in making the decisions. The information comes from both computer and noncomputer sources.

 Having established this framework, our task in this text is to explain the role of the computer. The computer portion of the complete information system contains each of the application areas—a data processing system, a management information system, decision support systems, office automation, and expert systems. Figure 1.17 shows this composite view. The data processing system processes the firm's accounting data, the MIS establishes an information resource that is directed at the needs of the organization, DSSs support individual managers in making separate decisions, office automation facilitates communications, and expert systems allow managers to apply higher levels of knowledge. All of these systems work together to provide the information for problem solving. We will use the term **computer-based information system** or **CBIS** to describe this overall system.

FIGURE 1.17
The Computer-Based
Information System in
Problem Solving

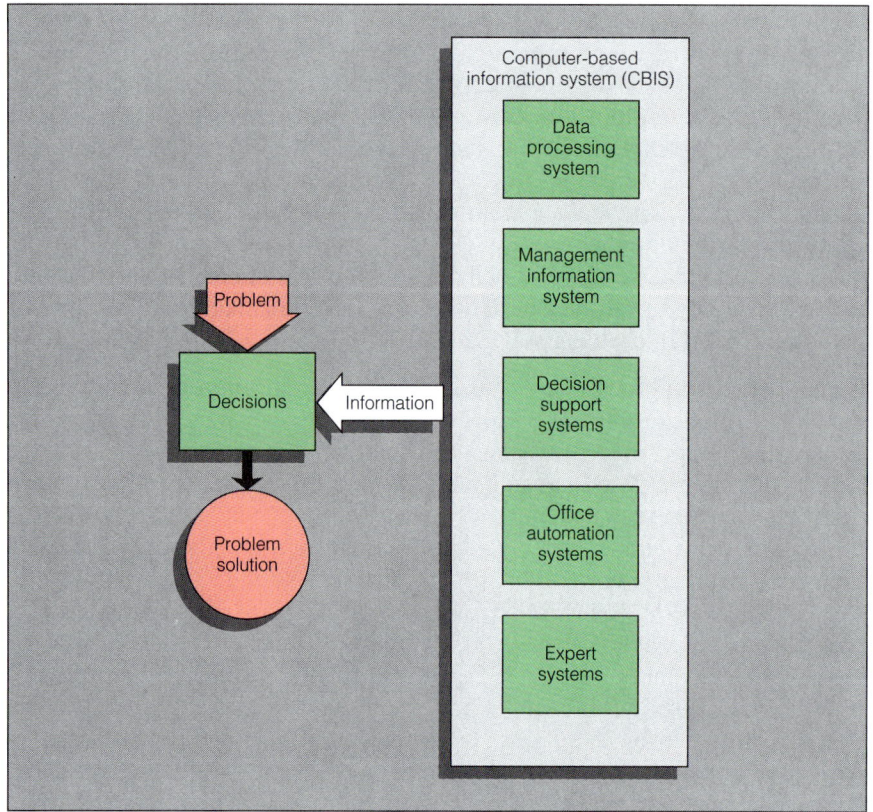

WHO USES THE COMPUTER IN A BUSINESS ORGANIZATION?

For the first twenty or so years of the computer era, only the information specialists were permitted to use the firm's computer. The firm usually had only a central computing facility, and it was off limits to noncomputer personnel.

This situation worked fine until the firm began to install terminals in user areas. The users could use the terminals to receive special reports and even perform mathematical modeling on the central computer. For the first time, the users could communicate directly with the computer without going through information specialists.

The next step came when microcomputers were placed throughout the firm. In some cases the users obtained their own micros, and in other cases the firm furnished them. Sometimes the micros were connected to the central computer. The micros and the mainframe formed a computer **network,** and the user could use the micro alone or as a terminal.

Many users recognized the potential power of the computing equipment and became proficient in its use. The term **end-user computing** was coined to describe this situation where the user can use the computer without assistance.

The trend is definitely toward end-user computing. More and more users know how to prepare their own computer programs and to use routines that have been written by others. In addition, the computing equipment is becoming easier to operate. Some people believe that the trend will mean the end of information specialists. That is unlikely.

Users will continue to do more and more of their own work, but there will be computer applications that they either cannot or will not attempt themselves. These will be applications that others, the information specialists, are better qualified to do. No users are likely to attempt to implement their own data processing systems; they will let the information specialists do that for the entire firm. Also, no users are likely to attempt extremely sophisticated systems such as complex mathematical models. Many users are qualified to take on such projects but their responsibilities do not permit them to devote the amount of time that would be required.

There will always be a need for information specialists. The users will implement some systems alone. The information specialists will work with the users in implementing other systems. In no cases, however, should the information specialists implement systems without the involvement of the users. The users are the only ones who know what is needed, and they are the ones who both must pay for and live with the systems.

EVERYONE NEEDS COMPUTER LITERACY

As it became more and more apparent that an understanding of the computer is important, the term *computer literacy* gained widespread use. Stated simply, **computer literacy** means an understanding of the computer. There are at least four features of the understanding:

1. Understand key computer terminology
2. Know what a computer can and cannot do
3. Understand the costs and benefits of using a computer
4. Be able to use the computer

A person who is computer literate knows the meaning of terms such as byte, kilobyte, RAM, ROM, and modem. The person also understands that it is impossible to know all of the terms since there are so many and new ones crop up almost daily. He or she therefore does not hesitate to ask for a definition when a new term is encountered.

The computer-literate person recognizes that the computer cannot do everything and usually can decide whether a potential application is feasible. This knowledge of capabilities and limitations carries with it an understanding that using the computer costs money. Perhaps the computer can do a job, but the cost is too high.

The fourth ingredient, being able to use the computer, is stimulating much argument today. Some people believe that the person should be able to code a **program**—the list of instructions that causes the computer to carry out its duties. You probably have heard of the more popular languages used in programming—FORTRAN, COBOL, and BASIC. This is the traditional way to get the computer to work for you.

Another group believes that programming is not required, but being able to use prewritten, packaged programs is. There are thousands of such packages available, especially for microcomputers, and they cause the computer to do a wide variety of tasks without the necessity of programming.

We are going to straddle the fence on this issue and give you the opportunity to learn how to create your own programs, how to use prewritten software, or how to do both. Chapter 2 is devoted to a description of the process of developing custom programs and Chapter 3 explains the options involved in using prewritten software. We will leave it up to your instructor to decide which route you are to follow in gaining computer literacy.

MANAGERS ALSO NEED INFORMATION LITERACY

If a person is to take full advantage of the many technological marvels available in today's world, computer literacy is a must. But, the manager needs something in addition—**information literacy,** which is an understanding of how to apply the computer in problem solving. Here are six major ingredients of information literacy:

1. Appreciate the importance of information in problem solving
2. Know the information sources
3. Know how to gather information
4. Understand the need to validate information
5. Recognize the importance of sharing information with others
6. Know how to use information in problem solving

The information-literate manager will realize that information is necessary for problem solving, will appreciate that information comes from many sources, and will know how to obtain information from those sources.

The information-literate manager will know that information must be validated before it is used. That is, its accuracy must be checked. Information is not accurate just because it is printed by a computer. Many managers have a keen sense of numbers—they can look at a column of figures and know when they are incorrect. This ability comes from their knowledge of the area of the business that the figures represent.

Being an information-literate manager and knowing the value of information in problem solving will encourage managers to share information. When one manager has information that can be valuable to others, that information is passed along. There is much of this information sharing in a firm—especially at the upper levels.

Information literacy boils down to being able to use information in solving problems. Notice that we did not say *computer* information. We mean *all* types of information. Information literacy goes beyond computer literacy and use of computer-produced information.

THE IMPORTANCE OF INFORMATION LITERACY IN A CAREER

At the beginning of the chapter we explained how the terms business and manager are used so broadly. We recognize that many types of organizations are businesses and that persons in charge of these organizations are managers. With this view, managers of all types—presidents, supervisors, preachers, coaches, and orchestra leaders—need information literacy.

It is also necessary that specialists who work with users in problem solving should be information literate. The specialist cannot be of much help if he or she knows little about why the information is needed and how it will be used.

So, if you plan to become a manager in a profit-seeking organization, a manager with another title in a nonprofit organization, or an information specialist, a big step toward maximizing your career potential is to achieve information literacy.

SUMMARY

A problem can be something good as well as something bad. The process of reacting successfully to both opportunities and challenges is called problem solving. Business problems can be caused by factors in the firm or its environment. Environmental influences include the world and national economy, government actions, competitor actions, supplier actions, and information provided by customers. Internal influences center on limited resources and the behavioral differences of the employees.

Problems are solved by managers, nonmanagers, and specialists. The specialists come from within the firm and from the environment. Problem solving is a group activity, directed by the manager. The manager enlists all of the help that is available in order to reach the best solution.

Problems are solved by following a series of steps: understand the problem, evaluate alternate solutions, implement the best solution, and follow up. Multiple decisions must be made at each step, and information helps the manager make the decisions. The manager can supplement his or her knowledge and experience by obtaining information from the firm's files of paper documents and from the computer system, and by gathering new information.

A complete information system is one that gathers information from both internal and environmental sources and uses both written and verbal media. Both formal and informal systems are used. A formal system is spelled out in writing; an informal one is not. The information from the system describes past, present, and possible future activity of the firm. Such a system is called a complete information system.

The computer can be an element in an information system. Computers have evolved through various sizes, but they all contain a CPU, one or more input units, some type of secondary storage, and one or more output units.

The computer transforms data into information. In some cases, the data is held in the database until it is needed. Data in the database exists in a hierarchy—file, record, and data element. The computer makes the information available in four basic forms—periodic reports, special reports, and the outputs from mathematical models and knowledge-based systems.

There are five major computer application areas, and each plays a unique role in the firm's information system. The data processing system processes the accounting transactions. The MIS provides an overall information system for the entire firm. DSSs are tailored to the needs of individual managers. Office automation is aimed at improving communications both within the firm and between the firm and its environment. Expert systems offer the opportunity to expand decision support beyond the capabilities of the managers by incorporating the problem-solving skills of experts. All five of these application areas comprise the computer-based information system (CBIS).

Whereas computers were used only by information specialists in years past, the user of today has access by means of terminals and micros. End-user computing is achieved when the user is self-sufficient and does not have to rely on information specialists.

Everybody needs computer literacy, but managers and information specialists also need information literacy. A manager and an information specialist form a team, applying computer techniques to problem solving.

KEY CONCEPTS

The broad interpretation of what constitutes a business organization

The fact that a problem can mean something good as well as something bad

The way that the environment can cause problems for the firm

The group nature of problem solving—involving managers, nonmanagers, and specialists

The role that information plays in problem solving

The encompassing nature of an information system, including all sources, all media, both formal and informal systems, and information relating to the past, present, and future

How computer use can be classified into five major application areas—data processing, MIS, DSS, OA, and expert systems

The difference between computer literacy and information literacy

KEY TERMS

Problem
Manager
Information specialist
Decision
Complete information system
Data
Information
Periodic report
Special report
Mathematical model
Simulation
What-If game
Knowledge-based system
Artificial intelligence
Electronic data processing (EDP), data processing
Management information system (MIS)
Decision support system (DSS)
Office automation (OA)
Expert system
Computer-based information system (CBIS)
End-user computing
Computer literacy
Program
Information literacy

QUESTIONS

1. Name four types of organizations in the firm's environment that can cause problems.

2. What distinguishes a manager from a nonmanager?

3. Give seven examples of specialists who help the manager solve problems.

4. What are the four basic steps of problem solving?

5. What is the difference between decision making and problem solving?

6. What is meant by the term "complete information system"?

7. What are the four basic sizes of computers?

8. Why does a computer need secondary storage? What does it contain?

9. Which would be read by the computer's input devices—data or information? Which would be produced by its output devices?

10. What is the three-tier hierarchy of data in the database?

11. What are the four basic ways that the manager receives information from the computer?

12. Which basic computer application addresses the information needs of the entire organization? Which is tailored to single decisions made by specific managers? Which is like a consultant? Which emphasizes communication?

13. Which types of computer applications will be developed jointly by managers and information specialists? Which will be developed by information specialists alone?

14. Could you have information literacy without having computer literacy? Explain your answer.

15. Can you name three occupations that do not require information literacy? Are these high-paying occupations? What does this tell you?

CASE PROBLEM

Wellesley Furniture

The ad for the new position of computing department manager had run in the Boston paper for five weeks. Wellesley had been in business for over one hundred years and had finally decided to get a computer. Top management felt that the first step should be to bring someone on board to manage the new activity. The response to the ad was underwhelming—only three applications were received, and one was from some college students who had submitted a resume for their professor.

Top management was beginning to feel desperate when Albert Williams, the external auditor who recently had audited the firm's accounting records, indicated that he might be interested. Albert seemed to be a legitimate candidate—college degree, well dressed, and a good knowledge of Wellesley's business.

An appointment was made for Albert to meet with Wellesley's president and three vice presidents for an interview. The five took their seats in the conference room, and Anita Browning, the president, asked "Albert, why would you like to be our new computer manager?"

Albert responded immediately "Because Wellesley is going places. Your profits have increased 15 percent each year for the past five years. You don't have any real problems, and I wouldn't have to spend my time putting out fires. I could concentrate on giving you the best accounting system in New England."

Bill Brownkamper, the vice president of finance, said "Then, you must not see a need to use the computer in the area of problem solving?"

"That's right," Albert replied. "Like I said, you don't have any problems to solve. Instead, I see the real pay-off in the accounting area. Every firm must have a good accounting system. It's important that when the auditors come in, you get a clean bill of health." Alice Muse, the vice president of marketing, took her turn. "You mentioned that we don't have any problems. Could you expand on that?"

"Sure, you're right in the middle of the part of the country that has shown the greatest recovery from the economic slump. There is no unemployment to speak of in New England. Sales are booming. You don't have anything to worry about, in my opinion."

"Well, Albert," John Martinez, the vice president of manufacturing, asked, "I've heard a lot about word processing. Maybe we could do that."

Albert did not hesitate to respond. "Oh, there's no doubt about it. Word processing can do you a world of good. From what I've seen, your methods of preparing correspondence are pretty primitive. You should get into word processing, but I wouldn't want a computer department of mine to get involved in that type of activity. It's not computing. It would only distract me from my main mission."

Anita Browning spoke up "Let me ask one final question. Would the computer system that you envision be able to provide our management team with information?"

"Oh, definitely. We would prepare all of the standard accounting reports. You know, the balance sheet and income statement. In addition, we would prepare a complete set of management reports. In fact, I've already begun to make a list of the reports that you need. If I get the job, we'll start cranking out those reports in no time."

Anita thanked Albert, and asked him to leave the room. She turned to the others and asked: "Well, what do you think?"

1. Do you think that Wellesley is going about the computer project the right way? Explain.

2. What do you think about Albert's plan to limit the applications to accounting?

3. Is it true that Wellesley does not have any problems? Explain.

4. What do you think about Albert's attitude toward word processing?

5. Do you believe that Albert's system will give the managers the information that they need? Explain.

6. Assuming that Albert is the only acceptable candidate and he is offered the job, what advice would you offer him as he begins his duties?

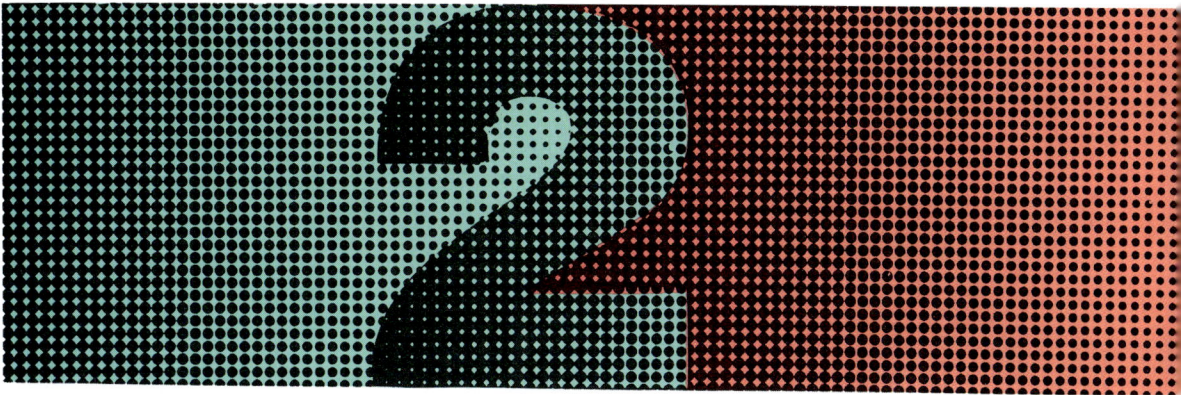

Introduction to Computer Software

In Part 1 you were introduced to the basic computing equipment that is called hardware. The instructions that guide the hardware, tailoring it to the specific firm's activities, are called software.

For the first twenty or so years of the computer era, the firm's own information specialists developed the software that was needed. More recently an alternative approach has become popular—purchase of prewritten software.

Part 2 is devoted to these two basic approaches. Chapter 2 explains how you can develop your own software and Chapter 3 provides an overview of the prewritten software that is available. These two chapters contain the important fundamentals that are necessary for learning and using problem-solving software.

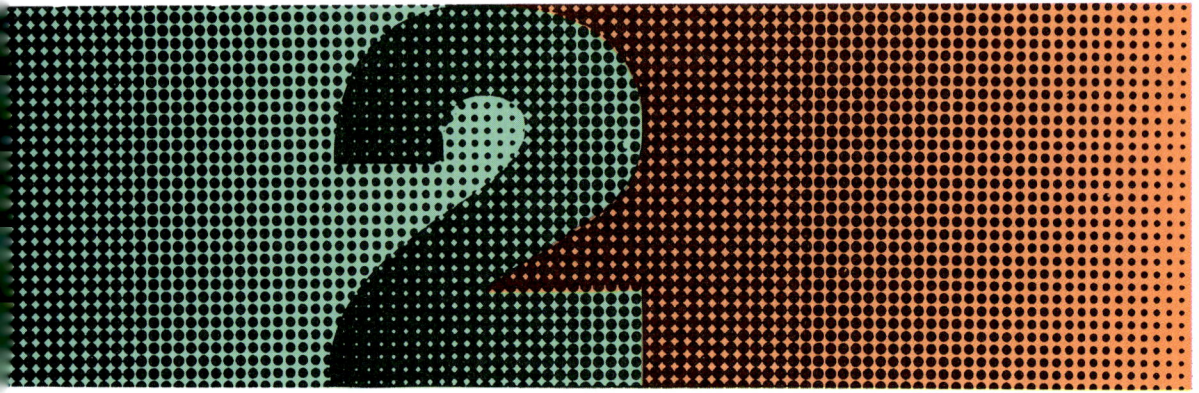

Developing Your Own Software

- Understand that software tailors general-purpose hardware to specific processing needs
- Appreciate the importance of a programming ability to a computer user
- Understand the stored-program concept
- Know the main features of the statements that are combined to produce the program
- Know the primary types of computer languages
- Understand the steps that are followed in developing a program, and who takes each step
- Have a fundamental understanding of what is meant by structured programming

OVERVIEW

This chapter introduces you to the traditional way of causing the computer to perform the desired processing—the development of a program. A distinction is made between hardware and software, and the role of the software in tailoring the hardware to a specific job is explained. While it is not an absolute necessity that the problem solver know how to program, there are certain advantages.

A computer program consists of a number of instructions that are called statements. The format of statements is explained as well as the basic types and how they are arranged in a program.

A brief description is offered of the major programming languages, and a single problem is solved using four of the languages for comparison purposes. The subject of program translation is explored, and the differences between the three types of translators are explained. Attention is also given to the process of preparing a program—a process that can be performed by information specialists working with end users, or by end users alone.

An important part of the chapter is an introduction to the programming approach that is receiving the most attention currently—structured programming.

After reading this chapter, you should be ready to learn a specific programming language such as BASIC (described in Appendices B and C).

THE CONCEPTS OF HARDWARE AND SOFTWARE

The most widely used computer terms probably are hardware and software. Nobody knows who coined these terms, but they have been around since the beginning of the computer era.

What Is Hardware?

Hardware is all of the equipment that comprises a computer system. In most cases, there are multiple units as we saw in Chapter 1. A small computer, such as a micro, will contain as few as two, three, or four units—interconnected by electrical cables. A large computer, such as a mainframe or supercomputer, will contain from perhaps twenty to several hundred units.

In the case of the large computer, many of the units are located in a central computing facility, called a **computer room**. Figure 2.1 shows a typical computer room. The major units—the CPU, secondary storage, and selected input and output units—are located in this central computing facility.

Other units such as terminals and micros can be located throughout the organization, perhaps hundreds or thousands of miles from the central facility. The terminals are connected to the central computer by such data communications circuits as telephone wires or cables, fiberoptic cables, or even microwave signals relayed by earth stations or bounced off of satellites. This computer network can also contain microcomputers, minicomputers, and even other mainframes.

What Is Software?

Most people use the term **software** to mean the programs that cause the computer to perform particular jobs. A broader interpretation also includes other items that are required to use a computer—manuals, supplies, user

FIGURE 2.1

A Computer Room

education, hardware maintenance, and so on. We will use the term in its narrow sense—to mean computer programs.

Tailoring General-Purpose Hardware to Fit Specific Needs

The term **hardware vendors** has been coined to describe the computer manufacturers. The hardware vendors make **general-purpose hardware**—a wide variety of organizations can use it for a wide variety of jobs. For example, the IBM Personal Computer (PC) is used to perform thousands of different types of jobs. This strategy of producing general-purpose hardware enables the manufacturers to mass produce the units.

When you first obtain a computer, its storage is blank. Before you can use the computer, you must load a program into its primary storage. You use a different program for each job that you want the computer to do.

It is the computer program, or software, that tailors the general-purpose hardware to the user's specific processing requirements.

Custom Software versus Prewritten Software

Early computer users had no choice but to prepare their own software, custom tailored to their needs. Over time, however, software was developed to solve problems faced by large numbers of firms. At first this software, which was called **prewritten software, packaged software**, and **off-the-shelf software**, was developed by the hardware vendors. More recently, the hardware vendors have been joined by a new category of firms called **software vendors** who specialize in software.

The prewritten software is always less expensive than the custom software, but usually the prewritten software does not meet the firm's exact needs. In those situations the firm must change its procedures to fit the software, change the software to fit the procedures, or find better software.

The size of the operation of the firm is one factor in determining whether prewritten or custom software is used. A small firm may have no choice but to use prewritten software because of limited funds. A large firm with its own staff of information specialists will use prewritten software when it meets the firm's needs, and will prepare its own custom software when that is the only option. These are general guidelines that apply in most, but not all, cases.

THE IMPORTANCE OF A PROGRAMMING ABILITY TO THE USER

You do not have to know how to program to use the computer. There are many user-friendly prewritten software packages that are available. However, an ability to program provides the user with two distinct advantages—more processing power, and an ability to communicate better with information specialists.

More Processing Power

Each of the prewritten packages is aimed at a rather narrow type of processing. A programming language, on the other hand, can be applied in a much broader way. With a programming language, you can build practically any type of computer solution that you might need.

The user who can both program *and* use prewritten software has more computing power available than does the user who can use only the prewritten packages.

Better Communication with Information Specialists

Even when the user will not do the programming personally, an ability to program is helpful when working with information specialists. The user can play a more active role in designing the computer solution to a problem. The user and the information specialist can work together, since they both speak the same language.

THE STORED PROGRAM CONCEPT

One of the most important principles of computing is the **stored program concept**. This means that the program is stored in the computer's primary storage, along with the data. This concept is illustrated in Figure 2.2.

The general-purpose hardware can be transformed into special-purpose hardware quickly and easily simply by loading a new program. When you load a new program, the previous one is erased.

A COMPUTER PROGRAM CONSISTS OF MULTIPLE STATEMENTS

The person who codes, or writes, the program is called the **programmer**. The program consists of a list of orders or directives to the computer that

FIGURE 2.2

The Program Being
Run Is Stored in
Primary Storage
Along with the Data

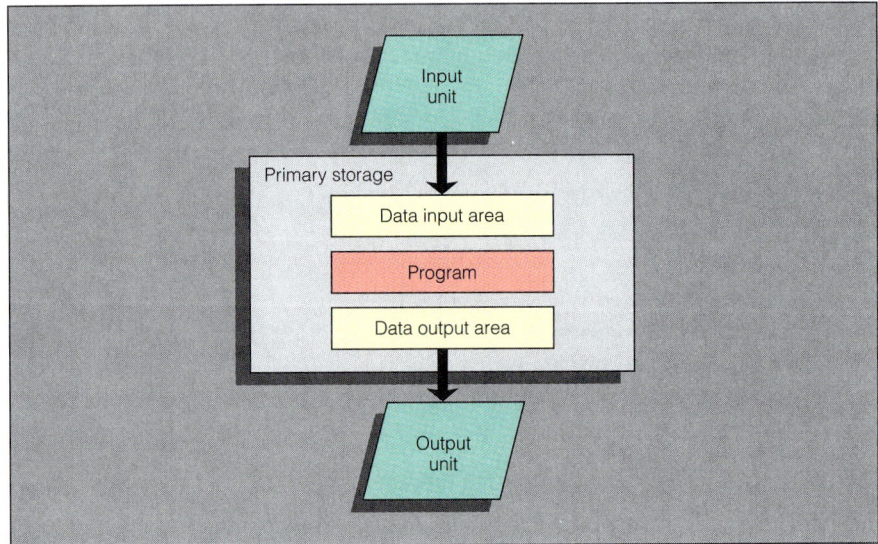

are called statements. A very small program can include less than ten state-ments, whereas a large one can include several thousand.

A statement consists of a verb and (in most cases) an object. The verb specifies the action to be performed—such as READ. The object elaborates on the verb and specifies what is involved—such as EMPLOYEE.NAME. The statement READ EMPLOYEE.NAME, written in the BASIC language, tells the computer to obtain that particular data element for processing.

Not all statements include a single object. Some have more. Take, for example, the BASIC statement PRINT EMPLOYEE.NUMBER, EMPLOY-EE.NAME, TOTAL.EARNINGS. This statement tells the computer to print an employee's number, employee's name, and the total amount of payroll earnings.

Some statements have only the verb. The END statement, for example, simply tells the computer that the BASIC program is completed.

FUNDAMENTAL TYPES OF STATEMENTS

A programming language such as BASIC or FORTRAN or COBOL includes a specific group of statements, called a **statement set**, for the pro-grammer to use. These statements perform very fundamental operations such as read, print, compute, and move. It is the responsibility of the pro-grammer to:

1. Select the statements necessary to accomplish the job.
2. Arrange the selected statements in the proper sequence.
3. Add the needed modifiers—the objects.

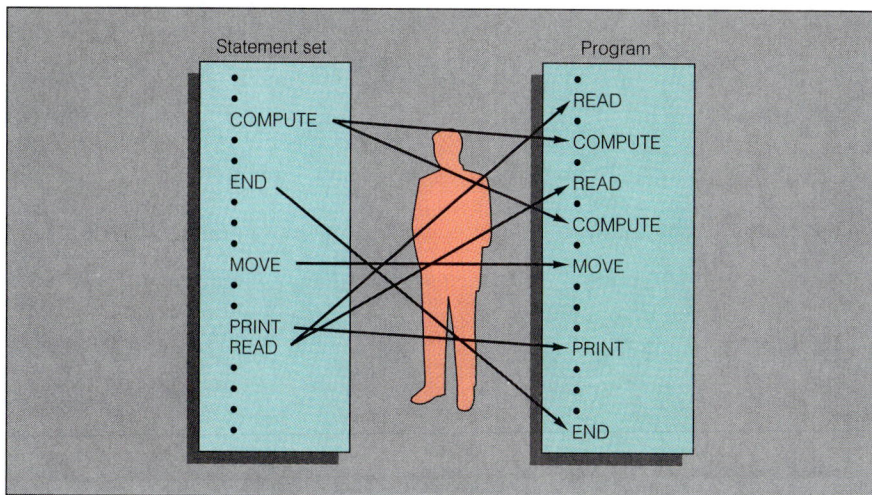

FIGURE 2.3

The Programmer Assembles the Statements in the Proper Order

The situation is analogous to playing a game of Scrabble. The Scrabble set contains an assortment of letters that you assemble to form words. The computer programmer, as shown in Figure 2.3, assembles the statements of the statement set to form a program.

Although the number of different statements in a statement set will vary depending on the language, there are only five fundamental types—input/output, data movement, arithmetic, logic, and control.

Input/Output

Input/output statements enter data into the computer's primary storage to be processed, and exit the results after the processing. The input can be from either input units or secondary storage. The output can be to either output units or secondary storage. Figure 2.4 shows this input and output.

Data Movement

It is often necessary to move the data around inside the primary storage. For example, we might want to move the employee's number from the input area of storage to the output area. The **data movement statements** accomplish this task as shown in Figure 2.5.

Arithmetic

You have heard about the marvelous things that computers do. They guide spaceships to the moon, design automobiles and homes, and even forecast the weather. Although many mathematical computations usually are involved, those computations are accomplished with only five basic operations—addition, subtraction, multiplication, division, and exponentiation (raising a number to a power). The statements that provide this ability are called **arithmetic statements**.

FIGURE 2.4
Input and Output

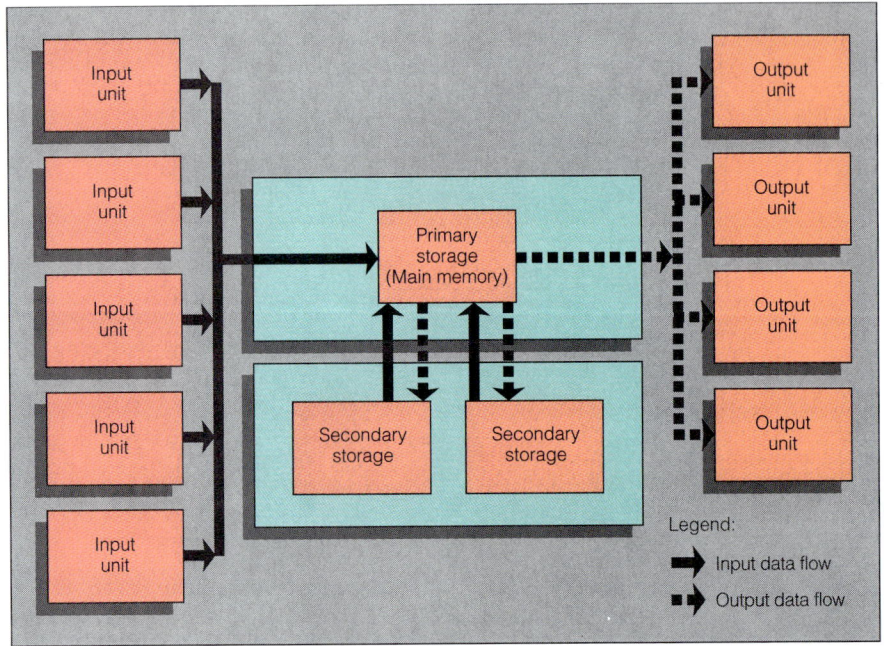

FIGURE 2.5
Data Movement

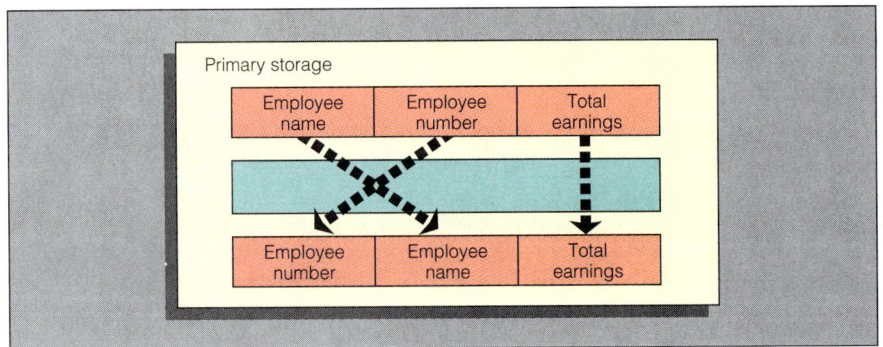

Sometimes a statement will perform only a single arithmetic operation, such as the COBOL statement:

```
COMPUTE NET-PRICE = GROSS-PRICE - DISCOUNT.
```

The minus sign separating GROSS-PRICE and DISCOUNT specifies a subtract operation.

You can also perform multiple arithmetic operations in a single statement. An example is the FORTRAN statement:

```
EXPAY = (HOURS - 40) * HRRATE * 1.5
```

This statement computes an employee's overtime pay by paying time-and-a-half (HRRATE * 1.5) for all hours worked over forty (HOURS – 40). The asterisks represent multiplication. The parentheses are used to control the sequence of the arithmetic, causing the subtraction to be performed first.

Logic

Logic statements enable the computer to make decisions. An example is the overtime decision in a payroll system. Overtime pay is computed only when more than forty hours are worked. Otherwise, only regular pay is computed. The logic statement written in COBOL could appear as:

```
IF HOURS > 40 THEN PERFORM OVERTIME-PAY-ROUTINE
ELSE PERFORM REGULAR-PAY-ROUTINE.
```

The computer can make this decision, relieving a payroll clerk of that responsibility.

Control

Normally the computer executes the statements in the same sequence as they appear in the program—one after the other. There are times, however, when you want to alter this sequence. **Control statements** are used for this purpose. An example is the GOSUB statement in the BASIC language. This statement says, in effect: GO to the SUBroutine (or set of statements) at a certain location in storage, and execute the statements.

Figure 2.6 is a BASIC program containing four of the five statement types. It does not contain a move statement.

THE STATEMENTS PERFORM FUNDAMENTAL TASKS

Although it is possible to arrange the program statements in an almost infinite number of patterns, they typically are grouped to perform certain fundamental tasks—initialization, input, processing, and output.

Initialization

Before you use the computer, you often have to prepare it to run your program. This preparation may involve making certain that the primary storage positions do not contain data from a previous program. If you do not reset these positions to zero before trying to use them to accumulate totals, then the totals will be incorrect.

This preparatory work is called **initialization**—you must initialize the computer, and this is accomplished by a set of statements that are included at the beginning of the program.

FIGURE 2.6

A BASIC Program Containing Input, Output, Arithmetic, Logic, and Control Statements

```
            10   'COMPUTE SALES COMMISSIONS
            20   '**********DRIVER MODULE**********
Control ──→ 30   GOSUB 100      'INITIALIZE STORAGE
            40   GOSUB 200      'PROCESS SALES DATA
            50   GOSUB 300      'PRINT FINAL TOTALS
            70   END
            100  '*******INITIALIZE STORAGE********
            110  LET TOTAL.SALES = 0
            120  LET TOTAL.COMM = 0
            130  RETURN
            200  '*******PROCESS SALES DATA********
            210  LET RESPONSE$ = "YES"
            220  WHILE RESPONSE$ = "YES"
            230      GOSUB 400      'READ DATA
            240      GOSUB 500      'PROCESS DATA
            250      GOSUB 600      'PRINT DATA
            260  WEND
            270  RETURN
            300  '*******PRINT FINAL TOTALS********
            310  LPRINT
Output ───→ 320  LPRINT "FINAL TOTALS", TOTAL.SALES, TOTAL.COMM
            330  RETURN
            400  '**********READ DATA************
            410  CLS
            420  PRINT "ENTER SALESPERSON NUMBER"
Input ────→ 430  INPUT SALESPERSON.NO
            440  PRINT "ENTER SALES AMOUNT"
            450  INPUT SALES.AMT
            460  RETURN
            500  '**********PROCESS DATA**********
Logic ────→ 510  IF SALES.AMT > 1000
                     THEN LET COMM.AMT = 100 + (SALES.AMT - 1000) *.15
                     ELSE LET COMM.AMT = SALES.AMT * .1
Arithmetic→ 520  LET TOTAL.SALES = TOTAL.SALES + SALES.AMT
            530  LET TOTAL.COMM = TOTAL.COMM + COMM.AMT
            540  RETURN
            600  '**********PRINT DATA***********
            610  LPRINT SALESPERSON.NO, SALES.AMT, COMM.AMT
            620  PRINT "DO YOU WISH TO CONTINUE (YES/NO)"
            630  INPUT RESPONSE$
            640  RETURN
```

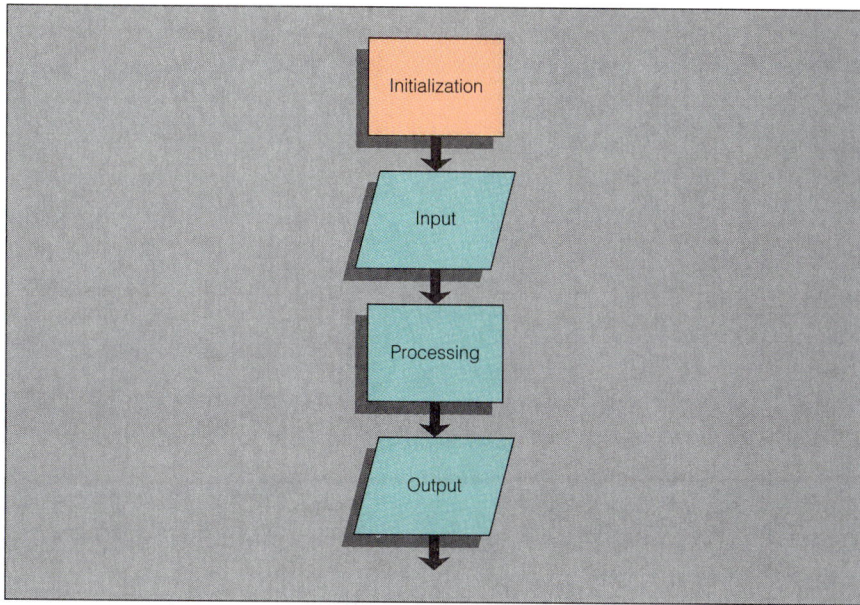

FIGURE 2.7

The Fundamental Tasks of a Computer Program

Input, Processing, and Output

There are large programs and there are small programs, however they all have one characteristic in common. Once initialization has been accomplished, there is a sequence of three basic operations that take place—input, processing, and output. First, one or more statements cause data to be entered into primary storage. That is the **input**. With the data in storage, one or more statements then manipulate the data in some way. That is the **processing**. With the processing completed, one or more statements make the results available to the user. That is the **output**.

A program therefore contains the groups of statements, arranged in the sequence shown in Figure 2.7. The figure is a simple program flowchart. A **flowchart** is a diagram composed of symbols that show the sequence of processes. The rectangle is used for initialization and processing. The parallelogram represents an input or output operation.

One or More Loops

If you want to process only a single record, such as the payroll data for a single employee, the structure of the program looks like Figure 2.7. You perform the operations in sequence and then the program is completed. However, programs typically are written to process many records, and the input, processing, and output are repeated for each one. For example, if a firm has 120 employees, the input, processing, and output portion of the payroll program is executed 120 times—once for each employee. It is usually not necessary to repeat the initialization.

FIGURE 2.8

A Loop Enables
Processing to Be
Repeated for Each
Record

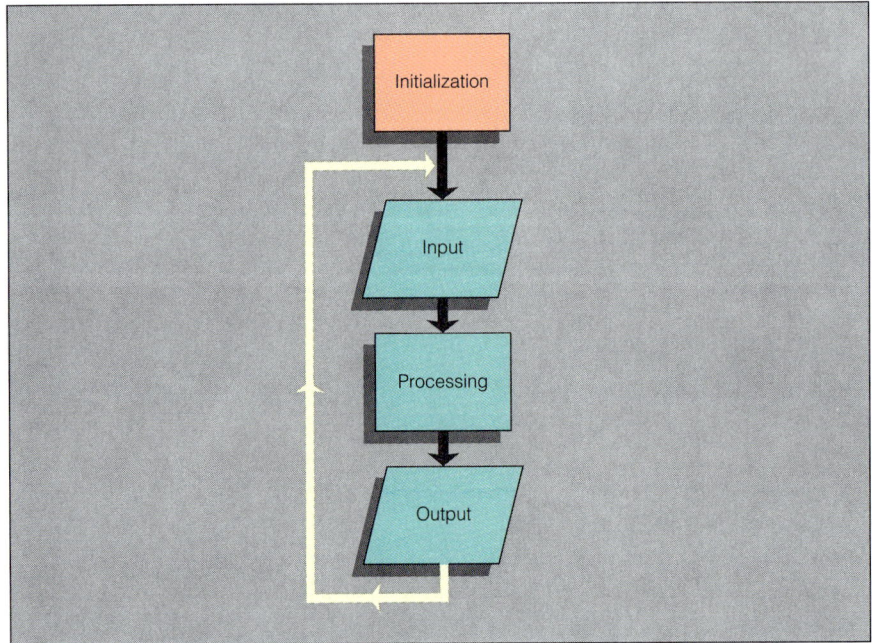

The program is written in such a manner that it incorporates a **loop**, as pictured in Figure 2.8. After the output from the first record is produced, the program loops back around and repeats the processing for the next record. This looping is repeated as many times as necessary to process the records.

PROGRAMMING LANGUAGES

Many programming languages have been devised during the computer's relatively short history—at least several hundred. Only a few, however, have achieved widespread use. We have mentioned the most popular—BASIC, FORTRAN, and COBOL. Others include PL/I, Pascal, C, APL, Lisp, Prolog, and Ada.

Each language has been developed to perform a particular type of processing. FORTRAN and APL are intended to solve problems that involve a large amount of mathematics. COBOL and PL/I solve problems that involve large volumes of input and output data. Lisp and Prolog are ideal for expert systems. BASIC was intended initially to be used with a terminal, but now is a general-purpose language that is popular with micros.

Machine Language

The main reason that the languages were developed is that the computer responds only to **machine language**—a series of zeros and ones that appear meaningless to a human. The zeros and ones are the **binary coding**

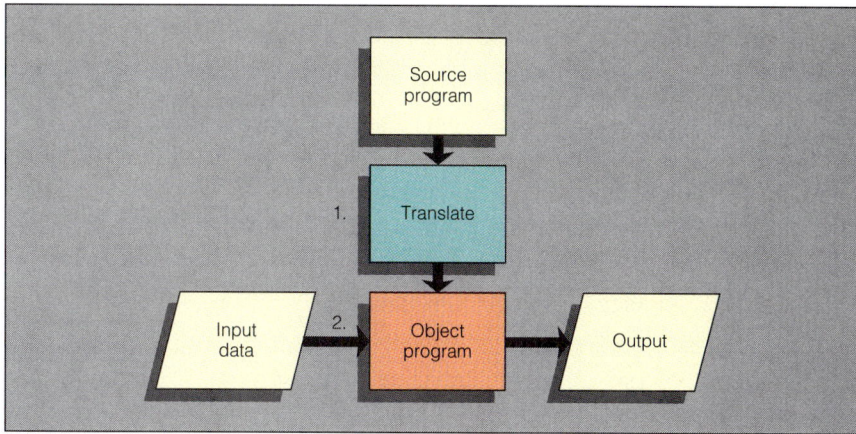

FIGURE 2.9

The Program Is Translated Before the Data Is Processed

system that the computer uses to represent data and instructions. This binary system is suited to the electronic nature of the computer whereby a one can represent an electronic switch that is *on*, and a zero can represent a switch that is *off*.

The first computers were programmed in machine language, but it quickly became clear that there must be a better way. The better way consists of a computer program that lets the programmer use a language more like English and mathematics that is translated into machine language. The computer program that does the translation is called a **translator**. This approach makes both the programmer and the computer happy—the programmer uses a meaningful language, and the computer gets its zeros and ones.

The program written by the programmer is called the **source program**. The translator translates the source program into a program in machine language that is called the **object program**. The computer then uses the object program to process the input data to produce the required output. This sequence of events is illustrated in Figure 2.9.

Statements versus Instructions

Earlier in this and in Chapter 1 we have used both the terms statement and instruction. Many people use these terms interchangeably but we will make a distinction. A **statement** is an order, written in the format of a particular programming language, that the programmer includes in the source program. An **instruction** is the order, coded in machine language, that the translator includes in the object program. The translator translates statements into instructions.

Assembly Language

The first translators were called **assemblers**, and they permitted the programmer to use an **assembly language**. Each computer had its own

FIGURE 2.10

A Program Written
in Assembly
Language

```
BEGIN     START   0
INFILE    DCB     DDNAME=INFILE,MACRF=GM,BLKSIZE=80,
                  LRECL=80,DSORG=PS,EODAD=EOF
OUTFILE   DCB     DDNAME=OUTFILE,MACRF=PM,BLKSIZE=80
                  LRECL=132,DSORG=PS
          BALR    12,0
          USING   *,12
          OPEN    INFILE,OUTFILE
READ      MVC     LINEOUT,SPACES
          GET     INFILE,CARDIN
          MVC     SALNOT,SALNO
          PACK    COMM,SALES
          AP      TOTSAL,SALES
          CP      COMM,=P'1000'
          BNL     PREM
REG       MP      COMM,=P'10'
EDIT      AP      CSUM,COMM
          MVC     COMMOUT,PATTRN
          ED      COMMOUT,COMM+1
          MVI     COMMOUT,C'$'
          MVC     LINEOUT(51),DETAIL
          PUT     OUTFILE,LINEOUT
          B       READ
PREM      SP      COMM,=P'1000'
          MP      COMM,=P'15'
          AP      COMM,=P'100'
          B       EDIT
EOF       MVC     LINEOUT+19(8),PATTRN2
          ED      LINEOUT+19(8),TOTAL
          MVC     LINEOUT+27(3),CENTS
          MVC     LINEOUT+32(7),PATTRN3
          ED      LINEOUT+32(8),CSUM
          PUT     OUTFILE,LINEOUT
CSUM      DC      PL4'0'
SPACES    DC      C' '
LINEOUT   DS      CL132
COMM      DS      PL4
CARDIN    DS      OCL80
SALNO     DS      CL15
SALES     DS      CL3
          DS      CL62
TOTSAL    DC      PL4'0'
DETAIL    DS      OCL51
          DS      CL10
SALNOT    DS      CL15
          DC      CL4' '
          DC      CL2'$'
DOLLARS   DS      CL3
CENTS     DC      CL10'.00'
COMMOUT   DS      CL7
PATTRN    DC      X'402020214B2020'
PATTRN2   DC      X'4020202020202021'
PATTRN3   DC      X402020214B2020'
          END     BEGIN
```

assembly language and assembler. You could not run an assembly language program on a computer other than the one for which it was designed. The assembly languages were said to be **machine-oriented languages** because of this hardware dependence.

An assembly language performs the translation on a "one instruction for one statement" basis. In other words, if the source program contains 250 statements, then the object program will contain 250 machine language instructions. While this might seem quite logical, we will soon see that it is not always the case.

An example of a program written in assembly language appears in Figure 2.10. We will include samples of different languages and each solves the same problem. The problem involves the computation of a sales commission for the firm's salespersons. Salespersons receive a 10 percent commission for the first $1,000 of merchandise that is sold. When sales exceed $1,000, the commission is 15 percent for the portion over $1,000. The BASIC program in Figure 2.6 solves this same problem.

Problem-Oriented Languages

During the first decade of the computer era, existing computers were made obsolete by new ones on almost a daily basis. This was costly for the users since the programs were machine oriented. A new set of programs had to be developed for each new computer.

A new breed of languages began to appear, called problem-oriented languages. **Problem-oriented languages** are not oriented to particular computers, but to particular types of problems. FORTRAN was the first such language, and we have seen that it is oriented toward mathematical problems. A FORTRAN program appears in Figure 2.11. COBOL was the next major problem-oriented language. It is oriented toward business problems. A COBOL program appears in Figure 2.12.

Compilers

Most of the translators in use today are for problem-oriented languages. A different name is used for most of the problem-oriented translators—**compiler**. You compile a problem-oriented source program into a machine-oriented object program. Some of the problem-oriented statements are very powerful compared to the assembly language statements. In many cases a single problem-oriented statement is compiled into several machine-language instructions. For example, a single WRITE EMPLOYEE-RECORD statement might generate fifteen machine-language instructions. The term **macro** (meaning large) is used to describe a statement that generates multiple machine-language instructions. The macro feature is one reason why the problem-oriented languages are so powerful, and so popular.

Interpreters

The BASIC language is an exception to the rule. BASIC is a problem-oriented language, but the most popular BASIC translators are called

FIGURE 2.11   A Program Written in FORTRAN

```
C       COMPUTE SALES COMMISSIONS
C       * * * * * * * * * * * * * * * * * * * * * * * *
C
C       VARIABLES
C               TSALES - TOTAL SALES
C               TCOMM  - TOTAL COMMISSION
C               SALES  - INDIVIDUAL SALES
C               COMM   - INDIVIDUAL COMMISSION
C               ID     - SALESPERSON IDENTIFICATION
C
C       INITIALIZATION
C
        TSALES = 0.
        TCOMM = 0.
C
C       INPUT SALESPERSON'S ID AND SALES
C
        WRITE(6,*) '        NUMBER', '   SALES', '            COMMISSION'
C
  5     READ(5,*,END=10) ID,SALES
C
        IF (SALES.GT.1000) THEN
           COMM = 100 + (SALES-1000) * .15
        ELSE
           COMM = SALES * .1
        ENDIF
C
        WRITE(6,*) ID,SALES,COMM
C
        TSALES = TSALES + SALES
        TCOMM = TCOMM + COMM
        GO TO 5
C
  10    WRITE(6,*)
        WRITE(6,*) 'TOTALS   ',TSALES,TCOMM
        STOP
        END
```

FIGURE 2.12   A Program Written in COBOL

```
IDENTIFICATION DIVISION.

  PROGRAM-ID.           SAL037.

  AUTHOR.               R Wayne Headrick.


ENVIRONMENT DIVISION.

  CONFIGURATION SECTION.

  SOURCE-COMPUTER.    ZENITH-248.


DATA DIVISION.

  WORKING-STORAGE SECTION.

    01   INPUT-DATA-ITEMS.
         05   SALESPERSON-NUMBER-IN     PIC 9(5).
         05   SALES-AMOUNT-IN           PIC 9(6)V9(2).
         05   IS-MORE-INPUT-DESIRED     PIC X  VALUE "Y".
              88  NO-MORE-INPUT-IS-DESIRED         VALUE "N"
                                                   FALSE "Y".

    01   OUTPUT-DATA-ITEMS.
         05   SALESPERSON-NUMBER-OUT    PIC ZZZZ9.
         05   SALES-AMOUNT-OUT          PIC ZZZ,ZZ9.99.
         05   COMMISSION-AMOUNT-OUT     PIC ZZZ,ZZ9.99.
         05   SUMMARY-TOTALS-OUT.
              10   TOTAL-SALES-OUT      PIC ZZZ,ZZZ,ZZ9.99.
              10   TOTAL-COMMISSIONS-OUT PIC ZZZ,ZZZ,ZZ9.99.

    01   ACCUMULATORS.
         05   TOTAL-SALES-ACCUM         PIC 9(9)V9(2).
         05   TOTAL-COMMISSIONS-ACCUM   PIC 9(9)V9(2).

    01   MISCELLANEOUS-DATA-ITEMS.
         05   COMMISSION-AMOUNT         PIC 9(5)V9(2).
         05   ACC-CTRL-1                PIC X(50)
              VALUE "LOW, REVERSE, TAB, NO BEEP, PROMPT".
         05   ACC-CTRL-2                PIC X(50)
              VALUE "LOW, REVERSE, UPDATE, NO BEEP, PROMPT".


PROCEDURE DIVISION.

  MAIN-PROGRAM-DRIVER.
       PERFORM UNTIL NO-MORE-INPUT-IS-DESIRED
           PERFORM GET-INPUT-DATA-ROUTINE
           PERFORM CALCULATE-COMMISSION-ROUTINE
           PERFORM DISPLAY-COMMISSION-ROUTINE
       END-PERFORM
       PERFORM DISPLAY-TOTALS-ROUTINE
       STOP RUN.
```

```
GET-INPUT-DATA-ROUTINE.
    DISPLAY "CALCULATE/ACCUMULATE SALES COMMISSIONS"
                LINE 3  POSITION 22  HIGH  ERASE
            "Enter salesperson number:"
                LINE 6  POSITION 25  LOW
            "Enter sales amount:"
                LINE 8  POSITION 25  LOW
    ACCEPT SALESPERSON-NUMBER-IN
                LINE 6  POSITION 52  CONTROL ACC-CTRL-1
    MOVE SALESPERSON-NUMBER-IN TO SALESPERSON-NUMBER-OUT
    DISPLAY SALESPERSON-NUMBER-OUT
                LINE 6  POSITION 52  HIGH
    ACCEPT SALES-AMOUNT-IN
                LINE 8  POSITION 48  CONTROL ACC-CTRL-1
    MOVE SALES-AMOUNT-IN TO SALES-AMOUNT-OUT
    DISPLAY SALES-AMOUNT-OUT
                LINE 8  POSITION 47  HIGH.

CALCULATE-COMMISSION-ROUTINE.
    IF SALES-AMOUNT-IN IS GREATER THAN 1000
        SUBTRACT 1000 FROM SALES-AMOUNT-IN
            GIVING COMMISSION-AMOUNT
        MULTIPLY 0.15 BY COMMISSION-AMOUNT
        ADD 100 TO COMMISSION-AMOUNT
    ELSE
        MULTIPLY SALES-AMOUNT-IN BY 0.10
            GIVING COMMISSION-AMOUNT
    END-IF
    ADD SALES-AMOUNT-IN TO TOTAL-SALES-ACCUM
    ADD COMMISSION-AMOUNT TO TOTAL-COMMISSIONS-ACCUM.

DISPLAY-COMMISSION-ROUTINE.
    MOVE COMMISSION-AMOUNT TO COMMISSION-AMOUNT-OUT
    DISPLAY "Commission amount:"
                LINE 11 POSITION 25  LOW
            COMMISSION-AMOUNT-OUT
                LINE 11  POSITION 47  HIGH
            "Do you want to continue (Y/N)?"
                LINE 16  POSITION 25  LOW
    ACCEPT IS-MORE-INPUT-DESIRED
                LINE 16  POSITION 56  CONTROL ACC-CTRL-2.

DISPLAY-TOTALS-ROUTINE.
    MOVE TOTAL-SALES-ACCUM TO TOTAL-SALES-OUT
    MOVE TOTAL-COMMISSIONS-ACCUM TO TOTAL-COMMISSIONS-OUT
    DISPLAY "Total sales:"
                LINE 6  POSITION 25  LOW  ERASE
            "Total commissions:"
                LINE 9  POSITION 25  LOW
            TOTAL-SALES-OUT
                LINE 6  POSITION 45  HIGH
            TOTAL-COMMISSIONS-OUT
                LINE 9  POSITION 45  HIGH.
```

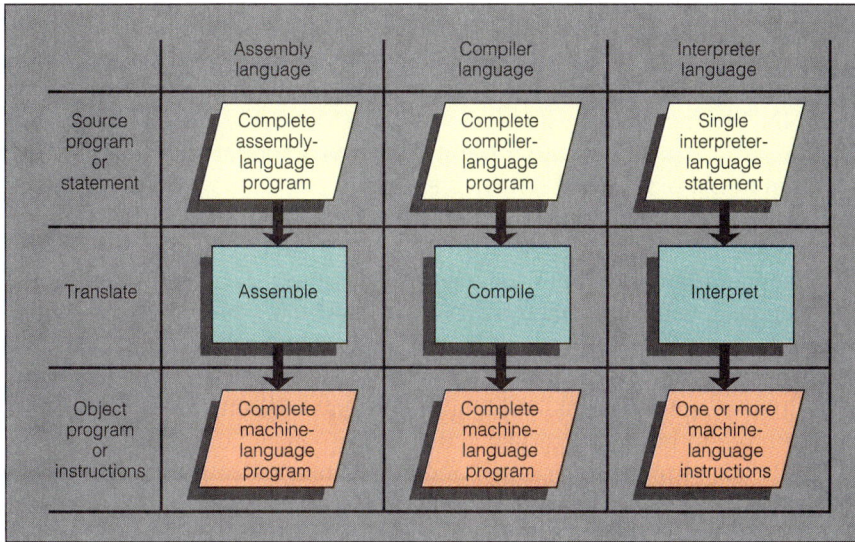

FIGURE 2.13

The Translation Process

interpreters. An **interpreter** does the same thing as a compiler, but it does it one statement at a time.

A compiler goes through the entire source program, statement-by-statement, and converts it into a complete object program. An interpreter, on the other hand, translates a statement and then executes it. Then it translates another. You do not end up with a complete object program when an interpreter is used.

Summarizing the Translation Process

Figure 2.13 summarizes the translation process. A translator converts a source program written by the programmer into an object program. The source program consists of programming-language statements. The object program consists of machine-language instructions.

When the programmer uses an assembly language, an assembler performs the translation. When a problem-oriented language other than BASIC is used, a compiler performs the translation. When BASIC is used, either a compiler or interpreter can perform the translation.

Fourth-Generation Languages

If you read the computer literature and talk with computer people, sooner or later you will hear the term *generation*. Computer hardware evolved through a series of **generations**—first the circuitry consisted of electronic vacuum tubes, then transistors, then silicon chips, and so on. During the 1970s the improvements in technology became less dramatic than in the earlier years, and the hardware generations began to blur. The interest in keeping track of the hardware generations subsided, and you do not often hear the term used that way any more.

The term lives on, however, in relation to software. The term **fourth-generation language**, abbreviated to **4GL**, currently is receiving attention. A 4GL offers a step beyond the problem-oriented languages in ease of use. While some of the problem-oriented statements are much like English and math, the programmer must assemble a large number of statements to perform a task. As an example, if the user wants a special report, a COBOL program might require 200 statements.

Fourth-generation languages were developed so that users can obtain information more easily—perhaps with a dozen orders or directives. The fourth-generation languages are also called **natural languages** since they are even more natural in their syntax or format than the problem-oriented ones.

The term **nonprocedural language** is also used to describe a fourth-generation language. When assembling the orders or directives of a 4GL, you do not have to be so concerned with the sequence. Such freedom is not characteristic of machine-oriented and problem-oriented languages, where the sequence of the statements must be exact. For this reason the machine-oriented and problem-oriented languages often are called **procedural languages**.

A fourth-generation language is really not a language as such. It does not have the lengthy statement set. You direct the computer by entering orders that are more powerful than statements. The powerful orders are called **commands**. In some cases, you only have to press two or three keys on the keyboard to cause things to happen.

The term **user friendly** is used to describe this new type of software. Most of the software that you hear about today falls in this fourth-generation, user-friendly category. Software such as Lotus 1-2-3 and dBASE III Plus are examples of 4GL.

Figure 2.14 illustrates the few lines of commands that are entered into the INQUIRE fourth-generation language to produce the illustrated report. The user specifies that the report is to include the employees grouped by department, with each department's employees listed in descending order based on their salary.

Most of the activity today is in the 4GL area, and this activity is expected to continue. The fourth-generation languages are the wave of the future, and we will return to them in the next chapter when we address prewritten software.

PROGRAM DEVELOPMENT

When a firm decides to develop its own software, there are a series of steps that must be taken. The process involves the user, and can involve the information specialists. In end-user computing the user performs all of the steps alone. Otherwise, the user and information specialists work together.

The steps are diagrammed in Figure 2.15. The diagram is a special type of flowchart, called a system flowchart. A **system flowchart** shows the pro-

FIGURE 2.14   An Example of the INQUIRE Fourth-Generation Language

```
Input

SCAN, TAB NAME CURTITL CURSAL CURDEPT, HEADER 'EMPLOYEES GROUPED

BY DEPARTMENT' " 'AND ORDERED BY SALARY', TITLE 'EMPLOYEE NAME'

NAME (JOB TITLE) CURTITL 'SALARY' CURSAL (CURRENT DEPT) CURDEPT,

SORT CURDEPT (A) CURSAL (D).


Output

                 EMPLOYEES GROUPED BY DEPARTMENT              PAGE    1
                                                              09/15/89
                       AND ORDERED BY SALARY

        EMPLOYEE NAME           JOB          SALARY      CURRENT
                               TITLE                     DEPT
        -----------------------------------------------------------

        JEAN CHING       SR STATISTICIAN       $24,500.76    201

        SAM JACKSON      GRP LDR SYS DEVELOPMENT  $24,000.00  201

        RICHARD HOPKINS  SR SYSTEMS PROGRAMMER   $23,584.75   201

        JANICE PARKS     SR PROGRAMMER          $22,055.79    201

        PAT FLEMING      PROGRAMMER-ANALYST     $19,759.31    201

        JOHN H. WHITE    MGR-CUSTOMER SUPPORT   $27,895.34    316

        BILL APPLE       PERSONNEL MANAGER      $25,485.50    316

        JANET WILLIAMS   SR SYSTEMS ANALYST     $23,500.00    316

        NANCY W. MOORE   SR SYSTEMS PROGRAMMER  $22,565.77    316

        GEORGE MILLER    COST ANALYST           $21,800.00    316

        JAMES GLEASON    ASST MGR-CUST. SUPP.   $21,475.85    316

        SALLY SCHUSTER   SYSTEMS ANALYST        $19,480.00    316

        JAMES P. HILL    APPLICATIONS GRP LDR   $19,259.99    316

        ROBERT P. KELLY  PROGRAMMER             $13,600.00    316

        FRED SMITH       RECEPTIONIST            $9,000.00    316

        JOE DECKER       CHEMIST                $16,445.00    384

        WAYNE RUIZ       MGR PERSONNEL TRAINING $27,845.50    401
```

FIGURE 2.15

The Programming Process

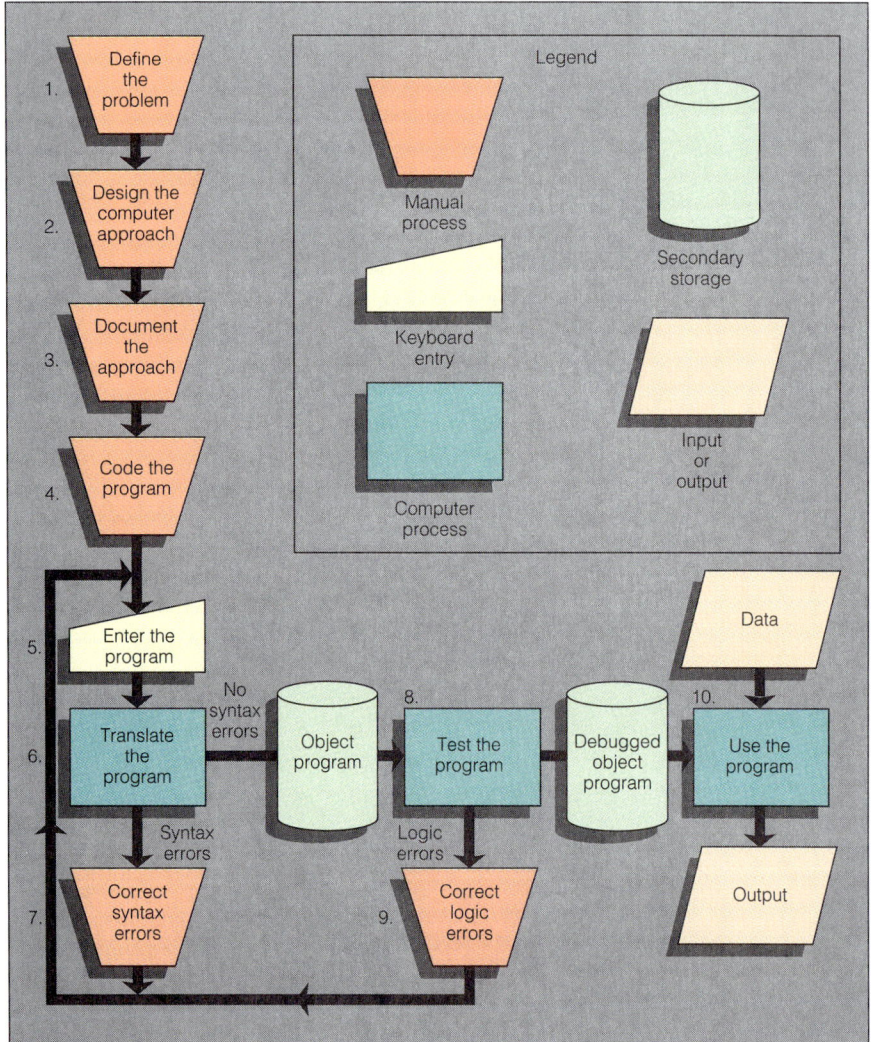

cessing steps for an entire system such as payroll, sales analysis, or inventory. The legend in the figure explains the meaning of the symbols.

1. *Define the problem.* There is a problem to be solved. Let us use the salesperson commission system as an example. Assume that the current, manual system frequently computes the commissions and bonuses incorrectly, and the checks often are late. Management decides to put the application on the computer. This is the type of data processing application that is developed jointly by users and information specialists. The information specialist who has the responsibility of working with the user in defining computer solutions is the **systems analyst**. The systems analyst knows both com-

FIGURE 2.16

A System Flowchart
of the Salesperson
Commission System

The figure shows a system flowchart with the following labeled elements:

- Sales order forms (paper document, top)
- 1. Enter sales order data → Sales order forms
- 2. Compute sales commission
- 3. Place sales order forms in file
- Sales commission report
- Sales order form file

Legend

- A paper document
- A document storage file (such as a file cabinet)

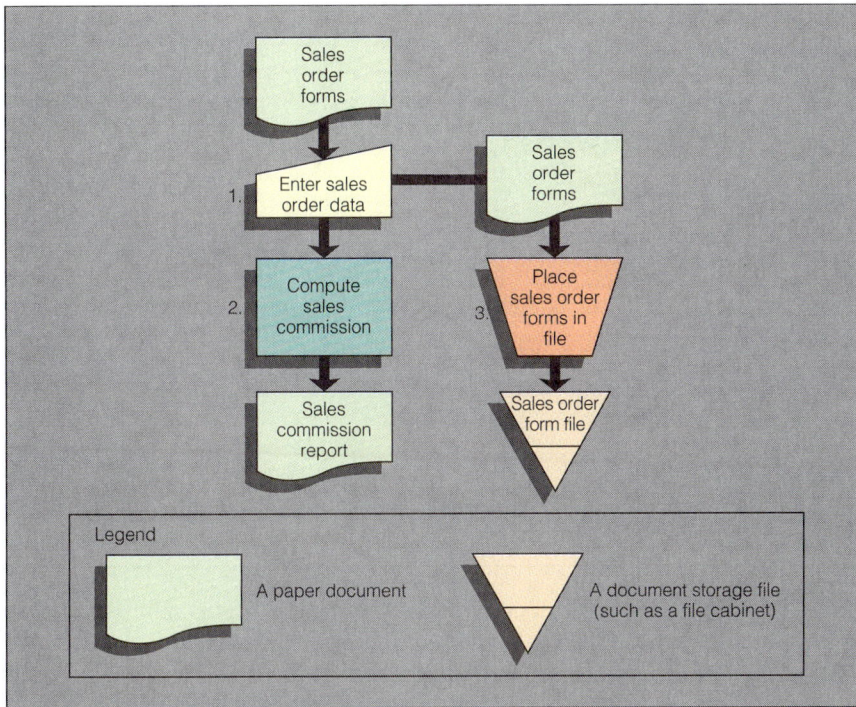

puting and business systems. The user and the systems analyst
jointly discuss the problem until the user is satisfied that the analyst
understands it thoroughly.

2. *Design the computer approach.* The systems analyst determines the
best way for the computer to handle the new application. For example, will sales data be entered from terminals in the sales department, or from terminals in the computer department? Should the
output be printed on the printer or displayed on the screen? The
systems analyst considers the advantages and disadvantages of each
alternative, and identifies the approach that appears to be best for
the user.

    The analyst reports the findings and recommendations to the
user, and the user either approves or disapproves. This relationship,
where the systems analyst advises and the user decides, is the
proper one when these two professionals work together.

3. *Document the approach.* The systems analyst prepares written documentation to give to the programmer. The documentation describes
the task that the computer is to perform, and can take several forms.
The documentation might be a simple narrative, or it might be a system flowchart as shown in Figure 2.16. The system flowchart is the
big picture.

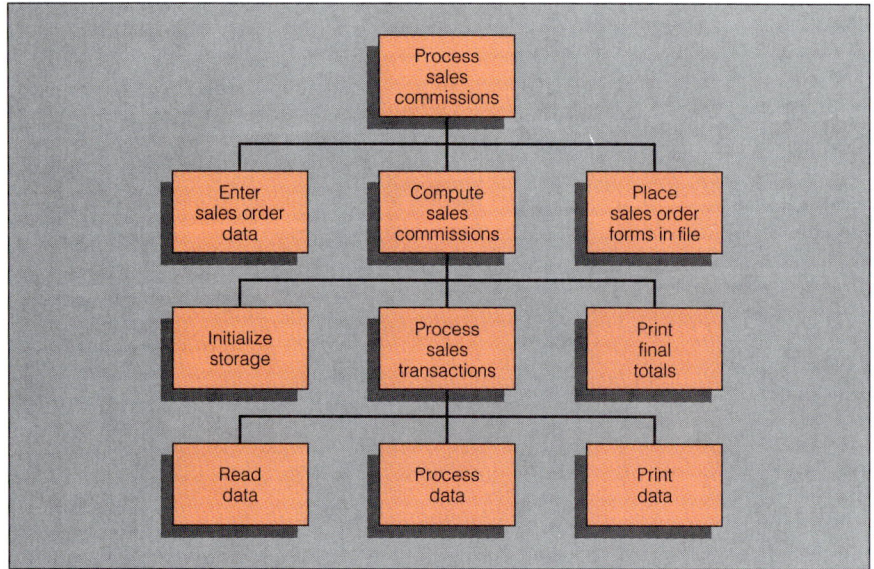

Another form of documentation that the systems analyst can use
is a **structure chart**, also called a **hierarchy diagram**. A structure
chart has the same general appearance as an organization chart, and
is illustrated in Figure 2.17. The overall process, or system, is represented by the rectangle at the top, which is subdivided successively
into component parts on lower levels.

The systems analyst gives all of the documentation to the programmer, who has the task of using the chosen programming language to convert the design into the source program.

4. *Code the program.* If the system is a simple one, the programmer may
code the program directly from the systems analyst's documentation. Most likely, however, the programmer will prepare documentation that is more detailed.

One example of more-detailed documentation is the program
flowchart illustrated in Figure 2.18. The **program flowchart** illustrates each major step that the computer must take in a single program.

Another documentation technique that is rivaling the program
flowchart in popularity is **structured English**. A sample appears in
Figure 2.19. Structured English looks like computer language but it
is not. The programmer uses structured English to rough out the
logic that is then transferred into the appropriate language.

This is the manner in which the logic of a computer program
evolves. You begin with a general description of what the system
will do, and the description is gradually made more specific. The
term **top-down design** has been used to describe this manner of

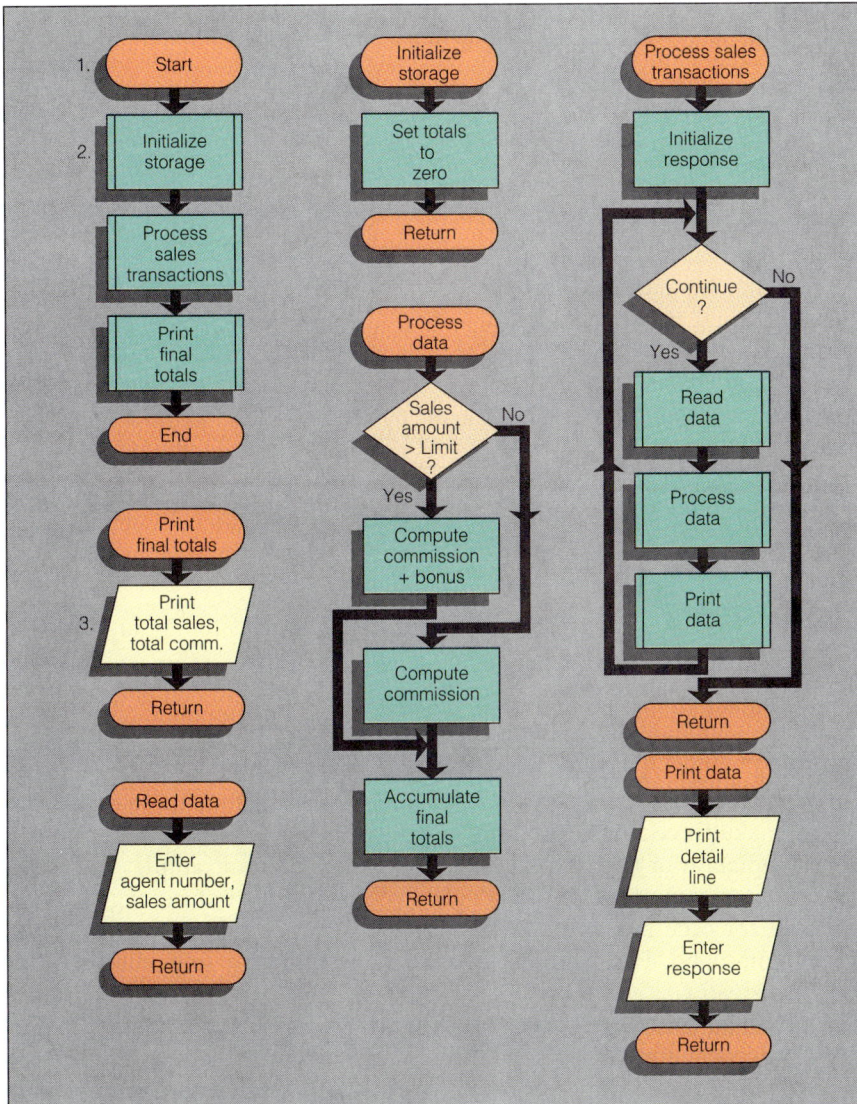

FIGURE 2.18

A Program Flowchart of the Salesperson Commission System

starting with the overall system and then designing the subsystems to integrate properly. The term **structured design** is also appropriate.

5. *Enter the program.* After the programmer has coded all of the statements, the source program is keyed into the computer, using either the keyboard of a small computer or a terminal connected to a large computer.

6. *Translate the program.* A translator is used to translate the source program into the object program.

FIGURE 2.19   Structured English Documentation of the Salesperson Commission Program

```
Initialize-storage
    TOTAL.SALES, TOTAL.COM = 0
Process-sales-data
    WHILE more records
        Do read-data
        Do process-data
        Do print-data
Final-totals
    PRINT TOTAL.SALES, TOTAL.COM
Read-data
    INPUT SALESPERSON.NO, SALES.AMT
Process-data
    IF SALES.AMT > 1000
        THEN COMM.AMT = 100 + (SALES.AMT - 1000) * .15
        ELSE COMM.AMT = SALES.AMT * .10
    Accumulate TOTAL.SALES, TOTAL.COM
Print-data
    PRINT detail line
    Determine if more records
```

7. *Correct the syntax errors.* There are two kinds of errors that you can make in coding a program—syntax and logic. A **syntax error** is a violation of the language's format rules. As an example, you leave out a comma or put in a space where it does not belong. A **logic error** occurs if you code a command properly, but it is the wrong command. For example, you want to subtract a sales discount but instead you add it.

   The computer detects the syntax errors during translation, and displays **error messages** on the screen or prints them on the printer. The programmer corrects the errors, and the translation process is repeated until a program with no syntax errors is obtained. The term **debugging** is used to describe the process of correcting program errors—both syntax and logic.

8. *Test the program.* When there are no syntax errors, the program can be executed with **test data** that checks the logical paths and arithmetic operations in the program.

9. *Correct the logic errors.* The programmer and the systems analyst examine the test results and make any necessary corrections. The modified program must be translated again by repeating Steps 5 through 8.

10. *Use the program.* When the logic errors have been corrected, the object program is used to process the firm's data. The user and systems analyst monitor the performance to ensure that the program accomplishes what was intended.

11. *Maintain the program.* The new system may be used for years, however situations change. Perhaps the government changes a tax law, the firm adds a new product line, or a supplier changes the way it computes trade discounts. These changes must be reflected in the computer programs. The activity that keeps the system current is called **program maintenance**. A significant portion of a firm's programming activity usually is devoted to such maintenance. This step is not included explicitly in Figure 2.15 because all of the steps (1 through 10) must be repeated.

No Need to Reassemble or Recompile

Before we leave this discussion of the programming process we should recognize an important point. Once a program written in an assembly or a compiler language is debugged, the object program is used to process the data. There is no need to assemble or compile each time. However, an interpreter is different. Each time the source program written in an interpreter language is used, it must be interpreted. The program written in the interpreter language generally takes longer to run than a program written in an assembly or compiler language for this reason.

THE STRUCTURED PROGRAMMING APPROACH

For the first 20 or so years of the computer era, each programmer could code the program in the manner that he or she preferred—as long as the program accomplished its job. As a result, the format of each program tended to be unique.

This approach had two serious weaknesses, and they both affected program maintenance. One weakness was the lack of a standard format. Each time a programmer maintained a program, time was spent in understanding the format. In most cases, the programmer doing the maintenance was not the same programmer who created the program. The other weakness was the influence of program size on complexity. The many paths in a large program had to be retraced by the maintenance programmer in order to understand the logic.

These were serious problems for a firm that had to maintain perhaps hundreds of programs. It was this difficulty of maintenance that provided the main stimulus for a new approach to programming.

In the mid-1960s, the new approach first appeared. The new approach, called **structured programming**, is a technique for developing a program that subdivides the program into modules, which are arranged in a hierarchy. In addition, the processes within the modules are arranged in three fundamental constructs.

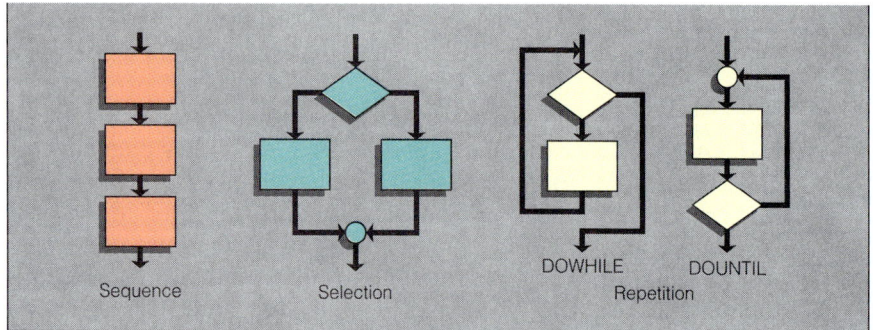

Modules Arranged in a Hierarchy

The structure chart in Figure 2.17 illustrates the hierarchy concept. Each rectangle represents a portion of the program called a module. A **module** is a series of statements that accomplish some particular processing.

Fundamental Constructs

A structured program uses only three constructs. A **construct** is the pattern in which statements are executed. The three constructs are sequence, selection, and repetition, and they are illustrated in Figure 2.20.

The **sequence construct** consists of a series of statements that are executed one after the other.

The **selection construct** consists of a logical decision that determines which of two paths the processing will follow. The diamond in the figure represents the decision point.

The **repetition construct** consists of a loop that is executed a certain number of times. The number depends on the results of the logical decision either at the beginning of the loop or the end. When the decision is made at the beginning, the loop is called a **DOWHILE loop**—the processing in the loop is repeated while a certain condition exists. When the decision is made at the end, the loop is called a **DOUNTIL loop**—the processing in the loop is repeated until the decision is made to stop.

Why Structured Programming Should Be Used

Most firms require their programmers to use structured programming when developing business programs. Large programs become more manageable and program maintenance is performed easier.

If the user engages in end-user computing, then he or she has the option of using structured programming or some other, less-disciplined technique. However, the choice should be structured programming. The standard format simplifies the programming task by providing a guideline to follow, the coding proceeds more rapidly, and the chance of error is minimized. Also, if structured programming is used, the program can be maintained by the information specialist more easily.

Many Unstructured Programs Are Still in Use

Before we leave the topic of structured programming we must recognize an important point. Many of the programs that are in use today were created before structured programming was developed. Firms are converting the older programs to the structured format gradually, but the volume is so large that it will take years to finish the task.

SUMMARY

The computing equipment is called the hardware, and the programs that cause the hardware to perform specific tasks are called the software. Firms must decide whether to make their own custom software or buy prewritten software.

The user benefits from a programming knowledge by achieving more processing power and being able to communicate better with information specialists.

One of the basic fundamentals of computing is the stored program concept. Simply stated, it means that the program is stored in primary storage along with the data that is being processed. This concept enables the user to tailor a computer to a specific task.

All statements include a verb, and they can include an object. Some statements have no objects, some have one, and some have several. There are five primary types of statements—input/output, data movement, arithmetic, logic, and control. All of a computer's arithmetic ability is provided by addition, subtraction, multiplication, division, and exponentiation.

Before you use a computer to accumulate totals, you should initialize those storage positions. Then, the program can perform input, processing, and output. If you want the program to process multiple records, you incorporate a loop into it.

Programming languages have evolved from the early machine-oriented assembly languages to the problem-oriented languages such as FORTRAN, COBOL, and BASIC. The programmer uses a programming language to prepare a source program which a translator converts into an object program in machine language. The source program consists of statements, whereas the object program consists of instructions.

The translator that converts an assembly language program is called an assembler. The translator that converts an entire problem-oriented program in one process is called a compiler, whereas the translator that performs the same operation a statement at a time is called an interpreter. Most BASIC translators are interpreters. Once a program written in assembly or compiler language is debugged, its object program is used to process the data.

A new breed of languages has come onto the scene—the fourth-generation languages, or 4GL. Actually, these are not languages in the true sense because they do not have lengthy statement sets. Instead, they use more powerful commands. The 4GL are more natural for the user to use, prompting the term user friendly. In addition, the 4GL do not have to adhere to the same strict sequence requirements of a programming language.

Development of a computer program consists of ten steps that are performed by the user alone, or with the help of the systems analyst and the programmer. The user and the analyst begin with the big picture that is gradually made more specific, prompting the term top-down approach. This process is reflected in the documentation. The documentation prepared by the systems analyst tends to be general whereas that of the programmer tends to be specific. The programming process is repeated when maintenance is performed.

The first programs had no standard format, and that feature made maintenance difficult. The modern approach is structured programming that subdivides a program into modules that are arranged in a hierarchy. In addition, only three constructs, or patterns, are used in arranging statements in a module.

KEY CONCEPTS

The difference between hardware and software

How software tailors a general-purpose computer to specific tasks

How a computer program consists of initialization followed by three basic operations—input, processing, and output

How a program processes multiple records by means of a looping action

The necessity of translating a source program into an object program

The distinguishing features of an assembler, a compiler, and an interpreter

KEY TERMS

Hardware
Software
Prewritten software, packaged software, off-the-shelf software
Stored program concept
Programmer
Initialization
Flowchart
Loop
Machine language
Translator
Source program
Object program

Statement
Instruction
Assembler
Assembly language
Machine-oriented language
Problem-oriented language
Compiler
Macro
Interpreter
Fourth-generation language (4GL), natural language, nonprocedural language
Command
User friendly

Systems analyst
Top-down design, structured design
Syntax error
Logic error
Structured programming
Module
Sequence construct
Selection construct
Repetition construct

QUESTIONS

1. How does a computer-using firm tailor general-purpose hardware to its specific needs?

2. When would a large firm with its own programming staff purchase prewritten software? Why would they do it?

3. Why should a user know how to program?

4. What are the five fundamental types of statements?

5. When is it necessary that a program contain an initialization module?

6. What three operations are repeated for each record to be processed? What is incorporated into the program to cause this repeating process?

7. What is the only language that the computer uses to process data? What two digits are used to represent this language?

8. Explain why you would not find an instruction in a source program.

9. Name three types of translators. In what ways do they differ?

10. Why would a user prefer to use a 4GL rather than a problem-oriented language?

11. At which step in program development does the programmer first participate? Which information specialist is involved prior to this step?

12. What distinguishes the tools used by the programmer from those used by the systems analyst?

13. When debugging a program, which type of error does the computer catch? Which type do the programmer and systems analyst catch?

14. What feature of an interpreter causes it to process data slower than do an assembler or compiler?

15. Why should a user use structured programming?

CASE PROBLEM

Feldman's Department Store

It did not take you long to start your own computer consulting business after receiving your MIS degree. One day, the phone rang, and it was Arnold Feldman, president of the largest department store in Moline. You had met Arnold at a concert, and told him of your new company.

Arnold explained that he was not happy with his computing operation and wanted you to take a look. You said "Sure," and were on your way. After a brief orientation chat, you interviewed Betsy Colgan, the manager of programming.

"Betsy, Arnold tells me that you have had a hard time keeping programmers—they leave just as soon as they become trained. Is that true?"

"That's right," Betsy explained. "I guess it's because of the maintenance programming. Most of our new hires have no programming experience and they think it's going to be a piece of cake. When they find out about the maintenance they look for companies where there is more new programming to do."

You asked Betsy if you could take a look at the program documentation, and she told you that they didn't have any. Then, you asked her if they were using structured programming. She explained that all of their programs were written before structured programming came along. They have been so busy maintaining the old programs that they have not had time to write any new ones, using structured techniques. Betsy doesn't even include structured programming in her in-house training program.

With all of this good news, you said "Good bye," and headed for Norman Lamb's office. He is the vice president of finance, and you wanted to interview a user. You got right to the point with "Norman, what is the status of end-user computing here at Feldman's?" You were surprised when Norman said "What's end-user computing?" You thought everyone knew that. Norman went on to explain that he and some of the other managers would like to get more out of the computer, but that the computer department could not get around to the managers' jobs. "They are so short-handed that it is all they can do just to keep the accounting applications running."

You figured that there was no reason to continue your conversation with Norman, and that you had a good enough picture to get back with Arnold. When you sat down in front of Arnold's desk, you looked him in the eye, and said: "Arnold, you have good reason to be concerned."

1. Who is responsible for the programmer turnover—Arnold, Betsy, or Norman? Support your answer.

2. Is there anything that Betsy can do to reduce the amount of time spent on maintenance? If so, what?

3. Should any changes be made in the hiring and training policies as they relate to programmers? If so, what? What benefits would you expect from the changes?

4. What can be done to provide the managers with better computer support? Assume that the size of the programming staff cannot be increased.

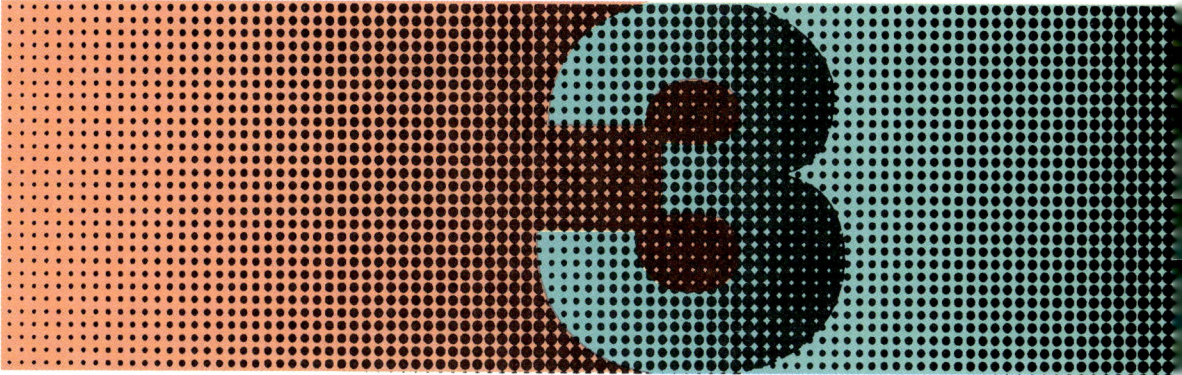

Using Prewritten Software

LEARNING OBJECTIVES   After studying this chapter, you should:

- Have an understanding of how prewritten software has evolved
- Know how to classify the different types of prewritten software into major categories and subcategories
- Know the main features of each type of prewritten software
- Understand how software can be made user friendly

OVERVIEW

In Chapter 2, our attention focused on the process of writing your own programs. In this chapter, our attention shifts to the other fundamental way of obtaining information from the computer—using prewritten software. The chapter begins with a brief review of how prewritten software evolved, and then the major categories and subcategories of prewritten software are identified and explained. Examples are offered of the different types of software that are available for each subcategory. The chapter concludes with a description of two popular ways software can be made more user friendly.

THE EVOLUTION OF PREWRITTEN SOFTWARE

The volume and variety of prewritten software keeps increasing each year. There was no prewritten software available for the first generation of computers. The firm's programmers had to create their own programs. The situation gradually improved as such hardware vendors as NCR, Burroughs, and Univac began to understand the needs of business users.

First There Were the Translators

The first prewritten packages were the language translators described in Chapter 2. Up until the early 1960s, these translators provided most of the prewritten software selection. They were used on mainframes, and came free-of-charge with the hardware.

Then Came Application Software

The hardware vendors then began to recognize the unique data processing needs of such industries as manufacturing, insurance, and banking. Software packages began to appear that could perform some of the most important applications in these industries. For example, packages could maintain the inventory for a manufacturer, handle the daily policy accounting for an insurance company, and maintain checking and savings account records for a bank.

Now there were two categories of prewritten software—the translators and the data processing packages. The translators became known as **system software** since they were necessary to make effective use of a particular computer. The data processing packages became known as **application software** since they performed the firm's data processing applications.

The main difference between system and application software is that the application software processes the user's data, and the system software does not. The system software is required to use both the hardware and the application software. All firms using the same computer can use the same system software, but application software is useful only to those firms for which it is intended. For example, an insurance company and an auto parts distributor may both use the same FORTRAN compiler but use different application software. The insurance company's application software emphasizes policyholder accounting, whereas that of the parts distributor emphasizes inventory management.

In 1964, IBM announced a new type of system software. The software could perform many of the functions previously done by human operators. The new software was called an operating system. An **operating system** is a master control program that manages many of the activities involved with using a computer. We will provide a more detailed description of the operating system later in this chapter.

The next big breakthrough in prewritten software came as a result of the microcomputer revolution. The hardware vendors who pioneered the early micros—Apple, Commodore, and Tandy—recognized that many users could not afford to hire programmers. The solution was to furnish all of the software that would be needed. A complete line of microcomputer software was developed—application software to perform the primary accounting functions as well as system software.

Then Came Application-Development Software

While the micro users were receiving most of the attention, the mainframe users were attempting to implement databases and were having a difficult time. The programming required to keep the files current was very complex. Both hardware and software vendors came to the rescue with software that was intended to manage a firm's database. The term **database management system** or **DBMS** was coined.

The DBMSs were not system software, and they were not application software—at least not the traditional type. These new packages were not geared to any particular application such as payroll or inventory, but they were used in processing a firm's data by maintaining the data in the database. The DBMSs could assist the users in developing their applications. The mainframe DBMS was the first example of what we call **application-development software**.

Five major classes of application-development software have evolved—database management systems, electronic spreadsheets, graphics packages, office automation packages, and expert systems. You have heard of many of the brands—VisiCalc, dBASE, WordStar, Lotus, Rbase, and WordPerfect. These are only a few of several hundred such packages.

The greatest amount of activity in the computing field today is in the area of application-development software for micros. The market is dominated by the software vendors—firms such as Microsoft, Borland International, and Lotus Development Corporation.

Figure 3.1 is a structure chart that shows how prewritten software is organized into categories and subcategories. We will use this framework as a basis for the discussion that follows.

SYSTEM SOFTWARE

There are three fundamental types of system software—operating systems, language translators, and utility programs.

Operating Systems

The most important type of system software is the operating system. The operating system is a type of gatekeeper, as shown in Figure 3.2. The user must go through the operating system to get to the computer.

Another way to think of the operating system is as an outer box, enclosing all other software. Have you ever opened a gift package only to find another package inside? The relationship between the operating system and other software can be viewed in this way, as shown in Figure 3.3. The

FIGURE 3.1

The Organization of
Prewritten Software

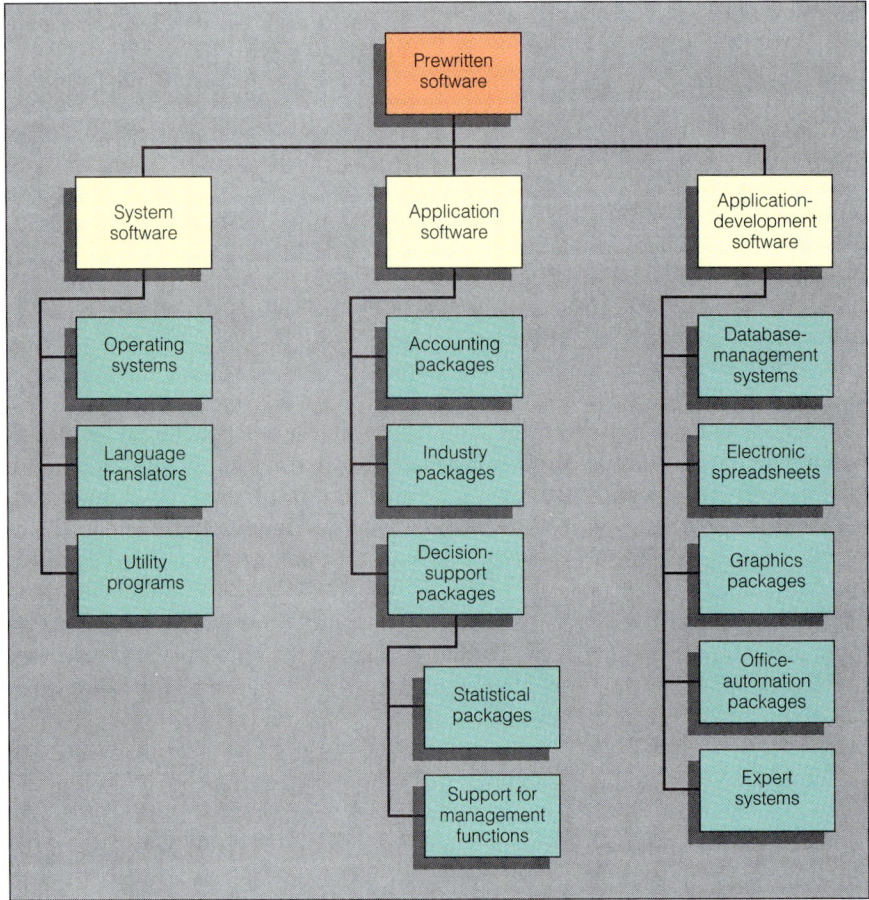

operating-system box must be opened to get to the inner boxes—the translators, the application software, and the application-development software.

**Component Parts
of an Operating
System**

The operating system is not one program, but several. The programs are too large to fit all of them into the computer's primary storage, so the most important part is stored there and the other parts are kept in secondary

FIGURE 3.2

The Operating
System as a
Gatekeeper

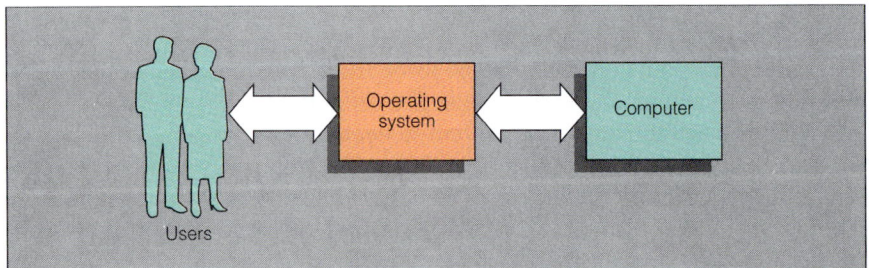

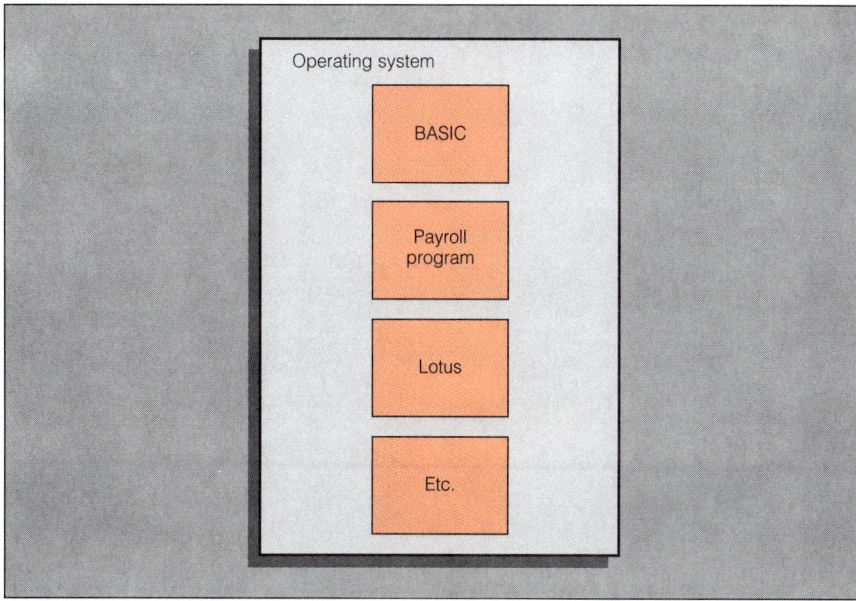

FIGURE 3.3
The Operating System as the Outer Box

storage. The parts in secondary storage are read into primary storage when they are needed.

The most important part is the **supervisor**, also called the **monitor** or the **executive routine**. The supervisor stays in primary storage all of the time. The term **main-memory resident** is used to describe the supervisor since it resides in the main memory. The other parts are called **transient routines** since they are maintained in secondary storage and transferred into primary storage when needed. One of the transient routines is **IOCS**, which stands for **Input-Output Control System**. This is the software that handles all of the exchange of data between the CPU and the input units, output units, and secondary storage.

The transient routines share the same area of primary storage, called an **overlay area.** When a transient routine is needed, it is read into the overlay area. The new routine is overlaid on top of the previous routine, erasing it. In this manner, the transient routines reside in primary storage only when they are being used.

Figure 3.4 shows the contents of primary and secondary storage as an application program is being run.

An operating system can perform as many as six basic functions:

Operating System Functions

1. *Schedule jobs.* The operating system can determine the sequence in which jobs are run, using a set of priorities established by the firm. The more important programs are run before the less important ones. This scheduling was performed by the human operator before the operating system came along.

FIGURE 3.4

The Operating System Resides in Both Primary and Secondary Storage as an Application Program Is Being Run

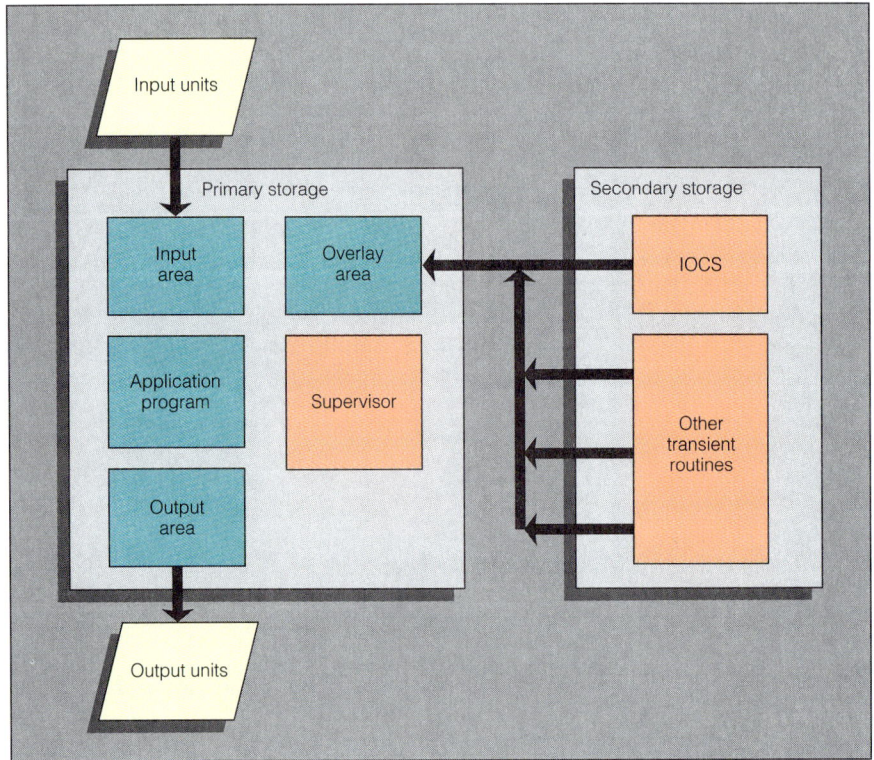

2. *Manage the system's hardware and software resources.* The operating system causes the user's program to be run by loading it into primary storage and then causing the various hardware units to perform as specified by the program. IOCS becomes involved when the program requires that data be read from input and secondary-storage units or written to output or secondary-storage units.

3. *Provide security.* The operating system can require the user to enter a **password**—a group of characters that identifies the user as one authorized to have access to the computer. This is one of the ways that the computer's programs and data are protected from persons who might inflict damage of some kind.

4. *Enable multiple users to share the computer.* The operating systems for some computers can handle the programs for many users simultaneously—a feature called **multiprogramming**. Actually, the computer can run only a single user's program at a time. The computer will execute a few instructions from one user's program, then execute a few instructions from another user's program, then another, and so on. Eventually the computer will return to the first program and execute a few more instructions. In this manner, programs are executed a

few instructions at a time rather than all at once. The operating system controls the switching back and forth between programs.

5. *Handle interrupts.* An **interrupt** is when one program wants to use the computer while another program is running. The operating system temporarily suspends processing the running program and handles the interrupt. In many cases the interrupt is a user request for information from the database. The operating system loads the application program that handles the request and causes the program to be run. Then the operating system resumes processing the interrupted job.

6. *Maintain usage records.* When multiple users share the computer, the operating system maintains records of the amount of time and the particular units that each user utilizes. The firm often charges the users' departments for this expense to maintain accountability for the system.

Both mainframes and micros have operating systems, but the systems perform different tasks or perform them differently. For example, the operating system for the mainframe permits multiprogramming, but most microcomputer operating systems do not. The mainframe operating system keeps usage records, but most micro operating systems do not.

Mainframe versus Microcomputer Operating Systems

```
//PAYROLL   JOB (N142.102D,S05,002,BI),'PROGRAM1'
//*MAIN        USER=N142BI.ORG=RCC
//*PASSWORD********************************************
//*TAMU        HOLDOUT,PRTY=5
//STEP1      EXEC NCBCLG,REGION.GO=512K,PARM.GO='SIZE=448K'
//COB.SYSLIB   DD DSN=USR.B49K.XX.PAYLIB,DISP=SHR
//COB.SYSIN    DD DSN=USR.N142.BI.PAYLAB,DISP=SHR
//GO.MASTER    DD DSN=USR.B49K.XX.PAYMAST,DISP=SHR
//GO.REPORT01 DD SYSOUT=A,DCB=(BLKSIZE=133,RECFM=FA)
//GO.REPORT02 DD SYSOUT=A,DCB=(BLKSIZE=133,RECFM=FA)
```

FIGURE 3.5

An Example of a Job-Control Language

Another area where mainframe and micro operating systems differ is in the area of user friendliness. As a rule it is more difficult to use the mainframe operating system than that of a micro. To get past the operating system gatekeeper of a mainframe, the user must enter identification codes and specifications of what is to be done. These codes are entered into the terminal keyboard in a special language called **job-control language** or **JCL**. The JCL for a mainframe can be very complex. Figure 3.5 is a sample. The JCL for a single-user micro, however, is very easy to use, contributing to its user friendliness.

There are several such features that distinguish mainframe and micro operating systems, but they are becoming less distinct as micro operating systems become more sophisticated. As an example, some newer micro operating systems permit multiprogramming.

Language Translators

When a programmer wants to translate a program, the statements are entered into the computer as described in the previous chapter. The JCL identifies the translator to be used. The supervisor obtains the appropriate translator from secondary storage, and the translation is performed.

In a multiprogramming environment, multiple programs can be translated at the same time, using different translators. The operating system will translate part of one, then translate part of another, and so on.

Utility Programs

Utility programs perform functions that are needed by all users of a particular computer. For example, utility programs for mainframe computers permit users to read a file of records from magnetic tape and print the records on the printer. This is a **tape-to-printer** utility. Similar utilities exist for **disk-to-printer, tape-to-disk**, and so on. Other utilities **sort** a file of records into a certain sequence, and **merge** two or more files into one. The utilities perform the functions without the need for programming.

Utility programs for microcomputers enable the users to perform certain functions involving the small, flexible magnetic **diskettes** that contain programs and data. Figure 3.6 illustrates a diskette. The diskette utilities

FIGURE 3.6

Microcomputer Utility Programs Facilitate the Use of Diskettes

enable you to perform operations such as copy a diskette, compare the data on two diskettes, and erase files from a diskette.

APPLICATION SOFTWARE

The second basic type of prewritten software is the application software that processes the firm's data. Application software exists for all computer sizes, but the packages for the larger computers are very expensive. Mainframe packages that perform major portions of a firm's data processing can cost $100,000 or more. The packages for micros cost much less—perhaps $300 or $600 each.

Three basic categories of application software have emerged—accounting packages, industry packages, and decision-support packages.

Accounting Packages

The accounting packages enable a firm to computerize its accounting system. Some packages perform the processing of the entire system, whereas some address the processing of certain subsystems such as payroll, inventory, and general ledger. There is a wide variety of this software available, especially for microcomputers.

Figure 3.7 is a flowchart of several accounting subsystems that function together as an integrated system, which we call the **distribution system**. Any company such as a retailer, wholesaler, or manufacturer that distributes or sells a product will have the subsystems pictured in the figure.

The process begins with the screening of customer sales orders by the **order-entry subsystem**. Then the data flows to the **inventory subsystem** where the inventory records are checked to determine whether the ordered items are in stock. If they are in stock, the **billing subsystem** prepares bills that are sent to the customers to collect the money. The bills are called **invoices**. The **accounts-receivable subsystem** follows up on the billing operation by preparing statements that remind the customers that money is owed, and processes customer payments when they are received. The **general-ledger subsystem** accumulates data from the inventory subsystem, accounts-receivable subsystem, and other accounting subsystems to produce standard accounting reports for management. The income statement, pictured in Figure 1.13, is an example of the output of the general ledger subsystem.

Industry Packages

You find the accounting subsystems in practically all types of firms. However, in some firms you will find subsystems unique to that particular industry. Prewritten software has been created to meet the needs of such industries as ranching and agriculture, real estate, retailing, manufacturing, trucking, and health care. Although this software is available for all sizes of computers, there are many more packages for micros than for mainframes.

FIGURE 3.7

The Distribution
System

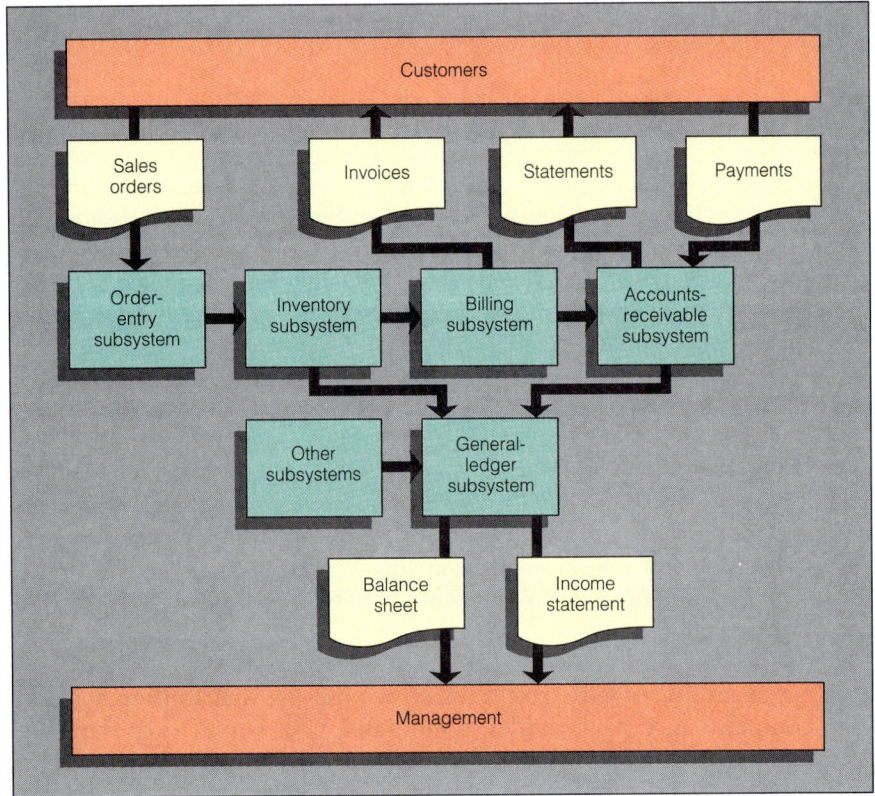

Many of the industry packages simply tailor the standard accounting procedures to the industry. For example, a construction-industry package might include a payroll program that is especially well-suited to how the earnings of construction workers are computed. Some of the industry packages, however, include programs that the manager can use in problem solving. Those programs are examples of the MIS and DSS application areas that were identified in Chapter 1.

DECISION-SUPPORT PACKAGES

The third category of application software includes decision-support packages. There are two major types of these packages—statistical packages, and packages that enable the managers to perform the basic managerial functions of planning, organizing, staffing, directing, and controlling.

Statistical Packages

Software packages have been available for performing basic statistical analyses since the early years of the computer. The statistical packages analyze large volumes of data and compute such basic statistics as the arithmetic mean and standard deviation. In addition, they compare sets of numbers and use such tests as the t test and the chi-square test to determine how similar or different the sets are. The more sophisticated routines of multiple regression and analysis of variance are also included.

These packages initially were prepared only for mainframe computers, but they are now available for the larger micros. Examples of mainframe statistical packages are SAS, SPSS-X, and BMD.

This software is not likely to be used personally by the manager. The reason is the great amount of mathematical or statistical knowledge that is required. Managers have tended to rely on specialists called **management scientists** or **operations researchers** to use the software. The specialists interpret the results and make recommendations to management.

Support for Management Functions

Although managers perform several basic functions, the computer always has done the best job in the planning and control areas.

There are many **forecasting packages** that enable the manager to project what might happen in the future. The packages use data describing what has happened in the past as the basis. For example, if past sales have increased in relationship to the number of salespersons, this relationship can be stated in mathematical terms. The forecasting packages can produce the projection in the form of a report or a graph such as the one pictured in Figure 3.8. You should understand that some forecasting packages do a better job than others, and no package is 100 percent accurate.

Another category of planning software includes **project management packages** that enable managers to plan such projects as construction of new facilities, introduction of new products, and acquisition of a computer. One such package is Project Scheduler 5000 Plus Graphics. It computes the

Planning

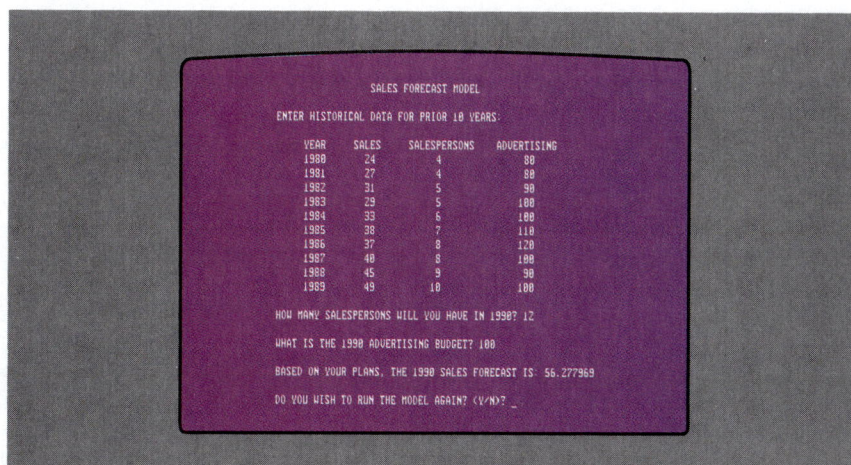

FIGURE 3.8

Using the Number of Salespersons to Project Future Sales

FIGURE 3.9

A Gantt Chart
Produced by a
Project Management
Package

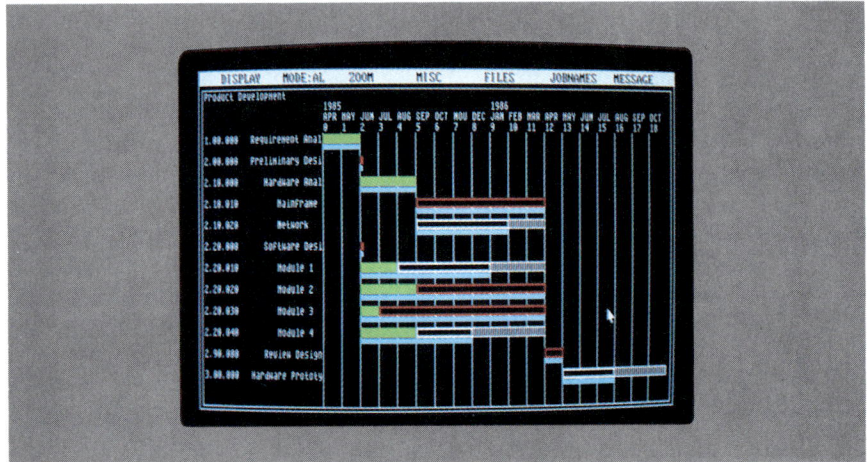

critical path (the sequence of tasks taking the longest time to complete), and displays the output in the form of a **Gantt chart**, or bar chart. Such a chart is shown in Figure 3.9.

Controlling

The best examples of control software are the packages that produce and maintain the **operating budget**. Most firms have a budget that is prepared each year to control expenditures. Limits are set for each department on such expenses as salaries, telephone, travel, and supplies. Managers receive periodic reports each month that compare the actual expenses with the budget. A typical budget report is illustrated in Figure 3.10.

Putting Application Software in Perspective

Some of the application software plays a direct role in problem solving, and some plays an indirect role. The accounting packages and many of the industry packages are designed for data processing, and any management information is only incidental. These systems play an indirect role in decision support by creating and maintaining the important database that can provide much of the input to the decision-support software.

Some industry packages, however, have a decision-support capability. They can produce information in a variety of forms, and some even have a modeling capability. These packages, plus the decision-support packages, provide direct support to the manager in solving a wide range of problems.

APPLICATION-DEVELOPMENT SOFTWARE

The third major category of prewritten software is application-development software. It enables firms to develop their own applications, and includes five types of packages—database management systems, electronic spreadsheets, graphics packages, office automation packages, and expert systems.

FIGURE 3.10 A Budget Report

BUDGET REPORT

Timberline Construction, Inc.   Job Cost Budget Report   9-17-89   Page 1

		Original Budget	Addl Budget	Total Budget	Pct Comp	To date Budget	To date Cost	Over Budget	Under Budget	Pct
50.10 Kruseway Plaza										
1	GENERAL REQUIREMENTS									
1.050 *	Field Engineering	128,993.00		128,993.00	100	128,993.00	136,424.20	7,431.20		5.76-
1.060	Regulatory Requir	11,483.00	1,550.00	13,033.00			6,264.17	6,264.17		48.06-
1.200	Project Meetings	28,708.00	3,876.00	32,584.00	39	12,764.64	12,764.64			
1.500 *	Const Fac/Temp Cn	8,574.00		8,574.00	100	8,574.00	9,162.10	588.10		6.86-
1.600 *	Material & Equipm	22,201.00		22,201.00	100	22,201.00	21,468.37		732.63	3.30
	GROUP TOTAL *	199,959.00	5,426.00	205,385.00		172,532.64	186,083.48	13,550.84		6.60-
2	SITEWORK									
2.210 *	Grading Rough/Fin	90,639.00	12,237.00	102,876.00	100	102,876.00	103,494.05	618.05		.60-
2.220 *	Excav/Bkfll/Compa	98,730.00		98,730.00	100	98,730.00	89,822.67		8,907.33	9.02
2.230	Base Course	102,861.00	7,611.71	110,472.71	23	25,640.57	96,119.44	70,478.87		63.80-
2.240	Soil Stabilizatio	7,839.00		7,839.00	28	2,193.60	6,585.69	4,392.09		56.03-
2.270	Slp Protct/Erosn	3,171.00		3,171.00	85	2,695.35	2,935.51	240.16		7.57-
	GROUP TOTAL *	303,240.00	19,848.71	323,088.71		232,135.52	298,957.36	66,821.84		20.68-
3	CONCRETE									
3.210	Reinforcing Steel	31,557.14	2,717.21	34,274.35	26	9,019.54	29,002.97	19,983.43		58.30-
3.220	Welded Wire Fabri	30,520.00		30,520.00	75	22,890.00	19,090.57		3,799.43	12.45
3.310	Structural Concre	130,734.00		130,734.00	75	98,050.50	105,372.21	7,321.71		5.60-
3.345	Concrete Finishin	24,854.00	1,839.20	26,693.20	75	20,019.90	18,986.05		1,033.85	3.87
3.360	Specially Plced C	8,855.00	654.28	9,509.28	75	7,131.96	6,771.23		360.73	3.79
	GROUP TOTAL *	226,520.14	5,210.69	231,730.83		157,111.90	179,223.03	22,111.13		9.54-
	JOB TOTAL *	729,719.14	30,485.40	760,204.54		561,780.06	664,263.87	102,483.81		13.48-

Database Management Systems

The database management system or DBMS helps the firm manage its data resource. The DBMS performs three basic functions. It stores data in the database, it retrieves data from the database, and it controls the database—keeps it secure.

Storage

Data is stored in the computer's secondary storage media. The media most often used on mainframe computers are magnetic disks and magnetic tapes that have the capacity to store millions or billions of characters. The media most often used with microcomputers include diskettes and small metal disks called **hard disks**. The hard disks have a much larger capacity than do the diskettes.

Retrieval

A major benefit of using the computer to manage the database is speed of retrieval. The user only has to enter a few commands, and the DBMS retrieves the information in a few seconds or minutes, depending on the complexity of the request. The information can be displayed on the screen or printed on the printer in the form of both special and periodic reports.

Control

The DBMS can be designed to screen each request and determine that the requester is an authorized user and approved to access the requested data.

The DBMS can require the user to enter a password in addition to the one required by the operating system. The DBMS password identifies the user as someone who is authorized to use the database. If the user passes this first screening, the DBMS then can scan a **user directory** that specifies the portion of the database that the user can use. In this manner, a user has access to only that portion of the database that is needed for the job.

How the DBMS Is Used

We have seen that the operating system is a type of gatekeeper of the computer system. We can think of the DBMS as a similar type of gatekeeper for the database. Figure 3.11 captures this idea.

The DBMS is involved each time data is to be read from the database or written to it. For example, assume that a payroll application program reads employee records from the database, computes the new amounts, and then writes the updated records back to the database. When the "read data base" instruction in the program is reached, the DBMS reads the appropri-

FIGURE 3.11

The DBMS is a Gatekeeper of the Database

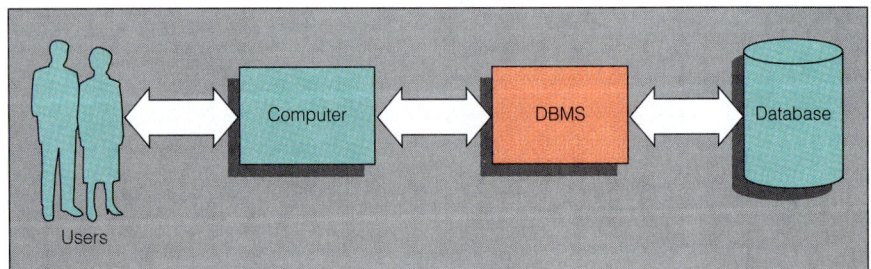

ate record into primary storage. In a similar fashion, when the "write data base" instruction is reached, the DBMS writes the updated record in the appropriate area of the database.

Another example is when a user enters a request for information from the database. The user uses a special language called a query language. A **query language** is a part of the DBMS that facilitates retrieval. It enables the user to retrieve database contents without having to write a program. The report prepared by the 4GL INQUIRE package in Figure 2.14 is a good example of how a query language is used. The query language is a 4GL, and is an effective way to prepare special reports.

There are many DBMSs on the market. The first were available only for mainframes. More recently, versions have been developed for micros. The first successful micro-based DBMS was dBASE II. It has since been upgraded to dBASE III, dBASE III Plus, and dBASE IV. Other popular micro DBMSs include Rbase 4000, Rbase 5000, and Rbase System V.

Electronic Spreadsheets

During the years when organizations used manual systems to keep their records, data was posted to large paper sheets in the form of rows and columns. The sheets were called **spreadsheets**, and they did a good job of reflecting the status of the organization.

As data processing systems evolved from manual to punched card systems and then to computer systems, the spreadsheet almost became forgotten. Then, in 1979, a software package that used the microcomputer's storage as a spreadsheet hit the market. The spreadsheet was named an **electronic spreadsheet**, and the product was VisiCalc. The timing was perfect because Steve Wozniak and Steve Jobs had just introduced the Apple computer. The combination of the Apple and VisiCalc was exactly what was needed to popularize the microcomputer as a problem-solving tool.

For the first time managers clearly could see how a microcomputer could be used for decision support. VisiCalc set sales records, but did not monopolize the market very long. Other electronic spreadsheets were developed by competitive firms. The most successful was Lotus 1-2-3, which achieved world-wide use.

There are also electronic spreadsheets available for mainframes, but they have not enjoyed the same acceptance as the micro versions. The most popular mainframe version is IFPS, for Interactive Financial Planning System. A micro version of IFPS is also available.

An electronic spreadsheet provides a matrix of storage locations consisting of rows and columns. The intersection of a row and column is called a **cell**, and can contain data or a formula. When you make a change to one cell, the software automatically reflects the change in the entire spreadsheet.

How Electronic Spreadsheets Are Used

Assume that you have a spreadsheet such as the one pictured in Figure 3.12 that displays an abbreviated income statement. In this example the revenue and expenses are based on the number of employees. When the number of employees is changed, the revenue, expenses, and profits (revenue

FIGURE 3.12

Using an Electronic
Spreadsheet to Play
the What-If Game

```
                        EMPLOYEE PLANNING MODEL


        INPUT DECISION:

            NUMBER OF EMPLOYEES                      144


        OUTPUT RESULTS:

            SALES REVENUE                      $38,523.75


            EXPENSES:

                MANUFACTURING                  12,457.10

                MARKETING                      15,534.91

                ADMINISTRATION                  4,890.55

            TOTAL EXPENSES                     $32,882.56


            PROFIT BEFORE TAXES                 5,641.19


            TAXES                               2,190.00


            PROFIT AFTER TAXES                 $3,451.19
```

less expenses) also change. The manager can enter various numbers of
employees, and see the effect of each on the profits. In this manner the
manager uses the electronic spreadsheet not only to prepare the income
statement, but also to try out various decision strategies.

Graphics Packages

We have seen in Figures 3.9 that a computer can produce information in a
graphic form. Early mainframe configurations frequently included a special output unit called a plotter that was used to print graphs. In addition,
special software was required to put the data into the correct form for the
plotter.

Plotters are still used but you do not have to have one to print a graph on a micro. If you have the proper printer, called a **graphics printer**, you can print both character and graphic output. Most micro printers manufactured today have this graphics capability.

Computer graphics were never very popular until Lotus came along. Lotus is the most popular graphics software because it does a good job, is easy to use, and works in conjunction with the electronic spreadsheet. There are many other graphics packages for both micros and larger computers.

Graphs are especially useful in identifying and understanding problems. Graphs can represent the distillation of large volumes of data, and often can show trends and relationships that become lost in the data. A manager can use a graph to signal a problem or potential problem, and then use a report, printed in a tabular form of letters and numbers, to provide more detail.

How Graphics Packages Are Used

Office Automation Packages

Several office automation applications require the use of a computer, and therefore require software. The most popular of these applications are electronic mail, electronic calendaring, and word processing. The packages are popular because they address a problem common to all types of organizations—communications.

Electronic mail is the use of a computer network to send, store, and receive messages. The sender keys a message into his or her terminal or microcomputer keyboard. The message is placed in the recipient's **electronic mailbox** in the secondary storage of the central computer. The recipient uses his or her terminal or micro to retrieve the message and display it on the screen. The electronic mail software controls the input, storage, and display.

Electronic Mail

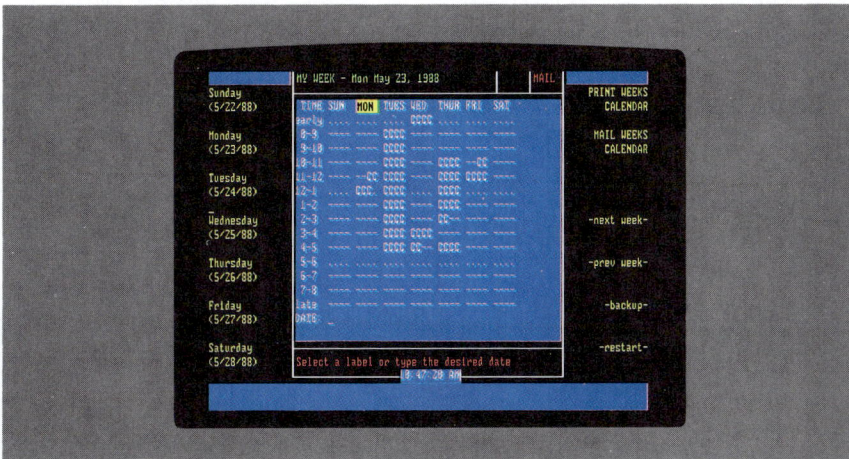

FIGURE 3.13
An Electronic Calendar

Electronic Calendaring

Electronic calendaring is the use of a computer network to store a manager's appointments calendar in secondary storage. The manager can enter appointments, make changes, and review the calendar using a terminal or micro. When it is acceptable to the manager, other persons in the organization can access the manager's calendar. The other persons use their own terminals or micros to schedule meetings, trips, tours, and so forth with the manager. Figure 3.13 illustrates a manager's electronic calendar.

Word Processing

Word processing is the use of an electronic device that automatically performs many of the tasks involved with preparing typed or printed documents. The electronic device comes in two basic forms: a system called a **dedicated word processor** that is specially designed to perform nothing but word processing tasks, or a computer. A dedicated word processor achieves its capabilities primarily through hardware—the equipment is designed so that tasks are performed when keys are pressed. When a computer is used, it achieves its word processing capabilities through software. A computer of any size can be used. The user enters the text using either a terminal or a microcomputer keyboard.

The microcomputer software area has been the hotbed of activity since the entry of the first widely accepted package—WordStar. Today, there are several hundred word processing packages for micros. The package that is stimulating the most current interest is WordPerfect.

How Office-Automation Software Is Used

All of the office automation applications are intended to improve communications. Electronic mail is an alternative to printed letters and memos. Electronic calendaring provides a new capability for making appointments and scheduling meetings for the purpose of communicating information. Word processing improves the quality of such printed documents as memos, letters, procedures, and policies. The value of these communications to problem solving can be just as great, or more so, than the information provided by other subsystems of the CBIS.

Expert Systems

The least developed of the prewritten software areas is the expert systems package. A prewritten expert system is called an **expert system shell**. Much of the expert system success has been achieved in medicine, where expert systems have been designed to help physicians diagnose patients' ills.

How Expert Systems Can Be Used

It seems logical that if a physician can use an expert system to diagnose a human patient, a manager should be able to do the same for an organization. Perhaps someday expert systems will enable managers to do a better job of finding out the real causes of the firm's illnesses. We describe expert systems in Chapter 15.

Putting the Application-Development Software in Perspective

The term 4GL can be used to describe this area of application-development software. When we introduced fourth-generation languages in Chapter 2, we recognized that they are not true programming languages. They more properly fit into the prewritten software category. They represent a modern, user-friendly alternative to programming.

Application-development software processes the firm's data, but it is not aimed at specific applications. Instead, it is designed to perform such specific types of processing as maintaining a database or creating an electronic spreadsheet. It is left to the imagination and creativity of the user to apply these packages to specific business problems.

ACHIEVING USER FRIENDLINESS IN SOFTWARE

Designers of software to be used in end-user computing attempt to make the software as user friendly as possible. Several techniques can be used, but two very popular ones are help screens and menus.

Help Screens

If a user encounters difficulty while using software, it may be possible to request a display that explains how to overcome the difficulty. The display is called a **help screen** or **help message**. Software that offers this capability often reserves a particular key on the keyboard for use in requesting the help, and the key is called the **help key**.

Figure 3.14 illustrates a help screen that displays an explanation of a data element that is used by a mathematical model. The bottom of the screen includes instructions for resuming processing after the help screen has been viewed.

Menus

You know from your restaurant experience that a **menu** is a list of choices. The term is used the same way in the computer field. Software displays a list of choices from which the user makes a selection, enabling the user to specify what is to be done. A software package that makes frequent use of menus is said to be **menu driven**.

Menus can exist in several different forms. Figure 3.15 shows two examples. The upper menu consists of five numbered choices, arranged vertically. The user makes a selection by entering the appropriate number. For example, if the user wants to run the inventory program, a 2 is entered and the inventory program is read into primary storage from secondary storage.

The lower menu consists of five choices arranged horizontally. The software has positioned a pointer, called a **cursor**, on the leftmost choice. In

How a Menu Is Used

FIGURE 3.14

A Help Screen

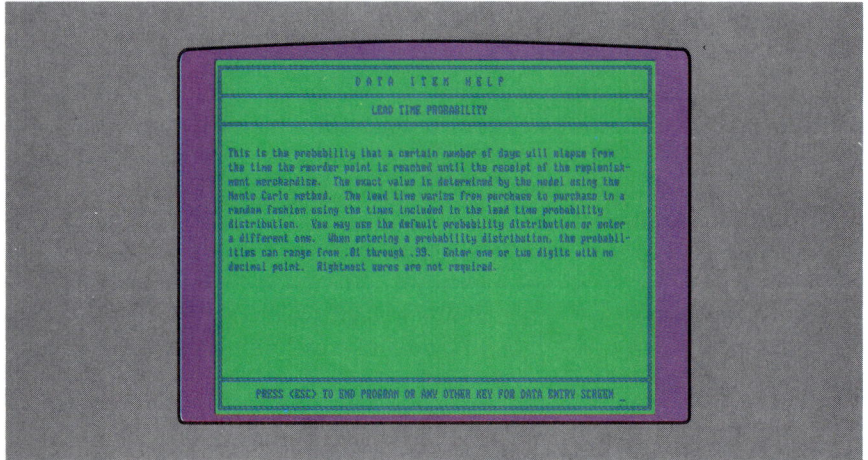

FIGURE 3.15

Two Examples of Menus

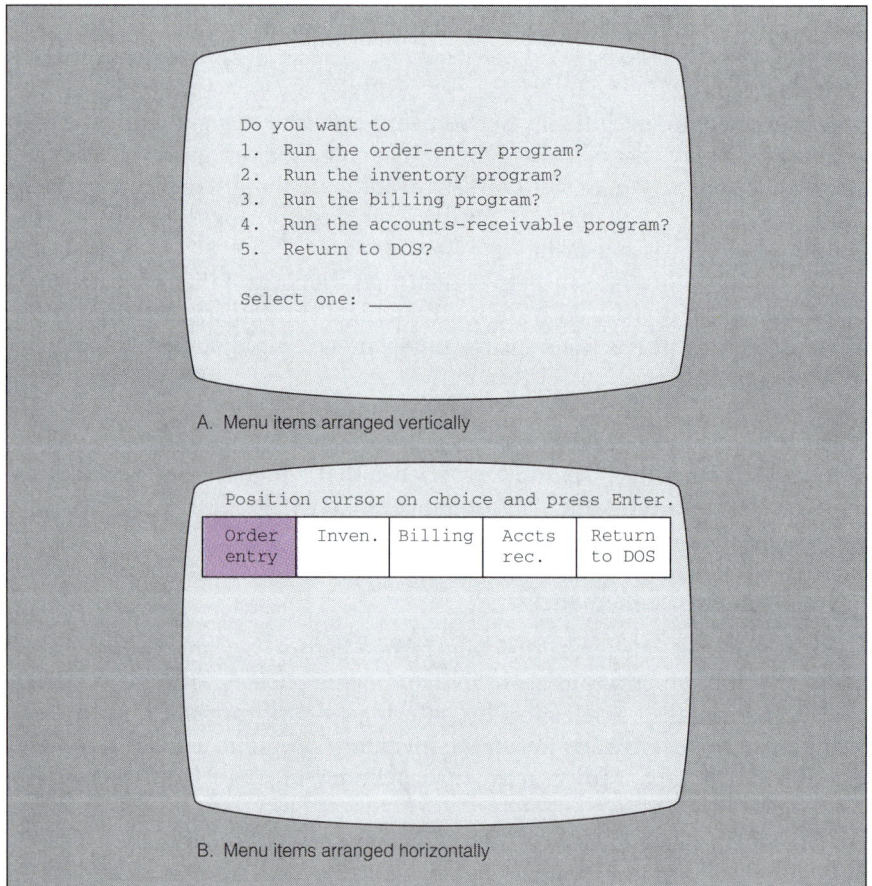

Do you want to
1. Run the order-entry program?
2. Run the inventory program?
3. Run the billing program?
4. Run the accounts-receivable program?
5. Return to DOS?

Select one: ____

A. Menu items arranged vertically

Position cursor on choice and press Enter.

| Order entry | Inven. | Billing | Accts rec. | Return to DOS |

B. Menu items arranged horizontally

menus of this type, the cursor is a bright rectangle, called a **highlight bar**. The user can move the highlight bar to other choices and can select a choice by pressing certain keys on the keyboard.

Menus can be used in a hierarchy. For example, the first menu selection causes a second to be displayed, the selection from the second menu causes a third to be displayed, and so on. Figure 3.16 illustrates the top-down selection from four menus arranged in a hierarchy. The first, top-level, menu asks whether an application or system program is to be run. The user

Levels of Menus

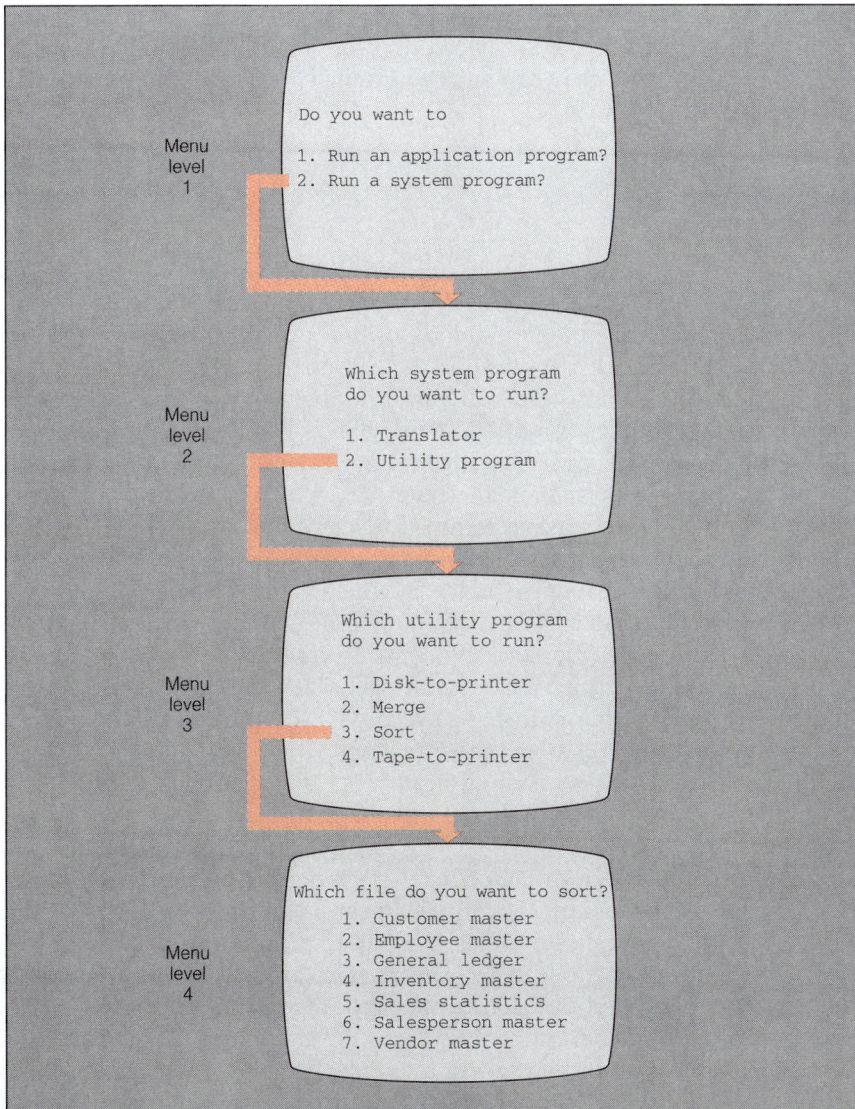

FIGURE 3.16

Menus in a Hierarchy

Menu level 1

```
Do you want to

1. Run an application program?
2. Run a system program?
```

Menu level 2

```
Which system program
do you want to run?

1. Translator
2. Utility program
```

Menu level 3

```
Which utility program
do you want to run?

1. Disk-to-printer
2. Merge
3. Sort
4. Tape-to-printer
```

Menu level 4

```
Which file do you want to sort?
     1. Customer master
     2. Employee master
     3. General ledger
     4. Inventory master
     5. Sales statistics
     6. Salesperson master
     7. Vendor master
```

selects system program by entering a 2. A second-level menu is then displayed, asking whether the system program is a translator or utility program. The user enters a 2 to select a utility program. A third-level menu then asks which of four utility programs is to be run. The user enters a 3 to specify a sort program. Finally, a fourth-level menu lists the files that exist in the database. The user enters the number of the file that is to be sorted.

In this example the sequence of menus enables the user to specify that a particular file is to be sorted. The specification is entered quickly and accurately. Menus make it unnecessary for the user to learn a series of commands that can be very tedious to use. The software leads the user through the specification process in a step-by-step manner.

Many of the techniques for achieving user friendliness originated with software vendors, but they can be used just as effectively by programmers and even users.

SUMMARY

The area of prewritten software has grown steadily since the early days of the computer, with a big stimulus coming from the microcomputer boom. There are three major categories of prewritten software—system software, application software, and application-development software.

The three types of system software are operating systems, language translators, and utilities. An operating system is a master control program that serves as a gatekeeper to the computer system. The most important part of the operating system is the supervisor, which is main-memory resident. Other parts, the transient routines, are kept in secondary storage and are read into an overlay area in primary storage when they are needed. One of these transient routines is IOCS, which controls the input and output. The operating system for a mainframe computer can perform six functions—schedule jobs, manage the computer's hardware and software resources, provide security, enable multiple users to share the system, handle interrupts, and maintain usage records. An operating system for a micro might not perform all of these functions.

The user uses a JCL to communicate with the operating system. As a rule, the JCL for a microcomputer is more user friendly than that of a mini or mainframe.

Utility programs perform functions that are needed by all users of a particular computer. For microcomputer users, the utilities relate to the diskettes—making duplicate copies, comparing diskettes, and erasing files.

There are three categories of application software—accounting packages, industry packages, and decision-support packages. The accounting packages perform the standard accounting jobs for most firms. These packages permit the computer to be used in the data processing application area. Some industry packages tailor the accounting applications to particular industries. Other industry packages include decision-support capabilities. The decision-support packages are the ones that are intended primarily for use in solving the manager's problems.

Five types of application-development software have emerged. The DBMS manages the firm's data resource, performing the functions of storage, retrieval, and control. Electronic spreadsheets manipulate data in rows and columns, and enable the user to play the What-If game. Graphics packages are used to display output in graphic form on the screen or print it using a graphics printer or a plotter. The office automation applications featuring electronic mail, electronic calendaring, and word processing are intended to improve communications. The final category is expert systems, which have the potential for aiding the manager in diagnosing a firm's ills. The term 4GL can be applied to application-development software.

Software of any type can be made more user friendly by using help screens and menus.

KEY CONCEPTS

How prewritten software can be classified into categories and subcategories

The manner in which the supervisor of the operating system resides in primary storage and the transient routines reside in secondary storage

How multiple users can share the computer at the same time—multiprogramming

How a complete accounting system consists of integrated accounting subsystems

How application software can provide both indirect and direct support for decision making

The manner in which help screens and menus contribute to user friendliness

KEY TERMS

System software
Application software
Operating system
Application-development software
Supervisor, monitor, executive routine
Main-memory resident
Transient routine
Overlay area
Password

Multiprogramming
Interrupt
Job-control language (JCL)
Utility program
Help screen, help message
Menu
Cursor
Highlight bar

QUESTIONS

1. What distinguishes system software from application software? What distinguishes application software from application-development software?

2. Which software area is receiving the greatest amount of attention from vendors? What type of vendors dominate this area?

3. Name the three types of system software.

4. In what ways do operating systems and database management systems function as gatekeepers?

5. How does the computer handle an operating system that requires more primary storage than is available?

6. Is JCL a programming language? Explain.

7. Name three operations that microcomputer utility programs perform.

8. What are the three types of application software?

9. What are the subsystems of the distribution system? Which ones receive input from customers? Which produce output for customers? Which produce output for management?

10. Which management functions are supported the best by prewritten software? Give an example of software for each function.

11. How does prewritten software provide indirect support for decision making?

12. Name the five types of application-development software. Which one includes a query language? Which one facilitates the What-If game?

13. A DBMS performs three main functions. What are they?

14. What are the different ways that graphic information can be produced?

15. What are two ways that choices can be selected from a menu?

CASE PROBLEM   Northwest Camping Products, Inc.

Dear Lynn,

Welcome aboard. We are looking forward to benefitting from your college education in computing. As one of the nation's leading manufacturers of camping supplies, we feel that we are in the right position to maintain our leadership in a growing industry. And, an important part of that growth will be our implementation of a computer!

Yes, your recommendation has been approved. The top-management committee met yesterday and decided to go along with your recommendation to implement a computer to perform data processing, office automation, and decision-support applications. However, your recommendation that a networked mini be implemented was not approved. Instead, the decision was made to go with a single micro. In addition, it was decided that we would use prewritten programs entirely. There are no plans to hire programmers or systems analysts, but we will have one full-time operator. It will be your responsibility to get the applications "on the air."

The committee has requested that you provide them with a list of the *types* of prewritten software that we will need. We want a computerized accounting system and want to provide our managers with a What-If modeling capability and support in the planning and control areas. However, keep in mind the lack of mathematical skills that exist in our present organization. The managers also would like to be able to query the database and obtain special reports. Finally, we want to get into office automation to the fullest extent possible with our particular computer configuration.

As soon as you prepare the list, let us get together and discuss it before we take it to the committee.

Sincerely,

Alex Weston
Administrative Vice President

1. Provide the list that the committee has requested.

2. Write a memo to Mr. Weston, addressing the decision to go with a single micro instead of a networked mini. List any constraints that the decision will cause in achieving the full capabilities in each application area.

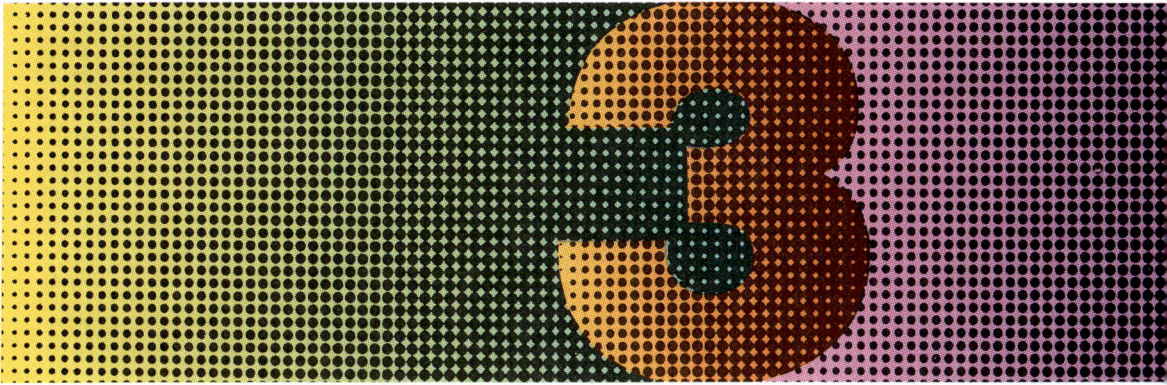

Business Problems and Problem Solvers

We recognized in Chapter 1 that everybody in an organization solves problems—managers such as presidents and supervisors, nonmanagers such as secretaries and plant workers, and specialists such as internal auditors and consultants. Some of the problems are those of the individuals as they carry out their duties, whereas other problems are those of the firm.

Problem solving is important on each organizational level, but its impact on the firm's operations becomes greater as you move up the hierarchy. The managers on the upper levels solve problems that determine the firm's future. A review of any organization's history usually reveals a few key problems that were faced by the upper-level managers. The ones that were solved became the keys to continued growth; the ones that were not solved led to deteriorating operations and possibly even to bankruptcy.

In Part 3 we focus our attention on the problem solvers, their organizations, the types of problems they solve, and the tools they use. In the course of the discussion we will introduce a concept that is important in problem solving—the concept of a system. We will see that it is beneficial for the problem solver to view an organization as a system and to use the tools that have been developed for systems analysis and design.

We will not assume that any particular technology, such as the computer, is used. Rather, we describe a methodology that can be used by all types of managers in all types of organizations in solving all types of problems. An understanding of these principles is important in incorporating the computer into the problem-solving process. That topic is the subject of Part 4.

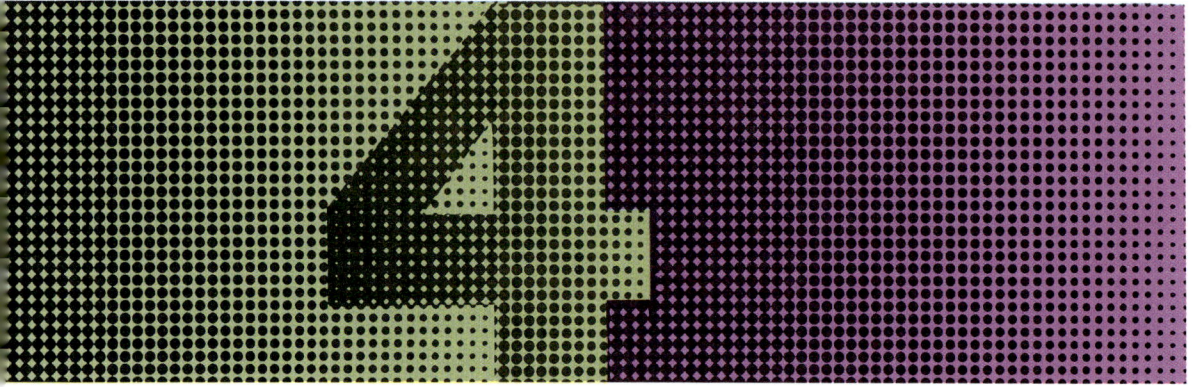

Business Organizations and Systems

LEARNING OBJECTIVES   After studying this chapter, you should:

- Understand the different types of organizations that provide the setting for problem-solving activity
- View an organization as a collection of both physical and conceptual resources
- Be familiar with the typical way in which businesses are organized, and understand the influence the structure has on problem solving
- Recognize the common elements that exist in organizations of different types
- Understand the basic systems concepts and how they relate to a business organization
- Be familiar with one way to classify elements in the environment of the firm, and view their relationships with the firm in terms of resource flows
- Appreciate why a systems view of the organization is helpful in problem solving

---

OVERVIEW

In this chapter we describe the setting where problem solving takes place—the organization to which the problem solver belongs and the environment of that organization. The organization can be a business or a nonbusiness type, and if it is a business it can be profit-seeking or nonprofit.

We will pay special attention to how personnel and other resources are allocated among the various units within the organization. Most organizations are subdivided into units that specialize in certain functions such as obtaining and allocating the necessary finances, producing the products and services the organization sells, and selling and distributing those products and services.

There are certain features common to most types of organizations, making it possible to develop an approach to problem solving that is applicable to a wide variety of situations. One such approach is to view the organization as a system and to make decisions that enable the system to meet its objectives.

WHAT IS AN ORGANIZATION?

An **organization** is a group of resources established for a particular purpose. A person or a group of persons recognizes a need for a particular product or service, and an organization is established to meet that need.

Public and Private Organizations

Organizations can be classified according to whether they are intended to meet the needs of the entire population or just a portion, and whether profit is an objective. Figure 4.1 shows this classification. Organizations exist in either the public or the private sector of the economy. **Public organizations** include the governments on the federal, state, and local levels. Their objective is to provide the services necessary to satisfy the needs or protect the interests of the general public. Examples are the U.S. Postal System, the military, state universities, and fire and police departments. Public organizations are nonprofit in nature. Revenues are raised, from sales, taxes, and tuition, but they are intended to cover only the costs of operation.

Private organizations are those founded and operated by individuals who may or may not be influenced by the profit motive. The broad term **business organizations** can also be used.

Profit and Nonprofit Organizations

In most cases the motivation for creating private organizations is profit. The operators strive to sell the products or services for more than they cost. These are **profit-seeking organizations**.

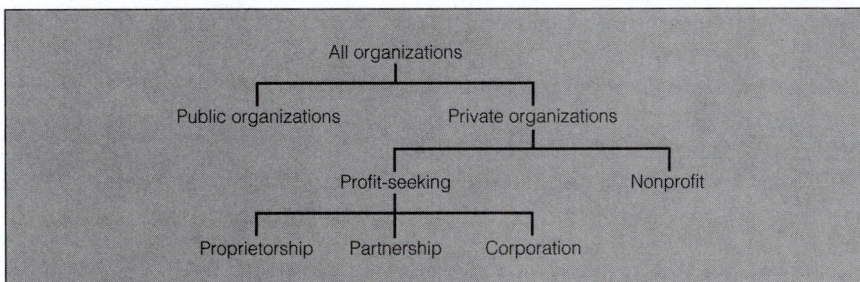

FIGURE 4.1
Types of Organizations

There are three basic types of profit-seeking private organizations—proprietorships, partnerships, and corporations. When the organization is founded and owned by an individual, it is called a **proprietorship**. When several persons band together to form the organization, it is called a **partnership**. When the founders comply with the rules of incorporation for a particular state, the organization is called a **corporation**. The owners of a corporation are the **stockholders**, and they are represented by a **board of directors** that sets policies and solves problems.

Nonprofit organizations are established to meet some need rather than provide the owners with a return on their investment. A good example is an educational TV station. Its fund-raising efforts are intended solely to cover the expenses necessary to provide the programming service. The Salvation Army and churches also fit into this category.

Organizational Resources

All organizations employ the same *types* of resources. The two basic types are physical and conceptual. **Physical resources** are those that exist physically and include personnel, facilities, equipment, materials, and money.

The first four of these resources are valuable because of their physical attributes. The personnel are the most valuable physical resource because of their unique skills and the fact that they direct the use of the other resources. The facilities are valuable because of their location, size, and construction. The equipment is valuable because of the processes it can perform, and the material is valuable because it is used in producing the firm's products and services. Money is a special type of physical resource. It is not important because of its physical properties but because it is used to obtain the other physical resources.

Conceptual resources are those that are valuable not because of their physical nature but because they *represent* physical resources. The best examples are data and information. It is true that these resources exist physically in the form of marks or characters printed on paper, magnetized spots on a computer storage medium, or material stored in a person's brain. But, like money, the physical properties are unimportant. What *is* important is how persons in the organization can use the data and information to understand and control the physical resources.

Many personnel in an organization work primarily with the physical resources. This normally occurs on the lower organizational levels. Employees in the receiving department inspect arriving materials and transport them to storage areas, plant workers operate and maintain machines to transform the materials into products, fork-lift truck operators transport the products to the shipping department, and truck drivers deliver the products to the organization's customers.

Others in the organization work primarily with the conceptual resources. Managers, secretaries, clerical personnel, and information personnel fall in this category. It is the responsibility of the secretaries, clerks, and computer specialists to create and maintain the conceptual resources

FIGURE 4.2
Personnel Are an
Organization's Most
Valuable Physical
Resource

needed by the managers. Many managers regard information as their most valuable resource since it enables them to manage the physical resources.

Organization Administration

When an organization is created, the necessary resources must first be assembled and then coordinated so that they all contribute to the organization's purpose in an efficient manner. An **administrative element** is established that accomplishes the assembly and coordination. This administrative element is the organization's management.

FIGURE 4.3
Managers Use
Information to
Understand and
Control the Physical
Resources

Regardless of whether the organization is public or private, profit-seeking or nonprofit, managers are necessary to ensure that the resources are applied toward a common goal—meeting the organization's objectives. Even though the leaders may have such titles as colonel, pastor, and coach, they are managers and they use the same management principles to direct the activity of other persons.

FUNCTIONAL ORGANIZATION STRUCTURE

As an organization increases in size, the administrators see the necessity of subdividing the resources into separate units. A typical approach is a **functional organization structure** consisting of units that specialize in similar activity. The organization chart that we studied in Chapter 1 (see Figure 1.4) shows this subdivision and also the hierarchical levels within each functional area.

All of the resources involved with handling the organization's monetary activity are assembled to form a **financial function**. Since every organization is financed with monetary resources, the financial function is found in every type of organization. The financial function frequently is called a finance division or department. The accounting department is a subunit within the financial function. The person who is in charge of the financial function is the **vice president of finance** or the **controller**.

All of the resources involved in interfacing with the organization's customers and promoting the use of the products and services are assembled to form a **marketing function**. In a business organization, the person in charge of the marketing function typically has the title of **vice president of marketing** or perhaps **sales manager**. Although all organizations do not have a separate marketing division or department, they all perform marketing *activity*. The TV commercials urging you to pursue a military career are examples of such marketing activity, as are Salvation Army bell ringers at Christmas time.

All of the resources used by manufacturing organizations in transforming raw materials into finished goods or products represent the **manufacturing function**. This function is called the manufacturing division or perhaps the production department, and is managed by a person with the title of **vice president of manufacturing** or perhaps **production superintendent**. Even though nonmanufacturing organizations do not have a formal manufacturing unit, many are involved with manufacturing in a broad sense. For example, McDonald's "manufactures" hamburgers, insurance companies "manufacture" policies, and banks "manufacture" loans.

The financial, marketing, and manufacturing functions are only three of the functional areas. Other functions include information services, engineering, R & D (research and development), and human resources.

Some types of firms use special names to describe their functions, such as underwriting department and claims division in an insurance company. But all types of organizations, public as well as private, have embraced the functional structure and it is the most popular type.

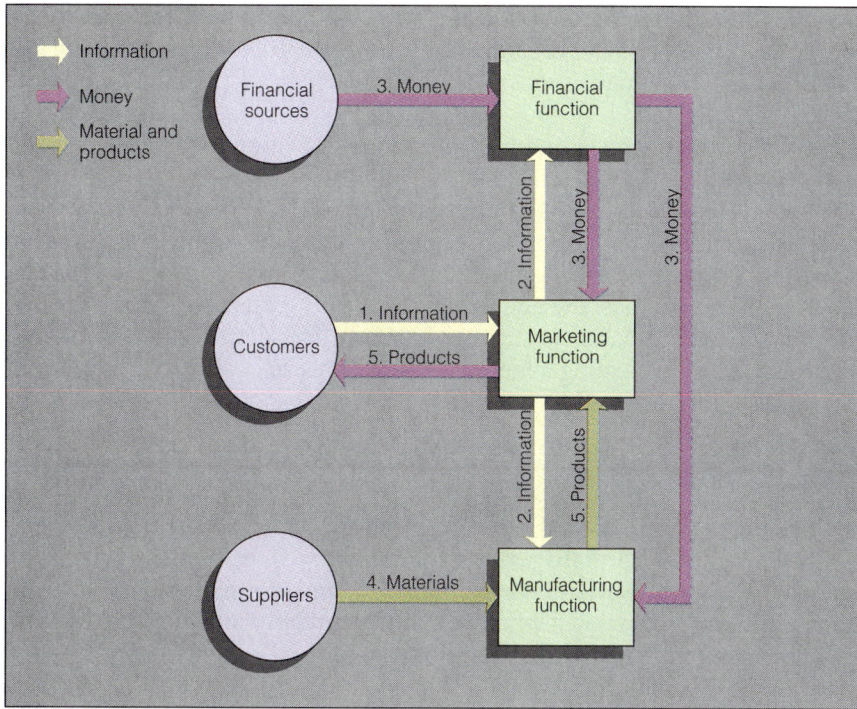

FIGURE 4.4

Interaction of Functional Units in the Firm

The Influence of Functional Structure on Problem Solving

The fact that the functional structure works is a miracle of sorts considering the complex interaction that exists among the functions. Figure 4.4 shows how some of the resources flow between the functions. The numbers in the narrative below correspond to the numbers in the diagram, and indicate the order of events.

1. The marketing function gathers information describing customers' needs.
2. Marketing transmits information to both the financial and manufacturing functions advising them of the needs.
3. The financial function obtains money from such financial sources as banks, and makes it available to marketing and manufacturing so they can acquire resources and meet the customers' needs.
4. Manufacturing acquires the raw materials from suppliers to produce the finished goods, or products.
5. Manufacturing makes the products available to marketing, which distributes them to the customers.

If the resources are to flow in the manner shown in the figure, all of the functional areas must work together. Sometimes the managers and employees of a functional area place their own interests above those of the overall organization. In such a situation the persons have a **functional attitude**, and it is difficult for the organization to meet its objectives. Many of the problems faced by managers are caused by lack of cooperation among the functional areas.

When the managers and employees place the interests of the organization above those of their units then the objectives are more easily met. The personnel are said to have a **company attitude** and top management devotes much of its attention to developing this environment. One reason Japanese firms have been so successful is the feeling of closeness that is created for the employees; the employees think of themselves as members of a family. United States firms such as IBM and Hewlett-Packard also have been successful in creating a family-like atmosphere.

SIMILARITIES AMONG ALL TYPES OF ORGANIZATIONS

We have recognized that all types of organizations employ the same types of resources, that all managers follow the same management principles, and that all types of organizations are structured along functional lines. In addition, all organizational structures are hierarchical and all types of organizations are concerned with revenue collection and expense control.

Hierarchical Structure

Employees in an organization are grouped in a hierarchical manner. Figure 4.5 illustrates this structure in the form of a pyramid. The upper levels consist of managers while the bottom level consists of nonmanagers.

The person at the top is usually the **president** or **CEO** (**chief executive officer**). In a proprietorship or partnership the CEO is an owner. In a corporation the CEO is appointed by the board of directors and is accountable to them. The president or CEO is responsible for the entire organization.

Reporting to the president or CEO are several **vice presidents**. As we have seen, each vice president is usually responsible for a single functional area. Within each functional area there are multiple levels of managers with such titles as director, manager, and supervisor. These managers are responsible for the operations in their particular units.

The idea of organizational levels does not mean that certain employees are better than others. It simply means that different levels of responsibility and reporting relationships exist. For example, the vice president of marketing, reporting to the president, is responsible for all marketing activity. The sales manager, reporting to the vice president of marketing, is responsible for all activity in the sales department. A sales office manager, reporting to the sales manager, is responsible for the sales office, and so on.

Revenue Collection and Expense Control

All managers realize that their revenues must be equal to or greater than their expenses. If they are not, the organization will cease to exist. All man-

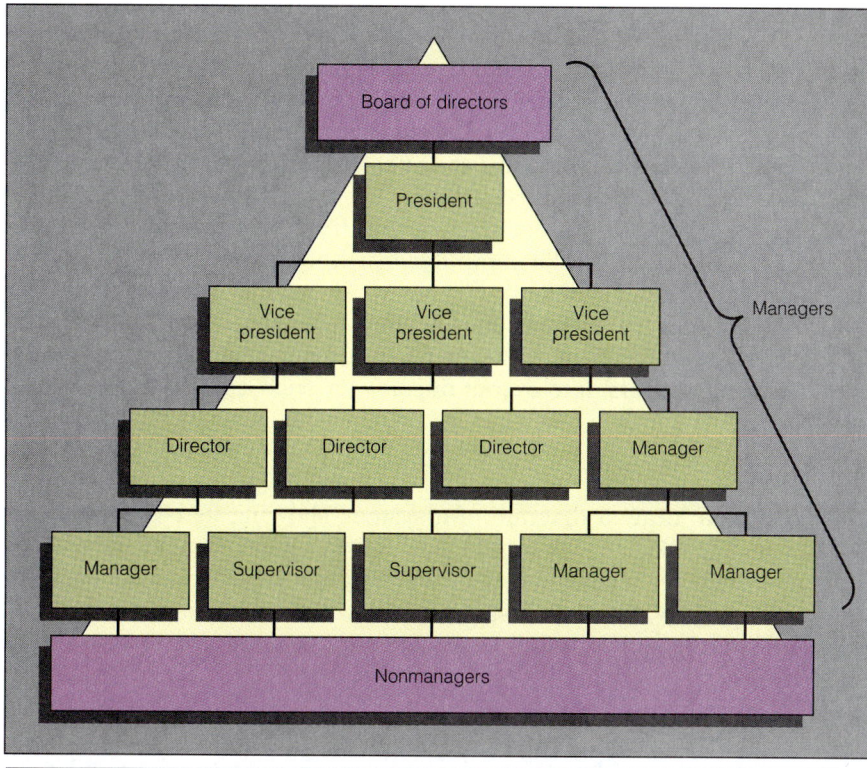

FIGURE 4.5

The Organization's
Personnel Are
Arranged in a
Hierarchy

agers therefore work to stimulate revenues and to keep expenses under control. Revenues are stimulated by engaging in such marketing activity as advertising and promotional campaigns. Most organizations seek to control expenses by establishing limits on how much can be spent for various items such as salaries and rent. The limits represent the **operating budget**, or simply the **budget**. Most organizations prepare a new budget for each financial year, called the **fiscal year**.

Many of the problems faced by managers relate to stimulating revenues and controlling expenses.

THE BUSINESS ORGANIZATION AS A SYSTEM

During recent years the term *system* has been used to an increasing degree in business literature. Managers are urged to "regard the firm as a system," and to take the "systems approach" to problem solving. The systems approach is the topic of Chapter 7, but we can learn to view the firm as a system here.

What Is a System?

A **system** is a group of elements or parts that are integrated for the purpose of achieving some objective. The type of system that first comes to mind is a **physical system** consisting of tangible elements or parts. Computers and air conditioners are good examples of physical systems. Some physical systems are not mechanical, but consist of people. Good examples are basketball teams, orchestras, and office staffs.

When thinking of a system, it is best to think of one that transforms some input into output. The computer transforms data into information that is used in solving problems. The air conditioner uses fuel to transform warm air into cold air that provides comfort to the occupants. In a simplified sense, an office staff transforms input documents, such as time sheets and sales orders, into output documents, such as payroll checks and invoices.

A Model of a System

It is possible to draw a diagram of a system, showing its basic parts and activity. Such a diagram, or model, appears in Figure 4.6 and shows that input resources are transformed into output resources. Flowcharting symbols developed by information specialists are used in the diagram. A parallelogram represents input and output operations, and a rectangle represents processing.

Open Systems

Every system exists within some type of environment that both provides the input resources and receives the output resources. The environment of the computer consists of the employees of the firm who prepare the input data and use the output information. The environment of the air conditioner consists of the supply of input fuel and air as well as the occupants who enjoy the cool temperature. The environment of the office staff is the firm and the outside organizations and individuals with which they interact.

Figure 4.7 shows the system within its environment. Such a system is called an **open system**. The system is *open* in that resources flow through it. All systems are of this type; there are no true closed systems.

The Control Element

The systems pictured in Figures 4.6 and 4.7 do not have a separate **control element** that makes automatic adjustments in the operation. Some systems

FIGURE 4.6
A Model of
a System

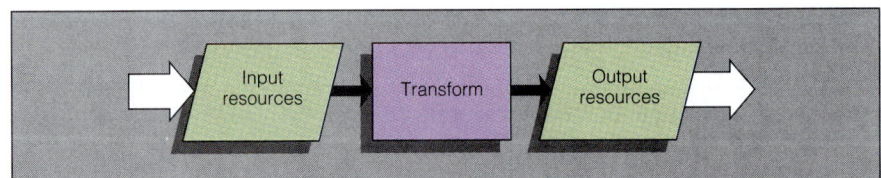

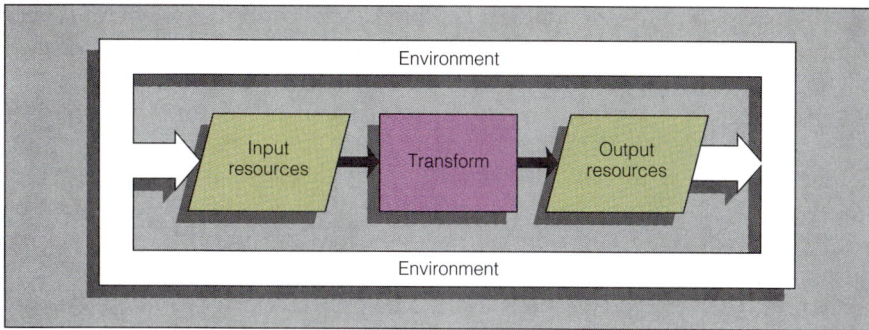

FIGURE 4.7
An Open System

are of this type. An example is an electric space heater that you plug into a wall outlet and turn on. It continues to put out heat until you turn it off.

On the other hand, many systems have control elements. The computer, air conditioner, and office staff are of this type. The program, thermostat, and office manager control the individual parts so that the system meets its objective.

Figure 4.8 shows the added control element, along with a feedback loop and performance standards. The **feedback loop** directs signals from the system output to the control element. The signals represent the level of output, such as the room temperature. The control element compares the feedback to the **performance standards** that the system is to meet, and adjusts the system input accordingly. For example, if the room temperature is higher than that entered into the thermostat (the performance standard), then the unit is turned on to produce more cool air. When the temperature is lowered to the thermostat setting, the unit is turned off. Such a system that includes a feedback loop, control element, and performance standards is called a **closed-loop system**. The feedback loop is closed. The level of out-

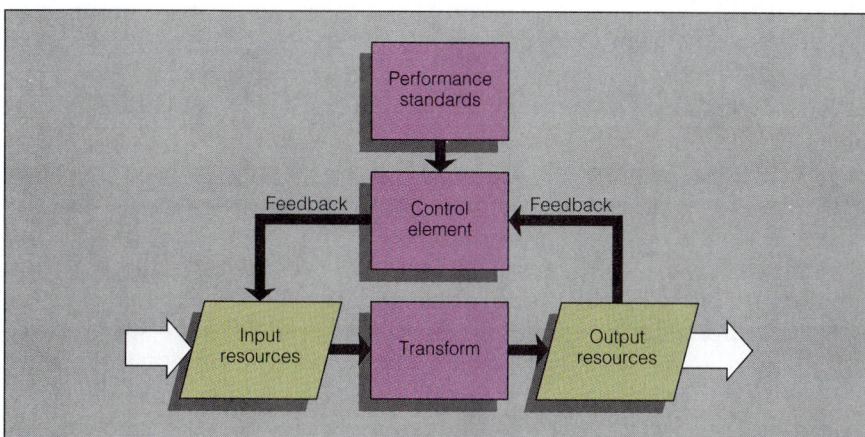

FIGURE 4.8
A Closed-Loop System

put is used to make adjustments in the input, which produces more output.

When a system does not have a feedback loop, control element, and performance standards it is called an **open-loop system**. The electric space heater is an open-loop system.

System Objectives and Standards

Before we proceed further, you should understand the difference between the system's objectives and the performance standards. The **objectives** are what the system is to accomplish, and they usually are stated in broad terms. For example, the objective of the air conditioner is to keep the occupants cool, the objective of the computer is to meet the informational needs of the users, and the objective of the office staff is to maintain a particular portion of the firm's overall conceptual system. The **standards** are measures, usually quantitative, that are intended to gauge how well the objectives are being met. An air conditioning standard might be a temperature range of seventy-six to seventy-eight degrees, a computer standard might be a maximum of one error in every 100,000 records, and an office staff standard might be the complete handling of a customer inquiry with no more than a single telephone call. The assumption is that the system will accomplish its objectives if it meets the standards.

Viewing the Firm as a System

It is easy to see the firm in a systems context. We have recognized the physical resources that contribute to the objectives. Input resources in the form of raw materials flow into the firm from its environment, and the manufacturing function transforms them into the finished products. The marketing function distributes the products to the customers in the environment.

The firm's management serves as the control element, comparing the production output to standards that have been set. The standards can relate to production volume, quality, cost, profit, and other measures. When management determines that performance is not up to standard, decisions are made that result in some changes to the organization. The changes are intended to solve the particular problems that prevent the output from meeting the standards.

A supermarket is a good example of a firm as a system. The input resources consist of the many food and nonfood items obtained from suppliers. The transformation consists of unpacking the items and displaying them on shelves, cutting and packaging meats, perhaps baking cakes and pies, and so on. The output resources are the products that the customers buy. The store's management serves as the control element, monitoring sales and adjusting the volume and mix of products accordingly. When products do not sell, they are removed from the shelves. When customers indicate a strong demand for a certain class of product, more space is provided and a wider selection of brands is offered. The store managers are guided by standards that specify the level of sales and expenses expected to lead the firm to the desired performance.

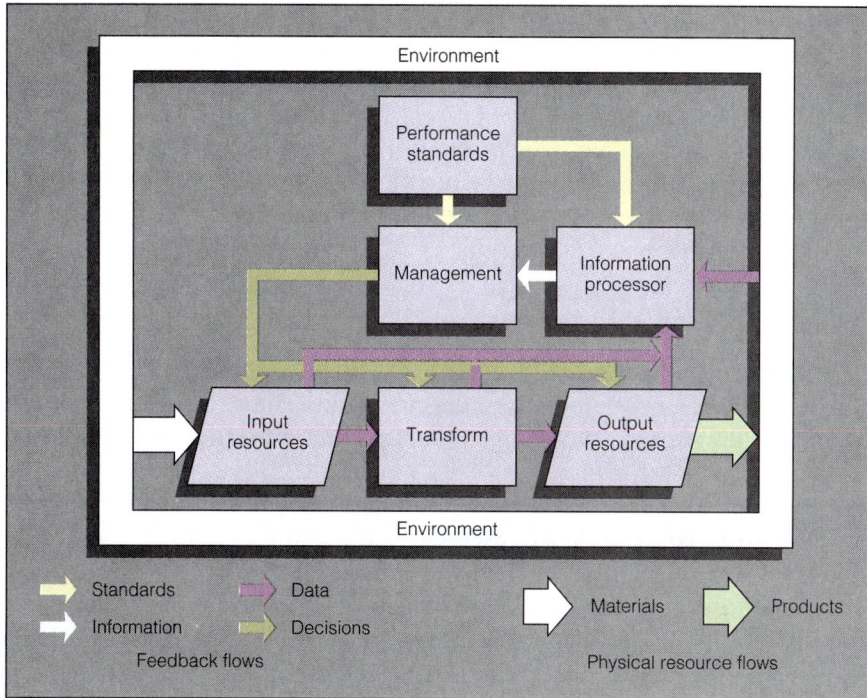

FIGURE 4.9

The Firm as
a System

Figure 4.9 shows the firm in this systems context. The feedback loop has been modified to include an **information processor** that transforms data gathered from the physical system and from the environment into information. The information processor can be a computer or any other device or activity that produces information from data. The information is made available to the manager who makes decisions that are communicated back to the physical system. The feedback loop therefore consists of three media: data, information, and decisions.

Data is gathered describing not only the output but also the input and the transformation processes. Management wants to know how *all* of the system is functioning. If any part is defective, decisions are made that relate to that particular part—input, transformation, or output.

You will note that the performance standards are made available to the information processor as well as to management. This enables the information processor to relieve management of much of the work involved with comparing actual performance to the standards. The information processor can assume some of the monitoring responsibility of the management.

The feedback loop includes three key elements that function together to control the physical system of the firm. These elements are the management, the standards, and the information processor. We will use the term **conceptual system** to describe these three elements. The data, information, and decisions flowing through the conceptual system *represent* the physical system, and are used to control the physical system.

This is the manner in which management controls the firm and ensures that all of the resources are working toward the objectives. You can see the important role played by information. It provides the basis for solving problems that arise in any area of the firm's operations. If the information does not flow as it should, management will not know that problems exist or cannot understand them once they become known.

THE ENVIRONMENT OF THE BUSINESS ORGANIZATION

Figure 4.9 recognizes the input flow of materials from the firm's suppliers, and the output flow of products to the customers. These are only two of the environmental elements with which the firm interfaces; there are six others:

- Organized **labor**
- **Government**
- The firm's **stockholders or owners**
- The **local community** where the firm resides
- The **financial community** of banks and other monetary institutions
- The firm's **competition**

Some of these environmental elements represent resources and some represent constraints. The suppliers furnish material resources, while labor and the local community furnish personnel resources. The stockholders, financial community, and customers furnish money resources. In some cases the government furnishes money resources in the form of research support, grants, and subsidies. In other cases the government serves as a constraint as it enforces the various laws and regulations that relate to business. Competition is a special type of environmental element in that it is the only one that is dedicated completely to constraining the firm.

The firm's management must operate within the resource limitations and constraints of the environment. We recognized in Chapter 1 that problems often are caused by something that happens in the environment. A manager must be alert to the environment so that current problems can be solved and potential problems can be prevented.

Environmental Resource Flows

Physical resources flow from the environment to the firm and from the firm to the environment as shown in Figure 4.10. We have recognized the input personnel, material, and money flows, as well as the output product flow. In this figure the firm's products are seen as a type of material flow.

These flows in turn stimulate other flows. The firm must pay the suppliers for the materials, and the customers must pay the firm for the products. Therefore, money flows must be added. There is a two-way money flow connecting the firm and the government, stockholders, and financial community. The government provides certain funds and receives tax payments,

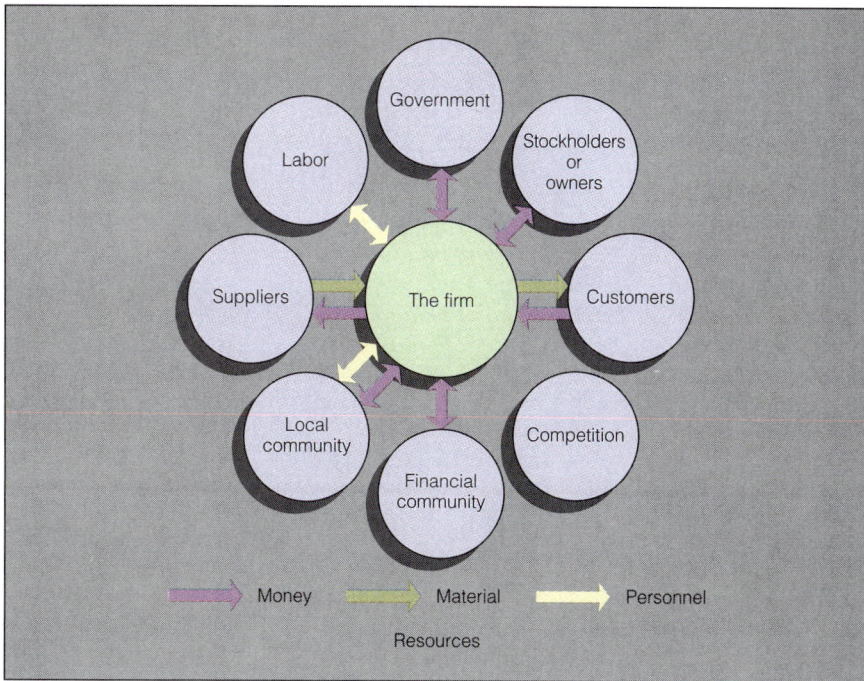

FIGURE 4.10
Environmental
Flows of Physical
Resources

the stockholders buy stock and receive dividends, and the financial institutions make loans that are repaid. The firm does not make direct money payments to organized labor, and does not pay money to the local community specifically for the labor flow. Most firms recognize their responsibilities to the local community and support local charities, hospitals, symphonies, and the like.

An important flow not pictured in Figure 4.10 is that of information. The firm strives to maintain an *incoming* information flow from *each* of the elements as a means of monitoring environmental activity. If the firm is to gather this environmental information in many cases it must provide information in return. If the firm expects local bankers to supply information on financial trends, the firm must be willing to provide the bankers with information on their own operations. Therefore, the firm actively participates in an *outward* information flow to all elements *except competition*.

Management recognizes that flows of environmental information are just as important as internal flows, and strives to maintain the flows at the desired level.

A MODEL OF A BUSINESS SYSTEM

We can integrate all of the topics in this chapter with the graphic model in Figure 4.11. The colored arrows represent the resource flows for each environmental element. The resource flows within the organization are shown

FIGURE 4.11

A Model of a Business System

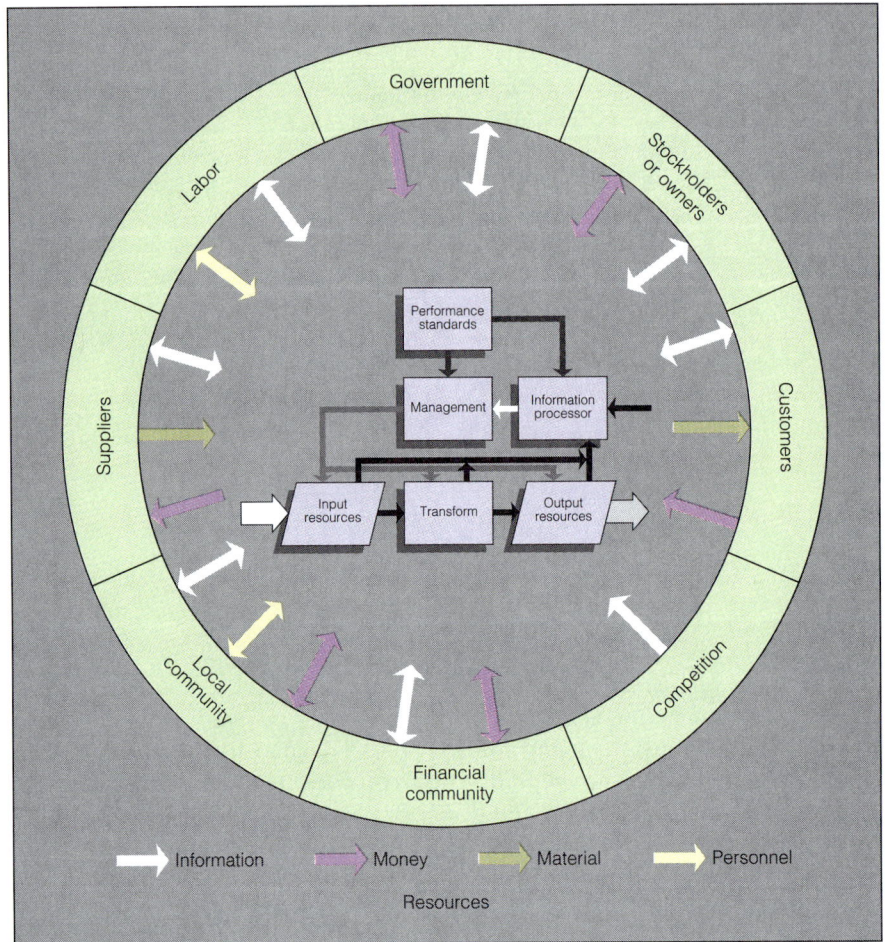

also. This model represents the problem-solving scene. The manager is presented with problems when both physical and conceptual resources do not flow as intended. Incoming flows of both environmental and internal information are necessary for problem solution.

BENEFITS OF VIEWING ORGANIZATIONS AS SYSTEMS

Certain aspects of the organization are visible to the eye. Most organizations maintain organization charts to show the functional and hierarchical relationships between units and people. The functional organization structure is especially easy to see. Names on doors label the units in a functional manner such as Marketing Division and Accounting Department.

However, these visible structures actually can hinder the problem-solving process. They create a situation where the problem solver cannot "see the forest for the trees." Since many of the levels and functional areas become involved in a particular activity, it is difficult to identify exactly where the problem lies. Everyone appears to be involved. This situation is made even more difficult when functional attitudes exist and result in finger pointing to other areas as the cause.

Viewing the firm as a system makes clear the importance of an information flow. If the manager is to control the system, then information must flow from all of the internal units as well as each element in the environment. In addition, a communication network must enable the manager to issue decisions that change the system's operation. These information flows enable the firm to function as a controlled, closed-loop system.

The Systems View of Problem Solving

In Chapter 1 we identified four basic steps in problem solving:

1. Understand the problem to be solved
2. Evaluate alternate solutions
3. Implement the best solution
4. Follow up to make certain that the solution is working

These steps are easier to take when the manager adopts a systems view. The manager can make certain that incoming information exists to signal existing and potential problems and also to facilitate understanding the problems (step 1). This same incoming information flow can also be used to evaluate alternate solutions (step 2). The communication network enables the manager to transmit decisions back to the units of the firm during the implementation period (step 3). The incoming information flow can also be used to follow up on the solution to ensure that it is working (step 4).

As an example of how the feedback loop is involved in problem solving, consider the following scenario. A manager views a periodic report and sees indications that a problem might exist. A request is entered into the manager's terminal to produce a special report that provides additional information. With an understanding of the problem, the manager identifies several possible solutions and uses a mathematical model to evaluate each one. The manager plays the What-If game to identify the solution that appears to be best, and uses the office automation system to communicate instructions to those persons responsible for solution implementation. Finally, a set of periodic reports keeps the manager informed concerning the effectiveness of the solution.

Do Managers Adopt a Systems View?

If you were to survey managers and ask them if they view the firm as a system as they solve problems, many would either say "No" or ask "What's a systems view?" This does not mean that they do not do it; it simply means that they are not *aware* that they do it. Few managers were introduced to systems fundamentals in school, and they have made no conscious efforts to incorporate them into their thought processes.

The systems fundamentals are very logical, and their benefits become evident through a process of trial and error. Good problem solvers are those who know their environment and have built effective information-gathering systems. They have recognized the necessity of good standards of performance and communications networks with their employees. These are all ingredients of adopting a systems view. We use the term **systems concept** to represent this view.

SUMMARY

The term organization is used to describe the group of resources established for a particular purpose. Organizations can be public or private, and they can be profit-seeking or nonprofit. Public organizations are the federal, state, and local governments. Profit-seeking private organizations can be corporations, where ownership is open to everyone through the purchase of stock. The stockholders are represented in decision making by a board of directors. Other forms of profit-seeking private organizations are owned by the founders who are either proprietors or partners, and they make the major decisions.

You can think of an organization of any type as a network of resource flows. Some of the resources are physical—personnel, facilities, equipment, materials, and money. Other resources are conceptual in that they *represent* physical resources. Examples of conceptual resources are information and data. The conceptual resources are especially important at upper-organizational levels where the managers often are isolated from most of the physical resources. When the organization is viewed in terms of resource flows, the main responsibility of management is to assemble the needed resources and keep them working toward the objectives of the organization.

The most popular way to organize a business is along functional lines. The primary functions are financial, marketing, and manufacturing. This functional structure often inhibits the solution of problems relating to resource flows since many of the flows cross functional boundaries. Top management works continuously to create a company attitude within the organization so that functional influences are minimized.

Although there are many types of organizations, all employ the same types of resources, the managers follow the same principles, the structures are generally functional in nature, the employees and their units are arranged in a hierarchy, and there is uniform concern for revenue collection and expense control. These common features make it possible to apply the same problem-solving techniques regardless of the organization type.

A firm can be viewed as an open system, receiving resources from the environment, transforming those resources, and making the outputs available to the environment. The firm is controlled by management serving as a control element, obtaining information from an information processor, and comparing this information with standards. These three elements—management, information processor, and standards—are the conceptual system. When performance must be altered, management makes decisions that travel along the feedback loop to the system units. When the feedback loop is closed in this manner, the firm is a closed-loop system.

The environment of the firm can be classified into eight elements—suppliers, customers, labor, government, stockholders or owners, local community, financial community, and competition. Resources flow between each element and the firm. In most cases there is a two-way information flow in addition to various physical flows. However, in the case of competition the firm seeks to establish only an incoming information flow.

When a firm is viewed as a system, the need for standards and a feedback loop becomes clear. The systems concept also makes it easier to understand the real causes of problems without being misled by functional influences. Although many managers do not consciously implement a systems-oriented style, it becomes their choice through trial and error.

KEY CONCEPTS

Influences of organizational structure on problem solving

Physical and conceptual resources that flow through the firm

How functional organization can hinder problem solving

The similarities that exist among organizations of all types

The business organization as a closed-loop, open system

How the conceptual system is used to manage the physical system

The relationship between the firm and its environment expressed in terms of resource flows

KEY TERMS

Physical resource	Physical system	Information processor
Conceptual resource	Open system	Conceptual system
Functional organization structure	Feedback loop	Systems concept
	Closed-loop system	
Functional attitude	Open-loop system	
Chief executive officer (CEO)	Objective	
System	Standard	

QUESTIONS

1. List five physical resources. Which one is the least valuable because of its physical properties?

2. What is a conceptual resource? Give an example.

3. Why might a president place a higher value on conceptual resources than would a lower-level manager such as the supervisor of the welding department?

4. How does a functional attitude impede problem solving?

5. List five characteristics that all types of organizations have in common.

6. Why would a nonprofit organization be concerned with increasing its revenues?

7. Explain why your watch is an open system. Are there any inputs? If so, what are they? What about outputs?

8. Is your watch a closed-loop system or an open-loop system? Explain.

9. What are the three media that flow through the feedback loop of a business firm?

10. Which three elements control the physical system of the firm? What name is used to describe these elements?

11. What conditions in a firm could contribute to it being an open-loop system?

12. Which environmental elements are connected to the firm by means of two-way money flows?

13. Why must two-way information flows exist between the firm and most of the environmental elements?

14. Explain the role of the feedback loop in:

   a. Understanding the problem.
   b. Implementing the solution.
   c. Following up on the solution.

15. What do we mean when we say that a manager has a systems view of the organization?

CASE PROBLEM — Polar Bear Coolers

Polar Bear Coolers is a Montgomery, Alabama, manufacturer of commercial refrigeration units such as those found in the frozen-foods sections of supermarkets. Their president, Dorothy Ramos, has just returned from a seminar sponsored by the American Management Association on management information systems. Polar Bear has used a computer for years, but mainly for data processing. The managers receive very little computer-produced information. In fact, they receive very little formal information, most of it coming from observation and personal conversations. Ramos calls a meeting of the executive committee, a group composed of herself and the vice precedents of finance (Alice Kimbrough), manufacturing (Bill Powell), and marketing (Jeff Akers). The executive committee makes all of the key decisions in the company.

Ramos: The reason I called this meeting was to tell you a little bit about the AMA seminar. I am really enthused about implementing a management information system, and want to get your reactions.

Kimbrough: I think it's long overdue. We've got a sound accounting system. The data is there. All we have to do is print it out. Our computer department is caught up on their projects, and they have hardware resources that they haven't even used yet. They should jump at the chance.

Ramos: Do you think that our computer people have the skills necessary to implement an MIS? You should know, the computer department is in your area.

Kimbrough: Well, probably not. But they can learn. We've got money in the budget to send them to school. They certainly have good computer skills.

Ramos: One thing that you should all be aware of is that if we do implement an MIS, it will take a lot of your time. You will have to spend time with the computer people explaining what information you need.

Powell: Well I'm not so sure that I can oblige. I've got my hands full getting the new R-5000 cooler off the production line. That project has all of my staff tied up. I'd just as soon pass for now. Why don't you all go ahead and implement the MIS. Maybe manufacturing can participate in a year or so when we get caught up.

Akers: Bill, you'll never get caught up. I've been here fifteen years and you've always had a crash project. I don't think that we can count on manufacturing to participate.

Ramos: Jeff, can I count on you?

Akers: Sure. You know us marketers. We're always ready to take on something new.

Ramos: Well, let me think it over. We can discuss it again at our next meeting.

1. Does Polar Bear need an MIS? Explain.

2. Do they have all of the resources necessary to implement an MIS? Explain.

3. What problems do you think that they will encounter if they go ahead and implement the MIS without manufacturing's participation?

4. Assume that you are a friend of Ramos' who owns a consulting business. She calls you, explains the situation, and asks for advice. What do you suggest that she do right now?

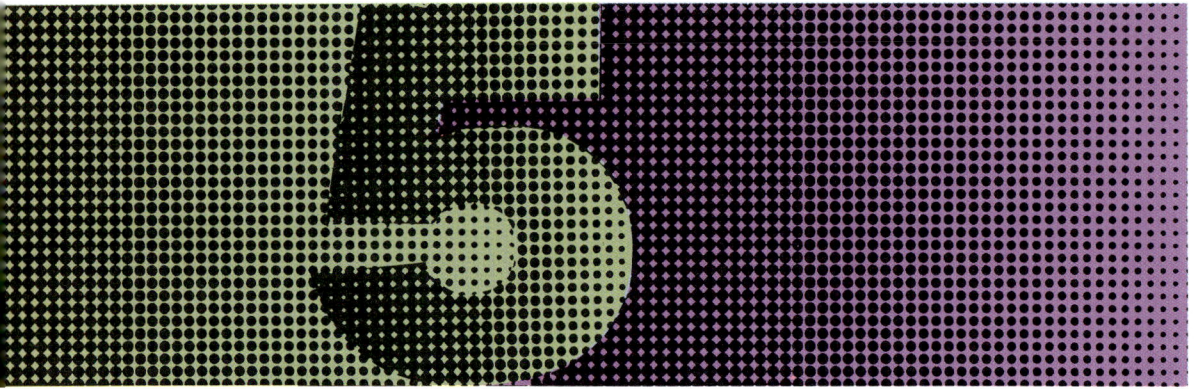

Business Problems

LEARNING OBJECTIVES   After studying this chapter, you should:

- Understand the time-consuming nature of problem solving and the need to respond to problem signals quickly
- Be able to distinguish between formal and informal systems for generating problem signals
- Learn to follow a chain of symptoms leading to the root cause of the problem
- Know the ingredients necessary to achieve a good solution
- Understand the effect of problem structure on decision making
- Become more familiar with how the computer can be used to solve problems relating to the physical resources
- See how problem structure influences the degree of problem-solving support the computer can provide

---

OVERVIEW

Now that we have described the setting in which problems are solved, let us direct our attention to the problems themselves. We first examine the manner in which the time dimension affects problem-solving and then we identify each basic activity in that process. A key factor is the distinction between problem symptoms and causes.

The problem-solving process consists of eight ingredients—a problem, a problem-solver, standards, information, solution criteria, alternate solutions, internal constraints, and a solution.

The manager's confidence in the solution is influenced by the structure of the problem. Problem structure is one of the underlying constructs upon which the concept of the decision support system, or DSS, has been built.

The solutions the manager reaches can be either optimizing or satisficing. The manager plays the What-If game in reaching satisficing solutions, and evaluates both satisficing and optimizing solutions before they are implemented.

We conclude by giving examples of how managers solve some typical business problems and by explaining ways the computer can be used.

IMPORTANCE OF THE TIME ELEMENT

Business is conducted at a more rapid pace today than ever before. Modern technology has made it possible to perform business activities much faster than anyone would have dreamed just a few years ago.

This increased pace can be seen in the process the firm follows in transforming raw materials into finished products. The firm often can place orders for raw materials by entering the order data directly into the supplier's computer system. The supplier can ship the materials by airfreight, and computerized materials-handling systems can speed the flow of the material through the plant. Much of the production process is automated, often utilizing factory robots. Once the finished goods have been fabricated they can be speeded to the firm's customers by airfreight.

Not only have there been increases in the speed with which the physical

FIGURE 5.1
A Factory Robot Speeds the Production Process

resources flow through the firm, but the flow of communications has increased as well. This is the feedback loop of the firm as a system. Information can be communicated electronically using office automation applications. Electronic mail enables the firm's employees to send messages to each other using their computer terminals. Voice mail permits the storage and transmission of audible messages using a combination of telephones and the computer. When the communication must be in the form of paper documents, specialized delivery firms such as Federal Express and UPS can deliver written messages overnight to almost anywhere in the world. It is also possible to transmit copies of documents over great distances in only a few seconds using facsimile transmission, or FAX.

These communication technologies represent the nervous system of the firm. Signals are sent to management, advising of a problem or potential problem. Management, in turn, sends signals to the various units within the organization to produce a corrective action. As firms seek a competitive edge in the marketplace, managers look for ways to respond more quickly to problem situations. The time required to solve a problem can be just as important as the solution achieved. A solution coming too late is no help at all.

PROBLEM-SOLVING ACTIVITIES

The time required to solve a problem is composed of four basic activities: generate a problem signal, understand the problem, select the solution, and implement the solution.

Generate a Problem Signal

Management likes to learn of problems *before* they cause any harm. **Problem-sensing systems** therefore are devised to be on the alert for problem signals. A **problem signal** is any type of indication that a problem exists now or might exist in the future. The signal can take any form—verbal, written, electronic, or some physical movement or condition. An example of a verbal signal is a telephone call, a written signal could be a memo or a report, and an electronic signal could come in the form of a message displayed on the manager's computer screen. A physical signal might be a line of customers waiting to be served, an empty shelf in the inventory storeroom, or a disassembled production machine awaiting repair parts.

The problem-sensing systems that managers devise can be formal or informal. A **formal system** is one that is planned in advance and is used according to a schedule. For example, a committee consisting of the firm's top-level managers meets each Monday to review the previous week's activity and plan for the coming week. Committee members can evaluate how previously implemented solutions are working and whether new problems need attention. Other examples of formal problem-sensing systems are periodic reports and tours of facilities. Some managers make it a practice to tour their areas at least once daily to look for problems to solve.

FIGURE 5.2

Physical Conditions
Often Serve as
Problem Signals

An **informal system** is one that is not used according to a schedule; it is called into play on an as-needed basis. An example is a telephone call from a salesperson advising the sales manager of new competitive activity.

Although many problem signals are generated by informal systems, the conditions that trigger the signals often are ignored or go undetected. As an example, the salesperson might not ask customers about competitive activity or might not take the time to alert the sales manager. For that reason, managers prefer to install formal systems so that little is left to chance.

Problem-sensing systems are devised to generate problem signals as quickly as possible. Messages that are communicated face-to-face, by telephone, and by computer networks are preferred over those in a written form sent through the mails.

A Computer-Based Problem-Sensing System

An example of a problem signal generated by the computer is a report prepared each day listing the inventory items with balances that have dropped to the reorder point. The **reorder point** is the inventory level that triggers an order of replenishment stock. Firms attempt to avoid a **stockout** condition of no inventory by anticipating the need to place an order when stock becomes low. It takes suppliers time to fill an order, and if the firm waits until no stock exists to place an order the stockout condition will last for several days, weeks, or even months. Considerable sales revenue can be lost during this period.

Figure 5.3 is a diagram showing how the reorder point signal works for a single inventory item. The diagram assumes a constant daily sales rate of

FIGURE 5.3

The Reorder Point Is
a Problem Signal

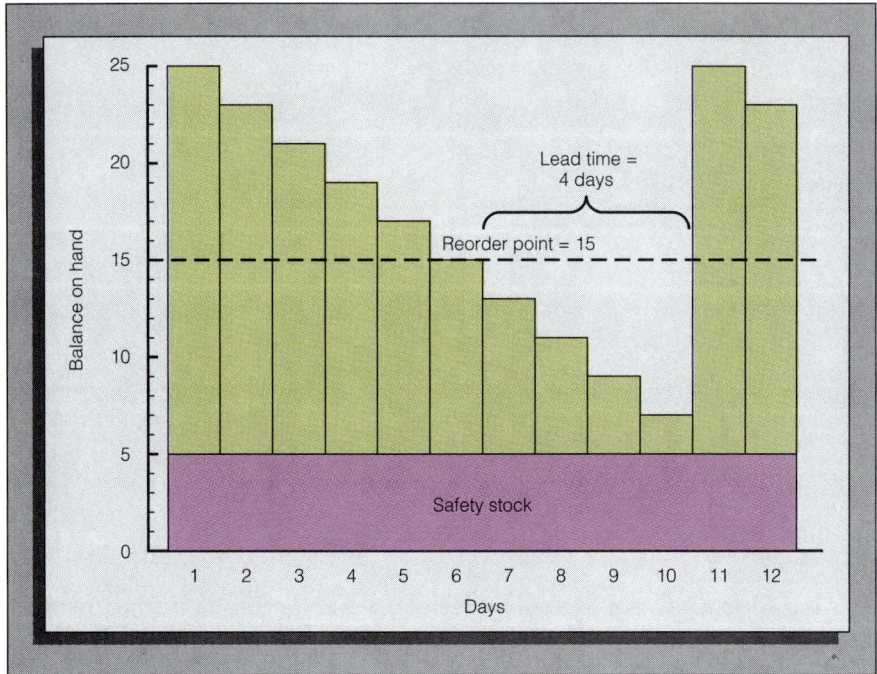

FIGURE 5.3

The Reorder Point Is a Problem Signal

two units. The **balance on hand** is twenty-five on day 1 and reaches the reorder point of fifteen on day 6. This signal causes a purchase order to be placed with the supplier.

The supplier requires four days **lead time** to fill the order. During that time the balance on hand continues to drop. On day 11 the balance has dropped to five when the replenishment shipment arrives. The receipt causes the balance on hand to be increased to twenty-five units.

You will notice that the firm has established a **safety stock** of five units to guard against a stockout. In the unpredictable world of business nothing can be anticipated with complete certainty. For example, the sales rate of two units per day will not always occur, or the supplier will require more than four days to fill the order.

Understand the Problem

Once the signal has been issued, it takes time to understand the problem. It might be necessary to gather additional information and data by conducting interviews or searching data files.

Management must ensure that it reacts to *problems* rather than to *symptoms* of problems. A problem **symptom** is an *indication* that a problem exists; it is not the problem itself, but often serves as a problem signal.

The situation is similar to that of a dentist who is confronted with a patient with a toothache. The toothache is not the problem; it is only a symptom. The dentist must find out the cause, such as a cavity, a fracture, or an infection. By reacting to the problem rather than the symptom, the dentist possibly can solve the problem without the need for an extraction.

The manager reacts in the same manner. The symptom might be a decline in profits. The manager must learn the cause of the decline. Perhaps it is due to the sales of a new product not living up to expectations. In that case what is the reason? Perhaps the product does not perform as advertised and constantly breaks down. If so, what is causing the breakdowns? Maybe it is a poor quality-control program in the plant. Then what is that cause? It might be high turnover of quality-control inspectors, the people who verify the quality of items as they are produced. The manager then would seek the cause of the excessive turnover. The salary level for quality-control inspectors might be less than at other firms. If that is the **root cause** then corrective action can be taken.

In this example the manager followed a **symptom chain** as shown in Figure 5.4 that eventually led to the root cause. The sales decline, poor product performance, poor quality control, and high turnover were only symptoms. The real problem was the low salary level.

Select the Solution

Once the root cause has been identified and the problem is understood, the manager must identify and evaluate the alternate solutions. It might be necessary to gather additional information and data in order to evaluate each alternative by comparing its advantages and disadvantages. The alternative that appears to be best-suited for solving the particular problem is selected for implementation.

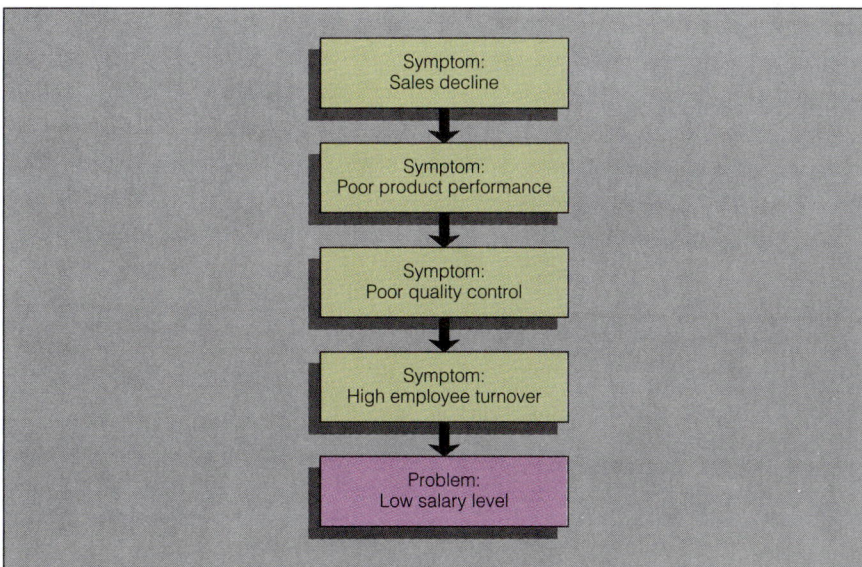

FIGURE 5.4

The Manager Can Follow a Symptom Chain

Implement the Solution

Once the solution has been identified, it must be implemented. Directives must be communicated down through the ranks to those who will put the solution to work. In some cases employees must be advised of changed company policies, or in-house educational programs must be conducted.

This is an area where office automation can speed the flow of communications. The manager can use word processing to prepare memos to be sent to the employees through the company mail. The manager can also use the computer system to transmit the messages as electronic or voice mail.

The manager is aware of how lengthy the problem-solving process can be, and devotes much attention to putting into place those systems that perform each of the steps as rapidly as possible.

INGREDIENTS OF THE PROBLEM-SOLVING PROCESS

The first necessary ingredient in problem solving is a problem to solve. Then you need a problem solver. There are other ingredients as well, as illustrated in Figure 5.5. Most of the ingredients exist within the problem-solver's organization. Only two, environmental information and environmental constraints, are external to the organization.

Standards

These are the performance standards that we identified in Chapter 4. They specify the **desired state** the system is expected to attain.

Information

The manager must have information available that describes the current performance level of the system—the **current state**. The current state is compared to the desired state to determine if a problem exists.

Information is gathered describing both internal and environmental activity. A good source of **internal information** is the firm's accounting system. The **environmental information** describes situations that can influence the resource flow between the elements and the firm. For example, firms often conduct customer surveys to identify unsatisfied needs, or to reveal attitudes about current products.

Solution Criteria

The manager must specify the improvements in performance that will be necessary to solve the problem. These are the **solution criteria** that bring the current state in line with the desired state. For example, if the performance standard is a production rate of 1,200 units per day and the firm is producing 1,050 units, the rate will have to be increased by 150 units.

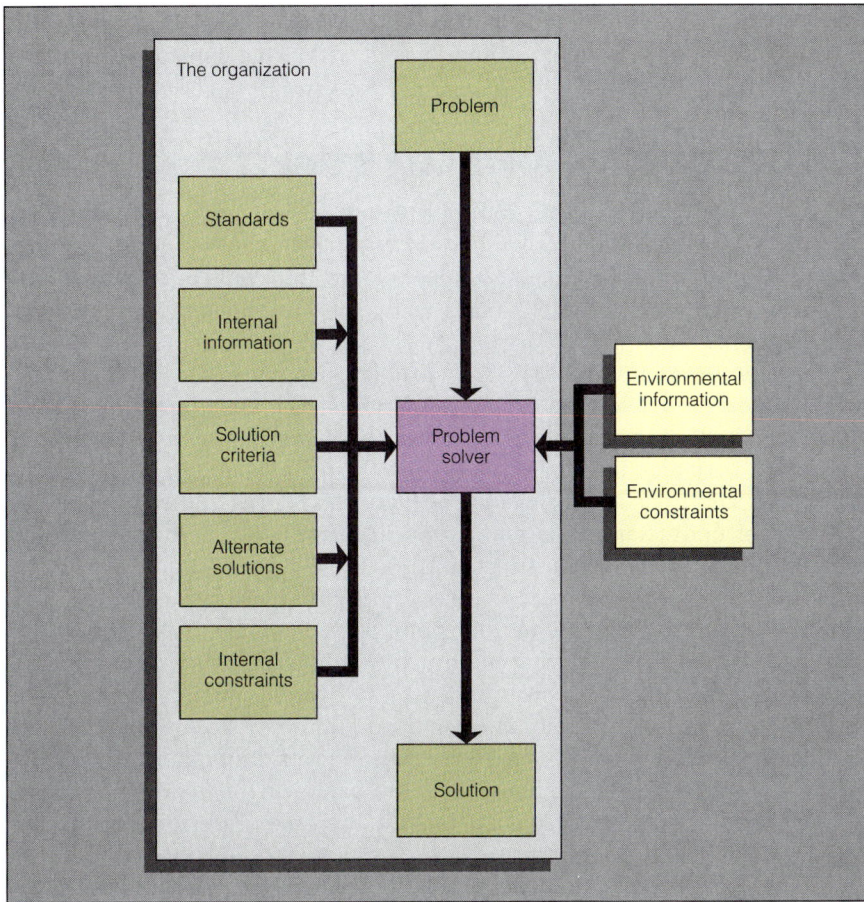

FIGURE 5.5

Components of the Problem-Solving Process

Alternate Solutions

Various ways to solve the problem must be identified and evaluated if the manager is to be assured that the best solution is reached.

Constraints

In all problem situations there are factors that constrain the problem solver. These constraints can originate both internally and in the environment. **Internal constraints** are those imposed by persons within the firm or by limited resources. For example, a manager specifies that the operating cost of the new system must not exceed that of the current system. Or, perhaps there are not enough sales representatives to market a new product.

   Environmental constraints can also be imposed by each element in the environment. Government laws, interest rates, and competitor activity are examples.

All of these elements affect the solution process. Standards, information, solution criteria, and alternate solutions contribute to a good solution. The manner in which the problem solver works within the constraints also has an influence.

THE CONCEPT OF PROBLEM STRUCTURE

There seems to be an almost unlimited variety of problems for managers to solve. Some of the same problems occur over and over, but new ones crop up nearly every day. The manager responds to this challenge by grouping similar problems into categories and using the same general approach for each category.

One way to classify problems is by problem structure. By **problem structure** we mean how well the problem is understood. If the manager knows all or almost all of the ingredients, or **variables**, that make up the problem, how these variables interrelate, and how they can be measured, then the problem is said to be a **structured problem**. Usually when the manager has this level of understanding a mathematical formula can be developed and used in solving the problem. An example is the EOQ formula.

The **EOQ** or **economic order quantity** is the quantity of an item that should be ordered when the reorder point is reached. The EOQ is intended to balance the costs of ordering too much with the costs of ordering too little. Certain **maintenance costs** are incurred when too much is ordered. The large inventory must be maintained in a warehouse or storeroom and there are such related costs as personnel, insurance, taxes, pilferage, and obsolescence. **Purchasing costs** also are incurred each time a purchase order is placed with a supplier. These costs include the time of persons in the purchasing department, telephone expense, forms costs, and so forth.

Persons who have studied the problem of inventory ordering have identified the key variables and have developed the EOQ formula:

$$EOQ = \sqrt{\frac{2\,PS}{M}}$$

Where: $P =$ Purchasing cost (in dollars per purchase order)
  $S =$ Annual sales of the product (in units)
  $M =$ Maintenance cost (in dollars per unit)

As an example of how the formula is used, assume that a computer store sells 260 Mac computers per year. If the annual maintenance cost is $3 per unit and the cost of a purchase order is $65, the EOQ is:

$$\sqrt{\frac{2 \times 65 \times 260}{3}} = \sqrt{11{,}267} = 106$$

Each time the store places an order for more Macs, it orders 106.

Few business problems are as well structured as the inventory ordering problem. By the same token, however, very few can be classified as **unstructured problems**. The manager usually is able to identify and perhaps measure *some* of the variables. Most problems, therefore, are **semistructured problems**.

An example of a semistructured problem is the one relating to building a new plant. One of the decisions involves selecting the location. Some of the variables influencing that decision can be measured—land costs, costs to ship raw materials into the plant, costs to ship the finished products out, taxes, and insurance. These variables represent the structured portion of the problem.

Other variables, although known, are difficult to measure. Firms prefer to build plants in communities that will facilitate recruiting and retaining the needed employees. Firms prefer locations with good climates, schools, churches, shopping, and recreation. Although the quality of life offered by a particular community can be subjectively evaluated, it is difficult to measure it quantitatively. That portion of the problem has little structure, producing an overall problem that is semistructured.

The Decision Support System Concept

In Chapter 1 we recognized how Gorry and Scott-Morton originated the decision support system (DSS) concept. They identified the area of semistructured problems as the one needing attention as shown in Figure 5.6.

A structured problem can be solved by the computer alone, following a programmed routine supplied by the manager. In solving semistructured problems, the manager enlists the power of the computer to address the structured portion while the manager subjectively considers the portion with little or no structure. If a problem has no structure at all, the computer can provide no help and the manager must reach a solution subjectively.

The DSS concept has provided the most popular approach for using the

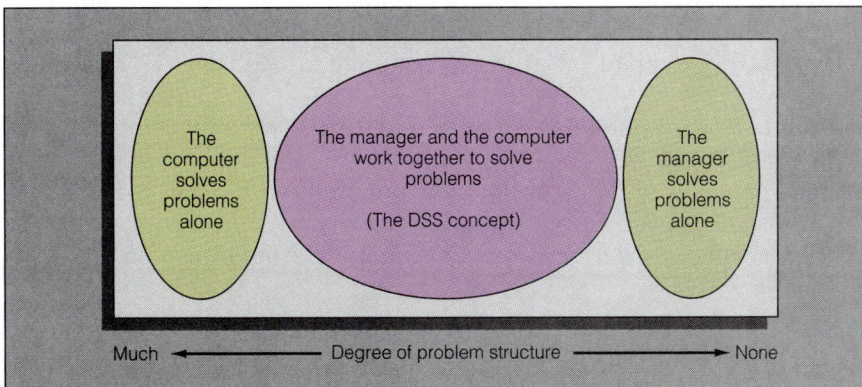

FIGURE 5.6

The DSS Is Intended to Be Used in Solving Semistructured Problems

The computer solves problems alone

The manager and the computer work together to solve problems

(The DSS concept)

The manager solves problems alone

Much ← ——— Degree of problem structure ——— → None

computer in problem solving during the 1980s. Managers have recognized that they can work *with* the computer as a problem-solving team.

TYPES OF SOLUTIONS

Sometimes the manager will identify a solution that she or he knows to be the best one. These solutions are called **optimizing solutions**. At other times the manager will identify a solution that may or may not be the best; it is simply *a* solution. Such solutions are called **satisficing solutions**; they satisfy the manager even though it is not known whether they are the best. Sometimes the manager, not wanting to invest any more time or money in the problem-solving process, will settle for a satisficing solution. At other times too little information is available for an optimizing solution.

Linear Programming

Certain mathematical techniques have been developed to produce optimizing solutions. As a rule, these techniques work only when the problems are well structured. A good example is **linear programming**, or **LP**. LP can solve two basic types of problems—routing and mix. It can determine the best route for city buses or salespersons to follow in covering their territories, and can determine the best mix of ingredients that go into such products as sausage or cement. In the case of LP, the best solution is the one that maximizes something, such as profit, or minimizes something, such as cost. For example, the best route for a city bus might be the one that carries the most riders in a twenty-four hour period. The best sausage mix might be the one costing the least, yet producing the taste consumers prefer.

The manager knows that the LP solution cannot be improved upon—it is an optimizing solution.

Playing the What-If Game

The solutions the manager reaches by playing the What-If game tend to be satisficing solutions. The problem is semistructured and the model does not address all the variables. The model produces an output, but the manager must apply subjective evaluation in deciding whether to implement a particular solution. Although it is possible that the solution might be improved upon, the manager is satisfied that it will solve the problem—it is a satisficing solution.

The necessary mathematics such as LP have been available to solve structured problems since the beginning of the computer era. Since semistructured problems occur more frequently, the DSS concept was developed. Today, the manager can use the computer in solving problems, even when all of the variables cannot be identified and measured.

EXAMPLES OF PROBLEM SOLVING

In Chapter 4 we identified the basic physical resources as personnel, facilities, equipment, materials, and money. In the section below we give examples of how managers use the computer in solving problems relating to each of these resource types.

Solving Problems Relating to Personnel[1]

The firm must determine the types and numbers of personnel needed to accomplish its objectives. Then it must obtain those resources and retain them in the firm as long as they are needed and are performing satisfactorily. The term **human resource information system** or **HRIS** has been coined to describe the computer-based system that supports the manager in solving problems relating to the personnel flow. Most large firms have a formal HRIS that may be used in establishing staffing levels, in recruiting, selecting, and placing new employees, and in counseling and promoting existing employees.

One of the most interesting applications is **job profile matching**. Each job in the company is studied to determine the tasks performed and the amount of time spent on each. Jobs often consist of a hundred or more tasks. The list of tasks and times represent the **job profile**.

All of the job profiles are matched by the computer to determine the degree of similarity between jobs. Similarity is measured in terms of profile **overlap**—the total percentage of time spent on the same tasks for each pair of profiles.

Figure 5.7 is a diagram that shows the overlap between jobs in the computer operator job family. The arrows connecting the job titles are labeled with the overlap percentage. The solid arrows indicate that an individual should be able to progress from one position to the next given the training and experience gathered in the lower-level position. The dotted arrows indicate that the progression to the higher-level position would require education or training not typically received in the lower-level position. This type of information is useful in counseling employees on possible career paths. For example, a series of higher positions can be identified that involve many of the tasks now being performed by the employee. When the employee is promoted, only the new tasks must be learned. The result is good job performance, possibly more frequent promotions, and high morale.

Solving Problems Relating to Facilities[2]

Much progress has been made in using the computer to design such facilities as plants and office buildings. Industrial engineers use special plant layout software to determine the most efficient arrangement of production machines. Architects use other software packages to design entire build-

---

[1] Material for this section was contributed by Dwain R. Boelter of Personnel Decisions, Inc. of Minneapolis, and P. R. Jeanneret of Jeanneret & Associates, Inc. of Houston. The author also acknowledges the assistance provided by Richard D. Arvey and Gerardine DeSanctis of the University of Minnesota.

[2] Material for this section was provided by Ric Guenther of the architectural firm Sikes Jennings Kelly & Brewer of Houston.

FIGURE 5.7

Job Overlap Helps
to Identify Career
Paths

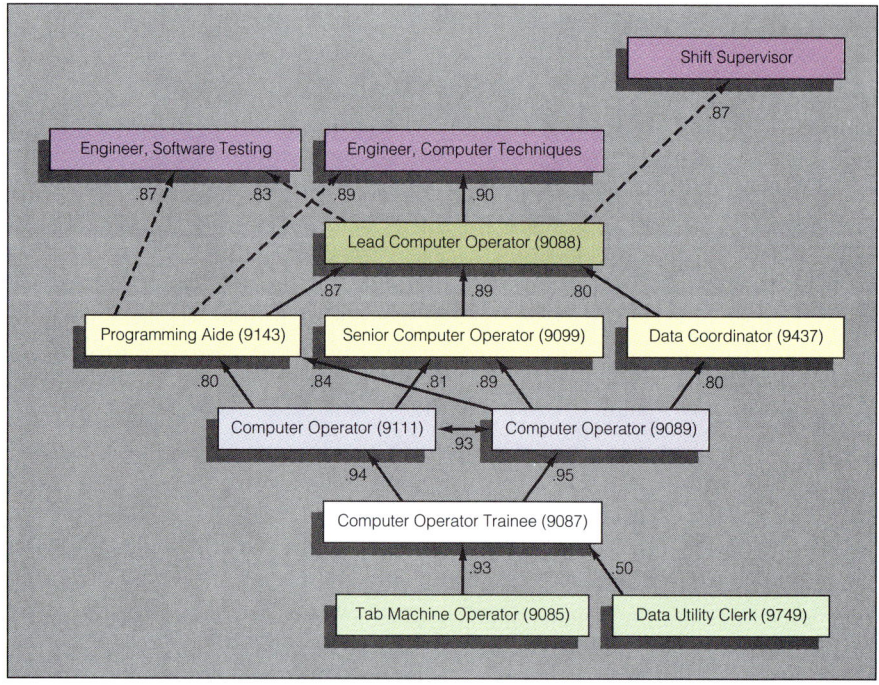

FIGURE 5.8

The Computer Can
Relieve the
Architect of Much
Drawing Time

ings and to determine the layout of offices and even the furniture arrangement.

Figure 5.8 illustrates a layout of a floor of an office building prepared by the computer. The output is printed on a plotter. Prior to the availability of

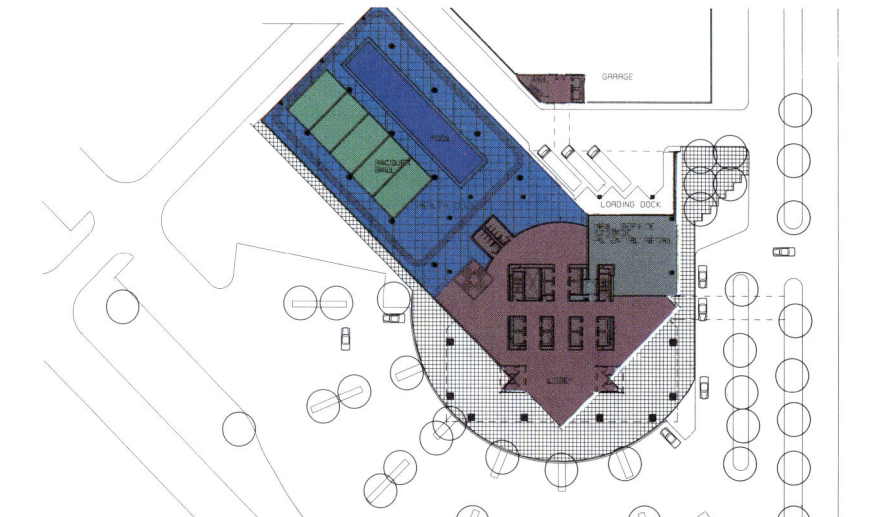

design software, much of the architect's time was spent in preparing and revising drawings. The software relieves the architect of much of the drawing time, providing more time for the more creative design activity and for working with clients.

Solving Problems Relating to Equipment[3]

Some equipment requires little or no maintenance. A personal computer is a good example. The general practice is to use it until something breaks and then get it fixed. Other equipment, however, must be maintained on a periodic basis. A good example is a large mainframe computer. It is common practice to set aside one or two hours each day for **preventive maintenance**, called **PM**, that is intended to prevent breakdowns. PM includes such activities as cleaning and oiling the mechanical parts, and checking and replacing electronic parts.

Production management uses PM as a way to minimize **breakdown hours**—the time machines are out of service awaiting repair. The computer can help production management solve this problem by printing a maintenance report as shown in Figure 5.9.

When production management feels that the breakdown hours listed in the center column are too high for a given machine, its maintenance can be

FIGURE 5.9

A Maintenance Report

EQUIPMENT MAINTENANCE SUMMARY

EQUIPMENT NUMBER	DESCRIPTION	SCHEDULED HOURS	RUNNING HOURS	BREAKDOWN HOURS	PARTS COST	LABOR COST	MAINTENANCE COST PER RUNNING HR.	COST GRTR 0.15?	TOTAL MAINTENANCE COST
1103	BURGMASTER DRILL	330.0	315.0	15.0	130.0	75.0	0.6508	*	205.0
1161	WARNER SWAZEY LATHE	495.0	400.0	95.0	60.0	1350.0	3.5250	*	1410.0
1178	CINCINNATI MILL	495.0	490.0	5.0	3.0	60.0	0.1286		63.0
1183	MAZAK N/C LATHE	330.0	328.0	2.0	5.0	10.0	0.0457		15.0
1195	FISCHER N/C LATHE	495.0	450.0	45.0	70.0	50.0	0.2667	*	120.0
2015	EXCELLO WORK CTR	495.0	420.0	75.0	700.0	100.0	1.9048	*	800.0
2113	EXCELLO BORING MILL	165.0	160.0	5.0	10.0	45.0	0.3438	*	55.0
2205	LINCOLN WELDER	330.0	330.0	0.0	0.0	0.0	0.0000		0.0
2213	FROREIP VERT LATHE	495.0	470.0	25.0	40.0	30.0	0.1489		70.0

[3] Material for this section was provided by Joseph Munn of Texas A & M University.

performed more often. When breakdown hours are minimal, maintenance can be performed less often, freeing mechanics for other work.

Production management can also use the report in deciding when it is time to purchase replacement equipment. The right-hand column that lists the total maintenance cost can be used in making this decision.

Solving Problems Relating to Materials

All firms have inventory problems of one sort or another. The problems are especially acute for a manufacturing organization that must have an adequate supply of raw materials for the production process.

The manager can use a mathematical model to estimate the impact of certain decisions on the inventory. For example, if the firm can find another supplier that can replenish the stock in three days rather than four, what will be the effect on inventory level and investment?

Figure 5.10 is a printout from such a mathematical model showing the activity for a single raw material item. A line is printed for each day show-

FIGURE 5.10

An Inventory Simulation

```
DATE:05/19/89         INVENTORY SIMULATION FOR 100 DAYS      PAGE 1

ITEM NUMBER:    25-100732
ITEM NAME:      CROWN MOLDING 3 1/2 IN.

          BEGIN                          END      ORDER     ANTICIPATED
  DAY    BALANCE    RECEIPTS    USAGE   BALANCE   QUANTITY   RECEIPT DATE
  ======================================================================
    1      800                    40      760
    2      760                   160      600
    3      600                    80      520
    4      520                   140      380
    5      380                   140      240       475           8
    6      240                   140      100
    7      100                   180       80-
    8       80-      475         120      275       475          10
    9      275                   140      135
   10      135      475           80      530
   11      530                   140      390
   12      390                   120      270       475          15
```

```
   98      290-     475         140       45       475         100
   99       45                  120       75-
  100       75-     475         120      280       475         114
```

ing the beginning balance, the receipts (the arrival of replenishment stock from the supplier), the usage (the number of units used in the manufacturing process), the ending balance, the order quantity, and the anticipated receipt date. Figure 5.11 shows the summary output from such a simulation that lists the various costs of a particular strategy.

Managers in the manufacturing function use such models in controlling the flow of resources through their area.

Solving Problems Relating to Money

Money flows into the firm from the environment as stockholders make investments, customers make purchases, and the financial community makes loans. Money flows back to the environment in the form of dividends to stockholders, payments to suppliers for purchases, and loan repayments to the financial community. Profit-seeking firms want the incoming flow to exceed the outgoing flow, and nonprofit firms want the

FIGURE 5.11

A Management Summary Produced by an Inventory Model

```
DATE:05/19/89        INVENTORY SIMULATION FOR 100 DAYS      PAGE 3

                           SUMMARY REPORT


==================[ S C E N A R I O    D A T A ]==================

UNIT CARRYING COST:  $1.35    UNFILLED SERVICE % COST:  $2,000.00
BEGINNING INVENTORY   800     ORDERING COST             $   85.00

==================[ D E C I S I O N    D A T A ]==================

ORDER QUANTITY        475     REORDER POINT                  335

========================[ R E S U L T S ]========================

       SERVICE LEVEL                      COST ANALYSIS

QUANTITY ORDERED     12,100    CARRYING COST        $     195
QUANTITY BACKORDERED  6,315    SERVICE COST         $106,000
SERVICE PERCENT        0.48    ORDERING COST        $  1,870
AVG INVENTORY LEVEL     144    TOTAL COST           $108,065


=================================================================
```

incoming flow to at least match the outgoing flow.

The seasonal nature of many firms' sales makes it difficult to achieve the desired flow rates. A manufacturer of surfboards is a good example. There is a high inflow of cash during the spring when the products are sold to wholesalers and retailers, but during the remainder of the year the expenses might exceed the sales.

The computer can perform a **cash-flow analysis** of the coming twelve-month period to show the monthly inflow and outflow. The output can be printed in the form of a **tabular report**, as shown in Figure 5.12, that presents the data in the standard fashion of rows and columns. It is also possible to print the output as a **graphic report** as illustrated in Figure 5.13.

With this information, financial management can make plans for loans during the deficit periods and for investments during the surplus periods.

FIGURE 5.12

A Cash-Flow Analysis in Tabular Form

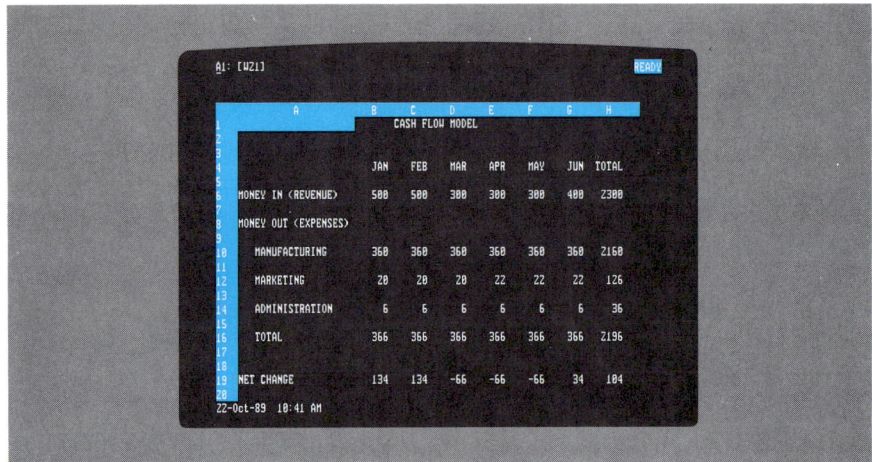

FIGURE 5.13

A Cash-Flow Analysis in Graphic Form

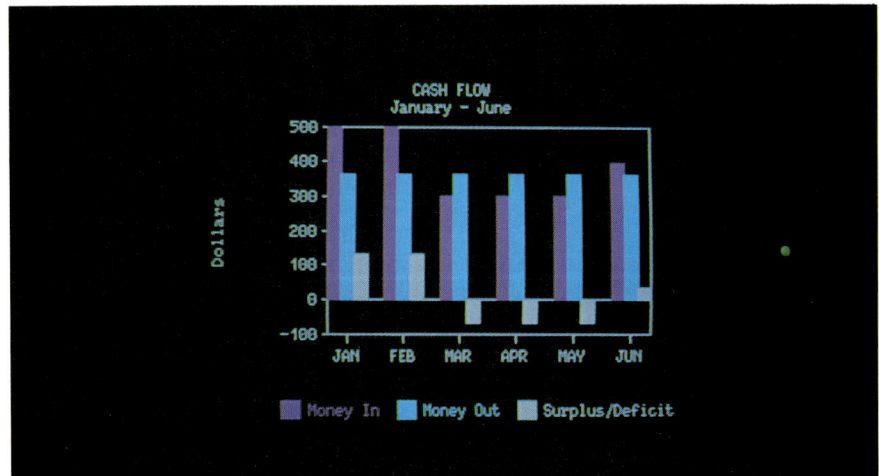

These are only a few of the many examples of how the computer can be used to solve problems relating to the firm's resources.

PROBLEM-SOLVING SYSTEMS

Some of the systems managers use to solve problems are quite simple, whereas others are complex. Steven L. Alter of MIT grouped systems into six classes based on degree of problem-solving support as shown in Figure 5.14.

Retrieve Data Elements

The simplest type of system is one that enables the manager to retrieve data elements. Perhaps the database contains precomputed figures showing the return on investment (ROI) for each of the firm's plants. The manager can request that the ROI for a particular plant be retrieved and displayed on the screen.

Analyze Entire Files

More support is provided when the system can analyze an entire file and produce the output in the form of a special or periodic report. For example, the computer can analyze a file of supplier data and print a report showing the volume of purchases during the past month from each supplier. Such a

FIGURE 5.14   Classes of Problem-Solving Systems

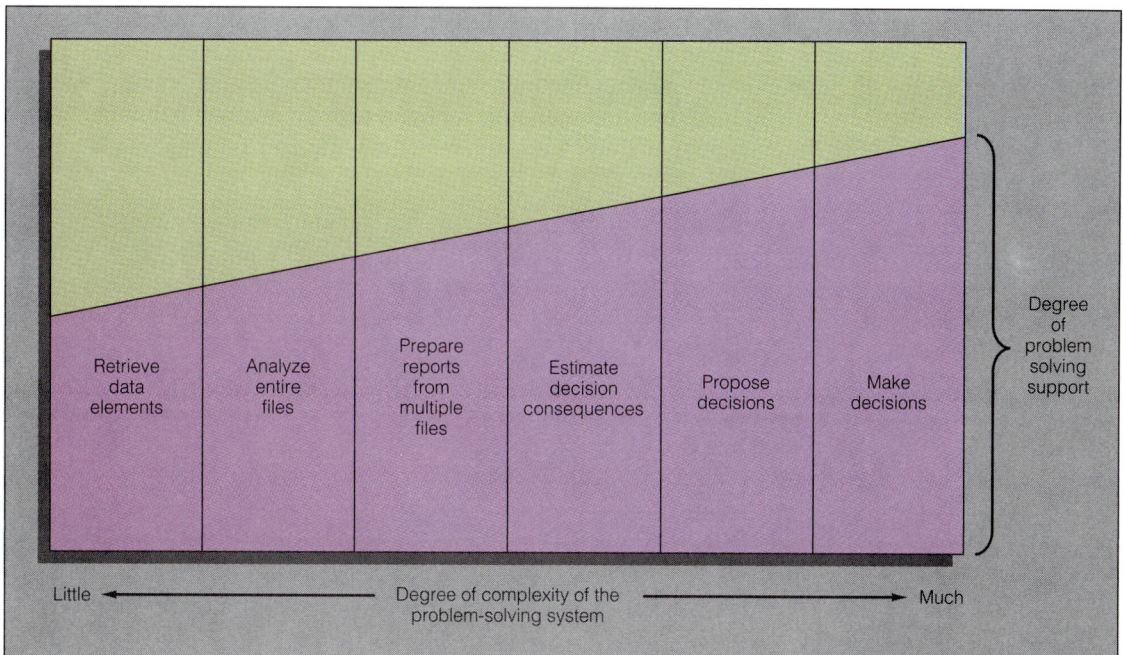

| Retrieve data elements | Analyze entire files | Prepare reports from multiple files | Estimate decision consequences | Propose decisions | Make decisions | Degree of problem solving support |

Little ← — Degree of complexity of the — → Much
problem-solving system

report would be helpful to buyers in negotiating quantity discounts from the high-volume suppliers.

Prepare Reports from Multiple Files

Many reports require that data be assembled from multiple files. A good example is the income statement illustrated in Figure 1.13. This report is a distillation of data from the inventory, accounts receivable, accounts payable, and other accounting files.

Estimate Decision Consequences

Up to this point, the problem-solving support has come from special and periodic reports. The final three system types involve the use of mathematical models.

The simplest model estimates what might happen if the manager makes a particular decision. An example is the output pictured in Figure 5.15. The model enables the manager to enter the price to be charged for a product during the coming year, and the projected results are printed for each quarter (three month period). In the example the manager enters a price of $5.00 and the quarterly after-tax profit is printed on the bottom line.

The model does not tell the manager that the $5.00 price is the best one; it simply shows what can be expected if such a price is charged. The manager can enter another price and see the results of the price change. In this way the manager uses the model to reach a satisficing solution.

Propose Decisions

When the structured portion of a problem is large, the system can identify the best decision. The linear programming model we discussed earlier is a model of this type.

However, we should recognize an important point concerning systems that facilitate an optimizing solution. Even though the best solution is identified, the manager does not implement it without first injecting a subjec-

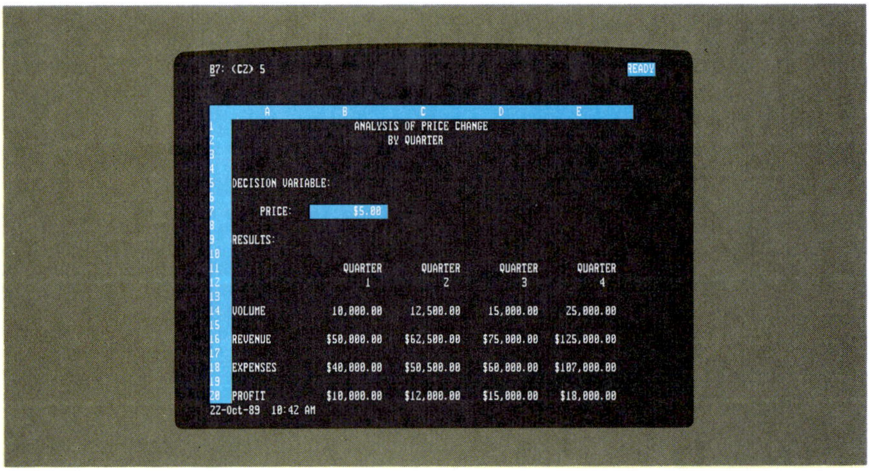

FIGURE 5.15

A Model that Permits the Manager to Estimate the Results of a Certain Price

tive evaluation. The manager knows that the model addresses only the structured part of the problem and that he or she is responsible for the unstructured part.

Make Decisions

When the problem is routine and a procedure for solving it has been worked out in detail, the manager will let the computer make the decision. This situation exists in the inventory area in the form of reorder point and order quantity formulas. The manager will not become involved except in such special situations as the order of very expensive items.

Problem structure influences the degree of problem-solving support that a system can provide. Better support is provided when the structured portion of the problem is large. There is also a relationship between systems complexity and the degree of support. The systems offering the greater support tend to be more complex.

ACQUIRING PROBLEM-SOLVING SYSTEMS

It is easy to get the idea that the manager only has to turn on the computer to obtain the necessary problem-solving information. Such a view is a misconception. Even when prewritten software is used the manager and perhaps the information specialist must spend days, weeks, or even months in studying the problem and deciding how it can be solved. It is only when this understanding exists that the necessary software can be purchased or prepared. When custom programming is necessary, several additional months might be required to do the coding and testing.

In addition to the time required to make available the necessary software, the data the software uses must be stored in the computer's storage units. In some cases the time required to create the database can exceed that of software preparation.

In Chapter 6 we examine the steps the manager and the information specialist take in developing computer-based problem-solving systems.

SUMMARY

Managers must respond to problem signals more quickly now than ever before. The time required to solve a problem consists of four activities—the time required to generate a signal, understand the problem, select the solution, and implement the solution.

Problem-sensing systems can be formal or informal. A computer-based system that detects inventory reorder conditions is an example of a formal system. A telephone call that advises the manager of a problem or potential problem is an example of an informal system. Much of the time spent in understanding the problem is devoted to separating symptoms from the root cause.

In solving a problem, the problem solver compares the current state to the desired state. Both internal and environmental information is used in understanding the current state. The solution criteria specify how much the current system must be improved. The evaluation of the alternate solutions must consider the constraints.

The concept of problem structure provided the foundation for the DSS concept. The DSS is aimed at semistructured problems.

Problem-solving systems can produce either optimizing or satisficing solutions. The What-If modeling technique is used most often in identifying satisficing solutions.

The computer can be used in solving problems relating to each of the resources. The simplest problem-solving systems enable users to retrieve data elements. The systems become successively more complex when they analyze entire files, prepare reports from multiple files, estimate decision consequences, propose decisions, and make decisions. Even with prewritten software, it can take months to implement computer-based systems.

KEY CONCEPTS

The difference between problem symptoms and the root cause

How solution criteria are derived from a comparison of the desired state and the current state

Problem structure

How solutions can be optimizing or satisficing

Variations in the degree of support that problem-solving systems can provide

KEY TERMS

Problem signal
Symptom
Root cause
Desired state
Current state
Solution criteria
Structured problem
Unstructured problem

Semistructured problem
Optimizing solution
Satisficing solution
Human resource information
    system (HRIS)
Tabular report
Graphic report

QUESTIONS

1. What are the four problem-solving activities?

2. What form does the problem signal take?

3. What is the difference between a formal and an informal problem-sensing system?

4. Assume that a company has established reorder points for each of its inventory items. What two unexpected events could cause stock-outs?

5. Which would be encountered the most often while solving a single problem—symptoms or root causes? Explain.

6. How does the manager know the current state of the system?

7. What is the name given to the difference between the current state and the desired state?

8. What features characterize a structured problem?

9. Is the DSS aimed at the types of problems that managers encounter frequently? Explain.

10. When would a manager settle for a satisficing decision rather than an optimizing one?

11. How can job profile matching contribute to improved employee morale?

12. Would a nonprofit organization be interested in cash-flow analysis? Explain.

13. Does a problem-solving system have to make computations on the data? Explain.

14. Why would a manager evaluate an optimizing solution before it is implemented?

15. Why does it take time to implement a problem-solving system even when prewritten software is used?

**CASE
PROBLEM**   Big Sky Sportswear

Big Sky Sportswear of Bozeman, Montana, manufactures outdoor clothing such as skiwear, swimsuits, and hunting and fishing apparel. They sell directly to wholesalers located across the United States, and the wholesalers sell to retailers such as department stores, sporting goods stores, and clothing stores. Product sales are very seasonal. For example, the retailers sell most of the skiwear during October through February. That means that the retailers buy the skiwear from the wholesalers during August and September, and the wholesalers buy it from Big Sky during June and July. Big Sky's main production months for skiwear are April and May.

Margie Rea is manager of the skiwear line and is responsible for everything relating to that product—planning, design, production, and distribution. During recent years, as competition increased, Big Sky has seen their skiwear profits drop. Big Sky either underestimates the sales impact of new styles and loses sales that could have been made had the stock been available, or overestimates the impact and is forced to sell the surplus stock at a loss.

One day Margie asks Bill French, the manager of the computer department, to come to her office. Margie presents the dilemma to Bill, who is thoroughly familiar with it. Margie explains that she is desperate for a solution, and thought that maybe the computer department could help.

Bill says "Well, it's clear that what we need is some kind of problem signal. If we had some way of knowing what is selling and is not selling at the retail level, we could set the level of our production accordingly. It wouldn't be necessary to produce so much early in the season; we could hold back and produce more if necessary."

"Bill, that sounds good, but I can see some difficulties. The special production runs would cost more than one big run in the spring."

Bill responds "But they probably wouldn't cost as much as the lost profits and the clearance sales. We could produce just enough in the spring to determine how the products will be received at the retail level. If we get the signal that sales are not going well, we don't produce any more. When sales go great, we produce more stock and get it right out to the wholesalers, maybe by airfreight."

Margie seems pleased with Bill's analysis, and says "Well, what we need is a problem signal of some sort. We also need to know who will issue it and what form it will take."

"And," interrupts Bill, "we also need to give some thought to what we can offer to the companies who will give us the signals. This is going to take some of their time, and they need to think that it is worth it."

Just then Margie's telephone rings. After a brief conversation she hangs up and says "Bill, I've got to go now. Let's continue this later. I think we're onto something."

1. Who would be best suited to issue the signals—the wholesalers or the retailers? Explain.

2. Should it be a formal or an informal system? Explain.

3. What are three ways that the signal could be communicated to Big Sky?

4. If the retailer initiates the signal, should it go to the wholesaler or to Big Sky? Why do you feel that your selected alternative is best? Does the other alternative have any advantages?

5. How could such a problem-sensing system benefit the retailers and wholesalers in terms of their material flows? What about their money flows?

Business Problem Solvers

LEARNING OBJECTIVES   After studying this chapter, you should:

- Understand that managers do not solve problems alone
- Become familiar with two ways to classify managerial activity
- Recognize the organizational influences on information source and form
- Become familiar with a way to classify managers based on their attitude toward problems
- Understand two techniques that can be used in generating problem signals—management by exception and critical success factors
- Recognize some of the problem-solving skills managers should possess
- See how the computer can be used in most of the problem-solving steps
- Learn who the information specialists are, the roles that they play in problem solving, and how the manager can take full advantage of their help
- Gain a familiarity with end-user computing—what it is, why it evolved, its strengths and weaknesses, and how firms are dealing with it

---

OVERVIEW

The main objective of this chapter is to learn more about the problem solvers. First we recognize that both the problem solver's organization as well as individual personal characteristics influence how problems are solved. In solving problems, the manager uses certain skills and employs concepts that have been developed to best utilize the manager's time. Two concepts are management by exception and critical success factors.

The computer can play an important role in problem solving, and the manager can use it alone or can be assisted by persons who are specialists in applying the computer as an information system. The various information specialists are described, and guidelines the manager can follow in working with the specialists are presented.

WHO IS THE PROBLEM SOLVER?

In Chapter 1 we recognized that problems can be solved by managers, non-managers, and both internal and environmental specialists. Managers seldom solve problems alone. They readily seek assistance from anybody that can help. **Group problem solving** is a popular approach, especially when the stakes are high. Several managers, staff assistants, and perhaps outside specialists can serve on a committee to solve a particular problem over a period of time. The terms **task force** and **project team** are often used to describe this type of group.

WHAT DO MANAGERS DO?

Two management theorists have received worldwide publicity for their classifications of what managers do. Henri Fayol, a Frenchman, in 1916 developed a list of management functions, and Henry Mintzberg, currently a professor at McGill University in Canada, in the early 1970s developed a list of managerial roles.

Management Functions

According to Fayol, all managers perform the following **management functions**:

- **Plan** what is to be done
- **Organize** the unit to accomplish the plan
- **Staff** the organization with the necessary personnel
- **Direct** the staff as they carry out their duties
- **Control** the staff to ensure proper performance

Although *all* managers perform *all* functions, managers on the upper-hierarchical levels spend much time planning and organizing, whereas those on lower levels spend much time staffing and directing. The control function is especially important to middle-level managers.

It is interesting that problem solving is not one of the functions. Perhaps problems arise when one or more of these functions are performed poorly. For example, when a unit exceeds its operating budget perhaps the reason is poor planning. Or, it might be that poor control was exercised.

The computer has provided excellent support as managers carried out the planning and control functions. Managers routinely use the computer to forecast future activity and to compare actual performance to the standards. However, the support for organizing, staffing, and directing has not been as good.

Management Roles

Mintzberg believes that the managers' authority and status enable them to play ten **management roles**. The roles fall into three categories—interpersonal, informational, and decisional—as illustrated in Figure 6.1.

Interpersonal roles

The interpersonal roles include figurehead, leader, and liaison. **Figurehead** includes ceremonial duties such as giving visiting dignitaries tours of the facilities. As **leader**, the manager maintains the unit by hiring and training the staff and providing motivation and encouragement. In the **liaison** role, contacts are made with persons outside the manager's own unit—with peers and others in the unit's environment.

Informational Roles

The informational category recognizes information as an important resource. As a **monitor**, the manager scans both internal and environmental activities for information bearing on the performance of the unit. When the manager receives valuable information to be passed along to others *in* the unit, he or she serves as a **disseminator**. The manager serves as a **spokesperson** by passing information to those *outside* the unit—superiors and persons in the environment.

FIGURE 6.1

Mintzberg's Managerial Roles

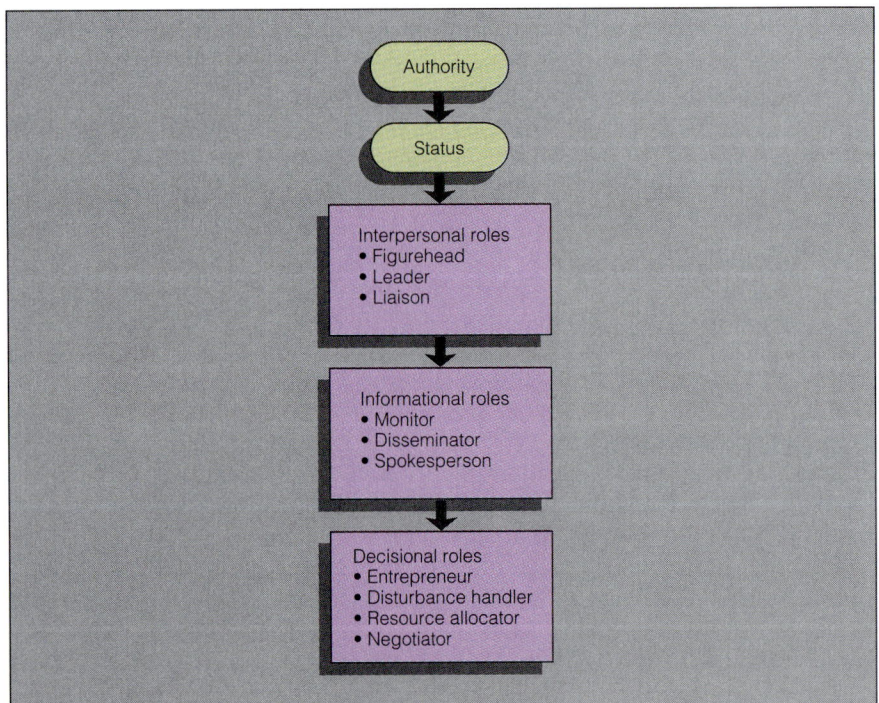

Authority

Status

Interpersonal roles
• Figurehead
• Leader
• Liaison

Informational roles
• Monitor
• Disseminator
• Spokesperson

Decisional roles
• Entrepreneur
• Disturbance handler
• Resource allocator
• Negotiator

The third role category recognizes the manager as a problem solver. The manager must serve as an **entrepreneur**, making improvements to the unit of a fairly long-lasting nature such as changing the organizational structure. As a **disturbance handler** the manager reacts to unanticipated events such as the announcement of a new product by a competitor. As a **resource allocator** the manager controls the purse strings of the unit, determining which subsidiary units get what resources. The last role sees the manager serving as a **negotiator**, resolving disputes both within the unit and between the unit and its environment.

Decisional Roles

Mintzberg's classification is more applicable to problem solving than is Fayol's since it emphasizes information and decision making. The four decisional roles can be used to classify the basic *ways* managers solve problems. Problems are solved by making improvements to the unit, handling disturbances, allocating resources, and negotiating.

INFLUENCES ON MANAGERS' PROBLEM-SOLVING STYLES

As managers gain experience in problem solving, they adopt certain unique styles. The organizational level as well as the personal characteristics of the managers can influence these styles.

Organizational Level

Managers usually are grouped into three organizational levels—top, middle, and lower. The board of directors, president, and vice presidents occupy the **top level**; the superintendents, directors, and managers of large organizational units such as plants, sales forces, and divisions occupy the **middle level**; and managers, group leaders, and supervisors of departmental units and subunits are on the **lower level**.

What determines the level? Although many factors are involved, the one most often cited is the manager's planning horizon. By **planning horizon**, we mean the future time period for which the manager has a planning responsibility. Managers on the lower level are concerned primarily with the current year, as pictured in Figure 6.2. Managers on the middle level are responsible for what will happen beyond the current year to a point three to five years in the future. Managers on the top level must plan for the time period that begins from five to seven years from now.

These planning horizons do not mean that upper-level managers are disinterested in what is happening currently. *All* managers become involved in solving today's problems.

Environmental information is more important to managers on the upper levels than on the lower. The reason is that the environmental influences affect the firm as a whole, not just units within the firm. These environmental influences must be anticipated and the strategy of the firm decided upon. That activity is the responsibility of upper-level managers.

The Influence of Level on Information Source

FIGURE 6.2

Planning Horizons

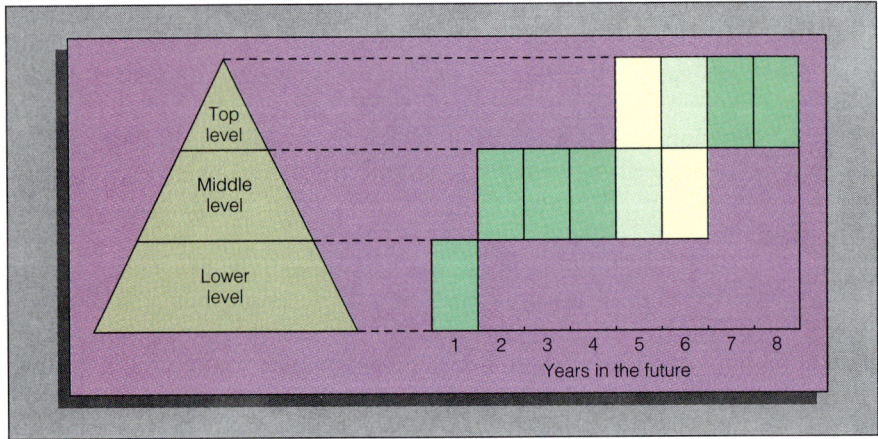

Figure 6.3 shows that most, but not all, of the information gathered by upper-level managers pertains to the environment. Likewise, most of the lower-level managers' information pertains to internal operations.

The Influence of Level on Information Form

Managers on the upper levels generally prefer to obtain information in a summarized form. This is because their areas of responsibility are so large that it is easy to become inundated with details. Lower-level managers, on the other hand, can use specific facts such as which employees worked overtime last week, which machines need repair, and how many days will be required to receive shipment of an ordered item. You can see in Figure 6.4 that upper-level managers receive *some* detail information and lower-level managers receive *some* summary information.

You must realize that these influences on information source and form are characteristic of *most* managers but not *all*. There are upper-level managers who like details of internal operations just as there are lower-level managers who use environmental summaries.

Personal Characteristics

Managers usually are pictured as aggressively seeking problems to solve. This picture applies to some managers but not to all.

The manager who looks for problems to solve is a **problem seeker**.[1] This person generates his or her own problem signals and often spots potential problems before they become serious.

Another type of manager is slightly less aggressive, but does not hesitate to face problems head-on. This person is the **problem solver**. He or she is alert to problem signals but does not seek them out. When a problem or potential problem becomes evident, the problem solver will tackle it with the same vigor as does the problem seeker.

[1] This classification was derived from Andrew D. Szilagyi, Jr., *Management and Performance* (Santa Monica: Goodyear Publishing Co., 1981), pp. 220-225.

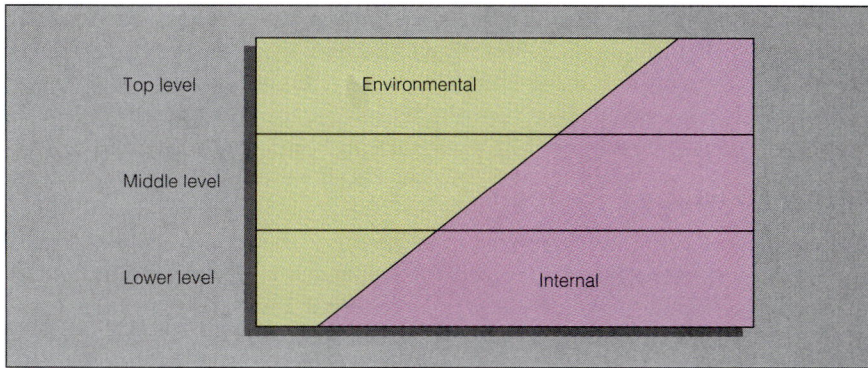

FIGURE 6.3
Influence of
Management Level
on Information
Source

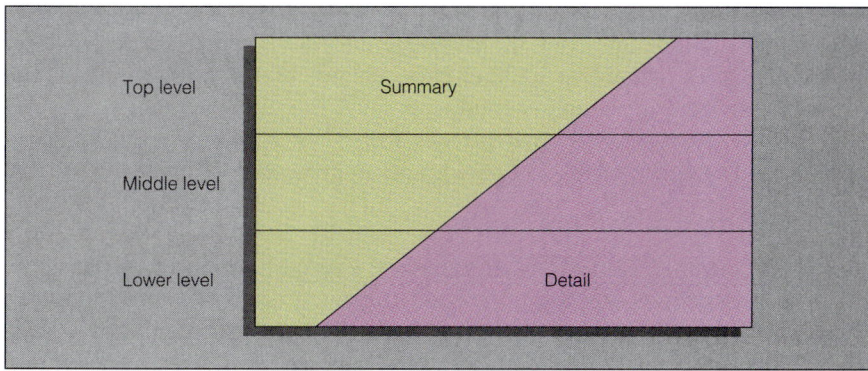

FIGURE 6.4
Influence of
Management Level
on Information
Form

A third type of manager is the **problem avoider** who prefers not to engage in problem-solving activity. This person does not want to know of problems, and problem-solving occupies little of his or her time.

The key point is that no two managers are exactly alike in how they solve problems. What works well for one manager might not work for another. For that reason, a standard set of problem-solving tools cannot be prescribed. A manager will consider the available tools and choose those best suited to the individual's particular style.

TECHNIQUES FOR GENERATING PROBLEM SIGNALS

The problem avoider will go to no special effort to generate problem signals. The problem seeker and the problem solver, on the other hand, want problems to be signaled when the symptoms first appear.

Some problem seekers and problem solvers want to receive all problem signals. There comes a point, however, when the signals become too numerous to handle. In such situations, the managers design systems that signal problems only in those situations where the manager's involvement is absolutely necessary. Two techniques have been developed for use in such a manner—management by exception and critical success factors.

Management by Exception

Frederick W. Taylor, an American management theorist who lived at the same time as Henri Fayol, devised the approach called **management by exception**, whereby the manager is only concerned with things that are *not* going according to plan. The manager spends time only on exceptional activity that is proceeding either worse *or better* than planned.

Management by exception requires the manager to establish a zone of acceptable performance as shown in Figure 6.5. Perhaps the zone relates to daily sales units. Sales should be between 800 and 1,100 units. As long as they remain within this zone the manager addresses other problems, however when sales rise above 1,100 or drop below 800 the manager seeks the cause. When activity is below the lower level the manager takes action to prevent its recurrence. When activity is above the upper level the manager takes action to effect such good performance more often.

Critical Success Factors

In 1961 D. Ronald Daniel of McKinsey & Company, one of the nation's largest consulting companies, coined the term **critical success factors** (shortened to **CSF**). He felt that a few key activities spell success or failure for any type of organization. The key activities are the CSFs, and they vary from one organization to the next. Daniel felt that the best way to manage an organization was to identify the CSFs and then monitor them very

FIGURE 6.5

Only Exceptional Performance Receives Management Attention

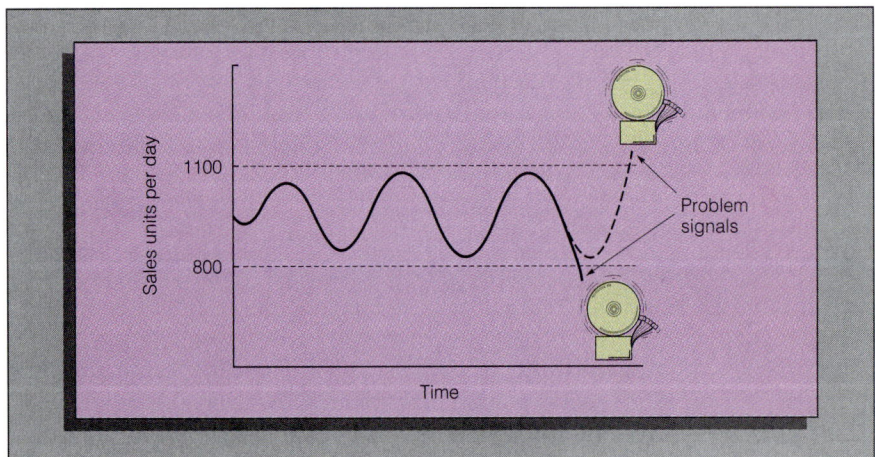

closely. It is a form of management by exception, but the activities receiving the manager's attention are always the same—the CSFs.

The CSF concept has received much attention recently, and efforts have been made to identify the CSFs for certain industries. In the automobile industry the CSFs are believed to be styling, an efficient dealer network, and tight control of manufacturing cost. In the food processing industry, new product development, good distribution, and effective advertising are the CSFs. In life insurance they are the development of agency management personnel, control of clerical personnel, and innovation in creating new insurance products.[2]

Managers who embrace the critical success factors concept establish problem-sensing systems to monitor each of the CSFs and provide a steady flow of information describing their status. The managers react to fluctuations and take action to ensure good performance for each CSF.

PROBLEM-SOLVING SKILLS

Managers acquire the skills necessary for problem solving from formal education and from job experience. College programs in management can be followed up with courses offered by such organizations as the American Management Association. The skills that appear to be the most critical to achieving success as a problem solver are described briefly below.

General Business Knowledge

The manager should understand the principles of economics, such as the interaction of supply and demand, and how they affect a business organization. In addition, he or she should be well schooled in accounting fundamentals as well as the principles of finance and marketing.

Knowledge of the Organization

The manager should know the *history* of the firm—how it was founded, and how it evolved over the years. This knowledge is valuable in understanding current problems and in projecting where the firm might go in the future. In addition, the manager should understand the firm's particular *industry* such as banking, retailing, health care, or transportation. Finally, the manager should understand the *people* within the firm—managers on higher levels (**superiors**), managers on the same level in other areas (**peers**), and personnel reporting to the manager (**subordinates**). The manager should know as much as possible about these persons' interests, motivations, and capabilities.

Knowledge of the Organization's Environment

In Chapter 4 we recognized the importance of the environment to the business system. All managers should understand the national economy and

---

2 The CSFs quoted here are from John F. Rockart, "Chief Executives Define Their Own Data Needs," *Harvard Business Review* 57 (March-April 1979): 85.

how it works. Special attention should be paid to how influences by the federal government can affect the firm, and how to be a good citizen of the local community.

Managers in certain functional areas should have a special understanding of the environmental elements with which their functions interface. Managers in the financial area should be expert in understanding the financial community and stockholders, manufacturing managers should specialize in suppliers and labor, and marketing managers should concentrate on the customers and competition. These areas of specialization are shown in Figure 6.6.

Communication Skills

The manager should possess strong verbal communication skills, since performance of all of the roles involve a personal interaction with others both inside and outside the unit. In addition, strong written communication skills can be an asset. The manager cannot rely entirely on a secretary to prepare written communications. Modern office automation applications such as electronic mail and word processing are involving the manager more directly in written communications than ever before.

Analytical Skills

The manager should understand the process of solving a problem. Much of this understanding is acquired from experience, but the fundamentals can be acquired in college courses. This topic will be the subject of Chapter 7.

FIGURE 6.6

Functional Areas Interface with Certain Environmental Elements

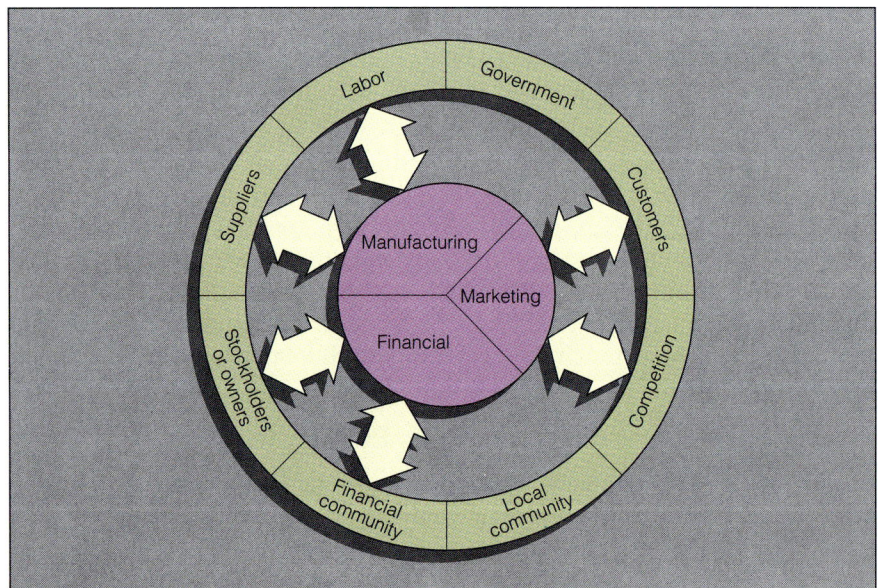

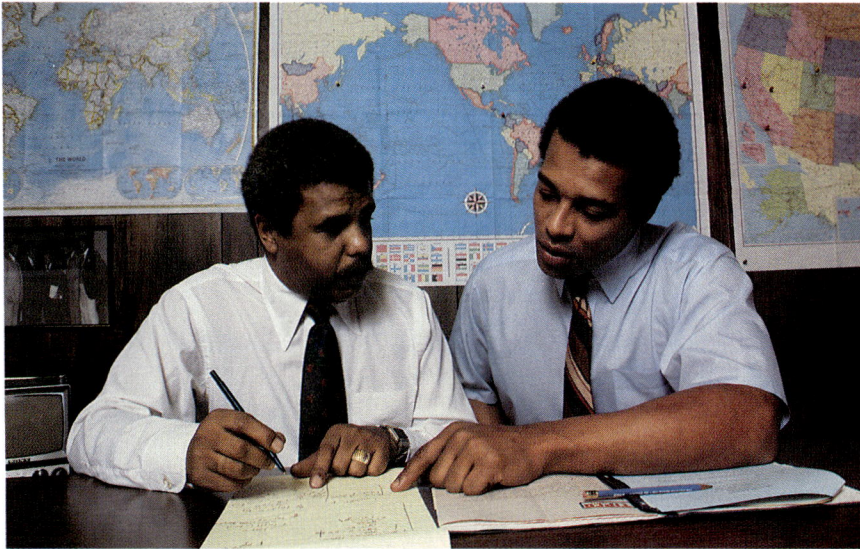

FIGURE 6.7
Communication
Skills Are Key to
Good Management
Performance

Intuitive Skills

More and more attention is being given to the role played by intuition in management decision making. **Intuition** is the ability to understand something quickly without consciously following steps of rational thinking and inference. Intuition is especially useful when addressing the unstructured parts of problems. One would think that intuition is a natural gift, but experts believe that it can be developed by believing in it, practicing it, and creating an environment where it can be practiced.

Information Literacy

Finally we come to the skill that we identified in Chapter 1. The manager must understand the role of information in problem solving, and how to design, implement, and use information systems. When built upon a computer literacy, information literacy enables the manager to incorporate the computer into the information systems when appropriate.

Few, if any, managers excel in all of these skill areas. Nevertheless, the areas represent good goals to work toward, and many managers spend their entire careers actively strengthening their weaker skills.

THE ROLE OF THE COMPUTER IN PROBLEM SOLVING

The computer can be used at each step of the problem-solving process.

Signal Problems or Potential Problems

We have seen how a computer can be programmed to determine when it is time to reorder an inventory item. The computer can be directed to issue similar signals concerning other phases of the firm's operations. For the computer to have this ability, it is necessary that standards of performance be established and made a part of the computer database. The computer can then compare actual performance to the standard. Used in this manner, the computer assists the manager in employing techniques of management by exception and critical success factors. This type of computer support is best provided by periodic printed reports and by special reports displayed on the screen at the manager's request.

Facilitate an Understanding of the Problem

Once the problem has been signaled, the computer can provide additional information to facilitate an understanding. This type of support usually comes in the form of displayed special reports.

Evaluate Possible Solutions

The computer has not enjoyed much success in *identifying* alternate solutions—that task usually is left to the manager. Once the alternatives have been identified, however, the manager can use the computer to measure the advantages and disadvantages of each. For example, the computer can compute the projected costs and revenues expected from each alternative and provide the information in the form of special reports. When much information must be reported, printed reports are excellent since the manager can easily flip back and forth among the pages, compare figures, make marginal notes, and so on. Screen displays are best when the amount of information is small and can be shown on a few screens.

Recommend a Solution

We saw in Chapter 5 that the computer can be programmed to identify the best solution when the problem is highly structured. An example is an evaluation that computes *point scores* as shown in Figure 6.8. Each alterna-

FIGURE 6.8

The Computer Can Compute a Score for Each Alternative

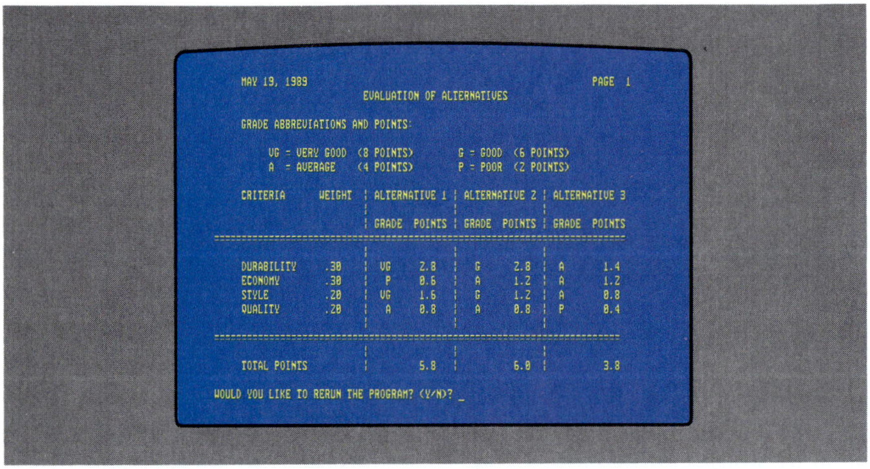

tive is evaluated using the same criteria, and the criteria are weighted to reflect their relative importance. Grades are assigned to each criterion, and the grades are multiplied by the weights to produce the scores. As in our other examples where the computer recommends a solution, the manager supplements the scores with a subjective evaluation. This application calls for the use of mathematical models or expert systems.

Facilitate Implementation of the Solution

The computer can be used to communicate the decision to those persons who have the responsibility of implementing it. While the computer can never replace personal communication, it can be used as a supplement. Office automation applications can produce many of the needed high-quality written and oral communications.

Track the Effectiveness of the Solution

Once the solution has been implemented, the computer can provide feedback describing how well the solution is, or is not, working. The manager can devise a system of periodic reports to provide this information.

Information literacy helps a manager use the computer in the above manner. The manager must understand not only the steps of problem solving but also the abilities and limitations of using the computer at each step. If the manager knows what information is needed, in most cases the computer can provide it.

THE ROLE OF INFORMATION SPECIALISTS IN PROBLEM SOLVING

It is not necessary that the manager assume all of the responsibility for using the computer. Persons in the organization who specialize in applying the computer to business problems can provide valuable assistance. An **information specialist** is a person whose *primary* responsibility is to contribute to the design, implementation, and operation of systems that provide information. The specialist contributes by providing technical knowledge. Such a wide variety of this technical knowledge is required that several types of information specialists have evolved. The information specialists must also possess a variety of skills in applying the tools of their trade.

In a small firm, all of the specialized functions are performed by a single individual, perhaps on a part-time basis. In a large firm, the employees are grouped by area of specialization and arranged in a hierarchy structure such as that pictured in Figure 6.9. We use the term **information services** to describe the unit, but other names such as **information systems**, **MIS department**, and **computer department** are popular.

The manager who has overall responsibility for the unit can also be given several titles. Sometimes it is **vice president of information services**

FIGURE 6.9

An Information
Services
Organization

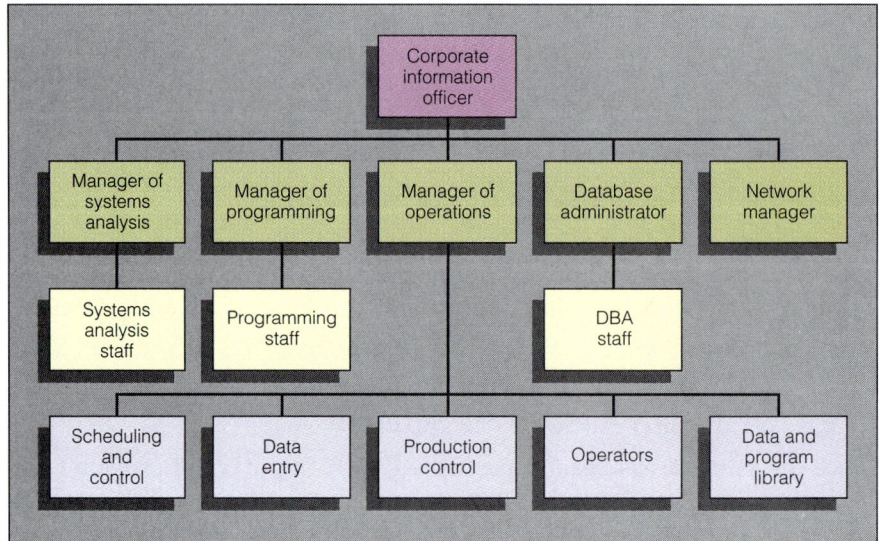

or **director of management information systems**. A new term, **chief information officer**, or **CIO**, is gaining popularity in larger firms such as banks and insurance companies.

Types of Information Specialists

Each of the information specialists is described briefly.

Systems Analysts

The person who works directly with the user is the **systems analyst**. The systems analyst helps the user to identify and understand the problem, and then considers different ways the problem can be solved. Each approach is documented using primarily graphic diagrams, and the approach that appears to be the best is recommended. The user decides whether to implement the systems analyst's recommendation.

Programmers

The **programmer** is the person who uses the systems analyst's documentation as a guide and prepares the program statements that cause the computer to perform the necessary processing.

Operations Staff

A small computer requires only a single **operator** but a large one can require a large and diverse staff. Not only are persons required to operate the equipment by pressing keys, changing paper forms, tapes, and disks, but other persons are required to schedule jobs, enter data, control the input and output, and manage libraries of storage media.

Database Administrators

For the first fifteen years or so of the computer era, the above positions were the extent of the information services operation. Then, in the early 1970s, the increasing interest in databases became so great that a new position was created. The **database administrator**, or **DBA**, is responsible for creating and maintaining the database. Not every firm has a DBA, but in a large organization several persons can have this title.

Another new position has been added in those organizations that have critical data communications needs. The **network manager** is an expert in the specialized area of data communications and recommends the hardware and software needed. The network manager also guides the implementation and maintenance of the systems.

Network Manager

The popularity of decision support systems has produced two new positions that usually exist at the top-management level. A **coach** is a person who provides the technical expertise to assist a manager in developing and using a DSS. The coach does not do the work for the manager but provides the necessary guidance.

Coaches and Chauffeurs

Once a DSS has been designed the manager may or may not use it personally. In those cases where the manager does not want to operate the equipment, a specialist called a **chauffeur** "drives" the equipment for the manager. For example, the chauffeur enters instructions and decisions into a model and obtains the output. The manager evaluates the output and perhaps requests that the chauffeur produce additional simulations.

The coaches and chauffeurs may be a part of information services or they may be members of the user's staff.

Most large organizations have a staff of **internal auditors** who ensure that the firm's data processing systems conform to the accepted accounting practices. The internal auditing organization is not a part of information services, but usually reports directly to the CEO or the board of directors. Some of the internal auditors are skilled in computer-based systems, and are called **EDP auditors**. (The term EDP stands for electronic data process-

EDP Auditors

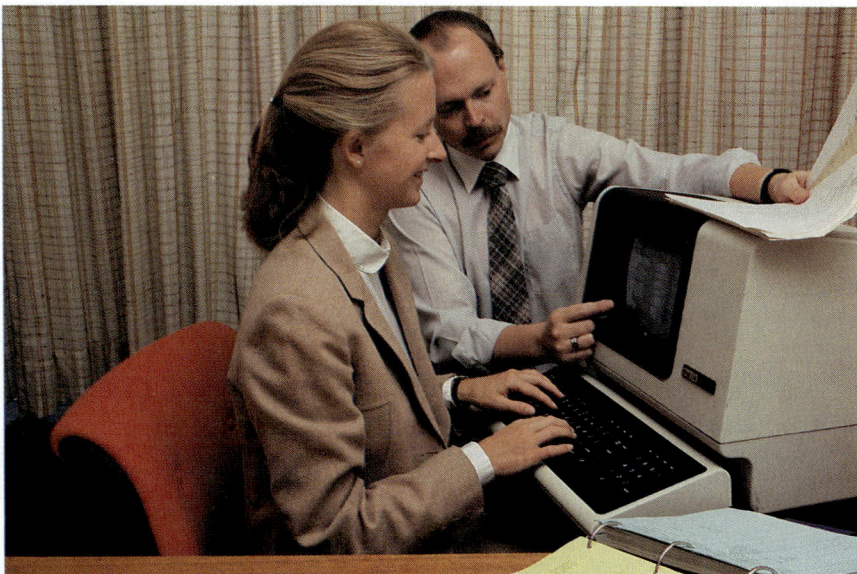

FIGURE 6.10
The Coach Assists the Manager in Developing a DSS

ing, and was used during the early years of the computer to distinguish it from other types of processing.)

How Do Information Specialists Help?

Information specialists can provide assistance at each step of the problem-solving process.

Identify Problems

This is the area where the least support is provided. It is usually the user who first notices the problem signals since he or she is on the scene.

Help Users Understand Problems

Once problems have been identified, information specialists can help the users understand them. Systems analysts perform most of this work, but database managers and network managers can be involved when the problems relate to their areas. Internal auditors can provide a similar service for data processing systems, and coaches can help managers understand problems requiring a DSS.

Develop Problem Statements

Once problems have been understood it is often difficult for the user to describe the problem in such a way that it can serve as a basis for solution. The systems analyst is skilled in preparing the systems documentation that forms the blueprint of the solution. We will describe the more popular documentation tools in Chapter 7.

Implement Systems for Users

For the first twenty-five years of the computer era, the sole responsibility of information specialists was to implement systems for users. The specialists supplied the technical knowledge that the users either did not possess or were unable to supply for various reasons. This type of activity still accounts for a majority of the information specialists' time. The specialists implement all of the data processing systems, the larger and more complex MIS and DSS designs, the organization-oriented office automation systems, and all expert systems.

Help Users to Implement Their Own Systems

A new area of responsibility for the information specialists is being stimulated by the users' increasing computer and information literacy. As users become more self sufficient in computer use they are developing their own applications. This is called **end-user computing**. In this environment the systems analyst functions as a consultant and an educator, leaving most of the work to the user.

GUIDELINES FOR WORKING WITH INFORMATION SPECIALISTS

The manager who wants to make full use of the computer in problem solving will develop an end-user capability, but will not attempt to implement all of the systems alone.

There are several actions that the manager can take to make certain that the information specialist resource is available when needed, and use the resource in the most effective way.

Cultivating the Information Services Resource

Upper-level managers decide the scale of the firm's computing resource—the number and sizes of computers, the number and variety of information specialists, and so on. However, managers on all levels can support such a resource by using it to its fullest extent and by continually promoting a strong computing capability within the organization.

Using the Information Services Resource Effectively

The best arrangement is when the user assumes control of the systems project from the beginning and maintains control each step of the way.

Since the user recognizes problem signals more often than does the information specialist, it is the user's project from the beginning. In addition, it is the user who will benefit from the system and in many cases pay for it.

Initiate and Maintain Project Control

There should be a clear understanding between the user and the systems analyst *before* the system is designed concerning what it will do. This **objective statement** should be in writing, and the systems analyst can help in its development.

Clearly Define System Objectives

It is easy for the user's enthusiasm to fade as the work proceeds. One way to avoid this trap is to develop a project plan with periodic **checkpoints** that give the manager an opportunity to verify progress. The information specialist can provide the user with written reports that are used in deciding whether to continue the project.

Maintain Participation throughout the Life of the System

Information specialists possess a wide range of skills. The systems analysts are experts in dissecting a systems problem and devising an effective solution. Programmers often are skilled in the use of modeling languages and techniques. The DBA knows how to create the valuable data resource. Network managers know how to solve problems involving widespread operations. Coaches and chauffeurs can design and operate DSSs that are especially valuable to upper-level managers.

Fully Utilize the Information Specialists' Capabilities

When these personnel resources are available, the manager should use them to the fullest extent.

A CLOSER LOOK AT END-USER COMPUTING

End-user computing at first appears to be a panacea. It makes the user more self-sufficient and it provides a degree of relief to the firm's scarce information specialist resource. End-user computing also eliminates the need for the often-difficult communication between the user and the information specialist. But there can be some real problems. In the following sections, we explain why this movement evolved, identify some of the negative consequences, and describe some of the solutions that firms have adopted.

The Evolution of End-User Computing

The increasing volume of end-user computing is due to several factors.

Application Backlogs

In the past the information specialists had such a heavy workload that they could not respond to all user requests. Backlogs of waiting jobs built up, and it sometimes took as long as three years to get them on the computer. During that time users sought other alternatives. Some users took their work to computer service firms that performed the processing for a fee. Other users were attracted to the notion of doing their own work and learned how to access the firm's mainframe from terminals, or acquired their own microcomputers.

Increasing Computer Literacy

During this same time period users were becoming more computer literate. Persons entering management ranks for the first time had received formal education in college, high school, and, in some cases, even elementary school. These computer-literate managers could implement their own applications without assistance from the information specialists.

More User-Friendly Software

Even in light of the increasing computer literacy, it is doubtful that end-user computing would have become a reality had it not been for user-friendly software. Software utilizing menus and help screen, as described in Chapter 3, does not require a programming knowledge and in most cases can be learned in a matter of hours or a few days.

Personal Computers

Not only has the software become more available, but the hardware as well—in the form of low-priced personal computers. Firms usually furnish personal computers to employees when a clear need exists. Very often these small systems provide the manager with all of the problem-solving support that is needed.

Disadvantages of End-User Computing

The most serious drawback of end-user computing is that the firm can lose control over the computing activity. Users are motivated to implement the applications that satisfy their own needs without regard to other users or the organization as a whole. In some cases users acquire hardware and software that is not well suited to the job, or already exists within the organization. The result is inefficient use of resources.

In addition, users often create their own databases without first checking to see if the data already exists, with little regard for accuracy, and with little effort to maintain security. Of all the disadvantages, the data issue is potentially the most harmful since it can affect everyone who uses the data.

Responses to End-User Computing

Firms have responded to end-user computing in a number of ways in an effort to reestablish control.

Information Centers

An **information center** is an area of the firm that houses computing equipment that anyone in the organization can use. The equipment usually includes terminals, microcomputers, letter-quality printers, and plotters. A selection of user-friendly software such as database retrieval and graphics packages are available. A small staff is on hand to help the users.

FIGURE 6.11
An Information
Center

The information center enables users to engage in end-user computing without buying their own hardware and software.

The MIS Steering Committee

Many firms establish an **MIS steering committee** that is responsible for evaluating requests for new computer applications. The committee consists of representatives from the major user areas plus information services. Such committees give the users a strong voice in determining which applications are given priority.

The Chief Information Officer

Historically the persons in charge of the firm's computing resource have had little influence outside their own areas. Although they often have had the title of vice president, in many cases they reported to another vice president, not to the president or CEO. The reason for this relative lack of influence was because many of the computer managers rose through the ranks because of technical knowledge and not managerial skills. Their peers looked upon them as technicians.

This situation seems to be changing, although slowly. In recognizing that information is a vital resource, some firms have designated a **chief information officer**, or **CIO**, to have the same level of influence as the functional vice presidents. The CIO not only sets policy in the information services area but assists the other top-level managers in setting corporate policy as well.

Information Resource Management

The above measures can be implemented individually or as an integrated program of **information resource management**, or **IRM**. When a firm adopts IRM it reflects the following characteristics:

- The firm uses its information resources to achieve competitive advantage

- The information services organization is regarded as one of the major functional areas of the firm
- The chief information officer participates in strategic decision making that affects the firm's overall operations
- A strategic plan for information resources spells out how all of the information resources will be applied in the next several years
- The strategic plan for information resources includes a plan for stimulating end-user computing, yet providing a central control

All of these developments are intended to increase computer use in the firm, but at the same time ensure that high levels of efficiency, accuracy, and security are maintained.

THE IMPORTANCE OF USER LEADERSHIP

Prior to end-user computing, the real key to effective computer use was *user participation*. The successful installations were those where users worked with the information specialists. When users did not participate, the information specialists designed the systems to provide the information that they thought the managers needed. Today, however, mere participation is not enough. The user must provide *leadership* by making all of the key decisions as the system is designed and implemented. You can see the importance of information literacy if this leadership is to be exercised.

SUMMARY

Not only do managers enlist the help of specialists when solving problems, but several managers often solve problems jointly.

Henri Fayol's management functions provide a classification of the basic jobs that managers perform. Information systems can be designed to provide problem-solving support in each area. Henry Mintzberg's classification of management roles can be used in the same way, and is especially helpful since it recognizes the importance of information and decision making.

Both a manager's organizational level and personal characteristics can influence problem-solving style. Managers on upper levels usually, but not always, make primary use of environmental information and prefer summary reports. Personal characteristics can cause managers to be problem seekers, solvers, or avoiders.

In an effort to conserve valuable time, some managers respond only to signals that things are not going as planned (management by exception) or only to signals relating to certain key performance measures (critical success factors).

For a manager to apply the maximum variety of skills to problem solving, he or she should have a good business knowledge, know the organization and its environment, have good communication and analytical skills, be able to utilize intuition, and have information literacy.

The computer can provide strong support in all steps of problem solving except one—identifying possible solutions. While at times some support can be provided, that step is usually the task of the problem solver.

Information specialists can lend assistance during the process of solving a problem. The specialists can implement systems for the problem solver or enable that person to engage in end-user computing. Users can ensure an adequate computing resource by promoting that resource within the organization. Users can benefit the most from the computing resource when they initiate and maintain control of projects, clearly define systems objectives, maintain participation throughout the project, and take full advantage of the information specialists' skills.

End-user computing is an outgrowth of several factors—some positive such as increasing computer literacy, and some negative such as application backlogs. When controlled, there are no disadvantages of end-user computing. Firms seek to maintain control by establishing information centers, forming an MIS steering committee, appointing a CIO, or implementing a comprehensive program of IRM.

KEY CONCEPTS

The group nature of problem solving

Management activity as a set of functions or roles

Each manager's unique style of gathering information and solving problems

How both computers and information specialists can contribute to problem solving

KEY TERMS

Group problem solving	Management by exception	EDP auditor
Management function	Critical success factors (CSF)	Information center
Management role	Operator	MIS steering committee
Planning horizon	Database administrator (DBA)	Chief information officer
Problem seeker	Network manager	(CIO)
Problem solver	Coach	Information resources management
Problem avoider	Chauffeur	(IRM)

QUESTIONS

1. Which of Fayol's management functions are best supported by the computer?

2. Which decisional role does the manager play when he or she:
   a. Makes changes in company policy?
   b. Settles a disagreement between two employees?
   c. Determines the funds necessary to operate the unit during the coming year?
   d. Sells some of the firm's investments in response to an unexpected rise in interest rates?
3. What is the president's planning horizon?
4. Why do top-level managers place such a value on environmental information?
5. What distinguishes a problem seeker from a problem solver?
6. Why would a manager respond to something that is going better than anticipated?
7. In what way is CSF a form of management by exception?
8. Which of the environmental elements are of special importance to marketing managers? Financial managers? Manufacturing managers? Which two are the responsibility of all managers?
9. Which of the problem-solving steps does the computer support the least?
10. Which information specialist is most likely to work directly with the user in formulating a computer-based problem solution?
11. What is the difference between a coach and a chauffeur? On which management level would they most likely be found?
12. Which of the problem-solving steps does the information specialist support the least? Why?
13. How could the potential harm of inaccurate end-user databases be greater than inefficient use of hardware and software?
14. What kind of hardware would you find in an information center? What kind of software?
15. Who belongs to the MIS steering committee?

CASE PROBLEM   Calgary Chemicals

Calgary Chemicals, located in Calgary, Alberta, Canada, produces a line of industrial cleaning solvents. There are three buyers in the purchasing department—Bill Malone, Murray Rosen, and Al Matocha. They are close friends and one day they were in the coffee shop.

Al opened the conversation with "You're not going to believe this, but last week I called the computer department and asked them to send me somebody to talk over a new computer application. Well, they sent this fellow who obviously doesn't know anything about purchasing. As soon as I said that I needed some information about our suppliers he told me that we don't carry any environmental data in our database. He was about to walk out when I told him to sit down and let's talk about it. I've been thinking about how nice it would be to get a printout each time we must select a supplier for a reorder. You know, the printout could list the suppliers we have used in the past and give information like the price we paid, how long it took to get the shipment, whether the promised date was met, and things like that. Well, to make a long story short, he told me that it could probably be done but it would be next year before we could get around to it. Next year! Can you imagine that? Do you know what I did? Well yesterday I went down to that computer store on Market Street and bought me one of those IBM Personal System/2s. You know, that's a good one and they were on sale. I'm going to charge it to the department; we've got money in the budget for it. They even threw in Lotus at no extra charge. It should be delivered next week. I'm going to produce my own reports. I'm going to mail a questionnaire to all of the suppliers that I do business with and build my own database. I can key the data in myself. But listen, you guys can use it too if you like. If I'm going to all of that trouble, we might as well get as much use out of it as we can. We all buy from the same suppliers."

Al paused to take a sip of coffee, and Bill took advantage of the lull in the action. "The same thing happened to a friend of mine in Shipping. This computer expert, it was probably the same guy, told him he needed a detailed report because he was on the bottom management level. The nerve of the guy. Well, my friend brought in his computer from home. It was an Atari that his kids had been using for games and they got tired of it. He's doing his own computing now and loves it. His daughter even keys in all of his data. She's taking typing at school and needs the practice."

"You know, that's probably happening all over," Murray said. "I've been tempted to do the same thing but I can't type. Sure, I'd like to go in with you—especially if I can use your data."

"That's great," Al said, clapping his hands. "What about you, Bill? Are you in?"

Bill shrugged and said "Sure, why not. What have we got to lose?"

1. Was the systems analyst correct in recognizing Al's information needs as being environmental rather than internal? Explain.

2. What mistake did the systems analyst make when talking with the Shipping manager?

3. Assuming that this situation is common throughout Calgary Chemicals, what are the potential harmful effects?

4. What steps could Calgary Chemicals take to prevent these harmful effects from occurring

Problem-Solving Processes and Tools

LEARNING OBJECTIVES   After studying this chapter, you should:

- Gain a fundamental understanding of the systems approach
- Gain a fundamental understanding of some popular problem-solving tools
- See how prototyping facilitates communication between the user and the information specialist.

OVERVIEW

In this chapter we cover three main topics. First we describe the process that problem solvers follow in solving problems. Then we explain some of the more popular documentation tools. We conclude with a description of how computer-assisted software engineering tools facilitate a new approach to system development.

The process described is called the systems approach, and it represents an orderly way of addressing a problem. The systems concept (being able to view the organization as a system) is an integral part of the approach.

The documentation tools evolved to help systems analysts in analyzing and designing systems. Most of the tools are graphic design aids that produce written documentation. There is a trend, however, toward tools that are software based.

Both the systems approach and the tools can be used by the manager and the information specialists in problem solving.

SYSTEMATIC APPROACHES TO PROBLEM SOLVING

In Chapter 1 we listed four steps that are taken in solving a problem:

1. Understand the problem to be solved
2. Evaluate alternate solutions
3. Implement the best solution
4. Follow up to make certain that the solution is working

There is nothing magical about these steps. They represent the common-sense way to solve a problem. In fact, it would be difficult to identify any other approach that a rational problem solver would follow. It would be foolish to begin solving a problem before you know what the problem is. Also, you should not simply pick the first solution that comes to mind without giving the other alternatives a chance. Finally, you should stick with the problem until it is solved.

The Scientific Method

Business problem solvers were not the first to study the problem-solving process. That honor goes to such physical scientists as physicists and chemists, and to such behavioral scientists as psychologists and sociologists. These scientists studied problem solving as a means of conducting controlled experiments. For example, a chemistry experiment conducted in a laboratory was viewed as a problem to be solved. A series of steps called the **scientific method** was developed for conducting such experiments. The steps, still followed by laboratory scientists, include:

1. Observe the phenomenon being studied
2. Formulate a hypothesis
3. Predict what will happen in the future
4. Test the hypothesis

For example, scientists might *observe* that rats that are handled physically by researchers learn faster than those left alone. The scientists state the *hypothesis* that "Physical handling facilitates learning." The scientists *predict* that rats that are handled physically will learn faster than those not handled. The scientists *test* the hypothesis by designing an experiment in which some rats are handled and others are not.

The Systems Approach

Business managers, seeking a similar orderly approach to problem solving, applied the scientific method. Their efforts produced the **systems approach**—a series of steps that can be followed in solving any type of problem. The problem is identified and understood, alternate solutions are identified and evaluated, the best solution is selected and implemented, and the problem solver makes certain the solution works as intended.

We will expand these basic steps to a larger number in order to obtain a finer breakdown of the required activity. Also, we will subdivide the steps into three types of effort: the **preparation effort** that the problem solver can take prior to the problem signal; the **definition effort** that is taken to understand the problem; and the **solution effort** that is taken to solve the problem. These three types of effort, called *phases*, and their subsidiary steps are illustrated in Figure 7.1.

PREPARATION EFFORT

Preparation effort is a state of mind. It is a way of viewing an organization so that problems can be solved in the most efficient and effective manner. The three steps of preparation effort include: view the firm as a system, recognize the environmental system, and identify the firm's subsystems. We laid the groundwork for taking these steps in Chapter 4 by describing the firm in systems terms, providing a way of viewing the firm's environment as eight elements connected to the firm by resource flows, and recognizing the functional organization structure.

Step 1: View the Firm as a System

The firm should be viewed as a controlled, open system as pictured in Figure 7.2. The conceptual system that consists of performance standards, management, and an information processor controls the physical system.

When viewed in this manner, it is clear that the firm must know where it wants to go, be well managed, and have a good information system and communication network that provide the information flow between the physical system and management.

FIGURE 7.1

Phases and Steps
of the Systems
Approach

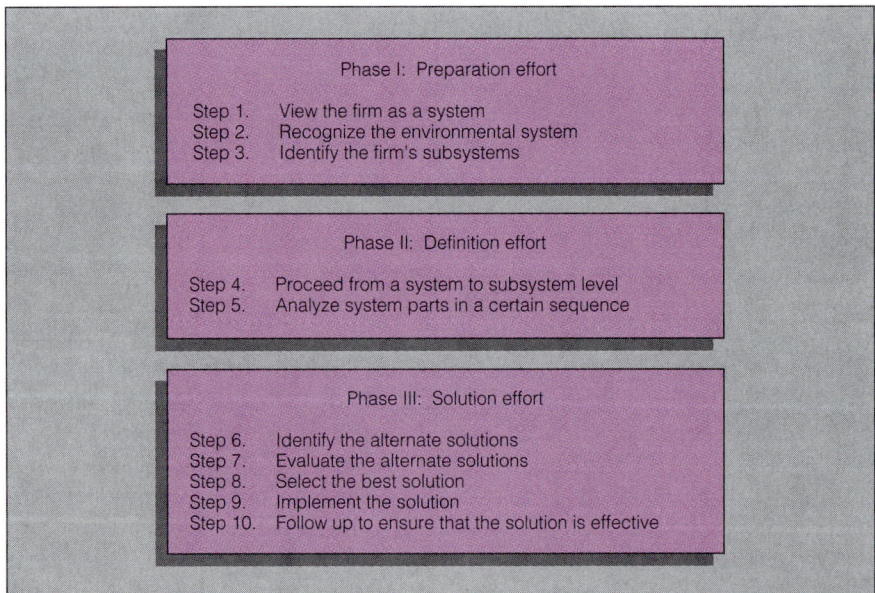

Phase I: Preparation effort

Step 1.   View the firm as a system
Step 2.   Recognize the environmental system
Step 3.   Identify the firm's subsystems

Phase II: Definition effort

Step 4.   Proceed from a system to subsystem level
Step 5.   Analyze system parts in a certain sequence

Phase III: Solution effort

Step 6.   Identify the alternate solutions
Step 7.   Evaluate the alternate solutions
Step 8.   Select the best solution
Step 9.   Implement the solution
Step 10. Follow up to ensure that the solution is effective

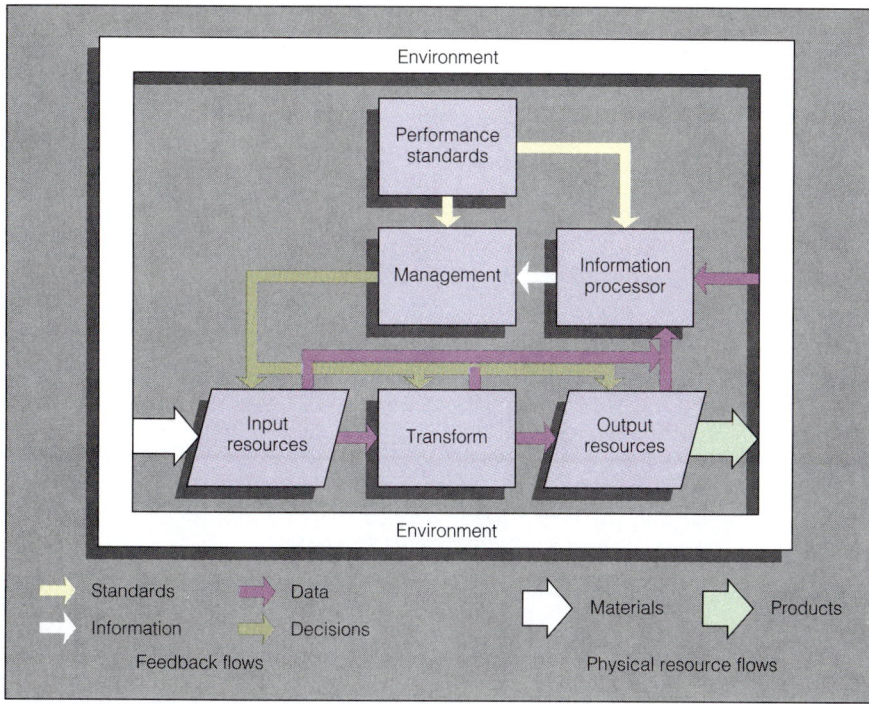

FIGURE 7.2

The Firm as a System

Step 2: Recognize the Environment of the Firm

Most firms have a special responsibility to two elements in the environment—customers and stockholders. All firms exist to meet defined customer needs, and profit-seeking firms also must reimburse the stockholders or owners for their investment. The other elements of the environment either assist or constrain the firm as it meets these two responsibilities.

Figure 7.3 shows the firm in its environment, connected to each of the elements by resource flows. All of these resource flows must exist for the firm to meet its objectives.

Step 3: Identify the Firm's Subsystems

A **subsystem** is a system within a system. In Chapter 4 we explained two ways to subdivide the firm—by functional area and by management level. Each functional area is a subsystem of the firm, but it is also a system. The manufacturing function, for example, has its own physical system of inputs, transformations, and outputs, and its own conceptual system consisting of manufacturing standards, manufacturing management, and manufacturing information. You can also think of each management level as a separate system.

Other approaches used to subdivide the firm involve the firm's products and geographic areas. General Motors is a good example of how products

FIGURE 7.3

The Firm in Its
Environment

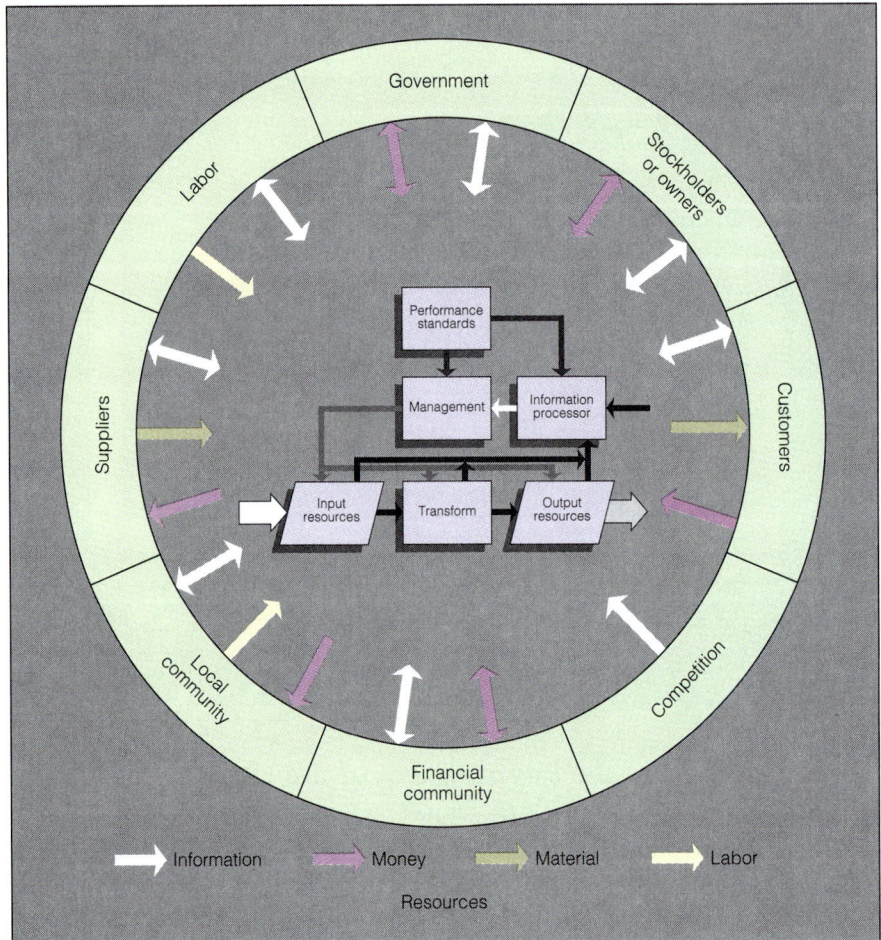

can be used. Its automobiles—Chevrolet, Pontiac, Buick, Oldsmobile, and
Cadillac—are produced by separate divisions. Each division is a physical
system with its own conceptual system. Geographic areas provide an effective way to subdivide firms with widespread operations. Firms might
divide their markets into such sales regions as the Western Region,
Midwestern Region, and Eastern Region. Each region is a separate physical
system and conceptual system.

By viewing the firm as a system, recognizing its environment, and identifying the subsystems within the firm, we have established a hierarchy of
three systems levels. The environment of the firm is on the top, the firm
itself is in the middle, and the subsystems of the firm are on the bottom.
The firm is a subsystem within the environmental system, and the subdivi-
sions of the firm are subsystems within the firm.

This systems hierarchy is important because we want to take a **top-down approach** to problem solving. We want to start with the big picture and gradually narrow our focus to a specific problem area. By following this process we will have a thorough understanding of the problem setting, and will be led directly to the problem.

You can begin to develop preparation effort now—in this course, reading this text. It is a frame of mind that prepares you for problem solving.

DEFINITION EFFORT

When a problem is signaled, the problem solver must gain an understanding of the problem. This is the **analysis phase** of problem solving; the problem solver analyzes the problem to understand it. That understanding can be gained by proceeding from system to subsystem level and by analyzing the system parts in a certain sequence. As the problem solver takes these steps he or she seeks to locate the problem—not solve it. Solution activity comes later.

Step 4: Proceed from System to Subsystem Level

The problem solver first addresses the environment of the system being studied. If the problem solver is a top-level manager such as the president, and the system being studied is the firm, then the environment is that of the *firm*.

If, however, the problem solver is a lower-level manager such as a functional vice president, then the environment is that of that *function*. In the case of the marketing function, for example, the environment includes such elements external to the firm as customers and competition, but it also includes elements *within the firm*—the other functional areas. The same situation applies on still-lower levels.

As the problem solver addresses the environment, the objective is to identify the elements and the resource flows connecting the elements to the system being studied. For example, an advertising manager would identify the firm's advertising agency as a supplier. Advertising ideas, strategies, art, and copy flow from the agency to the firm, and money flows back to the agency.

After understanding the environment, the problem solver addresses the system, examining the elements that must be present. Then, the subsystems are given the same treatment. The purpose of this top-down analysis is to identify the system *level* where the root cause of the problem exists.

Step 5: Analyze System Parts in Sequence

In the process of identifying which system level is defective, the problem solver determines which *element* on that level is causing the problem. The system elements are examined in the sequence shown in Figure 7.4.

First, the problem solver examines the system *standards*. Good standards must exist. If not, that problem must be solved before proceeding.

FIGURE 7.4

Each Part of the
System Is Analyzed
in Sequence

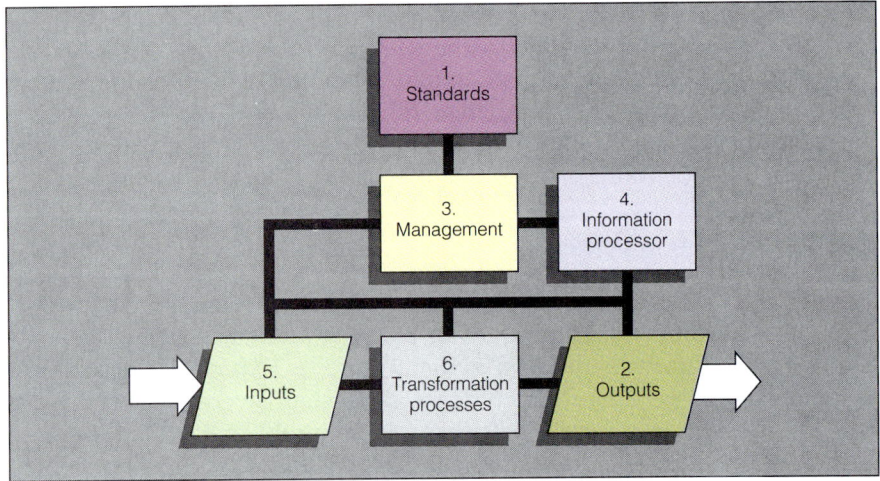

FIGURE 7.4

Each Part of the
System Is Analyzed
in Sequence

When the system has good standards, the next element to be examined consists of the system *outputs*. Are the outputs measuring up to the standards? If they are, there is no problem to solve. If they are not, the task of the problem solver is to find out why.

In most cases *management* will be the reason why the output is not meeting the standards. It is management's responsibility to create the system to produce the output. Perhaps there are not enough managers or they do not have the necessary skills. If management is perceived to be the problem, then that problem must be solved.

When management checks out O.K., the problem solver next focuses attention on the *information processor*. Perhaps management is not receiving the necessary information. In that case an information processor must be implemented that meets management's needs.

When no problems exist in the conceptual system, the physical system can be examined. First, a judgment is made concerning the *inputs*. Does the system have enough physical resources to do its job? Are the resources of the proper quality? If an input problem exists, it is solved. Finally, the *transformation processes* are studied and any defects there are corrected.

The problem solver reacts to the problem signal by analyzing the system to determine which element on which level is defective. As soon as the problem level and element are identified, additional data is gathered to fully understand the problem.

SOLUTION EFFORT

The terms **design phase** and **synthesis phase** have been used to describe this sequence of steps that produces the problem solution. During the analysis phase, the systems analyst subdivided the system into subsystems for the purpose of understanding the problem. During the design phase, the new or improved subsystems are synthesized to form the new system.

Step 6: Identify the Alternate Solutions

The manager attempts to identify all of the feasible alternatives. This is a point in the process where group problem solving is especially valuable. The manager often calls on specialists to help in the identification.

In many cases there are more alternatives than the manager can study in detail. Therefore the list is culled to select only those that are feasible. **Feasibility** is the ability of the system to be implemented and used as planned. There are five types of feasibility:[1]

- **Technical**—sufficient technology, such as hardware and software, must exist to solve the problem.
- **Economic**—the solution must be sound from an economic standpoint. The firm must be able to afford it, and it must represent a good return on investment.
- **Legal**—the solution must comply with the applicable laws and regulations.
- **Operational**—the solution must be workable. It must be one that the persons working within the system will support and be capable of performing.
- **Schedule**—the solution must be one that can be implemented within the time constraint that might be imposed.

Step 7: Evaluate the Alternate Solutions

The first step in evaluation is to identify the **evaluation criteria**, or the factors used to measure each alternative. For example, if the problem is an inadequate information processor, three alternatives might be: upgrade the existing computer system, install a larger computer, or install a microcomputer network. The problem solver decides to evaluate the alternatives based on cost of operation, user training, responsiveness, data security, and ability to adapt to changing user needs. Table 7.1 shows how each of the alternatives measures up to the evaluation criteria. The advantages and disadvantages of selecting each alternative are identified.

The evaluation criteria in the table are only an example. The problem solver will identify criteria based on the situation.

Step 8: Select the Best Solution

The overriding concern when evaluating the alternatives should be how well each one enables the system to meet its objectives. The alternative that does the best job within the constraints is the *best* solution. It is possible that the analysis will not identify an alternative that is clearly the best. In

---

[1] This classification was taken from John Burch and Gary Grudnitski, *Information Systems: Theory and Practice* (New York: John Wiley & Sons, 1986), pp. 49-50.

TABLE 7.1

Evaluation of Alternatives

	Alternative 1: Upgrade existing system	Alternative 2: Install larger system	Alternative 3: Install microcomputer network
Advantages	1. Small increase in cost of operation 2. No user training required 3. Provides maximum data security	1. Very responsive to information requests 2. Good data security 3. Easily adaptable to changing user needs	1. Slight decrease in cost of operation 2. Slightly adaptable to changing user needs
Disadvantages	1. Moderately responsive to information requests 2. Not easily adaptable to changing user needs	1. Large increase in cost of operation 2. Much user training required	1. Some user training required 2. Only moderately responsive to information requests 3. Presents data security problems

that case, the problem solver might request that additional data be gathered, or might make a selection based primarily on intuition.

Step 9: Implement the Solution

Implementation involves not only communication of the solution to those persons who will make it work, but also the necessary educational programs and other activity that may be required. In some cases physical facilities will have to be constructed or special equipment obtained and installed. In addition, details might have to be coordinated with elements in the environment such as suppliers, customers, or the federal government.

Step 10: Follow Up to Ensure that the Solution Is Effective

The problem solver should establish a procedure for following up on the solution. The procedure can include formal components such as a set of periodic reports, and informal components such as tours of the area where the system has been implemented. This feedback becomes a permanent part of the manager's information system, and is continued until it produces a signal that the system is no longer working as intended. Then, a new problem-solving process begins.

This is the manner in which the problem solver follows the systems approach in solving a problem. The defective system part is identified and the solution that best enables the system to meet its objective is implemented. All problems can be solved in this manner.

AN EXAMPLE OF THE SYSTEMS APPROACH

Assume, for example, that you are a Houston management consultant and that you are invited by the Armadillo Motors board of directors to determine why their market share has been declining. Armadillo Motors (AM) is the largest manufacturer of recreational vehicles in America.

An Example of Preparation Effort

It is easy for you to see AM as a system. Its many factories and assembly plants perform the transformation function. Input raw materials, parts, and subassemblies are supplied by hundreds of firms. The AM network of dealerships distributes the output to government, business, and individual buyers around the world. Thousands of managers on numerous levels perform the control function, using information from computers of all sizes as well as other types of information processors.

With this view of AM as a system, you update yourself on its environment. You study the worldwide automobile market—reading articles that have appeared in such business publications as *Business Week, Fortune*, and *The Wall Street Journal*. You review government legislation that affects AM's operations and study the more important court cases in which AM has been involved. You contact a friend who is an expert in labor law and ask her to supply you with information concerning AM's relationships with organized labor. You also obtain statistics from the federal government that address the issue of imports and exports, and review the most recent AM annual reports to study the financial condition. As a final step, you visit several automobile showrooms in the Houston area—those selling not only U.S. autos but those from other countries as well. You feel that you have a good feeling for the environment in which AM operates.

As a last step before beginning your on-site work, you ask the AM president to supply you with copies of organization charts and the policy manual. From this information you can identify the subsystems within AM and understand their interrelationships.

An Example of Definition Effort

Now you are ready to define the problem. You begin by interviewing top managers. You first ask to see copies of their objectives and performance standards. You are impressed that standards have been established for all levels of the organization—from AM as a whole to the smallest dealership.

Next, you obtain computer printouts that show how well the standards are being met. You notice that the division having the most difficulty in meeting its market share objectives is the MiniVan Division. You shift your focus from AM as a system to the MiniVan Division subsystem.

You obtain more detailed information concerning the MiniVan standards and outputs. For example, you learn which models are selling well and which are not. It is no surprise that the least-expensive models are having the greatest difficulties. That is the market segment where the competition is the keenest.

You interview several top MiniVan managers and obtain information concerning their management team. You are permitted to examine personnel records that list educational background, skills, and so on. You conclude that the management resource is there—it possesses the required technical knowledge and managerial skills.

You next turn to the information processors available to the MiniVan Division. The hardware and software resources are impressive, and the information specialists use leading-edge techniques. However, the managers are not receiving all of the information they need. Specifically, not enough information is available on government and business organizations that buy competitive automobiles. Without this information, AM is unable to tap those particular market segments.

You have identified the problem as the information processor within the MiniVan subsystem of AM. There is a need for management information that is not being met.

An Example of Solution Effort

The task is to create a system that will provide MiniVan management with the needed information and keep it current. Two basic alternatives are identified. The MiniVan marketing research department could gather the information and enter it into the MiniVan computers, or an outside marketing research firm could be hired to perform the same tasks.

A cost/benefit analysis is conducted of the two alternatives and it is decided to do the work inhouse. The main determining factor is the greater control that MiniVan can exercise to keep the information current.

A system is implemented that automatically notifies marketing research when it is time to gather new data, and provides the system output in the form of periodic reports. In addition, MiniVan management can obtain special reports from the database upon demand. As a control to ensure that the system continues to function, the MiniVan MIS steering committee establishes a schedule of quarterly reviews that will include user suggestions.

In this manner, a top-down approach is followed in defining the problem—focusing first on AM as a system and then on the MiniVan Division as a subsystem. On each system level the system parts are studied in sequence. Once the problem is identified with the MiniVan information processor, it is solved by considering the possible alternatives, evaluating each, implementing the one that appears best, and following up.

DOCUMENTATION TOOLS

Documentation tools produce a written record of the system design. The tools can be used at two points in the problem-solving process—during the definition effort when analyzing the existing system (Steps 4 and 5), and during the solution effort when implementing the solution (Step 9).

Reasons for Using the Tools

There are two basic reasons why the problem solver uses the tools—understanding and communication.

The written documentation helps the problem solver understand the problem or system by presenting the details in various forms.

Understand the Problem

It is necessary that the problem solver communicate both the problem details and the solution to others who participate in the problem-solving process. The tools provide a common ground for communication.

Communicate the Problem and the Solution

Types of Tools

There are two basic types of documentation tools—graphic and narrative. We begin by describing three graphic tools—system flowcharts, program flowcharts, and data flow diagrams. Then we describe two narrative tools—the data dictionary and structured English.

SYSTEM FLOWCHARTS

A **system flowchart** shows the step-by-step processing that is performed by a single *system*. Special symbols are used to represent processes and data files. The processes are diagrammed in the sequence of the data flow, and the files used by each process step are included. A plastic **flowchart template** can be used to draw the symbols, or special flowcharting software can be used.

Refer back to Figure 2.16 for a sample system flowchart. This flowchart shows how sales commissions are computed.

Process Symbols

There are four process symbols—for manual processes, offline keydriven processes, online keydriven processes, and computerized processes.

A **manual process** is one that is performed without the aid of any type of mechanical, electrical, or electronic device. The following symbol has been filled in with a description that identifies the particular process.

Manual Processes

Open
the
mail

Keydriven machines are operated by pressing the keys. There are two types of such machines—offline and online. **Offline** devices are not connected directly to the computer, and examples are cash registers, pocket

Offline Keydriven Processes

calculators, and typewriters. The following symbol illustrates the use of a typewriter to prepare a shipping label.

Prepare shipping label

Online Keydriven Processes

An **online** device is connected to the computer. A good example is a keyboard terminal. The following symbol is used to show only the *input* using the device. The example illustrates the entry of sales order data using a terminal. A separate file symbol is used to show output from an online device.

Enter sales order data

Computerized Processes

A **computerized process** is *any* process performed by a computer, ranging from a program that prints a simple report to a complex mathematical model. The following symbol represents *one* program.

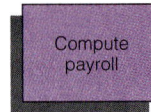

Compute payroll

The suggested direction of data flow from one process to the next is top-to-bottom or left-to-right. The arrows that connect the symbols show the direction. It is also suggested that the process steps be numbered in the order in which they are performed.

File Symbols

The file symbols identify the storage media used. File names are entered in the symbols for identification purposes.

Magnetic Tape

A data file contained on one or more reels of magnetic tape is illustrated with the following symbol.

Inventory file

The following symbol is used to illustrate a data file stored on one or more disks or diskettes. **Magnetic Disk**

Any type of document that is printed on paper is illustrated with the following symbol. The document can range from a form that is filled out by hand to a report or graph that is printed by the computer. **Printed Document**

When output is displayed on a screen it is illustrated with the following symbol. **Screen Display**

The magnetic tape and disk symbols are used for online storage. The tape and disk units are connected to the central processing unit. When data is stored offline, such as in a file cabinet, the following symbol is used. **Offline Storage**

The file symbols are added to the process symbols to complete the picture of the system.

PROGRAM FLOWCHARTS

A **program flowchart** shows the step-by-step processing that is performed by a single *program*. The sample in Figure 2.18 computes the sales commission, and was identified as Step 2 of the system flowchart in Figure 2.16.

In Chapter 2 we recognized five types of programming statements—input/output, data movement, arithmetic, logic, and control. Parallelograms are used for input and output, rectangles are used for data movement and arithmetic, diamonds are used for logic, and control is illustrated with arrows.

Input and Output Operations

All computer input and output is illustrated with the following symbol.

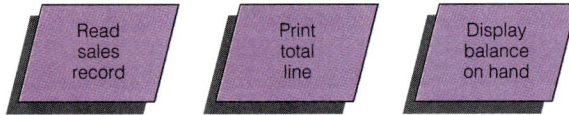

Read sales record · Print total line · Display balance on hand

Data Movement and Arithmetic

The rectangles illustrate both data movement and *any* type of arithmetic operation—addition, subtraction, multiplication, division, exponentiation, or any combination.

Move employee number to output · Compute EOQ

Predefined Process Symbol

In a structured program the steps of the driver module are illustrated with the following symbol.

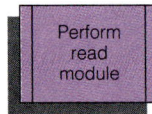

Perform read module

This symbol is called a **predefined process symbol** and it is used to refer to a process included somewhere else in the flowchart.

Logic

The logic decision a computer makes is illustrated with the diamond. In most cases there is only a single input and two outputs. The outputs represent true or false, or yes or no, paths.

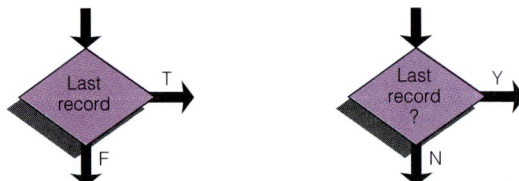

Last record — T / F · Last record ? — Y / N

In this example, if the last record has been reached the processing follows the T or the Y path. If not, processing continues along the F or the N path. The exit arrows can leave the diamond at the sides or the bottom.

Control

When it is necessary for processing to deviate from a sequential pattern, arrows are used to show the choice of logical paths (as shown in the logic example) or the looping action.

Other Symbols

Three other symbols are used. Connector symbols can be used in either a system or program flowchart, but terminal symbols are used only in a program flowchart.

Sometimes there is a need to draw a long line on the page to connect two symbols. The long lines add an undesirable clutter that can be eliminated by using **on-page connectors**. Figure 7.5 provides an example. Any letter or number can be entered into *both* symbols to indicate they are connected.

Connector Symbols

In a similar fashion, connections can be made from a point on one page to a point on another page by using **off-page connectors**. See Figure 7.6.

The beginning and end of each module of a structured program is illustrated with the oval. The beginning and end of the driver module are often labeled Start and End respectively. The beginning of a subsidiary

Terminal Symbol

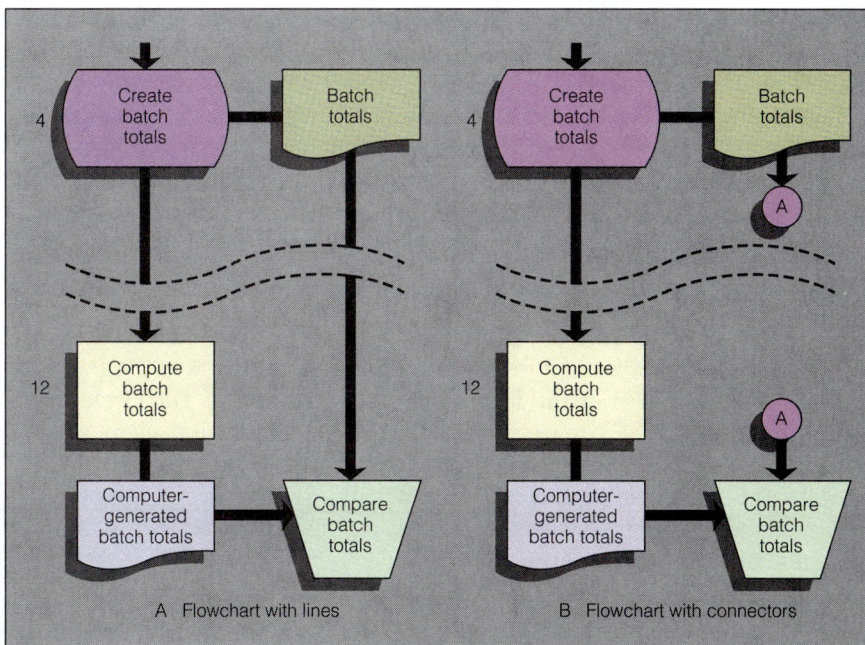

FIGURE 7.5
Use of On-Page Connectors

A   Flowchart with lines

B   Flowchart with connectors

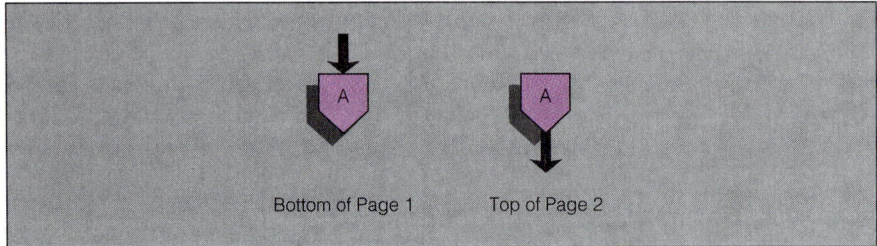

Bottom of Page 1 Top of Page 2

module includes the module name and the end is labeled Return. Figure 2.18 provides examples.

System and program flowcharts traditionally have been the primary documentation tool of the information specialist. Managers who design and implement their own systems can first draw a system flowchart to show the overall system structure, and then draw the necessary program flowcharts to serve as guides for the coding. Managers who prefer to let information specialists handle the design and implementation can also benefit from a knowledge of flowcharting. The knowledge makes it easier to explain the problem and understand the solution. It also gives the manager a better appreciation for the work done by the information specialist.

DATA FLOW DIAGRAMS

If you were documenting a system, one of the most natural methods would be to draw circles to represent the processes and connect the circles with arrows to show the direction of the work flow. Such diagrams are called **data flow diagrams**, or **DFDs**.

Two features of DFDs have accounted for their popularity. First, they are good for taking a top-down, structured approach to documentation. The DFDs exist on multiple levels in a hierarchy with each lower level providing additional detail. Second, the concept is very simple. There are only four symbols and there are few rules.

The Context Diagram

The top-level DFD is called a **context diagram**—it shows the system in the context of its environmental interfaces. Figure 7.7 is a context diagram of a payroll system. Three of the four symbols are included. The circle represents the system, the square represents the environmental element with which the system interfaces, and the arrows show the data flows.

All context diagrams include only a single circle. It contains a short description of what the system accomplishes. The description consists of a verb and an object, or the system name.

The number of environmental elements that can appear in a context diagram depends on the system. Systems with two, three, or four environmental elements are common.

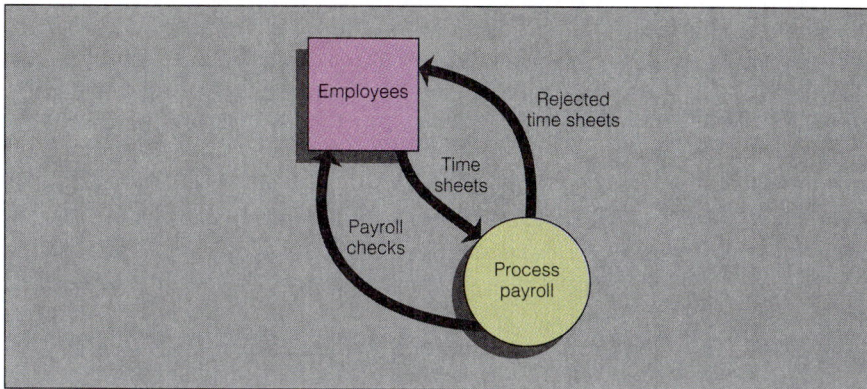

FIGURE 7.7
A Context Diagram

The arrows show the direction of the data flows. In this system the employees provide the system with time sheets and the system provides the employees with rejected time sheets and payroll checks.

The First-Level DFD

Since the context diagram illustrates the entire system with a single circle, it is necessary to drop down to a lower level to show more detail. The DFD that is one level below the context diagram is called the **first-level DFD**. Figure 7.8 is a first-level DFD of the payroll system.

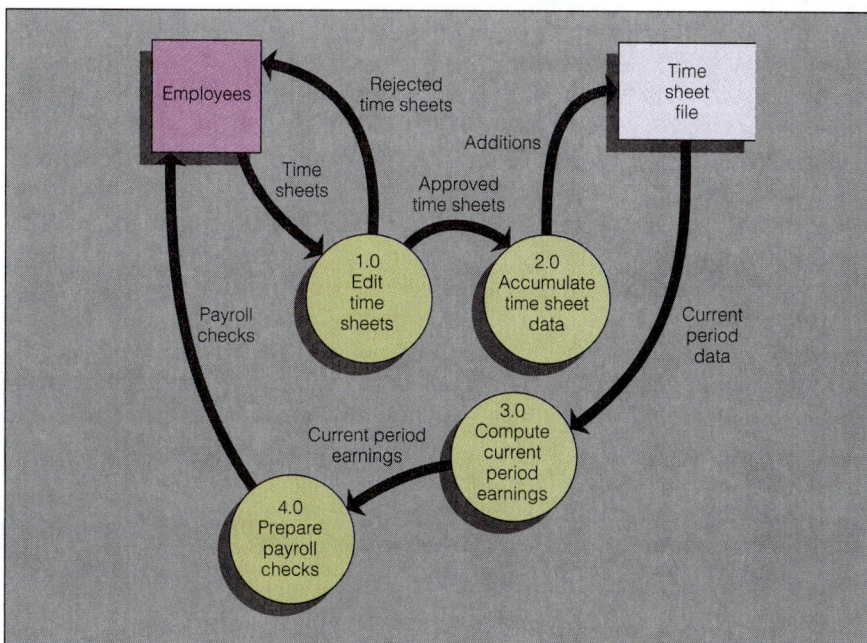

FIGURE 7.8
A First-Level DFD

Essentially, the first-level DFD "explodes" the single circle of the context diagram into multiple circles that represent the main processes. The payroll system consists of four processes. Processes on this and all lower levels are identified with verb-plus-object descriptions, or subsystem names. Each process is also numbered. It is common practice to number the first-level processes 1.0, 2.0, and so on.

You will notice that the figure contains a new symbol—an open-ended rectangle. This is the fourth DFD symbol, and it represents a data store. A **data store** is a data file or database. You label the symbol with the file or database name. Data stores can be included in any DFD except the context diagram.

Each data flow contains a name to identify the data. If the data is a document, such as a Sales Order form, that name is used. A data flow can also represent a single data element or a few elements that travel together. When only a single element is involved, the arrow is labeled with the element name. In the case of a few elements, the analyst devises a name such as "Customer Credit data" or "Reorder data."

In the Figure 7.8 example, the time sheets are edited upon receipt from the employees. Sheets not filled out correctly are returned to the employees. Data is then accumulated from the approved time sheets, and the sheets are added to the file. At some specified time, such as the end of the month, the contents of the file are used to compute the current period earnings. Then, the payroll checks are prepared and sent to the employees.

The DFD does not specify *who* performs each process, nor does it specify any technology that might be involved. For example, you cannot determine from a DFD whether a computer is used.

A Second-Level DFD

The first-level DFD usually does not include all of the processing details. For example, the Figure 7.8 DFD does not indicate the specific editing that takes place in process 1.0. In order to show the necessary detail, you must draw a DFD on a still-lower level. Figure 7.9 is an example of a **second-level DFD**—one that is two levels down from the context diagram. This example "explodes" process 1.0 and shows that three types of editing occur. Note the numbering system used—showing that these are three subsets of processes 1.0. Lower-level processes are numbered in this same manner.

This example shows that all three process steps return rejected time sheets to the employees when particular errors are detected. The three data flows converge to form a single flow. This is an acceptable DFD technique. You can also show a single flow splitting apart to form multiple flows.

You continue to draw lower-level DFDs until you feel that you have incorporated as much detail as is possible, using a DFD.

The Need for Accompanying Documentation

It usually is necessary to supplement DFDs with other documentation to provide the details of both data and processes. The data dictionary pro-

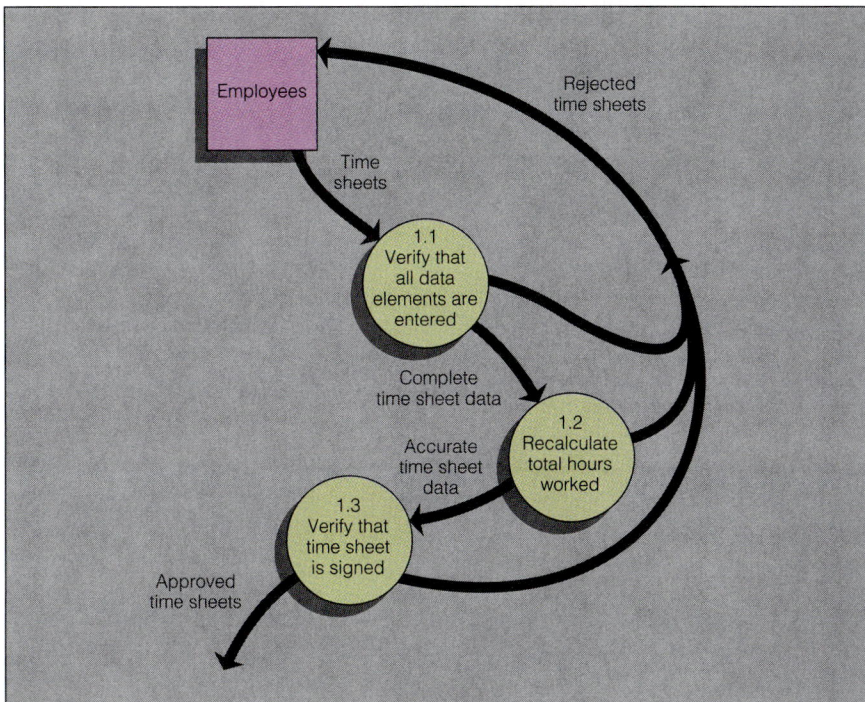

FIGURE 7.9
A Second-Level
DFD

vides the data detail, and structured English provides the process detail. These three tools—DFDs, data dictionary, and structured English—form a package that can be used to document modern, structured systems.

THE DATA DICTIONARY

The **data dictionary** is a description of each data element used in a system. The dictionary can exist in a *paper form* with each sheet representing a data element, or it can be recorded on a *computer storage medium*.

Figure 7.10 shows a paper form called a **data element dictionary entry** used to describe each data element in a thorough manner.[2] There is no standard format. Managers and analysts can even design their own forms.

When a computer-based data dictionary is used, the elements can be sorted in various sequences and printouts prepared that reveal various characteristics. For example, a **where used list** can list each of the data elements and identify the system processes where each is used. Very often a database management system will include a data dictionary capability.

---

[2] The general format of the dictionary forms illustrated in this section came from James Senn, *Analysis and Design of Information Systems* (New York: McGraw-Hill, 1984), pp. 125-134.

FIGURE 7.10

A Data Element
Dictionary Entry

DATA ELEMENT DICTIONARY ENTRY

Use: To describe each data element contained within a data
structure, data flow, and data store.

ELEMENT NAME: Employee number

DESCRIPTION: The identification number that is assigned to each
                   employee

TYPE: Numeric

LENGTH: 6 positions

ALIASES: Man number
                   I.D. number

VALUE RANGE: 100000 - 999999

TYPICAL VALUE: None

LIST OF SPECIFIC VALUES (IF ANY):
                   None

OTHER EDITING DETAILS
                   None

Additional Data Dictionary Forms

When the data dictionary is used to supplement a DFD, additional forms
are used to describe the data stores, data structures, and data flows.

Figure 7.11 is a **data store dictionary entry** illustrating the time sheet file
of the payroll system. Since a data store is a file, the data structures listed
are the different types of records contained in the file. In the example there
is only a single record type. An example of a data store with multiple structures would be an Inventory Transaction file containing an issues record

FIGURE 7.11
A Data Store
Dictionary Entry

DATA STORE DICTIONARY ENTRY

Use: To describe each data store, or file, on a data flow diagram.

DATA STORE NAME: Time sheet file

DESCRIPTION: An accumulation of all time sheets filled out by
the employees for the week. Sheets entered in the
file have been edited for accuracy.

DATA STRUCTURES: Time sheet

VOLUME: 350-360

ACCESS: The file is kept locked except during working hours.
Only the payroll clerk has access.

and a receipts record. Both structures would be listed on the data store dictionary entry form.

Do not confuse the number of structure *types* with the number of *records*. A data store might have only a single structure type but contain hundreds of individual records—all with the same structure.

A **data structure dictionary entry** form is used to provide additional detail about each structure. Figure 7.12 describes the time sheet structure. The contents listed in the center of the form are the data elements.

FIGURE 7.12
A Data Structure Dictionary Entry

DATA STRUCTURE DICTIONARY ENTRY

Use: To describe a formal data structure, such as a record or document.

STRUCTURE NAME: Time sheet

DESCRIPTION: The form that is filled out by each hourly employee for the week

CONTENTS:
Week ending
Department number
Employee number
Time in*
Time out*
Number of hours worked*
Approval signature

* Appears on form seven times (one per day)

The fourth data dictionary form is the **data flow dictionary entry** used to describe each arrow in a DFD. The form in Figure 7.13 describes the arrow labeled "Current period data" in Figure 7.8.

STRUCTURED ENGLISH

When users first began coding their own programs, they often rebelled against the tedious effort required to create the program flowcharts. They searched for an easier way to plan programs, and they developed a type of

FIGURE 7.13
A Data Flow
Dictionary Entry

DATA FLOW DICTIONARY ENTRY

Use: To describe each data flow (arrow) on a data flow diagram.

DATA FLOW NAME: Current period data

DESCRIPTION: The employee data for the current pay period (week)
that is used to calculate the payroll amounts

FROM PROCESSES:

TO PROCESSES: 3.0 Compute current period earnings

DATA STRUCTURES: Time sheet

shorthand that became known as pseudocode. **Pseudocode** is a narrative description of a program that looks like computer code, but is not.

Pseudocode became so popular that efforts were made to establish some guidelines. The result was structured English. **Structured English** is a shorthand narrative of a procedure that has the following features:

- Each step of the process is described with a verb and one or more objects.
- Like a computer program, the steps are listed in the sequence in

which they are performed.
- All of the data names that are used are described in the data dictionary, and the names appear in uppercase.
- Uppercase is used for words that describe input and output operations (READ, PRINT, and so on) and selection (IF, THEN, ELSE, WHILE, and so on).
- Only the three constructs of structured programming (sequence, selection, and repetition) are used.

Figure 7.14 is an example recorded on a form called a **process dictionary entry**. The special form is not necessary. The example shows how the current period earnings are computed in the payroll system.

COMPUTER-AIDED SOFTWARE ENGINEERING

The backlog of jobs waiting to be placed on the computer has prompted both software and hardware vendors to develop software-based documentation tools, code generators, and prototyping tools that facilitate software development. The entire set of tools is called **computer-aided software engineering**, or simply **CASE**. **Software engineering** is the application of such scientific principles as the systems approach and structured programming to the software development process. The term **productivity tools** has also been used to describe this overall set of software intended to increase the productivity of the system developers.

Software-Based Documentation Tools

The software-based documentation tools, often called **analyst workbenches** and **analyst tool kits**, relieve the systems analyst of much of the work in preparing graphic systems descriptions such as flowcharts and data flow diagrams. Figure 7.15 is a data flow diagram drawn with a CASE tool. In addition, the CASE tools can assist the analyst in designing screen displays and report formats.

Code Generators

A **code generator**, also called a **programmer workbench**, can create code from program specifications, produce accompanying documentation, provide data dictionaries, and perform error checking. Some of the generators can also maintain a **central repository** of previously generated code modules that can be reused when they are needed. The repository approach is much more efficient than creating each new program from scratch.

Prototyping Tools

A problem that has plagued system developers since the beginning of the computer era has been the difficulty of specifying exactly what the user needs. The user might not know or cannot put the description into words.

```
START
READ first record
DO WHILE [there are records]
    IF [HOURS.WORKED > REG.HOURS]
        COMPUTE CURR.GROSS = (REG.HOURS * WAGE.RATE) +
            ((HOURS.WORKED - REG.HOURS) * 1.5 * WAGE.RATE)
    ELSE
        COMPUTE CURR.GROSS = HOURS.WORKED * WAGE.RATE
    ENDIF
    IF [CURR.GROSS < TAX.BREAK0]
        SET INC.TAX = 0
    ELSE
        IF [CURR.GROSS < TAX.BREAK1]
            COMPUTE INC.TAX = CURR.GROSS * TAX.RATE1
        ELSE
            IF [CURR.GROSS < TAX.BREAK2]
                COMPUTE INC.TAX = CURR.GROSS * TX.RATE2
            ELSE COMPUTE INC.TAX = CURR.GROSS * TX.RATE3
            ENDIF
        ENDIF
    ENDIF
    IF [(YTD.GROSS + CURR.GROSS) > FICA.MAX]
        IF [YTD.FICA = (FICA.RATE * FICA.MAX)]
            SET FICA = 0
        ELSE
            COMPUTE FICA = (FICA.RATE * FICA.MAX) - YTD.FICA
        ENDIF
    ELSE
        COMPUTE FICA = FICA.RATE * CURR.GROSS
    ENDIF
    COMPUTE CURR.NET = CURR.GROSS - INC.TAX - FICA
    READ next record
END WHILE
STOP
```

Reverse side

PROCESS DICTIONARY ENTRY

Use: To describe each process included on a data flow diagram.

PROCESS: 3.0 Compute current period earnings

DESCRIPTION: Gross pay is computed for both employees
                working overtime and not working overtime.
                Income tax and social security tax are computed
                and subtracted from gross pay to produce net pay.

INPUT: Current period data

OUTPUT: Current period earnings

LOGIC SUMMARY   See reverse

Front side

FIGURE 7.14

Structured English Recorded on a Process Dictionary Entry Form

FIGURE 7.15

A Data Flow
Diagram Drawn
by a CASE tool

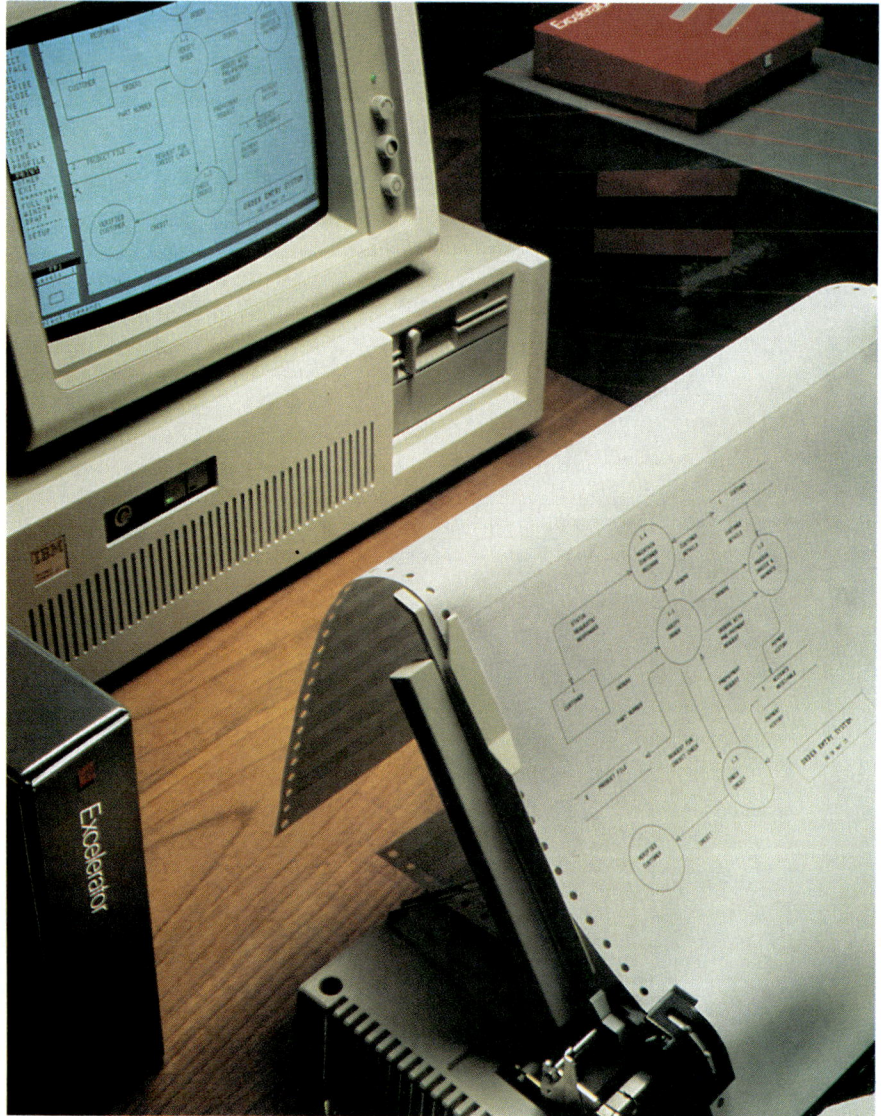

An approach aimed at solving this problem is the rapid development of a
prototype system that gives the user an idea of how the system will function, but without performing all of the necessary tasks. The software prototype is used in the same manner as the three-dimensional models that provide automobile engineers with a view of a new design.

   The manager views the system prototype and tells the systems analyst
why it is unsatisfactory. A second prototype is prepared and shown to the
user so that more suggestions might be obtained. This iterative process is
repeated until a satisfactory system is produced. At that point, the information specialists have the choice of implementing the final prototype as the

operational system or developing an operational system from the prototype specifications. This process of using system prototypes to develop design specifications is called **prototyping**.

Prototyping is made possible by CASE software. The software enables the rapid development of screens and reports used by the user to interface with the system. The software also can generate the code that does the internal processing.

Documentation tools and code generators have been in use for several years, but complete CASE software is just now evolving. It holds the promise of improving the software development process in the form of reduced costs, earlier implementations, and higher levels of system quality.

PUTTING THE PROBLEM-SOLVING TOOLS IN PERSPECTIVE

System flowcharts, DFDs, and software-based documentation tools are the tools of the systems analyst. Program flowcharts, structured English, and code generators are the tools of the programmer. Both the systems analyst and programmer benefit from the data dictionary and the CASE tools.

When the manager engages in end-user computing, he or she can use all of the tools. It is easy to think of end-user computing as simply such user-friendly software as Lotus or dBASE. Often overlooked is the need to define the problem and design the solution before the software comes into play. The systems approach, the documentation tools, and CASE are intended to ensure that a system is designed that provides the needed problem-solving support.

SUMMARY

Physical and behavioral scientists developed an approach to conducting experiments called the scientific method. Business problem solvers adapted the approach to business and called it the systems approach. The systems approach consists of three phases of effort—preparation, definition, and solution.

Preparation effort requires that you take a systems view of the firm, its environment, and the subsystems within the firm. Definition effort involves starting with the top system level and working down, and examining the system parts in a certain sequence on each level. Solution effort requires that you identify feasible solutions. The types of feasibility are technical, economic, legal, operational, and schedule. You next evaluate the alternatives and select the best one. The best solution is the one that contributes the most to the firm as it works toward its objectives. The solution is implemented, and you follow up to make certain that it performs as intended.

Documentation tools have been developed that permit understanding and communication. Graphic tools include system flowcharts, program flowcharts, and data flow diagrams. Narrative tools include the data dictionary and structured English. A wide variety of software tools, called CASE, enable the problem solver to use the computer to prepare documentation, generate and maintain repositories of code, and engage in prototyping.

Users can follow the systems approach and use the documentation tools when engaging in end-user computing.

KEY CONCEPTS

The systems approach, consisting of the three main phases of effort

The efficient top-down and element-by-element approach to systems analysis

Levels of documentation detail, as provided by DFDs

How DFDs, the data dictionary, and structured English together provide a complete system documentation

How prototyping facilitates definition of user needs

KEY TERMS

Systems approach
Preparation effort
Definition effort, analysis phase
Solution effort, design phase, synthesis phase
Subsystem
Top-down approach
Feasibility
Evaluation criteria
Documentation tool
System flowchart
Program flowchart
Data flow diagram (DFD)

Context diagram
Data store
Data dictionary
Structured English
Computer-aided software engineering (CASE), productivity tool
Software engineering
Analyst workbench, analyst tool kit
Code generator, programmer workbench
Prototype

QUESTIONS

1. What are the three types of effort involved with using the systems approach? Which one is the design phase? The analysis phase?

2. On which system level do you begin when you take a systems approach to defining a problem?

3. Which part of the system—conceptual or physical—is most likely to contain the root cause of the problem? Explain your reasoning.

4. What are the five types of feasibility?

5. Which is the *best* solution alternative?

6. What happens when follow-up activity indicates that a system is no longer functioning as it should?

7. What are two reasons for using the documentation tools?

8. What are the four types of processes shown by a system flowchart?

9. What do the four data flow diagramming symbols represent?

10. What is the name of the highest-level DFD? Which type of symbol does it *not* include?

11. What are the four data dictionary entry forms?

12. How does structured English differ from pseudocode?

13. What is the name of the dictionary entry form that contains structured English?

14. Name three basic capabilities of CASE software.

15. Which of the tools is the systems analyst most likely to use? The programmer? The user who is involved in end-user computing?

PROBLEMS

1. Draw a system flowchart of the following inventory system.
    a. Inventory clerks fill out physical inventory sheets that show the quantity of each item in the warehouse.
    b. The warehouse supervisor compares the physical inventory sheets with a computer-prepared inventory listing showing what should be on hand. Any items with quantities that do not agree are marked with an asterisk.
    c. The supervisor's secretary types an inventory adjustment form for each asterisked item on the physical inventory sheets, and files the physical inventory sheets in an Inventory Sheet file.
    d. A data entry operator reads from the inventory adjustment forms and keys the data into a keyboard terminal. The adjustment forms are then filed in an Adjustment Form file.
    e. A computer program prints an Inventory Adjustment report to be used by the plant manager.

2. Draw a data flow context diagram and first-level DFD of the inventory system. Hint: Start the first-level DFD with a process symbol rather than an environmental element. The inventory clerks are a part of the system.

3. Draw a system flowchart of the following sales order system.
    a. Customer sales orders are received from customers.
    b. A sales-order clerk keys the sales-order data into a terminal.
    c. The computer writes the data onto a magnetic disk as the Sales-Order file.

   d. The sales-order data on the disk is sorted into inventory item number sequence, and the output is a Sorted Sales-Order file.
   e. The Sorted Sales-Order file is used to update the Inventory Master file, also on magnetic disk. The same program prints a Sales-Order listing, and records a Sales-Order History file on magnetic tape.

4. Draw a context diagram and a first-level DFD of the sales order system.

CASE PROBLEM   Ace Toys

You are a little nervous as you enter Jim Pelzer's office. He is the superintendent of the Newark plant and this is your first assignment as a systems analyst. He motions you to sit down and then explains why he called the information services department for help. It seems that the new compressed-paper skateboards have not been holding up as well as expected. Retailers report that customers are returning the boards because the wheels have pulled loose. Refunds will have to be made to the retailers and this will reduce Ace profits.

Confused, you ask Pelzer how this affects you. After all, you are a computer specialist, not a production expert. You recall your college professor telling you that you would work with conceptual systems, not physical ones.

"Because," replied Pelzer, "I think we can solve this problem with better information. You probably don't know much about production, but we have a quality control department in the manufacturing division. The department consists of quality control inspectors who monitor each step of the production process, looking for things that might cause defects. Maybe the cause is poor raw materials or a machine that is out of adjustment. However, the inspectors don't have any way of knowing how the boards hold up after they are shipped. This is where you come in. I want you to design a system that provides the quality control inspectors with feedback information—information from the retailers and maybe even the kids who buy the boards. With the additional information the inspectors can be more alert to things that might be causing trouble. The inspectors need feedback. Feedback—that's a term that you computer folks understand. Right?"

You nod, and Pelzer motions you to the door with the instructions to "Go find out what information the inspectors need, and come back when you have something." As you feel the pressure of Pelzer's hand in the middle of your back, you turn and ask "Is it all right if I talk with people in addition to the inspectors?" Pelzer says "Definitely not. We don't have time for a wall-to-wall study. We've got to get this problem solved before the retailer credits kill us. Get right to the problem. Don't waste anybody else's time." With that, he slams the door.

1. Is Pelzer correct in recognizing a need for feedback information? Explain your answer.

2. Does Pelzer want you to follow the systems approach? Explain why or why not.

3. Make a list of the system levels involved with the problem. Start with the top-level system. Identify with an asterisk the level where Pelzer wants you to limit your data gathering.

4. Using Figure 7.4 as a diagram of Ace Toys, which system part does Pelzer want you to study?

5. Assume that you decide to recommend to Pelzer that a different approach be followed. Make a list of the steps you would recommend. Do not just copy the steps from the book. Relate the steps to the Ace problem.

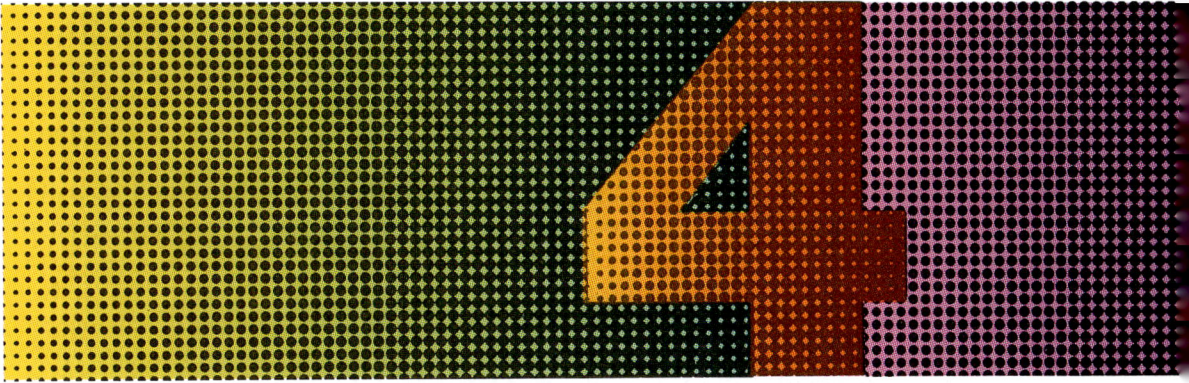

The Computer as a Problem-Solving Tool

In Chapter 1 we recognized that managers use a complete information system in solving the organization's problems. The complete system obtains information from both environmental and internal sources, and makes the information available in the form of both written and verbal media. When the computer is included in this complete system, the computerized portion is called the computer based information system, or CBIS.

You were introduced to some computer fundamentals in Chapter 1. We identified the different computer sizes (supercomputer, mainframe, minicomputer, and microcomputer), as well as the basic types of components found in all computers. The components include the central processing unit (CPU), one or more input and output units, and some form of secondary storage.

In Part 4 we recognize that the CPU contains an arithmetic and logic unit and a control unit in addition to primary storage. Key terms relating to primary storage (byte, kilobyte, RAM, and ROM) are explained. The secondary storage of the PC is the diskette, and data is recorded in the form of tracks and sectors. We also explain the use of the keyboard as an input device, as well as how to set up the printer to obtain printed output.

Assuming that you are familiar with these computer fundamentals, you can use this part of the text to gain a better understanding of computer hardware and software. In Chapter 8 we describe the computer input and output units in greater detail and explain the fundamental approaches to terminal use. We also discuss the critical issues of economic justification, computer security, and ethics in computer use. Chapter 8 concludes with a description of the process the problem-solving manager and the information specialists follow in implementing a computer system.

Chapters 9 and 10 round out Part 4. Chapter 9 deals with secondary storage, the relationship of storage to the type of processing performed, the database, and the database management system (DBMS). In that chapter we also recognize the need for database security. Chapter 10 introduces you to the fundamentals of data communications—the hardware and software used to link widespread computing resources, the possible types of networks, standard network architectures and protocols, security considerations, and the role of data communications in problem solving.

An understanding of the material contained in this part of the text contributes to your computer literacy. This literacy and an accompanying information literacy are the prime ingredients in building and using a CBIS.

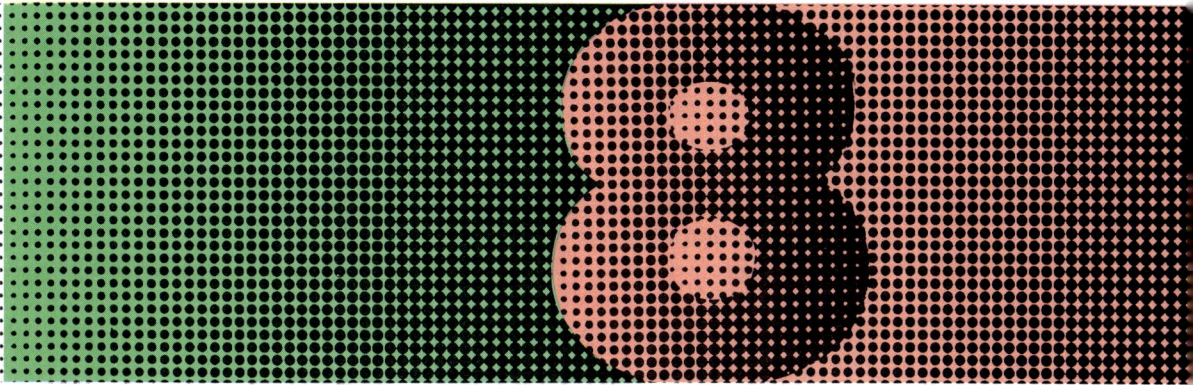

Fundamentals of Computer Processing

LEARNING OBJECTIVES   After studying this chapter, you should:

- Have an appreciation for the variety of input devices used to enter data into a computer, as well as the different types of output devices that can record the results of the processing
- Know the different ways to enter data using a keyboard terminal or a microcomputer keyboard
- Know some techniques for keeping input errors to a minimum
- Appreciate the difficulty of economic justification of computer use and know some alternate methods that can be used
- Recognize the importance of incorporating security measures into a computer system
- Recognize the responsibility to use the computer in an ethical manner
- Be familiar with a set of steps the manager and the information specialists can take in developing a computer system

OVERVIEW

In this chapter we supplement the computer fundamentals presented in Chapter 1. More information is provided on input and output devices. Special attention is paid to those devices that the problem solver uses directly—terminals connected to a computer of any size, and the keyboard and screen of a microcomputer. The fundamental ways of using these devices are covered.

The remaining topics in the chapter do not relate specifically to hardware. Although complete error avoidance is impossible, three techniques for keeping errors to a minimum are presented. The issue of economic justification of computer use is addressed, as well as the important role that computer security plays. It is also recognized that computer use carries with it an ethical responsibility to safeguard the rights of everyone affected by the system. The chapter concludes with a description of the steps that lead to the implementation of a computer-based information system.

THE EXPANDING SCOPE OF COMPUTER USE

The federal government has always been a leader in the use of data processing devices. The first punched card machines were installed in the Bureau of the Census in 1890, and the first mass-produced computer, the Remington Rand UNIVAC I, was installed by the same agency in 1951. The large scale of operations was a primary reason why the government led the way. However, it did not take private industry long to follow suit. The punched card machines provided much of the data processing capability for larger business organizations during the first half of this century, and the installation of a UNIVAC I by General Electric in 1954 marked the beginning of computer use in processing business data.

Up until the minicomputer and microcomputer made their impact in the 1970s, computer use was restricted to only the larger organizations—government as well as business. The systems were very expensive by today's standards. A small computer leased for as much as $5,000 per month, and the fee for large computers was in the $25,000 to $75,000 per month range. The systems were so expensive that the practice was to lease them rather than purchase them outright. The rapid development of new technology, causing the early computers to quickly become obsolete, also contributed to the popularity of leasing.

The minicomputer and then the microcomputer had a dramatic effect on the cost of computing. Today an organization of any size can afford a computer—and it is not a stripped-down model. An inexpensive microcomputer system, *purchased* for as little as $1,000, contains more processing punch than the giant systems of twenty years ago.

Therefore the question firms ask today is not "Can we *afford* a computer?" Rather, it is "Do we *need* a computer?"

Hardware Cost Is the Tip of the Iceberg

Even though the purchase price of a computer is within reach of any organization, that is not the only cost. The purchase price of the hardware may

FIGURE 8.1

The First Mass-Produced Computer—the UNIVAC I

be only the tip of the iceberg, with other, less obvious, costs being much higher. The *software* cost can be substantial if a large number of prewritten packages must be purchased or if a programming staff must be hired to create custom software. The other *information specialists*, such as systems analysts and operators, also add to the cost. While the trend has been toward lower hardware costs, the personnel costs have escalated. Other costs that should be considered include such *supplies* as paper, ribbons, disks, and tapes, as well as *furniture and fixtures*, and such *facilities* as computer rooms. A cost that never appears on the company's books is the *user's time* that is necessary to implement a computer system.

Many managers without good computer backgrounds have been attracted to the low computer prices and have made purchases without first determining a need and considering all of the potential costs. These managers have learned the hard way that there is no shortcut to the benefits of computer processing. The benefits come only after a dedication by top management to make all of the necessary investments in time and money.

THE COMPUTER SCHEMATIC

When the first computer class was conducted in the 1950s, the instructor most likely drew a diagram on the chalkboard similar to the one illustrated in Figure 8.2. The diagram is called the **computer schematic**, and it is just as applicable today as it was then. The symbols show the primary units, and the arrows represent such electrical connections as cables and circuits that permit data and control impulses to flow through the system.

The CPU houses the primary storage unit, the arithmetic and logic unit, and the control unit. The primary storage unit stores the program containing instructions and the values being processed. Primary storage in modern computers is in the form of tiny **metal-oxide semiconductor** or **MOS** chips such as the one pictured in Figure 8.3 that can contain over four million bytes of data. The **arithmetic and logic unit** (the **ALU**) performs the

FIGURE 8.2

The Computer
Schematic

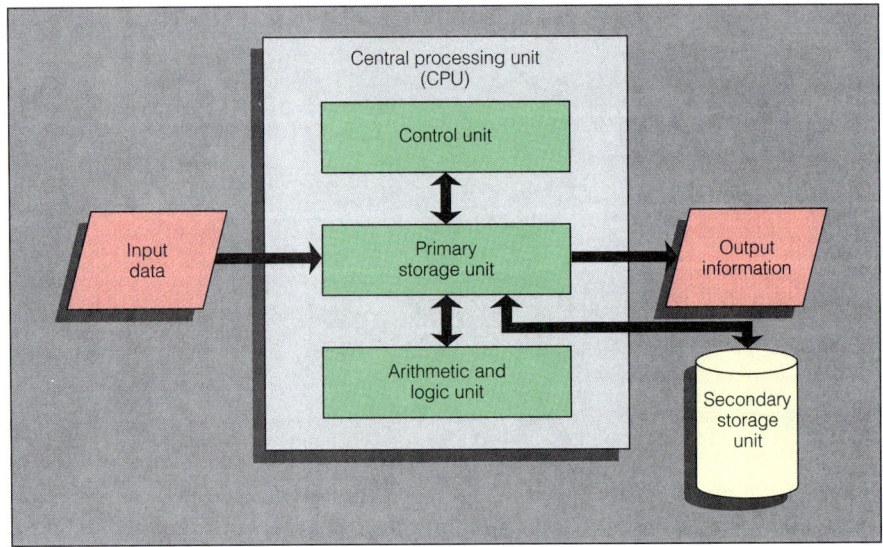

FIGURE 8.3

The MOS Chip
Provides Primary
Storage

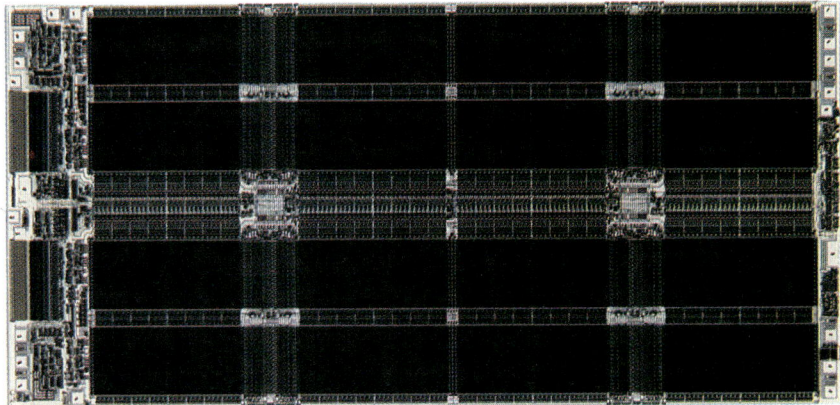

arithmetic and logic operations. The **control unit** causes the program
instructions to be executed in the proper sequence.

The computer schematic also includes one or more secondary storage
units and input/output units. Small computer systems include only a few
of these units; large systems can include hundreds.

An important point to recognize is the fact that a particular computer
configuration selection is based on the applications to be performed by the
organization. For example, the units comprising a hospital computer are
quite different from those for a bank or a supermarket.

The primary architecture of computers of all sizes is reflected in the computer schematic. It provides a good blueprint for learning the wide variety
of available hardware units. We will discuss input and output units in this
chapter and secondary storage units in Chapter 9.

INPUT DEVICES

There are four principal ways of entering data into a computer as illustrated in Figure 8.4. You can operate a keyboard terminal attached directly to the computer, you can operate a keydriven device that is not attached to the computer, the data can be read magnetically or optically from a document or an object, and you can speak to the computer.

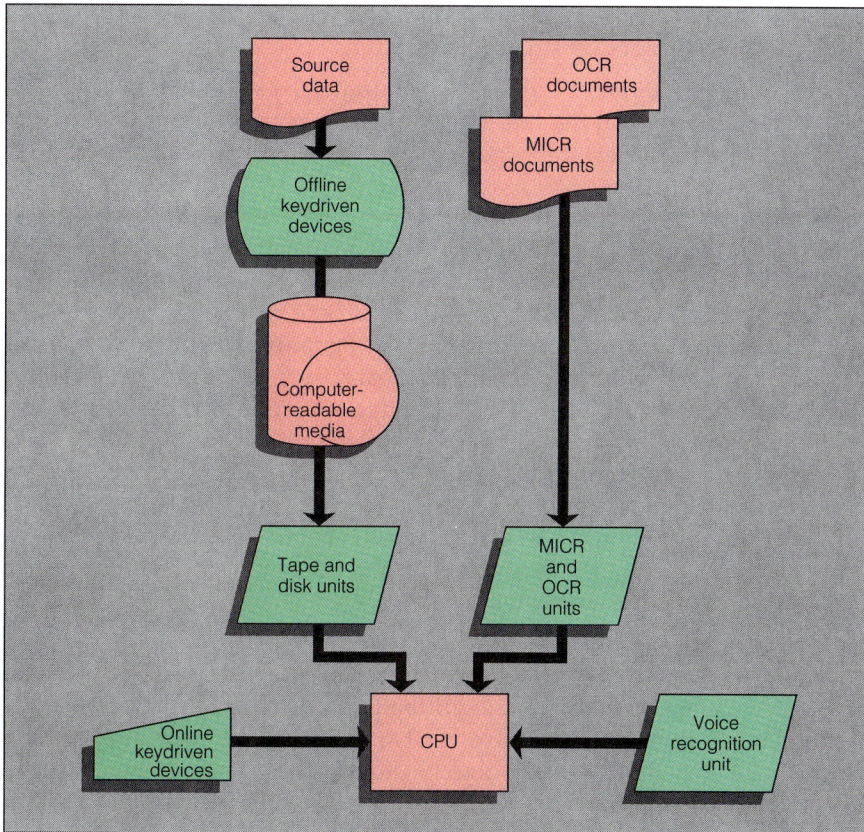

FIGURE 8.4
Input Options

Online Keydriven Devices

The most popular input option today is the keyboard terminal or the microcomputer keyboard. Both are **online keydriven devices** connected directly to the CPU. The **microcomputer keyboard** is connected to the CPU by a short cord, and the **keyboard terminal** is connected to a computer of any size by a data communications link such as a telephone line that might span thousands of miles. Data entered in the keyboard is transmitted to primary storage where it is processed.

In addition to entering data through the keyboard, other labor-saving features and devices often are available. Some terminal and microcomputer screens have a **touch screen** capability—you need only touch an area of the screen with your finger to issue a command or enter a data element. A similar technique employs the use of a **light pen**—a hand-held electronic pointer used to enter data through the screen. Other keyboards are supplemented by a **mouse**—a box about the size of a cassette tape that you can move on a flat surface. As you move the mouse, the cursor moves in an identical pattern on the screen. The mouse is especially well-suited to manipulating graphical patterns on the screen, providing a **graphical user interface**, or **GUI**, capability.

Offline Keydriven Devices

It is also possible to enter data into a computer by using an **offline keydriven device**. Up until the late 1970s the most popular input option was the **keypunch machine**, which created punched cards to be read by special **card readers**. The keypunch machines were offline, but the card readers were online.

For a brief period in the 1960s and 70s when offline creation of computer input was in vogue, **key-to-disk** and **key-to-tape** units were used in larger organizations. These units recorded the data onto magnetic disks or magnetic tape reels that could then be mounted on online **disk drives** or **tape units**. The main advantage of this approach over keypunching was the elimination of the punched cards. The keying operation was still very slow.

Today's offline keydriven devices consist mainly of cash register devices in retail stores that record transaction data on magnetic tape cassettes or diskettes for later processing.

The use of keydriven devices of all types is commonly referred to as the **input bottleneck** since the slow speed of the operators' fingers is a barrier to getting data into the computer.

Source Data Automation

One approach to eliminating the input bottleneck is to read the data directly from input documents or objects. The term **source data automation** describes how the document or object is automated by printing the characters so that they can be read by the computer. Two technologies are used—magnetic ink character recognition and optical character recognition.

Magnetic Ink Character Recognition

In the late 1950s the American Banking Association adopted a special type style to be used on checks. The type style, or **type font**, appears in Figure 8.5 and consists of the digits and four special characters. The characters are printed in a special ink containing magnetic properties that facilitate reading. This input technique is called **magnetic ink character recognition**, or **MICR**.

When you receive your checks from the bank they contain your account number, a number that identifies the bank, and the check number. The amount is added in magnetic ink by the first bank to process the check after it has been written. A keydriven device called an **inscriber** or **encoder** is

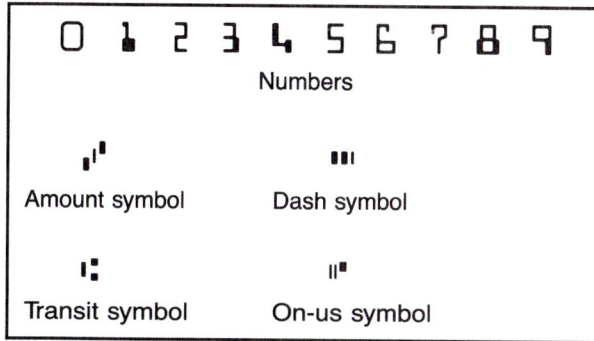

FIGURE 8.5
The MICR Type
Font

used to add the amount. The checks are then read by an input device called a **reader sorter**, which reads the data into primary storage.

MICR enabled banks to handle the increasing numbers of checks during the 1960s and 70s. In the 1980s a new approach, designed to reduce check volume, was taken. The approach is called **electronic funds transfer**, or **EFT**. The idea behind EFT is to handle deposits and withdrawals electronically. Automated teller machines, or ATMs, are examples of EFT.

The MICR font is called a **stylized font** in that the characters are specially shaped to facilitate the reading. In the search for a way to read characters that have a more normal shape, an approach was developed enabling a computer input unit to read the characters in much the same way as does the human eye. This approach is **optical character recognition**, or **OCR**. Depending on the model, OCR input units can read alphabetic, numeric, and special characters, as well as bar codes and such marks as true–false responses on a test-scoring sheet. Most units read machine-printed characters, but some can read characters printed by hand. It is possible to read practically any type font, and a special ink does not have to be used.

Optical Character Recognition

The most widespread example of OCR is the use of **bar code scanners** in supermarkets to read the **bar codes** on the grocery items. Similar OCR devices are used in department stores where sales clerks use a hand-held **wand** to read identifying codes from item tags. This use of OCR in retailing has been given the name **point of sale** recording, or **POS**. POS enables the clerks to handle transactions faster and more accurately, and reduces customer waiting time.

OCR has other uses as well. Credit card firms such as American Express and oil companies read the charge slips optically. OCR enables the companies to bill their customers faster, thereby speeding up the collection of the money. Federal Express uses OCR to read the air-bill number from labels on packages as a means of tracking the flow of packages through the system.

MICR, EFT, and OCR are ways that computer users have whittled away at the input bottleneck.

Voice Recognition

It is also possible to enter data and instructions into the computer by speaking into a microphone attached to a **voice recognition unit**. Prototype models were built in the late 1950s, but it was not until the 70s that units began to be mass produced. Two types of voice recognition units have been designed. A user enters a **vocabulary** into a **speaker-dependent system** by speaking the words several times. The system is thereby tailored to that speaker's voice. The other type of unit, a **speaker-independent system**, can recognize anyone's voice. Its design is still being refined—differences in accents is a difficult hurdle to overcome.

Voice recognition has not been accepted by business users as quickly as anticipated. It still remains largely an attraction to hobbyists for use with microcomputers. The technology will no doubt continue to be improved, and someday it might provide the primary means for communicating with the computer.

OUTPUT DEVICES

The end product of computer processing is some form of output, and Figure 8.6 illustrates the options—displayed, printed, graphic, microfilm, and spoken.

Displayed Output

The output device most popular with end users is the **display screen**, a **cathode ray tube** (often called a **CRT**) or a **monitor**. The rapid speed of the display is the main reason for the popularity, and the ability of some units to display graphics and use color also adds to the appeal.

Printed Output

The main disadvantage of the display screen is its inability to produce a paper copy, called a **hard copy**. Hard copy is necessary or preferred in four situations:

1. When information must be sent through the mails (such as an invoice or bill mailed to a customer)
2. When a historical record is required (such as a listing of this month's payroll checks)
3. When the volume of output is large (such as a lengthy management report)
4. When several people must use the information at the same time (such as in a conference)

Output devices called **printers** produce the hard copy. The first printers were called **line printers** since they printed so fast it appeared they were printing a line at a time. The early speeds were about 600 lines per minute (lpm) and most of the units in use today are in that same range, although speeds as high as 3600 lpm have been achieved.

FIGURE 8.6   Output Options

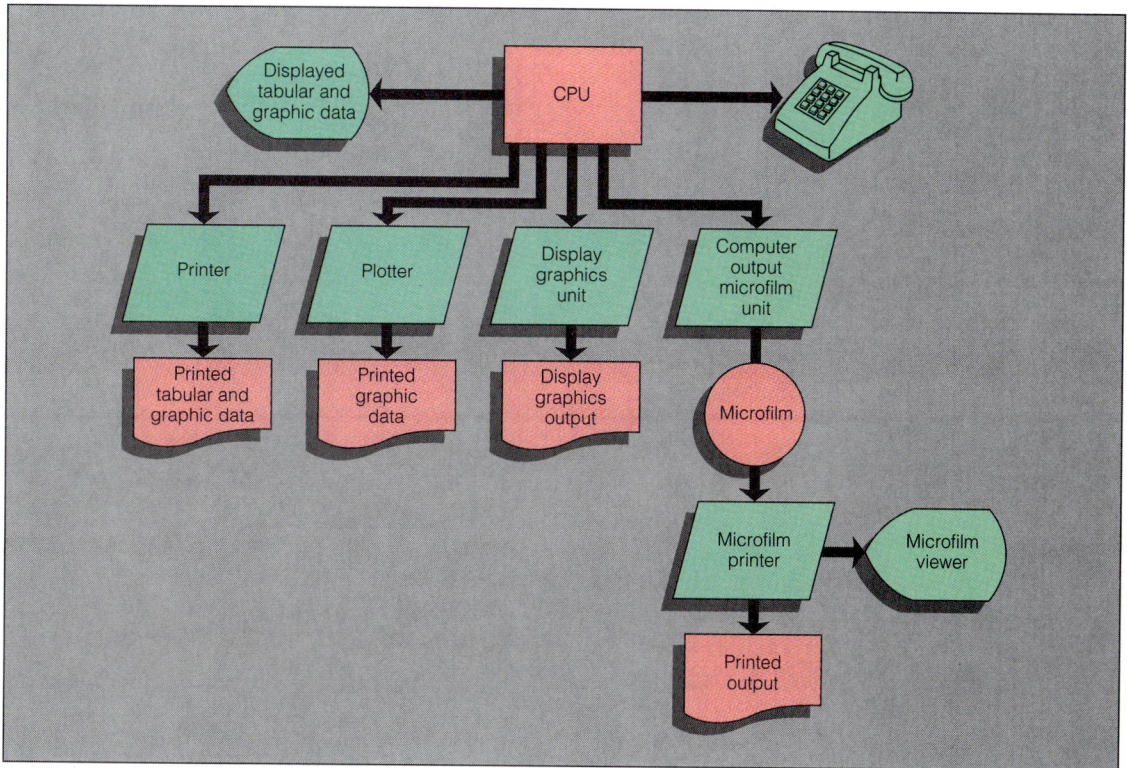

Other printers have been developed to achieve both faster and slower speeds. The fastest printers are **page printers** that can print in the 15,000 to 20,000 lpm range, and the slowest are the ones used on microcomputers, called **character printers** or **serial printers**, that print from 30 to 350 characters per second (cps).

Popular character printer technologies are the **dot matrix printer** the **daisy wheel printer** that uses a printing element like the one illustrated in Figure 8.7, the **ink jet printer** that sprays droplets of ink onto the paper to form the character shapes, and the **laser printer** that uses a laser beam to cause ink powder to adhere to the paper in much the same manner as a photocopying machine. The daisy wheel, ink jet, and laser printers can produce **letter quality** documents—just as attractive as those prepared on an electric typewriter. Some dot matrix printers can produce **near-letter quality** documents.

Graphic Output

Some of the first computer users such as engineers and architects recognized the need to produce graphic output. Special output devices named

FIGURE 8.7

A Daisy Wheel
Printing Element

plotters were designed to meet this need. Plotters, either attached to the CPU or operated offline, can produce black-and-white or color graphic output on regular-sized or over-sized paper. A map, drawn by a plotter using multicolored ink pens, is shown in Figure 8.8.

FIGURE 8.8

An Example of
Output Using a
Plotter

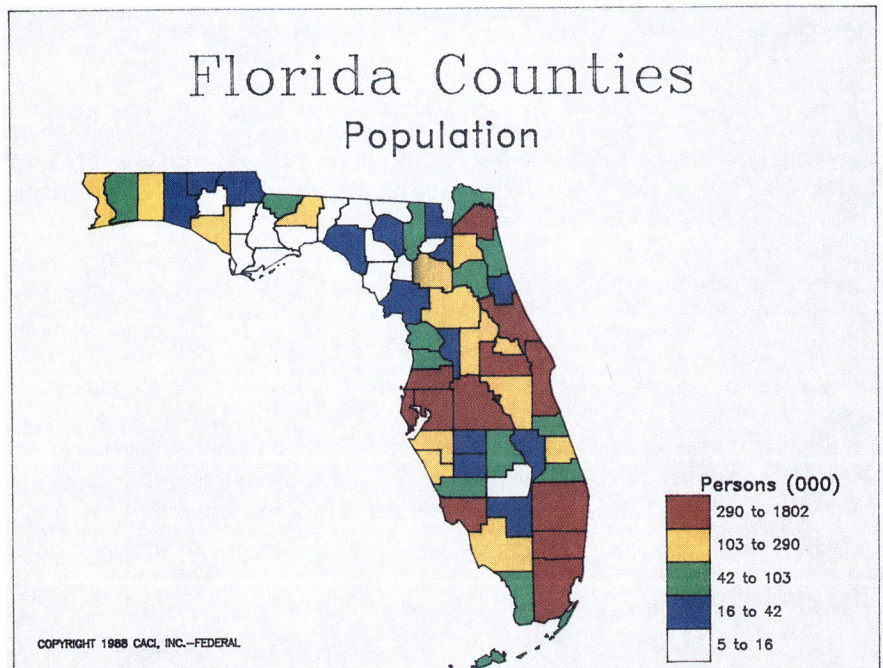

Florida Counties
Population

Persons (000)
290 to 1802
103 to 290
42 to 103
16 to 42
5 to 16

COPYRIGHT 1988 CACI, INC.—FEDERAL

A recent development in hard copy graphic output has been the **graphics printer**, a character printer with an ability to produce graphics as well as characters. Most microcomputer printers have this capability.

A manager can use graphic output in problem solving. In addition to producing the graphics in hard copy form by using a plotter or graphics printer, the graphics can also be displayed on the screen. Screen displays are especially effective when using a color monitor.

It is even possible for the computer to produce graphics, called **presentation graphics**, that can be used in making presentations to groups. For example, the graph in Figure 8.9 was produced by the computer in the form of a color slide for projection onto a screen. Presentation graphics are especially well-suited to group problem solving.

Microfilm Output

Companies with large document files often maintain them in a miniature form on photographic film. The name **microform** is given to all such technologies, with the term **microfilm** describing the film in a reel form, and **microfiche** describing the film in a sheet form. It is possible to record the images of a room full of paper documents on a few microform reels or sheets that can fit into a drawer.

The computer can use a **computer output microfilm (COM)** unit to create either microfilm or microfiche. Special offline **microfilm viewers** are used to display the filmed documents. **Microfilm printers** can be used to produce hard copies. Perhaps you have used this equipment in the library.

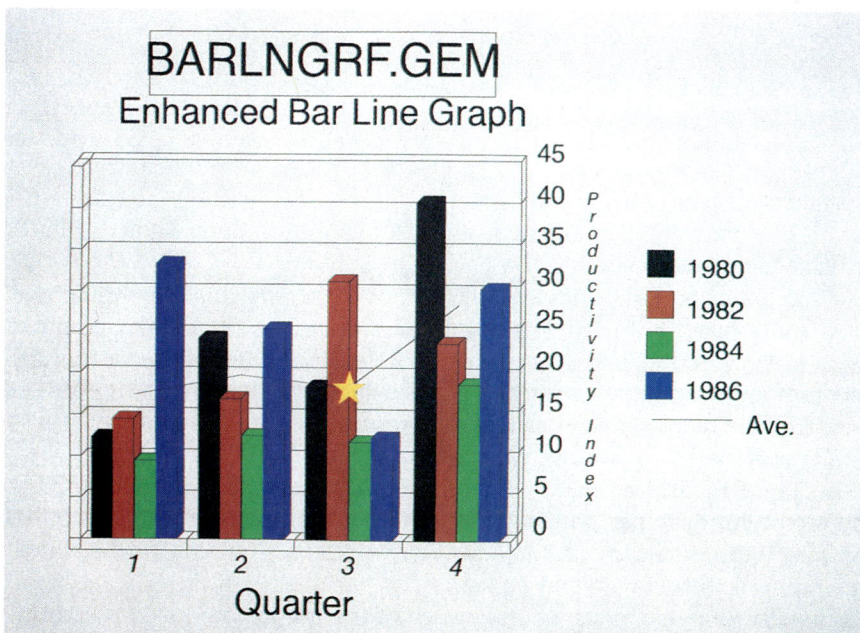

FIGURE 8.9

An Example of Presentation Graphics

A major problem that has plagued microfilm-based systems has been retrieval. The computer can be used to store the location of microfilm reels but that has been the extent of the contribution. The end result is a hybrid system—one using both microfilm and computer technology. This problem is being solved by replacing the microfilm with compact disks (CDs), also known as laser or optical disks. We describe CDs in Chapter 9

When document images are stored in a CD form, the computer not only identifies the location of the image but also retrieves it. CDs are expected ultimately to replace microfilm as the dominant image storage technology.

Audio Output

Even though voice recognition has been slow to catch on, audio output has been used for specialized applications for some time. An **audio response unit** can select prerecorded words to form an audible computer output that can be transmitted over a communications channel. When you dial a telephone number and receive the message "I'm sorry. The number you dialed is no longer in service. The new number is . . . ." that message is most likely produced by an audio response unit that combines the prerecorded explanation with computer-assembled numbers—each individually recorded.

Audio response enables a user to use a push-button telephone to key an information request into the computer and to receive a response. While this approach has not been embraced by managers in retrieving information for problem solving, it is used by nonmanagers. For example, a salesperson in a customer's office can use the customer's phone to determine the inventory status of an item that the customer wants to buy.

THE ROLE OF INPUT AND OUTPUT DEVICES IN PROBLEM SOLVING

It is easy to see how the manager can use a keyboard terminal and perhaps a printer and plotter in problem solving. The devices provide the communication link between the manager and the computer. Such devices play a *direct role* in problem solving.

What about the other devices? The input devices such as the MICR and OCR units provide the means of entering data into the database, either while a transaction is occurring or shortly after. The database thereby becomes an up-to-date conceptual representation of the physical system of the firm. The manager can use this data resource in problem solving. These input units play an *indirect role* in problem solving.

In a similar fashion, many of the output devices affect problem solving indirectly. For example, a manager might ask a staff member to glean information from microfilm records and then present a summary of that information in the form of a typed report.

The fact remains, however, that much of the output produced by a computer is aimed at satisfying data processing, not decision support, needs.

PRIMARY APPROACHES TO KEYBOARD INPUT

Three primary approaches have been devised that enable the user to enter instructions and data into the computer using an online keydriven device. The approaches are questions and answers, form filling, and menu display.

Questions and Answers

When the computer requires input from the user, a question or instruction can be displayed on the screen. The question or instruction is called a **prompt**. The user responds by keying in the response. If more input is required, the computer displays another prompt. Figure 8.10 shows how the **questions-and-answers technique** enables the manager to enter the data required by a mathematical model. The user therefore does not have to memorize the procedure for entering data into a program. The computer guides the user, step-by-step.

The prompts are not limited to simply specifying what data is to be entered, but can also specify the format. For example, a prompt might read:

```
ENTER CLIENT'S NAME IN THE FORMAT:
Lastname, Firstname Initial
```

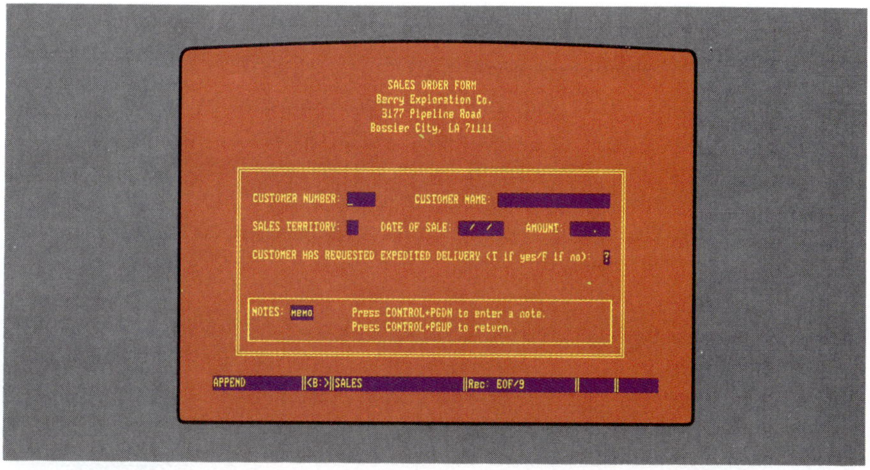

FIGURE 8.10

The Questions-and-Answers Technique

Form Filling

It is possible to display a form on the screen with blanks to be filled in by the user. The **form-filling technique** is used by moving the cursor to the appropriate blank and then keying in the data. Figure 8.11 shows how data is entered into a dBASE III Plus database by keying the data for the fields into blanks called **templates**. The size of each template is the exact size of the field.

FIGURE 8.11

The Form-Filling Technique

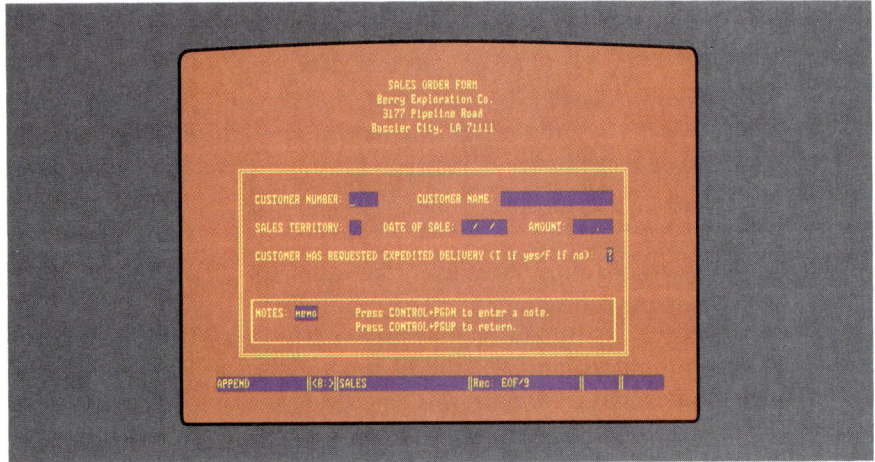

Menu Display

Currently the most popular way for managers to interact with the computer is the **menu-display technique**. It is used by many large-selling software packages such as Lotus, and that factor has contributed to its popularity. We explained menus in Chapter 3.

Very often the menus are displayed in one or more rectangular-shaped areas on the screen called **windows**.

An example of this **windowing technique** appears in Figure 8.12. This example illustrates the format that was made popular by Macintosh. The user uses a mouse to make selections from the menu at the top of the screen, and the selections cause windows to appear below. The windows frequently make use of symbols, called **icons**, which represent operations to be performed. The Macintosh screen format has been so widely accepted

FIGURE 8.12

An Example of the Windowing Technique

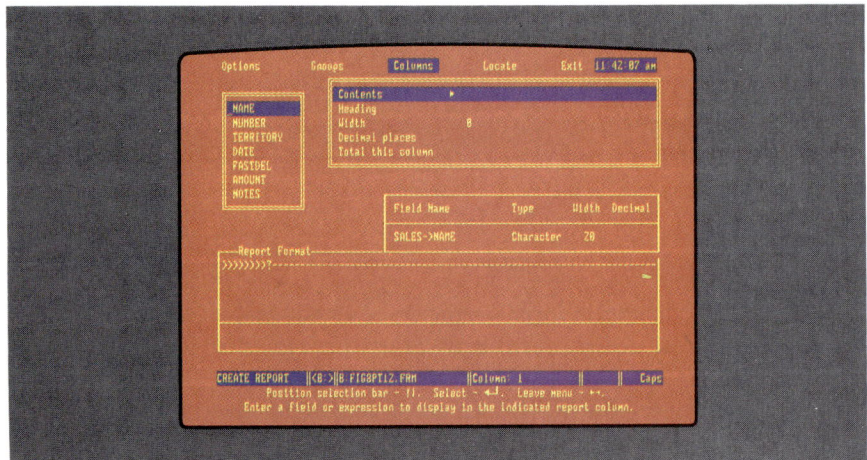

that it is made available in essentially the same form in the Microsoft Windows graphical user interface.

KEEPING INPUT ERRORS TO A MINIMUM

Even with all of the techniques that have been devised to assist the user in data entry, it is still possible for the user to make errors. Typographical errors are just as easy to make with a computer as with a typewriter. In other cases the user simply enters the wrong data. All of these errors can be detected by the user immediately after they are made or later, when the output of the processing is analyzed.

Software can be designed to provide error prevention by making it impossible for the user to make certain types of errors. The software can also assist the user in error detection by catching many of the errors that are made. The software typically does not perform error correction, but can make it easier for the user to perform that task.

Error Prevention

Two approaches to error prevention are the protected screen format and the ability to cancel a command before it is executed.

It is possible to design an input screen so that certain displayed data cannot inadvertently be changed by the user. The user cannot move the cursor to those locations. Such data fields are said to have a **protected format**.

Lotus and dBASE III Plus use the Esc key as a means of **command cancellation** to let the user back out of an error. WordPerfect uses the F1 function key for the same purpose. Perhaps after making three successive menu selections, you realize that you are on the wrong track. Each time the Escape key is pressed, you are returned to the previous menu level.

Error Detection

The computer can be programmed to screen data for errors as it is being entered, or after it is stored in primary storage.

The best place to catch an error is when the data is being entered. The software can include **input screening routines** that detect when the wrong type of data is entered. For example, if you try to enter an alphabetic letter in a numeric field, the software can issue an audible alarm, display an **error message** on the screen, or both.

Programmed **edit routines** that check stored data for errors can be quite thorough. For example, a payroll amount can be rejected if it is too large for the employee's job classification, or a sales order for a particular item can be rejected when there is no such record in the Inventory Master file.

Error Correction

Some software (BASIC and Lotus are examples) includes an **edit command** that the user can use to correct errors. The cursor is moved to the error position and characters can be added, deleted, or changed without rekeying the entire entry.

WordPerfect has an ability to **recall deleted data**. Its unique undelete feature "remembers" as many as three changes that you make to your copy. You are able to reinstate versions that were previously deleted.

These are the more commonly used techniques for keeping input errors to a minimum. Together, they contribute to the high levels of accuracy characteristic of computer processing. You should realize, however, that regardless of how much thought goes into error prevention, detection, and correction, errors still will be made. It is impossible to completely eliminate errors. Error controls incorporated into a system add to its cost, and a system designed to be completely error free would be so expensive that no organization could afford it. Rather than attempt complete error elimination, firms strive to keep errors to an acceptable minimum.

ECONOMIC JUSTIFICATION OF COMPUTING EXPENDITURES

Managers always like to have an **economic justification** for their expenditures. They like to feel that the money will earn an even larger amount in return. That philosophy forms the basis for everything the manager does, from the purchase of stocks and other investments to the construction of new plants and the purchase of computers.

Costs of the Computer Investment

Computer costs are relatively easy to identify and measure. Earlier we identified the major cost areas—hardware, software, personnel, supplies, furniture and fixtures, and facilities. Information specialists can accurately estimate these costs for a prospective computer user.

Returns from the Computer Investment

There are several ways that computer use can produce a return on the investment. Companies can install computers with the intention of avoiding clerical costs, reducing inventory investments, increasing productivity, and improving decision making.

Avoidance of Increases in Clerical Costs

The first computers were installed with the intention of achieving a **cost reduction**. The managers planned to replace clerks with the computer, but that happened only rarely. Invariably there were other jobs in the company for the replaced clerks to perform and they were simply transferred.

Very few computers have been economically justified based on a clerical cost reduction. However, computers *can* have an effect on *future* costs by eliminating or postponing the need to hire additional clerical employees. **Cost avoidance** is a more realistic goal than cost reduction.

Reduced Inventory Investments

Another area where the computer has had a measurable economic impact is inventory. By establishing computed reorder points and economic order quantities, as described in Chapter 5, the inventory level can be lowered, reducing the required investment. The funds representing the reduction can be used elsewhere. For example, if a firm can reduce its inventory valued at $10,000,000 by only 5 percent, the reduction would be $500,000. If this money is simply invested at a 10 percent interest rate it will earn $50,000 per year.

Possibly the most widely used motive for justifying computer use is the increase in productivity that can be achieved. This productivity can be realized in both the manufacturing and clerical areas.

Increased Productivity

Figure 8.13 shows a design engineer using a light pen to sketch a design on the computer's screen. This is an example of **computer aided design (CAD)**. Computers can also control production machines such as lathes and drill presses as shown in Figure 8.14. This application is called **computer aided manufacturing**, or **CAM**.

While CAD/CAM has boomed in the manufacturing area, similar inroads have been made in the clerical area. First, *computer based data processing* permitted the performance of accounting tasks faster and more accurately than was possible with the earlier manual, keydriven machine, and punched card machine systems. More recently, *office automation* has provided an opportunity to increase the productivity of all office workers, managers and clerical employees alike.

The main theme of this text is use of the computer to provide information for decision making. The concepts of the management information system, decision support system, and expert system reflect the popularity of this approach. Historically, however, this has not been the primary reason for implementing a computer. Rather, the firm has based the computer deci-

Improved Decision Making

FIGURE 8.13
Computer Aided Design (CAD)

sion on manufacturing and data processing productivity. The decision support has been icing on the cake—something to be achieved with the equipment in addition to the productivity benefits.

Measures of Information Value

It is easier to place a value on the costs of using a computer than the benefits. The benefits of avoided clerical costs and increased productivity can be projected, but it is difficult to prove that they actually are achieved. Too many influences other than the computer enter the picture over time.

Placing a value on information for decision making is even more difficult. So many information sources, noncomputer as well as computer, are called upon in making decisions that it is nearly impossible to determine the role played by any particular one. Also, information value is difficult to measure in monetary terms. For example, what is the dollar value of a monthly sales report, a response to a database query, or a What-If solution provided by a mathematical model?

Factors Contributing to Information Value

In spite of these difficulties, we can identify four factors that contribute to information value—relevancy, accuracy, timeliness, and completeness.

Relevancy

Information has **relevancy** when it relates specifically to the problem at hand. The manager should be able to select information that is needed without wading through a volume of information on other subjects.

Accuracy

Ideally, all information should be accurate, but features that contribute to system accuracy add to the cost. For that reason, firms often settle for less than perfect accuracy. Applications involving money, such as payroll, billing, and accounts receivable, demand 100 percent accuracy. Other applications, such as statistical reporting, often can be just as useful when the data contains a few errors. For example, management might use a summary report of past sales statistics as one of the inputs to the strategic planning process. Since management uses the report as a general guideline and supplements it with considerable judgment, any efforts to ensure complete data accuracy are not considered to be worth the cost.

Information should be available before crisis situations get out of hand or opportunities are lost. The manager should be able to obtain information that describes what is happening now—not what happened in the past.

Timeliness

The manager should be able to obtain information that completely describes a problem or a solution. However, systems should not drown the manager in a sea of information. The term **information overload** recognizes the harm that can come from too much information. The manager should be able to determine the amount of detail that is needed.

Completeness

Nonmonetary Measures of Information Value

Because of the difficulty of placing a monetary value on information, managers often use other measures. Two approaches are perceived value and surrogate measures.

The **perceived value** of information by the user probably is a more effective measure than what the information is actually worth. If users *think* a system is producing valuable information, they will use it. Conversely, if the system is viewed negatively, it will not be used even if it is an excellent system. Some firms conduct surveys to determine users' perceived values.

Perceived Value

Peter G. W. Keen, a consultant who specializes in decision support systems, identifies four levels of nonmonetary benefits that the computer can attain.[1] These benefits can be observed after implementation, often months or years later. In the following order, computer use leads to:

Surrogate Measures

1. *Management action*
2. *Management change* in such functions as planning and controlling
3. *Increased use of decision-support tools*
4. *Organization change* in terms of its structure and personnel

When management can see that the computer is causing certain *action* to take place, and when the computer influences how the managers perform their *functions*, there is evidence that the computer is producing a return on investment. When managers make greater use of documentation and software *tools*, such as those described in Chapter 7, there is added justification. Finally, when there is evidence that the computer has provided information that was used in making *fundamental changes* in the firm's policies, strategies, and organization structure, the money spent for computing is justified.

It has always been the responsibility of the systems analyst to support the recommended system design with some type of justification. In most

---

[1] Peter G. W. Keen, "Computer-Based Decision Aids: The Evaluation Problem," *Sloan Management Review* 16 (Spring 1975): 20–22.

cases an economic justification is impossible, and the analyst and the manager must use other measures.

SECURING THE COMPUTING RESOURCE

The firm values its computing asset very highly for two reasons. First, the *amount of the investment* can be substantial—a million dollars or more for a large firm. Second, the computer plays an *indispensable role* in the firm's operations. Most companies could not continue to operate if the computer were out of service for any length of time. The computer is valuable not only for its physical properties, but for its conceptual qualities as well—how it *represents* the physical system of the firm. The firm seeks to secure its computing resource from threats that might cause damage or destruction.

There are four primary types of threats—natural disasters, accidental damage, intentional damage, and computer crime. A variety of measures have been taken to either prevent or minimize the harmful effects that can be inflicted.

Natural Disasters

A natural disaster such as a flood, earthquake, lightning, or tornado can wipe out an entire company, including its computing facility. It did not take too many of these disasters to make early computer users aware of the harmful effects of computer loss on the organization. Firms quickly learned the importance of devoting attention to **computer site decisions** as a means of minimizing the damage from natural disasters. Today, you rarely find computers installed in basements of buildings next to rivers or near areas where combustible materials are stored. In California, recent earthquakes are causing firms to consider that threat when determining the location of their computing facility.

Accidental Damage

The main cause of accidental damage is employee carelessness. For example, a fire can result from a cigarette thrown into a wastebasket, or an electrical malfunction can occur when a soft drink is spilled onto the top of a computer unit. It is even possible for data errors to occur when dust, cigarette ashes, or other contaminants come in contact with magnetic recording media such as tapes and diskettes.

Computer users have responded to these threats of accidental damage by taking certain **environmental precautions**. Efforts are made to keep the computer rooms clean, and smoking is prohibited. In addition, the rooms are maintained within the temperature and humidity ranges specified by the manufacturer, and fire extinguishers are kept handy.

Intentional Damage

Early computer users showcased their computers as evidence of their progressive nature. You could walk down the sidewalk in any large city and look through large picture windows at a firm's computers, only a few feet away. Then in the late 1960s when antiwar sentiment was high and there was much social unrest, several computer rooms were bombed. Companies began to safeguard their installations.

Today firms take **physical security measures** to guard against damage that might be intentionally inflicted. Such damage can be caused by former employees who were fired, by customers who feel that they were mistreated, or by organized groups who regard the firm and its products as some type of threat. The security measures are generally aimed at making the physical computing facility inaccessible to unauthorized persons, and include:

- Locating the computing facility in a remote area
- Controlling access to the area of the building where the computer is located
- Using security guards
- Installing locks on computer room doors

In some cases it is necessary to go through several locked doors to obtain access, and the doors can be opened only with the proper key, combination, magnetically encoded badge, or even thumbprint.

Computer Crime

Much publicity has been devoted to **computer crime**, which most often takes the form of theft of the firm's assets through manipulations of the computer system. Financial institutions such as banks and savings and loan associations are especially vulnerable. Both employees and outsiders can gain access to the database or library of programs and transfer funds to their own checking or savings accounts.

Computer crime is a form of intentional damage, but it is unique in that it is not necessary for the criminal to be on the firm's premises. The criminal can be miles away and gain access to the database by means of the data communications network.

A type of computer crime that potentially is more costly than the theft of money is the theft of the firm's strategies and trade secrets. An unethical competitor can learn of a company's plans or modify the database and software library so that they are unusable. To date there have been few such incidents reported, but the threat remains.

Theft of Information

Firms guard against all forms of computer crime by taking the physical security precautions described above. In addition, steps are taken to protect the database and the data communications network from unauthorized entry. We address **database security** in Chapter 9 and **data communications security** in Chapter 10.

CONTINGENCY PLANNING

In addition to the security measures described above that are intended to prevent or minimize damage, the firm also gives attention to planning the recovery from such damage. In the event that the firm loses its computing capability for any reason, a plan exists for the company to resume operations quickly.

The key feature of such planning is the provision for backup facilities. Backup facilities can range from equipment that generates emergency power to complete computer installations.

Emergency Power Backup

Some firms install emergency power generators in another part of the building to provide electricity to the computer in case the city power is shut off.

Cooperative Arrangements with Other Users

If another firm in the area uses the same type of computer, an arrangement can be worked out whereby one firm can use the other's computer in an emergency. Most firms are receptive to such cooperative arrangements.

Hot Sites and Cold Sites

More elaborate backup arrangements are available. Firms can subscribe to commercial services that provide emergency computer facilities. It is like an insurance policy. The firm pays a monthly fee, and in the event that its computer becomes inoperative, the emergency facilities can be used.

The facilities take two forms—hot sites and cold sites. **Hot sites** are complete computer centers that include all of the necessary hardware. The computer is typically one of the most popular mainframes. When a firm loses its own computing capability it can use the hot site.

A **cold site** is a facility without the computer. The term **empty shell** is also used. In an emergency, the firm obtains the computer from the vendor and it is installed in the cold site. Some firms maintain their own hot sites or cold sites.

FIGURE 8.15

A Backup Computer Facility Called a Hot Site

Contingency Plans

A firm's disaster plans can be documented in a formal, written **contingency plan** that spells out in detail the steps to be taken when disaster strikes. The plans can be very complete, including such measures as evacuation procedures intended to protect the safety of the employees. Firms even conduct disaster drills so that all participants know their roles.

You should understand that not all firms have implemented the security precautions described here. In many cases it takes a disaster to make management aware of the importance of securing the computing facility.

ETHICS IN COMPUTER USE

In the vast majority of cases, organizations have used their computers in an ethical manner. Overall, the computer has had a positive influence on society, contributing to improved health care, law enforcement, employment opportunities for the handicapped, education, and so on. There have been instances, however, when the computer has been used unethically. For example, both government and industry have been criticized for gathering and maintaining data on individuals that has no bearing on the organization's mission. In the area of consumer credit, there have been situations where firms have been unwilling to correct erroneous or outdated information. These instances have been numerous enough to prompt federal legislation aimed at protecting the individual's **right to privacy** concerning computer data storage and use. The Fair Credit Reporting Act of 1970 and the Privacy Act of 1974 were passed with this objective in mind.

Computer Ethics and Problem Solving

As the manager strives to use the computer in an ethical manner, attention should be given to each element in the firm's environment. For example, how can computer use comply with the firm's ethical obligations to its suppliers? One example is the unauthorized copying of prewritten software diskettes. Most prewritten software systems are accompanied by a **license agreement** that prohibits or restricts copying. When the user accepts the software the license agreement is accepted as well. Unauthorized duplication of diskettes is unethical and should not be condoned by firms or by their employees.

Another example of an ethical obligation relates to competition. The firm should not obtain competitive data in an unethical manner such as by tapping into a competitor's computer network.

As each computer system is designed and used, the users and information specialists should ensure that it does not infringe on the rights of the firm's employees, or individuals and organizations in the environment.

IMPLEMENTING A COMPUTER BASED SYSTEM

In Chapter 6 we described the information-literate user as one who engages in end-user computing, yet also utilizes the expertise of information specialists. Both avenues to computer use require a series of steps to be taken to implement the information system.

Life Cycle Phases

The steps have been labeled the **system life cycle**, which consists of four phases—planning, analysis and design, implementation, and operation. Figure 8.16 shows the primary roles played by the manager (the user) and the information specialists during each phase. During the planning phase

FIGURE 8.16

The Cooperative System Development Process

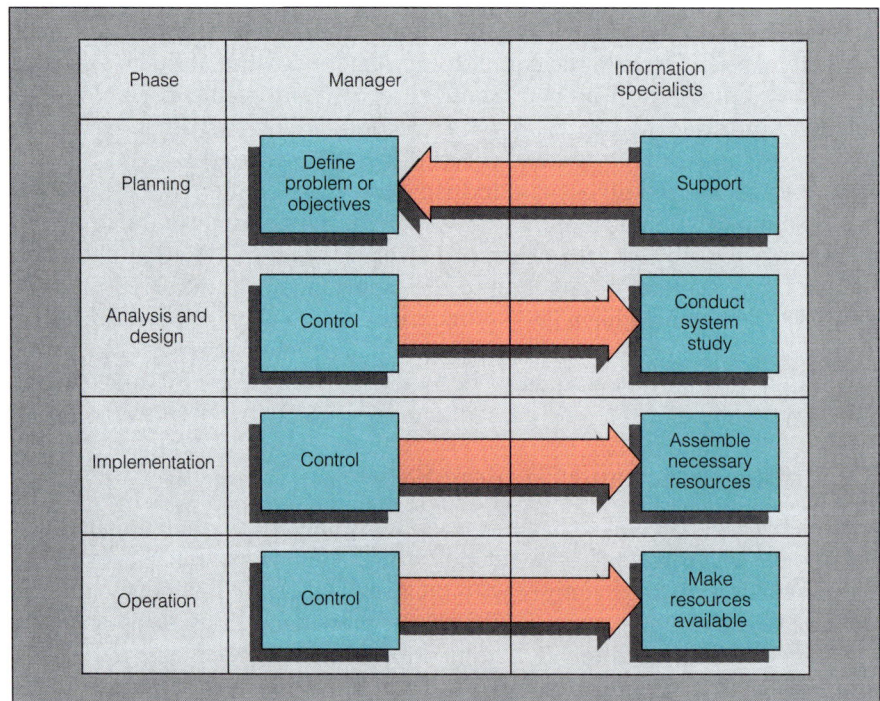

Phase	Manager	Information specialists
Planning	Define problem or objectives	Support
Analysis and design	Control	Conduct system study
Implementation	Control	Assemble necessary resources
Operation	Control	Make resources available

the manager defines the problem to be solved, and the information specialists lend support. During the next three phases the information specialists perform the technical work of conducting a system study, assembling the necessary hardware, software, and other resources, and making those resources available to the user. When managers engage in end-user computing, they assume responsibility for each of these phases.

Diagrams are included in the following sections that show the steps of each phase. You will be able to see the similarity between the system life cycle and the systems approach, described in Chapter 7. The system life cycle is simply an application of the systems approach to the implementation of a computer system.

The Planning Phase

The first four steps are the main responsibility of the manager as shown in Figure 8.17. The manager is assisted by the systems analyst in (1) recogniz-

FIGURE 8.17

Steps in the Planning Phase

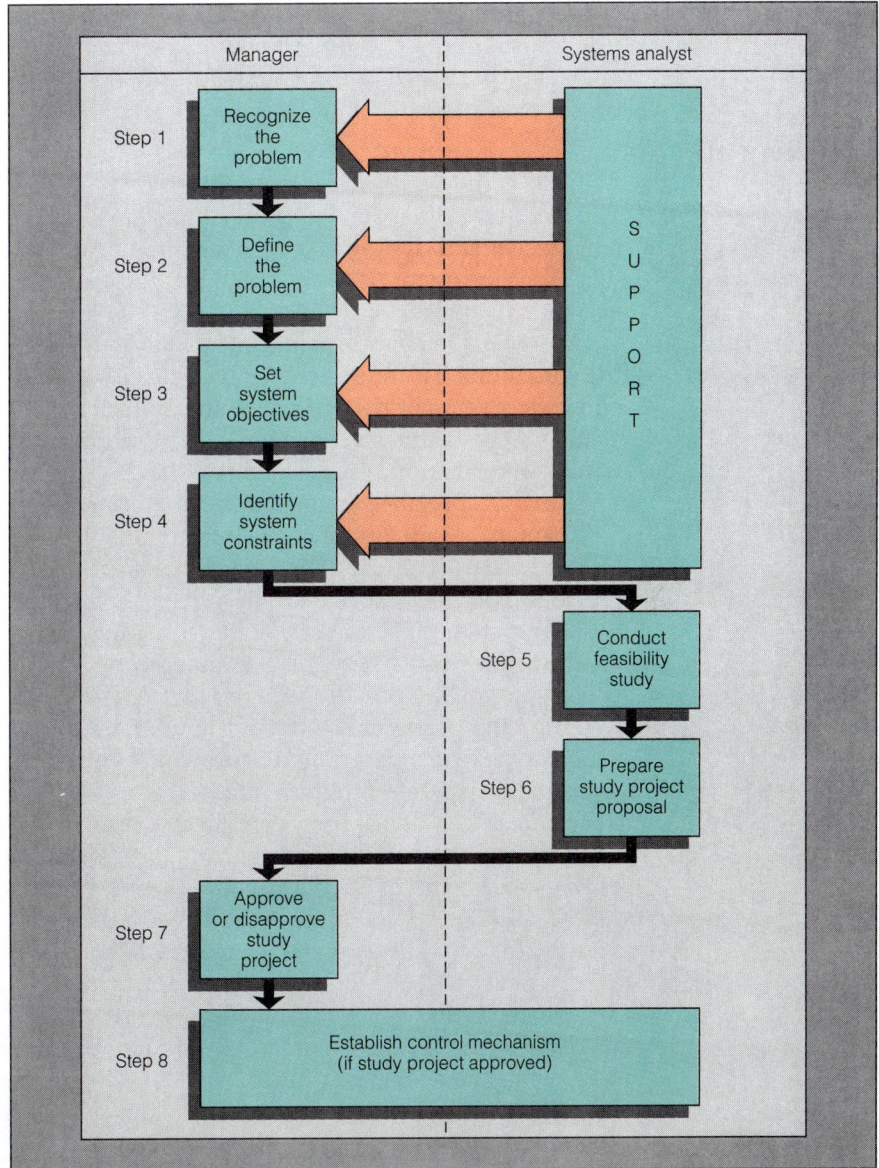

ing the problem, (2) defining the problem, (3) setting the objectives that the new system must achieve, and (4) identifying any constraints that might apply. With the problem understood, the systems analyst (5) conducts a feasibility study and (6) prepares a written **study project proposal** that describes the suggested solution in a general way. At this point the systems analyst has not gathered enough data to present a specific solution. The manager (7) evaluates the proposal and either approves or disapproves the project. The manager makes a **go/no-go decision**. In the event that approval is given, the manager and information specialists (8) jointly establish a control mechanism that will guide them the rest of the way. A **control mechanism** might consist of a plan to meet weekly to discuss past progress and map out the next steps, and to utilize such visual aids as planning charts and diagrams.

The Analysis and Design Phase

The steps that the manager and systems analyst take in analyzing the current system and designing a new one are illustrated in Figure 8.18. During this phase the analyst can be assisted by the database administrator and the network manager.

Once management gives the approval to proceed, it is important that (1) the intentions be announced to the employees. This step minimizes the employees' fears of the unknown and solicits their support in the detailed **systems study** of the current system. The scope of the project might require that the information services organization (2) acquire additional staff members such as specialists in the defined application areas.

The manager (3) describes the information needs to the analyst, and they (4) jointly define the **system performance criteria**. These are examples of the solution criteria that were described in Chapter 5—they specify what the new system must do to meet the user's needs.

This is the point where the information specialists might develop system prototypes as described in Chapter 7. The prototypes enable the manager to define the performance criteria and communicate them to the systems analyst. The firm's programmers become involved at this point if the prototypes require custom programming.

The next four steps are accomplished primarily by the systems analyst with the manager providing a control. The systems analyst (5) designs each of the subsystems in detail, (6) identifies alternate types of hardware that can be used, and (7) evaluates each alternative. The analyst (8) selects the configuration that appears to best satisfy the performance criteria. Prototyping can help the manager and systems analyst narrow down the design alternatives.

The systems analyst (9) prepares a written proposal for the manager that documents the design in a formal manner. The proposal is called an **implementation project proposal**, and it provides the justification for proceeding to the next phase. Although the systems analyst recommends a system design, it is the manager who (10) approves or disapproves it.

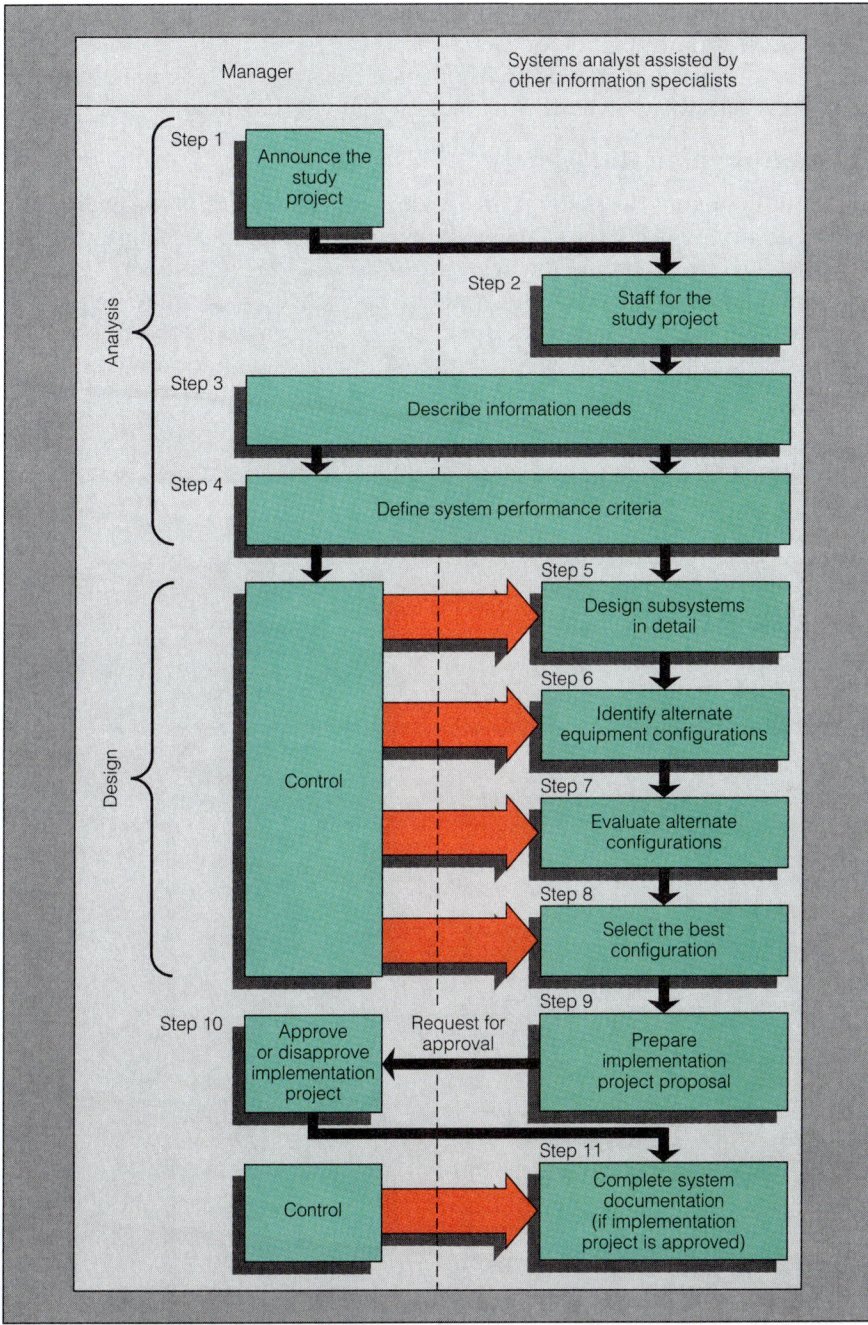

FIGURE 8.18

Steps in the Analysis and Design Phase

This is the second go/no-go decision point in the life cycle. The manager thereby maintains control over the entire project, giving the go-ahead only after successful completion of each phase.

When approval is granted to implement the system, the systems analyst (11) completes the system documentation that was begun in Step 5.

The Implementation Phase

Up until this point the systems analyst has provided most of the computing expertise in designing the system. The other information specialists become involved in implementing the design as illustrated in Figure 8.19

Both the manager and the information specialists (1) plan the implementation—specifying *what* is to be done, *when* it is to be done, and *who* will do it. The organization's management then (2) makes an announcement to the employees that brings them up to date and asks for their support in the

FIGURE 8.19   Steps in the Implementation Phase

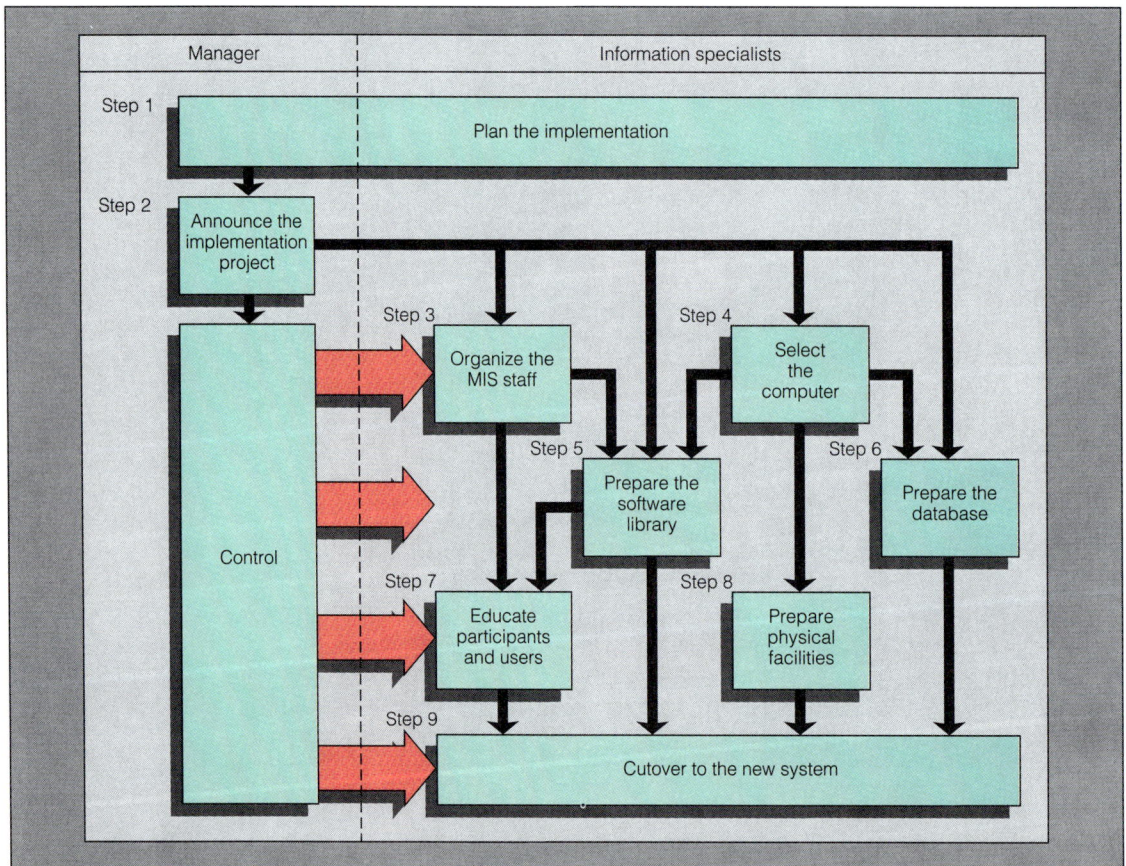

implementation. The remainder of the steps are taken by the information specialists with the manager providing control.

The information services group (3) organizes for the effort—acquiring new staff members, assigning staff to particular projects, and perhaps conducting inhouse training programs. If it is necessary to acquire a new computer or additional hardware, (4) the configuration and brand are determined. The firm's programmers (5) prepare the software, the database administrator assisted by the computer operations staff (6) prepare the database, and the systems analysts (7) educate the people who will work with the system and use its output. Once (8) the physical facilities are ready, the computer is installed and the (9) cutover to the new system is accomplished.

A comment is in order concerning the sequence in which hardware and software are acquired in Steps 4 and 5. In the event that you elect to purchase prewritten software, you first identify the software that meets your needs, and then you acquire the hardware that uses the software. Step 4 becomes "Purchase the software library," and Step 5 is "Select the computer."

The Operation Phase

Only three activities are included in the operation phase. First, shortly after cutover, a **postimplementation review** is conducted that evaluates how well the system is satisfying the performance criteria. This evaluation can be made by the manager or by an unbiased third party such as an internal auditor or consultant. Information specialists should not be expected to evaluate their own work.

The second activity involves system **use** by the manager. This use can continue for years. During this period, minor modifications are made to keep the system current. For example, a tax rate in a payroll system is changed to reflect a change in a tax law. This third activity is called **system maintenance** and can account for a large portion of the information services staff time.

At some point the system will need major repair or even replacement. In those cases the life cycle is repeated to produce the improved system.

The time required to complete the life cycle can vary. It might take months or even years to take all of the above steps for a big project. A small project, such as implementation of a new software package for a microcomputer, might require only a few days or weeks. Another key point is that not all of the steps have to be taken for every project. Some steps, such as the acquisition of additional staff, are skipped when they are not necessary.

Even though the sequence of steps is flexible, it is important to recognize that system implementation is a logical process. The systems approach provides the fundamental structure of first defining what the system is to do, evaluating possible system designs, and following up to ensure that the system performs as intended.

SUMMARY

Computer prices have dropped to a point where any organization can afford one, but other costs are involved. Managers should be aware of all of the potential costs when deciding to implement a computer system.

All computers fit the computer schematic. The CPU includes the primary storage, the ALU, and the control unit. Input devices include online key-driven devices, offline keydriven devices, MICR and OCR readers, and voice recognition units. The variety of output devices is also large, consisting of screen displays, printed output, graphics, microfilm, and audio response.

The manager personally uses some of the input and output units in problem solving, and others can play an indirect role. The input devices enable the database to stay current, and the output devices can be used by subordinates to synthesize information for the manager.

Three approaches can be used in entering data into a keyboard unit. The questions-and-answers technique consists of prompts displayed on the screen in the form of questions and instructions. The manager responds by keying in the required data. The form-filling technique requires the manager to key data into displayed blanks or templates. The menu-display technique involves selections from menus that often are displayed in windows.

Although computer based systems are not immune from errors, high levels of accuracy can be achieved by incorporating measures aimed at error prevention, error detection, and error correction.

When seeking economic justification of computer expenditures it is easier to measure the costs than the benefits. Rather than attempt to reduce clerical costs, a more realistic approach is to avoid future increases. Other benefits involve lower inventory levels as well as productivity increases in the manufacturing and clerical areas.

Of all the application areas, the value of information used in problem solving is the most difficult to measure. One approach is to use users' perceptions, and another is to use surrogate measures. The surrogates include evidence that the computer is helping managers take action, causing managers to change how they perform their functions, stimulating use of decision-support tools, and leading to major changes in the company's policies, strategies, and structure.

Early computer users recognized the importance of protecting their systems from natural disasters and accidental damage. However, social unrest and vulnerable databases of financial and strategic data have given rise to other threats—intentional damage and computer crime. Users seek to minimize the exposure to these risks through a combination of computer site decisions, environmental precautions, physical security measures, database and data communications security, and contingency planning.

When designing computer based systems, users and information specialists should consider the rights of each environmental element and also the firm's own employees to ensure that these rights are not violated by unethical computer use.

Regardless of whether users implement their own system or work with information specialists, a life cycle of steps must be taken. The four major phases are planning, analysis and design, implementation, and operation. When the manager has primary responsibility for a step the information specialist provides support. When the information specialist has responsibility, the manager provides control.

KEY CONCEPTS

How hardware costs are only one of the costs of using a computer

The manner in which computers of all sizes fit the computer schematic

How source data automation affects the input bottleneck

How input and output devices play direct and indirect roles in problem solving

Ways of justifying expenditures for the computer as a problem-solving tool in light of the difficulty in measuring the value of information

The system life cycle

KEY TERMS

Graphical user interface(GUI)
Input bottleneck
Source data automation
Magnetic ink character recognition (MICR)
Electronic funds transfer(EFT)
Optical character recognition (OCR)
Point of sale (POS)
Cathode ray tube (CRT)

Hard copy
Letter quality
Near-letter quality
Presentation graphics
Prompt
Questions-and-answers technique
Form-filling technique
Menu-display technique
Window

Computer aided design(CAD)
Computer aided manufacturing (CAM)
Information overload
Contingency plan
Right to privacy
License agreement
Go/no-go decision
Systems study
System performance criteria

QUESTIONS

1. Name seven categories of computer cost.

2. What two technologies make source data automation possible?

3. Why do banks use inscribers or encoders? Do they create an input bottleneck?

4. Name an everyday use of OCR where characters are read from objects rather than from documents.

5. Why has voice recognition been more difficult to achieve than audio response?

6. When is printed output necessary or preferred?

7. Name three ways to produce graphic output.

8. List the input and output devices that play a direct role in management problem solving.

9. What is the difference between cost reduction and cost avoidance?

10. What are the counterparts to CAD/CAM as means of increasing clerical productivity?

11. List the primary types of threats to the computing resource. List the measures the firm can take to guard against the threats.

12. Why is the potential cost of unauthorized manipulation of the database and software library so great? Answer in terms of problem solving.

13. Would a small firm using a single microcomputer be concerned about backup facilities? Explain your answer.

14. Where does prototyping fit into the system life cycle?

15. What is the relationship between the system life cycle and the systems approach?

CASE PROBLEM   National Chemicals

The story had made all of the papers and was on network TV. The snow had piled up on the roof of the National Chemicals plant in Omaha and weakened the steel structure. The roof over the computer room had caved in, ruining all of the company's computing equipment. Luckily, backup data records were kept in another part of the building. It took three weeks to acquire new equipment and get back on the air. National's computer is the only one of its type between New York City and Los Angeles, and the computer manufacturer had to build a new one especially for National.

Jim: You all know why I called this special meeting of the board of directors. The loss of the computer almost wiped us out. We just cannot afford to let that sort of thing happen again. The computer facilities we reconstructed are only a temporary measure. We're going to have to build a new facility, and I want us to give a lot of thought to doing things in the best way. I'm sure that we all want a computing facility we can rely on.

Andy: Jim, what exactly are we trying to guard against?

Jim: Certainly the threat of a natural disaster such as the snow, but also the possibility that somebody might want to cause us some harm because of our Army contracts. I feel that we're lucky that that sort of thing hasn't happened before. Being in the chemical business exposes us to risks that many firms don't have. The way I see it, now is an opportunity for us to safeguard our computer from hazards of all kinds.

Al: Jim, what are our options?

Jim: I think we have two basic choices. We can rebuild here at the main plant site, or we can build in some remote area.

Ramona: Why a remote area?

Jim: I think that we could do a better job of securing it. It would be out of the way, and somebody would have to make a special effort to find it. We have that acreage up in Wyoming we could use.

Al: You talk about remote. The nearest town is thirty-five miles away and the nearest airport is ninety miles away in Casper.

Jim: That's right. We wouldn't have to publicize where our computer is.

Ramona: Wouldn't that cause us problems—our main operations being here and our computer being in Wyoming?

Jim: Not really. We could transmit all of the data electronically. The situation would be no different from companies that are spread out all over the country and have a single computer site.

Al: What about our computer staff? Could we get them to move to Wyoming? We have a high quality of life here in Omaha.

Jim: We're only talking about the operators. The rest of our staff would stay here. I've already thought that one over, and I don't think it would be wise to move everybody up there. All of the operators might not want to go, but we could hire and train a new staff in Wyoming.

Al: Why don't we vote on it?

Jim: We had better discuss it some more first. I think we need to look at the pluses and minuses of both options. I want us to have the best security that money can buy.

1. What primary threats exist at the Omaha location?

2. What threats would exist at the Wyoming location?

3. What security measures should National take should they decide to stay in Omaha?

4. What security measures would be appropriate in Wyoming?

5. Which location do you recommend? Briefly support your answer, citing your answers to the earlier questions.

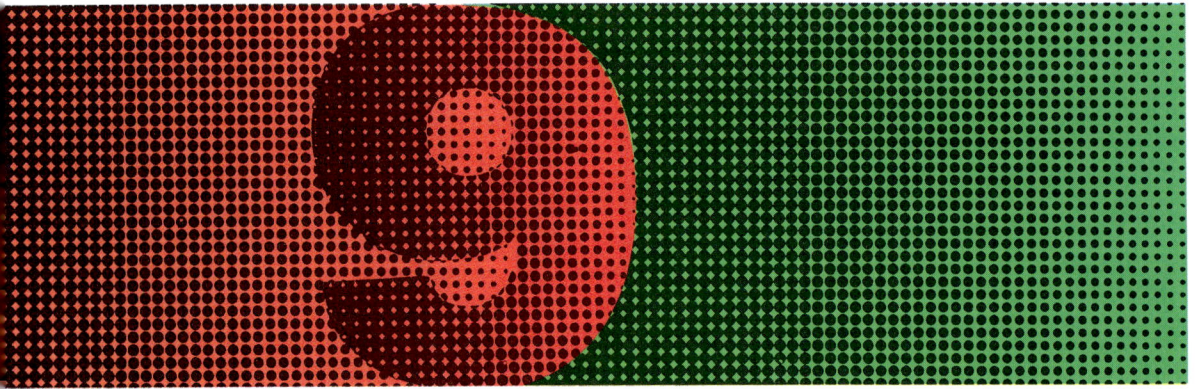

Secondary Storage and the Database

- Know the two basic types of secondary storage
- Understand how data is stored on magnetic tape and magnetic disk
- Understand the relationship between secondary storage media and the way that data is processed
- Be familiar with the database concept—how it evolved and its influence on problem solving
- Know what a database management system is—its fundamental structures, how it contributes to security, and its role in problem solving

OVERVIEW

In earlier chapters we have discussed all of the major computer units except secondary storage and data communications. In this chapter we address secondary storage—identifying the two basic types and giving examples of each. We also recognize the influence of secondary storage on the way data is processed.

Most of the emphasis in the chapter is on the database and the software that manages it—the database management system. The roles of both in problem solving are explained. Our attention to computer security is continued with a description of the features of the database management system that safeguard the data resource.

SECONDARY STORAGE

Secondary storage supplements primary storage. Even though the capacity of primary storage has increased dramatically over the years, it still is not large enough to contain all of an organization's data and software. The necessary capacity is achieved in the form of secondary storage attached to the CPU. There are two primary types of secondary storage—sequential and direct access. Direct access provides for immediate retrieval of individual records, but sequential storage does not.

Sequential Storage

When **sequential storage** is used the records must be processed in the same sequence as they appear in the file. The first record must be processed first, the second record second, and so on until the end of the file is reached. The mechanism that handles the reading and writing can only access the next record; it cannot jump forward or backward to access other records.

The punched card and magnetic tape files used by early computers were sequential. Although punched card files have practically all been replaced, magnetic tape remains as the only storage medium dedicated exclusively to sequential processing.

Most mainframe computer systems still include one or more **tape units** or **tape drives**, the units that read and write the tape data. Figure 9.1 pictures a magnetic tape unit. Large computer configurations can include several such units. The data is written onto the tape and read from it in much the same manner as sound is recorded onto and played from a cassette tape. The computer tape is wider, but is made of the same plastic material with a brown ferrous oxide coating that facilitates the recording of magnetic spots, called **bits**. Several bits make up a byte, or character.

All of the data elements that comprise a record are recorded one after the other along the length of the tape as shown in Figure 9.2. The name **field** is used to describe the space in the record where a data element is stored.

All of the bytes of a record are written onto the tape from primary storage in one process using a tape-write program statement. A tape-read statement causes all of the bytes of the record to be read from the tape into primary storage. Figure 9.3 shows how the multiple records of a file appear on the tape. Blank gaps separate the records.

A valuable feature of any magnetic recording medium such as magnetic tape is the ability to reuse it by recording new data on top of the old. The old data is automatically erased as the new data is recorded, just as with audio or video tape.

The files that provide the conceptual representation of the firm are called **master files**. There are Inventory master files, Customer master files, Employee master files, and so on. Each master file contains data about its particular subject. The master files are updated with data from transaction files. A **transaction file** contains data describing activities of the firm such as sales, purchases, and employee hours worked.

Magnetic Tape Records

Updating a Magnetic Tape File

FIGURE 9.1
A Magnetic Tape
Unit

FIGURE 9.2
A Magnetic Tape
Record

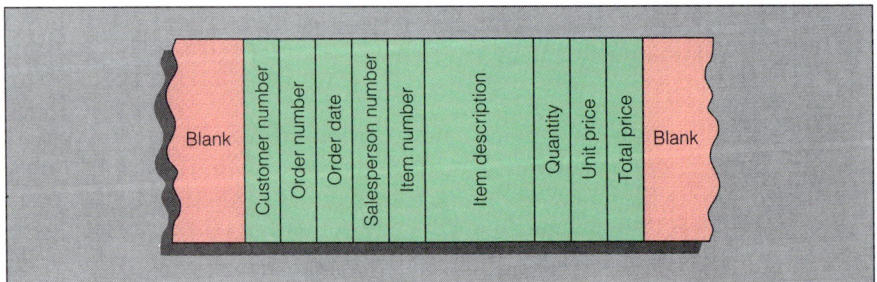

FIGURE 9.3   A Magnetic Tape File

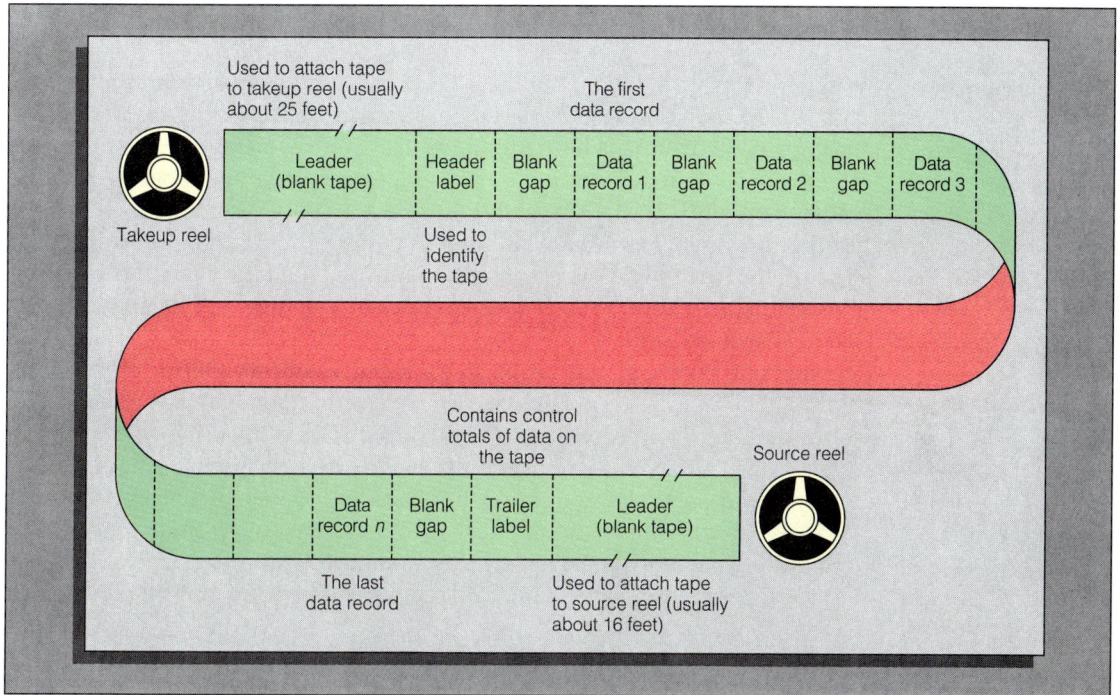

The process of updating a file is called **file maintenance**. File maintenance involves adding new records, deleting records, and making changes
to fields in records. When a magnetic tape master file is maintained it is not
possible to write the updated record back to the same area of the tape from
which the record was read. The updated record must be written onto
another tape. For that reason, file maintenance of a magnetic tape file pro-

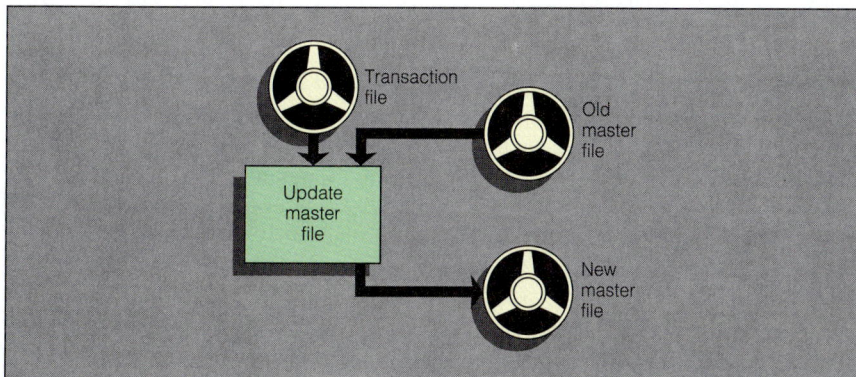

FIGURE 9.4

Updating a
Magnetic Tape File

duces a second, updated tape. Figure 9.4 illustrates the process. The names **old master file** and **new master file** distinguish the two master files. The records in the transaction file must be in the same sequence as those in the old master file.

Uses of Magnetic Tape

Magnetic tape provided all of the secondary storage in early computer configurations, but has been replaced to a great extent by other technologies. Today, magnetic tape is best suited for use as a **historical storage medium**. The firm can store accounting data on tape and retain the tape in a storage vault as an **audit trail**, or record of business activity. Magnetic tape is ideal for this use since more than 140 million bytes of data can be recorded on a single 2400 foot reel. A similar use of magnetic tape is as a **backup file** for a master file on a direct access storage device. This use will be explained in the next section.

Magnetic tape can also serve as an **input medium**. Offline key-to-tape units can be used to record transaction data onto magnetic tape reels or cassettes that are then processed by the computer. This approach is popular in retail stores where cash registers often include a magnetic tape unit that records data as sales are made. After the store closes, a central computer, perhaps in another city, automatically retrieves the data from the tape.

Finally, magnetic tape can serve as a **communications medium** that can be sent through the mails. Larger firms are required to submit their tax data to the IRS in this manner.

Direct Access Storage

A **direct access storage device**, called a **DASD**, enables the read/write mechanism to be directed to a certain record without a sequential search. Although several DASD technologies have been used, the most popular is the **magnetic disk**. The disks are made of metal that is covered with the same recording surface used on magnetic tape, and are mounted in a vertical **disk stack** as shown in Figure 9.5. Multiple disks are attached to a single spindle, and the disks rotate past a comb-like access mechanism. The disk stack is housed in a **disk drive** or **disk unit** attached to the CPU. The computer configurations of large firms include multiple disk drives to provide adequate online capacity.

During the 1970s disk drives were designed so that the disk stacks could be removed and replaced with other stacks. The removable disk stacks were called **disk packs**. As the capacities of disk storage increased and the costs decreased, it became less necessary to swap the disk packs, and today the disk drives feature permanently mounted disk stacks.

Magnetic Diskettes

The DASDs of microcomputers most often include one or two **diskette drives** that process data recorded on a small **diskette**. Until recently the most popular diskette size was a diameter of 5 1/4 inches, which had a 360 kilobyte capacty. A **kilobyte (KB)** is 1,024 bytes. Today the most popular diskette size is 3 1/2 inches, with a capacity of 1.44 megabytes. A **megabyte (MB)** is 1,000 KB or roughly 1 million bytes.

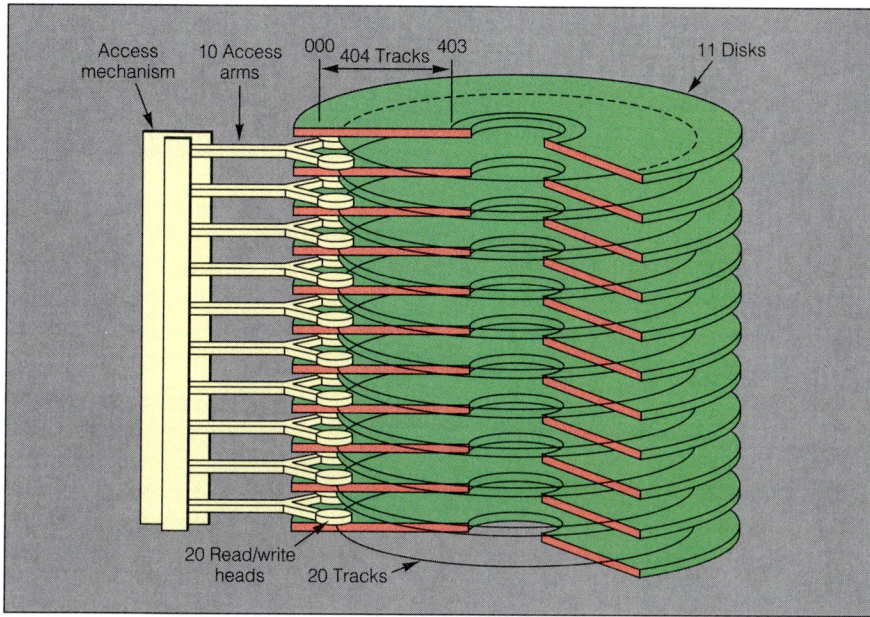

FIGURE 9.5

A Disk Stack

Additional capacity can be achieved in the form of a **hard disk,** which is permanently mounted in the main processor cabinet or a separate unit. Hard disk capacities typically are measured in 20 MB increments and can go as high as 1,000 MB, or 1 billion bytes—a **gigabyte (GB).**

The **access mechanism** in Figure 9.5 contains two **read/write heads** at the end of each **access arm.** All of the arms move in and out between the rotating disks in a synchronized fashion. One read/write head services the disk surface above, and the other head services the surface below. A disk-write program statement is used to write data from primary storage onto the disk in the form of circular **tracks** analogous to the grooves of a phonograph record. A disk-read statement is used to read data from the tracks.

When data is to be read from or written to a disk, it is first necessary to position the access mechanism on the proper track and then activate the proper read/write head. The computer program contains a seek-record statement that accomplishes the positioning.

Reading and Writing Disk Data

The capacities of the tracks are very large. This makes it possible to enter several records around the track—one after the other.

DASD Records

In order for the access mechanism to move to the proper location, it must be given the **address** where the record is located on the disk. The address specifies the track number and the read/write head number. In addition, the address might specify the record number on the track—record 1, record 2, and so on. Figure 9.6 illustrates one of several forms the DASD address can take.

The DASD Address

FIGURE 9.6
A DASD Address

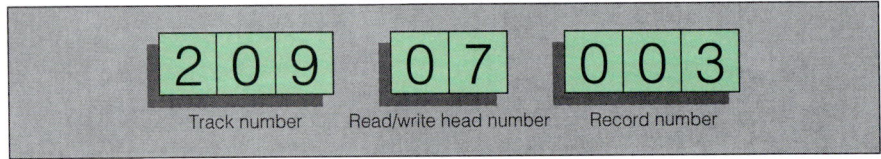

```
2 0 9      0 7      0 0 3
```
Track number   Read/write head number   Record number

Updating a DASD File

Since the access mechanism can be directed to any record for reading or writing at that location, it is not necessary to create a second file as with magnetic tape. Updated records are rewritten in their original location. Figure 9.7 illustrates how file maintenance is performed on a DASD based file. In this illustration the transaction data is entered through an online keydriven device. The transaction data could also be in the form of a magnetic disk or tape file. It is not necessary that the transaction data be in any particular sequence.

At this point we should recognize that a DASD can be used as sequential storage. In that case, the DASD records are read and written in the same manner as magnetic tape—one record following another.

Uses of DASD

DASD is perfect for use as a **master file medium**. The files can be updated as transactions occur, providing a current record of the firm's activity. Users can gain immediate access to this data from terminals. However, the lack of an automatic audit trail provided by an old master file encourages the user to periodically copy the DASD file onto magnetic tape. The tape serves as a **backup file** that is placed in a vault for safekeeping. As subsequent transactions are processed against the DASD master file, the changed master file records are copied onto a second magnetic tape file called an **audit file** or **transaction log.** If the master file becomes unusable for any reason, it can be reconstructed by reprocessing the audit file against the backup file.

Another popular use of DASD is as an **intermediate storage medium** to contain semiprocessed data. For example, data can be transferred from one

FIGURE 9.7
Updating a DASD File

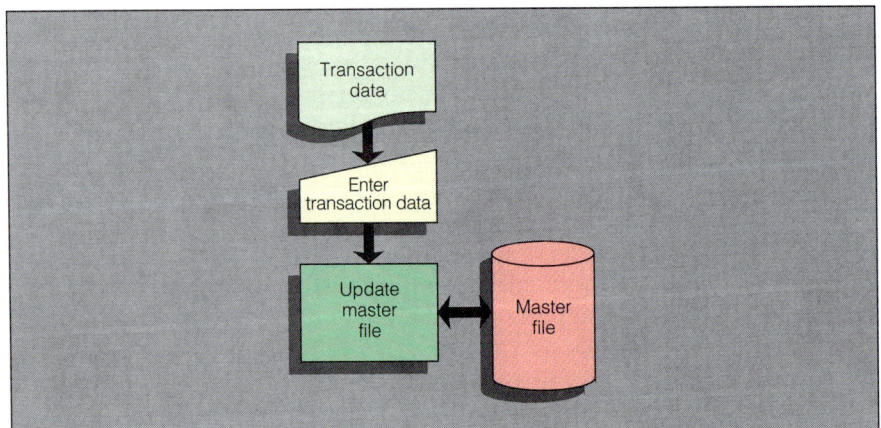

program to another in a disk form. DASD can also be used as an **input medium** in the same manner as magnetic tape. DASD is not good for historical storage since the disk stacks are too expensive, are more vulnerable to damage, and take up considerable space.

Thus far during the thirty-plus years of the computer era, magnetic disks have proven to be unbeatable in terms of performance and cost. Other technologies have been tried—such as magnetic drums, bins of magnetic tape loops, magnetic cards, magnetic bubbles, and MOS (metal-oxide semiconductor) chips, but none has caught on. The continued improvements in disks and diskettes indicate that they are likely to be around for a long time.

Other DASD Technologies

The emerging technology that appears to have the best chance of replacing magnetic disks is the laser disk. A **laser disk**, also called an **optical disk** or **compact disk**, is one that represents data by combinations of tiny pits (or blemishes) created on the surface by a laser beam. A less-powerful beam is used to read the pits or blemishes. The main advantage of laser disks is the large capacity; a single disk can contain as much data as fifteen reels of magnetic tape. Until recently, the main disadvantage has been an inability to erase the recorded data. The disks had only a write-once capability—termed **WORM (write-once, read-many)**. Laser disks are now available that can be erased and rewritten an unlimited number of times—a **write-many, read-many** capability.

Although laser disks are a DASD, they are most often mentioned as a replacement for magnetic tape. Used for historical storage, the write-once capability is perfect. The availability of a write-many capability perhaps will enable them to replace magnetic disks.

THE RELATIONSHIP OF SECONDARY STORAGE TO PROCESSING

There are two principal ways to process data. You can handle each transaction separately, or you can accumulate multiple transactions and process them together as a batch. When each transaction is processed separately it is known as **online processing**. The term **transaction processing** is often used but this creates confusion since the term is also used to describe data processing applications. To avoid the confusion we use the term online processing. When the transactions are processed in batches it is known as **batch processing**.

The primary influence on the type of processing is the firm's applications. The applications determine the type of secondary storage required. Then, with that storage attached to the CPU, the processing permitted by the storage is performed.

Batch Processing

Batch processing is the oldest of the two options, but is still used—especially for such data processing systems as payroll and accounts receivable.

FIGURE 9.8

Batch Processing

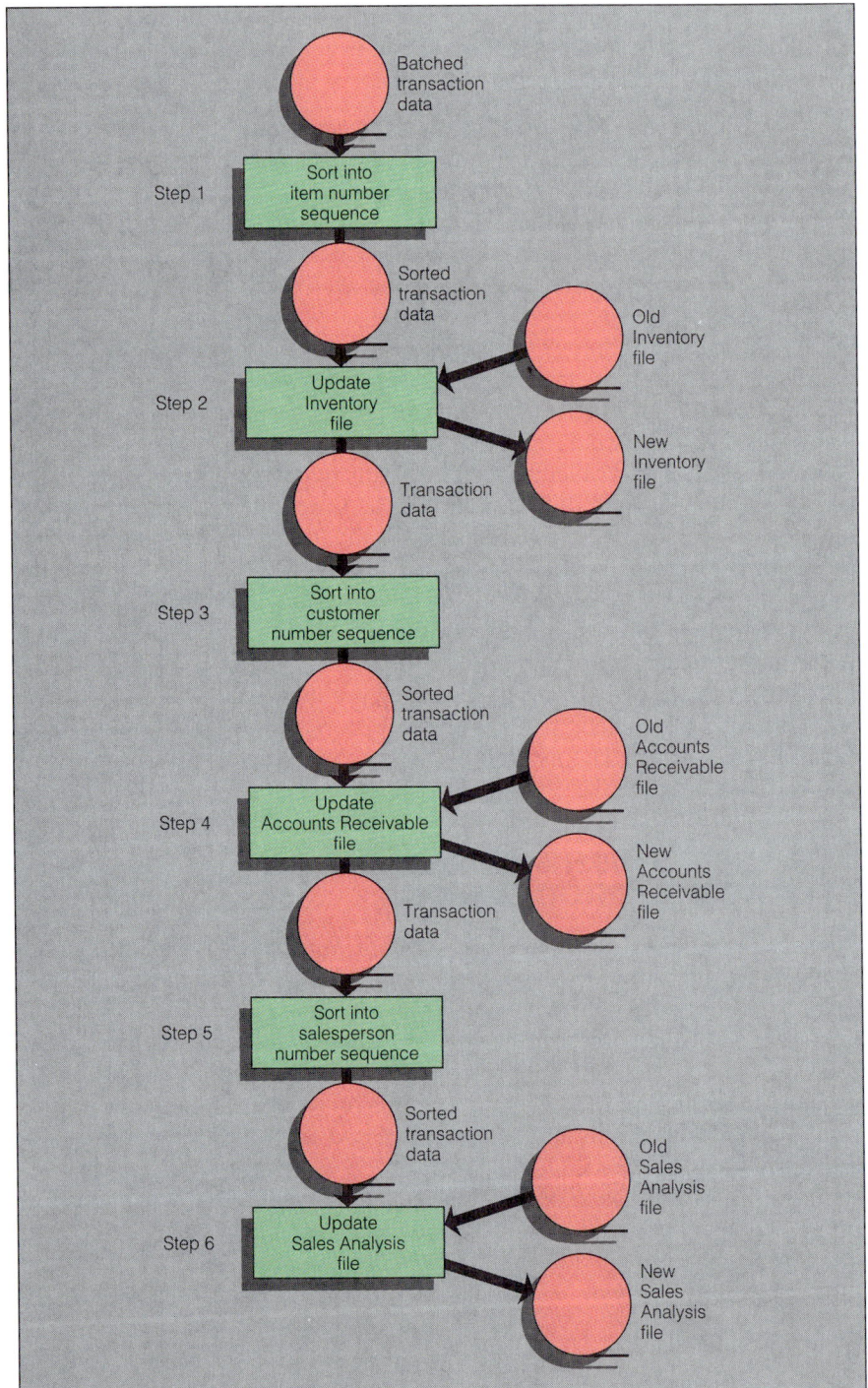

It is an assembly line approach, and makes efficient use of the computer.

Figure 9.8 is a system flowchart that shows how sales transaction data is processed in a batch. The objective of this system is to update three master files—Inventory, Accounts Receivable, and Sales Analysis. The circle at the top represents a reel of magnetic tape containing the sales transaction records that have been batched. Perhaps the records represent the previous day's sales. Firms typically update their batch files on a daily basis, called a **daily cycle**.

The first file to be updated is the Inventory file, which is arranged in item-number sequence. The term **key** is used to describe the data element that determines the sequence. In this case, item number is the key. The transaction records must be in the same sequence, so they are sorted in Step 1. The inventory file is updated in Step 2.

Steps 3 and 4 accomplish the updating of the Accounts Receivable file, and Steps 5 and 6 do the same for the Sales Analysis file. The Accounts Receivable file key is customer number, and the Sales Analysis file key is salesperson number.

The main shortcoming of batch processing is the fact that the file is only current immediately following the cycle update. For example, if the firm updates its Inventory file during the evening, the file becomes out-of-date during the next day as transactions occur. This means that management does not have available an accurate data resource.

Online Processing

Online processing was developed to overcome the problem of out-of-date files. The technological breakthrough that made online processing possible was disk storage.

Figure 9.9 illustrates the online approach to updating the same three files as in the batch example. Each transaction is processed *completely* while it is in primary storage. The appropriate Inventory master record is read into primary storage, updated with the transaction data, and then rewritten to the DASD. Then the Accounts Receivable master record is updated in the same manner, followed by the Sales Analysis record. All three files are updated before the next transaction is entered.

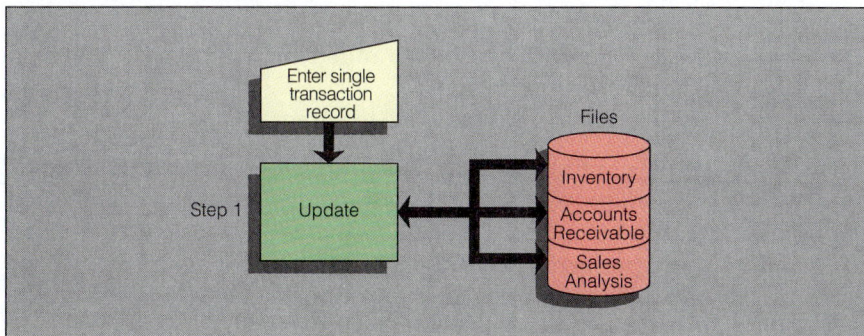

FIGURE 9.9
Online Processing

Online systems frequently use the computer to control the physical system of the firm in some manner. This requires that the computer respond quickly to the status of the physical system. Assume, for example, that you want to charge a department store purchase and you give the clerk your driver's license for identification. The clerk keys the license number into the POS terminal and the computer conducts a credit check. If your credit is O.K. the sale is made; if not, the sale is cancelled. A computer system that controls the physical system in this manner is called a **realtime system**.

For many years online processing was a luxury that only the larger firms could afford because of the cost of the DASDs and terminals. Today the prices are no longer a barrier. A small firm with a microcomputer can engage in online processing.

INFORMATION AND DATA MANAGEMENT

The term **information management** is used to describe the overall effort in a firm to create and maintain an information resource. Since data is the raw material from which information is derived, firms also engage in data management. **Data management**, a subset of information management, includes all of the activities involved in making certain that the firm's data is accurate and up-to-date.

Data Management Activities

The data management activities include:

- *Data collection*   The necessary data is gathered and recorded on a form called a **source document** that serves as input to the system. For example, data describing a sale is entered on a sales order form, and payroll data is recorded on a time sheet.
- *Verification*   The data is edited in some manner to verify its accuracy. Perhaps the data entry operator verifies the data visually as it is displayed on the screen. Any errors are corrected.
- *Storage*   The data is stored on some medium such as magnetic tape or magnetic disk.
- *Control*   While the data exists in storage it is controlled and secured to prevent destruction, damage, or misuse.
- *Organization*   The data can be arranged in various sequences to increase its information value.
- *Retrieval*   The data is made available to authorized users.

During the era of purely manual systems, all of these activities were performed by clerical employees. When data processing became mechanized through the use of punched card machines and early computers, many of the activities were performed by the machines. Today, when a firm has organized its data into an integrated data resource and has assembled the software necessary to manage that resource, it is possible to perform all of the activities on the computer.

THE HIERARCHY OF DATA

Firms traditionally have organized their data into files. You visit any business office and you see file cabinets, file drawers, file boxes, and file folders. A **file** is a collection of data *records* that relate to a particular subject. For example, there are billing files that describe the invoices the firm sends to its customers, purchase order files that describe the purchase orders the firm sends to its suppliers, and so on. A **record** consists of all of the *data elements* relating to a subunit within the file. For example, each record in a Payroll file relates to an individual employee. A **data element** is the smallest unit of data—it cannot be subdivided. In a payroll record you would find such data elements as name, employee number, social security number, hourly rate of pay, number of dependents, and so on.

Data, therefore, exists in a hierarchy:

- File
  - Record
    - Data element

The file is the highest level in the hierarchy and the data element is the lowest.

THE PREDATABASE ERA

During the first half of this century, as firms processed data manually and with keydriven and punched card machines, the data was managed on a piecemeal basis. As each data processing system was designed, the input data files needed by that system were created with little thought as to how those files affected other systems. Perhaps much, or even all, of the data in the new file already existed in another file. The result was much data **redundancy**, or duplication. This same situation existed during the first fifteen years or so of the computer era as these same firms converted their data processing systems to the computer. Each application with its data was regarded as a separate entity, with no overall data plan. This situation was characteristic of the predatabase era.

Something happened in the mid-1960s that caused firms to take a new look at their data. Most large firms had converted their data processing applications to the computer and were looking for new frontiers. Enter MIS. Managers and information specialists alike became interested in using the computer as a management information system. In addition to processing accounting data, the computer would prepare reports for managers to use in decision making.

As the firms began to implement their MISs they realized that they were constrained by the data. Take the example of a credit manager who wanted a report in salesperson sequence to provide information about customers who had not been paying their bills. Each line of the report would include all of the information needed for each customer—the customer name and address, the amount of money owed, the telephone number, and the name and address of the company salesperson responsible for the account. The credit manager intended to send each customer a letter asking for payment. If that did not work the manager would make a telephone call. If that did not work the manager planned to send a memo to the salesperson requesting that a personal call be made.

The data required to prepare the report resided in three files. The Accounts Receivable file identified the past-due accounts and provided the customer names and addresses. The telephone numbers were contained in the Customer master file, and the salesperson names and addresses were in the Salesperson master file.

The system flowchart in Figure 9.10 shows the steps necessary to prepare the report. In Step 1 a program selected the needed data from the Customer master and Accounts Receivable files. Since both files were maintained in customer-number sequence the selection was accomplished from both files at the same time and the data recorded on an intermediate file. However, the third file (the Salesperson master file) was maintained in salesperson sequence. Before the data from that file was selected the data from the intermediate file was sorted into salesperson sequence in Step 2,

FIGURE 9.10

The Predatabase Preparation of a Management Report

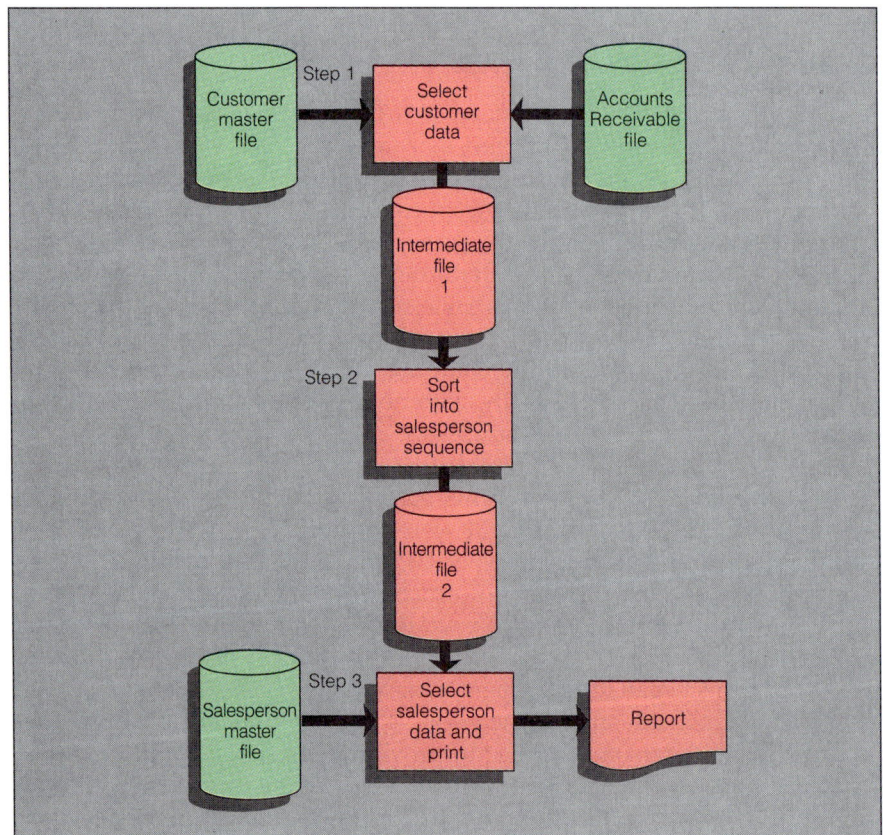

producing a second intermediate file. In Step 3 the data from the second intermediate file was combined with data from the Salesperson master file and the report was printed.

A separate program was needed for each step of the system. The sort program in Step 2 was a prewritten program obtained from the computer manufacturer, but the first and third programs had to be created by the firm's programmers. This programming might have taken weeks. The information specialists appeared to be unresponsive to the users' needs. They had good reason. They were constrained by the data.

THE DAWN OF THE DATABASE ERA

The data constraint was imposed as a result of the **physical organization** of the data—how the data was arranged in secondary storage. The information specialists sought ways to solve this physical organization problem. Their efforts led to the use of a **logical organization** of data that could integrate, or bring together, data from several different physical locations.

The logical organizational is how the **user** sees the data. For example, the credit manager sees the report information as fitting together logically—all of the fields relate to a past-due receivable. The physical organization, on the other hand, is how the **computer** sees the data—as separate files.

Techniques were developed to achieve a logical integration of data within a single file, and also a logical integration between multiple files.

Logical Integration within a Single File

Two approaches were developed that enabled the selection of certain records from a single file without the need to search the entire file. The two approaches were called inverted files and linked lists.

Inverted Files

An **inverted file** is a file maintained in a certain sequence, but an index has been prepared that enables records from the file to be selected in some other sequence.

The type of problem that the inverted file was designed to solve was the request by a manager for a report listing only certain records in a file. For example, a sales manager might want to see a listing of the sales made by salesperson 23. Each record in the file had to be examined by the computer to determine if it was a salesperson 23 record. If so, it was selected and used to print the report. A file containing thousands of records might include only a dozen or so records for salesperson 23, but *every* record in the file had to be scanned. It was very inefficient.

The information specialists realized they could create an index for the Salesperson master file that listed all of the records for each salesperson. Such an **inverted file index** is illustrated in Figure 9.11. When the index is needed, it is read into primary storage and the program scans the salesperson number column looking for salesperson 23. When that row is found the program can scan across to the right and pick up the needed record numbers. In the example there is a record for each of salesperson 23's customers

FIGURE 9.11

An Inverted File
Index

Salesperson number	Salesperson name	Customer 1	Customer 2	Customer 3	Customer n
16		17042	21096		
20		41854			
23		23694	25410	30102	30111
31		31002			
56		34107	13109		
92		20842			
98		61634			
104		10974			
110		16342	64210	51263	41782

who has made a purchase. If the Salesperson master file is DASD based, the needed records can be selected without searching the entire file.

Linked Lists

Another technique was used to achieve the same results. Assume that the same manager wants the same report. A separate field, the salesperson link, is added to each record in the file as pictured in Figure 9.12. The field contains a **link**, or **pointer**, that serves to tie together all of the records for each salesperson. A file containing such link fields is called a **linked list**.

Only the links for salesperson 23 are shown in the figure. The program selects the records by scanning each record in the file until the first record

FIGURE 9.12

A Linked List

Customer number				Salesperson number	Salesperson link
22504					
23694				23	25410
24782					
25409					
25410				23	30102
26713					
28914					
30004					
30102				23	30111
30111				23	*
30417					
31715					

Data record

for salesperson 23 is found. The link field in the first record is called the **head**, and it identifies the *next* record for salesperson 23. The next record is retrieved (again assuming a DASD capability), and its link field identifies the third record. This process is continued until the last record is retrieved. The link field in the last record contains a special code that identifies it as the **tail.**

Inverted files and linked lists provide a way to logically integrate data within a single file, but there is also a need to achieve the same results between multiple files.

Logical Integration between Files

In the mid-1960s General Electric modified COBOL to allow data to be retrieved from multiple files. Links were used to interconnect the records in one *file* to the logically related records in *other files*. GE's system was named IDS (for Integrated Data Store), and it was the first real step toward an integrated database of multiple files.

THE DATABASE CONCEPT

The **database** is an integrated collection of computer data, organized and stored in a manner that facilitates easy retrieval. Figure 9.13 shows how many of the firm's files can be logically integrated. The lines represent the

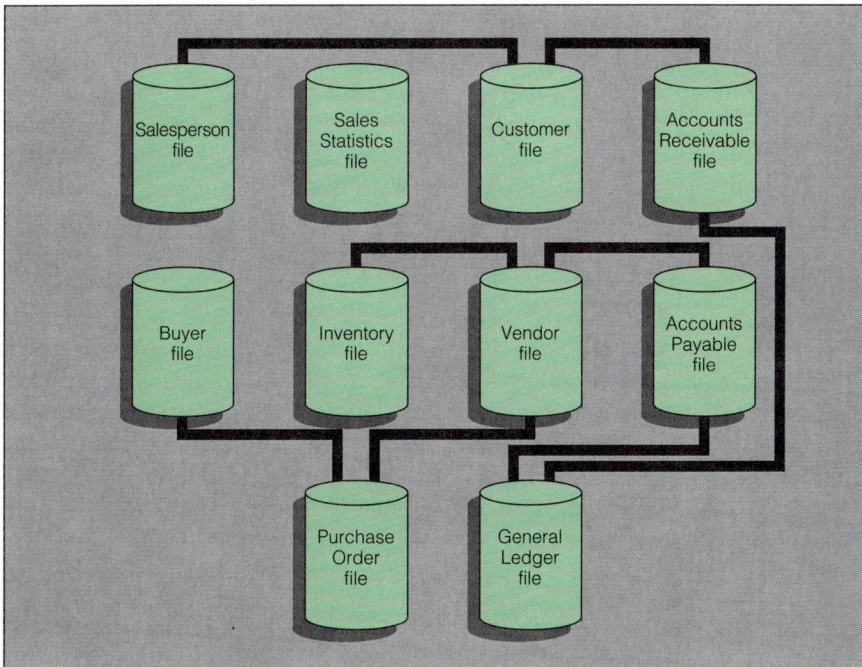

FIGURE 9.13

A Database Consists of One or More Files

logical integration. For example, contents of the Customer file and Accounts Receivable file can be combined to produce a report describing the customers who owe the firm money.

When a firm adopts the database concept, the hierarchy of data becomes:

- Database
  - File
    - Record
      - Data element

Separate files still exist, and they represent the major components of the database. However, the physical organization of the data does not constrain the user. Means are provided to integrate the contents of the files that have logical relationships.

DATABASE STRUCTURES

The logical integration of files can be achieved explicitly or implicitly.

Explicit Relationships

The inverted indexes and link fields we studied earlier establish **explicit relationships** between logically integrated data. The indexes and fields exist physically, and must be incorporated into the files when they are created. Otherwise, the manager's request for logically integrated information cannot be met easily.

Hierarchical Structure

Let us look at an example of a database using explicit relationships. Figure 9.14 shows how the records of four separate files can be integrated. Each salesperson has a *single* salesperson record that contains data such as that listed in the figure. Each salesperson has *multiple* sales statistics records—one record for each item sold to a customer. Each salesperson also has *multiple* customer records that provide information about each customer in the salesperson's territory. Finally, each of the salesperson's customers can have *multiple* accounts receivable records—one for each unpaid purchase.

The records in the figure are arranged in a hierarchy. Each record on one level can be related to multiple records on the next-lower level. When such a logical relationship exists between the records in different files it is called a **hierarchical structure**. A record on one level that has subsidiary records is called the **parent**. The records on the next-lower level are called **children**. In a hierarchical structure, a child can have only a single parent.

Another important feature of Figure 9.14 is the link fields establishing the explicit relationships. Once you retrieve a salesperson record (say for salesperson 23), the links can lead you to the other records *in other files* that are logically related to that salesperson.

Network Structure

Another structure is very similar to the hierarchical except that a child can have more than one parent. The structure is called the **network structure**

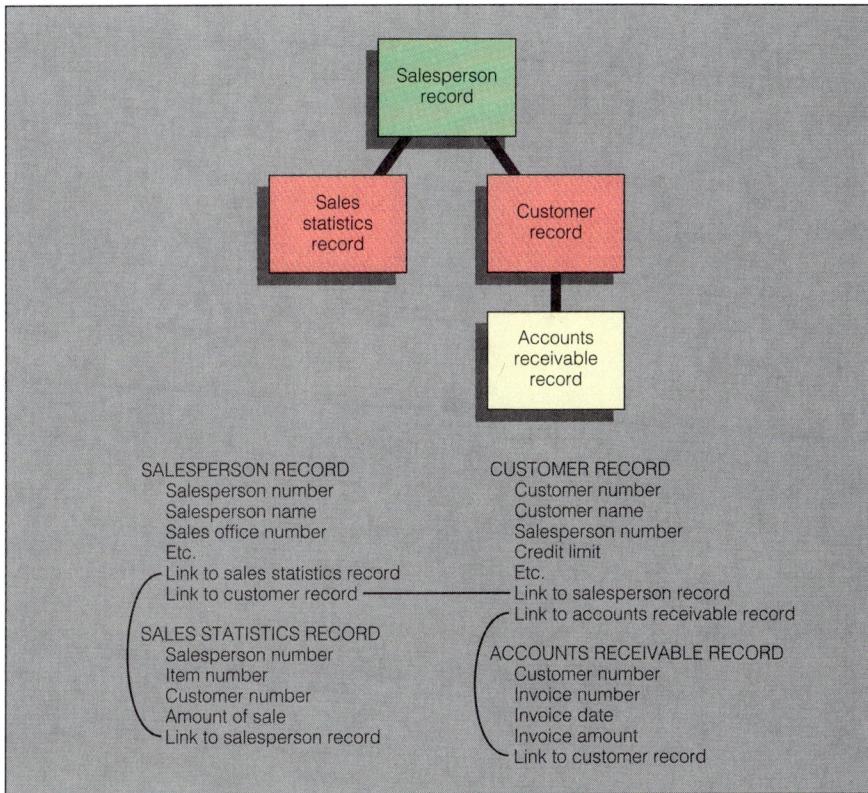

FIGURE 9.14
Explicit
Relationships
between Files

and an example appears in Figure 9.15. In this example, each buyer in the purchasing department is represented by a record. Each buyer is responsible for purchasing *multiple* inventory items, and each item is represented by a record. Each inventory item can be acquired from *multiple* vendors, and there is a vendor record for each. Multiple purchase order records exist for each buyer and for each inventory item. The purchase order records are unique in having two parents—buyer records and inventory records.

While the hierarchical and network structures that employ explicit relationships are a giant step toward eliminating physical constraints, the approach does not offer a complete solution.

The Limitation of Explicit Relationships

Figure 9.16 shows how the logically linked salesperson files (in the upper-right corner) appear in the database. There are other groups of logically linked files. All of the files in a particular group can be used together to provide integrated information; however, a file in one group cannot be used in another since the link fields have not been established. You can see the constraint this imposes on the user and the information specialist. It is necessary to identify the groups of files that must be used together *before* the database is created. This restricts the manager from making special **ad hoc requests** for combinations of information not previously specified.

FIGURE 9.15
A Network
Structure

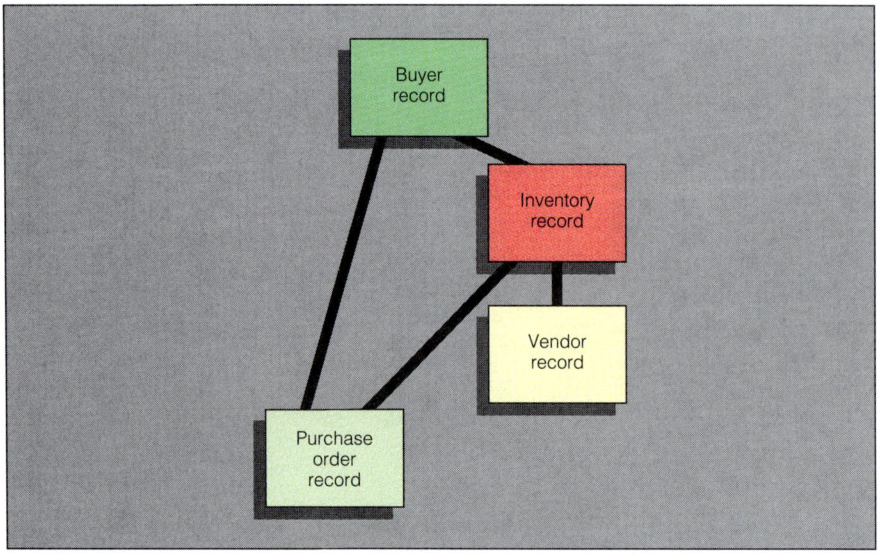

FIGURE 9.16
A Hierarchical
Database

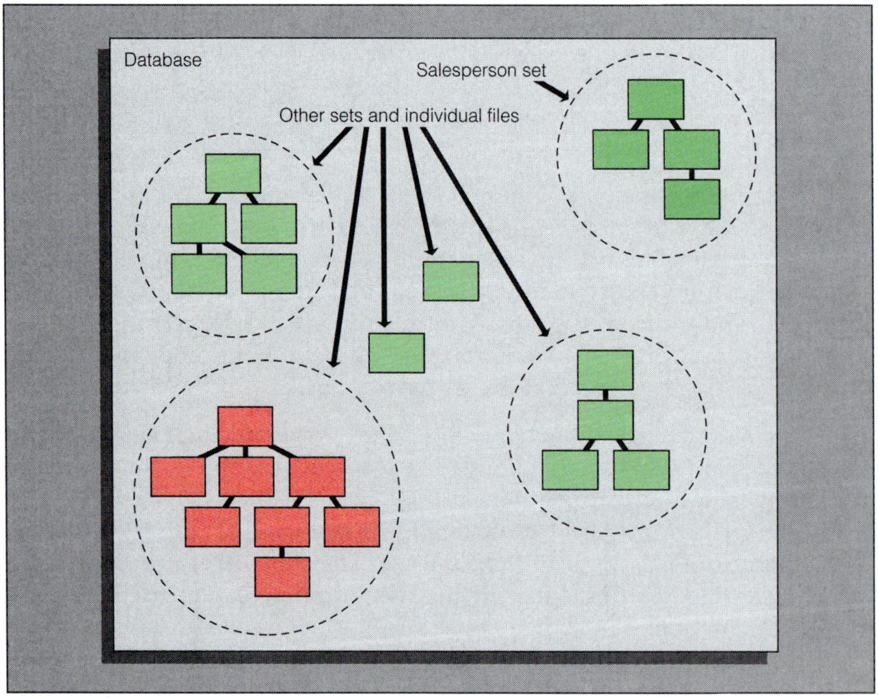

Implicit Relationships

In the early 1970s E. F. Codd and C. J. Date, working separately, developed an approach to establishing relationships between records that do not have to be stated explicitly. In other words, special link fields do not have to be included in the records. Their approach has been named the **relational structure**, and it uses **implicit relationships**—relationships that can be implied from the existing record data.

Assume we want to use two data tables to prepare a report. The data in a relational database is in the form of tables called **flat files**. The files are "flat" in that they are two-dimensional arrangements of data columns and data rows.

The two data tables that will be used to prepare the report appear in Table 9.1. We want the report to list the salespersons in territory 1, showing their salesperson numbers and their names. Both tables are needed; Table A provides the means of identifying the records for territory 1, and the salesperson names come from Table B. If you were told to prepare such a report you would need no special instruction. You would logically integrate the data, even though no explicit relationship exists. The implicit relationship is established by the salesperson number field in both tables. The salesperson number field ties together the territory numbers in Table A and the salesperson names in Table B. This is the way the contents of multiple files are logically integrated in a relational database.

TABLE 9.1

| Table A | | Table B | |
SALESNO	TERR	SALESNO	NAME
112	1	112	ADAMS
128	3	128	WINKLER
153	2	153	HOUSE
159	1	159	FRANCIS
162	1	162	WILLIS
166	2	166	GROVETON

DATABASE SOFTWARE

The software that establishes and maintains the logical integration between files, whether it uses explicit or implicit relationships, is called the **database management system**, or **DBMS**. GE's IDS was the first example of a DBMS, and it was followed by similar efforts of other giant firms such as IBM and North American Aviation. Software firms also got into the act. All of these initial efforts were aimed at mainframe users, since they had the most serious data problems.

The packages that enjoyed the widest acceptance were IBM's IMS (for Information Management System), Cincom's TOTAL, Software AG's ADABAS, Intel's SYSTEM 2000, and Cullinet's IDMS. IMS and SYSTEM 2000 are examples of the hierarchical structure. TOTAL and ADABAS use the network structure. These systems, still in use, were very expensive, costing $100,000 or so. However, the mainframe users felt that the solutions to their data problems justified the high prices. In the early 1980s, approximately 10,000 mainframe DBMSs were in use worldwide.

The next wave of DBMS innovation featured relational software. Again, the first packages were aimed at mainframe users. SQL/DS (Structured Query Language/Data System) and QBE (Query By Example) from IBM, ORACLE from Relational Software, Inc., and RAMIS II from Mathematica Products Group were representative of this first generation of mainframe relational DBMSs. About the same time, microcomputer sales were booming and a number of scaled-down DBMS packages were developed for that market. The first to make a big impression was dBASE II, a product of Ashton-Tate. It cost only a few hundred dollars and by 1985 over 300,000 copies had been sold.

Recently, practically all DBMS development has been in the microcomputer area. dBASE II was followed up with dBASE III, dBASE III Plus, and dBASE IV, now marketed by Borland International. Another successful line of microcomputer-based DBMSs has been the product offerings of MicroRim Corporation, which include the Rbase series.

CREATING A DATABASE

The first step in creating a database is to define the data that is to be included. This definition is documented with the data dictionary.

The Data Dictionary

The **data dictionary** defines each data element, identifying the name, type of data, number of positions, its source, how it is used in the system, and so on. The data dictionary can exist as either a notebook of paper forms or a computer file. An illustration of a paper **data element dictionary entry** form can be found in Figure 7.10.

When the data dictionary exists as a computer file, software is necessary to create and maintain the file and make it available for use. Such software is called a **data dictionary system**, or **DDS**. DDSs can be acquired as separate systems or as modules within a DBMS.

The Data Description Language

Once the data dictionary has been created, its descriptions must be entered into the DBMS. The DBMS includes a **data description language**, or **DDL**, used to describe the data. Figure 9.17 shows how the contents of the data dictionary are entered into the computer and the DDL produces the schema. The **schema** is the logical description of the database contents used

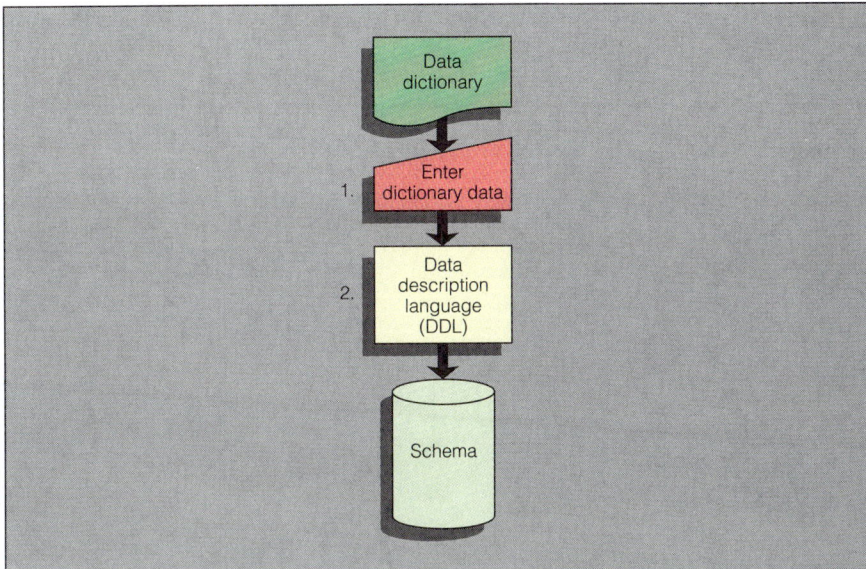

FIGURE 9.17
Describing the
Database Contents

by the computer. For example, the schema used by dBASE III Plus includes:

- The data element name
- The type of data (character, numeric, date, logical, or memo)
- The number of positions
- The number of decimal positions (for numeric data only)

It is important that you understand that the schema is not the data itself—it is the *description* of the data. The term **subschema** is used for the subset of the overall description that relates to a particular user. Each user must define specific data needs, and each of those descriptions are a subschema.

Once the schema and subschema have been created, the data can be stored in the database.

USING A DATABASE

A **database user** can be a *person* or an *application program*. The person usually uses the database from a terminal and retrieves data and information by using a query language. The term **query** is used to describe the request for information from a database. The user queries the database. A **query language** is a special, user-friendly language enabling the computer to respond to a database query. The response, on the screen or in hard copy form, can have the same general appearance as a report.

When an application program, such as a payroll program, retrieves data from the database or stores data in it, a special **data manipulation language**, or **DML**, is used. Figure 9.18 shows five lines of DML embedded in a COBOL program.

FIGURE 9.18   Data Manipulation Language Embedded in an Application Program

```
002530 9400-INSERT-SEGMENT SECTION.
002531
002532     MOVE ALL SPACES                 TO DP-TIME-SEGMENT.
002533     MOVE MID-SCREEN-EMPLOYEE        TO DP-TIME-EMPLOYEE.
002534     MOVE CONVERTED-SCREEN-DATE      TO DP-TIME-WORK-WEEK.
002535     MOVE CONVERTED-DATES (INDX)     TO DP-TIME-WORK-DATE.
002536     MOVE CONVERTED-HOURS (INDX)     TO DP-TIME-HOURS.
002537     MOVE DP-EMP-GROUP               TO DP-TIME-GROUP.
002538     MOVE MOD-SCREEN-LEV-REQ         TO DP-TIME-LEAVE-REQUEST.
002539     MOVE WORK-NONWORK-FLAG (INDX)   TO DP-TIME-TYPE-PRJ.
002540
002541     MOVE MID-SCREEN-PRJ-CD (INDX)   TO DP-PROJECT-ROOT-KEY.
002542     MOVE MID-SCREEN-PRJ-ID (INDX)   TO DP-PROJECT-ID-KEY.
002543
002544     CALL 'CBLTDLI' USING ISRT DPPROJECT-PCB
002545                               DP-TIME-SEGMENT
002546                               DP-PROJECT-ROOT-SSA
002547                               DP-ID-SSA
002548                               DP-TIME-INSERT-SSA.
002549
002550     IF DPPROJECT-STATUS-CODE = SPACES
002551     THEN
002552         NEXT SENTENCE
002553     ELSE
002554         MOVE 'Y'      TO IMS-ERROR
002555         MOVE '9400-1' TO BSM-PARA
002556         MOVE 'PRJ'    TO BSM-DB
002557         MOVE DPPROJECT-STATUS-CODE TO BSM-STATUS
002558         GO TO 9400-EXIT.
```

DBMS Events

The events that take place when an application program retrieves data from the database are illustrated in Figure 9.19. In Step 1 the DML specifies to the DBMS what data is needed. In Step 2 the DBMS checks the schema and subschema to verify that the data exists in the database and the application program is entitled to use it. In Step 3 the DBMS passes along the

FIGURE 9.19
DBMS Events

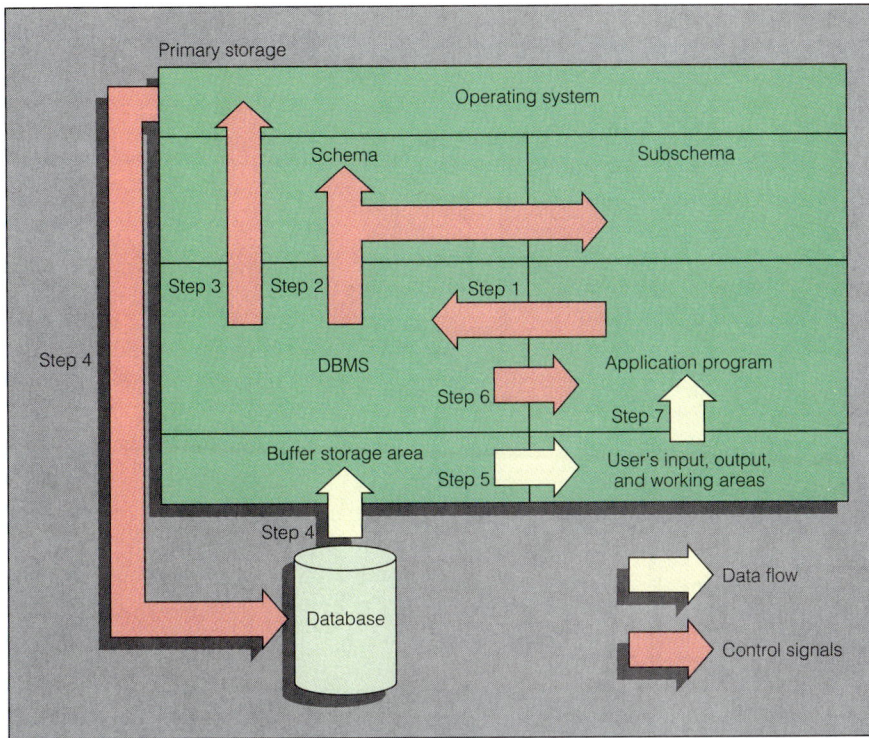

data request to the operating system, which retrieves the data in Step 4 and enters it in a special buffer storage area in primary storage. The data then is transferred into the application program's input area in Step 5. The DBMS returns control to the application program in Step 6, and the application program uses the data in Step 7.

The same series of events occur when a query language is used. In that case the query language is a subset of the DBMS and the retrieved information is displayed on the user's output device.

A MODEL OF A DBMS

Each DBMS performs data management in a unique way. For example, some utilize explicit relationships, whereas others utilize implicit. Some mainframe DBMSs include query languages and others do not. However, a model can be used to show the major components that potentially may be offered by a DBMS. Such a model is pictured in Figure 9.20.

Data Description Language Processor

The **data description language processor** transforms the data dictionary into the database schema. This is the DDL described earlier. All DBMSs have a DDL.

FIGURE 9.20

A DBMS Model

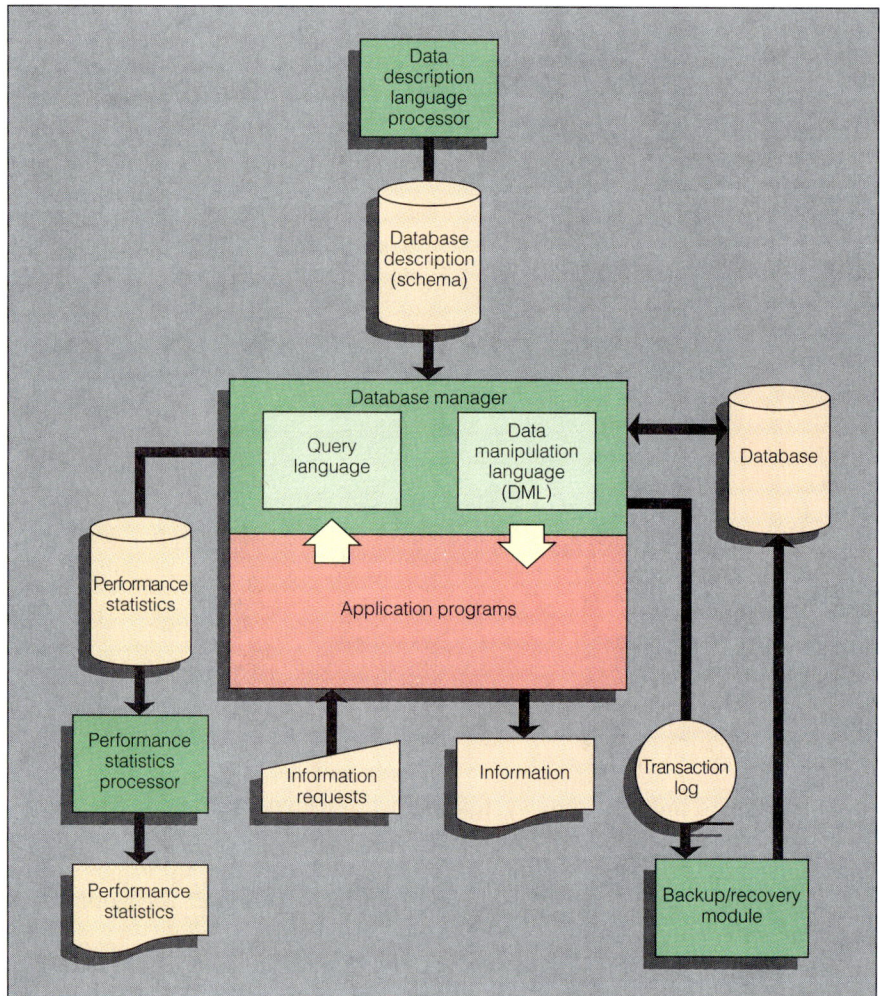

Performance Statistics Processor

The **performance statistics processor** maintains statistics that identify what data is being used, who is using it, when it is being used, and so forth. The DBA (database administrator) uses the statistics to monitor database use. Microcomputer based DBMSs typically do not include this component.

Backup/Recovery Module

The **backup/recovery module** is used to recover from a disaster that makes the database unusable. The **transaction log** enables the reconstruction of the database as described earlier in the chapter. This component also is not usually found in microcomputer DBMSs.

Database Manager

The **database manager** is the most important of the components in that it handles the users' data requests. The query language and the DML are a part of the database manager. All DBMSs include this component.

The database manager also produces the performance statistics processed by the performance statistics processor, and the transaction log processed by the backup/recovery module.

The database manager is the only DBMS component that remains in primary storage. The others are read into primary storage from a DASD when they are needed.

DATABASE SECURITY

DBMSs offer varying degrees of security for the databases they manage. Mainframe DBMSs utilize several methods in combination to ensure that only authorized users gain access. The early microcomputer DBMSs were lacking in this regard, but that weakness is being overcome. Today's microcomputer DBMSs such as Rbase System V, dBASE III Plus, and dBASE IV have many of the same security capabilities as do mainframe systems.

Security Levels

Someone likened database security to constructing a series of fences around the data resource—one fence inside the other. In order for a user to reach the data in the center, the gates in each of the fences must be opened. The *levels* of security offered by a DBMS are similar to the fences.

Mainframe operating systems typically require you to enter a unique **password**, or code, in order to use the computer. The password can be perhaps eight characters in length and should be known only to the user. This is the first, outer fence guarding the computer.   **Passwords**

DBMSs can have their own password fence. After gaining access to the computer, you might have to enter a special password to use the database.

After successfully satisfying the password requirement, the DBMS might check a **user directory**, a listing of all of the persons and programs authorized to use the database. The directory is maintained on a DASD and is brought into primary storage when needed. If a user is not listed in the directory, access is not granted.   **User Directory**

After passing the user checks, the DBMS can consult a **field directory** that identifies the data elements the user can access and how each can be used. For example, the field directory of a payroll clerk might allow the fields of an employee record to be *read* only, but the directory of a payroll supervisor might provide an ability to *make changes*.   **Field Directory**

The data can be **encrypted**, or coded, so that it is meaningless to an unauthorized user who is able to pass through the above fences. For example, a year-to-date gross earnings field containing 16,250.73 might appear as 6137205 in an encrypted form. The encryption is accomplished by a soft-   **Encryption** ware routine included in the DBMS. Authorized users provide an **encryption key** to decode the data.

Today's computerized databases are infinitely more secure than any type of data storage that previously existed, however the security is not 100 percent perfect. This challenge will stimulate information specialists to continue to develop new database security measures.

PUTTING THE DATABASE AND DBMS IN PERSPECTIVE

Not all firms have achieved the degree of logical integration of their computer data that we have described. Such an ability is not necessary as long as two conditions exist. First, if the firm is using the computer solely for data processing and not decision support, a predatabase hierarchy with files as the highest level can produce the desired results. Second, if there is no requirement to integrate the contents of multiple files, there is no need to adopt the database concept.

There are many firms using the computer in a very sophisticated way without a logically integrated database. In some cases these firms have purchased prewritten software systems to process their daily transactions. The prewritten systems maintain the files for the user, reducing the need for the integrated database and the DBMS.

While the integrated database and the DBMS are not an absolute necessity, there is no doubt that the trend is in that direction. This trend is most evident at the microcomputer level where the DBMS packages are both inexpensive and user friendly.

DBMS Advantages

Firms and individual users are attracted to the DBMS because it enables them to:

- *Reduce data redundancy*. The total number of files are reduced as duplicate files are deleted. There is also a minimum of common data among files.
- *Integrate data from multiple files*. The physical organization of data no longer constrains users in receiving information from multiple files.
- *Retrieve data and information rapidly*. Both the logical relationships and the DML and query language enable users to retrieve in seconds what is needed.
- *Improve security*. While the security fences of the DBMS can be incorporated into custom software, they seldom are. The data managed by the DBMS should be more secure than the other data in the firm.

DBMS Disadvantages

The advantages are not without their costs. A decision to use a DBMS commits a firm or user to:

- *Obtain expensive software.* The mainframe DBMSs remain very expensive. The microcomputer DBMSs, while inexpensive when compared to mainframe versions, can represent a substantial cost for a small organization.
- *Obtain a large hardware configuration.* The DBMSs often require larger primary and secondary storage capacities than are required by the application programs. Also, the ease with which the DBMS can retrieve information encourages the inclusion of more user terminals in the configuration than otherwise would be necessary.
- *Hire and maintain a technically trained staff.* Mainframe users often assemble a special staff of information specialists who are expert in DBMSs. This is the DBA portion of the information services organization described in Chapter 6. This disadvantage is less applicable to microcomputer users because of the user-friendly nature of those DBMSs.

The popularity of DBMSs among organizations of all sizes indicates that the users feel the advantages to be worth the costs.

THE ROLE OF THE DATABASE AND THE DBMS IN PROBLEM SOLVING

An up-to-date and accurate computerized database can be one of the most important resources of the problem solver. The database represents the raw material from which the problem-solving information is derived. Regardless of whether the information is presented in the form of a periodic report, a special report in response to a query, or the output from a mathematical model, the DBMS provides the data.

The DBMS is the **gatekeeper** of the database. The DBMS is used to create the database, maintain its contents, make the contents available to the user, and safeguard the data resource from unauthorized access.

We should recognize that neither computerized databases nor DBMSs are absolute prerequisites to problem solving. However, they can be valuable resources to the information-literate manager.

SUMMARY

The firm's database and software library are maintained in secondary storage, and the contents are retrieved when needed. Secondary storage devices are of two types—sequential and direct access.

Magnetic tape is the most popular form of sequential storage. When a magnetic tape master file is updated, it is necessary to create a new, complete file. The old file is used for backup. Magnetic tape is excellent for historical storage, and also serves as a DASD backup, an input medium, and a communications medium.

The most popular type of DASD is magnetic disk. Mainframes and minicomputers use permanently mounted metal disks. Microcomputers use diskettes and also permanently mounted hard disks. The access mechanism can be directed to any record in the file by providing an address that specifies the track number, the read/write head, and possibly the record sequence number. DASD is ideal for use as a master file medium, and can also serve as intermediate storage and as an input medium.

Laser disks are being used in place of magnetic tape for historical storage. They can be a good master file medium when a write-many technology is employed.

If your computer configuration includes sequential storage, you can process data in only a batch fashion. If, however, your computer includes DASD you can process data either batch or online. The name realtime is used to describe an online system that reacts to activity within the physical system and controls that system.

Data management is the subset of information management that performs the functions of data collection, verification, storage, control, organization, and retrieval.

During the predatabase era, firms paid little attention to their data resource. The hierarchy of data consisted of the file, record, and data element.

Firms began to overcome the constraints of the physical organization of data by using inverted files and linked lists. GE used links to logically integrate multiple files—the first example of the database concept. Logical integration can be achieved explicitly in hierarchical or network structures, and implicitly in relational structures.

The first step in creating a database is to define the data dictionary. That description is used by the DDL to produce the schema. Each user can have an individual subschema.

Either a person or an application program can be a database user. The person uses a query language and the program uses a DML.

Database security is achieved by building fences around the data resource that consist of passwords, directories, and encryption.

Although a logically integrated database and a DBMS are not an absolute necessity, they can represent a valuable resource in problem solving.

KEY CONCEPTS

The technique of retaining data and programs in secondary storage until they are needed

How a DASD can retrieve a record without the need for a sequential search

The relationship between sequential storage and batch processing

The hierarchy of data

Physical and logical organizations of data

How inverted files and linked lists facilitate the selective retrieval of records

The database concept

How hierarchical and network structures use explicit relationships to achieve logical organization

How the relational structure uses implicit relationships to achieve logical organization

The relationship between the data dictionary and the schema

How a database user can be an application program as well as a person

The levels of database security

How the database and DBMS are used in problem solving

KEY TERMS

Sequential storage
Field
Master file
Transaction file
File maintenance
Audit trail
Direct access storage device (DASD)
Disk stack
Kilobyte (KB)
Megabyte (MB)

Gigabyte (GB)
Laser disk, optical disk, compact disk
Online processing
Batch processing
Realtime system
Information management
Data management
Source document
File
Record

Data element
Physical organization
Logical organization
Explicit relationship
Implicit relationship
Database management system (DBMS)
Schema
Query
Query language
Encryption

QUESTIONS

1. What are the two kinds of computer storage? What are the two primary kinds of secondary storage?

2. What processes must be performed by file maintenance?

3. What capability of laser disks will increase their appeal as a master file medium?

4. What are the two types of processing?

5. What distinguishes a realtime system?

6. What is the physical organization of data? The logical organization?

7. Name two techniques used to select records from a file without the need to scan the entire file.

8. What is a database?

9. What are explicit relationships? Which database structures use them?

10. What is a serious disadvantage of explicit relationships to the problem solver?

11. What are implicit relationships? Which database structure uses them?

12. What is the relationship between the data dictionary, the DDL, and the schema?

13. Who are the database users? What languages do they use to obtain data from the database?

14. List the levels of security through which a user must pass in order to retrieve data from a well-secured database.

15. What is the difference between a data manager and a DBA?

CASE PROBLEM   Database Systems, Inc.

You are sitting at your desk reflecting on the name you chose for your new database consulting company, when the letter carrier pushes three letters through the mail slot in the door. As soon as you pick them up you know they are the first returns from your mail survey. You thought that a survey would be a good way to identify prospects. You plan to offer the expertise that top management needs in determining whether to implement a DBMS. If a DBMS is in order, you will urge your clients to hire a DBA and then you will work with that person, top management, information services personnel, and users in implementing the DBMS.

You open the three letters and extract the completed questionnaires. You are somewhat disappointed that none of the respondents enclosed a letter asking for your help. Oh well, that will come later. You glance over the questionnaires (9A, B, and C), and the wheels begin to spin.

1. Which company is the best prospect for a DBMS? Support your answer.

2. Which company is the worst prospect? Why?

3. If you were going to sell each of the three companies on implementing a DBMS, what would be your main argument for each?

4. Would it be necessary for any of the companies to acquire additional computing hardware to implement a DBMS? Be specific.

5. List the steps (no more than eight) that you will recommend that your best prospect take in implementing the DBMS. Use the systems approach as a general guideline, but do not simply copy those steps. Relate the steps to your prospect.

9A

Company Name: *Landmark Construction*

Size Computer: _____ Mainframe;   √ Mini;   _____ Micro

Secondary Storage: _____ Diskette;   _____ Mag. Tape;   √ Mag. Disk

Number of keyboard terminals in managers' offices: *3*

Number of keyboard terminals in nonmanagers' offices: *8*

Do you have a DBMS? _____ Yes;   √ No   DBA? _____ Yes;   √ No

Number of systems analysts: *6*   Number of programmers: *6*

Main Applications:

Data Processing: *Payroll, inventory, accounts payable, cost accounting, general ledger*

Management Information System: *Estimate project costs, schedule and control projects*

Biggest Current Computer Problem:

Can't combine data from several files in the format that we want

Future Computer Plans:

Want to provide managers with current information concerning actual vs. budgeted costs.

9B

Company Name: Citizens Bank

Size Computer: X Mainframe;   _____ Mini;   _____ Micro

Secondary Storage: _____ Diskette;   X Mag. Tape;   _____ Mag. Disk

Number of keyboard terminals in managers' offices: 0

Number of keyboard terminals in nonmanagers' offices: 85

Do you have a DBMS? _____ Yes;   X No   DBA? _____ Yes;   X No

Number of systems analysts: 25   Number of programmers: 40

Main Applications:

Data Processing: Primarily checking accounts, savings accounts, and installment loans.

Management Information System: Standard accounting reports.

Biggest Current Computer Problem:

No problems.

Future Computer Plans:

Want to be able to display accounting reports on accountants' screens rather than in hard copy form.

9C

Company Name: Fashion Bar Cleaners

Size Computer: _____ Mainframe;   _____ Mini;   xx Micro

Secondary Storage: xx Diskette;   _____ Mag. Tape;   _____ Mag. Disk

Number of keyboard terminals in managers' offices: Not applicable

Number of keyboard terminals in nonmanagers' offices: Not applicable

Do you have a DBMS? ? Yes;   ? No   DBA? ? Yes;   ? No

Number of systems analysts: 0   Number of programmers: 0

Main Applications:

Data Processing: We use a prewritten software package designed especially for laundry and dry cleaning operations.   Very good package.

Management Information System: The prewritten package produces a variety of reports on demand, but we haven't used that feature yet.

Biggest Current Computer Problem:

Nobody knows how to program.

Future Computer Plans:

Want to add Lotus to print some graphs.   Will probably hire college student part-time who knows Lotus.

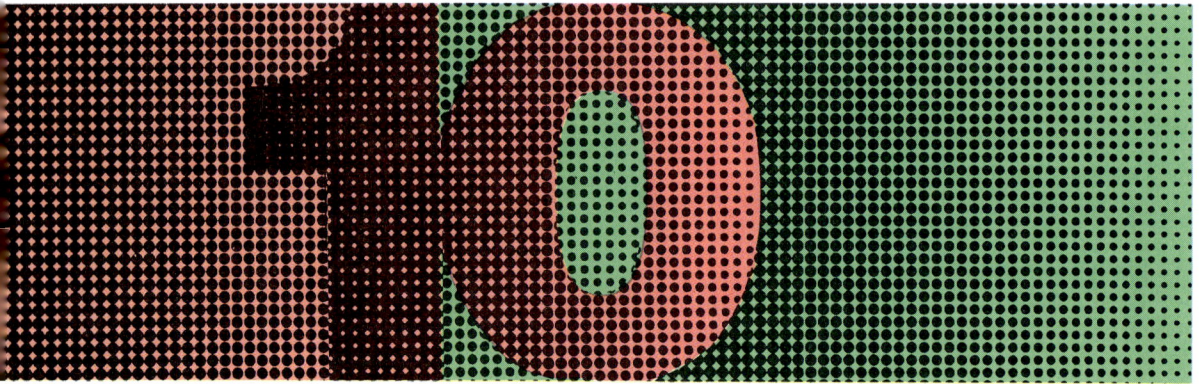

Data Communications

LEARNING OBJECTIVES After studying this chapter, you should:

- See how the basic communication model describing human communications also applies to data communications using computing equipment
- Become acquainted with the hardware and software used in a typical business data communications network
- Recognize the role of common carriers in data communications
- Learn the distinguishing characteristics of the more popular network uses and structures
- Gain a fundamental understanding of standard datacom protocols and architectures
- Appreciate the need to make the data communications network secure and learn how it can be done
- See the effect of data communications on decision making at both the organization and the individual levels

---

OVERVIEW

As the scale of business operations grows, it becomes necessary to gather data and disseminate decisions over a wider area. Data communications hardware and software enable the computer to perform that task.

The basic model that depicts communication between humans can serve as the starting point for a study of data communications. In this chapter you are introduced to both the devices and the software used in business data communications networks. Several different network configurations are possible, and we explain the more popular ones, such as the local area network, or LAN.

Attention is given to the topic of data communications protocols—why they are necessary and how they are being achieved through standard network architectures. We also recognize the importance of security in a data communications network and explain several measures that can contribute to that objective.

The chapter concludes with a discussion of how data communications can facilitate a policy of either centralized or decentralized decision making and how it makes the computing resource available to everyone in the organization.

THE BASIC COMMUNICATION MODEL

The most common form of communication is when one person speaks to another. This process can be illustrated with the diagram in Figure 10.1. The diagram is the **basic communication model**, and the two most important elements are the **sender** and the **receiver**. When one person speaks to another the sender uses his or her brain and voice as a **coder** to put the communication, or **message**, into a form that can be transmitted. The message must travel along some type of channel to reach the receiver. A **channel** is a pathway over which communications can flow. A verbal message communicated in face-to-face conversation travels in the form of sound waves through the air to reach the receiver. The air is the channel. When the message reaches the receiver, it must be decoded. The receiver's ears and brain serve as the **decoder**.

When one person talks to another person over the telephone, the sender's telephone is involved in the coding process, the telephone lines serve as the channel, and the receiver's telephone is involved in the decoding. This telephone communication fits the model in Figure 10.1 as does a situation where a speaker uses a public-address system as a coder to address a large group. The basic communication model represents *any* type of communication from a sender to one or more receivers.

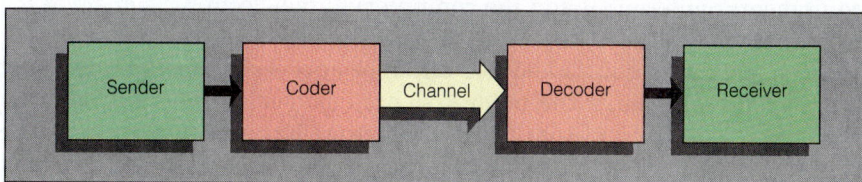

FIGURE 10.1

The Basic Communication Model

COMPUTER-BASED DATA COMMUNICATIONS

The basic communication model can also serve as the basis for a diagram that shows how data is communicated by computer. **Data communications** is the movement of coded data and information from one point to another by means of electrical or electromagnetic devices, fiber-optical cables, or microwave signals. Other terms used are **teleprocessing**, **telecommunications**, and **datacom**. We will use datacom.

Figure 10.2 shows the **basic data communications schematic**. This is the simplest form of computer communication. A single terminal is linked to a computer. This diagram differs from the basic communication model in that the communication can flow in either direction. The terminal can be the sender and the computer can be the receiver, or vice versa.

FIGURE 10.2

The Basic Data Communications Schematic

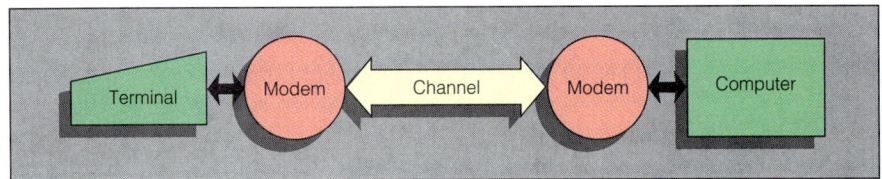

All datacom channels do not have this two-way capability. A channel that can transmit data in only one direction is called a **simplex channel**. A channel that can transmit in both directions, but only one direction at a time, is called a **half-duplex channel**. A channel that can handle two-way traffic simultaneously is a **full-duplex channel**.

All of the interconnected datacom devices are described by the term **network**. The devices form a data communications network. The devices are **networked** to achieve the communication.

As with communication between humans, the messages communicated in a computer network must travel along a channel. Many technologies are used in datacom channels, but the most common is the same telephone circuit used for voice communication. A **circuit** or **line** is the transmission facility that provides one or more channels. For example, a standard telephone line can provide twenty-four channels.

In order to use the telephone circuit, a special device must be included at each end. The device is called a **modem**, which stands for *mo*dulator-*dem*odulator. The modems convert the electronic signals of the computing equipment (the terminal and the computer) to the electronic signals of the telephone circuit, and vice versa. The engineers who design the computing and the telephone equipment use different approaches to code the data. Data is represented in a computer system in a *digital* form—the characters are coded using combinations of bits that have only two possible states—*on* and *off*. The telephone equipment, on the other hand, typically uses an *analog* form of signal that represents the characters with electrical waves of varying frequencies. The different tones you hear when you press the buttons of a push-button telephone are the sound frequencies of the various digits.

The modem on the sender end of the channel converts the digital computer signals to the analog telephone signals. The modem on the receiver end converts the signal back into its original form.

Perhaps you have seen a device similar to the one in Figure 10.3. It is called an **acoustic coupler**, and it is a modem that sometimes is used with microcomputers. The acoustic coupler enables the micro to communicate data to and from another computer. The acoustic coupler is attached to the micro, and you simply place the telephone handset in the modem holder after you have established a telephone connection. The connection is made by dialing the number of the computer on the other end.

A wide variety of datacom hardware and software has been developed, along with a special data communications terminology. For these reasons, the data communications field can be overwhelming at first. The basic data communications schematic is important since it provides the framework upon which a knowledge of data communications can be built.

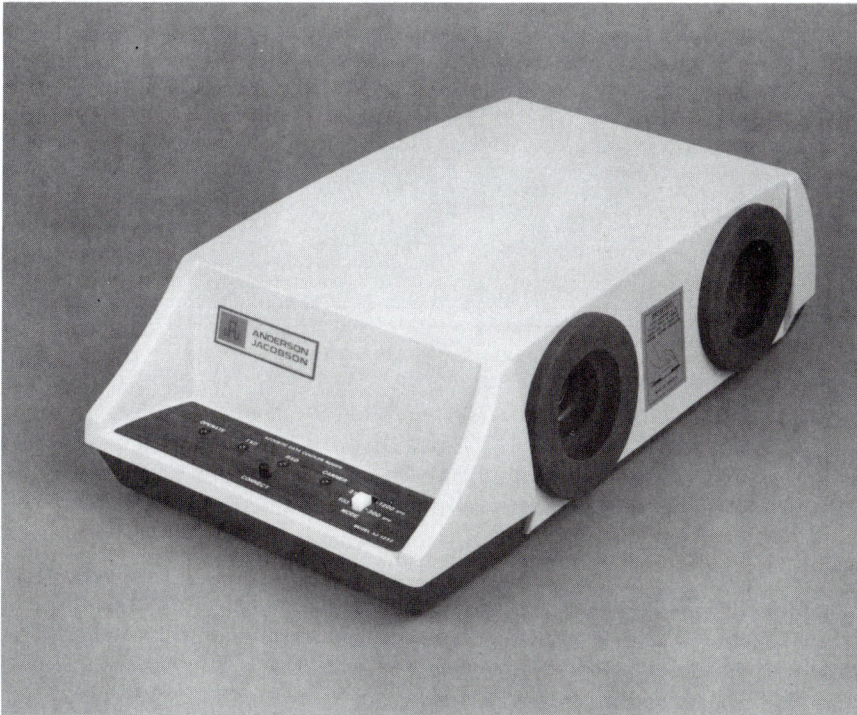

FIGURE 10.3

An Acoustic Coupler Is a Modem

DATA COMMUNICATIONS EQUIPMENT

We will first describe the variety of available datacom hardware, and then the software and how the hardware and software are used in problem solving.

An Expanded Datacom Network

Figure 10.4 illustrates an expanded datacom network. These are not all of the devices that can be included in a network, but they provide a good idea of how a datacom network might appear in a business organization.

One end of the channel includes multiple terminals. There may be a

FIGURE 10.4

An Expanded Data Communications Network

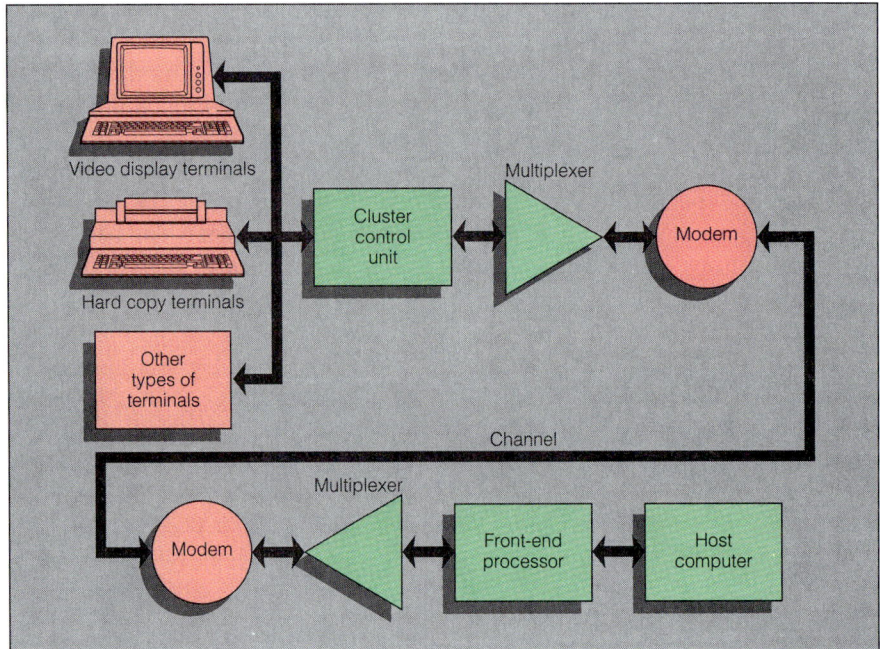

hundred or more, and they can be of various types. The other end of the channel includes two computers. One is called the **host computer**. It is usually the larger of the two, and is the one that processes the firm's data. It is the information processor in the firm's conceptual system. The other computer is especially designed to perform datacom tasks. It is named the **front-end processor**, and is used to connect the host to the communication channel.

Computers are designed to perform data processing, not data communications. When the volume of data communications activity is heavy, a front-end processor can be added to the network to relieve the host of much of the data communications workload.

Two other devices in Figure 10.4 require explanation. They are the cluster control unit and the multiplexer.

The **cluster control unit** is added to the network when there are a large number of terminals in one location, such as the accounting department. The cluster control unit controls the terminals so that they all have access to the channel and none of the terminals monopolizes the channel's use.

The **multiplexer** enables the channel to handle more than a single message at a time. It makes the channel look like a multiple-lane highway.

The other elements in the expanded network, the modems and the channel, are our old friends from the basic network.

We will begin at the user's end of the network and explain in more detail each of the units.

Terminals

In Chapter 8 we recognized the keyboard terminal as the most popular way to enter data into a computer. Actually, it is one of five types of terminals.

There are two types of keyboard terminals—those that display output on a screen, and those that print the output on paper. The terms **CRT terminal** (CRT stands for cathode ray tube), **VDT** (for visual display terminal), and **alphanumeric display terminal** are used interchangeably to describe the terminal that utilizes the screen display. The terms **hard copy terminal** and **teleprinter terminal** describe the terminal that produces the output in a paper form. A hard copy terminal appears in Figure 10.5. It is essentially a microcomputer character printer with a keyboard.

1. Keyboard Terminals

FIGURE 10.5

A Hard Copy Terminal

Keyboard terminals are popular with managers. The keyboard can be used to request reports, make database queries, and enter the data and instructions used by mathematical models. The hard copy terminal provides a permanent record of the output, and the CRT terminal displays the output very quickly.

2. Push-Button Telephones

In Chapter 8 we explained how a computer equipped with an audio response device can transmit messages that the user can hear on a telephone. Used in this manner, the push-button telephone (a rotary-dial telephone will not work) becomes the most readily available and least expensive type of terminal. The push buttons are used to transmit data and instructions to the computer. For example, a manager might be touring field offices and hear that an important customer's order is late in being filled. The manager can use a push-button telephone to query the database to determine the order status.

3. Point of Sale (POS) Terminals

In Chapter 8 we also recognized how **point of sale**, or **POS** terminals are used in supermarkets and other retail outlets such as department stores. The terminals provide a means of entering transaction data into the database as the sales are made. The terminals make possible a database that reflects the current status of the firm.

4. Data Collection Terminals

During the early years of the computer era, a type of terminal was designed for use by factory employees. The terminal was called a **data collection terminal** and it was used in attendance reporting and job reporting. **Attendance reporting** is accomplished by punching in when you come to work and punching out when you leave. **Job reporting** involves clocking on a production job when it is begun and clocking off when it is completed.

Today's data collection terminals, such as the one pictured in Figure 10.6, feature an OCR wand, a badge reader, and a keyboard. The OCR wand can be used to read characters from documents that travel with the job through the plant, facilitating job reporting. The badge reader reads data recorded on the workers' badges either as punched holes or as bits on a magnetic strip, facilitating attendance reporting.

FIGURE 10.6

A Data Collection Terminal

Today's data collection terminals are also used in other than the manufacturing area. They are commonly found in libraries, used to check out books. The librarian uses the OCR wand to read the identifying characters from the book and from your ID card.

As with the POS terminals, the data collection terminals enable employees to communicate data to the database describing what is happening in the firm.

Perhaps you have noticed special cash-register-like terminals in places like McDonald's, donut shops, and cafeterias. The terminals usually feature a large bank of keys—one key for each type of product. You purchase a Big Mac, a small fries, and a small Coke and the salesperson presses three keys. Such terminals are **special purpose terminals**—they have been designed for a specific use.

5. Special Purpose Terminals

A good example of a special purpose terminal is the Federal Express FED EX SUPER TRACKER Plus hand-held terminal shown in Figure 10.7. When the courier picks up a package, SUPER TRACKER is used to gather data to be used in tracking the package through the Federal Express system. Some of the data is optically scanned by SUPER TRACKER, and some is entered by the courier into the SUPER TRACKER keyboard. SUPER TRACKER then uses its microprocessor to determine the best route to the destination. The courier inserts SUPER TRACKER into a portable Astra printer, which prints a label that is attached to the package. The Astra label contains a barcode that identifies the destination, the type of service to be provided, and the routing.

When the Federal Express courier delivers a package, SUPER TRACKER optically scans the Astra label on the package. The courier then keys in the first initial and last name of the recipient. When the courier gets back to the truck, SUPER TRACKER is inserted into another terminal, which adds the date and time. The truck terminal then transmits the data by microwave to an area computer (there are about 150 across the United States, and also in London and Hong Kong). The area computer transmits the data to the main computer center in Memphis. Within two minutes after the package is delivered, the Memphis computer has a record of the transaction. The Federal Express system is an excellent example of how a firm can track resource flows on a global basis—in realtime.

Intelligent and Dumb Terminals

When a terminal can only send and receive data it is referred to as a **dumb terminal**. When a terminal has the additional ability to perform some type of processing it is called an **intelligent terminal**. The intelligence is provided by a microprocessor, and in some cases the terminal is actually a microcomputer. Any of the above terminal types, with the exception of the push-button telephone, can be either an intelligent or a dumb terminal.

To the user, the terminal is the most important part of the datacom network. It is the unit that the user sees and uses. All of the other devices are

behind the scenes. The user regards his or her terminal as *the system*. However, when an adequate network is not available to handle the datacom traffic, the time delay in waiting for a computer response can become irritating. When designing a datacom network, it is important that the information specialists assemble the hardware and software that are adequate to handle the firm's data volumes.

Cluster Control Unit

The cluster control unit establishes the connection between the terminals it controls (usually thirty-two or less) and other devices and channels. It enables the terminals to share a printer or to have access to multiple computers via different channels. The cluster control unit can also perform error checking and code conversion.

Multiplexer

When there is a need for multiple terminals to share the channel at the same time, multiplexers can be added to each end of the channel. The other portions of the network handle only single messages at a time. Multiplexers help to reduce transmission costs.

Modem

The communications companies, such as AT&T and GTE, are called **common carriers** since their facilities are available to the general public. Common carriers use a variety of technologies to transmit a message. The older technologies represent the data in an analog fashion described earlier.

The newer technologies use a digital approach. However, even when a digital signal is used, a modem is still required to shape the signal for transmission. The only exception is when a push-button telephone is used as a terminal. All other datacom channels include a modem of some type on each end.

Modems are designed to operate at certain speeds—usually 300, 1200, 2400, 4800, 9600 bits per second, and up. The modem speed determines the rate at which messages are transmitted.

The Channel

Up to this point, all of the datacom equipment is furnished by the firm—the terminals, cluster control unit, multiplexer, and modem. In most cases the channel is provided by one or more common carriers. Figure 10.8 shows how the channel can be subdivided into sections that perform the transmission function in different ways.

When the signals leave the sender's modem they travel along a **local loop** that provides the connection between the firm's equipment and the central   **The Local Loop**

FIGURE 10.8   The Common Carrier Portion of the Channel

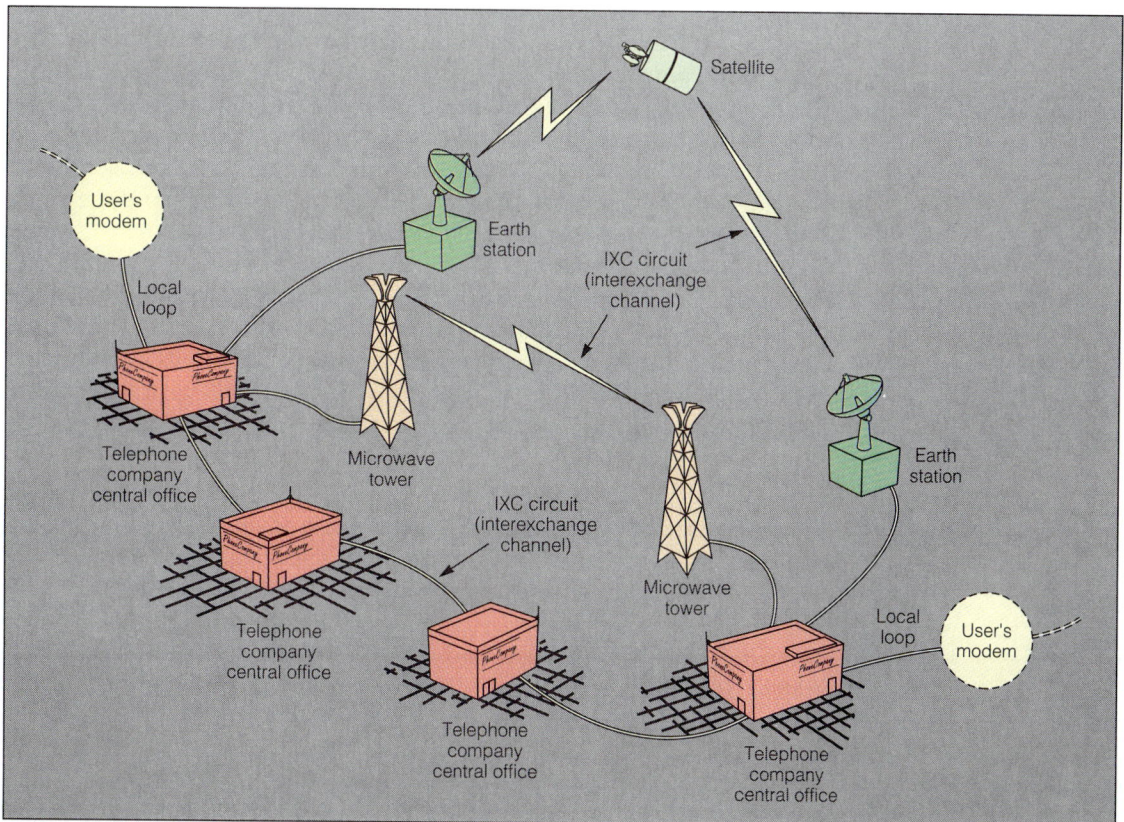

office of the telephone company in the sender's city. The local loop ordinarily consists of wires or coaxial cables. Four wires are necessary and they are twisted in pairs. The **twisted pair** is the most common type of circuit. A **coaxial cable**, or **coax**, consists of a single wire covered with insulation, and contained within an outer cylindrical shell. If you have cable TV, the round, black cable attached to your set is a coaxial cable. The coaxial cable used by the common carrier usually consists of several individual cables bundled together. A bundle two inches in diameter can handle as many as 20,000 calls at one time.

The Interexchange Channel

When the message reaches the telephone company central office a decision is made that determines which route it will follow on its next leg. The portion of the channel that spans the greatest distance is the **interexchange channel**, or **IXC circuit**. Originally, the IXC circuit existed in the form of wires strung on telephone poles or metal cables buried underground, connecting the central offices in the various cities.

The wire and metal cable channels still exist, but they are being replaced by fiber-optical cables and microwave signals. **Fiber-optical cables** consist of hair-thin strands of glass through which pulses of light are passed. The pulses are coded to represent the data. **Microwave signals** are very short electromagnetic waves transmitted in a line-of-sight manner and cannot bend to conform to the curvature of the earth. When the signals are transmitted on the ground they go from one **microwave tower** to another. The towers usually are spaced from twenty to thirty miles apart. The microwave signals can also be bounced off of a satellite that is 23,300 miles from the earth, orbiting at a speed that permits it to remain stationary in relationship to the earth. The transmission stations that both send and receive the satellite signals are called **earth stations**, and have the same appearance as the dishes used to receive satellite TV signals.

The decision of which IXC path to follow is made by a computer in the telephone company central office, and is based on the volume of traffic at that particular time. For example, if you place three calls from Philadelphia to Baltimore, the first might go by earth-bound microwave transmission, the second by satellite microwave, and the third by underground cable.

Billing Methods

The common carrier can use several billing methods to charge you for the channel use. The same methods are used for data communications as for voice. The simplest arrangement is a **dial-up circuit** that is established by dialing the receiver's number. A firm can make an unlimited number of local transmissions for a flat fee, and long-distance transmissions are billed separately. If there is much long-distance activity during the month, the firm can contract with the common carrier for **Wide Area Telecommunications Service**, a **WATS circuit**, which provides lower rates as the usage increases.

Both a dial-up circuit and a WATS circuit are **voice grade circuits**—they were designed to handle voice traffic. While the circuits are adequate for that purpose, they often do not offer the quality required to transmit the hundreds or thousands of data communications bits at a reasonable speed. The local loop equipment in some regions is very old and adds considerable noise to the circuit. Noise can also be added as the message is routed through the telephone company central offices where some of the circuits pass through mechanical relays. A firm can avoid the noise problem by leasing a **private circuit** or **private line** that can be used without restriction twenty-four hours a day, seven days a week. In addition, the common carrier can **specially condition** the circuit by adding such special devices as filters at the central offices. Such a specially conditioned circuit is called an **above-voice grade circuit**.

Receiving Modem and Multiplexer

The modem on the receiving end of the channel converts the signal back to the form of the computing equipment, and the multiplexer converts the multiple channels into a single one. This equipment, plus the remainder of the channel, is the property of the using firm.

The Front-End Processor

The front-end processor handles the incoming and outgoing data communications traffic for the host computer. Both computers can be of any type but a common configuration consists of a minicomputer that serves as the front-end processor and a mainframe that is the host.

The channel we have been describing up to this point is but a single path to the host. It is possible to have many, perhaps hundreds, of such channels, and each is connected to the front-end processor by means of a **port** as shown in Figure 10.9.

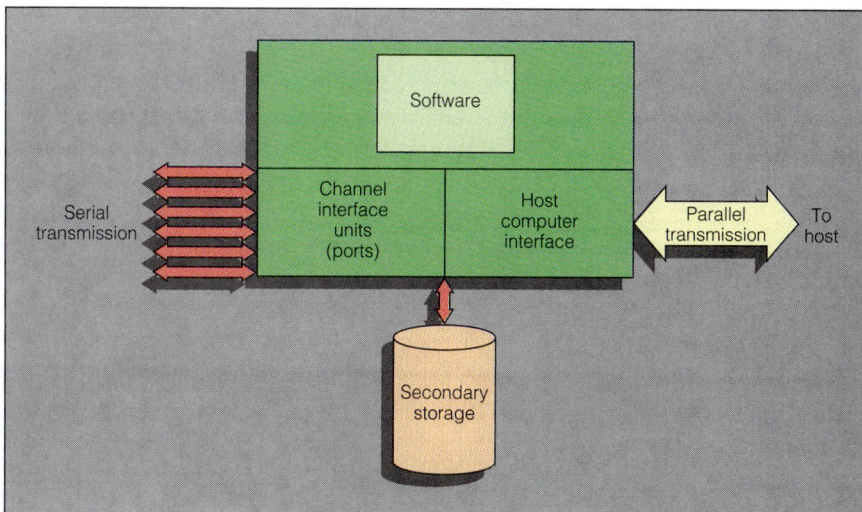

FIGURE 10.9

The Front-End Processor

The front-end processor functions as an input unit of the host by assembling the incoming messages and making that data available to the host. The front-end processor functions as an output unit of the host by receiving messages for transmission to the terminals.

While the transmission speed between the channel and the front-end processor can be relatively slow (in most cases the bits are transmitted **serially**, one after the other), the transmission speed between the front-end processor and the host can be fast (several bits can be transmitted at the same time—in **parallel**).

Some front-end processors perform a **message switching** function by routing messages from one terminal to another without involving the host. If, for any reason, the receiving terminal cannot receive the message (perhaps it is in use or is out of service), the front-end processor can hold the message in its secondary storage and send it later—a function called **store and forward**.

The Host

The host processes the incoming datacom messages in the same manner as data received from any other type of input unit. After the processing, messages can be transmitted back to the front-end processor for routing.

All datacom networks do not include the variety of hardware units we have described. Our descriptions are typical of larger organizations that use mainframes. Firms using minicomputers and microcomputers can use more modest configurations. Nevertheless, all network designs reflect the basic communication model.

NETWORK USES

There are two major approaches to using a datacom network—timesharing and distributed data processing.

Timesharing

A **timesharing** system is one consisting of a *single* computer shared by multiple users who gain access by means of terminals. This approach enjoyed its peak popularity during the late 1960s and early 1970s when firms sought to maximize their computing power by installing large computers at their headquarters. The first users were scientists and mathematicians who used the central computers to perform computations that required large systems. Figure 10.10 illustrates a timesharing system.

Distributed Data Processing

When small computers became popular, the firms changed their strategy and began *distributing* the minis and micros throughout the organization. When these systems are interconnected, the technique is known as **distributed processing** or **distributed data processing (DDP)**. It is important that you understand that even though small computers stimulated the DDP approach, such networks can include computers of all sizes.

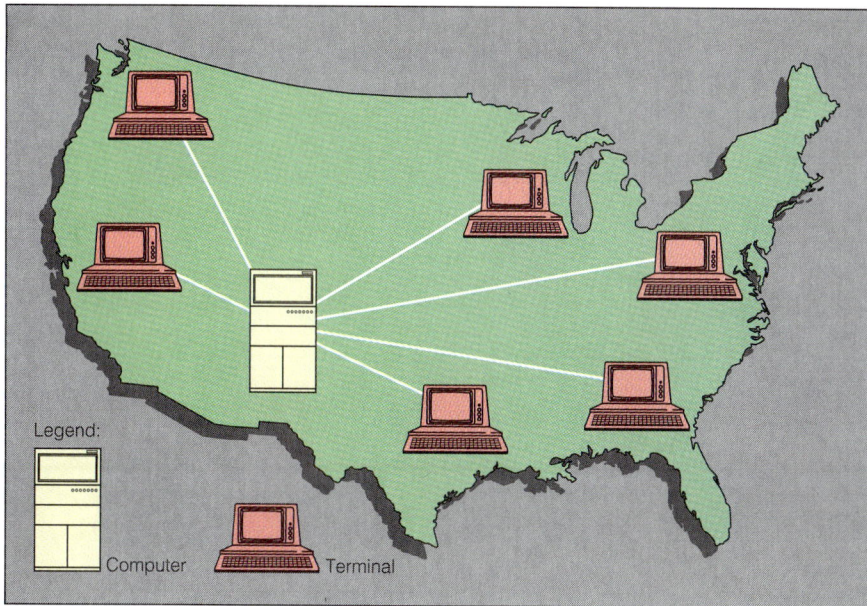

FIGURE 10.10

A Timesharing System

Legend:

Computer   Terminal

NETWORK STRUCTURES

When the network is used for distributed processing, the equipment can be interconnected in three types of patterns. The patterns are star, ring, and hierarchical. Timesharing networks take the form of the Star pattern.

Star, Ring, and Hierarchical Patterns

A **star network** includes a central computer as shown in Figure 10.11. The central computer is called the **central node**. A **node** is a point in the network where the circuits are interconnected by one or more units. The other nodes of the network can be computers of any size or they can be terminals.

When the network does not include a central node, the name **ring network** is used. Figure 10.12 shows a ring arrangement.

When more than two levels of computers exist in a hierarchy, as in Figure 10.13, the structure is a **hierarchical network** or **tree network**. This structure is especially applicable to firms with intermediate-sized computers installed in regional offices.

Within each of these three types of patterns, different datacom circuits and special network types can be used as described below.

Point-to-Point Circuit

The simplest type of circuit is the **point-to-point circuit**, and it consists of a single terminal or computer on one end and a single computer on the other. It could connect two nodes in a star or ring or hierarchical network. The basic data communication schematic in Figure 10.2 illustrates this type.

FIGURE 10.11
A Star Network

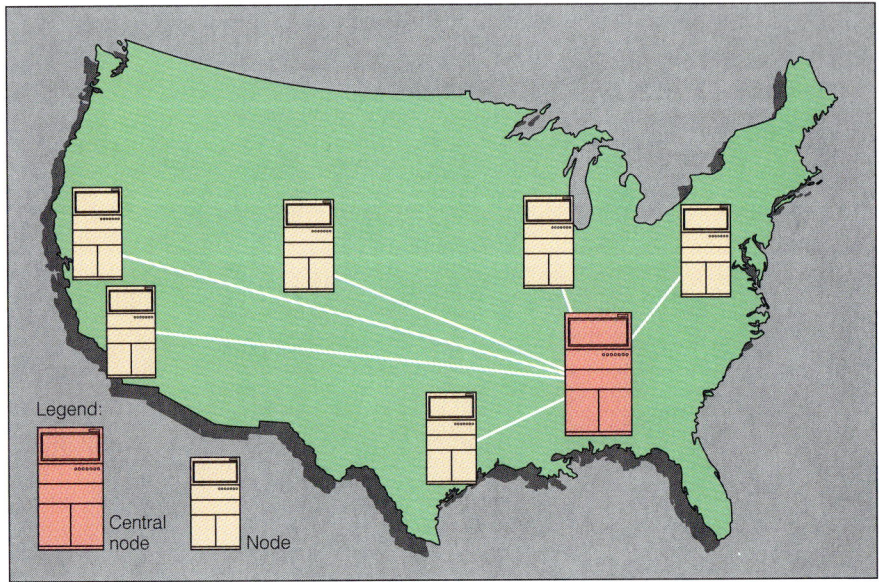

FIGURE 10.12
A Ring Network

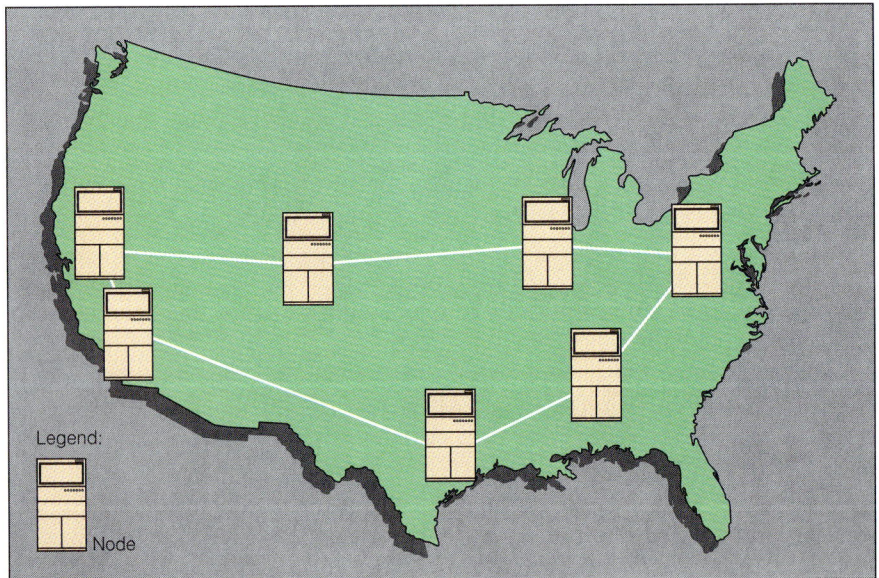

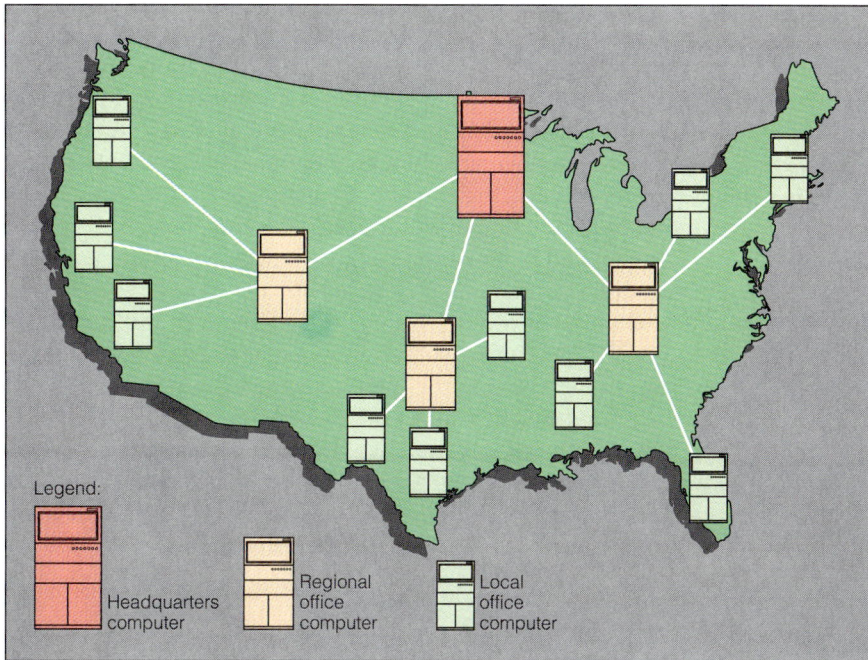

FIGURE 10.13
A Hierarchical, or
Tree, Network

Multidrop Circuit

A more common practice is to attach multiple terminals to the same channel. This configuration is called a **multidrop circuit** or **multipoint circuit** and is pictured in Figure 10.14. The front-end processor determines which terminal will use the channel at a given time.

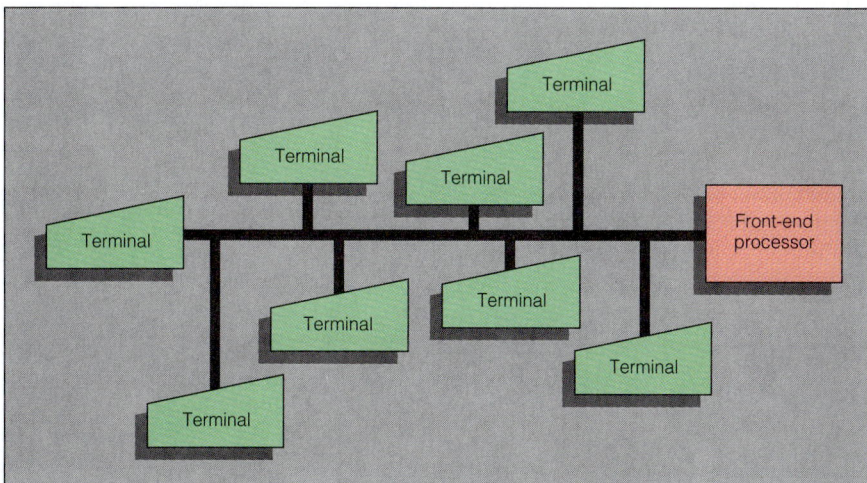

FIGURE 10.14
A Multidrop Circuit

Packet Switching

A firm with a large volume of datacom traffic can consider using a **packet switching network** as shown in Figure 10.15. Each circle represents a **switching node**, or **SN**, that includes a computer and software. The front-end processor uses **packet assembly and disassembly**, or **PAD**, software to subdivide messages into fixed-length blocks (of perhaps 128 bytes) called **packets**. The software enables the packets to be routed from one SN to another on their way to their destinations. Some of a single message's packets can follow one route, and some of the packets can follow another.

The decision of which route to use is based on the available channels and the traffic. If a portion of the network is out of service, another route can be used. As shown in the figure, some routes can consist of more than a single IXC. The multi-IXC routes are the ones with the heaviest traffic.

Packet switching is an efficient way to use a complex network such as a hierarchical structure. It offers the added security of alternate routes when part of the network is out of service. A firm can construct its own packet switching network by leasing private lines to serve as the IXC channels, or it can lease service from a **public packet switching network** such as Telenet or Tymnet.

Local Area Networks (LANs)

The type of network currently receiving the most publicity is the **local area network**, or **LAN**. All of the equipment and circuitry of a LAN are owned and operated by the firm. A common carrier is not involved unless the LAN interconnects with an IXC. In most cases the LAN is restricted to a single building or several buildings in the same area, but that is not an absolute requirement.

FIGURE 10.15

A Packet Switching Network

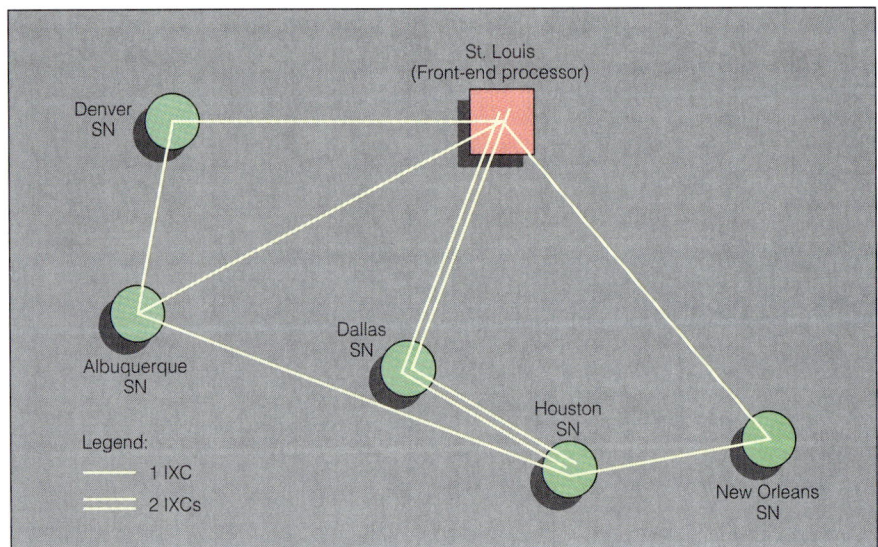

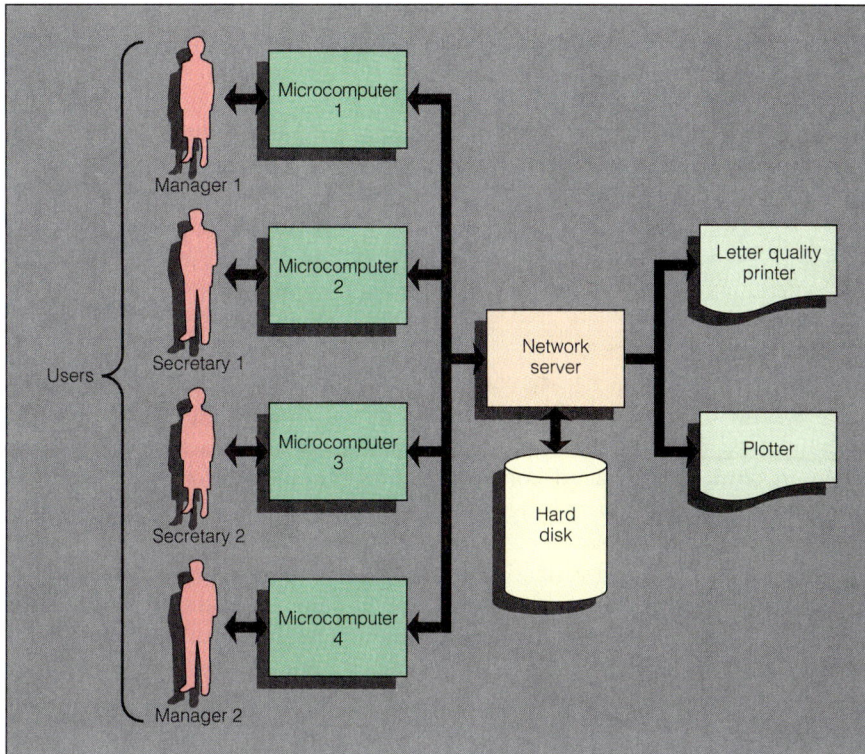

FIGURE 10.16
A Local Area
Network

One reason that LANs are so popular is because they are most often used for office automation. Figure 10.16 shows a LAN consisting of four microcomputers located in users' offices and a large micro called the network server. The **network server** includes a DASD and other devices such as letter quality printers that can be used by all of the micros in the network. For example, manager 1 can use expert system software stored in the network server DASD to prepare a graph that is plotted on the plotter. Manager 2 can use word processing software in the network server DASD to type a letter that is printed on the letter quality printer. The LAN enables the users to share the devices, thus saving money.

Three types of circuitry are available to connect the devices in the LAN. The firm can select between twisted pairs, coax, or fiber-optical cables. The choice is influenced by such factors as distance, susceptibility to interference on the circuit, and cost. Twisted pairs are the least expensive but have the most limited capability. Coaxial and fiber-optical cables can carry video signals that enable the firm to engage in teleconferencing, an office automation application that we discuss in Chapter 14.

Fiber-optical cables provide a high-quality channel and the costs are decreasing as the technology becomes more widely adopted. One advantage is that it is extremely difficult for a computer criminal to tap into the

LAN Circuitry

circuit. A datacom network utilizing fiber-optical cables thus has the potential of being more secure than a network composed of twisted pairs or coax. However, this difficulty of tapping can be a disadvantage when new users must be added to the network.

LAN Software

Special software enables workstations to share the peripherals. Most of the software is located in the network server, but some is located in each workstation. One of the most popular LAN software systems is NetWare, marketed by Novell, Inc. In a Novell network, the network server contains the NetWare operating system, and each workstation contains a NetWare shell. It is called a **shell** because it fits around the microcomputer's operating system.

LAN Control Methodologies

The way that messages transverse a LAN is determined by the type of LAN control that is used. Two popular control methodologies are the contention-based approach and the token-passing approach.

When **contention-based control** is applied, any microcomputer node that wants to transmit a message first listens to the network for a busy signal. When a signal is not detected, the node sends the message.

Since there is no centralized control, two or more nodes may attempt transmission at exactly the same time. This is called a **collision**. In order to avoid collisions, it is necessary to implement certain control schemes. With the contention-based approach, the network control is relatively simple, however network performance can quickly degrade when the transmission load becomes heavy.

Contention-based control is implemented in Ethernet, one of the earliest LAN designs that was developed jointly by Xerox, DEC, and Intel. Still very popular, Ethernet is based on a bus-oriented wiring scheme that enables data to be transmitted at speeds up to 10 mbps (million bits per second).

When **token-passing control** is employed, centralized network control is achieved by means of a token. A **token** is a set of data bits that are passed from node to node. A node can only send a message when it has the single token of the network. The method is similar to a track relay in which a runner can only run with the baton.

The network control is more complicated in token passing than in a contention-based scheme, but the token passing guarantees regulated access. Token-passing control is implemented in IBM's Token Ring Network and in General Motors' Manufacturing Automation Protocol.

Client/ Server Computing

An approach to network use that is currently stimulating much interest is client/server computing. **Client/server computing** is based on the notion that some functions are handled best on a local basis and some are handled best on a central basis. Therefore, client/server computing is a blend of the timesharing approach that features central use, and the distributed processing approach that emphasizes local use. Client/server computing can involve computers of any size in any network configuration, but the most common form is one or more interconnected LANs.

In a typical client/server computing network, application processing is shared between clients and one or more servers. A **client** is a user who accesses the network by means of a desktop computer. **Desktop computer** is the name given to a microcomputer that is used as a PC or a workstation. A **workstation** is a micro configuration that is tailored to a user's needs. Workstations are used by employees ranging from secretarial and clerical workers to executives. A **server** can be a computer of any size—a mainframe, a mini, a workstation, or even a micro—that provides a control function for the network.

Client/server computing is a much more complex hardware and software configuration than either timesharing or distributed processing. Any system in the network can access and use any other available systems. In this way, unused computing capacity in a desktop can be utilized by other desktops in the network, or work can be downloaded to the desktop from a sever. The key to client/server computing is the network server software that provides control points for critical functions such as hardware sharing, data sharing, database management, storing and forwarding, network management, batch processing, and the interconnection of multiple networks.

The current interest in client/server computing is a result of technological, economic, and organizational forces working together. The technological forces consist of advances in microcomputers and data transmission technologies, database management systems tailored to network use, and graphical user interfaces. Economic forces are applied by an international marketplace that demands maximum efficiency in the use of information resources. Organizational forces include the migration of many computing activities from the central computing center to user areas.

In the client/server environment the information specialists focus on the firm's main applications that run on the servers, and the end users develop applications to run on their desktops. In order to take full advantage of client/server computing, applications must be developed specifically to run in such an environment. The concept is so new that there are only a handful of applications today that were developed with such a specific use in mind.

DATACOM SOFTWARE

The datacom network can include many hardware units such as multiplexers and modems designed specifically for data communications, but it can also include general-purpose computers. Software enables the network units to perform the datacom tasks, and can exist at any point in the network. It is common practice to locate some of the software in the host, but most is located in the front-end processor. Additional software can be located in other units such as the cluster control units and terminals. Different names are used for the software, depending on its location.

Software in the Host

The name used to describe the datacom software in the host is **telecommunications monitor (TCM)**. This software supplements the portion of the operating system that handles the data transmission between the host and the front-end processor. Although the functions performed by the TCM software vary from system to system, it typically enables the host to:

- Put messages in a particular order based on their priorities.
- Perform a security function by maintaining a log of activity for each terminal and verifying that a particular terminal is authorized to perform the requested task.
- Interface the datacom network with the DBMS. Most mainframe DBMSs have versions that permit networked users.
- Handle minor disruptions in processing (such as the temporary loss of power) by periodically saving the status of primary storage. The term **checkpoint** is used to describe the point in the processing where the status is saved. When a disruption occurs, primary storage is restored to its condition at the previous checkpoint, and any subsequent processing is repeated. This is known as **checkpoint and restart** activity.

Software in the Front-End Processor

The name used for the datacom software in the front-end processor is **network control program (NCP)**. This software ordinarily performs the following functions:

- Determine if terminals want to use the channel. One approach is to **poll** the terminals. Various techniques can be used, with the most straightforward being **roll call polling** where each terminal is asked in sequence if it wants to use the channel.
- Maintain a record of channel activity by assigning a **date and time stamp** to each message, along with a unique serial number.
- Convert the codes used by one type of equipment (such as IBM) to another (such as DEC).
- Perform an editing function on incoming data by checking for errors and rearranging the format.
- Add and delete routing codes. Codes are added to outgoing messages to route them to the proper terminals, and codes are deleted from incoming messages before transmitting them to the host.
- Maintain a history file in secondary storage of messages handled during the past twenty minutes or so. The file can be used to recover from a disruption.
- Maintain statistics on network use.

These are only a few of the functions performed by software in the front-end processor. It is easy to see that it is the workhorse of the network.

PROTOCOLS AND NETWORK ARCHITECTURES

One of the characteristics of the datacom field since its inception has been the wide variety of hardware and software products on the market. The products are marketed by computing firms such as NCR and DEC, and by communications firms such as AT&T and U S Sprint.

This variety has been a blessing for datacom users since it has stimulated competition among the suppliers and made available a wide selection of models. However, the variety has been a burden in that it has made it difficult to interconnect the different suppliers' products.

In the datacom field the name **protocols** is used to describe the rules for interfacing, or interconnecting, the various units. The datacom devices follow the protocols in communicating with one another. This has been called shaking hands.

Luckily, some of the suppliers saw the problems coming before the situation got out of hand. IBM was among the first. In 1970 IBM was marketing 200 different datacom products that could be interconnected fifteen different ways. IBM management decided that a set of standards should be defined that could serve as a guide for future developments.

SNA

IBM named its system of protocols **Systems Network Architecture**, or **SNA**. In designing SNA, IBM considered all of the activities necessary in transmitting data through a network with a user at one end (called the **user node**), the host computer at the other (called the **host node**), and several **intermediate nodes** that consist of such other devices as the front-end processor and cluster control units.

IBM separated the *physical* activities that transmit the data from the *logical* activities that control the physical transmission. SNA was aimed at the logical activities.

SNA classified the logical activities into *layers*. The purpose of the layers was to insulate the user from changes in the datacom hardware and software. For example, the firm could convert from a network of dial-up lines to a LAN and the change would not affect the user or the user's software.

Other Manufacturers' Protocols

SNA was received so well that other computer manufacturers developed their own standards. For example, Burroughs announced its Burroughs Network Architecture (BNA), and Honeywell developed its Distributed System Environment (DSE). However, users did not regard the large number of manufacturers' "standards" as the solution to their problem. For example, IBM's SNA made it easy to interface IBM hardware and software, but it did not help the user who wanted to mix IBM products with those of other datacom suppliers.

The OSI Model

The problem of incompatibility between datacom products affected users on a worldwide basis, and in 1978 the International Standards

FIGURE 10.17   The OSI Model

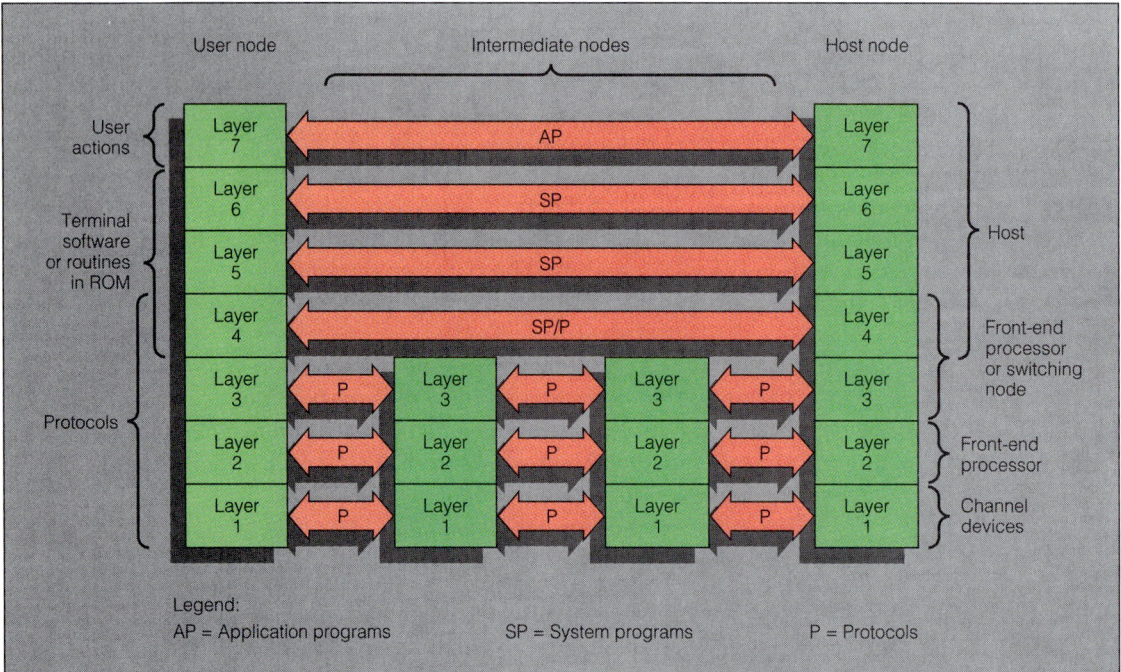

Organization announced a system of network protocols and named it the **Open Systems Interconnection**, or **OSI model**. The OSI model also uses layers to define the logical and physical activities.

Figure 10.17 illustrates the OSI model. The host node is at the right, the user node is at the left, and the intermediate nodes, such as those of the front-end processor and the cluster control unit, are in between. The bottom three layers appear in all nodes, but the upper four layers appear in only the host and user nodes.

The brackets at the right of the figure indicate which hardware units are used in performing the functions of the various layers. The brackets at the left indicate whether the functions are performed by user actions, terminal software or routines in the terminal ROM, or by protocols.

The arrows linking the nodes at each layer are labeled to indicate the form of the linkage—application programs (AP), system programs (SP), and protocols (P). A layer in one node "talks" to the corresponding layer in another node.

Each of the layers is described briefly:

1. *Physical layer*. Transmits the data from one node to another.
2. *Data link layer*. Formats the data into a record called a **frame** and performs error detection.
3. *Network layer*. Causes the data on the physical layer to be transferred from node to node.

4. *Transport layer.* Enables the user and host nodes to communicate with each other. It also synchronizes fast- and slow-speed equipment as well as overburdened and idle units.

5. *Session layer.* Initiates, maintains, and terminates each session. A **session** consists of all the data transmitted as a unit, including signals identifying the beginning and the end. A session is like a telephone call that begins with Hello and ends with Good-bye. Standard log-on and user identification routines are used to initiate datacom sessions.

6. *Presentation layer.* Formats data for presentation to the user or the host. For example, information to be displayed on the user's screen is formatted into the proper number of lines and number of characters per line.

7. *Application layer.* Controls user input from the terminal and executes the user's application program in the host.

How the Architecture Handles the User/Host Interface

Let us assume that the user wants to use a mathematical model located in the host to select the best pricing strategy. The user indicates that the pricing model is to be used by entering instructions in the terminal, under control of layer 7 (the application layer). Layer 6 (the presentation layer) changes the input data into the format used for transmission, and layer 5 (the session layer) initiates the session. Layer 4 (the transport layer) selects the route the message will follow in traveling from the user to the host node, and layers 3 and 2 (the network layer and data link layer respectively) cause the data to be transmitted through layer 1 (the physical layer).

When the message reaches the host node, control moves up the layers to the application program (the model) in the host. Communication from the host back to the user follows the same pattern—down the layers in the host node, across to the user node, and up the layers in the user node.

Some OSI Protocol Examples

An example of a protocol on the physical layer is the RS232c plug used to interconnect datacom hardware. The plug, pictured in Figure 10.18, is used by all manufacturers of datacom equipment.

An example of a layer 2 (data link layer) protocol is the format for a message frame, pictured in Figure 10.19. The flags identify the beginning and the end of the frame, and the address causes the message to be routed to its destination. The control field specifies the type of frame, and the frame check character field is used to detect (and possibly correct) errors.

Putting Datacom Protocols in Perspective

Because of IBM's large customer base, SNA has become an unofficial standard. Approximately three-fourths of the IBM mainframe users adopted SNA. DEC's Digital Network Architecture (DNA) also achieved a large following.

The OSI model has picked up support rather slowly. One reason is that protocols were not initially announced for all of the layers. Protocols for the

FIGURE 10.18
The RS232c Plug

FIGURE 10.19
A Message Frame

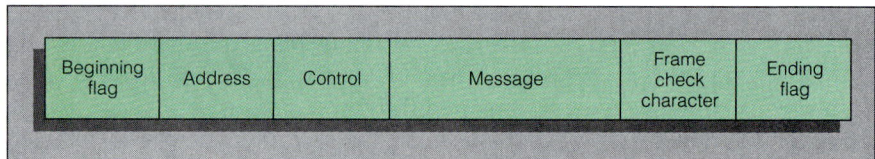

Beginning flag	Address	Control	Message	Frame check character	Ending flag

first three layers were announced in 1978 but did not receive widespread use until the mid-1980s. Protocols for all layers were not scheduled for definition until the early 1990s. By all rights, the OSI model should become the true datacom architecture standard. In the meantime, many users will continue to support the computer manufacturers' architectures, which may incorporate gateways to make them compatible with the OSI model.

DATACOM SECURITY

A networked computer is exposed to a much higher security risk than one located in a single room. The datacom channels and their terminals are open invitations to computer criminals, who can be thousands of miles away, to embezzle funds and steal trade secrets. When a firm implements a datacom network, special attention should be given to such security risks.

Firms recognize that complete datacom security is an impossibility, but various measures are used in combination to provide a level of security that is both affordable and acceptable. Datacom security precautions fall into five areas: organizational responsibility, software, hardware, facilities and procedures, and an overall datacom security plan.

Organizational Responsibility

Someone in the organization should have overall responsibility for the datacom activity. This is the **network manager** who reports to the CIO. The network manager was described in Chapter 6, and appears on the organizational chart of the information services unit in Figure 6.9. It is the responsibility of the network manager to incorporate security measures into the system and to monitor performance to ensure that the security is maintained. The network statistics provided by the front-end processor software play a big role in this monitoring activity. In a large organization the network manager will oversee a staff of data communications specialists who design, implement, and maintain datacom systems.

Software Controls

Users should be required to enter passwords in order to gain access to the system. Routines in the host computer can ensure that both the terminal and the user are authorized to engage in the requested activity. Then the front-end processor should maintain a log of each message. The log can identify the place, date, and time of entry into the system—useful information in catching computer criminals and identifying system weak points.

Hardware Controls

The manufacturers of datacom equipment recognize the importance of security, and design units aimed specifically at achieving that objective. Two examples are encryption devices and port protection devices.

Encryption Devices

In Chapter 9 we described how the database contents can be encrypted. The same coding precaution can be taken for data transmitted through the network. Special **encryption devices** can be incorporated in the network as shown in Figure 10.20. The hardware on the sending end codes the message by using an **encryption algorithm**, and the hardware on the receiving end decodes the message using the same algorithm. The algorithm is never changed, and, in fact, there is no real attempt to keep it secret. What is kept secret, however, is the key used by the algorithm to code and decode the message. The key is changed frequently—perhaps daily—as a way to thwart computer criminals who might intercept messages as they are transmitted through the network.

FIGURE 10.20   Encryption Devices in the Datacom Network

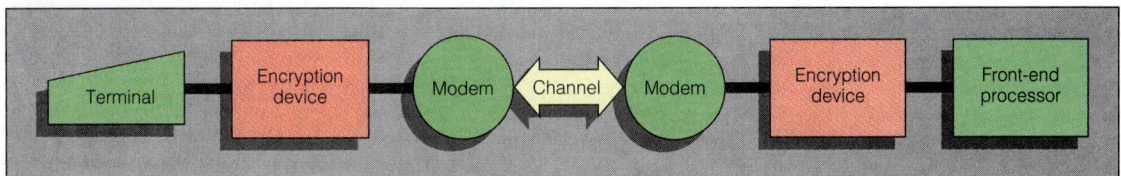

A **port protection device** is a microcomputer driven unit attached to the front-end processor to intercept calls dialed by users who wish to establish a link with the host. Some computer criminals randomly dial numbers and listen for the typical high-pitched tone usually emitted by the modem when a link is established. Then, they work to gain access to the system.

Port protection devices use several means to screen out unauthorized calls. Some devices replace the modem tone with a recorded human voice or simply silence. The computer criminal is then unaware that the computer number has been reached. Other devices can require the caller to key in a password. The caller hangs up while the host conducts a security check. Then the port protection device dials the caller's number to establish the connection. This ensures that the connection is made with the user's terminal—not one at another location belonging to a computer criminal. Port protection devices with this feature are said to have a **call-back ability**.

Facilities and Procedures

Rooms containing such datacom equipment as front-end processors, multiplexers, and terminals can be kept locked, and it is possible to lock the terminals themselves. You need a key to use a locked terminal just as you need a key to start your car. You can even enclose a terminal in a protective steel cabinet that is bolted to the floor.

In addition to facility controls, procedures can be established to add an extra measure of security at the point where users gain access to the system by establishing a dial-up connection. The telephone number of the computer center can be changed frequently, and calls can even be taken by human operators who identify the callers before access is granted.

Overall Datacom Security Plan

The network manager should identify each type of potential datacom security threat and design one or more measures to eliminate or minimize each one. A **datacom control matrix**, such as the one pictured in Figure 10.21, can be prepared. The components of the datacom network are listed down the left-hand side, and the threats are listed across the top. Attention is given to each cell, and specific security measures are identified for each. The numbers in the cell represent the measures. For example, number 7 can represent "Acknowledge the successful or unsuccessful receipt of messages." A cell with several numbers represents a portion of the system that is well secured against that particular threat. A cell with no numbers indicates a potential trouble spot.

When managers and information specialists consider the various security measures in Chapters 8, 9, and 10, and implement the appropriate mix, they can have confidence that the computing resource is well secured.

THE ROLE OF DATACOM IN DECISION MAKING

Datacom influences decision making in both an individual and an organizational way.

FIGURE 10.21   Datacom Control Matrix

		Threats								
		Errors and omissions	Message loss or change	Disasters and disruptions	Breach of privacy	Security/ theft	Reliability (uptime)	Recovery and restart	Error handling	Data validation and checking
C o m p o n e n t s	Host computer or central system	1, 2, 3, 4, 7	1, 2, 3, 4, 5, 7	1, 8, 11 13, 16	6, 8, 24	6, 8, 24	1, 13, 16			6, 24
	Software	1, 2, 3, 4, 7	1, 2, 3, 4, 5, 7	1, 8, 16	6, 8, 24	6, 8, 24	1			6, 24
	Front-end communication processor	1, 2, 3, 4, 7	1, 2, 3, 4, 5, 7	1, 8, 13, 16	6, 8, 24	6, 8, 24	1, 13, 16			6, 24
	Multiplexer, concentrator, switch	1, 2, 3, 4, 7	1, 2, 3 4, 5, 7	1, 8, 13, 16	6, 8, 24	6, 8, 24	1, 13, 16			6, 24
	Communication circuits (lines)	12		10, 15, 16 18			15, 16			
	Local loop	12								
	Modems	12, 18	18, 24	8, 9, 10, 11, 13, 14, 15, 16, 18	24	24	9, 10, 11 13, 14, 15, 16, 17, 18	9, 10, 11 14, 15	18, 19, 20 22, 23	
	People	5	5, 7		6, 8, 24	6, 8, 24				6
	Terminals/ distributed intelligence		2		6, 8, 24	6, 8, 24	1			6, 24

Individual Influence

Datacom makes the computing resource available to every person in the firm regardless of geographic location. This can be seen especially in time-sharing where the users share a centrally located computing resource. Assume that a firm with a nationwide operation has its headquarters and its central computer center in Minneapolis. A plant manager in Sunnyvale, California, has exactly the same amount of computer resource available as a manager at the Minneapolis headquarters.

In a similar way, datacom provides uniform computer support throughout the organization. Assume that our Minneapolis company replaces the managers' terminals with microcomputers that are interconnected to the central computer in a star network. Now the Sunnyvale manager has *some* computing power in her or his own micro, but also can tie in with the Minneapolis computer or other computers in the network when a larger or different computer configuration is needed.

Until datacom, the computer was a tool to be used personally by only the information specialists. Datacom is one of the reasons for the popularity of end-user computing.

Organizational Influence

Datacom enables a firm to pursue a strategy of either centralized or decentralized decision making. In a firm that stresses **centralized decision making** all of the important decisions are made by top management at headquarters. Datacom contributes to this arrangement by providing for the flow of data from the organization's widespread operations into the headquarters' computer where information is made available to top management. Datacom also contributes by providing a means of communicating top management's decisions throughout the organization.

In a firm that practices **decentralized decision making**, top management delegates the authority for making certain decisions to lower-level managers. In this scenario the lower-level managers can access the central computer and use the hardware, software, and data that typically reside at headquarters. The lower-level managers can solve their own problems by using the central computer in a timesharing manner or by using other computers in the network when distributed processing is practiced.

SUMMARY

The basic data communications schematic has the same general appearance as the basic communication model. All of the interconnected computer and communications devices are called a network. A fundamental network consists of a terminal and a computer that serve as sender and receiver, modems that code and decode the messages, and a channel. A more typical network consists of multiple terminals controlled by a cluster control unit. There are five types of terminals—keyboard, push-button telephone, POS, data collection, and special purpose. Terminals can also be either intelligent or dumb. Multiplexers are added to each end of the channel to enable the transmission of multiple messages at the same time. Modems are always needed, even when the channel transmits the messages in a digital, rather than analog, fashion. The channel consists of three major sections—a local loop, the IXC circuit, and another local loop. The IXC circuit can consist of wires, coaxial cables, fiber-optical cables, land-based microwave, or satellite microwave.

The front-end processor plays a key role in the network, coordinating the channel devices, selecting message routes, and converting the serial transmissions from the channel to a parallel form for the host and vice versa. It is possible for the front-end processor to perform some functions independent of the host, such as message switching.

Networks enable the computer to be used in two major ways—timesharing or distributed processing. A timesharing network includes only one computer; a DDP network includes more than one. Both timesharing and DDP networks can be arranged in a star, ring, or hierarchical pattern.

Different device configurations can exist within a network. The configuration that includes only a single device at each end is called a point-to-point circuit, and when multiple terminals are used it is called a multidrop circuit. Packet switching is used for very large message volumes. The LAN is gaining popularity as a way that the firm can install a complete, in-house network, including the channel. LANs are often used for office automation.

When firms are confronted with the dilemma of processing large jobs centrally and smaller user jobs in user areas, the remedy is client/server computing. A server, which can be a computer of any size, is connected to user terminals, which usually take the form of desktop computers or workstations. The client/server software enables work to be shifted from one computer to another so as to utilize available capacity.

Most of the datacom software resides in the front-end processor, but much can be in the host. It is also possible to locate software nearer to the user, such as in the cluster control unit and even the terminal.

In an effort to standardize the interfacing of datacom equipment, several network architectures have been developed. IBM introduced SNA, and was followed by the other mainframe manufacturers. ISO also announced its OSI model. These architectures typically view the logical tasks that control the physical movement of data as multiple layers and use combinations of hardware, software, and protocols to achieve the transmission.

Security is potentially the weak point of the datacom network. The firm can address the security problem by designating a network manager, using available software and hardware controls, designing facilities and establishing procedures that contribute to security, and establishing an overall security plan.

Datacom makes it possible for a firm to follow a strategy of either centralized or decentralized decision making. In a firm that uses datacom for data gathering and decision transmission, all problem solvers have access to the same computing resources.

KEY CONCEPTS

The basic communication model

The basic data communications schematic

How the computing and communications hardware and software work together to transmit data through a network

The distinction between timesharing and distributed processing

Client/server computing

How layers of logical datacom activities control the physical transmission of data

How a datacom control matrix provides the basis for an overall datacom security plan

The manner in which datacom influences problem solving in both an organizational and an individual sense

KEY TERMS

Channel
Data communications,
   teleprocessing, telecommu-
   nications, datacom
Network
Circuit, line
Modem
Host computer
Front-end processor
Dumb terminal

Intelligent terminal
Common carrier
Dial-up circuit
Wide Area Telecommunica-
   tions Service, WATS circuit
Timesharing
Distributed processing, distri-
   buted data processin (DDP)
Local area network (LAN)
Client

Server
Protocol
Systems Network Architecture
   (SNA)
Open Systems Interconnection
   (OSI) model
Datacom control matrix
Centralized decision making
Decentralized decision making

QUESTIONS

1. What are the five components of the basic communication model?

2. What device performs the coding and decoding function in a data-com network? Is it required when the channel handles data in a digital fashion?

3. What is the main role of the front-end processor in a datacom network?

4. List the five types of terminals. Identify with an asterisk the types a manager would use.

5. What role do multiplexers play in a datacom network?

6. What technologies can be used in the local loop to transmit data? What technologies exist in the IXC circuit?

7. Name two advantages to a firm that leases a private circuit.

8. What are the two major uses of a datacom network? What distinguishes the two?

9. What is the role of the network server in a LAN?

10. What technologies can be used to transmit data in a LAN? Which would be used if the firm wanted to engage in videoconferencing? Which offers the greatest security?

11. What is a protocol?

12. How many logical layers are in the OSI model? How many physical layers?

13. Why is it unnecessary to maintain the secrecy of the datacom encryption algorithm?

14. Who in the organization would have the main responsibility to develop a datacom control matrix?

15. Does datacom facilitate centralized or decentralized decision making? Explain.

COMPUTER THIEVES GET
$300,000 from Mission S&L

Depositors' Funds Safe, Mission President Says

Officials of Mission Savings and Loan reported Friday that an audit revealed that someone expert in computer theft gained access to their central computer and embezzled $300,000. A log of the computer's activity indicated that the act took place on Monday night and that a terminal located in the Southside branch office was used.

The thief, or thieves, transferred the money from several accounts to one that had been opened by a Fred Dugan only last week. On Tuesday morning the funds were withdrawn from the Eastside branch by someone posing as Dugan.

Mission employees were unable to provide police with a description of Dugan, saying only that he appeared nervous and as he left the branch he asked the security guard for "directions to the nearest Ferrari dealer."

Headquarters for Mission Savings and Loan is at their downtown location, and there are five branch offices in addition to the Southside and Eastside locations.

Amanda Stephens, Mission president, assures depositors that their funds are safe. Each depositor's funds are insured by the federal government and the theft will have no effect on any depositors' accounts, according to Stephens.

Officials described Mission's computer facilities as among the most modern in the Bay Area. From three to six terminals are located in each branch office, and there are approximately twenty-five terminals at the headquarters operation. Mission also has computer terminals located in the business offices of fifteen Little Miss Muffet Food Stores so that customers can make deposits and withdrawals as they shop. Little Miss Muffet employees operate the terminals for the customers.

Mission officials have taken steps to prevent a recurrence. All passwords used by Mission and Little Miss Muffet employees have been changed. Fred Berry, Mission's computer manager, told reporters that he was confident that the new passwords will provide complete security for the depositors. He stated that Mission plans to change the passwords periodically.

Stephens and the board of directors met yesterday to discuss additional security measures. According to Stephens, "We will take any steps necessary to prevent this from happening again."

1. Make a list of hardware devices that Mission can install to improve their security. Number each device—H1, H2, and so on.

2. List the security measures that can be performed by datacom software. Number each entry—S1, S2, and so on. The passwords required by the operating system and the log of activity maintained by the front-end processor are the only measures being utilized currently.

3. Prepare a datacom control matrix similar to Figure 10.22, but containing only a single column labeled Security/Theft. Down the left-hand margin list the system components: host, front-end processor, channel, terminals, people. Post the numbers from Questions 1 and 2 to the appropriate cells. Which portion of the network is secured the best? The least?

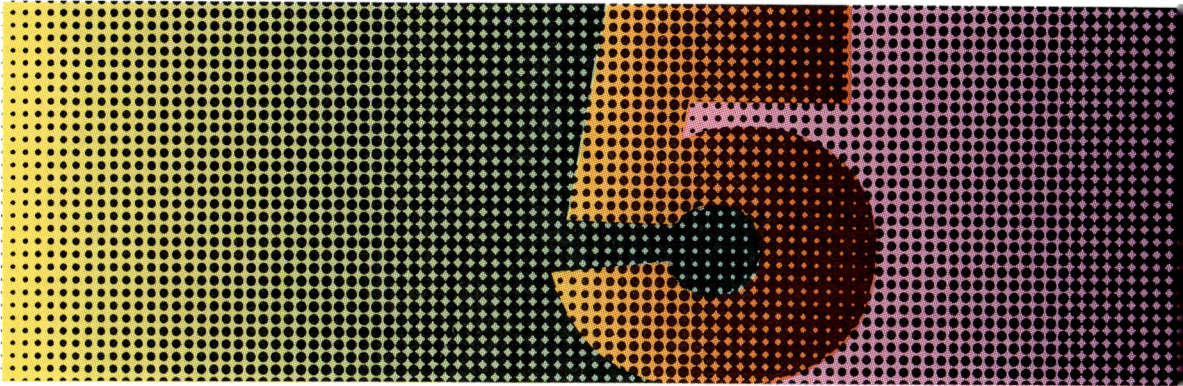

Problem-Solving Systems

The jobs that computers perform are called *applications*. Very often the term *systems* is used. In the beginning, the only computer application was *data processing*. The firm's data processing system consisted of such subsystems as payroll and inventory.

As the larger firms successfully implemented their data processing applications, new challenges were sought. The computer was recognized as a tool that could produce information for management decision making. First, there was the concept of the *management information system*, or *MIS*. Then, a refinement known as the *decision support system*, or *DSS*, appeared.

Today, additional areas of computer use are emerging, and they apply the computer in completely different ways. One, aimed at employing computer and other electronic devices for the purpose of improving the communication of information, is *office automation*. The other, aimed at using the computer for the purpose of duplicating human reasoning, is *artificial intelligence* and its subset *expert systems*.

In Part 5 we explore each of these five major application areas in separate chapters. The descriptions illustrate how the fundamentals you have learned in other parts of the text are applied by business organizations in using the computer as a problem-solving tool. We conclude with a look at the future, recognizing emerging trends that will influence computer use.

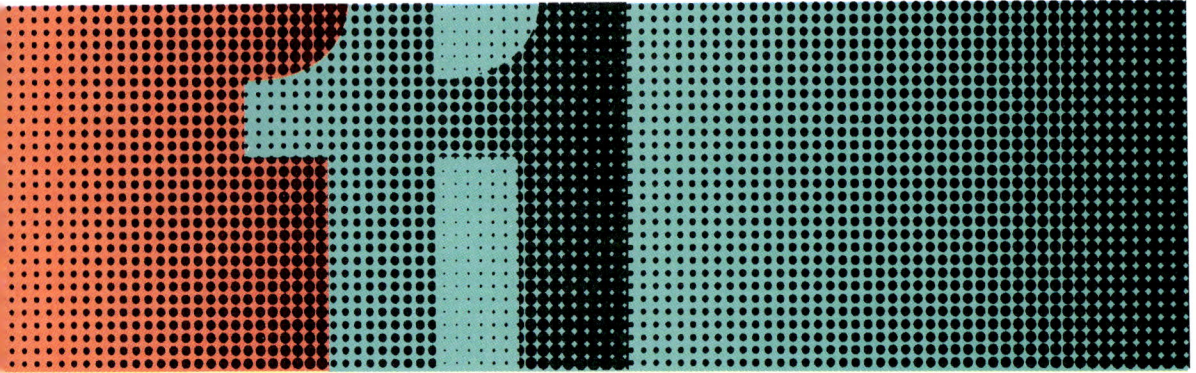

Data Processing Systems

LEARNING OBJECTIVES   After studying this chapter, you should:

- Understand what data processing is
- Have a fundamental familiarity with several primary data processing applications and how those applications can be performed by the computer
- Have an improved understanding of the variety of available prewritten data processing software
- Understand the role of data processing in problem solving

OVERVIEW

For the first decade of the computer era, firms only applied the computer to their accounting applications. This activity was called data processing. As computer use became more sophisticated, other applications were added—MIS, DSS, office automation, and expert systems. However, data processing remains the basis for the more advanced, problem-solving applications. The data processing system provides the storehouse of data used by the other applications.

In this chapter we define data processing and describe its main tasks. We explain how it differs from the other applications and how it is performed in a manufacturing, wholesaling, or retailing organization. The chapter concludes with a brief overview of prewritten data processing software and an explanation of how data processing supports problem solving.

WHAT IS DATA PROCESSING?

Data processing is the manipulation or transformation of such symbols as numbers and letters for the purpose of increasing their usefulness. Data processing includes all of the tasks involved with maintaining an accurate and up-to-date record of the firm's operations. The data processing tasks include gathering data that describes the firm's activities, manipulating the data into a usable form, storing the data until it is needed, and producing documents used by persons and groups both inside and outside the firm.

Figure 11.1 shows how the data is gathered from the input, transformation, and output parts of the physical system of the firm and stored in the database. The figure also shows how the documents are made available internally and to the persons and groups in the firm's environment who use the documents in their dealings with the firm. You notice in the figure that the data processing system has a responsibility to furnish documents to each environmental element except competition.

The environmental elements view the documents they receive from the

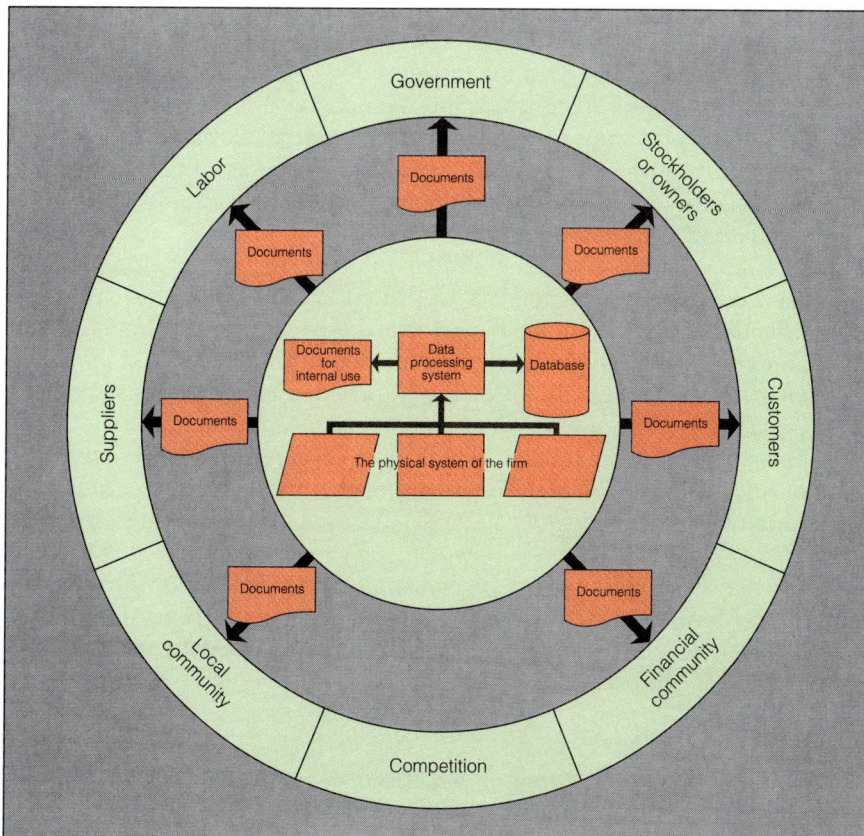

FIGURE 11.1

Data Processing Serves the Needs of Persons and Groups Both Inside and Outside the Firm

firm as containing *information*, but the firm views the documents as containing *data*. For example, the customers of a telephone company view the contents of the bills they receive as information—how much is owed, what long-distance calls were made, and when the bill is due. The telephone company, however, pays no particular attention to the hundreds or thousands of bills it prepares. The steps of printing the bills, inserting them in envelopes, and stamping the envelopes are most likely performed by machine. To the telephone company, the bills contain data.

The Data Processing System

The system performing the data processing tasks is the **data processing system**. In our view, the data processing system is the same as the **accounting system**. This view is based on the fact that early computers were applied only to accounting tasks, and the use was called **electronic data processing**, or **EDP**. In taking this view, we recognize that data processing can involve such nonaccounting activities as use of a mailing list to prepare form letters, preparation of statistical tables, and so on.

Over the years, four different types of data processing systems have been used:

- *Manual systems* The first systems were manual. They included only people, pens or pencils, and ledger books for posting the entries. The ledger books represented the record of the firm's operations.
- *Keydriven machines* The invention of such keydriven machines as the cash register, typewriter, and desk calculator provided a degree of relief in handling large data volumes. The machines enabled the firm's activity to be posted to the ledger books faster and more accurately than with manual systems.
- *Punched card machines* In a similar manner, the larger organizations recorded their transactions in punched card form and used the punched card machines to perform the necessary file maintenance and processing. The holes in the punched cards represented the status of the firm. Practically all of the punched card machines have been replaced by computers.
- *Computers* Most organizations today rely on computers to do a majority of their data processing. The record of the firm's activity exists in the form of magnetized spots on tapes, disks, or diskettes.

All of the firm's data processing systems do not lend themselves to the computer. Many such systems are too small or occur only infrequently. Therefore, the modern business organization processes its data using a combination of computer, keydriven machine, and manual methods.

The Objective of Data Processing

The objective of data processing is to produce and maintain an accurate and up-to-date record of the firm. Unlike the other major computer applications—MIS, DSS, OA, and expert systems—the firm does not decide whether it wants to perform data processing. The firm is required by law to maintain a record of its activity. Elements in the environment such as federal and state governments, stockholders, and the financial community demand that the firm engage in data processing. But even if the environment did not demand it, the firm's management invariably would implement data processing systems as a means of controlling the firm's activities.

DATA PROCESSING TASKS

Regardless of whether the data processing system is manual, keydriven, computer, or a combination, four main tasks are performed.

Data Gathering

As the firm performs its activities of providing products and services to its environment, each action is described by a data record. Each item purchased by a customer is described by a record, as is each job completed by a factory worker and each payment made to a supplier. When the action involves an environmental element, it is called a **transaction**. There are sales transactions, purchase transactions, stock transactions, loan transactions, and so on. For this reason, the term **transaction processing** is used.

The data processing system, therefore, is designed to gather the data that describes each of the firm's internal actions and its transactions with its environment.

Data Manipulation

It is necessary to manipulate the data in various ways to transform it into a usable format. The data manipulation operations include:

- *Classifying* Data elements are included in the records to be used as **codes** for identifying and grouping the records. For example, a payroll record includes codes that identify the employee (employee number), the employee's department (department number), and the employee's payroll classification (payroll class).
- *Sorting* The records are arranged in certain sequences, based on the codes or other data elements. For example, the file of payroll records is arranged so that all of the records for each employee are together and the records for each employee are in date sequence.
- *Calculating* Arithmetic and logic operations are performed on the data elements that produce additional data elements. In a payroll system, as an example, the hourly rate is multiplied by the hours worked to produce the gross earnings.
- *Summarizing* There is so much data that it is necessary to synthesize it, or boil it down, to produce totals and subtotals. Problem solvers usually work with summaries rather than detailed data. The summaries enable the problem solvers to "see the forest rather than the trees."

Data Storage

In a small firm there are hundreds of transactions and actions each day; in a large firm there are thousands. Epson, for example, claims that every ten seconds one of its customers installs an Epson computer or printer.

Each transaction is described by several data elements. For example, a sales record identifies *who* makes the purchase (the customer number), *what* is purchased (the item number), *how much* is purchased (the quantity), *when* it is purchased (the sales date), and the customer's *authorization* (the customer purchase order number). You can see how a data processing system can produce a large volume of data.

All of this data must be kept somewhere until it is needed, and that is the purpose of data storage. As explained in Chapter 9, the data can be stored on various magnetic media, such as tapes and disks, and these files are often called the database. Most of the data in the database is produced by the data processing system.

Document Preparation

The data processing system produces the outputs needed by persons and groups inside and outside the firm. The outputs are triggered by an action or a time schedule. An example of an output triggered by an action is the bill prepared each time a customer order is filled. An example of an output triggered by a time schedule is a payroll check prepared each week.

In most cases the outputs are in the form of printed documents; however, we saw in Chapter 8 that it is possible to produce computer output in several other forms as well.

Characteristics of Data Processing

There are several characteristics of data processing that distinguish it from the other computer applications. Data processing systems:

- *Perform necessary tasks* As explained, the firm does not choose whether it performs data processing. Data processing is a required activity.
- *Adhere to relatively standardized procedures* Regulations and accepted procedures spell out how data processing is to be performed. Organizations of all types process their data in basically the same manner. Accounting firms, such as Arthur Andersen and Price Waterhouse, audit the firm's books periodically to ensure that the proper procedures are followed.
- *Handle detailed data* Since the data processing records describe the firm's activities in a detailed way, they provide a means of reconstructing each action and transaction in sequence when that becomes necessary. Such a chronology of activities is called an **audit trail**.
- *Have a primarily historical focus* The data gathered by the data processing system generally describes what happened in the past. That is because many firms batch the transactions and update the files later. Online systems have the capability of also describing what is happening right now, but those data processing systems are still in the minority. In many cases management feels that the need for an up-to-the-minute accounting record does not warrant the expense. As hardware costs continue to decrease, more firms will implement data processing systems that reflect current activity as well as historical.

- *Provide minimal problem-solving information* The data processing system produces *some* information output for the firm's managers. The standard accounting reports such as the income statement (refer back to Figure 1.13) and the balance sheet (pictured in Figure 11.2) are examples. However, the information output is not the primary objective of the data processing system, as it is with the other application areas.

Whereas the line separating the other applications is often fuzzy, data processing can be distinguished by these listed characteristics.

CONSOLIDATED BALANCE SHEET		
Longhorn Plastics Industries, as of December 31		

FIGURE 11.2
A Balance Sheet

Assets		
Current assets:		
Cash and time deposits		$ 122,900
Accounts receivable, less allowances		772,800
Inventories		738,300
Total current assets		1,634,000
Investments		866,800
Properties, plants and equipment		2,687,300
Total assets		$5,188,100

Liabilities		
Current liabilities:		
Accounts payable	$	679,600
Accrued payroll and other compensation		134,400
Total current liabilities		814,000
Long-term debt		1,440,300
Commitments and contingent liabilities		2,254,300
Stockholders' equity:		
Capital stock		139,100
Retained earnings		2,794,700
Total stockholders' equity		2,933,800
Total liabilities and stockholders' equity		$5,188,100

A SAMPLE DATA PROCESSING SYSTEM

Let us look at a data processing system that we call the **distribution system**. This system would be found in a distribution type of organization, such as a manufacturer, a wholesaler, or a retailer. Many firms *distribute* products to their customers, so the distribution system is quite popular.

System Overview

Figure 11.3 is a context diagram of the distribution system. The context diagram is the data flow diagram that presents only the main features of the system. If you are unfamiliar with data flow diagrams (DFDs), you should read the description in Chapter 7 at this time.

The context diagram shows that the distribution system interfaces with three environmental elements—the firm's customers, management, and the purchasing/receiving system. By environmental we do not mean the environment of the *firm*, but the environment of the *system*.

The arrows show the data flow between the environmental elements and the system. Sales orders flow from the customers to the system; rejected sales order notices are sent to the customers when their orders are rejected for any reason. The system produces invoices and statements that flow to the customers, and payments flow from the customers to the system. The system also produces standard accounting reports that flow to management. The distribution system is connected to the purchasing/receiving system by the flows that describe items to be purchased and received. The purchasing/receiving system interfaces with the firm's suppliers.

FIGURE 11.3

A Context Diagram
of the Distribution
System

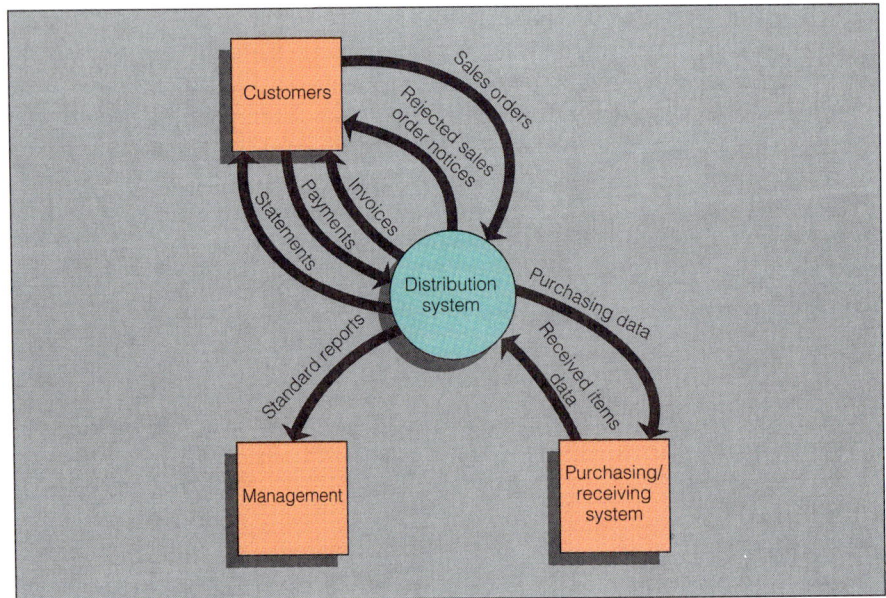

Subsystems of the Distribution System

A more detailed view of the system appears in Figure 11.4. This is a first
level DFD showing how the distribution system consists of the five main
processes, or subsystems, represented with circles. Each of the processes is
actually a complete system.

The **order entry system** screens customers' sales orders before entering
them into the system. When orders are accepted, the data flows to the
inventory system, which determines if the merchandise is available. If so,
the **billing system** is notified so that invoices can be prepared and sent to
the customers, charging them with their purchases. The billing system also
notifies the **accounts receivable system** that the customers owe money to
the firm. It is the responsibility of the accounts receivable system to process
the customers' payments. When customers do not pay on time, the
accounts receivable system prepares statements, which are sent to the customers as a reminder. The **general ledger system** gathers data from the
inventory and accounts receivable systems for the purpose of integrating it
into a complete description of the firm's activity. The reports that go to
management are produced by the general ledger system.

As the inventory system processes each item on a customer's order, a
check is made to determine whether the order caused the balance on hand
to drop to the reorder point, signaling a need to order replenishment stock.
When the reorder point is reached, the inventory system notifies the pur-
chasing/receiving system with purchasing data that an order for replenishment stock is necessary. The purchasing/receiving system notifies the
inventory system with received items data when the stock is received.

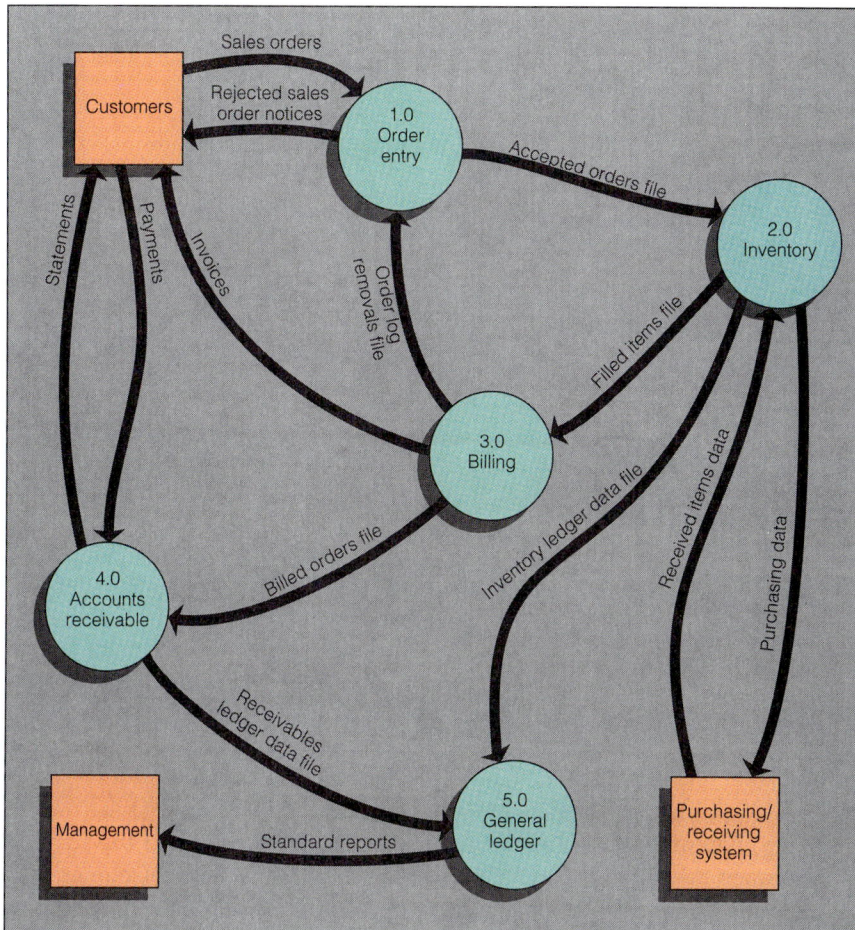

FIGURE 11.4

A First Level DFD of the Distribution System

You will notice that the five subsystems of the distribution system communicate with each other by means of data flows, which are actually data files. These files are necessary when the data is processed in a batch manner. When the data is processed online, it is possible that some or all of these files can be eliminated.

We will describe each of the subsystems separately, and document each with a second level DFD.

Order Entry

Figure 11.5 shows the four processes contained within the order entry system. Decimal positions are used in the process numbers to show that they are subsidiary to step 1.0 in Figure 11.4.

A document serving as the source of input data to a system is called a **source document**. The **sales order form** is the source document of the distribution system. It is designed to contain all the data needed to initiate

FIGURE 11.5

The Order Entry
System

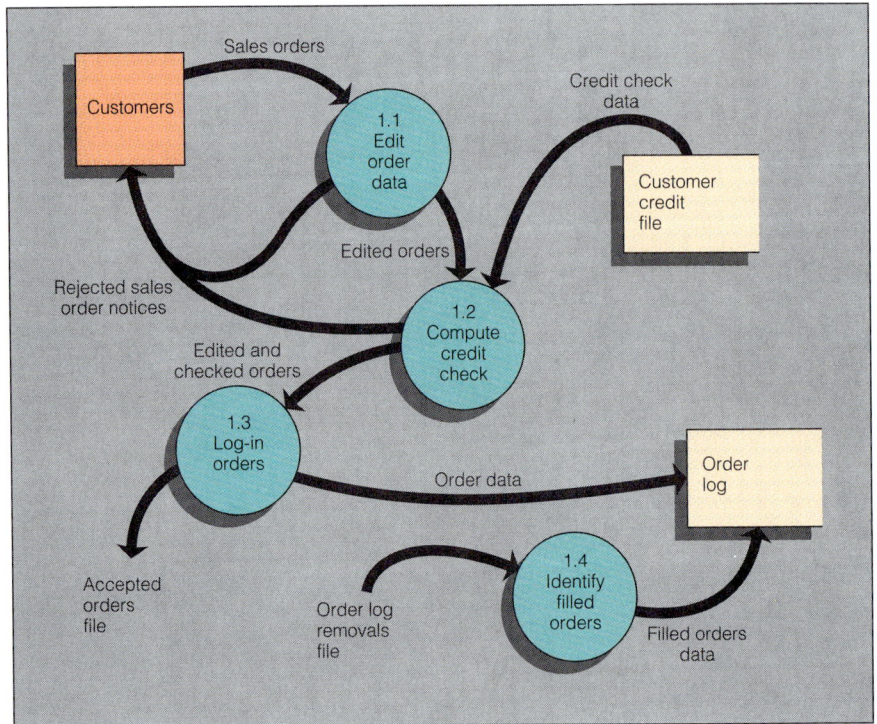

the processing of a sales order. A sample is included in Figure 11.6.

In some cases the customers mail the sales order forms to the firm. In other cases the firm has an order department where order clerks take orders over the telephone, filling out a form for each call. Some order forms are filled out by salespersons as they cover their territories.

1.1 Edit Order Data

The sales order form is checked for missing or incorrect data. Maybe the person filling it out forgot to include the customer number, or perhaps the item number does not match the item description. Errors are corrected when possible.

When error correction is not possible, a rejected sales order notice is sent to the customer, along with the rejected order. The notice explains why the order was rejected and asks that a corrected order be resubmitted.

The primary output from process 1.1 consists of the edited orders—the ones that pass the editing process. They serve as input to the next process.

1.2 Compute Credit Check

The order amount is added to the amount of the customer's accounts receivable—how much the customer owes for prior purchases. The receivable amount is obtained from a customer credit file as shown in the figure. The file also includes a credit limit for each customer. The amount of the current purchase plus the receivable amount is compared to the credit limit. When the credit limit is exceeded, the order is rejected. For example,

FIGURE 11.6	A Sales Order Form

L.L. Bean, Inc.
Freeport, Maine 04033-0001

Toll-Free Orders: 800-221-4221
24 Hours—7 Days a Week
100% Satisfaction Guaranteed
No Time Limit

FREE L. L. Bean Specialty Catalogs:
☐ Hunting Specialties #8589   ☐ Winter Sporting #8990
☐ Women's Outdoor Specialties #8985   ☐ Fly Fishing #8587 (Avail. 2/88)
☐ Home and Camp Specialties #8583   ☐ Spring Sporting #8584 (Avail. 3/88)

ORDERED BY: Phone(   )_____ ☐ Day ☐ Night
If name or address is incorrect please print correct information.

SC 7995 22
M G MC LEOD
1106 GLADE
COLLEGE STA   TX 77840

If a peel off label is available on the back cover, please attach it here.

GIFT ORDER or SHIP TO: Please print. Use only if different from "Ordered by".
☐ Mr.
☐ Mrs.
☐ Ms.

Street/Route   Box/Apt.

City   State   Zip

Gift Card—From

Federal Express Recipient Phone No.(   )_____

Page	Stock No.	Color	Size	Inseam	How Many	Description	Total Amount

If you need more space, please attach a separate sheet of paper.

PAYMENT METHOD

☐ MasterCard ☐ VISA
☐ American Express

Check or Money Order (Please, no Currency)
AMOUNT ENCLOSED $_____

Card Account Number

Month   Year
Expiration Date Required

Customer Signature

Item Total	
5% Sales Tax on Items Delivered in Maine	
Regular SHIPPING & HANDLING FREE within U.S.	Paid by L.L. Bean
Optional FEDERAL EXPRESS (See reverse side)	
SPECIAL SHIPMENT or Foreign Shipment (See reverse side)	
TOTAL	

if the customer already owes $1,200 and the credit limit is $1,500, any order in excess of $300 is rejected.

Orders that do not pass the credit check are returned to the customers, along with rejected sales order notices.

1.3 Log-In Orders

When orders are accepted, a brief identifying description of each is entered in an **order log**, which serves as a control to make certain that the orders are filled. For example, a customer might telephone and ask "Where is my order from last week?" The order log reveals whether the order was received. In a manual system the log is a ledger book and entries are made by hand. In a computer system the log might be stored in a DASD.

In addition to the log entries, records describing accepted orders are added to the accepted orders file, which provides the link to the next system in the chain—the inventory system.

1.4 Identify Filled Orders

The orders listed in the order log are unfilled. They are called **open orders**. When orders are filled, the billing system signals the order entry system with the order log removals file. The records for the filled orders are identified in some manner to indicate that they no longer are open. One approach is to add the date that the order is filled.

Inventory

When the customer orders are accepted, the next step is to determine if the merchandise is available. That is accomplished by the inventory system as illustrated in Figure 11.7.

2.1 Check the Balance on Hand

The item record is retrieved from the inventory file, and the balance on hand field is compared with the order quantity from the accepted orders record to see if adequate stock exists. If not, a backorder record is entered in the backorder file. A **backorder** means that "We can't fill the order now, but we will fill it later when we replenish our inventory."

When the order can be filled, the data to be used to bill the customer in the next system is extracted from the item record. This includes such data as item description, warehouse location, unit weight, and unit price.

2.2 Check the Reorder Point

When the order can be filled (the balance on hand is greater than or equal to the order quantity), a check is made to see if the new, reduced balance on hand caused the reorder point to be reached. Each item record contains a reorder point field. When the balance on hand drops below the reorder point, it is time to reorder. The reorder point is set high enough to allow sufficient time to receive the new supply before a **stockout** occurs (the stock is exhausted). When the reorder point has been reached, purchasing data is made available to the purchasing/receiving system.

FIGURE 11.7

The Inventory System

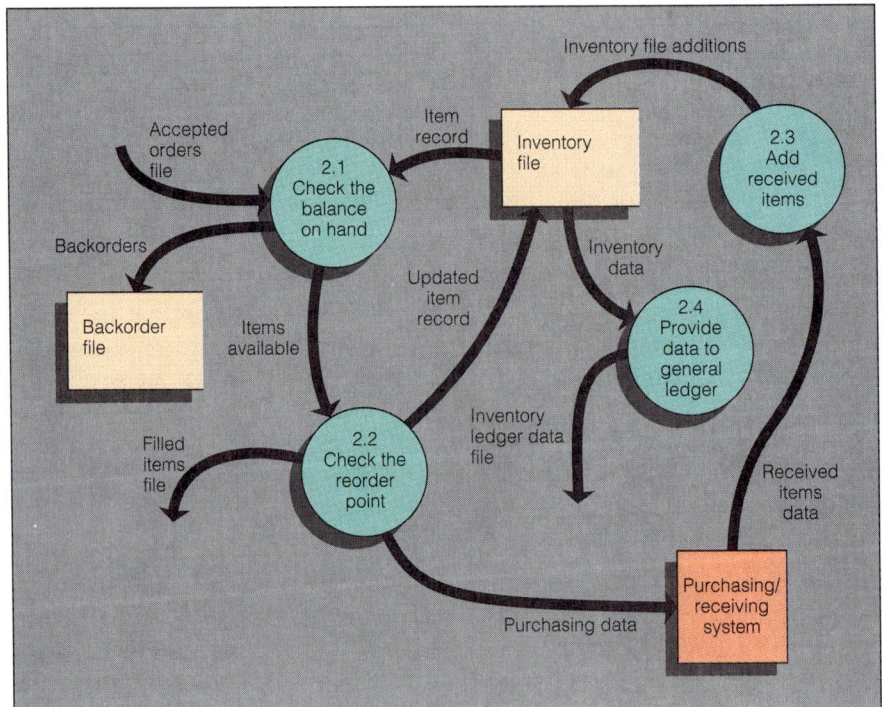

Records representing filled orders are written onto a filled items file for use by the billing system. Before the processing of the sales order is completed, the updated item record is written back to the inventory file. In those cases when the order is filled, the updated record contains the new balance on hand. In those cases when the reorder point is reached, the updated record also contains such data describing the purchase as the date and quantity of the order.

2.3 Add Received Items

The above processes reduce inventory balances to fill orders. Another process is necessary to increase balances when the replenishment stock arrives. This signal is provided by the purchasing/receiving system in the form of received items data. The balance on hand field in each received item record is increased by the quantity of the receipt.

2.4 Provide Data to General Ledger

As explained earlier, the general ledger system obtains data from several other subsystems within the data processing system. This step provides data from the inventory file.

Billing

The name **invoice** is used to describe the bill the firm sends to a customer. Figure 11.8 pictures a typical invoice. The system that prepares the invoices is the billing system, and its three processes are illustrated in Figure 11.9.

3.1 Obtain Customer Data

The data relating to the customer is extracted from the customer file. The data includes customer name and address, shipping instructions, and salesperson number.

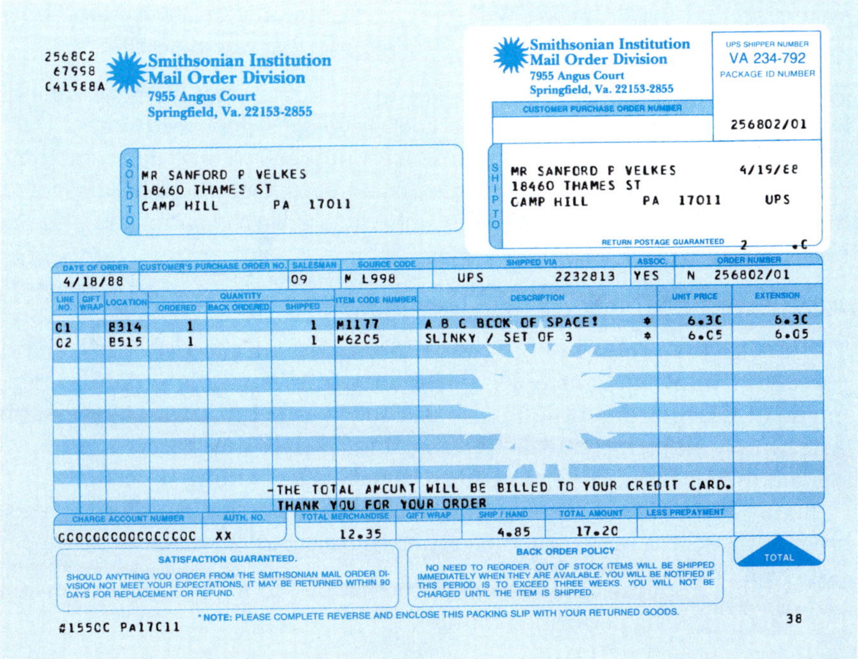

256802
67958
C419E8A

Smithsonian Institution
Mail Order Division
7955 Angus Court
Springfield, Va. 22153-2855

SOLD TO
MR SANFORD P VELKES
18460 THAMES ST
CAMP HILL PA 17011

Smithsonian Institution
Mail Order Division
7955 Angus Court
Springfield, Va. 22153-2855

UPS SHIPPER NUMBER
VA 234-792
PACKAGE ID NUMBER
256802/01

CUSTOMER PURCHASE ORDER NUMBER

SHIP TO
MR SANFORD P VELKES 4/19/88
18460 THAMES ST
CAMP HILL PA 17011 UPS

RETURN POSTAGE GUARANTEED 2 .C

DATE OF ORDER	CUSTOMER'S PURCHASE ORDER NO.	SALESMAN	SOURCE CODE	SHIPPED VIA	ASSOC.	ORDER NUMBER
4/18/88		09	M L998	UPS 2232813	YES	N 256802/01

LINE NO.	GIFT WRAP	LOCATION	QUANTITY ORDERED	QUANTITY BACK ORDERED	QUANTITY SHIPPED	ITEM CODE NUMBER	DESCRIPTION	UNIT PRICE	EXTENSION
C1		B314	1		1	M1177	A B C BOOK OF SPACE! *	6.30	6.30
C2		B515	1		1	M62C5	SLINKY / SET OF 3 *	6.05	6.05

-THE TOTAL AMOUNT WILL BE BILLED TO YOUR CREDIT CARD.
THANK YOU FOR YOUR ORDER

CHARGE ACCOUNT NUMBER	AUTH. NO.	TOTAL MERCHANDISE	GIFT WRAP	SHIP / HAND	TOTAL AMOUNT	LESS PREPAYMENT
C0C0C0C000C0CCC0C	XX	12.35		4.85	17.20	

TOTAL

SATISFACTION GUARANTEED.
SHOULD ANYTHING YOU ORDER FROM THE SMITHSONIAN MAIL ORDER DIVISION NOT MEET YOUR EXPECTATIONS, IT MAY BE RETURNED WITHIN 90 DAYS FOR REPLACEMENT OR REFUND.

BACK ORDER POLICY
NO NEED TO REORDER. OUT OF STOCK ITEMS WILL BE SHIPPED IMMEDIATELY WHEN THEY ARE AVAILABLE. YOU WILL BE NOTIFIED IF THIS PERIOD IS TO EXCEED THREE WEEKS. YOU WILL NOT BE CHARGED UNTIL THE ITEM IS SHIPPED.

*NOTE: PLEASE COMPLETE REVERSE AND ENCLOSE THIS PACKING SLIP WITH YOUR RETURNED GOODS.

#155CC PA17C11 38

FIGURE 11.8
An Invoice

FIGURE 11.9
The Billing System

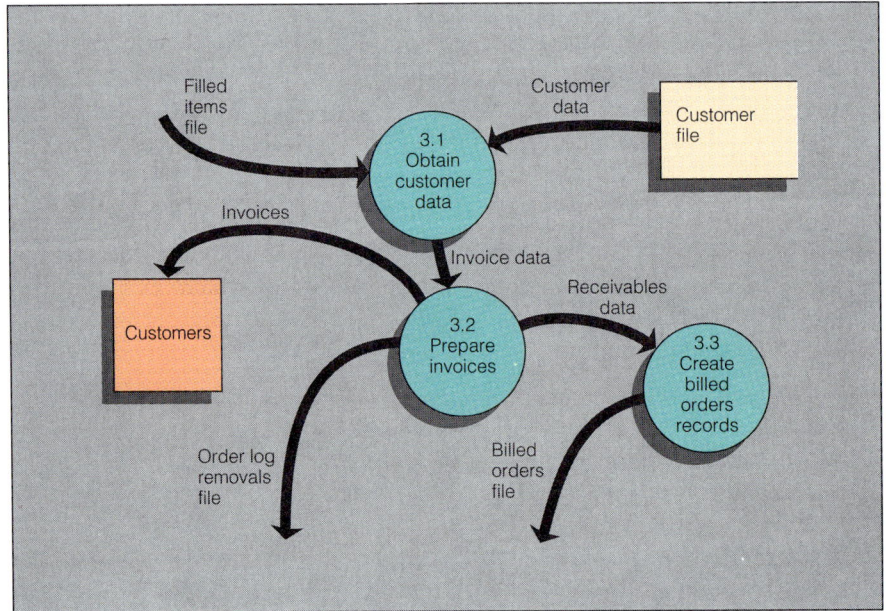

3.2 Prepare Invoices

Each item listed on the invoice is called a **line item**. The line items are **extended** by multiplying the unit prices by the quantities ordered. The extended amounts are accumulated to produce an invoice total. Perhaps a sales tax is computed and added. The invoices are mailed to the customers.

At this point we have filled the order and must notify the order entry system so that the order log will no longer show the order as being open. This notification is accomplished with the order log removals file.

3.3 Create Billed Orders Records

This process assembles the data to be entered in the accounts receivable file by the accounts receivable system. Each invoice is described with a billed orders record that includes the invoice number, invoice date, customer number, customer name and address, customer order number, salesperson number, and invoice amount. All of the billed orders records comprise the billed orders file.

Accounts Receivable

The invoice is the official notification to the customer to pay. It is common practice to allow the customer thirty days after the billing date to make payment. During this time the transaction is called a **current receivable**. After thirty days the transaction becomes a **past-due receivable**. Firms remind their customers of past-due receivables by mailing statements.

Figure 11.10 shows the accounts receivable system. The four processes are not linked in a sequence; each represents a separate activity.

4.1 Add New Receivables to the File

The records from the billed orders file are added to the accounts receivable file. This process is performed daily.

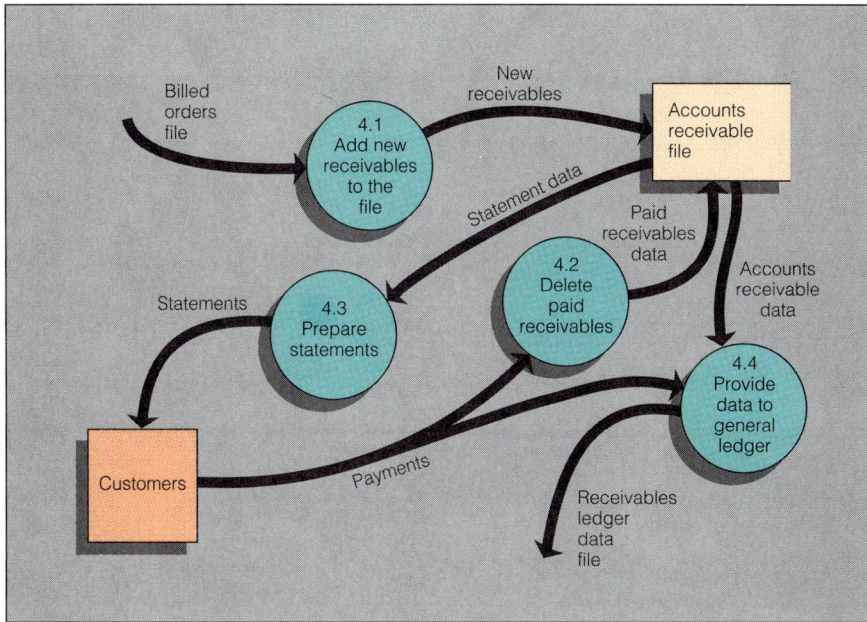

FIGURE 11.10

The Accounts Receivable System

Assuming that customer payments arrive each day, those receivables records are removed from the file on a daily basis.

4.2 Delete Paid Receivables

On a monthly cycle, **statements** are sent to customers with accounts receivable to remind them of their outstanding obligations. The statement usually contains only a single line entry for each **outstanding invoice**—one that has not been paid. The firm continues sending statements until each invoice is paid, or, in the case of unpaid invoices, the receivable is turned over to a collection agency or written off as a bad debt.

4.3 Prepare Statements

Also on a monthly basis, the receivables system supplies data to the general ledger system. The accounts receivable figure on the balance sheet (see Figure 11.2) comes from the accounts receivable system.

4.4 Provide Data to General Ledger

General Ledger

The general ledger system, as diagrammed in Figure 11.11, brings together the financial data describing the firm's activities.

The system consists of the general ledger file that includes such individual accounts as cash, finished-goods inventory, accounts receivable, and reserve for depreciation.

5.1 Maintain General Ledger

The inventory ledger data file was produced by the inventory system, and the receivables ledger data file was produced by the accounts receivable system. Additional inputs come from other systems not included in the distribution system.

5.2 Prepare Reports The standard reports (income statement and balance sheet) are prepared on a cycle basis—monthly, quarterly, or annually. These are periodic reports that the manager automatically receives.

FIGURE 11.11
The General Ledger System

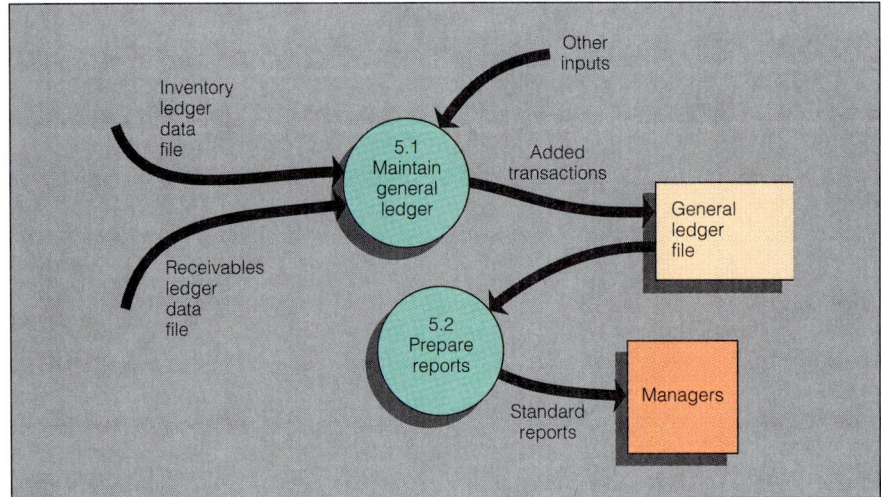

A COMPUTER-BASED DATA PROCESSING SYSTEM

The data flow diagrams show the steps necessary to accomplish the processing without showing the specific devices used. DFDs provide an excellent starting point for designing a system of any type—computer or noncomputer.

System flowcharts are a good way to document a system in a specific manner, showing the types of computing equipment used. If you are unfamiliar with system flowcharts, read that description in Chapter 7 before proceeding. Figure 11.12 shows how a DASD oriented computer configuration performs the distribution system activities. The steps below correspond to the numbered steps in the flowchart.

1. The sales order data is keyed into an online terminal. Only the data needed to process the order is entered—customer number, customer purchase order number, numbers of each of the items that are ordered, and quantities of the items. Data such as customer name and address is not entered since it already exists within the system.

2. The order entry program performs the processes described earlier. All of the input and output files are stored on a DASD. A printed output consists of rejected sales order notices mailed to the customers. The accepted orders file on a DASD provides the linkage to the inventory system.

3. The inventory system retrieves item records from the inventory file for items received and for accepted orders. Entries are made in the backorder file when a stockout condition exists, and in the purchas-

FIGURE 11.12

A System Flowchart of the Distribution System

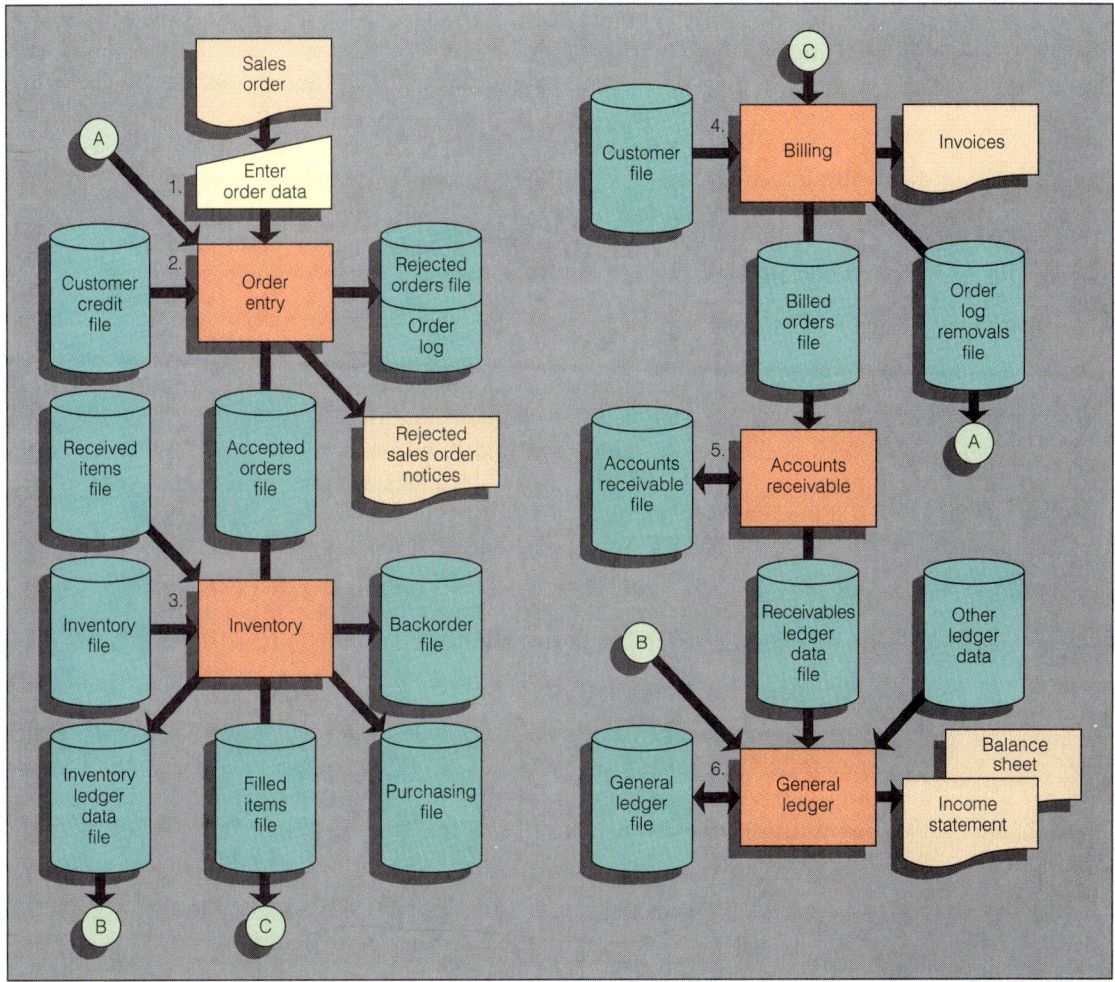

ing file when reorder points are reached. Data for the general ledger system is provided in the form of the inventory ledger data file. The filled items file provides input to the billing system.

4. The billing system prepares invoices and creates two files. The order log removals file is used to remove filled orders from the order log in Step 1, and the billed orders file provides input to the accounts receivable system.

5. The accounts receivable system updates the accounts receivable file with the billed transactions. Separate programs remove receivables records when payments are made and prepare monthly statements. Those programs are not shown.

6. The general ledger system receives input from the accounts receivable system, the inventory system, and other sources to maintain the DASD based general ledger file and prepare the reports.

In online processing, the first five steps (through accounts receivable) are taken for a single sales order before the next one is handled. Rather than batch the transaction data in the intermediate files connecting the systems as shown, the data is kept in primary storage and the systems are executed one after the other. This reduces the delay in preparing the invoices and filling the orders.

Even when online processing is used, the general ledger system typically processes data in a batch manner. In most cases, there is no need to update the general ledger accounts as transactions occur.

PREWRITTEN DATA PROCESSING SOFTWARE

A wider assortment of prewritten software is available for data processing than for any other application area. The reason is the standard way that most of the data processing applications are performed and the fact that all firms perform them. Most of the packages are written for microcomputers, but mainframe and minicomputer users are not neglected.

Prewritten data processing software can be obtained in two primary forms. One form consists of **accounting packages** designed to perform the main data processing tasks found in most organizations. The other form consists of **industry packages** tailored to specific industries.

Accounting Packages

Two approaches have been taken in producing accounting software. First, **separate application packages** are developed for each of the data processing subsystems such as inventory and purchasing. Second, **integrated accounting systems** are developed that include all, or most all, of the subsystems.

Separate Application Packages

Table 11.1 shows the approximate number of separate packages prepared for the IBM Personal Computer and the PC compatibles. There is quite a variation in the number of packages that are available. Inventory software is popular because the problem it solves is one of the most structured in business, and because it offers the opportunity to achieve significant reductions in inventory investment. Payroll software is popular because it is aimed at an application that every organization performs, although in a variety of ways.

Integrated Accounting Systems

There are about 125 integrated accounting systems designed so that data flows from one subsystem to the next. If a firm wants to computerize its entire accounting system, then the integrated approach is the way to go.

A good example of an integrated accounting package is **Champion Integrated Business Accounting Software: Business Accounting,** from Champion Business Systems, Inc. This package consists of the following modules:

Subsystem	Approximate number
Accounts payable	75
Accounts receivable	92
General ledger	90
Payroll	99
Inventory	126

Source: *The Software Encyclopedia 1992*, Volume 2 (New Providence, NJ: R. R. Bowker), pp. 1451–1969.

TABLE 11.1
Application Packages for the IBM PC

- General ledger
- Accounts payable
- Inventory
- Payroll
- Accounts receivable
- Job costing
- Job estimating.

The accounts payable module includes an ability to prepare purchase orders, and the accounts receivable module includes order entry and point-of-sale functions. There is an eighth module that enables users to prepare custom reports.

Prewritten data processing packages usually constrain the user in some manner—the maximum number of records that can be handled, the number of data fields per record, the maximum size of each field, and so on. Constraints such as these usually are easy for the small firm to live with. The constraints dealing with how the processing is performed can be more serious. For example, an inventory system that handles only a single storage location would be unacceptable to a furniture chain that has stock at several stores. If a package does not handle a transaction the same way the firm does, either the firm's practices or the software must be modified, or another package must be considered.

Prewritten Software Constraints

Industry Packages

Industry packages are those designed for particular fields such as law, agriculture, construction, and medicine. The support here is very uneven, with some fields receiving excellent support, and others receiving little or none.

Three industry packages are described below.[1]

Activity Tracker from Argos Software is a package designed to meet the needs of farmers and ranchers. There is considerable prewritten support in this area. Activity Tracker records all of the daily activities that a farmer or rancher is likely to incur, such as those dealing with crops, livestock, equip-

[1] These descriptions are based on those found in *The Software Encyclopedia 1992*, Volume 2 (New Providence, NJ: R. R. Bowker), pp. 1451–1969.

ment, employee actions, and meetings. The user defines codes that classify each activity in terms of When, Where, What, Who, and How information. When the user enters the transactions, the codes and descriptions are displayed on the screen to facilitate data entry. The database provides a wealth of information to the farmer or rancher concerning the operations.

Demand Deposit Analysis from Banker's Information Systems & Services Enterprises is designed to help banks treat all of a customer's accounts in an integrated manner. It can handle as many as sixty different banking services, such as checking account, savings account, and installment loans, and as many as twenty-five types of accounts for each customer. It prices and analyzes the cost of each service and provides management with output that is used to ensure adequate funds to cover the costs of all the services.

Construction Accounting Systems from CMA Micro Computer can be used by either a contractor or sub-contractor. It includes a general ledger system, a job cost and project management system, and a payroll system. The payroll system includes an ability to handle workers' compensation data. A capability is provided to prepare proposals and bids, and information output includes a trial balance, balance sheet, income statement, and detailed job cost reports.

Before we leave the industry packages we should make an important point. All of the packages do not address data processing exclusively. Many of the packages include decision-support features.

THE ROLE OF DATA PROCESSING IN PROBLEM SOLVING

Since data processing is characterized by large volumes of data, it is easy to get the idea that it can lend little support to problem solving. That is not true for two reasons:

1. Data processing systems *do* produce information output—usually in the form of standard accounting reports. These reports are especially valuable in the financial area of the firm and at top management levels.
2. The data processing system provides the rich database that can be used in problem solving. The database provides the input for periodic reports, special reports produced in response to management queries, mathematical models, and expert systems—the primary ways that the manager receives information from the computer.

Data processing is the foundation upon which other problem-solving systems, especially MIS and DSS, are built. The first step in providing the manager with computer support for problem solving is to implement a sound data processing system.

SUMMARY

The data processing system, or accounting system, maintains a detailed record of the firm's operations. The systems of most modern organizations consist of a combination of computer, manual, and keydriven machine methods. Unlike the other major computer application areas, the firm has no choice concerning data processing. It must be performed in order to provide the basis for control of the firm's operations by management and elements in the environment.

Data processing consists of four main tasks—data gathering, data manipulation, data storage, and document preparation. Data manipulation includes classifying, sorting, calculating, and summarizing.

There are several characteristics of data processing that distinguish it from the other application areas. Data processing performs necessary tasks, adheres to relatively standardized procedures, handles detailed data, has a primarily historical focus, and provides minimal problem-solving information.

A distribution firm uses five data processing subsystems to process customer orders—order entry, inventory, billing, accounts receivable, and general ledger. Each is a system that can be documented with data flow diagrams to show what is done, and documented with a system flowchart to show how the jobs are performed by the computer.

A wide variety of prewritten data processing software exists for computers of all sizes. The software comes in two primary forms—accounting packages and industry packages. The accounting packages can address separate data processing applications or several applications combined in an integrated fashion. The industry packages are aimed at the data processing applications in particular industries.

Data processing contributes to problem solving in two ways. It produces standard reports that summarize the firm's financial condition, and it provides the database of internal data used to prepare reports, respond to database queries, and simulate the firm's operations.

KEY CONCEPTS

How data processing captures the details of the firm's daily activity

How the main data processing tasks are unaffected by the methods used—manual, keydriven machine, or computer

Why data manipulation is necessary to make the data meaningful to users

The manner in which data flows from subsystem to subsystem in the process of filling a customer's order

The fact that it is not always necessary for the data processing systems to process data in an online manner

The constraints provided by prewritten software

The data processing system as the major contributor to the database

Data processing, transaction processing

Data processing system, accounting system

Transaction

Distribution system

Order entry system

Inventory system

Billing system

Accounts receivable system

General ledger system

Source document

Sales order form

Order log

Backorder

Invoice

Line item

Current receivable

Past-due receivable

Statement

Accounting package

Industry package

QUESTIONS

1. Who are the users of the output from the data processing system?

2. What four methods have been used to process data? Which one is obsolete? Which one(s) would you find in a firm such as American Airlines?

3. What can trigger an output from the data processing system?

4. What specific types of computer units (input, output, and secondary storage) would be necessary in order for the data processing system to reflect current activity?

5. What types of organizations use the distribution system?

6. What are the three environmental elements of the distribution system? Do they exist inside or outside the firm? Explain.

7. How many different source documents exist in the distribution system? Provide the name(s).

8. What checks are conducted before a sales order is accepted?

9. Distinguish between a backorder and a stockout.

10. Distinguish between an invoice, a bill, and a statement.

11. What numbers are multiplied together when a line item is extended?

12. When does a receivable become past-due?

13. Which file in the distribution system contains records representing outstanding invoices?

14. What distinguishes an accounting package from an industry package?

15. Name two ways the data processing system contributes to problem solving.

CASE PROBLEM

McCullin Brothers Wholesale Grocers

The traffic is pretty light as you drive to Computer City, the largest computer store in Waco. It's almost too good to be true. Not everybody has a chance to implement a brand new computer system from scratch—in a well-established, financially sound company. For as long as you can remember you have been aware of the sacrifices your parents made, and their parents before them, in founding McCullin Brothers Wholesale Grocers. For so many years the company didn't seem to change. The same small offices, warehouse that contained a thousand distinctive scents, and the three or four delivery trucks. You guess that it was the move to the big city that did it, putting McCullin Brothers right in the middle of a profitable market area.

Well, now it's up to you to continue the growth. Since you are the only member of the family who ever studied computers, you, Arnold McCullin, were the logical choice to implement the new computer system. With an unlimited budget from which to work, what more could anyone ask?

Earl: Welcome to Computer City. I'm Earl Gaston. Can I help you?

Arnold: You certainly can. I'd like to buy a computer and some software.

Earl: (Earl is seized by a sudden burst of energy.) Excellent! Are you with a company?

Arnold: Yes. McCullin Brothers.

Earl: I've seen the trucks. Do you know exactly what you want?

Arnold: I certainly do. I studied computers in college and have just finished an exhaustive study of the available micros. That's the size computer I want to start with. I've decided that the Toshiba T1100 PLUS is what I need. I noticed in the Yellow Pages that you carry them.

Earl: That's correct. But are you sure you want the Toshiba? We also carry the IBM Personal System/2. Most people want it. You might as well jump on the IBM bandwagon.

Arnold: I don't think so. The Toshiba is a PC compatible so I can use all of the PC software. I know I want the Toshiba.

Earl: O.K. I'll have a stock clerk get one from the storeroom and help you put it in your car. Now, you mentioned software . . .

Arnold: That's right. I would like for our first computer application to be Lotus. I studied it in college and want to use it to graph some accounting data. I think it will allow our managers to get a better handle on our financial situation. We can produce the balance sheet and income statement in a graphic form. I think the information would be much more useful that way than a bunch of numbers. Don't you agree?

Earl: Oh, definitely. We sell a lot of Lotus. You say that you want to graph accounting data? Where is the data going to come from? Are you going to put the accounting system on the computer?

Arnold: No, not yet. I'm anxious to get into decision support. I never could get too interested in accounting in college. We have an excellent accounting system, even though it is primarily manual. Our accounting department is growing with the company. We've learned that we must add a new accountant for about every five million dollars of additional sales revenue. But, there's an unlimited supply of accountants coming out of college, and they do excellent work. It takes them a little longer to close the books each month, but the books always balance. Our CPA says that's the important thing. I think I'll just leave the accounting system the way that it is and concentrate on decision support. That's my bag.

Earl: That's fine with me. We have some good accounting packages—some are designed specially for wholesaling—but I'll be happy to fix you up with Lotus. Step right this way and I'll write up your bill.

1. Can you give any reasons why Arnold is wise in beginning with decision support?
2. Can you give any reasons why he is not wise?
3. Assume that you were in several computer classes with Arnold and he calls you on the phone. He explains his situation and asks your advice (you made As and he made Bs). What would you recommend and what would your reasoning be? Be brief; it's a long-distance call.

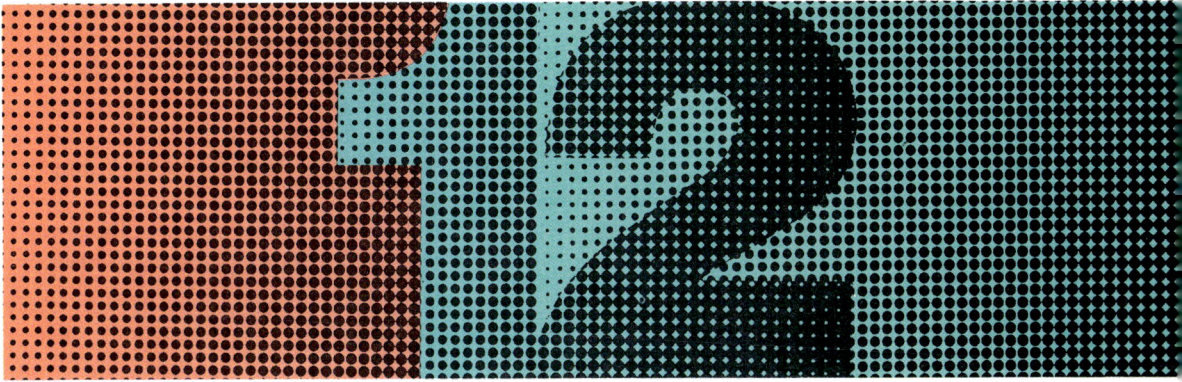

Management Information Systems

LEARNING OBJECTIVES   After studying this chapter, you should:

- Understand what a management information system (MIS) is and its main features
- Appreciate how the MIS can be subdivided into subsystems that recognize the specific information needs of managers in the functional areas
- Recognize that certain behavioral influences can affect the success of a computer project, and understand a fundamental strategy that can be followed in responding to those influences
- Understand the role of the MIS in problem solving

OVERVIEW

The first formal effort to build a computer-based system to provide the manager with problem-solving information was given the name *management information system*, or *MIS*. The MIS is a companywide information resource—shared by all managers on all levels and in all functional areas.

We begin the chapter with a definition of MIS and a model showing its major parts. The model depicts the MIS as a combination of resources—human, hardware, and software—that gathers data and information from both inside the firm and the environment. Data is stored in the system and is transformed into information. The information is made available to managers in the form of periodic reports, responses to database queries, and results of mathematical simulations.

Next we describe how the managers in the functional areas of marketing, manufacturing, and finance have created information systems that meet their particular needs. These functional information systems consist of subsystems that gather data and information, a database where the data and information are stored, and subsystems that transform the data into information made available to the managers.

We conclude the chapter by explaining how to overcome employee resistance to computer projects, and how the MIS supports problem solving.

WHAT IS AN MIS?

It was the mid-1960s, and most large firms had finally overcome the pains of implementing their first computers. It had been a difficult task since those organizations had accumulated huge volumes of data over the years and considerable effort was required to put the data in a form acceptable to the computers. The computer literacy within the firms was limited to the handful of information specialists, and those specialists had no real experience in guiding the implementation through the steps of the system life cycle. Accomplishments came slowly—by trial and error.

The firms had one factor on their side during those hard times: the computer was applied in exactly the same way as the keydriven and punched card machines had been—in performing accounting tasks. The tasks were well defined, and primarily affected the firm's accounting departments. Computer implementation consisted essentially of transforming the older routines into a computer form.

Early MIS Efforts

With the data processing systems on the air, both the firms' information specialists and the computer manufacturers wanted to keep the computer activity moving, and new application areas were sought. It did not take long to realize that the informational output of the data processing systems left much to be desired. For so many years the technology—the keydriven and punched card machines—had been incapable of providing management information. Now it became clear that the computer could fill that gap, and it looked as if it would be an easy task.

The firms who attempted the first MISs learned otherwise. The big barrier turned out to be the managers. As a group they knew nothing about the computer. They knew their jobs and they knew how to solve problems, but they had not given much thought to the role of information in problem solving. As a result, it was difficult for the managers to articulate exactly what they needed from the MIS.

This situation was frustrating to the information specialists. Since they knew little about management, they did not know what questions to ask. To the information specialists it appeared that the only solution was for them to design and implement systems to produce information that they *thought* the managers needed. This was done, and in many cases the systems analysts had guessed wrong and the systems were not used.

Over time the managers learned about the computer and about the processes they followed in solving problems. The information specialists also learned the fundamentals of management. The MISs were refined and expanded so that they more closely fit the managers' needs. The MIS eventually became established as a major computer application area.

A Definition of MIS

As firms refined their MIS efforts, the meaning of the term changed accordingly. Today, we can define the **management information system**, or **MIS**, as the formal and informal systems that provide past, present, and projection information in a written and oral form relating to the firm's internal operations and its environment. It supports the managers and employees and key environmental elements by furnishing information in the proper time frame to assist in decision making.[1]

For the most part, the terms in the definition are self explanatory. It is important, however, that two points be understood. First, the MIS consists of planned and documented formal systems, and informal systems developed "on the spot" to solve a particular problem at hand. Second, such elements in the firm's environment as customers, suppliers, stockholders, and the government also share the information output.

You can see from this definition that the MIS is quite broad. It is intended to provide *complete support* to *all managers* in solving *all types of problems*.

An MIS Model

Figure 12.1 illustrates the major components of the MIS. The arrows show the flow of data and information from both the physical system of the firm and from the environment. Data is directed to the **information processing resources**—the combination of hardware and information specialists that transform the data into information. The data and information can be stored in the **database**, and the data is transformed into information by the **software library** of computer programs.

Information from both internal and environmental sources is directed to the **users** who make decisions affecting changes in both the physical system of the firm and the information processing resources. Data does not go to the users directly, but is transformed into information by the information processing resources.

THE CONCEPT OF FORMAL MIS SUBSYSTEMS

As firms gained experience in implementing companywide MIS designs, managers in certain areas began tailoring the system to fit their own needs. These **functional information systems** received much publicity in some

---

[1]This definition paraphrases one by Walter J. Kennevan, which appeared in his September 1970 article in *Data Management*, titled "MIS Universe."

FIGURE 12.1

An MIS Model

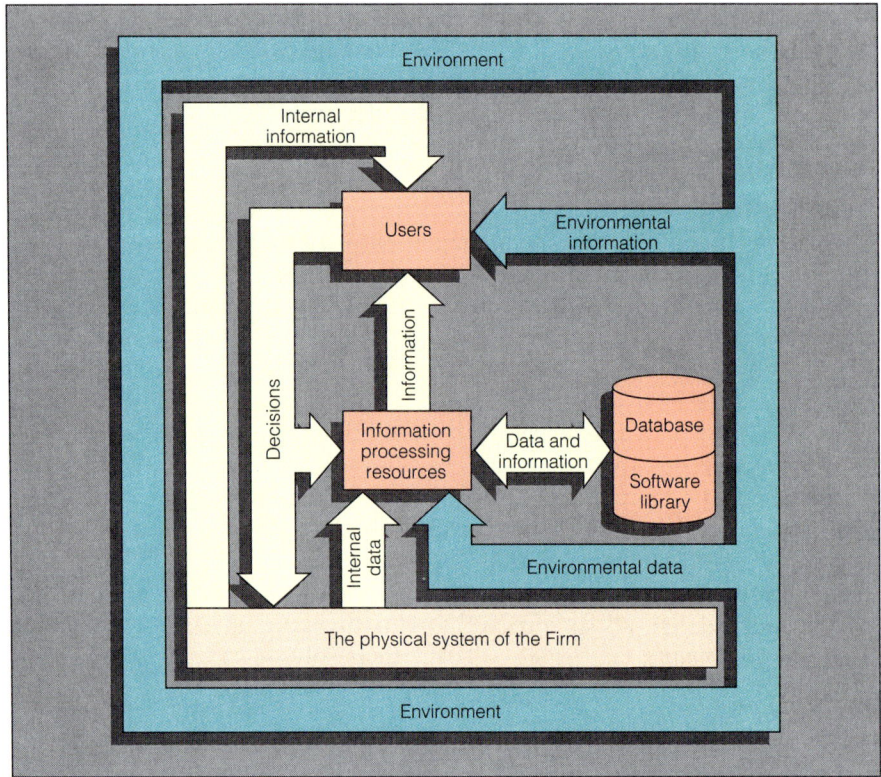

areas and not so much in others. Marketing was the first area to conceive the notion of a functional information system, and considerable effort was spent in preparing diagrams and descriptions of how the computer could be applied to the entire range of marketing operations.

In the following sections we address the MIS subsystems that represent the three major functional areas—marketing, manufacturing, and finance. There is nothing that separates the functional information systems *physically*. For example, much of the database used by one functional subsystem is also used by others, and many of the programs used in one system are used in others. Functional information systems are a *logical* way of thinking about the MIS rather than a *physical* separation.

THE MARKETING INFORMATION SYSTEMS

A **marketing information system** is a subset of the management information system providing information to be used in solving the firm's marketing problems.

We can illustrate the marketing information system with the model in Figure 12.2. We will use the same general model format for the other func-

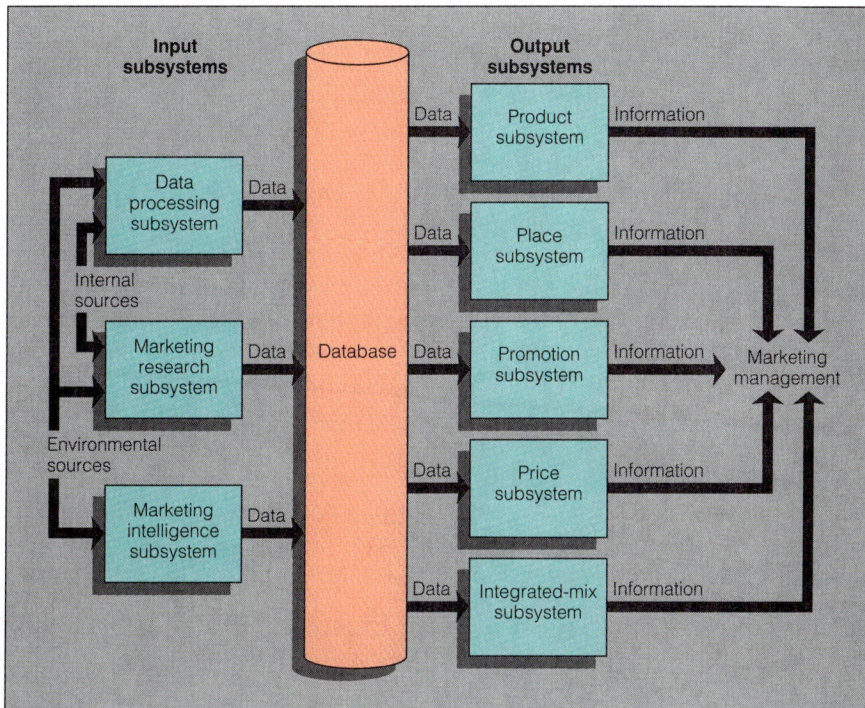

FIGURE 12.2

A Model of a
Marketing
Information System

tional information systems as well. The **input subsystems** gather data and
information that is entered in the database. The **output subsystems** consist
of computer programs that transform the data into information for the
functional managers.

Marketing Input Subsystems

All three functional information systems derive data and information from
the **data processing system** described in Chapter 11. The **marketing
research subsystem** gathers data primarily concerning the firm's customers
and prospective customers. Mail and telephone surveys as well as personal
interviews are used to gather the data. The **marketing intelligence subsystem** gathers data and information concerning the firm's competitors. This
system is usually very informal. For example, the firm's marketing representatives will shop at competitors' stores and attend open houses of competitors' offices and plants. Much competitor information is gleaned from
such publications as *The Wall Street Journal*, as well as from competitors'
annual reports. Marketing intelligence (as well as manufacturing intelligence and financial intelligence discussed later) is an ethical activity. It is
not to be confused with **industrial espionage**, which is a form of spying.

The data processing and marketing research subsystems gather data and
information from both internal and environmental sources. The marketing
intelligence subsystem gathers only environmental data and information.

Marketing Output Subsystems

All of the products and services offered by the marketing function are referred to as the **marketing mix**. They include the *product*, the *place* where the product is sold, *promotion* such as personal selling and advertising, and the product *price*.

The model uses the mix ingredients as a way to classify the output subsystems. All software that informs the manager about the product is included in the **product subsystem**. All software that describes how the product is distributed to the customers is included in the **place subsystem**. Likewise, the software that keeps the manager posted concerning personal selling and advertising is in the **promotion subsystem**, and all information about pricing is provided by the **pricing subsystem**. The manager can use these subsystems separately or in combination. The **integrated-mix subsystem** allows the manager to develop marketing strategies that use the mix ingredients in a combined manner.

Each output subsystem box in the model can represent multiple computer programs. There are programs that print or display periodic reports, programs that facilitate database queries, and programs that serve as mathematical models. Some of the boxes contain more programs than do others.

A Marketing Information System Example

An example of output from the product subsystem is the series of **sales analysis reports** produced from accounting transaction data. The accounting records used in preparing the invoices can be sorted into various sequences to provide management with information describing the firm's sales in terms of its products, customers, and salespersons. A **sales by product report** appears in Figure 12.3. The products are listed in a **descend-**

FIGURE 12.3

A Sales by Product Report

SALES BY PRODUCT
FOR THE MONTH OF JUNE 1989

PRODUCT NUMBER	PRODUCT NAME	CURRENT MONTH SALES	YEAR-TO-DATE SALES
129875	GASKET CENTER CASE	$ 5,090.23	$ 31,764.00
087235	MAINSHAFT	$ 4,760.01	$ 29,329.45
118320	1ST MOTION SHAFT	$ 1,789.45	$ 28,243.59
250067	OIL SEAL REAR	$ 11,560.24	$ 23,450.07
228203	LAYGEAR	$ 8,369.34	$ 14,709.03
576000	HUB 5TH	$ .00	$ 13,623.68
516012	SHIFT FORK 1-2	$ 450.95	$ 12,634.44
090407	SYNCHRO RING 2ND	$ 2,243.27	$ 9,963.58
282130	BUSH SHIFT LEVER	$ .00	$ 490.00
576301	OIL SLINGER	$ .00	$ 11.50

ing sequence based on year-to-date sales so that the highest selling products are listed first. This technique calls the manager's attention to the items contributing the most revenue. The same technique is used in the **sales by customer report** in Figure 12.4 to call the manager's attention to the best customers.

Reports such as these can be used in signaling problems or potential problems. They are especially useful to the problem-seeking manager described in Chapter 6. Such a manager can scan the reports, in printed or displayed form, looking for problems to solve.

```
                    SALES  BY  CUSTOMER
               FOR  THE  MONTH  OF  JUNE  1989


  CUSTOMER         CUSTOMER          CURRENT MONTH      YEAR-TO-DATE
   NUMBER           NAME                SALES              SALES

   98115      KEN'S AUTOMOTIVE SER    $12,359.50        $73,888.65
   97050      PROFESSIONAL CAR SVCS   $ 9,459.59        $62,782.09
   97051      TASCO WHEEL & TIRE CTR  $11,102.30        $62,689.99
   95025      BRYAN DRIVE TRAIN INC   $ 3,336.72        $54,091.27
   95026      MONTGOMERY AUTO SHOP    $      .00        $48,650.29
   97030      QUALITY USED CARS       $    487.23       $38,340.02
  108170      PLAGER TIRE & AUTO      $ 5,545.92        $32,784.27
     335      KOCHMANS AUTO REPAIR    $ 7,890.34        $26,840.10


  102678      BEALE AUTO SALES        $    450.95       $    450.95
   90305      AUTO DOCTOR             $      .00        $      8.89
```

FIGURE 12.4

A Sales by Customer Report

THE MANUFACTURING INFORMATION SYSTEM

Manufacturing managers make wider use of the computer than do other managers. In earlier chapters we have discussed computer aided design (CAD), computer aided manufacturing (CAM), and factory robots. Liberal use is also made of computers as information systems in scheduling production, controlling inventory, controlling production quality, and reporting on production costs.

These separate information system applications have been integrated in the model of a manufacturing information system in Figure 12.5. A **manufacturing information system** is a subset of the management information system used in solving the firm's manufacturing problems.

Manufacturing Input Subsystems

The data collection terminals described in Chapter 10 are an example of how the **data processing subsystem** is used in manufacturing. The terminals are located throughout the plant to record each major activity—from

FIGURE 12.5

A Model of a
Manufacturing
Information System

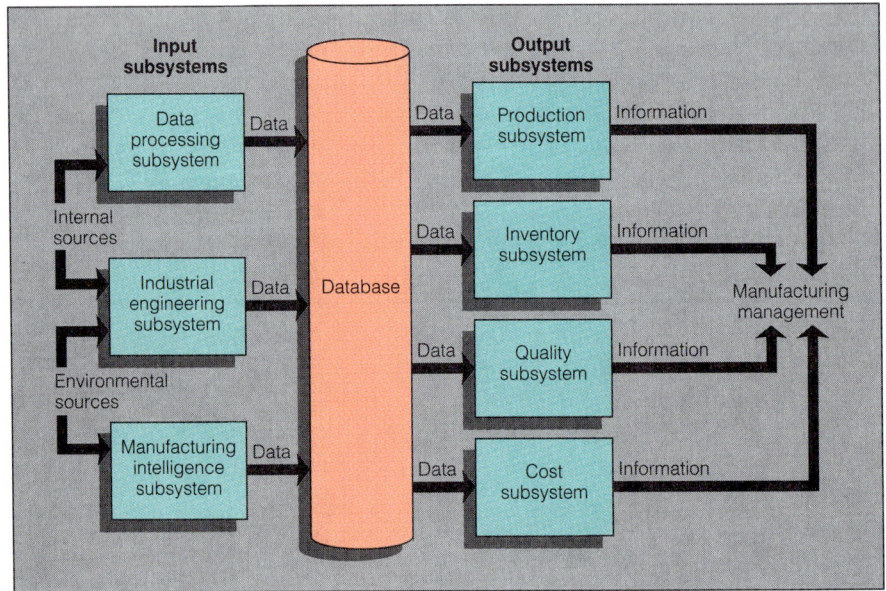

receipt of raw materials to shipment of finished goods. The terminals enable the computer to store up-to-the-minute information describing the physical manufacturing system.

In addition to the data processing subsystem, data describing internal manufacturing operations is provided by the **industrial engineering subsystem**. This subsystem consists of the industrial engineers, or IEs, who study production processes for the purpose of making them more efficient. IEs design *physical* production systems by deciding where to locate plants, how to arrange production lines, and what sequence of production processes to follow. The IEs also are involved in such *conceptual* systems as scheduling and inventory. The data and information provided by the IEs represents the industrial engineering subsystem.

Some of the data produced by the data processing subsystem relates to the environment—specifically to suppliers. Other environmental data and information is provided by the **manufacturing intelligence subsystem**. Like its marketing counterpart, it is largely informal. It provides supplier information not contained within the data processing system, and it also provides information on the labor element in the environment.

Manufacturing Output Subsystems

The four output subsystems each measure a dimension of the production process. The **production subsystem** measures the process in terms of *time*—tracking the work flow from one step to the next. The **inventory subsystem** measures the *volume* of production activity as the inventory is transformed from raw materials into work in process and finally into finished goods. The **quality subsystem** measures the quality of the materials as they are transformed. Raw materials are checked for quality when they are received from suppliers, quality control checks are made at different points in the production process, and a final check is made of finished goods before they are turned over to marketing for distribution to customers. The **cost subsystem** monitors the costs of production—primarily labor and material costs.

A Manufacturing Information System Example

As an example of how the production subsystem tracks the flow of a particular job, let us assume that a company manufactures bicycle flashlights—the type you strap on your leg so that the light bobs up and down as you pedal. A clear lens mounted on the front provides some light ahead, and a red lens at the rear warns the motorists behind.

It is necessary to identify the optimal quantity of flashlights for a single production run, or job. The quantity is called a **job lot**. A formula, called the **economic manufacturing quantity (EMQ)** or the **economic lot size**, avoids the high costs of producing too many or too few units. This formula is similar to the EOQ formula described in Chapter 5. We will assume that the optimum lot size is 2,200 flashlights.

Determine How Many to Produce

The lights are assembled from several parts. The list of the parts is called the **bill of material**, and it is like a recipe. An exploded view of the flashlight, along with its bill of material, appears in Figure 12.6. Only single quantities of each part are used, except for batteries. Each light uses two batteries.

Determine the Needed Raw Materials

If the plant is to produce 2,200 flashlights, raw materials sufficient for the entire job lot will be required. The quantities for each part listed on the bill of material are multiplied by the lot size. This is called **exploding the bill of material**. Figure 12.7 illustrates this process. The total numbers of each part are the **gross requirements**.

The inventory balance for each part is subtracted from the gross requirements to determine the **net requirements**—quantities that must be obtained from suppliers. This process is shown in Figure 12.8. You can see that all of the parts are available in the needed quantities except two: switches and bulbs. The firm needs 1,400 switches and 2,200 bulbs.

It is possible that additional purchase orders will be triggered by the net requirements computation. These orders are for in-stock items, but with a balance below the reorder point. The reflector is an example. There are enough reflectors on hand, but only four will be left after the flashlights are produced. The requirement for the flashlights should cause the reorder point to be reached if that situation has not already been encountered.

The production process cannot start until all of the parts are available. When the switches and bulbs arrive, data is transmitted to the computer from a terminal located in the receiving area. The computer then notifies management by transmitting messages to terminals in their offices.

Obtain the Raw Materials

FIGURE 12.6

Component Parts and Bill of Materials of a Finished Product

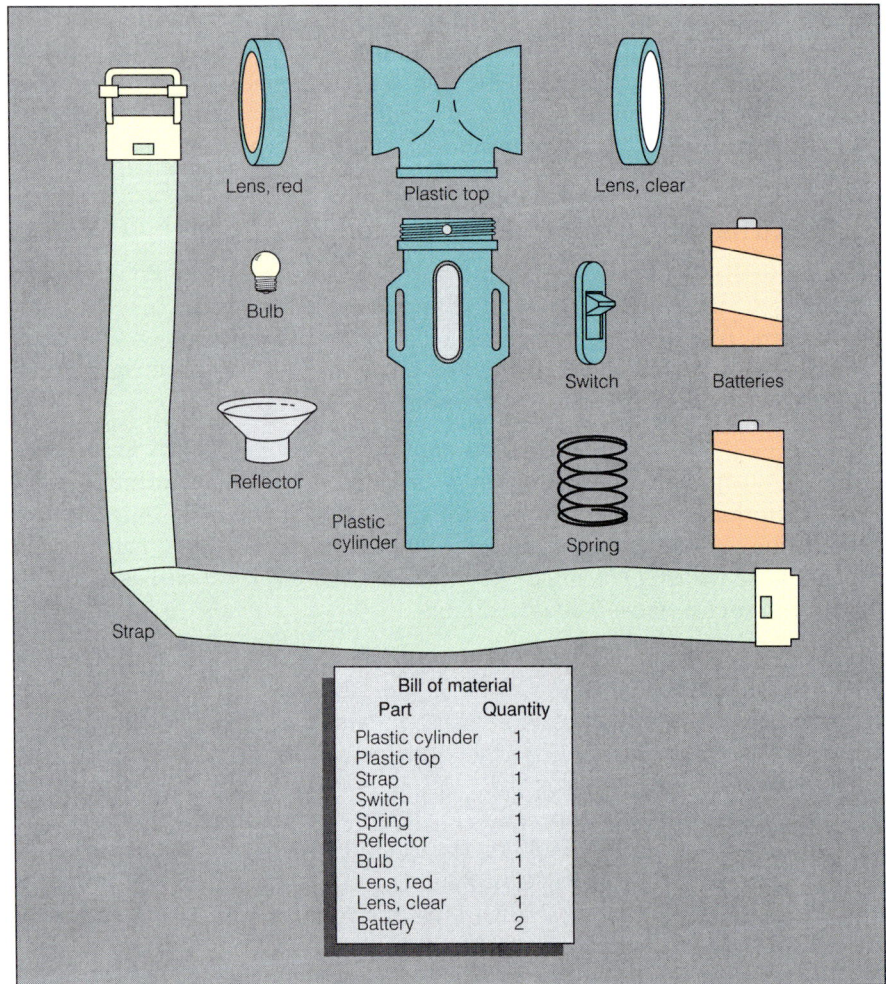

Lens, red

Plastic top

Lens, clear

Bulb

Switch

Batteries

Reflector

Plastic cylinder

Spring

Strap

Bill of material	
Part	Quantity
Plastic cylinder	1
Plastic top	1
Strap	1
Switch	1
Spring	1
Reflector	1
Bulb	1
Lens, red	1
Lens, clear	1
Battery	2

FIGURE 12.7

An Exploded Bill of Material

Part	Quantity per final product		Number of final products		Gross requirement
Plastic cylinder	1	×	2200	=	2200
Plastic top	1	×	2200	=	2200
Strap	1	×	2200	=	2200
Switch	1	×	2200	=	2200
Spring	1	×	2200	=	2200
Reflector	1	×	2200	=	2200
Bulb	1	×	2200	=	2200
Lens, red	1	×	2200	=	2200
Lens, clear	1	×	2200	=	2200
Battery	2	×	2200	=	4400

FIGURE 12.8
Net Raw Material
Requirements

Part	Gross requirements	Inventory on hand	Net requirements
Plastic cylinder	2200	3000	0
Plastic top	2200	2250	0
Strap	2200	6000	0
Switch	2200	800	1400
Spring	2200	2999	0
Reflector	2200	2204	0
Bulb	2200	0	2200
Lens, red	2200	3625	0
Lens, clear	2200	5500	0
Battery	4400	5005	0

Schedule Production

Figure 12.9 shows how the work flows through the plant. The flow begins by releasing the raw materials from inventory. In this example there are two main flows: one for assembling the cylinder and one for the top. Work can be done simultaneously on both units to reduce the length of time required for the job. The steps in the cylinder flow are numbered 1 through 4 and are circled. The steps for the top are numbered 5 through 8 and are enclosed in squares. In Step 9 the top assembly is attached to the cylinder assembly and the result is a finished flashlight that enters the finished goods inventory.

The production schedule determines when the steps of the production process will be taken. To create the schedule, the lot quantity must be multiplied by the performance standards for each step. For example, in the first step of attaching a battery spring to the cylinder (Step 1 in Figure 12.9), a special operator-controlled spring insertion machine is used. A standard insertion time of 0.16 minute per spring means that 352 minutes of both machine and operator time will be required to attach 2,200 springs. Similar computations can be made for each remaining step of the process to identify the total machine and employee requirements.

The computations can be seen in Figure 12.10. Some steps (1, 2, 5, 7, and 8) require machines and operators. The other steps are performed manually. Specific types of machines and employees are identified.

Once the machine and employee requirements have been determined, the production scheduling program can schedule the job. A production schedule appears in Figure 12.11. On the left-hand side the date and time are printed for the release of each of the ten parts from raw materials inventory. When the parts are released, they are transported to the workstation where they will be used.

The nine production steps are listed in the center, along with a start date and time for each. A production step is scheduled to begin no later than thirty minutes after the raw materials are delivered to the workstation.

The Production Process

The production subsystem triggers the production process. Information is made available to employees in the inventory and production areas, telling

FIGURE 12.9

Job Flow through
the Plant

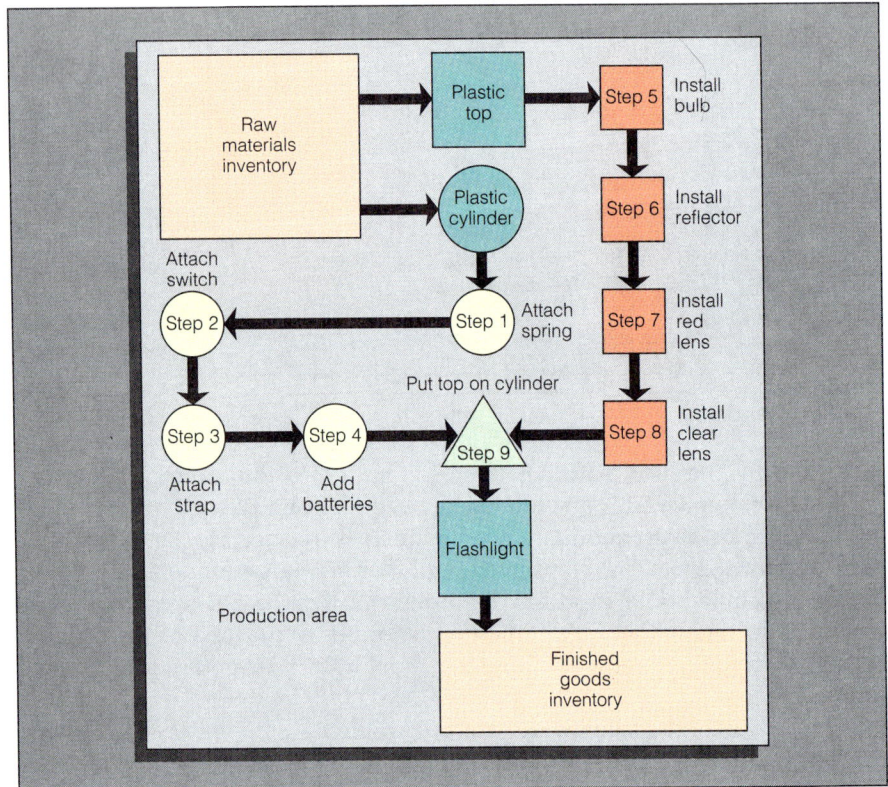

them what to do, when to do it, and (if necessary) how to do it. Perhaps the computer transmits instructions to terminals in the raw materials store-room and at the workers' workstations.

As work begins on a production step, the worker uses the terminal to advise the computer of:

- Job identification
- Step number
- Workstation
- Employee identification
- Start time

The first three items can be optically read from documents that accompany the job. The worker uses an OCR wand attached to the terminal to scan the documents. The worker accomplishes employee identification by inserting his or her identification badge in the terminal. Start time is recorded by the computer as the message is received. When the job step is completed, the worker again advises the computer by using the terminal. The computer enters the completion time, enabling the calculation of the time

```
              MACHINE AND EMPLOYEE REQUIREMENTS
PRODUCT--BICYCLE FLASHLIGHT

PRODUCTION QUANTITY--2200

               --------MACHINE------      -------EMPLOYEE------

   STEP          TYPE  STD.  TOT. TIME      TYPE   STD.  TOT. TIME

1--ATTCH SPRG    129   .16     352         0-129   .16     352
2--ATTCH SW      402   .30     660         0-402   .30     660
3--ATTCH STRP    ---   ---     ---         ASSY    .10     220
4--ADD BATTS     ---   ---     ---         ASSY    .08     176
5--INST BULB     202   .16     352         0-202   .16     352
6--INST REF      ---   ---     ---         ASSY    .30     660
7--INST LNSR     602   .20     440         0-602   .20     440
8--INST LNSC     604   .20     440         0-604   .20     440
9--ATTCH TOP     ---   ---     ---         ASSY    .16     352
```

FIGURE 12.10

Computation of Machine and Personnel Requirements

```
                    PRODUCTION SCHEDULE

JOB NAME      BICYCLE FLASHLIGHT
JOB NO.       79-133

  RAW            RELEASE     PRODUCTION       START        COMPLETION
  MATLS         DATE  TIME     STEP         DATE   TIME     DATE   TIME

CYLINDER       10-24  0800
SPRING         10-24  0800   1-ATTCH SPRG  10-24  0838    10-24   1430
SWITCH         10-24  1430   2-ATTCH SW    10-24  1500    10-26   0900
STRAP          10-26  0930   3-ATTCH STRP  10-26  0950    10-26   1330
BATTERY        10-26  1345   4-ADD BATTS   10-26  1404    10-26   1700
TOP            10-23  0900
BULB           10-23  0900   5-INST BULB   10-23  0930    10-23   1522
REFLECTOR      10-23  1530   6-INST REF    10-23  1600    10-25   1000
LENS RED       10-25  1030   7-INST LNSR   10-25  1100    10-26   0920
LENS CLEAR     10-26  0930   8-INST LNSC   10-26  1000    10-26   1620
                             9-ATTCH TOP   10-27  0800    10-27   1352
```

FIGURE 12.11

A Production Schedule

required to complete each step. This is the job reporting use of data collection terminals introduced in Chapter 10.

The production subsystem can inform manufacturing management when jobs move faster or slower than planned by printing or displaying exception reports. An **exception report** is a report prepared when something happens that is out of the ordinary. Such reports facilitate management by exception.

The production subsystem tracks the flow of work through the physical system as each process is performed. It is possible for manufacturing management to know the status of the physical system at all times. This is a good example of the value of a conceptual information system.

THE FINANCIAL INFORMATION SYSTEM

A **financial information system** is a subset of the management information system used in solving the firm's financial problems. It is pictured in Figure 12.12. An **internal audit subsystem** assists the **data processing subsystem** in providing internal data and information. Larger firms usually have a staff of **internal auditors** who are responsible for maintaining the integrity of the firm's accounting systems. Internal auditors who have a computer expertise are called **EDP auditors**.

As in the other functional systems, the **financial intelligence subsystem** gathers information from the environment. In this case, the environmental elements providing the information are the financial community, stockholders, and the federal, state, and local governments. As with the other intelligence systems, financial intelligence is largely informal.

FIGURE 12.12

A Model of a Financial Information System

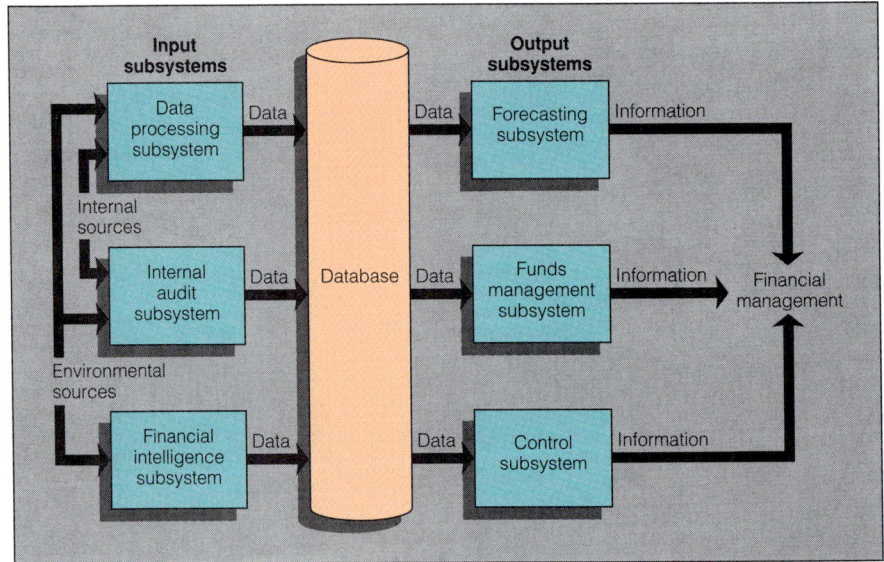

Output Subsystems

The **forecasting subsystem** forecasts company activity five to ten years into the future to provide the basis for strategic planning. The **funds management subsystem** projects the flow of money through the firm for a coming period, such as a year. Management wants to know in advance of possible cash surpluses and deficits. The **control subsystem** prepares the annual operating budget that specifies how much each unit can spend for certain expense categories. Feedback information is then provided to the unit managers so that they can monitor their performance compared to the budget.

A Financial Information System Example

The flow of money from the environment, through the firm, and back to the environment is important because money is used to obtain the other physical resources. The flow can be managed to achieve two goals: to assure that the inflow is greater than the outflow, and to assure that this condition remains as stable as possible throughout the year.

A firm could show a good profit on the year's activities, yet have periods during the year when expenses exceed revenues. This situation can be seen in Figures 12.13 and 12.14 where a manufacturer of garden equipment enjoys high sales to wholesalers in the fall and low sales in the spring. From March through May the monthly sales of $300,000 are not high enough to cover the monthly manufacturing expenses of $360,000. Money outflow during March through May exceeds inflow by $262,000, even though profit for the year is $1,908,000.

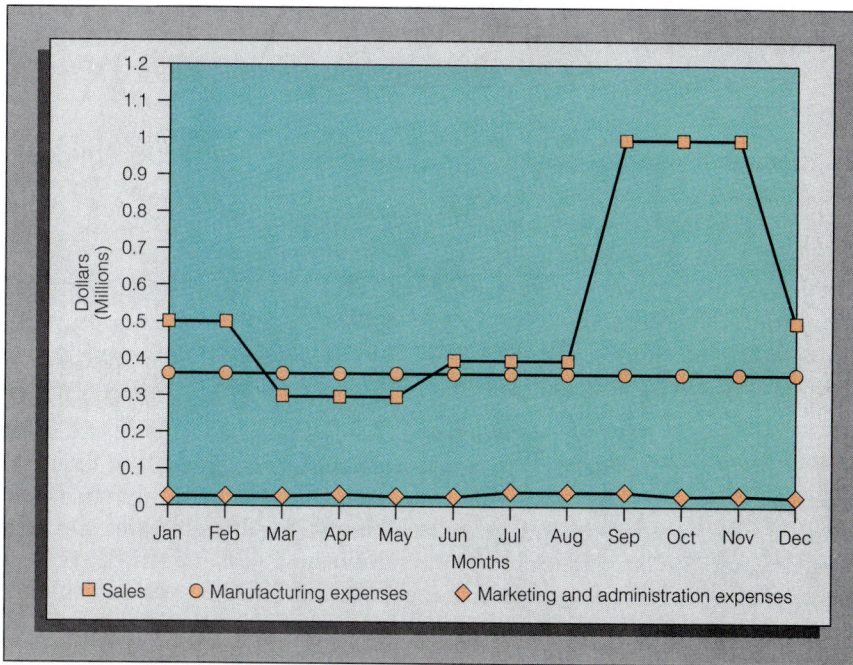

FIGURE 12.13

Fluctuating Sales Influence Monthly Profit

The funds management subsystem can perform a **cash flow analysis** that tracks the inflow and outflow by month. The software performing this task is called a **cash flow model**. The software can be a custom programmed mathematical model or application development software such as an electronic spreadsheet. The graph in Figure 12.13 was produced by Lotus PrintGraph, and the report in Figure 12.14 was produced by the 1-2-3 electronic spreadsheet software. Spreadsheets and the accompanying graphics are excellent for this type of analysis.

FIGURE 12.14   An Unbalanced Money Flow

	JAN	FEB	MAR	APR	MAY	JUN	JUL	AUG	SEP	OCT	NOV	DEC	TOTAL
MONEY INPUT													
SALES	500	500	300	300	300	400	400	400	1000	1000	1000	500	6600
MONEY OUTPUT													
MANUFACTURING													
EXPENSES													
WAGES	82	82	82	82	82	82	82	82	82	82	82	82	984
MATERIALS	220	220	220	220	220	220	220	220	220	220	220	220	2640
OTHER MFG.													
EXPENSES	58	58	58	58	58	58	58	58	58	58	58	58	696
TOTAL MANU-													
FACTURING													
EXPENSES	360	360	360	360	360	360	360	360	360	360	360	360	4320
MARKETING AND													
ADMIN. EXP.	26	26	26	28	28	28	40	40	40	30	30	30	372
NET CHANGE IN													
MONEY	114	114	-86	-88	-88	12	0	0	600	610	610	110	1908

Although the annual results of the garden equipment manufacturer are good, the money flow throughout the year is anything but stable. What can be done with the surplus during the winter months? What about the deficit during the spring and summer? One alternative is to develop a new product that would increase revenues during the slack period, but, because such a program can take several years to complete, it is not considered to be an immediate alternative. Other strategies that can produce results during the coming year must be considered.

First Simulation— Variable Production Schedule

One approach is to match production to sales rather than spend constant amounts for wages, materials, and manufacturing expenses. The financial manager uses the cash flow model to consider the effect of scheduling production for one month to equal the sales forecast for the next. This strategy, which would have to be approved by manufacturing management as well as top management, is illustrated in Figure 12.15. There is a peak manufacturing period during the summer and a slack period during the winter.

Second Simulation— Delayed Materials

The above change helped the situation during the first four months, but the money drain during May through August actually increased. The main reason is the high materials expenses for May through July. If the manager can shift these expenses to months with high sales revenues, the negative balances can be eliminated or reduced.

It probably would not be practical to shift the *acquisition* of materials to an earlier or later period, but the *payment* might be delayed. Materials could be acquired for the May–July production peak, and payment delayed until September–November. Suppliers probably would be receptive to such an arrangement if interest could be charged on the delayed payments.

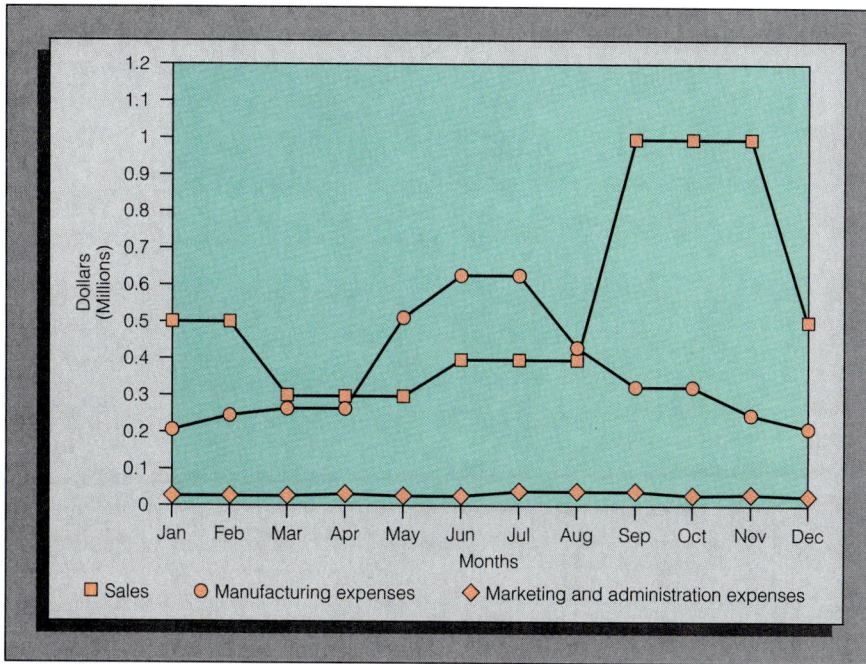

FIGURE 12.15

Modified
Production
Schedule

The finance manager can simulate this solution, which is illustrated in Figure 12.16. A four-month interest charge of four percent has been added to each month's material expenses to reflect the delayed payments. There is a positive cash flow each month except for very small negative flows from June through August. If this flow is satisfactory to the finance manager, no further simulations are performed.

The finance manager can use the cash flow model to evaluate strategies aimed at achieving the best use of money, and then can work cooperatively with other managers to select and implement the optimal strategy.

BEHAVIORAL INFLUENCES ON SYSTEM DESIGN

Each functional information system is used primarily by the managers in that area. However, in some cases other functional managers as well as the firm's executives also use the system's output.

At times the managers in one functional area do not want to share their information with others. Their reasoning is that they have gone to the expense of gathering the information and they should be able to control its use. While such attitudes are clearly not in the best interests of the firm as a whole, they are a reality of human nature.

The designers of information systems must be aware of how such **behavioral influences** can affect the success or failure of a system. Very often **fear** is the underlying cause of resistance to the implementation of a

FIGURE 12.16

Effect of Delaying
Payments to
Vendors

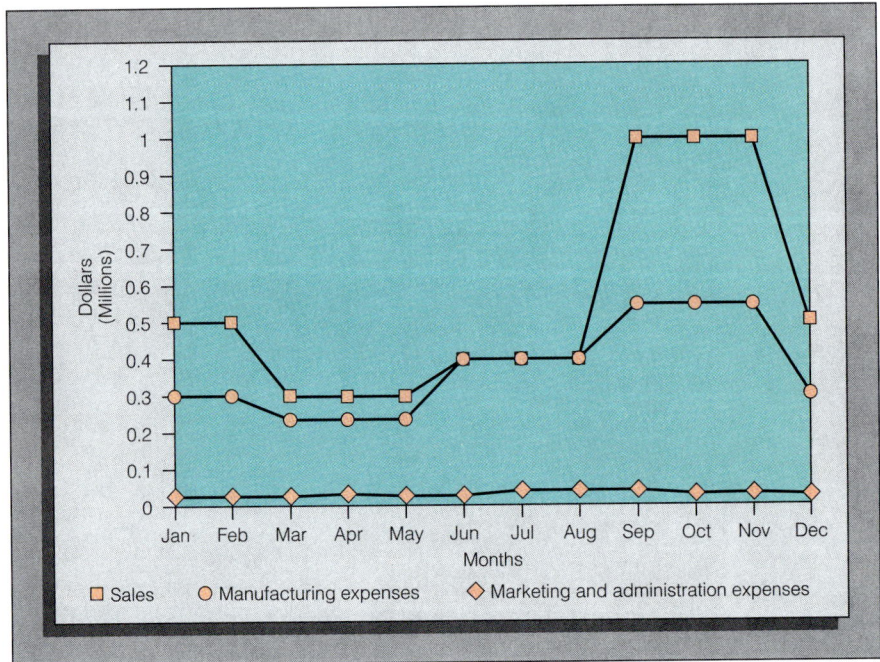

computer system. The functional managers fear interference by the other functions.

The employees of the firms that installed the first computers experienced fear. The fear was appropriate in those instances where the firms attempted to replace clerks with the computer. Even when management had no such intention, the employees still tended to be distrustful, and expected the worst.

When employees are afraid of the computer they can react in various ways. The healthiest situation is when the employees express their fears to management. That gives management the opportunity to respond and put the fears to rest. Many times, however, the employees will keep their fears to themselves and take action to sabotage the system. They will not cooperate with the designers during the implementation period or perhaps will attempt to inflict damage on the system once it becomes operational. Such cases are extremely rare, but the system designers should be alert to any signals that a problem or potential problem might exist.

The firm's management, assisted by the information specialists, can prevent or reduce fear by taking the following steps:

1. Use the computer as a means of achieving **job enhancement** by letting the computer do the redundant, boring work and letting the employees use their skills to their fullest in addressing the more challenging tasks.

2. Use *formal communications* in the form of memos, newsletter articles,

or even video tapes to keep the employees aware of the firm's intentions. . .

3. Build a relationship of *trust* among the employees, the information specialists, and management.

4. Align the individual *employee's needs* with the objectives of the firm. First, the employees' needs are identified. Second, the employees are motivated by being shown that work toward the firm's objectives also helps them to meet their own needs. Third, the employees work toward achievement of the firm's objectives, and fourth, the firm's objectives are met.

Information specialists can make a big contribution to overcoming employee fears. The specialists often observe resistance that the employees keep hidden from management. Information specialists, especially systems analysts, DBAs, and network managers who work directly with users, should be trained to recognize and respond to such resistance. These behavioral skills are just as important as technical skills.

THE ROLE OF THE MIS IN PROBLEM SOLVING

The MIS contributes to problem solving in two basic ways: it provides an organizationwide information resource, and it contributes to problem identification and understanding.

Provides an Organizationwide Information Resource

MIS is an *organizationwide* effort to provide problem-solving information. The information systems that comprise the MIS most often represent large-scale systems that provide information to groups of people, such as all of the managers in a department. The MIS is a formal commitment by top management to use the computer for more than data processing.

Contributes to Problem Identification and Understanding

The main idea behind the MIS is to keep a continuous supply of information flowing to the manager. During the early years of marketing information systems there was confusion concerning the distinction between the information system and marketing research. Some likened marketing research, with its surveys designed to gather timely data about specific activities, to a flash bulb. The surveys shed a bright light on a topic, exposing all of the features, but the information is current for only a short time. The information system, on the other hand, is like a candle. It does not provide as much information, but the information continues for a long time.

The *light* from the MIS is intended to provide the manager with signals of problems or impending problems. The manager then uses the MIS to gain a basic understanding of the problem—determining where it is located and what is causing it. In some cases, the MIS can support the manager through the remaining steps of the solution process.

The main weakness of MIS is that it is not aimed at the specific needs of the individual problem solvers. Very often the MIS does not provide exactly the information needed. The decision support system concept was created in response to that need, and we will address that approach in Chapter 13.

SUMMARY

Early MIS efforts were largely unsuccessful because of the difficulty the managers experienced in articulating their information needs. Over time the communication barrier between the managers and the information specialists was removed and firms implemented successful systems.

An MIS includes both formal and informal components that provide information on both internal operations and the environment. The information spans the past, the present, and the future, and is used by managers, nonmanagers, and elements in the environment. It is important that the MIS output be in the proper time frame so that it can be used for decision making. The main components of an MIS include information processing resources (both hardware and personnel), the database, the software library, and users.

The MIS concept was so well received that managers in the functional areas began incorporating software and data into the systems to meet their own needs. Functional information systems consist of input subsystems that gather data and information for entry in the database, and output subsystems that transform the data into information and present the information to managers. The marketing, manufacturing, and financial information systems all use data processing as an input subsystem. The three systems also include input subsystems (marketing research, industrial engineering, and internal auditing) that gather data internally, and intelligence subsystems that gather data from the environment.

The marketing output subsystems are based on the four ingredients of the marketing mix—product, place, promotion, and price—plus a subsystem that integrates the ingredients. Sales analysis reports are an example of the output of the product subsystem.

The manufacturing output subsystems inform management concerning four dimensions of production activity—time (the production subsystem), volume (the inventory subsystem), quality (the quality subsystem), and cost (the cost subsystem). The production subsystem uses an EMQ to determine the lot size, explodes the bill of material to obtain the net inventory requirements, schedules production using standard times for each production step, triggers the production process, and tracks the flow of work through the plant.

The financial output subsystems prepare long-range forecasts (the forecasting subsystem), control the flow of money through the firm (the funds management subsystem), and maintain a tight rein on the firm's monetary assets (the control subsystem). A cash flow model is an example of the funds management subsystem.

A synergism is produced when all of the functions develop information systems—the whole is greater than the sum of the parts.

Employees on all levels can experience fear when confronted by a new computer project. Top management combats this fear by dedicating the computer to job enhancement rather than job reduction or elimination, keeping the employees informed, creating an atmosphere of trust, and aligning individual needs with the organization's goals. The information specialists can be especially effective in overcoming negative behavioral influences.

The MIS is an organizationwide commitment to a quality information resource. The MIS is especially valuable in identifying problems and helping managers to understand them so they can be solved.

KEY CONCEPTS

How MIS represents a significant departure from data processing

The global nature of MIS in terms of the information provided, the systems that provide the information, and how the information is used

How an information system can be tailored to the special needs of groups of managers within the organization

How the intelligence subsystems specialize in gathering data from certain environmental elements

The production subsystem as a conceptual representation of the firm's physical production system

How a mathematical model can simulate future activity of the firm—such as its cash flow

How management and the information specialists can institute a formal program aimed at minimizing the behavioral influences that can threaten a computer project

KEY TERMS

Functional information system	Job lot	Gross requirements
Marketing information system	Economic manufacturing quantity (EMQ), economic lot size	Net requirements
Sales analysis report		Exception report
Manufacturing informatio system	Bill of material	Internal auditor
	Exploding the bill of material	Cash flow analysis
		Job enhancement

QUESTIONS

1. What factor minimized the task that the early computer users faced?
2. Why did so many early MIS efforts fail?

3. What are the four main ingredients of the MIS as shown in the MIS model?

4. What are the three sources of management information as illustrated by the MIS model? What are the two sources of data?

5. Is marketing intelligence a formal or informal system? Explain.

6. Which environmental elements provide data and information to the marketing intelligence subsystem? The manufacturing intelligence subsystem? The financial intelligence subsystem?

7. Why would you want to print a report in a descending sequence?

8. What is the difference between gross requirements and net requirements?

9. What data is scanned optically when a worker starts a job? What other data is recorded, and how?

10. What computing equipment is used by the production subsystem in keeping manufacturing management informed of production progress?

11. What are the two goals of using a cash flow analysis?

12. What is a prime underlying cause of resistance to computer projects? On what level(s) in the organization can that condition be found?

13. What are four strategies that can be employed in minimizing the negative effects of behavioral influences?

14. What two steps of the problem-solving process does the MIS support the best?

15. What is the main weakness of the MIS?

CASE PROBLEM   Columbine Life

It has been five years since Columbine Life implemented their marketing information system. It is very straightforward, consisting of a set of reports and graphs prepared each month by the central computer. Only four copies of the reports are prepared, and they are placed in three-ring binders. The information services department keeps one copy as a permanent record, and three copies are given to the marketing department. The vice president of marketing, Elizabeth Sayles, keeps one for her own use, gives one to the director of marketing operations, and one to the director of marketing administration.

By all measures, the system is a success. It has been Columbine's best effort at providing management information. The system came about as a result of the phenomenal sales growth of the early 1980s. There was great demand for the firm's products and it was necessary to add new salespersons. Marketing management was experiencing difficulty in controlling the larger sales force and Columbine president, Clarence Avery, decided that better information was the solution. The executive committee, consisting of Avery, Sayles, and the other vice presidents, agreed to implement the marketing information system.

At first Sayles was against the idea. She did not want details about marketing's operations spread around the company. Avery conceded and assured her that marketing would retain control of the information and decide when and how it would be made available to others in the firm.

After deciding to implement the system the executive committee never formally discussed it again. Also, there were no efforts to install similar information systems in other areas of the firm. Avery's rationale for not following up is that the firm is prospering and the managers seem to be doing a good job of managing. Why rock the boat?

During the time the system has been in operation, marketing has come to rely on it in their day-to-day operations. Bill Weese, director of marketing administration, says, "It helps us do a better job of managing."

The main weakness of the system is that its information output could be used by the firm's executives and other managers, but it is not made available to them. In fact, the executives and other managers are not even aware of the kind of reports and graphs that are prepared.

The situation came to a head in the spring. Rob Browder, the vice president of information services, wrote a paper describing the system for presentation at a computer conference. The paper concluded with the recommendation that the reports be distributed to each committee member. As a courtesy, Browder gave copies of the paper to the other members of the executive committee.

Avery had no sooner finished reading his copy when Sayles appeared in his doorway—rolled-up report in hand. She was visibly shaken. Avery motioned for her to sit down and she looked Avery straight in the eye and said "I've just read Rob's report and I assume that you have too." Avery nodded. Sayles continued "I just want you to know that I will not agree to making our information available to the others. You promised me long ago that we could control the dissemination, and I want you to keep your word. We have been using the information and doing a good job. What more could you ask? And why should marketing be singled out this way? There has been no effort to put information systems in the other departments. It's unfair. I'll guarantee you one thing. If you change the rules now, you can just forget about marketing cooperating on any future computer projects. There, I've had my say. Now, are you going to follow Rob's recommendations or not?"

1. Is the marketing information system an MIS? Why or why not?
2. Consider both the advantages and disadvantages of:
    a. Doing nothing; keeping the system the same as it is now.
    b. Forcing marketing to share its information.
3. Can you think of a better alternative? If so, describe it and list the advantages and disadvantages.

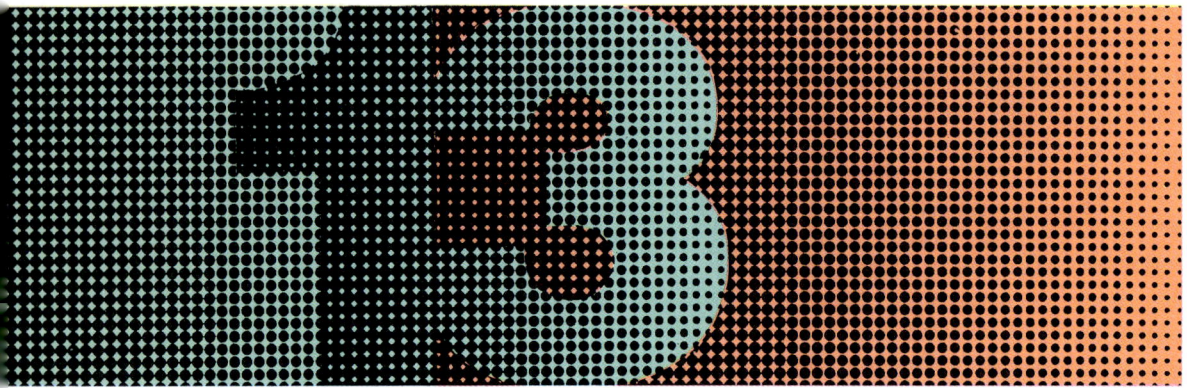

Decision Support Systems

LEARNING OBJECTIVES After studying this chapter, you should:

- Know the features that distinguish a decision support system from the MIS
- Have a better understanding of both periodic and special reports and know some techniques for making them more effective
- Know how to classify mathematical models and be familiar with the main modeling terms
- Understand the different software approaches to model building
- Know the key to successful model use

OVERVIEW

We begin the chapter by briefly reviewing the major fundamentals of decision support systems presented in other chapters. These fundamentals are supplemented with a list of characteristics that can be used to distinguish a decision support system from the MIS.

The major emphasis in the chapter focuses on the ways the manager obtains information from a decision support system. First the characteristics of both periodic and special reports are described and suggestions are offered for improving their information content. Then the subject of mathematical modeling is explored. The different types of models are identified, the main modeling terms are defined, and a sample model is explained. Attention is paid to model building by describing the available software approaches, and to model use by stressing the importance of being able to interpret the output.

The chapter concludes with an explanation of the role the decision support system plays in problem solving.

WHAT IS A DECISION SUPPORT SYSTEM?

We recognized at the end of Chapter 12 that the MIS does not always provide the manager with exactly the needed information. That is because the MIS is aimed at problems faced by the entire organization, or by units within the organization. The MIS is not intended to provide custom support for each manager. That shortcoming stimulated efforts that led to the decision support system concept.

The Gorry and Scott Morton Framework

The origin of the decision support system concept was an article by G. Anthony Gorry and Michael S. Scott Morton of the Massachusetts Institute of Technology (MIT) that appeared in a professional journal in 1971.[1] The article included a grid, reproduced in Figure 13.1, that viewed computer applications in terms of the degree of structure in the problems they are intended to solve and the management level that they support.

In Chapter 5 we discussed how problems can be structured, unstructured, and semistructured. When all of the ingredients, or variables, that comprise a problem are known, and when they can be measured quantitatively, the

Problem Structure

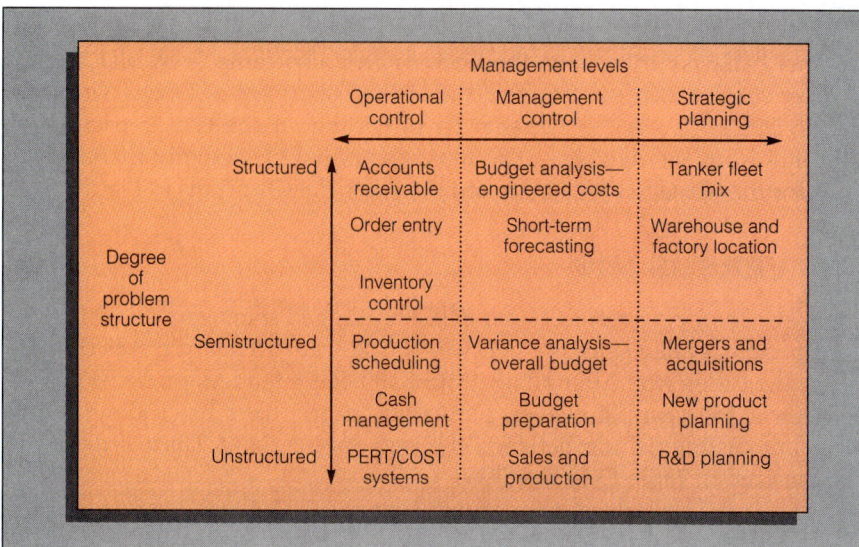

FIGURE 13.1
The Gorry and Scott Morton Grid

	Management levels		
	Operational control	Management control	Strategic planning
Structured	Accounts receivable	Budget analysis—engineered costs	Tanker fleet mix
	Order entry	Short-term forecasting	Warehouse and factory location
	Inventory control		
Semistructured	Production scheduling	Variance analysis—overall budget	Mergers and acquisitions
	Cash management	Budget preparation	New product planning
Unstructured	PERT/COST systems	Sales and production	R&D planning

Degree of problem structure

1"A Framework for Management Information Systems," *Sloan Management Review* 13 (Fall 1971): 55-70.

problem is structured. Few business problems are completely structured, and few are completely unstructured. Most are semistructured, with some variables being known and quantifiable, and some not.

Management Level

We discussed management levels in Chapter 6. The person credited with addressing this topic most effectively is Robert N. Anthony. He coined the names **strategic planning level** for the top level, **management control level** for the middle level, and **operational control level** for the lower level.

Structured Decision Systems

Gorry and Scott Morton sought to distinguish between the computer applications that had been successfully performed and those that had not. The horizontal dashed line across the grid separated the two groups. Each application above the line was being performed at that time in many companies, and was called a **structured decision system**, or **SDS**. The SDSs were aimed at the more structured problems faced by all levels.

The applications below the line were still on the horizon in 1971. Since they were aimed at less structured problems, they had been more difficult to implement. They were given the name decision support systems. DSS became the label for a new approach to computer use in problem solving.

Definition of Decision Support System

We define a **decision support system**, or **DSS**, as a computer-based system intended for use by a particular manager or a group of managers on any organizational level in making a decision in the process of solving a semistructured problem. The DSS produces output in the form of periodic or special reports or the results of mathematical simulations.

Alter's DSS Types

Another early contributor to the DSS concept also came from MIT. Steven L. Alter studied fifty-six firms and identified six types of DSSs.[2] The most simple DSS supports the manager by providing an ability to retrieve data elements from the database. The most complex DSS actually makes decisions for the manager. We illustrated the Alter classifications in Figure 5.14.

DSS VERSUS MIS

The distinction between DSS and MIS has nagged managers and information specialists alike since the DSS was introduced. To many, it was difficult to see any difference. After all, the MIS had been intended for decision support. Over the years, however, particular criteria have been identified as means of distinguishing between the two applications. These criteria are summarized in Table 13.1. The DSS:

- *Supports the individual* The DSS is tailored to specific problems faced by the individual manager or a small group of problem solvers,

---

[2] For more information, see Steven L. Alter, "How Effective Managers Use Information Systems," *Harvard Business Review* 54 (November–December 1976): 97–104.

TABLE 13.1

Comparing MIS and DSS

Criteria	MIS	DSS
Focus of support	The organization	The individual
Type of support	Indirect	Direct
Problem-solving phases supported	problem identification, problem understanding, and follow-up	All
Types of problems supported	All	Semistructured
Emphasis	Information	Decisions

whereas the MIS is intended to support an entire organizational unit.

- *Provides direct support* DSS focuses on a specific decision that is made to solve a specific problem. In some cases, as in Alter's more complex DSS types, the system can recommend or even make decisions. MIS support, on the other hand, is less direct. The manager must apply the information.

- *Supports all problem-solving phases* The DSS not only helps the manager identify and understand problems, as is the case with the MIS, but it can also provide strong support during the remaining steps of the problem-solving process. The DSS helps the manager to identify and evaluate alternate solutions, and to select the best. The DSS is not unique, however, in providing follow-up information. The MIS can do that as well.

- *Supports semistructured problems* The DSS focus is much narrower in terms of problem structure. It is aimed at only the semistructured variety. MIS, on the other hand, has never been aimed at any particular class of problem.

- *Emphasizes decision support* The DSS emphasizes decisions—recognizing that the manager makes many decisions in the course of solving a single problem. The decisions come first and the solution follows. The DSS is intended to help the manager make good decisions, thereby laying a firm foundation for problem solving. The MIS concept, on the other hand, emphasizes information—the fact that it is needed for problem solving.

The DSS concept did not experience early failures as did MIS. Most likely the main reason is the narrower scope of the DSS. The more modest approach of the DSS maximizes its chance of success.

OTHER POSSIBLE DISTINGUISHING FEATURES

Everyone does not distinguish between MIS and DSS in the above manner. To some, DSS is interactive, requiring the use of an online keyboard terminal. Conversely, the MIS is seen as a system producing information largely in the form of periodic reports.

The interactive use can involve both database queries and use of mathematical models. To many, the use of modeling is the key feature of DSS.

Another group associates the MIS with support for lower-management levels, and DSS with support for upper levels.

While these features might very well distinguish between MIS and DSS in terms of what has actually been *achieved*, they do not necessarily reflect how the concepts were *intended*. There is no reason why upper-level managers cannot receive information support from the MIS, or why periodic reports cannot be regarded as decision-support tools. This view is supported by the Gorry and Scott Morton grid that includes all management levels, and by Alter's nonmodeling DSS types.

A DSS MODEL

Figure 13.2 shows how the DSS supports the manager through each step of the problem-solving process. The steps are those of the systems approach as described in Chapter 7. The DSS consists of an information processor—the computer, database, and software library. Both internal and environmental data are stored in the database. The software enables the computer to provide information in the form of reports, responses to database queries, and simulations performed by mathematical models. The arrows show how the information in these basic forms is made available to a manager or specific group of managers for use in decision making at each problem-solving step.

Two comments are in order concerning the support for the steps. First, all steps are not supported to the same degree. As a rule, the first two steps that provide for problem identification and understanding are well supported. The support for identification of alternatives is usually very slight. Second, each information medium is better suited for supporting certain steps than others. Reports and database queries are used most often in problem identification and understanding. Simulation is most valuable in alternative evaluation. Reports are excellent for follow-up.

We will now address the ways that the CBIS provides information—periodic reports, special reports produced as a result of database queries, and mathematical modeling. These outputs are characteristic of both MIS and DSS.

PERIODIC AND SPECIAL REPORTS

If you were to pick up a report from a manager's desk, you probably could not tell whether it was a periodic report or a special report. They both can

FIGURE 13.2
A DSS Model

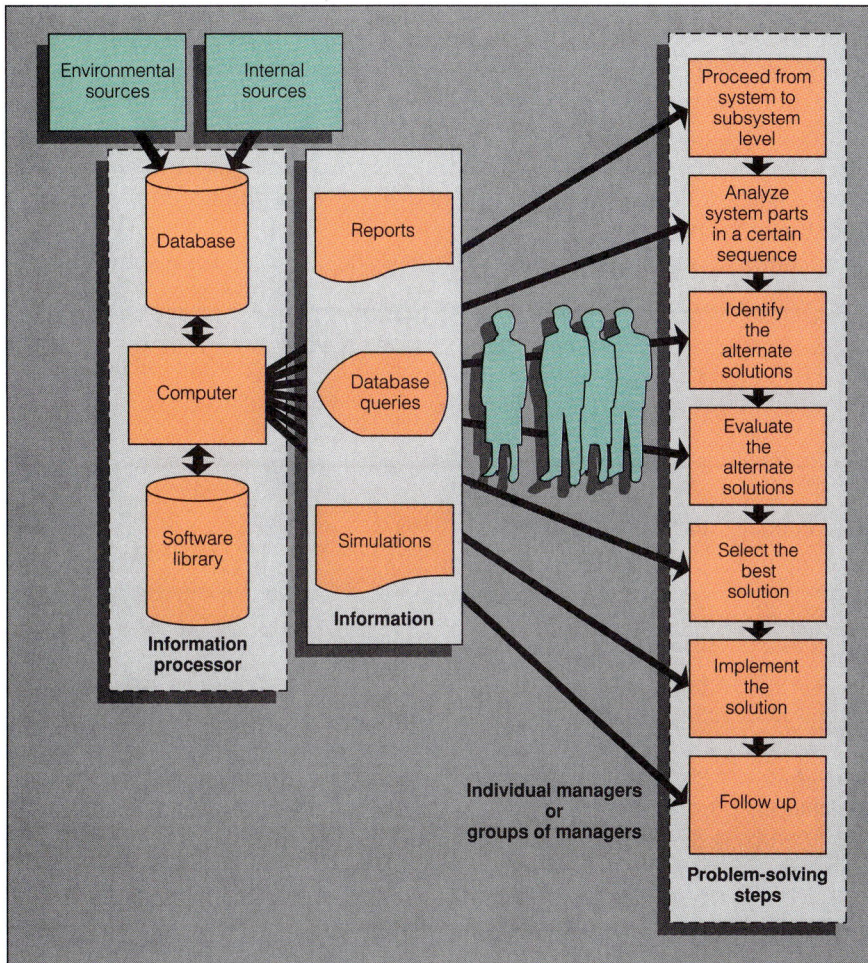

look exactly alike. What distinguishes them is the manner in which they are triggered. A **periodic report** is prepared according to a certain schedule, such as a monthly analysis of sales by customer. A **special report** is prepared when something special happens. For example, the firm might have a policy of preparing an accident report each time an accident occurs. Or perhaps a manager is confronted by an unexpected disturbance, such as a fall in interest rates, and needs special information. The manager can obtain the special information by making a database query. We use the term special report to include the response to database queries.

Printed and Displayed Reports

We recognized in Chapter 8 that reports can be printed or displayed. That option applies to both periodic and special reports.

Detail and Summary Reports

Both periodic and special reports can be detail or summary. A **detail report** provides specifics about each action or transaction. The lines representing the actions or transactions are called **detail lines**. The lines showing the accumulated amounts for a group of actions or transactions are called **total lines**. In the detail report illustrated in Figure 13.3, each detail line represents a sales transaction, and each total line shows the accumulated sales total for each customer.

In contrast, a **summary report** includes lines that can represent multiple

FIGURE 13.3

A Detailed Report

```
                                                              Page 1
                          SALES LISTING BY CUSTOMER
                            FOR THE MONTH OF JUNE

   CUSTOMER        CUSTOMER        SALES ORDER      SALE          SALES
   NUMBER           NAME             NUMBER         DATE          AMOUNT

    004329      KEN'S HAIR DESIGN     402398      06/05/89    $      89.23
                                      403871      06/13/89    $      11.14
                                      412289      06/21/89    $      23.15
                                      445491      06/30/89    $     145.67

        Detail lines                 Total line              $     269.19*


    005892      SHEAR CLASS           391432      06/01/89    $     222.59

                                                             $     222.59*


    015692      THE MANE ATTRACTION   423890      06/28/89    $   1,120.00
                                      445492      06/30/89    $     230.95

                                                             $   1,350.95*


    022451      LUNA'S HAIR BOUTIQUE  380429      06/01/89    $     650.00
                                      446499      06/30/89    $      12.00

                                                             $     662.00*


    023567      REGIS HAIR SALON      4789236     06/30/89    $   2,235.67

                                                             $   2,235.67*


    138935      THE FLAIR PLACE       4022644     06/09/89    $      75.60
                                      4022678     06/11/89    $     123.45
                                      4507812     06/30/89    $     123.45

                                                             $     322.50*


    146720      LA VILLA BEAUTY SHOP  4100234     06/15/89    $     145.87
                                      4101234     06/17/89    $   4,567.90

                                                             $   4,713.77*


                                                  TOTAL      $   9,776.67**
```

actions or transactions. Figure 13.4 is a summary report prepared from the same data as the detail report. The detail transaction data is not included.

We recognized in Chapter 6 that, in a general sense, detail information is used at lower-management levels whereas summary information is used at upper levels.

Report Organization

The three main areas of a report are the heading, body, and footing.

In the **heading area**, centered at the top of the page, is **fixed heading material** such as the name of the report. Also included is **variable heading material** such as date and page number.

In the **body area** are **column headings** that identify the **data columns** immediately below. The convention is to place **identification data** (such as numeric codes) on the left, **descriptive data** (such as alphabetic names) in the center, and **quantitative data** (such as dollar amounts) on the right.

In the **footing area** are **total amounts** accumulated while the report is printed. These totals can be **page totals** (separate totals for each page) and **final totals,** also called **overall totals,** for the entire report.

Some reports do not include totals of any type; they simply list actions or transactions. The terms **detail listing** or simply **listing** are used.

Report Sequences

Report lines usually are printed in some particular sequence to make the content more informative. A field in the data records is used to sequence

Page 1

SALES SUMMARY BY CUSTOMER
FOR THE MONTH OF JUNE

CUSTOMER NUMBER	CUSTOMER NAME	SALES AMOUNT
004329	KEN'S HAIR DESIGN	$ 269.19
005892	SHEAR CLASS	$ 222.59
015692	THE MANE ATTRACTION	$ 1,350.95
022451	LUNA'S HAIR BOUTIQUE	$ 662.00
023567	REGIS HAIR SALON	$ 2,235.67
138935	THE FLAIR PLACE	$ 322.50
146720	LA VILLA BEAUTY SHOP	$ 4,713.77
	TOTAL	$ 9,776.67*

FIGURE 13.4
A Summary Report

the records before the report is printed. The field is called a **key field** or **control field**, and can contain both numeric and alphabetic characters.

An **ascending sequence** is the most popular, with the lowest control field values (such as customer number 0001 or name Aardvark) listed first and the highest values (number 9999 or Zikmund) listed last. The other approach is a **descending sequence** that lists items with the highest control field values first. For example, items with the highest sales or with the most number of days since the last activity can appear at the beginning of the listing rather than at the end. We used a descending sequence in Figures 12.3 and 12.4.

Group Totals

Very often totals are printed for groups of records—when the control field changes. The point where this occurs is called a **control break**.

There can be more than one control field. The report in Figure 13.5 is arranged in sequence based on three control fields. The product class is the most important—it is called the **major control field**. The customer number is the least important—it is the **minor control field**. In between is the sales district—the **intermediate control field**.

Since there are three control fields there are three **total levels**. **Major totals** are printed when the major control field changes, **intermediate totals** are printed when the intermediate control field changes, and **minor totals** are printed when the minor control field changes.

FIGURE 13.5

A Report with Minor, Intermediate, and Major Totals

```
                          SALES FOR MONTH OF SEPTEMBER

                            PETROPLEX OFFICE SUPPLY

        PRODUCT     SALES      CUSTOMER       CUSTOMER           SALES
        CLASS     DISTRICT      NUMBER          NAME            DOLLARS
        ------------------------------------------------------------------
          12         14         102236     WOODY'S AUTO SUPPLY  $1250.00
                                134532     NATIONAL CENTER        454.50
                                226793     ABO'S GALLERY          723.75
                                                                $2428.25*

                     18         099235     ALEXANDER & CO.      $   10.00
                                                                $   10.00*

                     23         452988     BOULDER LABS         $  373.95
                                672098     HEINZMAN HARDWARE       5623.00
                                                                $5996.95*

                                                                $8435.20**

          24         32         957620     VARION METALS        $  245.00
                                                                $  245.00*

                                                                $  245.00**

          28         42         349566     ZALES DATA SYSTEMS   $1233.33
                                542863     MIDWEST HOME           890.90
                                694029     METRO NEWS CENTER       12.50
                                737322     SHANE COMPANY            5.00
                                                                $2141.73*

                                                                $2141.73**

             ***COMPANY TOTAL***                              $10,821.93***
```

IMPROVING THE INFORMATION CONTENT OF REPORTS

The value of reports as a problem solving tool can be enhanced by following a few simple guidelines.

- *Tailor reports to the user's needs* The most important point to keep in mind is to design reports to meet the needs of the user.
- *Prepare reports promptly* Reports should be prepared as soon after an activity occurs as possible. Ideally, periodic reports should be available the day after the end of the period. Special reports should be available within a few minutes when the manager uses a query language.
- *Report content should be focused* Periodic reports should address particular areas of the firm's operations, and special reports should shed light on topics of current importance.
- *Keep reports short* Use summaries whenever possible to make it easier to digest the contents.
- *Use screen displays whenever possible* Displayed reports can be retrieved faster and eliminate the storage bulk of printed reports.
- *Make reports easy to read* Use report and column headings, complete descriptions rather than abbreviations, and dates and page numbers. Use asterisks to identify the different total levels as in Figure 13.5. Do not include too much information on a single page.
- *Incorporate management by exception into reports* In Chapter 6 we explained how the principle of management by exception is used to inform managers of only activity that varies significantly from the norm. Management by exception can be incorporated into reports in different ways.

The overtime report in Figure 13.6 is prepared *only when an excep-*

```
                   OVERTIME EARNINGS REPORT

             FOR THE WEEK ENDING AUGUST 19, 1989


    --------------------------------------------------------------
                                        OVERTIME EARNINGS
    DEPARTMENT NO.   DEPARTMENT NAME     CURRENT MONTH    YEAR-TO-DATE
    --------------------------------------------------------------

       16-10         RECEIVING           $ 2,305.00      $ 5,319.20
       16-11         INSPECTION          $ 1,025.60      $ 4,386.12
       16-12         MATERIALS HANDLING  $ 3,392.50      $12,629.00
       16-13         TOOLING             $    78.00      $ 1,049.00
       16-14         ASSEMBLY            $     0.00      $   792.80
       16-15         PLATING             $ 3,504.90      $12,635.20
       16-16         SHIPPING            $ 5,219.16      $18,294.16


               TOTALS                    $15,525.16*     $55,105.48*
```

FIGURE 13.6

An Overtime Earnings Report

tion occurs. In this situation the managers have indicated that they want to know when employees must work overtime to get the work out.

The aged accounts receivables report in Figure 13.7 lists the exceptions (the receivables that are more than thirty days old) in *separate columns.* If the manager is interested in the receivables over ninety days old, that column is scanned to pick them out.

The sales by salesperson report in Figure 13.8 compares the current and year-to-date sales quotas to the current and year-to-date actual sales, and prints the differences in *variance columns.* The manager

FIGURE 13.7

An Aged Accounts Receivable Report

```
                                                                  PAGE 8
                      AGED ACCOUNTS RECEIVABLE REPORT
                           AS OF MAY 31, 1989

    -------------------------------------------------------------------
    -------CUSTOMER ----------    CURRENT   30-60    60-90   OVER 90   TOTAL
    NUMBER        NAME            AMOUNT    DAYS     DAYS     DAYS    AMOUNT
    -------------------------------------------------------------------
    51212   KELLY & MARLEY INC  1,003.10   20.26                    1,023.36
    51221   KENNEDY ELECTRIC      181.34                              181.34
    52472   KENYON MACHINERY      443.10                              443.10
    53204   KEPNER DANA CO                 153.26   114.14   11.12    278.52
    54233   KERITE CO             367.94   101.74                     469.68
    54574   KEYMAN ASSOCIATES                                432.71   432.71
    55081   KIMBULIANS             24.12   122.81                     146.93
    55430   KIRSCH CO              26.30                               26.30
    55943   KOEBEL & CO                     49.42                      49.42
    56247   KOPECKY & CO           31.29   192.52                     223.81
    57163   KUNKLE INC            217.82                              217.82
    58296   LANDE MFG CO          106.95                              106.95
    58342   LANGE CO                        869.40                     869.40
    58654   LARRABEE INC        1,196.35                            1,196.35
    59355   LAURIENTI MFG CO       21.93    1.94                      23.87
    60245   LEBEN DRILLING INC      1.10   476.93   174.96           652.39
    60772   LEEMONT INC            35.87    35.95                      71.82
```

FIGURE 13.8

A Sales by Salesperson Report

```
                          SALES BY SALESPERSON REPORT
                               MARCH 31, 1989

    ----SALESPERSON-----   -----CURRENT-MONTH----   -----YEAR-TO-DATE-----
      NO.      NAME        QUOTA  ACTUAL  VARIANCE   QUOTA  ACTUAL  VARIANCE

      0120  JOHN NELSON     1200   1083     -117      3600   3505     -95
     10469  LYNN SHERRY     1000   1162     +162      3000   3320    +320
     19261  DARVIN UPSHAW    800   1090     +290      2400   2510    +110
     20234  JANIE EVANS     1500   1305     -195      4500   4110    -390
     61604  TRAVIS BURKE    2000   2333     +333      6000   6712    +712
     62083  CATHY HAGER     1000    990      -10      3000   2319    -681
     63049  STEVE JENNER    1100   1250     +150      3300   2416    -884
     64040  SAM MOSELEY     1050    985      -65      3150   3020    -130

            TOTALS          9650  10198      548     28950  27912   -1038
```

scans the variance columns and picks out the very large or very small amounts—the exceptions.

Both the manager and the information specialist can incorporate these features into report designs.

THE ROLE OF REPORTS IN PROBLEM SOLVING

Reports are most helpful in signaling a problem or potential problem, and in providing information that explains a problem once it has been identified. Reports become less helpful when the manager becomes involved in the solution effort.

The objective of report design should be to achieve the same timeliness and focused nature of a memo prepared in response to a current matter.

MATHEMATICAL MODELING

A **model** is an abstraction of something; it represents some phenomenon—an object or an activity. The phenomenon is called the **entity**. If a model represents a firm, the firm is the entity. If a model represents the fluctuation in a firm's inventory, the inventory fluctuation is the entity.

Types of Models

There are four major types of models—narrative, physical, graphical, and mathematical.

You can describe an entity using spoken or written words. When the term *model* is used broadly, the words can be considered a **narrative model**. Narrative models are the most common type, but you know from experience that such models lose their effectiveness as the entity becomes complex. In that situation, the narrative must be supplemented with other types of models.

Narrative Models

One way to describe a complex entity is with a **physical model**—a three-dimensional representation that exists physically. Although you may not be aware of it, you most likely have used physical models. When you were a child you played with toy cars, dolls, and trains. Perhaps you made models—ship models or houses made of blocks. Architects use physical models to give their clients an idea of how a building will appear.

Physical Models

This text makes liberal use of **graphic models**—two-dimensional diagrams with appropriate labels—as a supplement to the narrative. The DSS model in Figure 13.2 is an example. Managers and information specialists make frequent use of graphic models in the form of charts, graphs, flowcharts, and data flow diagrams.

Graphic Models

Any mathematical formula is a **mathematical model.** The most basic business model is the **profit model**, $P = R - C$, where P stands for profit, R for revenue, and C for cost. The letters P, R, and C all represent some aspect of the firm's operations. They are **variables** that assume different values.

Mathematical Models

Some popular business models are not much more complicated than the profit model. The EOQ model explained in Chapter 5 is an example. Very complex mathematical models, however, can include hundreds of formulas and variables.

Types of Mathematical Models

The rest of our discussion will focus on mathematical models. They are the reason for the current interest in modeling as a problem-solving tool.

There are several different ways to classify mathematical models. They can be static or dynamic, probabilistic or deterministic, and optimizing or suboptimizing.

Static or Dynamic Models

A **static model** does not include time as a variable. It deals with a situation at a particular point in time, like a snapshot. A good example is the EOQ formula that computes the optimum order quantity using the values that exist currently for the variables.

A model that includes time as a variable is a **dynamic model**. The model represents the behavior of the entity over time, like a motion picture. The output of the inventory model shown in Figure 13.9 provides an example. This model simulates 225 days of activity, and prints a line for each.

Probabilistic or Deterministic Models

Another way to classify models is based on whether the formulas include probabilities. A **probability** is the chance that something will happen. Probabilities range from 0.00 (for something with no chance) to 1.00 (for something that is a sure thing). Probabilities often are presented as percentages. A weather forecaster says "There's a 30 percent chance of rain." A mathematician would say "The probability of rain is 0.30." A model that includes probabilities is called a **probabilistic model**.

A model that does not include probabilities is a **deterministic model**. The EOQ formula, for example, is a deterministic model.

Optimizing or Suboptimizing Models

An **optimizing model** is one that selects the best solution among the alternatives. For a model to do this, the problem must be very well structured.

A **suboptimizing model** permits a manager to enter a set of decisions and the model will project *an outcome*. The model does not identify the decisions that will produce the best outcome, but leaves that task to the manager who plays the What-If game. Suboptimizing models are often called **satisficing models**—they satisfy the manager. The additional precision that could be gained in identifying the optimum solution is not worth the manager's time.

Simulation

When a model represents its entity, the model is said to simulate the entity. The model is the **simulator**, and the process of using the tool is **simulation**. Just be certain that you do not make a common error by saying that you "simulate the model." You simulate the entity.

The Modeling Scenario

The setting in which a simulation occurs is called the **scenario**. For exam-

FIGURE 13.9

An Inventory Model

```
                  INVENTORY PLANNING MODEL
                      OCTOBER 11, 1989

                      SCENARIO:

             BEGINNING BALANCE:       200

             DAILY SALES UNITS:        20


                      DECISIONS:

             ORDER QUANTITY:          100

             REORDER POINT:           175

             LEAD TIME:                 3


                      RESULTS:
```

| | BEGINNING | | | ENDING | ORDER | RECEIPT |
DAY	BALANCE	RECEIPTS	SALES	BALANCE	QUANTITY	DUE DAY
1	200		20	180		
2	180		20	160	100	5
3	160		20	140		
4	140		20	120		
5	120	100	20	200		
6	200		20	180		
7	180		20	160	100	10
8	160		20	140		
9	140		20	120		
10	120	100	20	200		
11	200		20	180		
12	180		20	160	100	15
13	160		20	140		
224	120	100	20	200		
225	200		20	180		

ple, if you are simulating an inventory system, as shown in Figure 13.9, the scenario specifies the beginning balance and the daily sales units. Models can be designed so that the **scenario items**, the data elements that establish the scenario, are variables, thus enabling different values to be assigned.

Decision Variables

The input values the manager enters to gauge their impact on the entity are known as **decision variables**. In Figure 13.9 the decision variables include the order quantity, reorder point, and lead time (the time required for the supplier to furnish replenishment stock).

Simulation Technique

The manager executes an optimizing model only a single time; it produces the best solution using the scenario items and decision variables. However, it is necessary to execute a suboptimizing model over and over, searching for the combination of decision variables that produces a satisfying outcome. Each time the model is executed only one of the decision variables is changed so that its influence can be seen. For example, the manager manipulates the order quantity until its proper level is identified. Then the reorder point is manipulated, and so on.

Format of Simulation Output

It is a good practice to include the scenario items and decision variables on the same screen or page as the output, as shown in Figure 13.10. Then it is always clear which inputs produced the output.

A MODELING EXAMPLE

We will use an **integrated strategy model** as an example of how a model is used. This type of model would be used by the firm's managers in making four major decisions—the *price* to be charged for a product, the amount of *plant investment* needed to increase the capacity for producing the product, the amount to be invested in *marketing* activity such as advertising and personal selling in order to sell the product, and the amount to be invested in *R & D* (research and development) to improve the product. Managers on the firm's strategic planning (top) level would make these decisions.

The model simulates four quarters of activity and produces two reports—an operating statement that includes key *nonmonetary* values such as market potential (demand) and plant capacity, and an income statement that reflects the results in *monetary* terms. The model is dynamic, deterministic, and suboptimizing.

Model Input

Figure 13.10 shows the input screen used to enter the scenario items and decision variables. The values for the first quarter already have been entered. The top three lines contain the scenario for the *last quarter*. Some of the values relate to the firm—its plant capacity, the number of units produced, the dollar value of raw materials, and so forth. The others relate to the influence of the firm's environment (economic index, seasonal index, competitor price, and competitor marketing).

The fourth line contains scenario items for the *next quarter*. The managers indicate they want to simulate four quarters, and enter estimates for the economic and seasonal indexes, and for the competitor's price and marketing.

The fifth line includes the four decisions, with space at the right where the results in the form of after-tax profit will be displayed. The managers enter *trial figures* for the decisions so they can see the effect on operations *if* the decisions are put into practice.

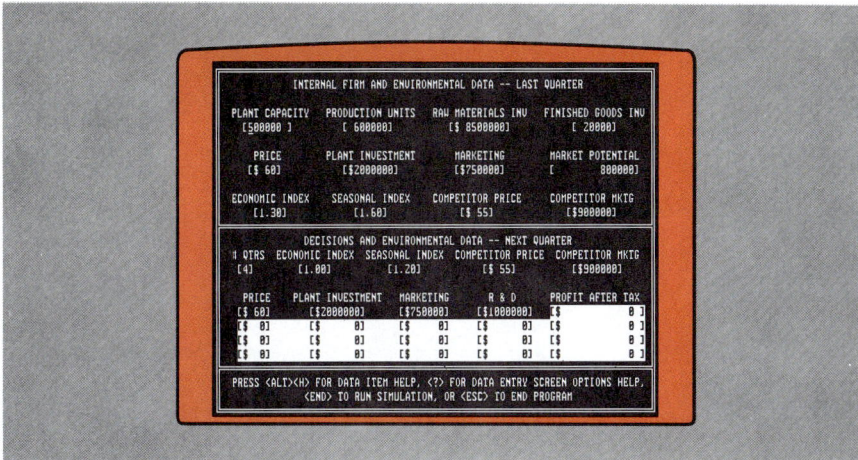

FIGURE 13.10
A Model Input
Screen

Model Output

The next quarter's activity (quarter 1) is simulated, and after-tax profit is displayed on the screen. The managers study the figure and decide on the set of decisions to be used in quarter 2. Those decisions are entered and the simulation is repeated. This process continues until all four quarters have been simulated. At that point the screen has the appearance shown in Figure 13.11. The decisions and resulting after-tax profit are listed in reverse sequence at the bottom of the screen. The figures for the fourth quarter are on top.

The managers can obtain more detailed output for the four quarters' activity in displayed or printed form. As you can see in Figure 13.12, the operating statement and income statement are displayed on separate screens.

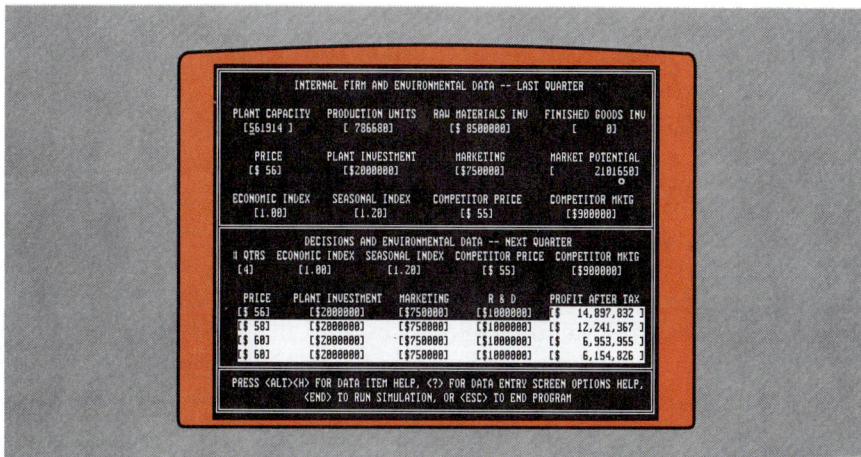

FIGURE 13.11
Summary Output
Is Displayed on
the Screen

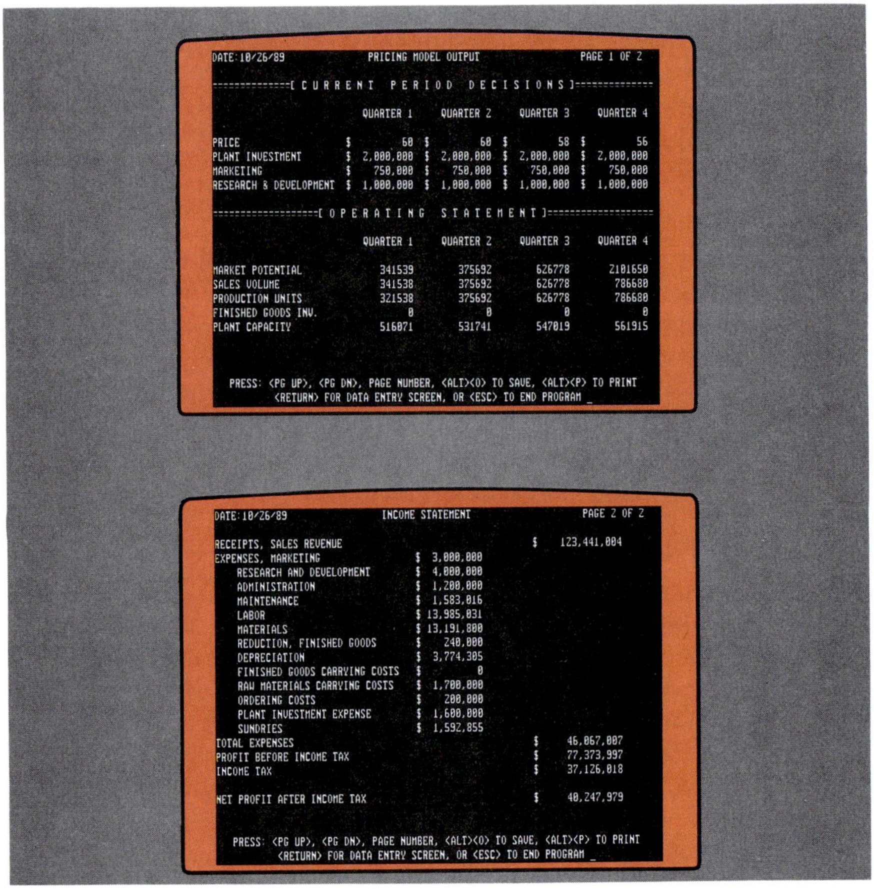

FIGURE 13.12

Detailed Output
Can Be Displayed
or Printed

The managers might enter dozens of sets of decisions in the process of finding the combination they believe to be best. In addition, the managers might try several scenarios—entering different scenario items for each quarter. When such a large volume of input data is required it might be a good idea to use a chauffeur, as described in Chapter 6.

MODELING SOFTWARE

The integrated strategy model is written in BASIC. The approach of using a **procedural language** has been the most common during the thirty-odd years of computer modeling.

Another avenue has also been available to modelers—the use of a specially designed **modeling language**. One of the first was GPSS (General Purpose Simulation System) developed by IBM in the early 1960s. Others came on the market, the most popular being DYNAMO, SLAM, SIMSCRIPT, GASP, and MODEL. These languages are especially suited to developing models but are not noted for being user friendly.

The approach currently receiving the most attention is the use of the

fourth-generation languages described in Chapter 2. Electronic spreadsheets fit into this category and make it easy for end users to develop their own models. Spreadsheets are not as flexible as procedural languages and are not ideally suited to all types of problems. However, in those cases where spreadsheets can be used, they produce a model more quickly and easily than using a procedural language.

THE KEY TO SUCCESSFUL MODEL USE

The key to successful model use is knowing how to evaluate the output. No model is perfect; they all incorporate certain assumptions and simplifications as a way of coping with the complexity of the real world. For example, the integrated strategy model requires the users to estimate the upcoming economic and seasonal indexes as well as the competitor's price and marketing. The users know that these inputs are only estimates, making the output only an estimate.

For this reason, managers never use model output without injecting their experience and intuition. This practice applies to optimizing as well as suboptimizing models.

THE ROLE OF MODELING IN PROBLEM SOLVING

Of the three ways to obtain information from the CBIS, only modeling takes a look into the future. That is where the manager believes the keys to success can be found.

You would think that the predictive ability of the model would make it a widely used management tool. Until recently, however, most managers avoided modeling due to the mathematical knowledge required. Feeling deficient in that regard, managers generally turned the modeling chores over to **management scientists** or **operations researchers**—persons skilled in applying quantitative techniques to business problems.

That situation changed dramatically during the 1980s. The availability of such user-friendly modeling tools as electronic spreadsheets has encouraged managers to develop their own models. These tend to be the simpler models. Management scientists and information specialists with modeling skills will continue to work with the managers in developing the more complex models.

THE ROLE OF THE DSS IN PROBLEM SOLVING

Whereas modeling has captured most of the decision-support attention, periodic and special reports should not be overlooked as means of obtaining information for problem solving.

We saw in Chapter 12 that the MIS is best suited to identifying problems and helping managers understand them. The DSS can extend this support through the remaining steps of the problem-solving process. This added capability is not because of the tools used, since MIS and DSS both employ the same ones. The reason for the more complete support is the fact that the DSSs are tailored to the specific needs of the individual managers.

SUMMARY

Gorry and Scott Morton conceived of the idea of a decision support system aimed at semistructured problems. These problems are faced by managers on all levels. Alter defined the DSS in terms of the support it provides—from single data elements to actual decisions.

It is not easy to distinguish DSS from MIS, but DSS more closely meets the needs of the individual, provides direct support, supports all phases of the problem-solving process, is aimed at semistructured problems, and emphasizes the role of decision making in problem solution.

Both the DSS and MIS can provide information in the form of periodic reports, special reports, or results of mathematical simulations. Both periodic and special reports can be printed or displayed; both can be detail or summary.

Reports are organized into heading, body, and footing areas. The information content of a report is influenced by the sequence. The basic sequences are ascending and descending. Minor, intermediate, and major totals can be printed when control fields change. The decision-support value of reports can be enhanced by tailoring them to the user's needs, preparing them promptly, focusing on topics of current importance, keeping them short, using screen displays when possible, making them easy to read, and incorporating management by exception.

There are four major types of models—narrative, physical, graphic, and mathematical. Mathematical models can be static or dynamic, probabilistic or deterministic, and optimizing or suboptimizing.

Model input consists of scenario items and decision variables. The manager changes one decision variable at a time to see the influence on output.

Mathematical models can be created by using a procedural language, a modeling language, or a fourth-generation language. Electronic spreadsheets are an example of a 4GL, and they are credited with the current popularity of end-user modeling. The key to successful model use is an ability to interpret the output—making adjustments when necessary so that the output more closely matches reality.

Models provide the manager with a look into the future, a type of decision support that neither periodic nor special reports can provide. A DSS provides a high level of decision support because it is tailored to a specific decision faced by a single manager or group of managers.

KEY CONCEPTS

The varying complexity of a DSS, ranging from retrieval of single data elements to models that make decisions

How DSS differs from MIS

How the information content of reports can be improved

Ways to classify mathematical models

How model input consists of both scenario items and decision variables

The importance of interpreting model output before using it in decision making

KEY TERMS

Detail report
Summary report
Listing
Ascending sequence
Model
Entity
Variable
Static model
Dynamic model

Probabilistic model
Deterministic model
Optimizing model
Suboptimizing model, satisficing
    model
Simulator
Scenario
Decision variable

QUESTIONS

1. Which management level(s) should the DSS support? Justify your answer using material from the chapter.

2. Which problem-solving steps does the DSS support better than does the MIS? Use the steps listed in Figure 13.2.

3. What are the three primary forms of information provided by a DSS or MIS?

4. When is a special report prepared?

5. What are the three main areas of a report? Which one is not found in a detail listing?

6. What causes a total to be printed? What are the three levels of totals?

7. List three ways to incorporate management by exception into reports.

8. What are the four types of models? Which is the most common type? Which has accounted for the current interest in decision modeling?

9. What name is given to the letters used in a mathematical model? Why is that name appropriate?

10. Which type of model is like a snapshot? Like a motion picture?

11. Why would a manager be satisfied with a model's output even though he or she knows that the output might not be the absolute best?

12. What distinguishes a scenario item from a decision variable?

13. Why is it a good practice to manipulate only a single decision variable at a time?

14. Why include the scenario items and decision variables on the model output?

15. What feature not found in periodic or special reports does modeling offer?

CASE PROBLEM   Racine Paper Products

"Ms. Vance? I'm Blanca San Miguel. I'm a systems analyst from information services, and we're conducting a survey of all the people who receive reports to see if there is any way they can be improved. According to our records you get the monthly product sales report. Is that true?"

Susan Vance, sales manager for Racine Paper Products, began to shuffle the papers on her desk and said "I think I have it around here someplace. I usually don't keep it, but I think I received one yesterday. I really don't use it. The person who was here before me ordered it and it just keeps coming. I've been meaning to call you people and tell you to stop, but I just never got around to it. Too busy, I guess."

"Do you mind if I sit down?" Blanca asked. "It looks like the report could use some improvement. I've got a copy here. Why don't you take a look at it and tell me what's wrong?"

Blanca placed the thick report in front of Susan. Looking at the top of the report, Susan said "Well, to begin with, this report is for the month of October and it's dated November 12. Why does it take twelve days to get it out? By the time I get it, it's past history."

"It's probably because it's so lengthy" Blanca replied. "We have a lot of reports like that, and it takes a long time to print all of the pages. Add to that the time required to route it through the company mails, and you've got a long delay. I grant you that we should be able to get it out sooner. All of the data is in the computer at the end of the month. Let me see what I can do to speed things up. Anything else?"

"As a matter of fact, yes. Isn't there some way to boil all of this down? That would certainly make the report easier to read. I suspect we have a lot of products that are just dead weight—we haven't sold any in ages and aren't likely to sell any more in the future. It would be best to just get rid of them. I know that if I spent several days going through this printout I could spot the nonprofitable items, but that seems to be a tremendous price to pay. I just don't have that kind of time."

"Oh, I am sure that we can give you a report that would help you make that decision without taking up all of your time," Blanca replied.

"What constitutes a product that isn't selling? Could you give us some guidelines?"

"Well, if it hasn't sold in six months I'd like to know about it. Could you tell me that?"

Blanca pulled a sheet of paper out of a folder and said "Here is the layout of the record we use to print the report. It doesn't have the date of the last sale in it, but I'm sure we could add it. Then it would be a simple matter to select those records that have been dormant for six months—or for any period."

Just then Susan's secretary walked into the room and said "Ms. Vance. They're ready for you in the conference room. Shall I tell them you will be a little late?"

"No. I'm on my way. Ms. San Miguel, I appreciate you taking the time to go over this report with me. If you could do some of the things we talked about, I'm sure I would use it more often. Why don't you work on it and get back with me?"

"One last question" Blanca asked as Susan headed toward the door. "Have you ever used the computer?"

"Oh no" Susan replied. "I'm no programmer."

1. Does it sound like Susan needs a special report or a periodic one? Explain your answer.

2. Should the report be a detailed listing or a summary? Explain.

3. What could be done to cut down on the delay in getting the report to Susan?

4. Would you recommend an ascending or descending sequence? What would be the control field?

5. How could management by exception be incorporated into the report?

6. Assume that the company decides to offer an inhouse course for managers in the use of a query language. What reasons could Blanca give Susan that she attend?

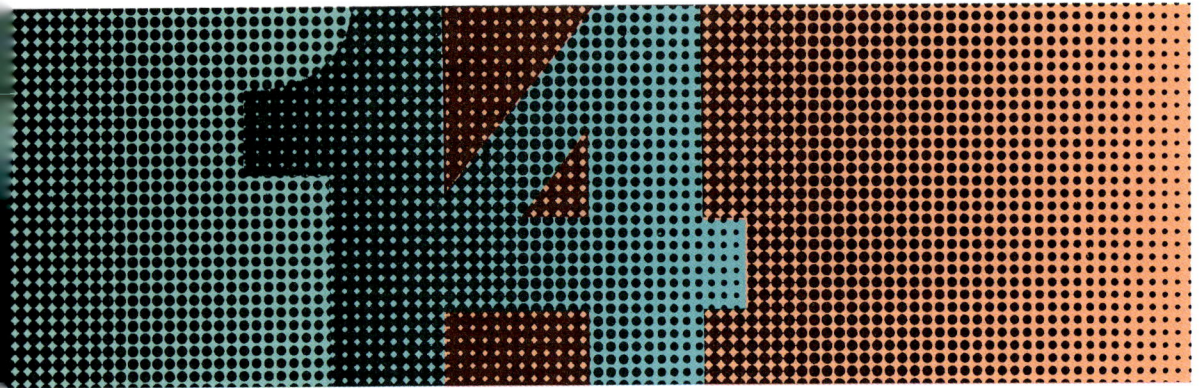

Office Automation

LEARNING OBJECTIVES   After studying this chapter, you should:

- Know the different application areas within office automation
- Understand the role that office automation plays in problem solving

---

OVERVIEW

Office automation is intended to increase productivity. When applied as a problem-solving tool, office automation enables managers to better communicate with each other while problems are being solved. The improved communications result in both better and faster decisions.

We begin the chapter by tracing the origin of office automation—recognizing that it has not always been linked with problem solving. Then the various office automation applications such as word processing and electronic mail are described. The chapter concludes with an office automation model that serves as a basis for tailoring office automation to the communication styles of individual managers.

AUTOMATION IN THE FACTORY

Automation is the use of machinery to perform physical tasks that normally are performed by human beings. The first applications of automation were in the factory. In the late 1950s production machines were designed so that they could be controlled by holes punched in paper tape. The application was called **numerical control**, and the machines could do the work faster and more accurately than when they had human operators. Then the machines were designed so that they could be controlled directly by a minicomputer—**direct numerical control**. More recently factory robots, CAM (computer aided manufacturing) and CAD (computer aided design) have contributed to automation in the production area.

Firms have regarded factory automation as a means of achieving greater productivity and thus competing better in world markets. During the 1970s firms spent an average of $25,000 for the purpose of increasing each factory worker's productivity. The investment paid off as productivity rose an average of 85 to 90 percent.[1]

OFFICE AUTOMATION

The picture in the office, however, has been different. During the 1970s the capital investment per office worker was in the $2,000 to $4,000 range, and productivity rose only 4 percent. When these figures were compared to those in the factory, managers realized that office productivity had been neglected.

Unplanned Growth

Although factory automation has been impressive, it has not followed any grand plan. As the innovations in technology came along, manufacturing managers simply took advantage of them. The same thing has happened in the office.

The origin of office automation can be traced back to the early 1960s when IBM coined the term *word processing* to describe the activity of its electric typewriter division. The term expressed the concept that office activity is centered around the processing of *words*. The intent was to draw the same attention to office products that had been achieved by computers and *data processing*.

The first tangible evidence of this new concept came in 1964 when IBM placed on the market a machine called the MT/ST. The letters stood for Magnetic Tape/Selectric Typewriter. The Selectric had been the name given to IBM's typewriter that featured the rotating-ball typing element. The MT/ST was a Selectric typewriter with a magnetic tape unit attached. As a form letter was typed, it was stored on tape. The letter could be typed over and over from the tape. The typist only had to type in the name and address of the person to receive the letter. The letter looked as if it had been typed especially for the person.

During the ensuing years other technologies were applied to office work—some involving computers and some not. All of the applications became known as office automation.

---

[1]The figures in this and the next section are from Nancy B. Finn, *The Electronic Office* (Englewood Cliffs, NJ: Prentice-Hall, 1983), pp. 8–9.

What Is Office Automation?

Office automation, or **OA**, includes all of the formal and informal systems primarily concerned with the communication of information to and from persons in the firm. The key word that distinguishes OA from data processing, MIS, and DSS is *communication*. OA is intended to facilitate all types of communication, both oral and written.

Who Uses Office Automation?

OA is used by people who work in offices. Since an office can include anything from a paneled executive suite to a cubbyhole in an inventory storeroom, the range of OA users is broad. Essentially there are four categories of OA users: managers, professionals, secretaries, and clerical employees.

FIGURE 14.1
Office Workers

We know who the managers are. The **professionals** are persons who do not manage others but contribute some special skill that distinguishes them from secretarial and clerical employees. Professionals usually are paid a *salary* whereas secretaries and clerical employees very often are paid on an *hourly* basis. Examples of professionals are buyers, salespersons, and such special staff assistants as marketing researchers, statisticians, and administrative assistants. The term **knowledge worker** has been applied to the managers and professionals—persons whose main contribution to their activities is their knowledge.

The secretaries and clerical workers support the knowledge workers. **Secretaries** usually are assigned to particular knowledge workers to perform a variety of duties such as handling correspondence, answering the telephone, and maintaining appointments calendars. **Clerical employees** perform tasks for the secretaries, relieving the secretaries of such activities as operating copying machines, assembling documents, filing, and mailing.

The Objective of Office Automation

Up until about 1980, OA was seen as a way of increasing the productivity of only secretaries and clerical employees. The OA products enabled these office workers to process more documents faster and better. Then it became apparent that the knowledge workers could benefit from OA as well. OA could make it easier for the knowledge workers to prepare *outgoing correspondence*. For example, the knowledge workers or their secretaries could use word processing to prepare letters, memos, and reports.

But the outgoing correspondence of one person is the incoming correspondence of another. Viewed as a means of stimulating *incoming correspondence*, OA becomes a tool to be used in obtaining information for problem solving. The recipient can benefit from the higher quality of the documents—they provide a better basis for decision making.

We recognized in Chapter 8 that firms can avoid future increases in clerical costs by using computers. This applies especially to OA where firms see the increased secretarial and clerical productivity as a means of delaying the addition of more personnel. Whereas these avoided clerical costs are good objectives, they are modest when compared to the potential benefits of using OA as a problem-solving tool. The improved decisions of the managers, which come as a result of the improved communications, have the potential of producing higher revenues for the firm in the form of increased sales and improved return on investments. The potential contribution to the firm's profits is much greater for the higher revenues than for the avoided costs.

Higher Revenues versus Cost Avoidance

The manner in which OA contributes to communications both to and from managers makes it especially applicable to group problem solving. We have recognized that managers seldom solve problems alone. They communicate throughout the steps of the problem-solving process, and OA can be used for some of the communication.

Group Problem Solving

As we recognize the role of OA in problem solving, we should also recognize that it has its limitations. It will not replace *all* traditional interpersonal communications—face-to-face conversations, telephone conversations, notes jotted on memo pads, and the like. Those informal communications will continue, since they are both convenient and effective. OA should have the objective of *supplementing* the traditional interpersonal communications, rather than replacing them completely.

A Supplement—Not a Replacement

OA Applications

At least eleven separate OA applications have been identified. They include:

- Word processing
- Electronic mail
- Voice mail
- Electronic calendaring

- Audio conferencing
- Video conferencing
- Computer conferencing
- Facsimile transmission
- Videotex
- Image storage and retrieval
- Desktop publishing.

We will discuss each of the applications below.

Word Processing

Word processing is the use of an electronic device that automatically performs many of the tasks necessary to prepare typed or printed documents. The electronic device comes in two basic forms: a system called a dedicated word processor, and a general-purpose computer. A **dedicated word processor** is a keydriven device designed to perform only word processing, and its specialized hardware and software work together as a unit. A general-purpose computer achieves its word processing capabilities through software. The computer can be a mainframe, a minicomputer, or a microcomputer. Most dedicated word processors have been replaced by general-purpose computers, especially microcomputers.

Figure 14.2 shows the primary units of a word processing system. The operator uses a keyboard to type the material, which is displayed on the screen. The operator can easily make changes to the displayed material—adding and deleting words, moving sentences around, adjusting the margins and spacing, and so on. Then the material is entered in secondary storage and printed.

The printed output can be used for making additional changes. The stored copy is retrieved and the changes are keyed into the system. Another printout is prepared, which allows for still further changes. This cycle is repeated until the user feels that the document is just right.

Word processing contributes to problem solving by enabling the manager to prepare more effective written communications to other members

FIGURE 14.2

A Word Processing System

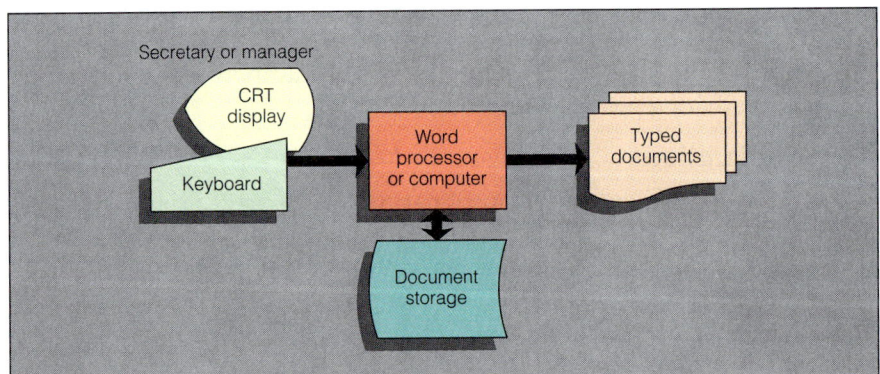

of the problem-solving team. The manager benefits as well when others, both inside and outside the firm, use word processing in preparing memos, letters, and reports for the manager.

Electronic Mail

Electronic mail is the use of a networked computer that allows users to send, store, and receive messages using the computer's terminals and storage devices. Figure 14.3 shows the system configuration. A user types a message using his or her terminal keyboard, and the message is placed in the recipient's **electronic mailbox** in computer storage. The message is retrieved at the convenience of the recipient, using his or her terminal and providing the proper password.

Electronic mail is intended to solve a problem called **telephone tag**—the game that you and someone else play when you alternately return calls and the other person is out or is unavailable.

Of course, electronic mail handles only one-way communications. If you wish to carry on a two-way conversation with someone, you must send multiple electronic mail messages back and forth.

Several options can be used in sending the messages, depending on the particular electronic mail software. If you want everyone in the firm with a terminal to read the message, it is placed on an **electronic bulletin board**, which everyone can access. If you want to receive a confirmation when the recipient retrieves your message, it can be sent as **registered mail**. If you do not want the recipient to route the message to others in the network you can send it as **private mail**.

Before electronic mail, managers would jot messages down on notepaper and the messages would then be typed in memo form by their secretaries. The memos would often be typed several times as the managers

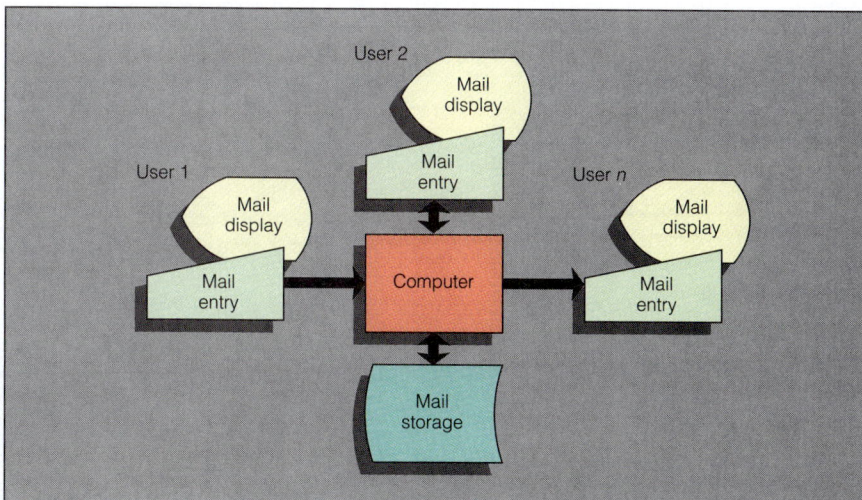

FIGURE 14.3

An Electronic Mail System

made corrections. This document preparation cycle can be speeded up considerably when managers key in their own electronic mail messages.

By using established electronic mail networks or by subscribing to electronic mail services, it is possible to communicate on a global basis. The major role of electronic mail in problem solving is the dissemination of information among members of the problem-solving team, regardless of their location.

Voice Mail

Voice mail is just like electronic mail only you send messages by speaking them into your telephone rather than typing them, and you use your telephone to retrieve messages that have been sent to you. Voice mail requires a computer with an ability to store the audio messages in a digital form and then convert them back to an audio form upon retrieval, as illustrated in Figure 14.4. Standard secondary storage units contain the user's **voice mailboxes**, and special equipment converts the audio messages to and from the digital form.

The main advantage of voice mail over electronic mail is that the manager does not have to type. Voice mail is not limited to inhouse use. If a manager wishes to communicate by voice mail with someone external to the firm, the manager only need reserve a voice mailbox for that person. The external contact can both send and receive voice mail messages using the manager's system.

Electronic Calendaring

Electronic calendaring is the use of a networked computer to store and retrieve a manager's appointments calendar as shown in Figure 14.5. The manager or manager's secretary can enter appointments, make changes, and review the calendar using a keyboard terminal. Figure 3.13 illustrates how a manager's calendar might appear in electronic form.

FIGURE 14.4
A Voice Mail
System

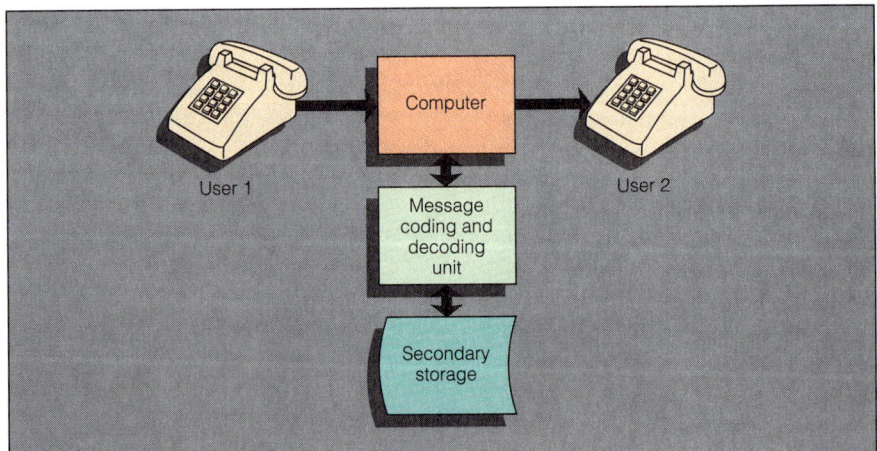

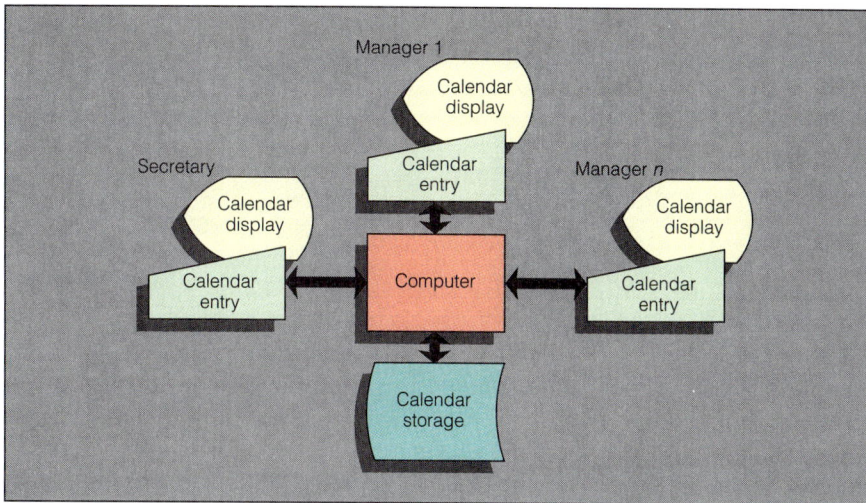

FIGURE 14.5

An Electronic
Calendaring System

It is possible to access other manager's calendars in addition to your own. If you want to schedule a meeting, the computer can check the other persons' calendars to pick a mutually convenient time. If you want to walk down the hall to talk with someone, you can check their calendar first to determine if they are available. If you prefer, you can prevent others from accessing all or part of your own calendar.

Electronic calendaring is unique among the OA applications in that it does not actually communicate information. Rather, it sets the stage for the communication. It is most useful to managers on upper levels who have complicated appointments schedules.

Audio Conferencing

Audio conferencing is the use of voice communications equipment to establish an audio link between geographically dispersed persons for the purpose of conducting a conference. The **conference call** that allows more than two persons to participate in a telephone conversation was the first form of audio conferencing and can still be used. However, much more elaborate systems are possible. Firms often install private, high-quality audio communications circuits between conference sites that can be established with the flip of a switch.

This is the first OA application discussed that does not require a computer. It only involves the use of a two-way audio communications facility as illustrated in Figure 14.6.

Audio conferencing appeals to firms that are spread over a wide area. Members of the problem-solving team can use the audio communications to exchange information and coordinate their activities.

Video Conferencing

Video conferencing supplements the audio signal with a video signal. Like

FIGURE 14.6

An Audio
Conferencing
System

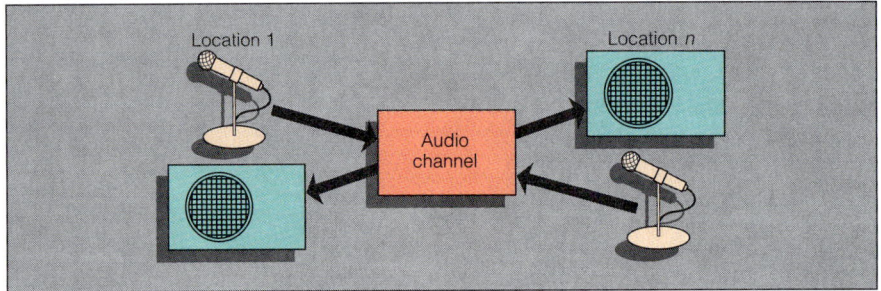

audio conferencing, video conferencing does not involve the use of a computer. Television equipment is used to send and receive the video and audio signals. Persons in one location can both see and hear persons in other locations as a conference is conducted. Figure 14.7 shows a video conference room where the images of participants in other locations can be viewed as the conference takes place. The firm can construct its own video conference rooms, or it can rent them from such organizations as telephone companies and larger hotel chains.

FIGURE 14.7

A Video Conference

One-Way Video and One-Way Audio

Video and audio signals are sent from a single transmitting site to one or more receiving sites. This is the most economical technique and has been in use for over thirty years, called a **closed-circuit telecast**. It can be used by a team leader to disseminate information to other team members.

One-Way Video and Two-Way

The two-way audio capability enables persons at the receiving sites to engage in conversation with persons at the transmitting site as all participants view the same video images.

Two-Way Video and Audio

The video and audio communications between all sites are two-way. This setup most closely resembles a conference where all participants are in the same room. However, it is the most expensive of the electronic aided conferencing approaches.

Computer Conferencing

Computer conferencing is the use of a networked computer to allow persons to exchange information during the process of carrying on a conference. This application is very similar to electronic mail. In fact, the same hardware and software are used for both applications. The diagram of electronic mail in Figure 14.3 applies to computer conferencing as well.

Computer conferencing is distinguished from electronic mail in that participation in a computer conference is confined to a well-defined group such as a committee, and exchanged information is confined to the activities of the committee.

Computer conferencing enables the exchange without the participants being involved at the same time—an **asynchronous exchange** of information. There have been instances where a computer conference member will enter a message at 2 o'clock in the morning or on a Sunday afternoon. Audio and video conferencing, on the other hand, require that all participants be on the scene at the same time in the traditional way—a **synchronous exchange**.

The term **teleconferencing** has been used to describe all three forms of electronic aided conferencing—audio, video, and computer conferencing. Teleconferencing can be used throughout the problem-solving process for exchanging information among the problem-solvers who are located in different cities. This capability enables persons who otherwise would be left out for reasons of geography to contribute to problem solution.

Facsimile Transmission

Facsimile transmission, commonly called **FAX**, is the use of special equipment that can read a document image at one end of a communication channel and make a copy at the other end, as diagrammed in Figure 14.8. A good name for the application would be long-distance copying.

The system is extremely easy to implement and operate. An ordinary voice-grade telephone line can serve as the channel and the equipment operation is no more difficult than that of a copying machine.

FAX contributes to problem solving by disseminating documents to members of the problem-solving team quickly and easily, regardless of their geographic location. Of special value to problem solvers is the ability to transmit graphic as well as textual material. Anything that can be copied on an office copier can be transmitted.

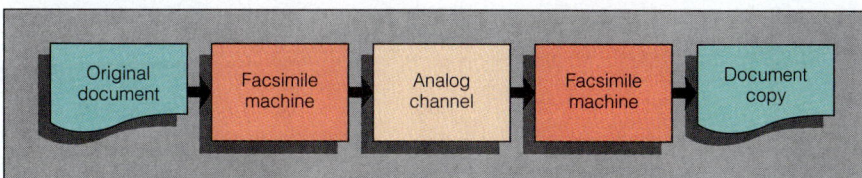

FIGURE 14.8
Facsimile Transmission

Original document → Facsimile machine → Analog channel → Facsimile machine → Document copy

Like voice mail, a manager can establish a FAX linkage with environmental contacts. The factor making this linkage possible is the set of FAX protocols that have been established on an international basis.

Videotex

Videotex is the use of a computer for the purpose of providing the display of stored information on a CRT screen. The information can exist in a narrative, tabular, or graphic form, and is stored in the computer's secondary storage. There are three basic sources of videotex material.

- Users can access material in the firm's *own computer*.
- The firm can subscribe to a *videotex service*, which enables users to access the storage of the service's computer.
- The firm can obtain access to the storage of *other firms*.

Thus far there has been little interest in the first and third approaches. Firms have been unwilling to go to the expense of creating their own videotex and they have been slow to realize the potential for shared information storage. A good example of the potential for shared storage is in the purchasing area. Suppliers could make their catalogs and price lists available to their customers' buyers in videotex form. The buyers would not have to maintain bulky catalogs as is now the practice, and would simply query the supplier's videotex storage as prices or specifications are needed.

Most of the videotex interest has centered around the second approach—the videotex subscription service. There are an increasing number of such services to which a firm can subscribe, in much the same manner as you subscribe to a newspaper or magazine. In fact, it is possible to receive the *New York Times* in videotex form. Two videotex services are of

FIGURE 14.9

A Videotex Display

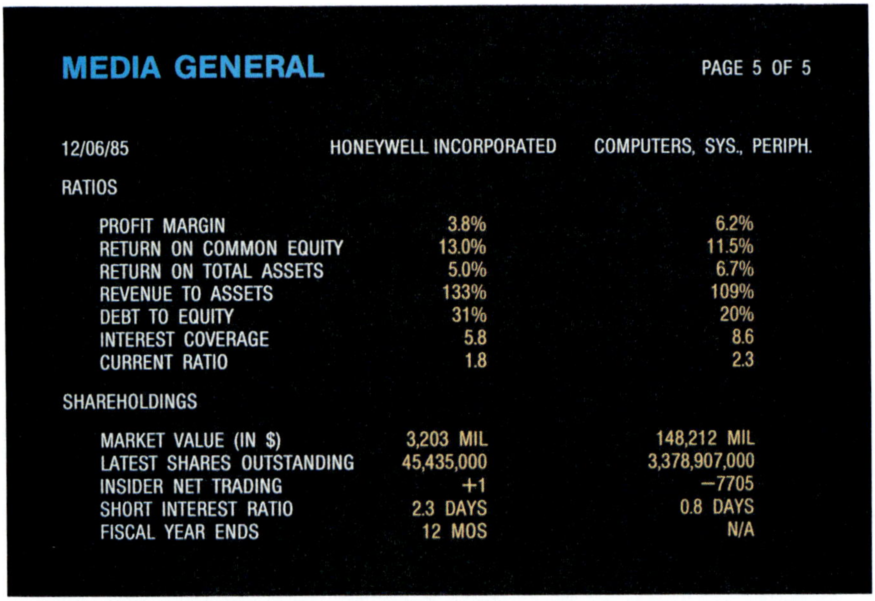

MEDIA GENERAL		PAGE 5 OF 5
12/06/85	HONEYWELL INCORPORATED	COMPUTERS, SYS., PERIPH.
RATIOS		
PROFIT MARGIN	3.8%	6.2%
RETURN ON COMMON EQUITY	13.0%	11.5%
RETURN ON TOTAL ASSETS	5.0%	6.7%
REVENUE TO ASSETS	133%	109%
DEBT TO EQUITY	31%	20%
INTEREST COVERAGE	5.8	8.6
CURRENT RATIO	1.8	2.3
SHAREHOLDINGS		
MARKET VALUE (IN $)	3,203 MIL	148,212 MIL
LATEST SHARES OUTSTANDING	45,435,000	3,378,907,000
INSIDER NET TRADING	+1	−7705
SHORT INTEREST RATIO	2.3 DAYS	0.8 DAYS
FISCAL YEAR ENDS	12 MOS	N/A

special interest to problem solvers—the Dow Jones News/Retrieval service and Datext.

- *Dow Jones News/Retrieval Service* Subscribers can use their terminals to access current or recent business information stored in the Dow Jones central computer. Two types of information are made available—business news items, and stock prices. The business news items are especially valuable in signaling problems or potential problems to all types of managers. The stock prices are especially valuable to financial managers.
- *Lotus One Source* This videotex service comes in the form of compact disks that the firm can use with its own computer. One of the disks is a videotex file named *CD/Corporate* that contains financial information on topics such as SEC filings, U.S. mergers and acquisitions, and U.K. public companies. Financial analysts can bring contents such as these up on their screens, and can transport the data into their electronic spreadsheets for additional processing.

After gaining initial acceptance in Europe, videotex began to make an impact in the United States. Its popularity will continue to increase as additional subscription services are offered and firms use videotex as a means to establish electronic linkages with their suppliers and customers.

Image Storage and Retrieval

We recognized in Chapter 8 that some firms have large volumes of documents, which they must maintain in files so that the information can be retrieved when needed. Initially, these files were maintained in paper form, but the space requirements became intolerable. The solution was to store an *image* of the document rather than the document itself, and microfilm provided a good medium. Today the microfilm is giving way to compact disk media as a way for the computer to perform both storage and retrieval functions.

This OA application has recently become known as **imaging,** the use of optical character recognition to convert paper or microfilm records to a digital format for storage in a secondary storage device. Once stored, the images can be retrieved for display or printing.

Imaging processes are performed by a **document management (DM)** system. The system consists of one or more optical character recognition (OCR) units for converting the document images to a digited form. Document management software is used to store the digitized data in compact disk storage, and make the images available to users who access the system from their workstations. The workstations are equipped with high-resolution screens.

Imaging is just getting off the ground, and the legal aspects are still being worked out. A few states have passed legislation that makes the digitized images admissable as evidence in court.

Imaging is used in problem solving when it is necessary to review historical documents for the purpose of understanding a problem. An operator accesses the DM system from a workstation, and produces a hard copy output for the manager.

Desktop Publishing

The newest member of the OA application family is desktop publishing. **Desktop publishing**, or **DTP**, is the preparation of printed output that is very close in quality to that produced by a typesetter. A DTP system consists of: a microcomputer with a high-resolution CRT screen, a laser printer, and DTP software. The high-resolution screen enables the operator to display the image in a form that is almost as clear and sharp as it will be printed—a feature called **WYSIWYG** (meaning "what you see is what you get"). The laser printer produces an output that is much better than that achieved with a dot matrix or even a daisy wheel printer. The laser printer can print as many as 300 dpi (dots per inch) compared to ninety-six by seventy-two dots per inch for a dot matrix printer. Figure 14.10 shows the results that are possible. The DTP software permits the selection of the type fonts and sizes, hyphenation and right-margin justification, addition of horizontal and vertical lines, and layout of pages (including graphics).

In some cases the DTP system can perform all of the publishing tasks, but in other cases it cannot. When professional typesetter quality is needed, the DTP system can produce a diskette that is used to drive the typesetter's equipment. When the layout includes special illustrations, such as halftone photos that the DTP software cannot produce or cannot import from other sources, blank areas can be left in the layout for the illustrations to be inserted by hand.

DTP applications fall into three areas: administrative, technical, and corporate graphics. **Administrative applications** include documents intended for such internal use as correspondence, reports, and newsletters. **Technical**

FIGURE 14.10

A Page Printed by a Desktop Publishing System

applications include such training materials as slides, overhead transparencies, and manuals. **Corporate graphics** include advertisements, brochures, and other documents intended for use outside the firm.[2]

The use of DTP as a problem-solving tool includes both administrative and technical applications. Members of the problem-solving team can use DTP to prepare proposals and reports to communicate among themselves and with others in the organization. The attractive, professional appearance of the documents adds to their communication effectiveness. In addition, slides and transparencies, produced from DTP documents, can be used in group problem-solving sessions.

THE ROLE OF OFFICE AUTOMATION IN PROBLEM SOLVING

Throughout the text we have emphasized the role of information in problem solving. Most of our examples have dealt with the use of the computer as an information system—making information available in the form of reports and simulations. However, we have also recognized that much of the information comes from noncomputer sources—primarily interpersonal communications. It is this area where OA shines. All of the OA applications we have discussed facilitate the communication of information among the members of the problem-solving team as they take the steps leading from the problem signal to the solution.

An OA Model

The communication potential of OA can be seen in the model pictured in Figure 14.11.[3] The rectangles represent the roles the manager plays. You recall that we discussed Mintzberg's managerial roles in Chapter 6. Information flows to and from the manager as the roles are played.

- When playing the *liaison role* the manager obtains information from the firm's environment, from other operating units in the firm, and from such internal support units as the information services department.
- When playing the *leader role* the manager obtains information from both superiors and subordinates.
- When playing the *monitor role* the manager passes the information along to others (the *spokesperson role* or *disseminator role*) or uses the information in decision making (the four roles at the bottom of the figure).

The circles in the model represent the individuals and groups with whom the manager exchanges information, and the parallelograms represent one or more OA applications that can facilitate the flow of information.

---

[2] This classification was taken from Pamela Jarvis, "Desktop Publishing: Is It for Every Office?", *The Office* 105 (June 1987): 65ff.

[3] This model is described in a more detailed fashion in Raymond McLeod, Jr. and Jack W. Jones, "A Framework for Office Automation," *MIS Quarterly* 11 (March 1987): 86–104.

FIGURE 14.11   An Office Automation Model

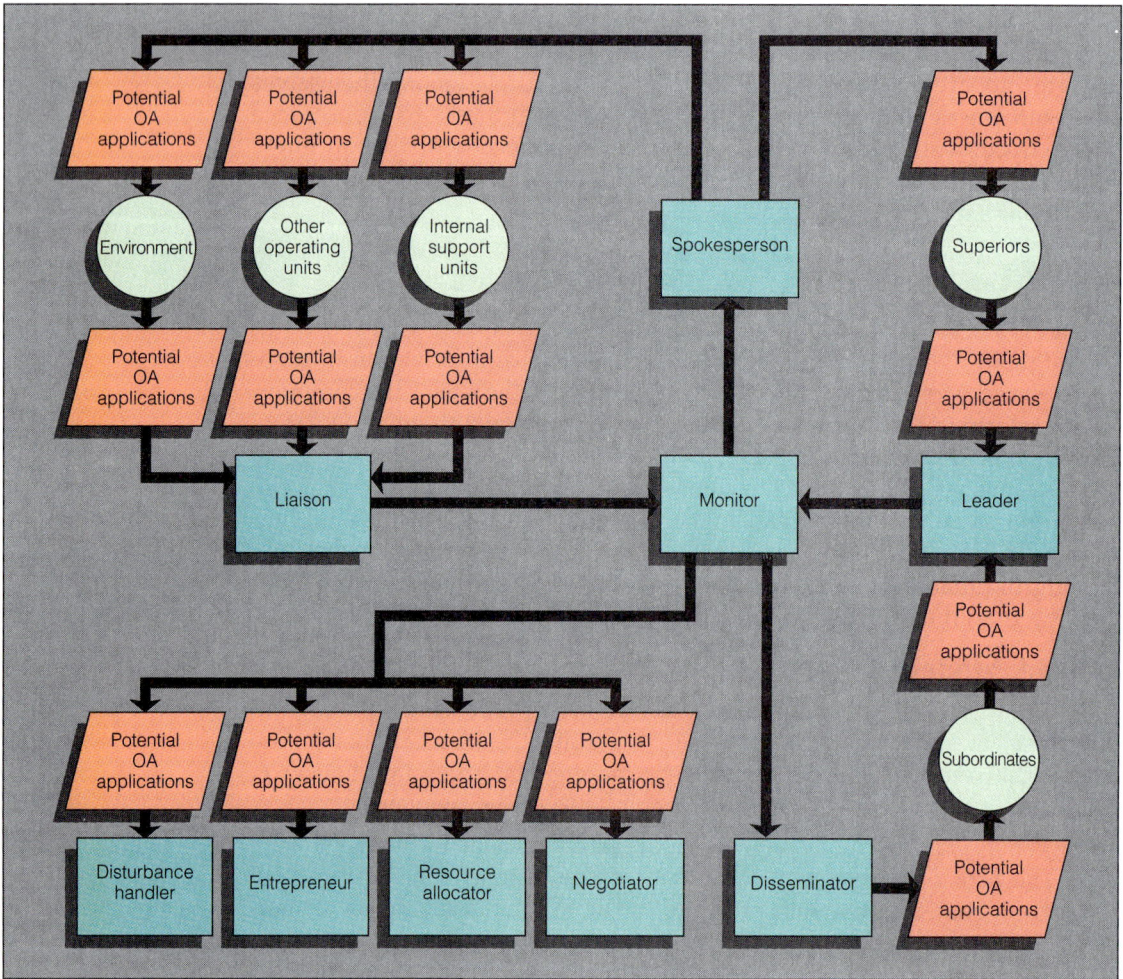

Selecting the Manager's "OA Mix"

The task of the manager (and of the information specialist working with the manager) is to select the OA applications to be used on each of the paths. Four factors influence the choice—the type of organization, other persons who are involved, available OA resources, and the manager's personal preferences.

Type of
Organization

As reflected in Table 14.1, a manager in a firm with only a single location can readily apply nine OA applications. A manager in a firm with geographically disbursed operations can utilize all eleven.

TABLE 14.1

The Influence of the Organization on the Manager's OA Mix

OA application	Firm with a single location	Firm with geographically dispersed operations
Electronic calendaring	X	X
Word processing	X	X
Electronic mail	X	X
Voice mail	X	X
Image storage/retrieval	X	X
Facsimile transmission		X
Videotex	X	X
Audio conference		X
Video conference		X
Computer conference	X	X
Desktop publishing	X	X

Another influence is the location of the other person or persons involved in the communication. Table 14.2 shows that all of the applications can be used for internal communications, but some are more established as communications from or to the environment than are others. Videotex can be used to gather information *from* elements in the environment, but it is unlikely that the managers would use it to communicate *to* the environment.

Other Persons Involved

TABLE 14.2

OA Application Choices for Internal and External Communications

OA application	Internal communications	Communication from the environment	Communication to the environment
Electronic calendaring	X	X	X
Word processing	X	Y	X
Electronic mail	X	X	X
Voice mail	X	X	X
Image storage/retrieval	X	Y	X
Facsimile transmission	X	Y	Y
Videotex	X	X	–
Audio conference	X	Z	Z
Video conference	X	Z	Z
Computer conference	X	Z	Z
Desktop publishing	X	Y	X

X = Under control of the manager   Z = Emerging use
Y = Not under control of the manager   – = Not Applicable

Four of the applications can facilitate environmental communication, but are not under the manager's control. In receiving communications *from* the environment, the environmental contact decides whether to use word processing, image storage and retrieval, facsimile transmission, and desktop publishing. If the manager wants to use facsimile transmission to communicate *to* the environment, the environmental contact also must have a FAX machine.

Available OA Resources

The manager is limited to the OA resources available in the firm—the necessary computing hardware, software, and special communications facilities. Like all other information-producing resources, however, they can be obtained when a need is shown.

Personal Preference

The information systems used by managers reflect their own personal preferences. Managers who prefer face-to-face communication are attracted to video conferencing and make good use of electronic calendaring. Those who like a written record use word processing, and those who spend a lot of time on the telephone are the best prospects for electronic or voice mail.

When considering OA applications to replace or improve traditional media, the grid in Figure 14.12 can be used. The traditional media are listed down the left-hand side and the OA applications are listed across the top. As an example, a manager who makes frequent use of memos can consider word processing, electronic and voice mail, image storage and retrieval, and FAX as ways to replace memos or to improve their content.

FIGURE 14.12

OA Applications that Can Replace or Improve Conventional Communications Media

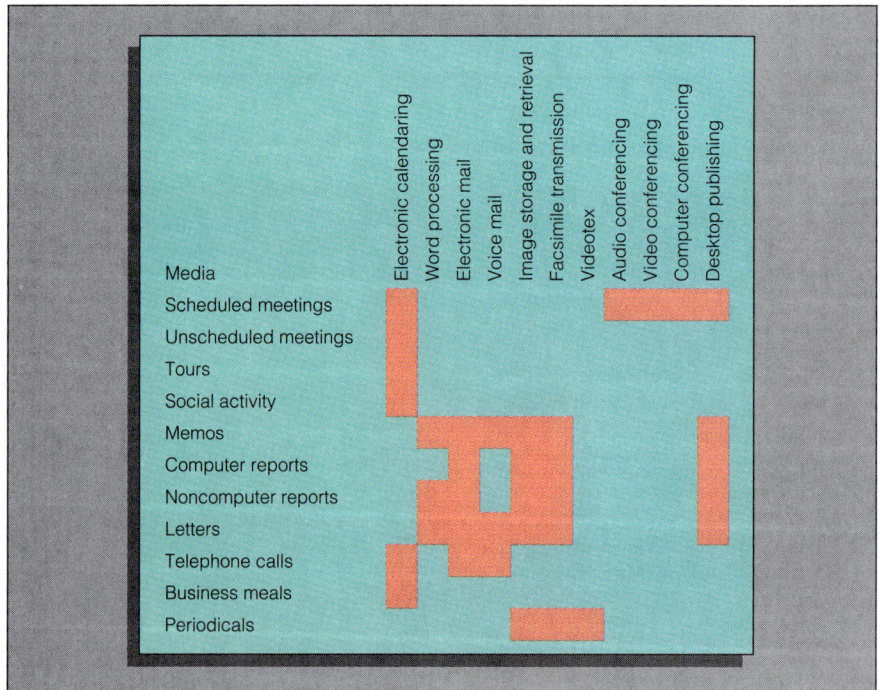

A Sample OA Mix

Figure 14.13 illustrates how a particular manager will work within the above influences to develop his or her unique OA mix.

Keeping OA in Perspective

In terms of its potential for supporting problem solving, OA is a sleeping giant. Too often it has been regarded as a secretarial tool since the manager does not always personally use the applications. This same criticism can be directed at all of the other problem-solving tools we have studied. The manager will not always code programs or personally query the database

FIGURE 14.13   A Sample Manager's OA Mix

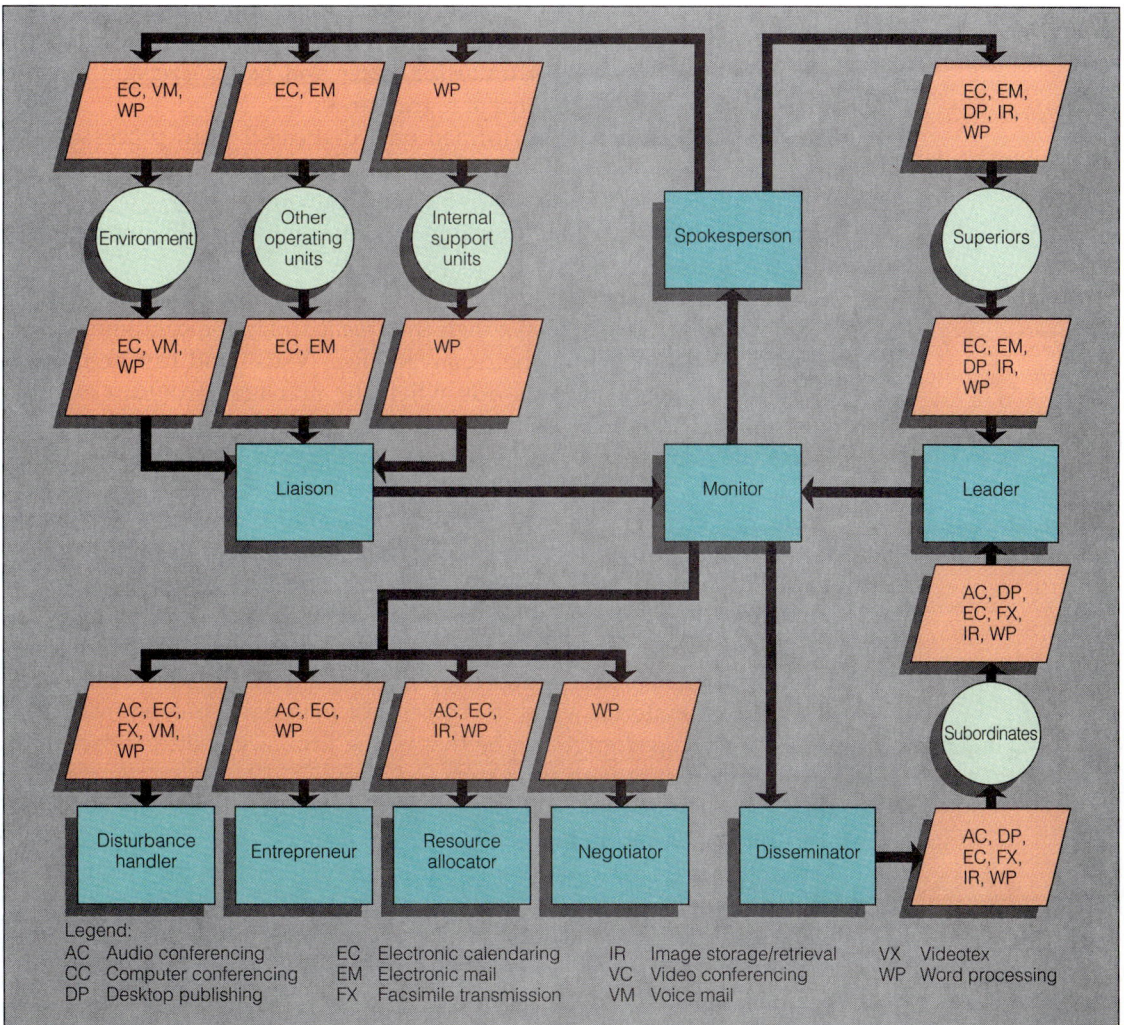

Legend:
AC	Audio conferencing	EC	Electronic calendaring	IR	Image storage/retrieval	VX	Videotex
CC	Computer conferencing	EM	Electronic mail	VC	Video conferencing	WP	Word processing
DP	Desktop publishing	FX	Facsimile transmission	VM	Voice mail		

and use mathematical models. However, this is not an issue. It does not matter who operates the equipment as long as the manager benefits.

Of all the information used in solving a problem, that provided by interpersonal communications accounts for a major portion. The manager and information specialist should view OA as a means of supplementing these interpersonal communications. In many instances OA offers the opportunity for better communications than are possible using traditional media.

SUMMARY

Factory automation led the way, and now office automation is stimulating interest. What began in 1964 as a single effort, called word processing, has blossomed into a booming industry with eleven separate application areas.

Most of the early OA attention was directed at secretarial and clerical activities. More recently the communication needs of managers and other knowledge workers have been recognized. The main objective of OA, regardless of who uses it, is increased productivity. For the problem solvers, OA offers the opportunity for faster and better decision making that benefits the firm in the form of higher revenues.

Word processing can be performed on a dedicated word processor or a general-purpose computer. Regardless of the hardware used, the main advantage of word processing is the ease with which changes to copy can be made. The writer is able to refine a document until it communicates exactly the desired message.

Electronic and voice mail were conceived as ways to combat telephone tag. In both cases the users have their own *mailboxes* in the computer's storage that they can check at their convenience. Voice mail can be used to gather environmental information when the manager provides external contacts with their own voice mailboxes.

Electronic calendaring enables a person in the firm to access the appointments calendars of others for scheduling meetings and visits.

There are three forms of teleconferencing—audio, video, and computer. Video conferencing can combine both sound and picture in both one-way and two-way configurations. Computer conferencing is like electronic mail except the participants and their topics are more restricted. Computer conferencing offers the opportunity for asynchronous communication.

FAX is long-distance copying that permits the transmission of graphic as well as textual material. Videotex consists of material retrieved from computer storage. The storage can be that of the firm, a videotex subscription service, or another organization such as a supplier.

Image storage and retrieval uses microfilm equipment or compact disks to store images in a form that facilitates retrieval.

Desktop publishing is the OA application that provides the "icing on the cake" by producing printed communications that look typeset.

One word describes the OA contribution to problem solving—communication. A systematic way to evaluate the communication potential of the OA applications is to consider how they could provide pathways to connect the managerial roles.

A manager will select the mix of OA applications based on characteristics of the organization, others who are involved in the communications, the resources available, and personal preferences. In some cases the OA applications are alternatives to traditional methods. Some applications offer new communications opportunities. Although OA was initially aimed at primarily internal communications, it has provided a means to link multiple firms to form interorganizational information systems. OA is a problem-solving tool even when the manager does not personally operate the equipment.

KEY CONCEPTS

How OA facilitates receiving information as well as sending it

The fact that OA will not replace the traditional communications methods

How a manager tailors an OA mix to fit personal needs within the resource constraints

KEY TERMS

Professional	Electronic bulletin board	Asynchronous exchange
Knowledge worker	Voice mail	Synchronous exchange
Word processing	Voice mailbox	Teleconferencing
Dedicated word processor	Electronic calendaring	Facsimile transmission (FAX)
Electronic mail	Audio conferencing	Videotex
Electronic mailbox	Video conferencing	Image storage and retrieval
Telephone tag	Computer conferencing	Desktop publishing (DTP)

QUESTIONS

1. What effect does increased productivity of secretaries and clerical employees have on the firm's profit? What about increased productivity of knowledge workers? Which approach offers the greatest profit potential?

2. In what ways are electronic mail and voice mail alike? In what ways are they different?

3. Which OA application is not used to directly communicate information?

4. What distinguishes computer conferencing from electronic mail?

5. Define asynchronous exchange. List the OA applications that use it.

6. Define synchronous exchange. List the OA applications that use it.

7. What are the three sources of videotex material?

8. How does the Dow Jones News/Retrieval Service differ from Datext in the way information is made available?

9. What two technologies are used to accomplish image storage and retrieval?

10. What are the three DTP application areas? Which are involved in problem solving?

11. Which OA applications involve the use of a computer?

12. What factors influence the choice of a manager's OA mix?

13. Which OA applications can contribute to an inflow of information from the environment? Of these, which are under the manager's control?

14. Which OA applications can be used to communicate information to the environment? Which one is not under the manager's control?

15. In a firm with only a single location, which OA applications could a manager consider for communication with subordinates?

CASE PROBLEM   North American Plywood and Gypsum

Edwin Kirby is corporate information officer for North American Plywood and Gypsum. P and G, as it is called in the construction industry, has its headquarters in Arlington, Virginia, and seven plants are located across the South, Southwest, and Far West. Each plant manufactures and ships a full line of building materials to retailers in its area. Kirby's major responsibility at present is the implementation of a new inventory system that will link the mainframe computer at headquarters with minis at the plant locations. The network will enable each plant to fill orders from stock at other plants when its own stock has been depleted. This is an additional application for P and G's computer network. All managers have terminals in their offices, and a WATS line makes telecommunications both fast and economical.

The inventory project has been underway for about three months and is approaching the design phase. The plan is to implement the new system one plant at a time. A headquarters implementation team will travel from plant to plant, providing assistance to the local information services personnel as needed. Implementation at the first plant is scheduled one year from now.

Each Monday morning at 8 A.M. Kirby and the top information services personnel at headquarters have a telephone conference with the managers of information services at the plants. The purpose of the conference is to review the previous week's progress and plan this week's activity.

"Is everybody here?" Kirby asks in a voice loud enough to be heard the telephone hookup. The four others seated around the conference table in Kirby's office are silent as the plant participants identify themselves, their voices coming from the speaker behind Kirby's desk.

When the final voice says "Sacramento's here," Kirby responds, "You sound like you're half asleep, Brenda." The voice replies, "No. Actually I'm *all* asleep. You forget that it's five o'clock in the morning out here. After this meeting I'm going to eat a good breakfast."

Kirby does not reply, but walks over to an easel that displays a large bar chart. "This might take some time today, people. I want to review the chart that Andy (Andrew Salem, the corporate manager of systems analysis) prepared. It shows the remainder of our implementation activity. I'd like to use it as the basis of our project planning. It shows each type of activity, such as local educational programs and database conversion, by plant and also by time period. I'm sure you know what it looks like. You've seen millions of bar charts and it's no different."

Kirby proceeds to explain the chart, but is continually interrupted by voices from the speaker: "Could you run over that again?" "I didn't get that, Ed." "Oh, I thought you meant *after* the team arrives." This went on for about twenty minutes and finally, in desperation, Kirby announces in an even louder voice "O.K. everybody. I've had enough. This is impossible. Listen, I'll have Andy make a copy of the chart for everybody and put them in the mail. You should all have it before the end of the week. We can discuss it in next Monday's meeting. We'll handle it that way from now on. Andy can send you an updated chart each week. It'll throw our planning about a week behind, but I don't want to go through this every time. Now, let's discuss what we did last week."

The telephone conference lasts for another forty-five minutes without any more incidents. After Kirby gives his usual "Let's hit it hard this week" farewell and presses the off button on the speaker, the others file out of the office. Kirby breathes a heavy sigh and sits down at his desk. His eyes focus on a magazine on top of his in basket. A question on the cover asks "Can OA Really Make Meetings More Effective?"

1. Assume that Kirby reads the article and becomes interested in OA. Which applications *that could be implemented on existing computing hardware* could Kirby use in communicating with the members of his project team? Make a list and, for each, include a brief explanation of how it would be used. The applications do not necessarily have to *solve* his communications problem; they only need to *contribute* to his communication ability.

2. Assume now that cost is not a limiting factor and Kirby decides to consider *all* OA applications, regardless of whether they require additional equipment. Make a list of the mix of OA applications you feel would provide the best support, and briefly explain each one.

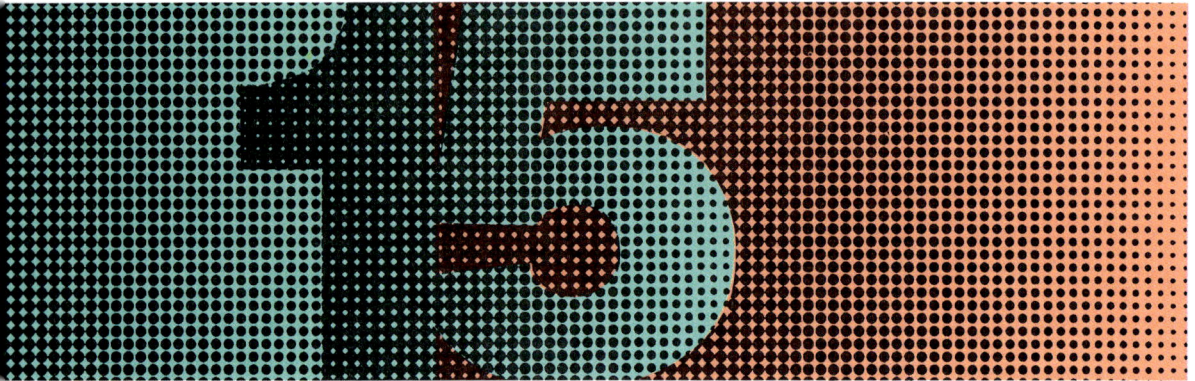

Artificial Intelligence, Expert Systems, and Beyond

LEARNING OBJECTIVES   After studying this chapter, you should:

- Know what is meant by the term artificial intelligence—how it evolved and what areas in addition to expert systems are included
- Understand the appeal of expert systems, how they compare with DSS, and when they should be used
- Know the component parts of an expert system, and the main features of each part
- Understand how an expert system is developed and how its security can be maintained
- Appreciate the potential role of the expert system as a problem-solving tool, and know its advantages and limitations
- Recognize that there will be other computer applications beyond expert systems, and have some idea of what they might be

OVERVIEW

This concluding chapter describes the major computer application area that is stimulating the most interest among information specialists—expert systems. Expert systems, a subset of artificial intelligence, is a progression beyond the applications we have traced in the previous chapters.

We begin by describing artificial intelligence—its purpose, how it evolved, and its major areas of activity. We then present a model of an expert system and describe each of its parts. This discussion includes the steps taken in implementing the system. Then we address the issue of security and explain the role of an expert system in problem solving, recognizing its weaknesses as well as its strengths.

The chapter concludes with a look into the future, projecting two possible application areas beyond expert systems as we know them today.

This look into the future is a fitting way to conclude our description of the computer as a problem-solving tool. With the foundation provided by the text, you should be able to apply its principles in your remaining college courses and in your career.

ARTIFICIAL INTELLIGENCE

For the past fifteen or so years there has been an increasing interest in using the computer for artificial intelligence. **Artificial intelligence**, or **AI**, is the activity of providing such machines as computers with the ability to display behavior that would be regarded as intelligent if it were observed in humans.[1] AI represents the most sophisticated computer application to date, endeavoring to duplicate some types of human reasoning. From all of the attention, one would think that AI is a brand new concept. The fact is that the seeds of AI were sown only two years after the first computer was installed for business use.

History of AI

In 1956 a meeting was held at Dartmouth College. It was attended by Marvin Minsky and John McCarthy of Dartmouth, Nathaniel Rochester of IBM, and Claude Shannon of Bell Laboratories. The term artificial intelligence was coined at this meeting, and the first AI computer program, called Logic Theorist, was announced. Logic Theorist was the product of work begun several years earlier at Carnegie Institute of Technology (now Carnegie-Mellon University) by Herbert Simon and Alan Newell. Simon and Newell had been investigating systems with a reasoning ability, and in 1956 were joined by J. C. Shaw of the Rand Corporation. Logic Theorist was the result. Its ability to prove calculus theorems encouraged the researchers to develop a program called the General Problem Solver (GPS) intended for use in solving problems of all kinds. The task turned out to be too much of a challenge.

AI research continued, but it took a backseat to the less ambitious computer applications, such as MIS and DSS. Over time, however, persistent research continued to push back the frontiers of using the computer for tasks that normally require human intelligence.

---

[1]This definition paraphrases one found in Clyde W. Holsapple and Andrew B. Whinston, *Business Expert Systems* (Homewood, IL:Irwin, 1987), p 4.

Areas of AI

A major subset of AI is expert systems. An **expert system** is a computer program that functions in the same manner as a human expert, advising the user how to solve a problem. The act of using an expert system is called a **consultation**—the user consults the expert system for advice.

In addition to expert systems, AI includes work in the following areas:

- *Perception* The use of visual images and auditory signals to instruct computers or other devices, such as robots
- *Learning* The ability of a computer or other device to acquire *knowledge* in addition to what has been entered into its memory by its manufacturer or by programmers
- *Automatic programming* The ability of a computer to code a program from instructions provided by the user in a natural language that resembles everyday conversation
- *Neural networks* Programmed routines that seek to duplicate the learning ability of the human brain

Each of these areas has the potential for benefitting business, but expert systems offer promise of achievements in computer based problem solving that have been impossible up until now.

THE APPEAL OF EXPERT SYSTEMS

Certain tasks require such specialized knowledge that experts are required. The concept of expert systems is based on the assumption that an expert's knowledge can be captured in computer storage and made available to others who have a need to apply that knowledge. The expert's knowledge enables the expert system to assume a larger portion of the problem solving task than is possible with other computer applications. Figure 15.1 illustrates the general trend toward increased computer support.

EXPERT SYSTEMS AND DSS

A DSS consists of routines that reflect how the manager believes a problem should be solved. The decisions produced by the DSS therefore *reflect* the manager's style and capabilities. An expert system, on the other hand, offers the opportunity to make decisions that *exceed* the manager's capabilities. For example, a new investments officer for a small life insurance company can use an expert system designed by a top financial expert with years of experience.

Another distinction between the expert system and DSS is the ability of the expert system to explain the line of reasoning followed in reaching a

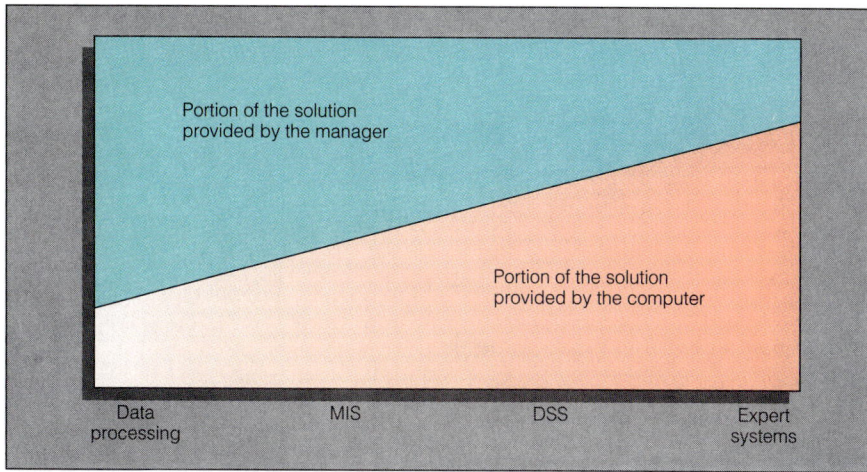

FIGURE 15.1

The Expanding Scope of Problem Support

Portion of the solution provided by the manager

Portion of the solution provided by the computer

Data processing   MIS   DSS   Expert systems

particular solution. Very often, the explanation of how a solution was reached is more valuable than the solution itself.

Deciding When to Use an Expert System

A DSS provides decision support in the form of periodic and special reports and the output from mathematical simulations. The data used by these DSS programs is primarily *numerical*, and the programs emphasize the use of *mathematical routines*. However, the data used by expert systems is more *symbolic*, often taking the form of a narrative text. The programs of expert systems emphasize the use of *logic routines*.

When confronted with a problem, you would favor an expert system over a DSS when:[2]

- The problem involves the diagnosis of a complex situation or the drawing of conclusions from a large volume of data.
- There is a degree of uncertainty in certain aspects of the problem.
- It is possible for a human expert to solve the problem in a reasonable amount of time.

In sum, an expert system should be used when the problem solution consists of a type of reasoning that normally is provided by the user, but can be defined and programmed into the computer.

PARTS OF AN EXPERT SYSTEM

A model of an expert system appears in Figure 15.2. The system consists of four main parts:

---

[2]These guidelines are based on those in *Personal Consultant Series Technical Report* (Austin, TX: Texas Instruments Incorporated, 1987), p. 4.

FIGURE 15.2

An Expert System
Model

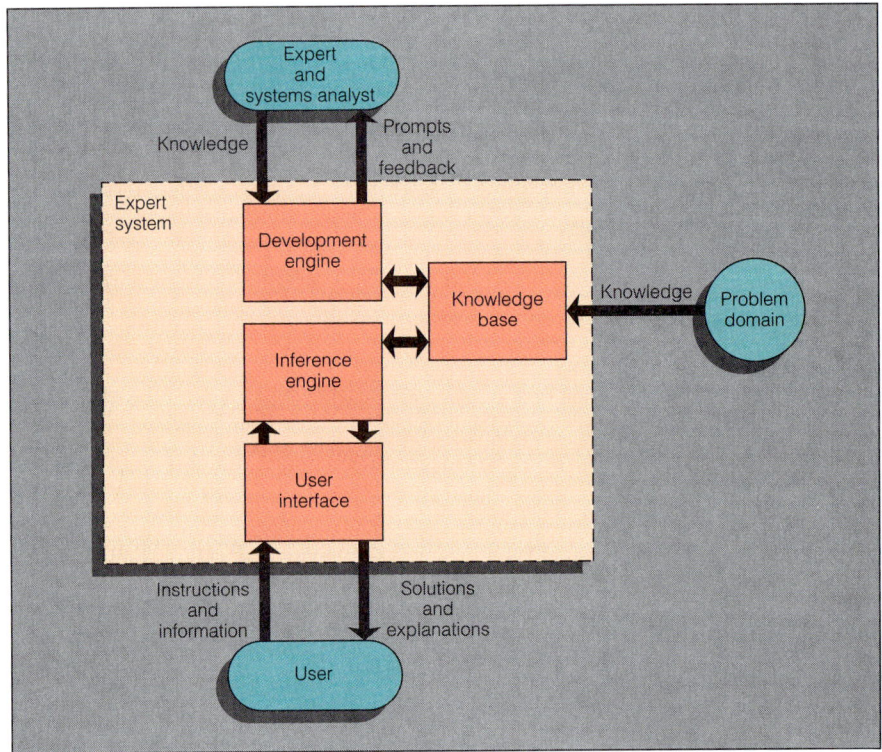

1. A **development engine** that the expert and systems analyst use to create the expert system
2. A **knowledge base** that houses the accumulated knowledge of the particular problem to be solved
3. An **inference engine** that provides the reasoning ability that interprets the contents of the knowledge base
4. A **user interface** that enables the user to interact with the expert system by means of a keyboard terminal.

THE USER INTERFACE

The user interface enables the manager to enter instructions and information into the expert system and to receive information from it.

The manager enters *instructions* to specify the parameters that guide the expert system through its reasoning process. The *information* the manager enters is in the form of values assigned to certain variables.

Methods for Entering Instructions and Information

The manager can use four methods to enter instructions and information:

- Menus
- Commands
- Natural language
- Customized interfaces

The menus are like those of Lotus, the commands are like the dot commands used with dBASE III Plus (LIST FILES ON A: LIKE *.*), and the natural language is like that used with a mainframe query language (WHO ARE THE EMPLOYEES IN OUR NEW YORK OFFICE WITH A COLLEGE EDUCATION).

The customized interfaces represent a new way to interact with the computer. Screens can be designed to vividly reflect particular aspects of the problem being solved. Figure 15.3 contains an example of a graphic developed by Ford Motor Company for use with the Texas Instruments Personal Consultant expert system in diagnosing robot problems.

Expert System Outputs

The ultimate objective of the expert system is to recommend a problem solution. This solution can be supplemented by two types of explanations.

1. *Explanation of questions* The manager may desire explanations while the expert system performs its reasoning. Perhaps the expert system will prompt the manager to enter some information. The manager asks why the information is needed, and the expert system provides an explanation.

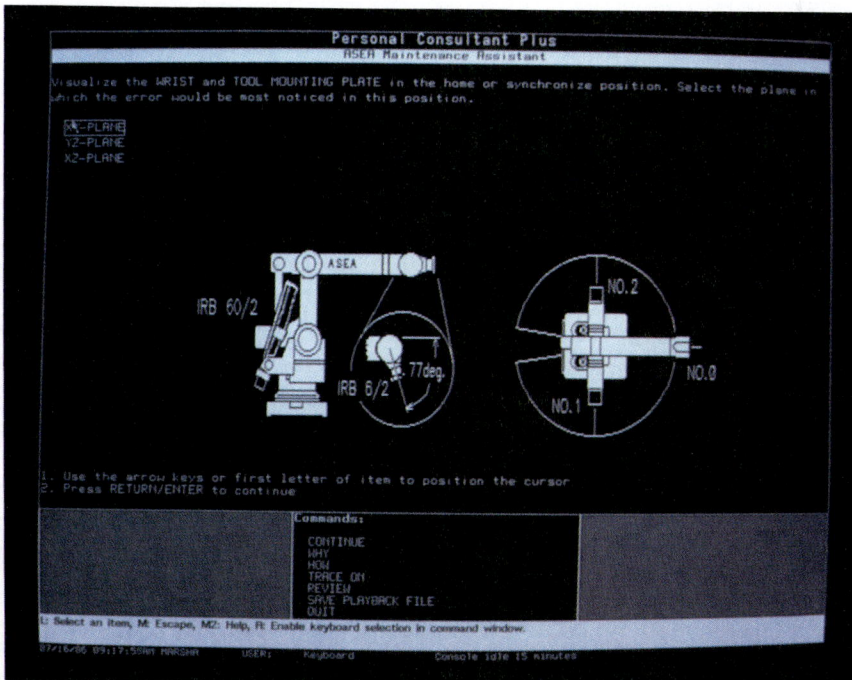

FIGURE 15.3

A Customized Interface

2. *Explanation of the problem solution* After the expert system provides a problem solution, the manager can ask for an explanation of how it was reached. The expert system will display each of the reasoning steps leading to the solution.

Although the inner workings of the expert system can be complex, the user interface is user friendly. A manager, accustomed to interacting with a computer, should have no difficulty in using an expert system.

THE KNOWLEDGE BASE

The knowledge base contains *facts* that describe the problem area, and *knowledge representation techniques* that describe how the facts fit together in a logical manner. The term **problem domain** is used to describe the problem area.

Rules

The most popular knowledge representation technique is the use of rules. A rule consists of two parts—a **condition** that may or may not be true and an **action** to be taken when the condition is true. The standard format of a rule is the same as an IF-THEN statement in a procedural programming language. An example of a rule is:

```
IF: ECONOMIC.INDEX > 1.20 AND
SEASONAL.INDEX > 1.30
THEN: SALES.OUTLOOK = "EXCELLENT"
```

All of the rules contained in an expert system are called the **rule set**. The rule set can vary from a dozen or so rules for a simple expert system to 500, 1000, or 5000 rules for a complex one.

Although it is not necessary, the rules usually are identified with numbers or names to facilitate creating, using, and modifying the rule set.

Networks of Rules

The rules of a rule set are not physically linked, but their logical relationships can be illustrated with a hierarchical diagram as in Figure 15.4. The rules at the bottom of the hierarchy provide *evidence* for the rules on the upper levels. The evidence enables the rules on the upper levels to produce *conclusions*.

The top level might consist of a single conclusion as shown in the figure, indicating that the problem has only a single solution. The term **goal variable** is used to describe the solution, which can be a computed value, an identified object, an action to be taken, or some other recommendation. For example, if an expert system is to advise top-level management whether to enter a new market area, a value of Yes or No would be assigned to the single goal variable MARKET.DECISION.

It is also possible for the top level of the hierarchy to include multiple conclusions, indicating that more than one solution possibility exists. An

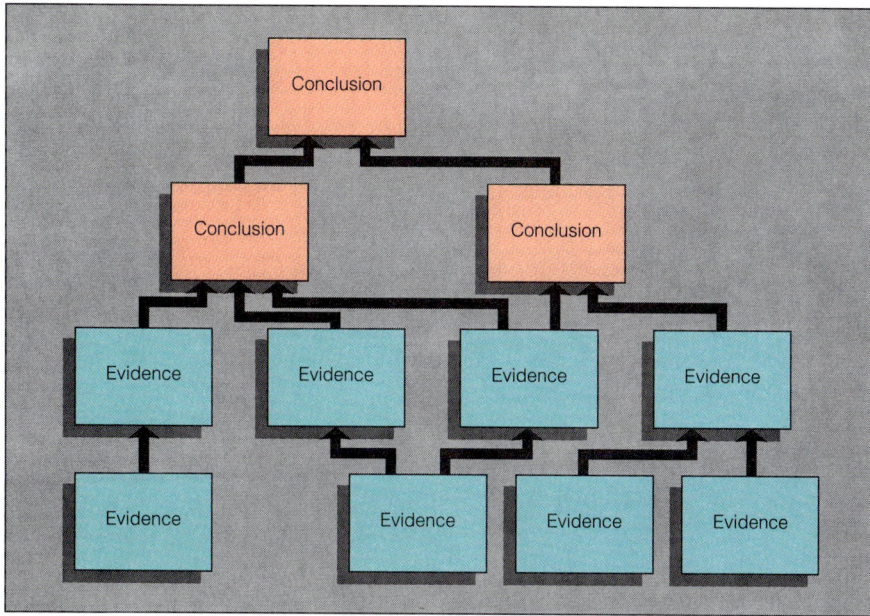

FIGURE 15.4

A Rule Set that Produces One Final Conclusion

example is an expert system that advises marketing management concerning the best strategy to follow in reacting to increased competitive activity. The system might select among possible strategies of improving the firm's products, investing more in advertising, or lowering prices.

The Problem of Rule Selection

The main difficulty of using rules to represent knowledge is that of efficient selection from the knowledge base. Oftentimes, only a subset of the total rule set is necessary to solve the problem. Take, for example, the expert system diagrammed in Figure 15.5. The seven animals listed across the top can be identified, based on the fifteen rules below. The rules are represented by circles, the rectangles below the circles are the conditions, and the arrows leading upward from the circles represent the actions or conclusions. Using this expert system, it is possible to identify an animal as a bird by using only rule R3 (it has feathers) or R4 (it flies and lays eggs).

The task is to condition the expert system so that it considers only the proper subset of rules. Several techniques can be used, but the most straightforward is for the user to enter parameters that narrow the rule selection. As an example, if the user specifies that the animal is a bird, only rules 13, 14, and 15 are necessary to identify the specific type of bird.

THE INFERENCE ENGINE

The inference engine is the portion of the expert system that performs reasoning by using the contents of the knowledge base in a particular sequence.

FIGURE 15.5 A Rule Set that Can Produce More than One Final Conclusion

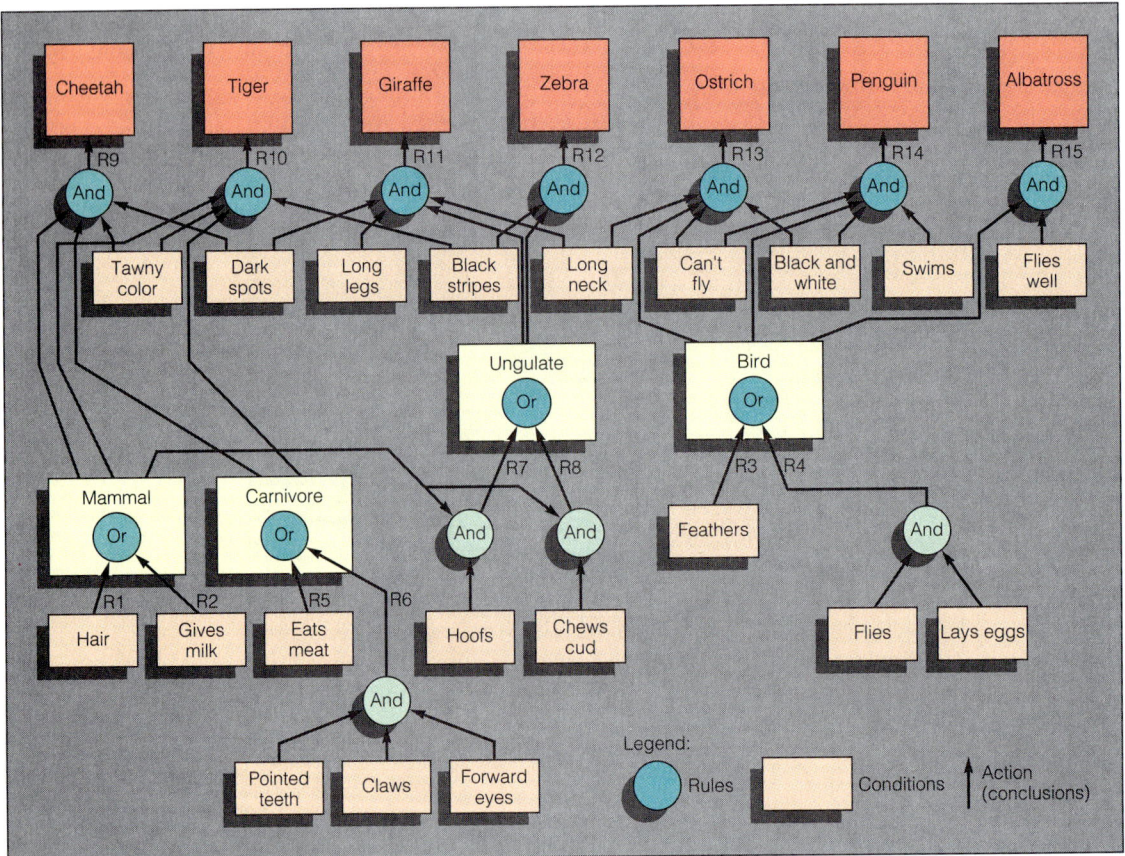

During the consultation, the inference engine examines the rules of the knowledge base one at a time, and when a rule's condition is true the specified action is taken. In expert systems terminology, the rule is **fired** when the action is taken.

There are two methods that the inference engine uses in examining the rules—forward reasoning and reverse reasoning.

Forward Reasoning

In **forward reasoning**, also called **forward chaining**, the rules are examined one after the other in a certain order. The order might be the sequence in which the rules were entered into the rule set, or some other sequence as specified by the user. As each rule is examined, the expert system attempts to *evaluate* whether the condition is true or false. When the condition is true, the rule is fired and the next rule is examined. When the condition is false, the rule is not fired and the next rule is examined.

It is possible that a rule cannot be evaluated as true or false. Perhaps the condition includes one or more variables with unknown values. In that case the rule condition is *unknown*. When a rule condition is unknown, the rule is not fired and the next rule is examined.

The process of examining one rule after the other continues until a complete pass has been made through the entire rule set. More than one pass usually is necessary in order to assign a value to the goal variable. Perhaps the information needed to evaluate one rule (such as the fifth one examined) is produced by another rule (such as the eleventh) that is examined subsequently. After the second rule (rule 11) is fired, the first rule (rule 5) can be evaluated on the next pass.

The passes continue as long as it is possible to fire rules. When no more rules can be fired, the reasoning process ceases.

Figure 15.6 shows the forward reasoning process. The rectangles repre-

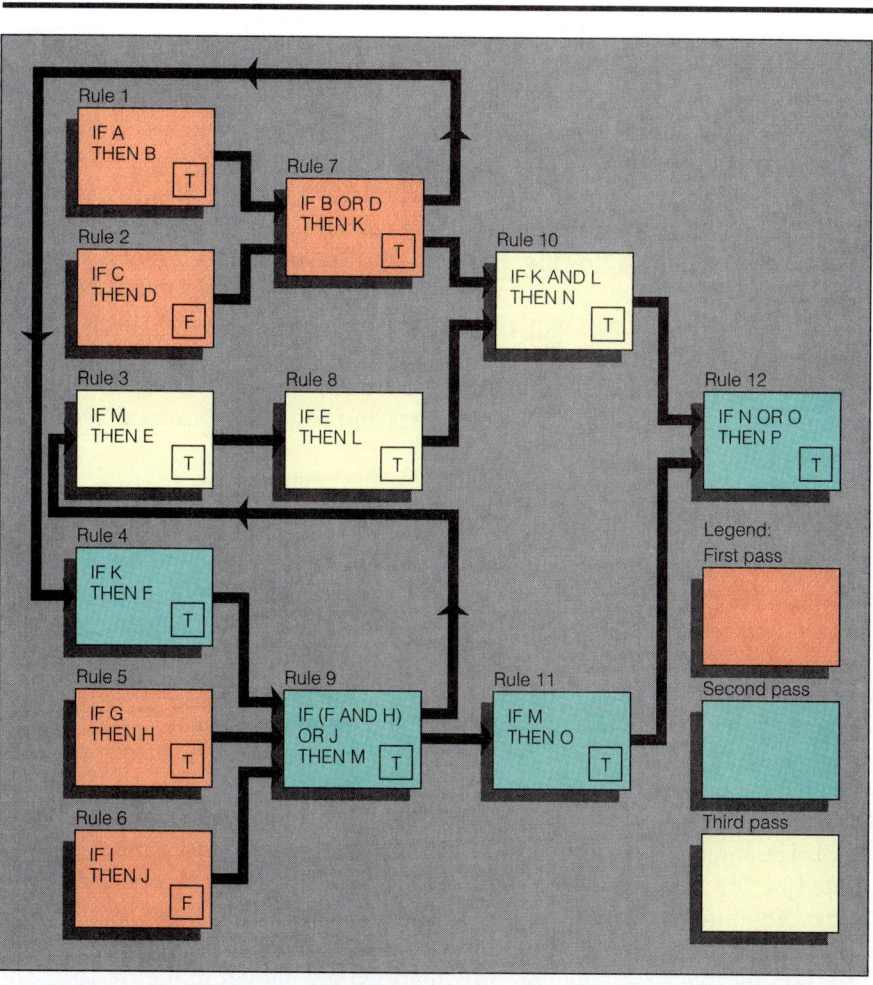

FIGURE 15.6

The Forward Reasoning Process

sent rules. The lines connecting the rules represent logical dependencies. For example, rule 4 cannot be fired until rule 7 has been fired.

Letters are used for the conditions and actions to keep the illustration simple. In rule 1, for example, if condition A exists, then action B is taken. Condition A might be THIS.YEAR.SALES > LAST.YEAR.SALES, and action B might be MARKET = "Growing". Likewise, in rule 2, if condition C exists, action D is taken.

You will note that some of the conditions include only one variable and others include two. When multiple condition variables are involved, they can be connected with the words *AND* or *OR*. These words have the same effect as when used in a programming language. In rule 7, if *either* condition B or D is true, the rule is fired. In rule 10, *both* condition K and L must be true for the rule to be fired.

The objective of the sample expert system is to compute a sales forecast. Rule 12 produces the forecast figure P, which is the goal variable. We will assume that the user provides the values for condition variables A, C, G, and I in rules 1, 2, 5, and 6 prior to the evaluation of the rules by the inference engine.

The colors in the figure indicate the pass during which the rules can *first* be evaluated as true or false. The rules in the orange rectangles are evaluated during the first pass, the green rectangles are evaluated in the second pass, and the tan in the third. The letters T and F identify whether the conditions are evaluated as true or false.

On the fourth pass no rules are fired and the reasoning process stops. If rule 12 has been fired, the value assigned to the goal variable P becomes the sales forecast. If the expert system was not able to fire rule 12, then insufficient information exists for a solution to the problem. In this example, rule 12 was fired on both the second and third passes. Condition O was determined to be true on the second pass and condition N was determined to be true on the third pass.

Reverse Reasoning

In **reverse reasoning**, also called **backward chaining**, the inference engine selects a rule and regards it as a *problem* to be solved. Using the same rule set as the previous figure, rule 12 is the problem since it assigns a value to the goal variable P. The inference engine attempts to evaluate rule 12, but recognizes that rule 10 *or* rule 11 must be evaluated first. Rules 10 and 11 become *subproblems* of rule 12 as shown in Figure 15.7. The inference engine then selects one of the subproblems to evaluate, and the selected subproblem becomes the new problem.

We will assume that rule 10 becomes the problem as shown in Figure 15.8. The inference engine then determines that rules 7 and 8 must be evaluated before rule 10 can be evaluated. Rules 7 and 8 become the subproblems. The inference engine continues to subdivide a problem into its subproblems in this manner, searching for a rule that can be evaluated.

The first five problems that are identified are shown in Figure 15.9. The

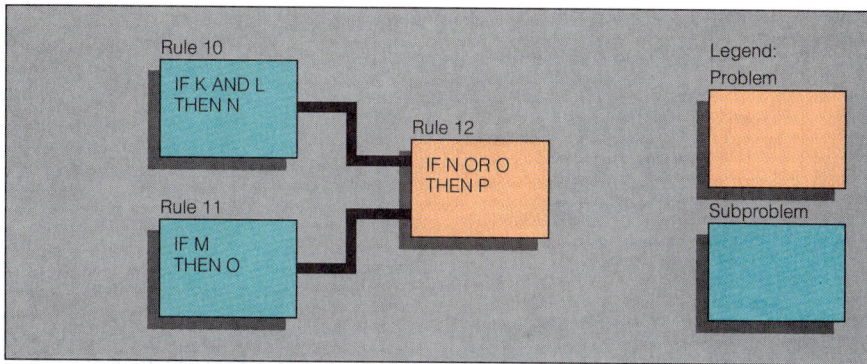

FIGURE 15.7

A Problem and Its Subproblems

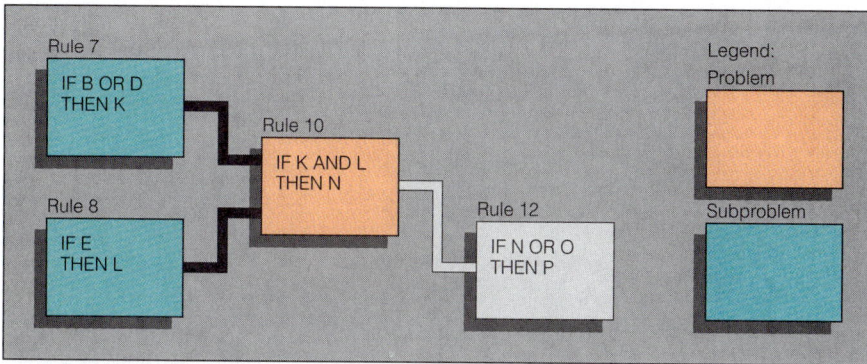

FIGURE 15.8

A Subproblem Becomes the New Problem

circled numbers and the blue arrows indicate the sequence in which the rules are examined. Since rule 1 is evaluated as true, it is possible to evaluate rule 7 as true without examining rule 2. With a value of true assigned to variable K, rule 10 can be reexamined. However, since rule 10 requires that *both* condition K and L be true, it is necessary to next evaluate rule 8. Rule 8 represents a dead end since its condition (variable E) cannot be produced by rule 3 until rule 9 is evaluated. In this situation, the inference engine addresses the other subproblem of rule 12—rule 11.

Figure 15.10 shows how the reasoning proceeds. Rule 9 becomes the problem and it can be evaluated using the outcomes of rules 4 and 5. Since both rules 4 and 5 are true, rule 9 can be evaluated as true without the need to examine rule 6.

Once rule 9 is fired, rule 11 can be fired as well. Since rule 12 is fired if either rule 10 *or* 11 is true, a value can be assigned to the goal variable P.

This is how reverse reasoning works. The inference engine identifies a problem and subdivides it into subproblems. It is a more logical process of selecting a reasoning path to follow and then sticking with that path until the problem is solved or a dead end is reached. In the case of a dead end, another problem is addressed.

FIGURE 15.9

The First Five Problems Are Identified

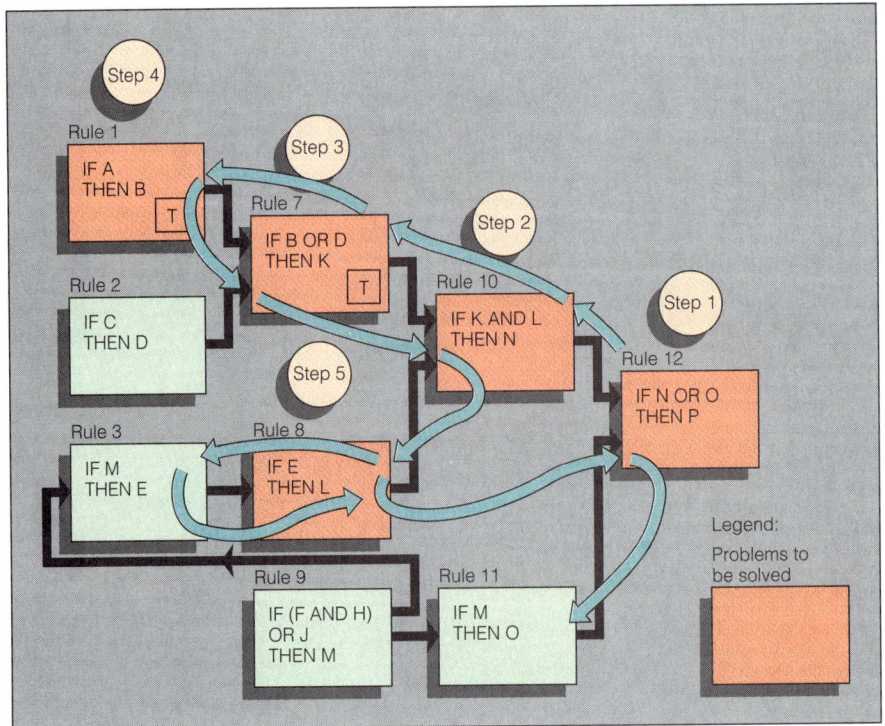

FIGURE 15.10

The Next Four Problems Are Identified

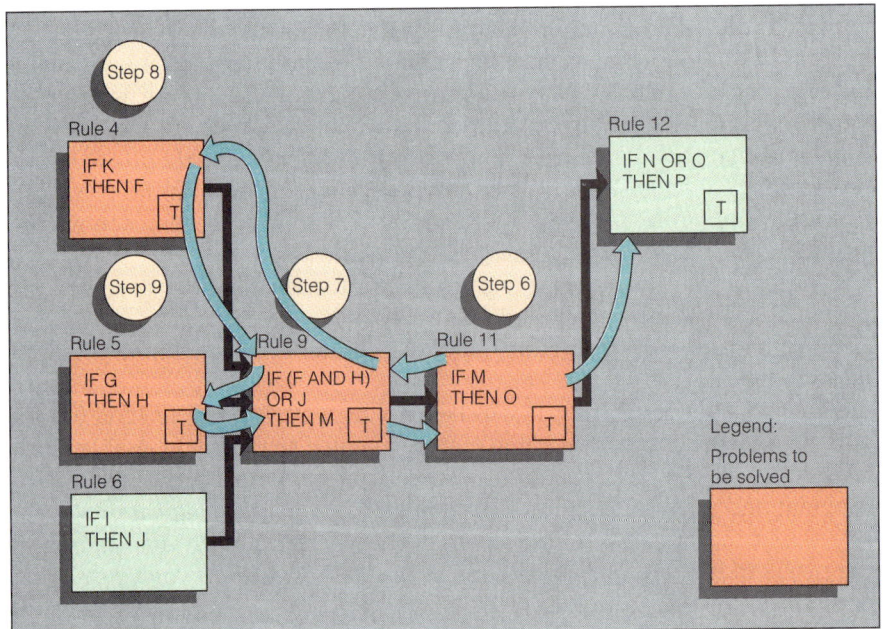

Comparing Forward and Reverse Reasoning

Reverse reasoning proceeds faster than forward reasoning since it does not have to consider all of the rules and does not make multiple passes through the rule set. However, forward reasoning is appropriate when *any* of the following conditions exist:

- There are multiple goal variables
- All or most all of the rules must be examined in the process of reaching a solution
- There are only a few rules

When an inference engine can perform both forward and reverse reasoning, the user can specify which method to use.

Providing Needed Information

As in the above example, the user can provide the inference engine with variable values at the beginning of the consultation. As the reasoning process proceeds, it may become necessary for the inference engine to obtain additional information. The inference engine can obtain the information from such other sources as databases, electronic spreadsheets, mathematical models, or other expert systems, or it can prompt the user for the needed information. Prompts can be designed to display such relevant data as graphs that assist the user in providing the needed information.

Figure 15.11 illustrates these various information sources. If the expert system is to provide the business user with full support, it should be able to interface with other problem-solving software in this manner. These additional software components can be built into the expert system, or it can interface with other commercially available systems.

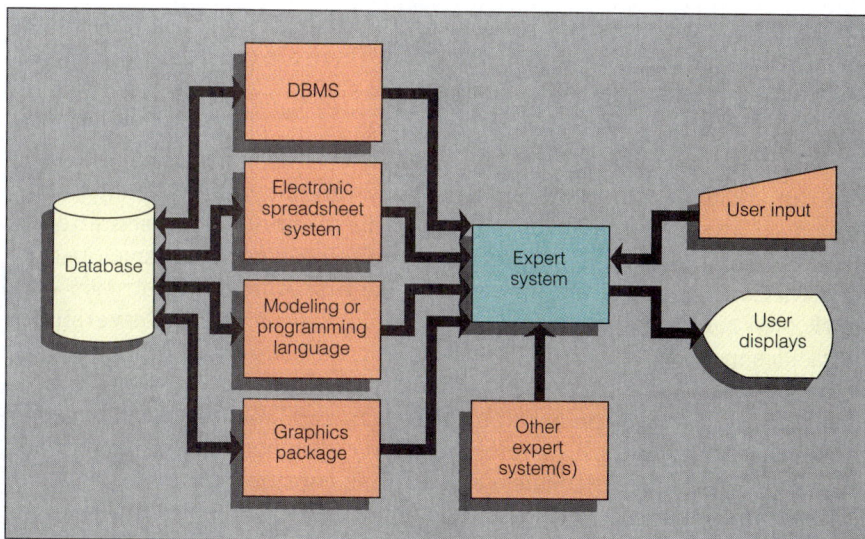

FIGURE 15.11

The Expert System Obtains Needed Information from Other Sources

How the Inference Engine Handles Uncertainty

There is not always 100 percent certainty about the information provided to the expert system. The uncertainty can apply to entire rules or to rule conditions. As an example of an **uncertain rule**, a system developer might not know for certain that a rule dealing with a raw material supplier's financial status has an influence on the material quality, but might be 80 percent certain that it does. As an example of an **uncertain condition**, a marketing manager using an expert system to project an economic forecast might be only 80 percent certain that the economic index for next year will be *strong*.

Expert systems use **certainty factors**, or **CFs**, to handle varying degrees of uncertainty. The CFs are analogous to the probabilities discussed in Chapter 13, and can range from 0, which represents complete uncertainty, to 100, which represents complete certainty.

In keeping with the notion that "a chain is no stronger than its weakest link" the expert system advises the user when the conclusion is less than 100 percent certain. For example, assume that four rules lead to a conclusion, and three of them can be evaluated with 100 percent certainty. However, the fourth rule has a CF of 80, meaning that the certainty of its action is 80. The expert system keeps track of the various rule CFs throughout the reasoning process and indicates the degree of certainty for the goal variable at the end of the consultation, such as:

```
SALES FORECAST = $12,450,500        CF = .80
```

The weak link approach is only one way to handle uncertainty. The user can select the method that best fits the particular situation.

THE DEVELOPMENT ENGINE

The development engine is used to create the expert system. Essentially this involves building the knowledge base. There are two basic approaches: programming languages, and expert system shells.

Programming Languages

You can create an expert system using any programming language, however, two are especially well suited to the symbolic representation of the knowledge base. These are Lisp and Prolog. Lisp was developed by John McCarthy (one of the members of the first AI meeting) in 1959, and work on Prolog was begun by Alain Colmerauer at the University of Marseilles in 1972.

For several years, Lisp enjoyed its greatest popularity in the United States, and Prolog was preferred by European and Japanese users. Recently, however, such geographic preferences have dimmed. Prolog has gained supporters in the United States, and there is considerable Lisp activity in Europe. The Japanese have cast their lot with Prolog, selecting it as the basis for their new generation of computers.

Expert System Shells

One of the first expert systems was Mycin, developed by Edward Shortliffe and Stanley Cohen of Stanford University with the help of Stanton Axline, a physician. Mycin was created to diagnose certain infectious diseases.

When the success of Mycin had been established, the developers looked for other ways to apply their accomplishments. They discovered that the Mycin inference engine could be tailored to another type of problem by replacing the Mycin knowledge base with one reflecting the other problem domain. This finding heralded the start of a new approach to building expert systems. It was realized that an **expert system shell**—a ready-made processor tailored to a specific problem domain through the addition of the appropriate knowledge base—can produce an expert system quicker and easier than by programming.

Today, most of the interest in applying expert systems to business problems involves the use of shells. The first commercial shell was KEE—for Knowledge Engineering Environment. KEE is designed for use on a computer designed especially for the Lisp language—a **Lisp machine**. Other large-scale shells have been designed for use on mainframes, such as the VAX 11/780. Some have been tailored to the IBM PC and PC compatibles.

When you use a shell to create an expert system, you can enter the rules by typing them in as you do when using a word processor. Another approach is to assemble the rule components by making selections from

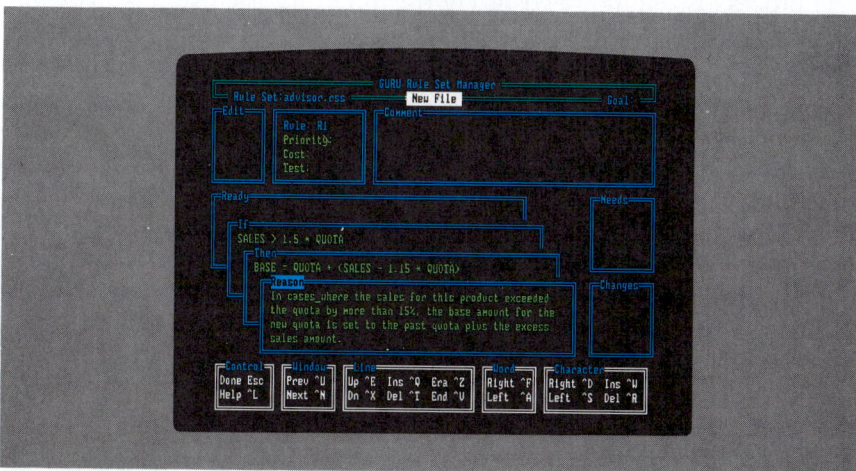

FIGURE 15.12

Assembling a Rule from Pull-Down Menus

pull-down menus. Figure 15.12 illustrates the pull-down menus of Guru, an expert system shell developed specifically for business by Micro Data Base Systems, Incorporated.

The Uniqueness of Expert System Development

The text and menu approach to rule building is much more user friendly than use of a programming language. The user friendliness does not, however, mean that the manager should develop an expert system alone. The key is not the ease of entering the rules but, rather, the identification of the rules. The rules are identified by a systems analyst working with one or more acknowledged experts in the problem domain.

The Role of the Systems Analyst

The term **knowledge engineer** has been used to describe the person who works with the expert. In a business organization, this person is likely to be the systems analyst. The systems analyst with the required skills *can* develop expert systems. In addition to the standard skills used in MIS or DSS work, the analyst must understand how experts apply their own knowledge in solving problems, and be able to extract a description of those processes from the expert.

The Role of Prototyping in System Development

The prototyping approach is ideal for the development of an expert system. The process is diagrammed in Figure 15.13 and each step is explained below.[3] The columns identify the responsibilities of the three participants—the systems analyst, the expert, and the user.

1. *Study the problem domain* The systems analyst studies the user's application area.
2. *Define the problem* The systems analyst and the expert work together to define the problem to be solved.
3. *Specify the rule set* The systems analyst can ask the expert questions to learn the logical steps of achieving a solution. The steps provide a basis for the rules. Or, the analyst can present various problem scenarios and the expert can respond with solutions, allowing the analyst to infer the rules from the responses.
4. *Test the prototype system* The prototype is subjected to tests. Perhaps a staff of domain experts evaluates the output. Steps 2 through 4 are repeated for each prototype.
5. *Construct the interface* When the developers feel the system does what it is supposed to do, the user interface is added.
6. *Conduct user tests* User testing first includes user education aimed at how to enter the inputs and how to interpret the outputs. When the users are familiar with the system, it is subjected to the type of use it will receive when it becomes operational. Unsuccessful tests require that Steps 2 through 6 be repeated.

---

[3]These steps are based on those found in Holsapple and Whinston, p. 160.

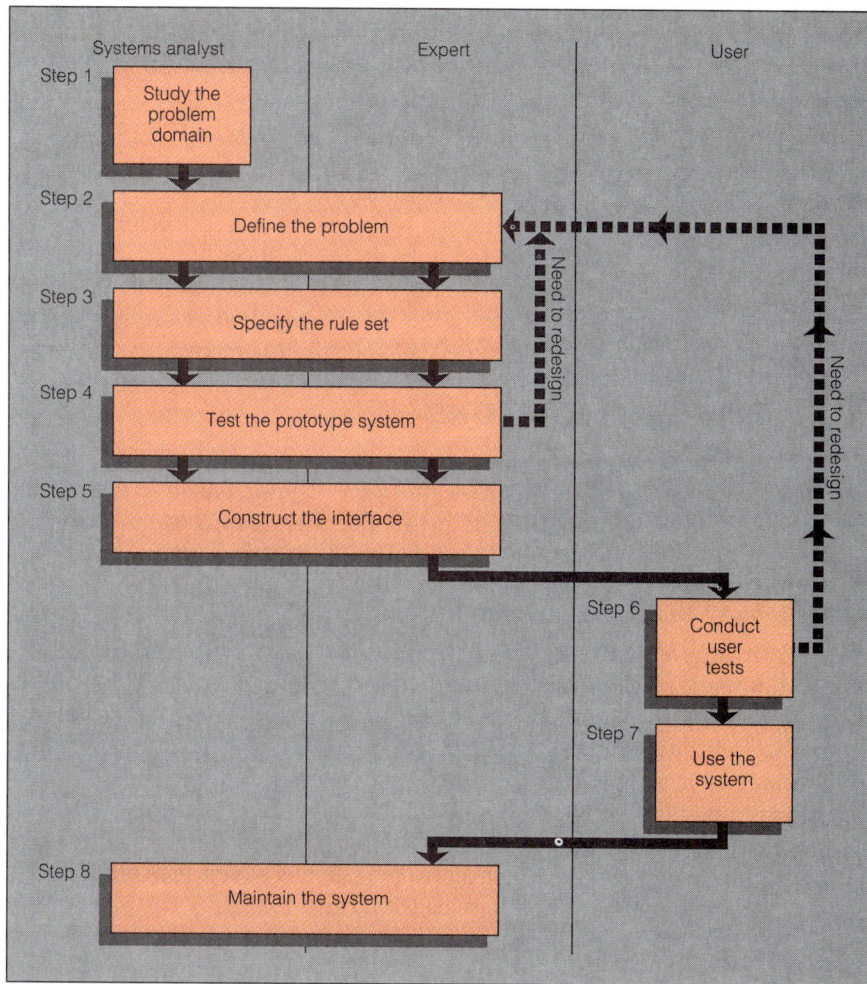

FIGURE 15.13

Implementation Steps

7. *Use the system* A successful user test means that the expert system can be put into everyday use. Either the prototype becomes the operational system or it is used as the blueprint for the operational system.
8. *Maintain the system* Like all computer applications, it is necessary to keep the expert system up-to-date so that it reflects the most current expert reasoning.

The development of an expert system usually takes longer than for other computer applications. It is not unusual to spend two or three years in specifying the rule set.

This concludes the description of the parts of an expert system. The remainder of the chapter focuses on key issues concerning its use.

EXPERT SYSTEM SECURITY

None of the other computer applications rival expert systems in terms of the importance of security. The expert system represents a distillation of the most valuable resource available to the firm—the knowledge of experts in how to solve the firm's problems. That knowledge must be protected.

As a minimum, the expert system should provide the same degree of security as that of a good DBMS—required use of passwords, directories that specify exactly what privileges each user enjoys concerning system use, and encryption of the knowledge base. In addition, the object code of the inference engine can be scrambled to make it unintelligible to a computer criminal. Since the majority of expert system shells were not specifically intended for business use, many fall short in this regard.

BUSINESS APPLICATIONS

Expert systems are so new that there are relatively few examples of how they have been applied to business problem solving. Most of the accomplishments have been in fields like medicine, chemistry, and geology. Two good business examples are XCON and Grain Marketing Advisor.

DEC's XCON

XCON was implemented by Digital Equipment Corporation to determine the components necessary to produce their VAX and PDP-11 computers. Data is entered from the customer order, and XCON (which stands for eXpert CONfigurator) uses over 4200 rules in a forward reasoning manner to consider over 400 possible computer components. One of the outputs is a room layout showing the cables needed to connect the different hardware cabinets. Another output serves as input to DEC's MRP (material requirements planning) system. DEC estimates that XCON saved the company $15 million in manufacturing costs between 1980 and 1985.

Mrs. Fields ROI

One of the reasons for the success of Mrs. Fields Cookies was the expertise of the founder, Debbi Fields. When her first store opened in Palo Alto, California, Mrs. Fields would bake a day's supply of cookies based on past experience and set sales goals for the day. When it appeared that sales might not match the goals, Mrs. Fields would give away free cookies to passersby to stimulate sales. When the organization grew to its present size of 700 cookie outlets it was impossible for Mrs. Fields to provide her experienced oversight to each store. Her husband had been a programmer for IBM and played a key role in computerizing most of the Mrs. Fields operations, including the development of an expert system called Retail Operations Intelligence, or ROI. ROI includes several modules that provide store managers with the same expertise that Debbi would apply if she were managing each store. The PC-based system worked so well that it was decided to form a software subsidiary, The Fields Software Group, which markets ROI to retailers of all types.

Potential Application Areas

The accomplishments of expert systems in business lie in the future rather than in the past. The areas of business where the potential for expert systems is greatest are those where:

- There are few experts
- The experts have so many responsibilities they cannot share their knowledge with everyone who needs it
- The experts are too expensive for some firms to afford

On the lower-management level, sales managers can use expert systems to set sales quotas, credit managers can establish credit limits, manufacturing managers can schedule production, and shipping managers can select transportation routes. On the upper levels, expert systems can be used to analyze financial statements, evaluate acquisitions of other firms, time the entry of products into markets, and consider investment opportunities.

EVALUATING EXPERT SYSTEMS IN BUSINESS

Interest in expert systems in business is on the rise. More and more firms are investing in expert system projects. Is this interest justified? Let us look at both the advantages and limitations of applying expert systems to business problems.

The Advantages of Expert Systems to Firms

Firms that implement expert systems can expect managers to perform at a higher level. The systems also provide a means of both developing management knowledge and maintaining it in the firm for a longer time.

Better Performance for the Firm

As the firm's managers extend their problem-solving abilities through the use of expert systems, the firm benefits from better overall performance. The firm is better able to meet its responsibilities to its environment.

Maintain Control over the Knowledge

Firms invest heavily in developing the specialized knowledge required by their employees. Expert systems afford the opportunity of making the experienced employees' knowledge more available to newer, inexperienced employees, and of keeping that knowledge in the firm longer—even after the employees have left. The stimulus for expert systems projects often comes when an experienced employee announces his or her intentions to retire.

The Advantages of Expert Systems to Managers

Managers who use expert systems can solve problems better, faster, and in a more consistent fashion.

Better Solutions

The main advantage of an expert system is its ability to outperform a human manager in a particular problem domain. The specialized reasoning of the expert usually is superior to that of the manager.

Faster Solutions

The computer can apply the knowledge required for problem solution at electronic speeds. This ability benefits the manager in two ways. First, it makes it possible for the manager to engage in problem-solving activity that heretofore has been impossible. For example, a financial manager who has been able to track the performance of only 30 stocks because of the volume of data that must be considered can track 300 with the help of an expert system. The second benefit of the increased speed is that it frees up the manager for other activities.

More Consistent Solutions

The computer does not have *good days* and *bad days* like the human manager. Once the reasoning is programmed into the computer, the manager knows that the same solution process will be followed for each problem.

Limitations of Expert Systems

Two characteristics of expert systems limit their potential as a business problem-solving tool. First, they cannot handle inconsistent knowledge. In business, few things hold true all of the time because of the variability in human performance—by persons both inside and outside the firm. Second, expert systems cannot apply the intuitive skills we recognized as characteristic of the human problem solver in Chapter 6.

The Bottom Line

Considering the time and money invested in exploring business applications of expert systems, the results are modest. The big constraint appears to be problem structure. For an expert system to be feasible, the problem must be highly structured, and we have seen that most business problems do not fit that mold.

There is no doubt that during the next few years effective expert systems will be built to solve business problems—even upper-level management problems. But the accomplishments will not come easy. It remains to be seen whether the enthusiasm of the designers will be great enough to persist over time in light of the difficulty of the task.

THE STEPS BEYOND EXPERT SYSTEMS

The immediate issue is whether expert systems will achieve widespread use as a business problem-solving tool. However, if the past is any clue, there will be other steps beyond expert systems. During the brief history of business computing, a progression of applications has captured the interest of managers and information specialists—first data processing, then MIS followed by DSS, then OA, and now expert systems.

If we could find a pattern in this evolution, we might be able to project the next steps. One approach is to evaluate the applications in terms of:

1. The type of problems they address
2. Whether they support the individual or the organization
3. The amount of problem-solving support they provide

Problem-Solving Space

Figure 15.14 shows how the five current applications compare in terms of these three dimensions. The dimensions produce a cube that represents a **problem solving space**—the area where support is needed.

Data processing applications are aimed at highly structured problems. The problem-solving support is very little and is aimed at organizational needs rather than those of individual managers.

Data Processing

The MIS occupies more problem solving space than any of the other applications. Its support can range from very little to very much, and the problems it supports can be both structured and semistructured. However, it is aimed more at supporting general information needs in the organization than those of individuals.

MIS

Like the MIS, the support provided by the DSS can range from very little to very much. Its problem solving area is not as large as the MIS since it specializes in only semistructured problems. The feature that distinguishes it from the MIS is the manner in which its support is brought closer to the individual managers.

DSS

OA applications are tailored to individual managers and are best suited to problems with little structure—where informal communications abound. Although OA provides problem-solving information, it is left to the manager to decide how to apply it.

Office Automation

The trend from data processing to MIS to DSS to OA is illustrated by the arrow in the figure. The trend has been one of shifting from:

Expert Systems

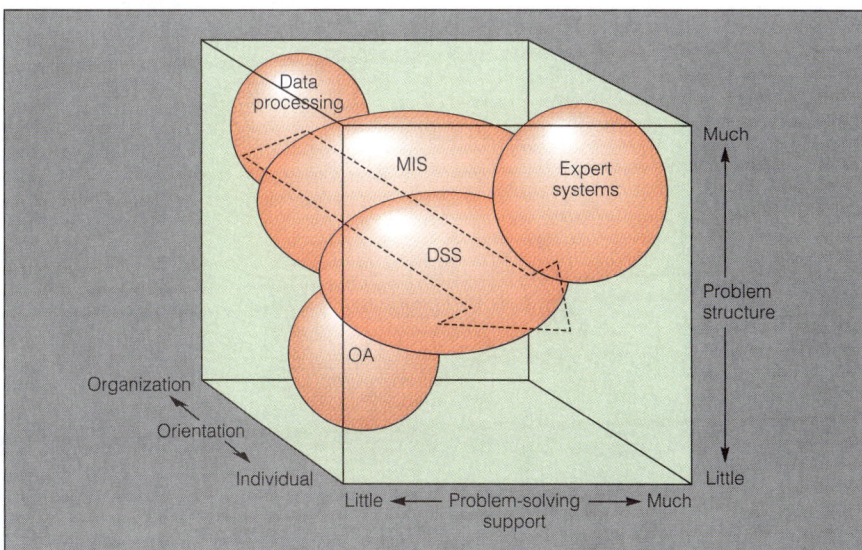

FIGURE 15.14
Problem Solving Space

1. Organizational to individual support
2. Little overall support to much
3. Structured to semistructured problems

Expert systems continue the first two trends but not the third. They are designed to meet the needs of specific managers and they provide a higher level of support than the earlier applications. However, they do not continue the trend toward problems with less structure. Instead, they revert back to problems that are highly structured.

Possible Future Applications

Where does this lead us? The area of the problem solving space that has been exploited the least is the bottom layer—problems involving little structure. It represents the area where future efforts can be aimed to increase the problem support of computer-based systems. Figure 15.15 shows two possible steps beyond today's systems. The first is a continuation of the DSS approach—supporting rather than duplicating the manager's reasoning processes. We call such a system a **minimally structured DSS**, or **MSDSS**. The MSDSS would be aimed at problems with very little structure such as those found at upper-management levels.

The second step is an expansion of the expert system concept to include less structured problems. We call it a **less structured expert system**, or **LSES**. The ability to handle uncertainty would appear to be key to achieving the LSES.

Whether these trends will come to pass is anybody's guess, but we can be sure of one thing. Managers and information specialists will continue to explore new ways to use the computer as a problem-solving tool.

FIGURE 15.15
Possible Next Steps

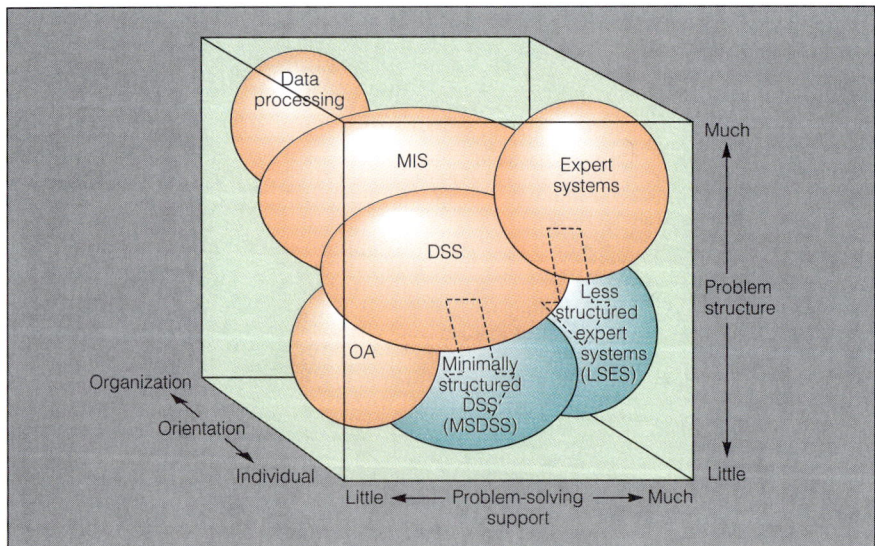

A FINAL WORD

When you begin your chosen career you will realize that all organizations do not apply the computer as we describe in this text. Many of our explanations have been *prescriptive* (what managers and firms should do) rather than *descriptive* (what they actually do).

We took the prescriptive route because of the *potential* of the computer to help managers solve problems. The fact that such support is not being used by all managers is no reason to refrain from encouraging it. Forward thinking college programs should prepare students to *improve* on today's methods rather than to simply *duplicate* them.

The discussion in this chapter shows that challenges still remain in the computer field. In fact, there are probably more challenges today than there were in 1954 when GE plugged in its UNIVAC I. Whereas today's managers and information specialists have far more hardware and software resources at their disposal, the challenges are much greater than those faced by yesterday's problem solvers.

While this may seem depressing, you must look at it in a positive way. This is the view taken by the manager who had a sign on the wall that read "Problems are opportunities in work clothes."

There are a lot of opportunities that remain in applying the computer as a problem-solving system.

SUMMARY

Artificial intelligence includes automatic programming, expert systems, the incorporation of perception and learning into computers and other devices such as robots, and neural networks. All of these areas can benefit business, but the concept of expert systems is intriguing since it offers a new approach to problem solving. An expert system is a program that incorporates the knowledge of a human expert. It affords managers the opportunity to make better decisions than they normally are able to make.

An expert system consists of four parts: the development engine used by the systems analyst and expert to create the system, the knowledge base that uses some means of knowledge representation such as rules to describe the problem domain, the inference engine that performs reasoning on the knowledge base, and the user interface that enables the user to enter information and instructions and receive solutions and explanations.

Rules consist of a condition and an action and comprise the rule set. The inference engine can examine the rules in either a forward or reverse manner, firing them when they can be evaluated as true. The inference engine assigns a value to the goal variable based on the fired rules.

The inference engine can obtain information from the user in addition to such sources as databases, spreadsheets, mathematical models, and other expert systems. The user can indicate the degree of certainty for both conditions and rules used in the reasoning process.

Early expert systems were created using programming languages. That approach is still followed, with Lisp and Prolog being the most popular languages. More recently, adapting an expert system shell to a specific problem domain has gained popularity—especially in business.

A systems analyst who understands management reasoning and can extract a description of that reasoning from the expert can participate in the development of an expert system. The difficulty of getting the reasoning right the first time dictates that a prototyping approach be followed. The user is not involved until the analyst and expert are satisfied that the system performs as intended. User tests can require further prototyping.

Expert systems should include all of the possible security features, since the expert knowledge represents such a valuable resource. The systems can be applied in areas where the experts are few, overworked, or too expensive. Both the firm and its managers can benefit from expert systems. The systems enable the firm to do a better overall job and maintain its resource of expert knowledge, and enable the managers to make better, faster, and more consistent decisions. The main limitations of expert systems are their inability to handle inconsistent knowledge and employ intuitive skills.

Many more accomplishments will be necessary before expert systems are established as an effective management problem-solving tool. In the meantime, work on DSSs should continue, gradually expanding their scope to include minimally structured problems. Assuming that expert systems as we know them today ultimately achieve success, efforts most likely will be made to expand their scope to include less structured problems. Much remains to be accomplished in applying the computer as a problem solving tool.

KEY CONCEPTS

How expert systems enable managers to perform on the level of experts

How a problem domain can be described by facts and rules in the knowledge base

The manner in which the computer performs reasoning by firing rules in a forward or reverse fashion

How the expert system handles uncertainty

The expert system shell as a means of system development

The fact that expert systems are not the end of the road in the evolution of computer applications in business, but represent only one stop along the way

KEY TERMS

Artificial inntelligence (AI)
Consultation
Development engine
Knowledge base
Inference engine
User interface
Problem domain
Rule set
Goal variable

Forward reasoning, forward
    chaining
Reverse reasoning, backward
    chaining
Certainty factor (CF)
Expert system shell
Minimally structured DSS (MSDSS)
Less structured expert system
    (LSES)

QUESTIONS

1. Is expert systems just another name for artificial intelligence? Explain.

2. When would you use an expert system rather than a DSS?

3. What are the two types of outputs produced by an expert system?

4. What is the main problem with using rules as a knowledge representation technique?

5. When is a rule fired? When is it not fired?

6. Why is reverse reasoning faster than forward reasoning?

7. List the situations where you would favor forward reasoning over reverse reasoning.

8. Where can the expert system obtain the information that it needs? Does it always obtain everything? Does that affect the reasoning process?

9. What are two primary approaches to developing expert system software? Which is more user friendly? Which is most popular in business?

10. What special skills does the systems analyst need in order to work with the expert in developing an expert system?

11. Who tests the expert system?

12. In what ways does the development of an expert system differ from that of an MIS or DSS?

13. What are the characteristics of business areas where the potential of expert systems is greatest?

14. Would an expert use an expert system that she or he had developed? Explain.

15. Do you think that a computer application will ever be developed for the purpose of replacing a manager?

Heritage Homes

   More and more young married couples are remodeling older houses
as a way of avoiding the high costs of new ones. The smart couple will
purchase a house with remodeling potential and then request bids from
contractors to do the work they cannot do themselves. In the
Wilmington, Delaware, area there are about a half dozen construction
firms specializing in remodeling. One is Heritage Homes, owned by
Alvin and James Bradberry. The Bradberrys have received more than
their share of the remodeling business because of their ability to come in
with lower bids than the other firms.
   When contractors receive invitations to bid, they meet with the owners to see first-hand the condition of the house. In order to make accurate
bids the contractors must be able to visualize from the owners' descriptions and their own observations the work that will have to be done and
then estimate the cost. Since the contractors know that they invariably
will encounter some unanticipated difficulties once work begins, they
add a cushion to their bids. The Bradberrys know their business so well
that they do not have to add much of a cushion. That is one reason for
their low bids.
   One rainy morning, when the Bradberrys could not work outdoors,
they were in the office talking about their computer. They use it in
preparing their proposals. Alvin has written some programs that compute certain materials costs, and James has developed a word processing
file used in preparing the written document.

Alvin: What do you think about us using an expert system to do our bidding? I've been doing some resding, and that seems to be the coming
thing. I doubt of any other contractors have such a system, and it might
help us keep our competitive edge.

James: I read the same article you did, and I'm still not convinced that an
expert system is as good as it's made out to be. For one thing, you need
an expert. Who are you going to use?

Alvin: Us. Wr'er the experts. We know this business better than anybody
else. We hit every bid right on the nose. All we have to do is get our
knowledge inside that electronic box and watch our smoke!

James: I'm not sure I could describe what goes through myhead as I
work up the bid. It just comes naturally.

Alvin: Oh, I think if you stick with anthing long enough you can do it. I wrote those materials cost programs with no sweat.

James: But you don't have time for a lot of programming. There are more important things for you to do.

Alvin: I could do it in my spare time. We're in no big hurry.

James: Well, it would be nice if we didn't have to spend so much time on the bids. If we could do it faster we could do more bidding and get more jobs. I'm convinced that there is an unlimited supply of remodeling jobs in Wilmingtom, and we've always talked about branching out to other cities.

Alvin: Exactly. Maybe over thhe next few months we could keep notes as we work up the bids–you know, write down what's going through our minds.

James: That's not a bad idea. We always carry a clipboard with us when we check out a house. We could just be more detailed in our not taking.

Alvin: After we accumulate a good set of notes, we might work up a form that we could fill out for each job–enter all of the data such as number of rooms, room size, condition of the wiring, plumbing,and so on. Then it would be a simple matter of entering the data from the form into the expert system.

James: Sounds good. Say, it's stopped raining. Let's get to work. We can daydream some other time.

1. Does this sound like a good expert system application? Support your answer.

2. Do you think that Alvin and James qualify as experts? What is your reason?

3. Do you think that Alvin qualifies to serve as the systems analyst on the project? Support your position.

4. Assuming that an expert system is produced, how could Alvin and James benefit?

5. What do you think about Alvin and James marketing their expert system to other contractors around the country?

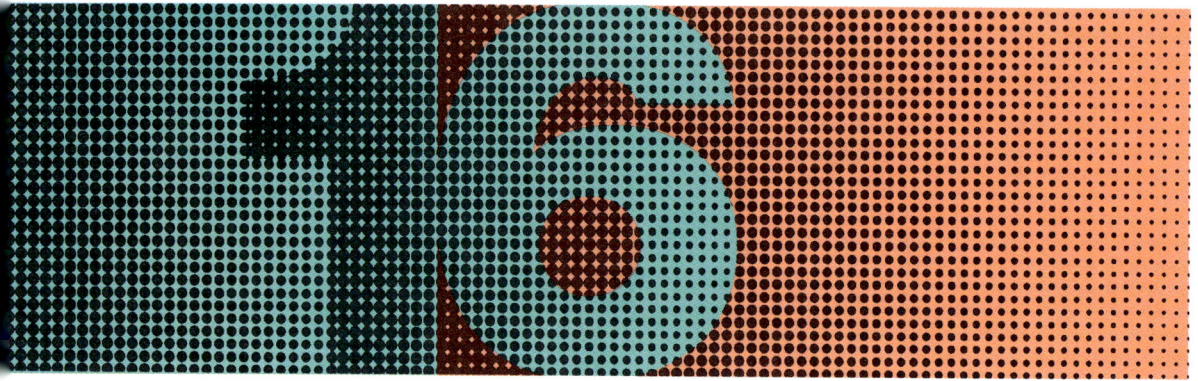

Emerging Trends in Information Systems

LEARNING OBJECTIVES After studying this chapter, you should

- Understand how the organization exerts an influence on development and use of computer-based information systems
- Be aware of two strategies that the firm's top-level executives are using to achieve competitive advantage with their information systems
- Know three strategies that information services can use when the firm engages in business process redesign

OVERVIEW

In the first fifteen chapters we have painted the picture of computer use in business. Many of the practices have been followed throughout the computer era, but changes, some subtle and some dramatic, are always under way. In this final chapter we address some changes that are just now beginning to exert an influence on computer use. Thus far, these changes have affected only a relatively small subset of business, perhaps the more innovative firms, but the trends and influences will become widespread by the year 2000.

The major feature of all of these changes is the influence of the organization. No longer are computer-based systems developed to meet the needs of users within the firm without considering how the sytems support the firm's long-term strategy. The organization exerts an influence by following concepts of information resources management, enterprise data modeling, and top-down project control. These concepts are facilitated by following strategies that involve interorganizational information systems, consolidation, downsizing, outsourcing, and insourcing.

All of these strategies are aimed directly at the firm's information resources. A practice that is affecting these resources in an indirect way is business process redesign.

This chapter provides you with a look at the picture of business computing in years to come.

ORGANIZATIONAL INFLUENCES ON BUSINESS COMPUTING

The big change that is presently under way in business computing is the increasing influence of the firm. This is a departure from the prevalent attitude throughout most of the computer era that systems should be designed to meet needs of individuals and groups within the firm. Even the MIS concept, which we have defined as an organizational system, was seldom implemented by following a grand plan intended to support the firm in achieving its long-term objectives. Today, information systems are developed in accordance with a strategic plan for information resources, a key element in achieving information resources management.

Information Resources Management

We introduced the concept of information resources management, or IRM, in Chapter 6 and recognized it as a reflection of the status of computing in a firm. When a firm practices IRM, several conditions exist:

- The firm uses its information resources to achieve competitive advantage.
- The information services organization is regarded as one of the major functional areas of the firm.
- The chief information officer participates in strategic decision making that affects the firm's overall operations.
- A strategic plan for information resources spells out how all of the information resources will be applied in the next several years, including a plan for stimulating and controlling end-user computing.

Figure 16.1 is an IRM model that shows how these conditions evolve in a top-down manner. The numbers in the figure correspond to the numbers below.

1. The environment of the firm exerts influences on executives as they strive to achieve competitive advantage.
2. The executives consider both environmental and internal influences when developing the firm's strategic plan. The internal influences reflect the degree to which the functional areas can support the firm's

FIGURE 16.1   An Information Resources Management Model

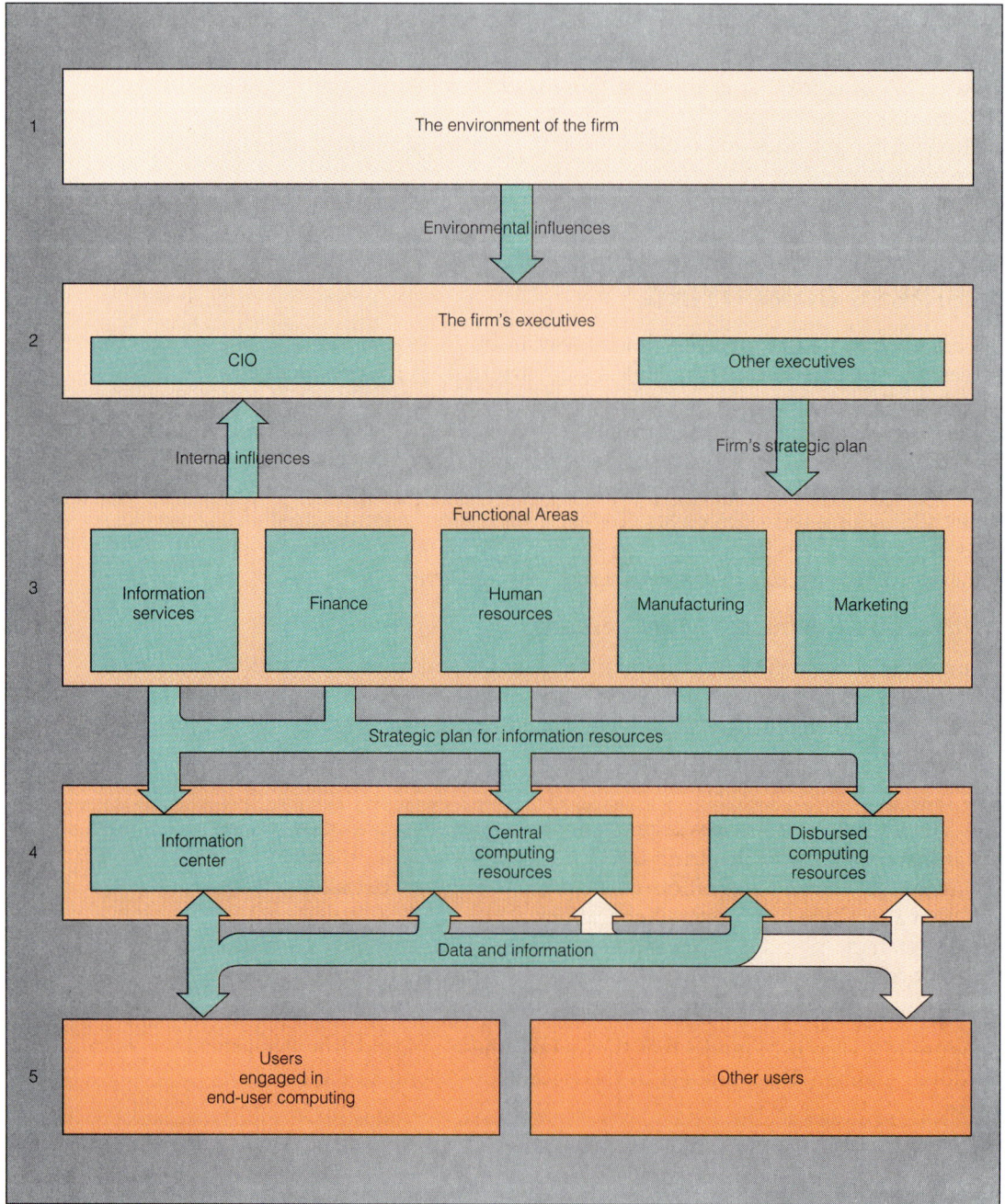

strategic objectives. The CIO is included in the group of executives who develop the firm's strategic plan.

3. With the firm's strategic plan in place, the functional areas work together to formulate strategic plans for their own areas. Information services has the primary responsibility for the strategic plan for information resources but is assisted by the other functional areas.

4. The strategic plan for information resources specifies how information resources will be used in three main areas: the information center, the central computing facility, and resources disbursed throughout the firm in user areas.

5. With the resources in place, users who engage in end-user computing use the resources in all three areas, whereas users who rely on information services for support use the central resources and those in their own areas.

This is the framework within which modern computer-based systems are developed and used.

Enterprise Data Modeling

Along with information resources management, another organizational practice is exerting an influence. Historically, information systems have been developed by focusing on the problems to be solved. *Problem* definition leads to an identification of the necessary *decisions,* which, in turn, produces a description of the needed *information.* The information needs lead to a determination of the necessary *processing* and, finally, a specification of the *data* needed for the processing. This chain reaction, illustrated in Figure 16.2, is called the **problem-oriented approach** to system development and remains extremely popular today.

Another approach began to exert an influence on information systems planning in the late 1980s. This approach, called the **enterprise data modeling approach,** begins at the executive level with a definition of the data needs of the enterprise, or firm. Figure 16.3 illustrates this top-down, data-oriented approach.

The figure shows how the description of the firm's overall data needs, the **enterprise data model,** is a product of strategic planning for information resources. This model, in turn, provides the blueprint for the firm's database. The underlying logic of the enterprise data modeling approach is that any information need can be met if the required data is in the database.

The enterprise data model can take a variety of forms, narrative or graphical, but the most popular is an entity-relationship diagram, or ER diagram. As the name implies, an **entity-relationship diagram,** or **ER diagram,** shows the relationships among entities that are described with data. An **entity** can be an environmental element, a resource, or a transaction.

Figure 16.4 is an example of a *portion* of an enterprise data model. This portion deals with those entities that are involved with purchasing raw materials from a supplier. The entities are represented with rectangles, and

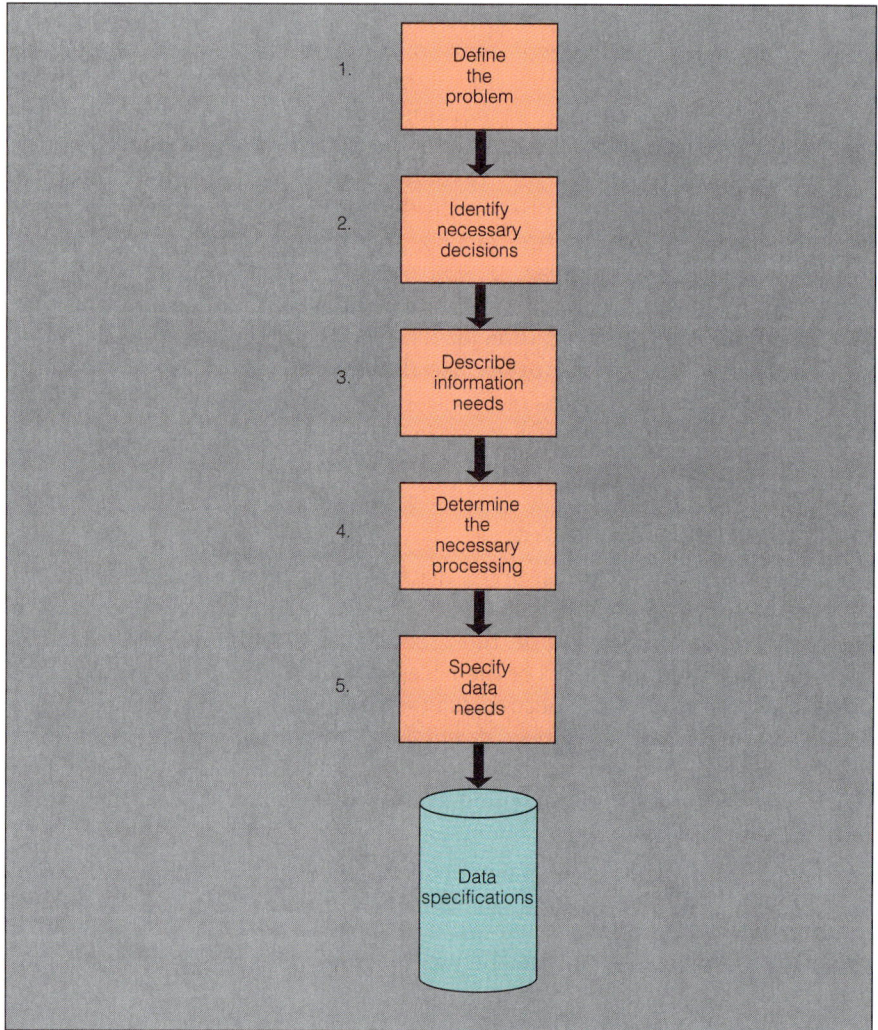

1. Define the problem
2. Identify necessary decisions
3. Describe information needs
4. Determine the necessary processing
5. Specify data needs

Data specifications

the relationships with diamonds. The relationships can involve either single or multiple entities. Single occurrences of an entity are shown with the digit 1 next to the rectangle, and multiple occurrences with the letter M. The figure shows how one supplier can fill many purchase orders, one purchase order produces one supplier invoice, and many invoices represent one accounts payable.

Once the entities and their relationships have been identified the data elements can be mapped to each entity as shown in the figure. The underlined data elements are called **identifiers,** since they identify the entities. The other elements are called **descriptors,** since they provide descriptive information.

FIGURE 16.3
The Enterprise Data
Modeling Approach
to System
Development

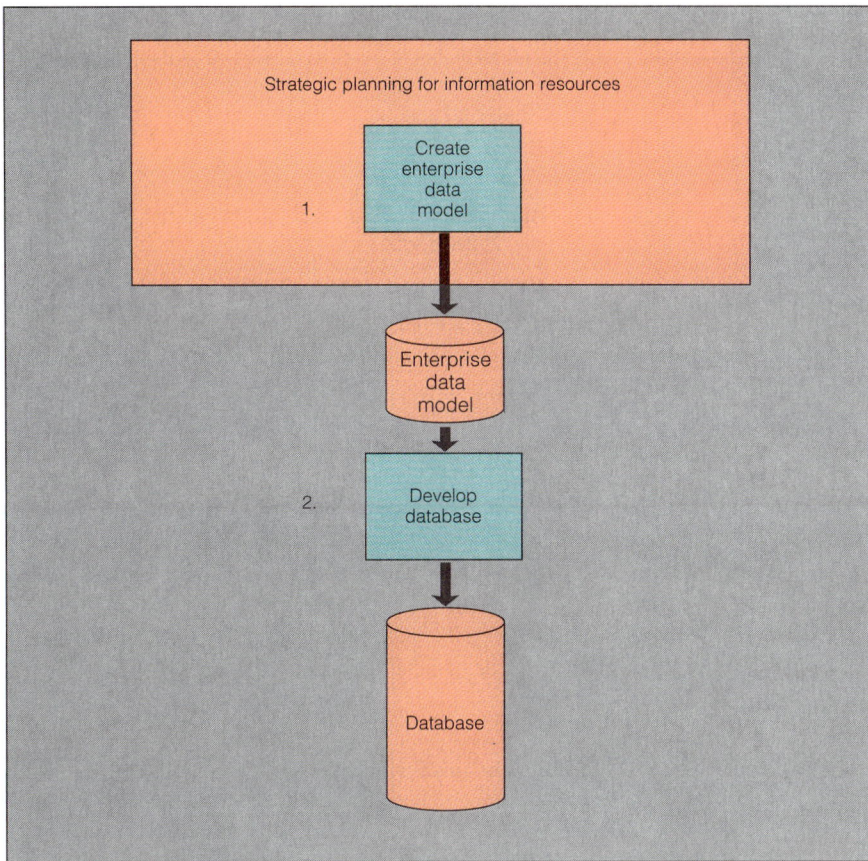

Enterprise data modeling is gaining popularity due, in part, to the increasing influence of the organization. The enterprise data model captures the data resource of the entire firm in a single, comprehensive description. The ER diagram is a popular data modeling tool because, once drawn, it represents the first step toward achievement of a relational database as described in Chapter 9.

Top-down Project Control

As soon as business computing gained momentum in the 1960s it did not take the information specialists long to recognize the value of working in project teams. Each project, such as the development of a payroll system, consisted of a mixture of systems analysts, programmers, and operations personnel, directed by a **project leader.** During the 1970s new information specialists such as database administrators and network specialists were added to the teams, along with users.

The control of these project teams was initially restricted to the information services organization, with the project leaders reporting to the CIO.

FIGURE 16.4   An Entity-relationship Diagram

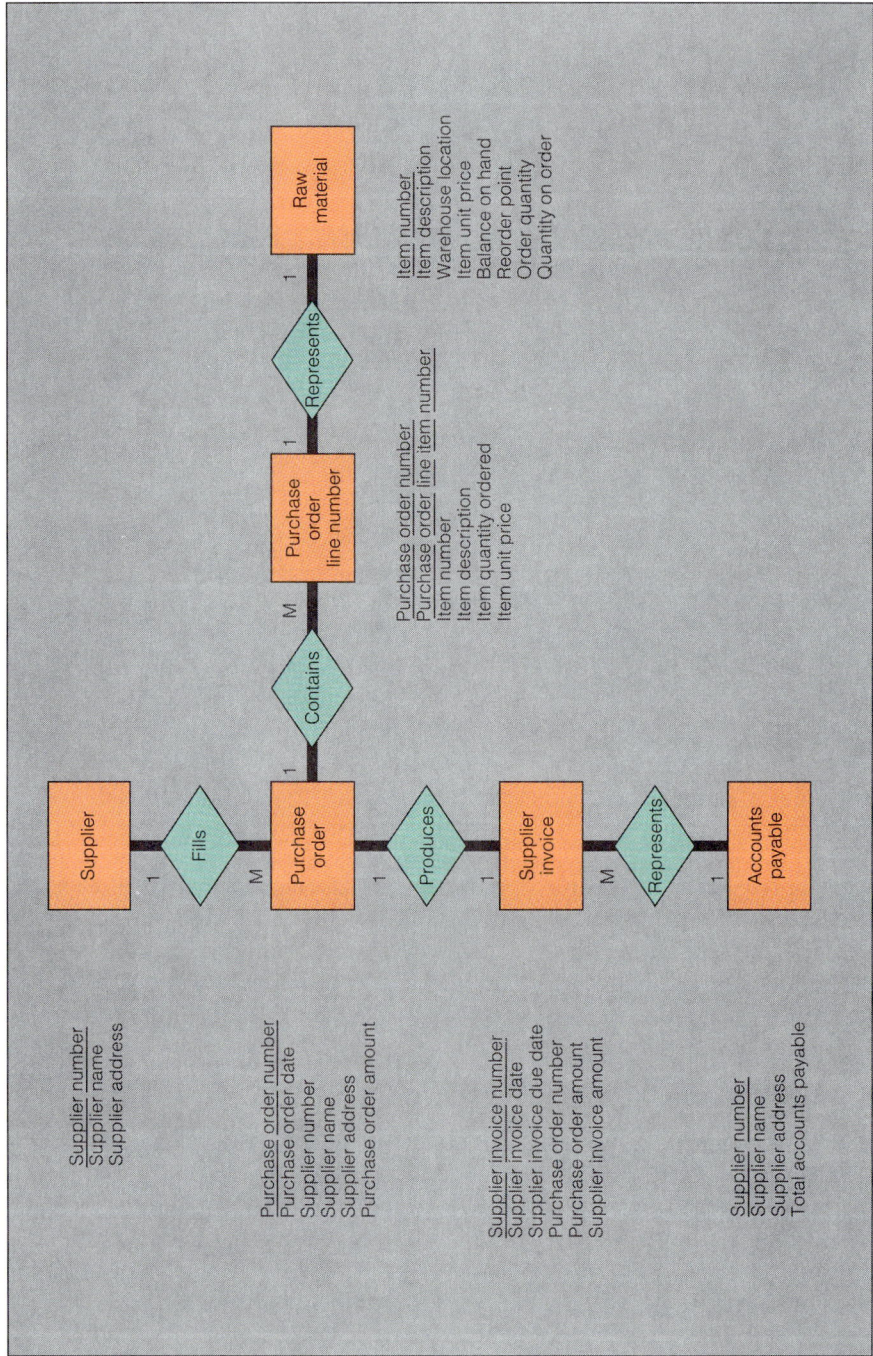

Toward the end of the 1970s, as the notion of organizational computing began to emerge, top management formed an **MIS steering committee** for the purpose of providing a central control point for all projects.

The MIS steering committee has always been accountable to the firm's executives, who usually function as an **executive committee.** Recently, however, the executives have been taking a more active part in project control by engaging in strategic planning that explicitly involves information resources. Today, control of systems projects begins at the executive level with strategic planning, as shown in Figure 16.5. The control of all ongoing projects is centralized in the MIS steering committee, and the control of each project team is in the hands of the project leaders. This top-down control ensures that the activities of each project support the overall strategic plan.

Organizational influence is a reality of modern-day computing. It reflects a recognition by top management that information is a valuable, strategic resource, and it results in an active involvement by top management in enterprise data modeling and project control. This organizational influence is expected to intensify in the future.

ORGANIZATIONAL INFORMATION STRATEGIES

The executives and the MIS steering committee accomplish the long-range business plan by pursuing strategies, which are intended to gain a favorable competitive position for the firm in its environment. Two such strategies are the formation of interorganizational information systems and reduction of computing costs.

Interorganizational Information Systems

An **interorganizational information system (IOS)** is a combination of multiple firms that are integrated by information flows. Such IOSs began as linkages between a firm and its customers, such as those achieved by American Airlines, American Hospital Supply, and McKesson Drug. American Airlines allowed travel agents to access the American reservations database; American Hospital Supply permitted hospitals to place orders directly to the American Hospital computer, and McKesson Drug followed the same strategy with drug stores. The success of these customer-oriented IOSs led to an expansion of the concept to include all organizations that participate in the flow of materials from the suppliers to the firm, and from the firm to its wholesalers, retailers, and, ultimately, customers.

When the IOS linkages consist of electronic data transmissions among the firm's computers, the arrangement is referred to as **EDI,** for **electronic data interchange.** For example, when a firm orders raw material from a supplier, all of the traditional paper forms can be replaced with electronic

FIGURE 16.5 The Top-down Approach to Project Management

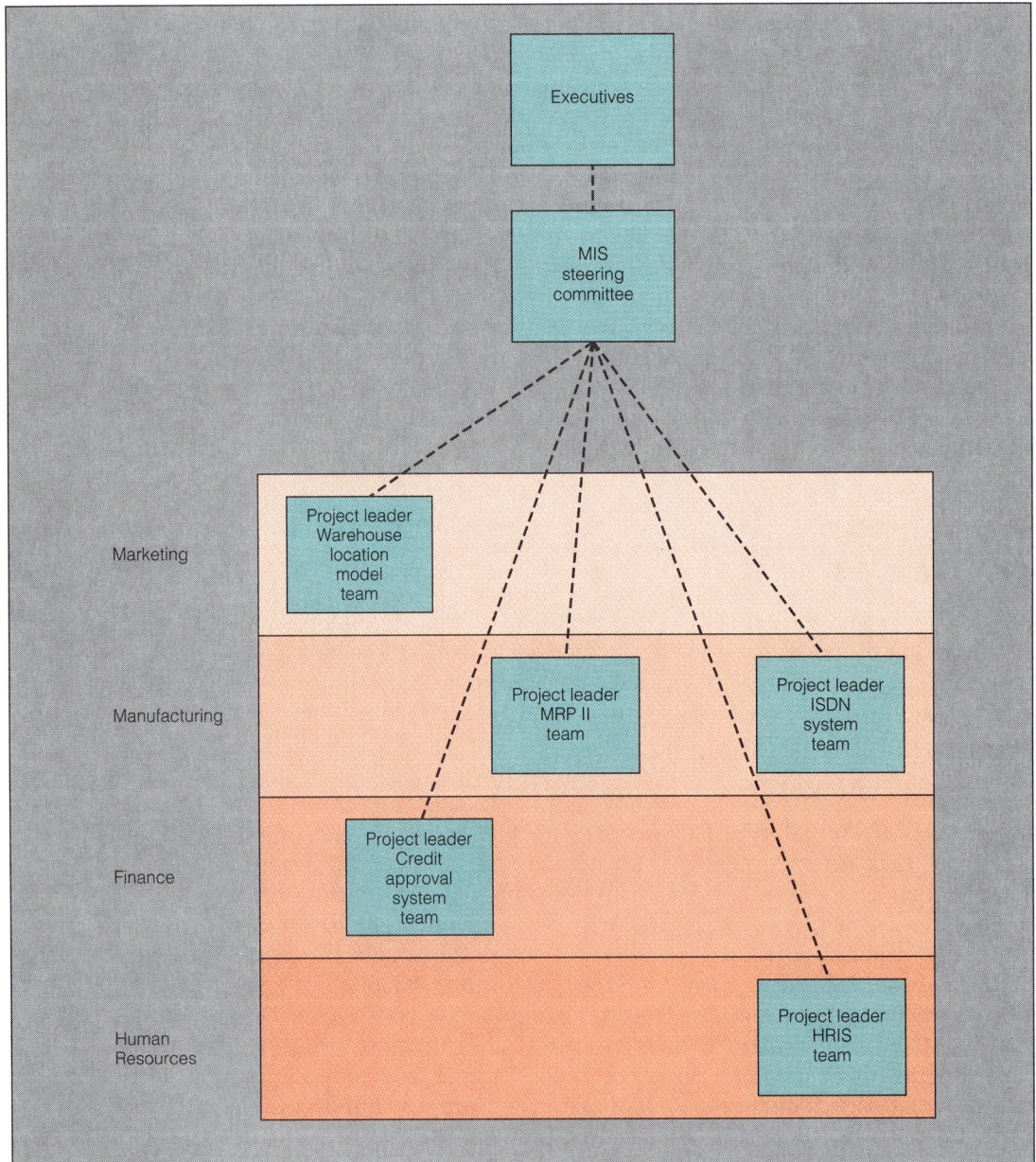

transmissions as shown in Figure 16.6. Standard formats have been established for requests for quotations (RFQs), price quotes, purchase orders, and so on.

Firms that are linked electronically produce a synergism that enables each to compete better in the marketplace. The strategic value of the IOS is easily seen, but the effect on systems development is less obvious. When firms enter into an IOS, their systems projects no longer are staffed by only their own personnel. When an IOS is developed, the project team can include representatives of the other firms. Certain guidelines that once were appropriate for intrafirm development no longer apply. For example, a firm with a single location previously would not consider audio or video conferencing but now can use these office automation systems to facilitate communication among the IOS participants.

Interorganizational information systems add another influence on system development to that now being exerted by the organization. Modern systems must reflect not only the needs of the firm but also the needs of other firms in the IOS network.

Strategies to Reduce Computing Costs

You would think that since top management has recognized the strategic value of information, they would be willing to pay whatever it costs. Such an attitude might be possible when a firm enjoys a position of monopoly and is not pitted against competitors. However, since such an arrangment seldom exists in today's global economy, top management must include information systems in its cost control measures. Several strategies are currently receiving attention. Among them are consolidation, downsizing, outsourcing, and insourcing.

Firms that decentralized or distributed their information resources in the 1960s, 70s, and 80s are now considering the possible benefits of consolidating certain operations. A good example of this strategy is the **information**

Consolidation

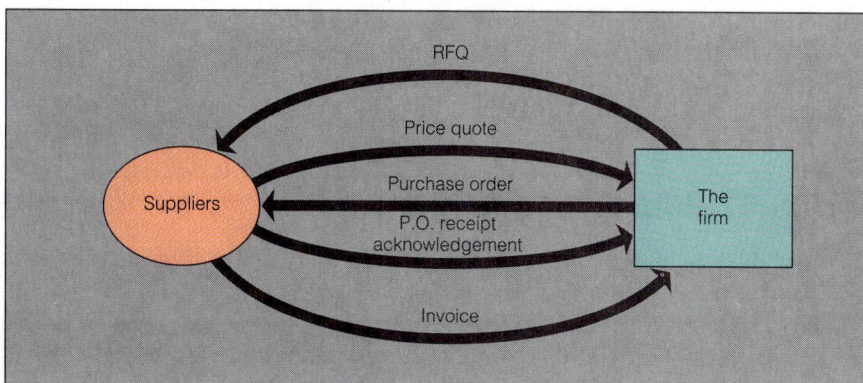

FIGURE 16.6

Standard Formats Have Been Established for Basic Electronic Data Interchange Transaction

center, described in Chapter 6, which consolidates hardware, software, and information services support personnel. The information center facilitates end-user computing without allocating information resources to each user.

Downsizing

The phenomenal increase in the capabilities of microcomputers has stimulated management to consider these units for processes that previously were performed by minicomputers and even mainframes. Many firms are following a **downsizing** strategy by tranferring processes to smaller, less expensive processors. Some firms are considering replacement of their central computing facility, featuring large computers, with one or more local area networks.

Outsourcing

For some time, firms have been farming out some of their information processing activities to outside firms, a strategy known as **outsourcing.** In 1989 the whole world took notice when Kodak, an organization regarded as a leader in applying computer technology, decided to go the outsourcing route. In the Kodak case, IBM assumed responsibility for running the Kodak computer operations; Anderson Consulting took over development of new systems, and Digital Equipment Corporation began to manage the Kodak networks. Firms that perform another firm's information processing for a fee, in accordance with a long-term contract, are known as **outsourcers.** The fees can be enormous, as was the case with a $2.1 billion agreement between Continental Airlines and Electronic Data Systems.

Insourcing

Sometimes firms enter into outsourcing agreements and then realize that they made a mistake. When a firm reacquires processing that previously has been assigned to an outsourcer it is known as **insourcing.** In 1987 NHP Incorporated of Washington, D.C. engaged in insourcing as a way to reduce their annual computing budget by 52 percent. In 1981 National Liberty Insurance insourced as a way to regain control of its computing operation rather than being "held hostage" by the outsourcer's pricing policies.

These cost control strategies are proof that top management will take drastic steps to keep costs in line. No longer does the CIO call all of the shots when determining how the firm's information dollar will be spent. The decision is made on the highest organizational level, involving executives from noncomputing areas in addition to the CIO.

BUSINESS PROCESS REDESIGN

No part of the business is safe from the eyes of the executives as they look for ways to improve the firm's operations. Fundamental processes, many of which have been followed for fifty years or more, are being considered for major overhaul. For example, an energy company such as Texaco is examining the way it drills for oil, refines the oil, transports the refined petroleum, and markets the products to its customers. This examination of fundamental processes for the purpose of achieving improved economies or efficiencies is called **business process redesign,** or **BPR.** The term **business process reengineering** is also used.

When a firm engages in BPR the results are bound to affect the computing operation, which is invariably integrated with the redesigned processes. Information services can follow three strategies in applying BPR to existing systems. The strategies are called the **three Rs,** and they include restructuring, reengineering, and reverse engineering. Figure 16.7 shows how the three Rs are positioned in the system life cycle.

Restructuring

When an information system must be redesigned it is often necessary to convert it to a structured form. Many systems were implemented prior to structured programming and exist in the form of a tangled mass of GO TO statements, an arrangement called **spaghetti code.** The transformation of an unstructured system to a structured format is called **restructuring.** As shown by the U-shaped pattern in the upper right-hand corner of Figure 16.7, an operational program can be restructured by repeating the implementation phase, and then putting the structured program back into use.

The other U-shaped patterns on the top row illustrate how the process of restructuring can apply to each developmental phase. The design can be restructured, as can the analysis leading to the design, and even the plan-

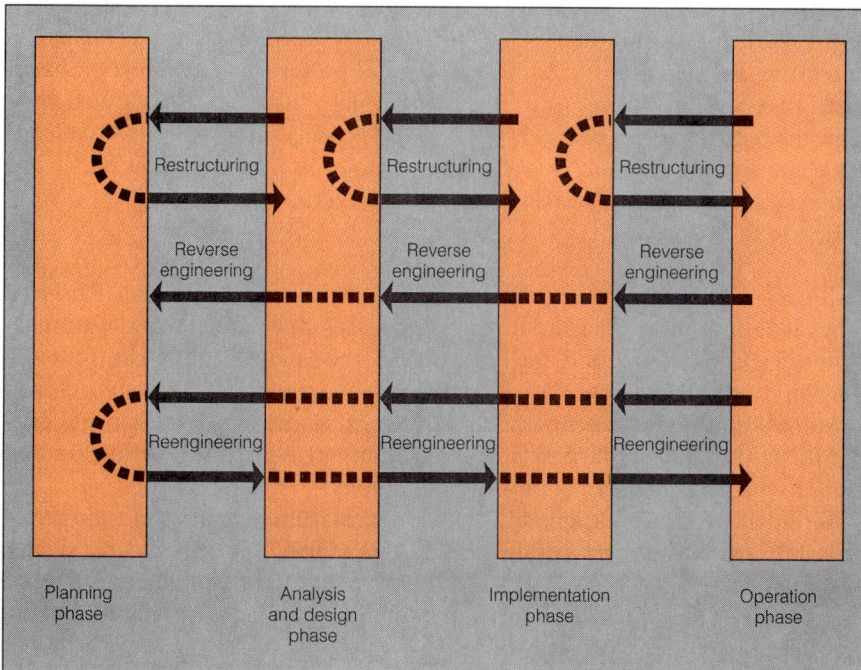

FIGURE 16.7

Business Process Redesign Strategies for Information Systems

ning. A system can be completely structured, one phase at a time, moving in a reverse sequence.

When you engage in restructuring, you do not attempt to change the **functionality** of the system—what it does. You strive only to achieve a structured format. Restructuring is a feasible strategy when a system has good functional quality but poor technical quality due to its unstructured format.

Reverse Engineering

An existing system might suffer from a problem other than lack of structure; there may be little or no documentation. When a firm decides to produce missing documentation that should have been prepared when a system was initially implemented, the process is known as **reverse engineering.** The figure shows that you can begin with the operational system and backtrack through the system life cycle, preparing the documentation as you go. First the program documentation is prepared, perhaps in the form of program flowcharts or structured English. Next the system documentation is prepared, perhaps in the form of data flow diagrams. Data documentation, such as ER diagrams and data dictionary entries, can also be prepared.

Like restructuring, reverse engineering has no affect on functionality. The objective is restricted to documentation.

Reengineering

When a system has poor functional quality it is necessary to change not only how it works but possibly *what* it does. Such a fundamental change is known as **reengineering.** As shown by the pattern in the figure, a backward progression through the complete system life cycle is followed by a forward progression. The purpose of the backward progression is to relearn the details of the system in order to facilitate its redesign. The backward progression can consist of restructuring or reverse engineering or a combination of the two.

Business process redesign is both good news and bad news. The bad news is that firms have fundamental processes that need to undergo massive overhauls. The good news is that perhaps firms have brought the development of new, innovative systems under control. New system development is no longer exerting such a drain on resources that attention cannot be paid to its established processes, many of which were implemented prior to the emergence of computer technology.

BPR adds a new responsibility for information services. No longer is activity restricted to new system development and maintenance of existing systems. Existing systems will also have to be completely reengineered because of basic changes that are made to the physical systems that the conceptual systems represent.

SUMMARY

Modern computer-based information systems are developed to meet the needs of users both inside and outside the firm, within constraints applied by the organization. Information resources management (IRM) is a concept that reflects the attitude of top management toward information. When a firm's executives embrace IRM, they use information as a means of achieving competitive advantage; they regard information services as a major functional area and the CIO as a top-level executive, and they insist on a strategic plan for information resources, which, among other things, spells out a strategy for end-user computing.

The strategic planning process produces an enterprise data model, often represented with an entity-relationship diagram, which reflects the overall data needs of the firm. This enterprise data modeling approach is replacing a problem-oriented approach in many firms.

Another reflection of the increasing involvement of executives in managing the firm's information resources can be seen in project control. Project leaders report to the MIS steering committee on a frequent basis to keep that committee informed of progress during the development period. The steering committee, in turn, keeps the executive committee informed. The executives ensure that project progress enables the firm to achieve its strategic objectives.

Two strategies that the firm can follow in using its information resources for competitive advantage are participation in interorganizational information systems (IOSs) and cost control. An IOS links the firm with its suppliers and channel of distribution by means of information flows. Electronic data interchange (EDI) replaces paper documents with electronic transmissions. Costs can be controlled by consolidation, downsizing, outsourcing, and insourcing.

As firms reach a plateau in implementation of new technologies they turn to their basic processes as a means of achieving additional economies and efficiencies. This activity is called business process redesign (BPR). BPR invariably causes existing computer-based systems to be redesigned, and this can be accomplished by restructuring, reverse engineering, or reengineering.

A FINAL NOTE

In a way, computer applications in business are like the carrot on a stick held in front of a donkey. The donkey never reaches the carrot. Firms have been implementing computer-based systems for almost forty years, and no firm has yet reached the saturation point. There are always additional ways to apply the computer, and there is no indication that this situation is about to change. What this means is that you are not entering the business field too late to contribute to ways that the computer can be applied. In fact, there are probably more opportunities for innovative computer use today than when General Electric first plugged in its UNIVAC-I in 1954. Whether you become an information specialist or a user, you will play a key role in the exciting world of business computing.

KEY CONCEPTS

How IRM reflects a positive attitude of top executives toward information and the people who provide it

The problem-oriented approach to system development

The enterprise data modeling approach to system development

Top-down project control, beginning on the executive level with the strategic plan

The interorganizational information system (IOS)

Business process redesign (BPR)

KEY TERMS

Enterprise data model	Consolidation	Restructuring
Entity	Downsizing	Reverse engineering
Electronic data interchange (EDI)	Outsourcing	Reengineering
	Insourcing	

QUESTIONS

1. How can you determine whether a firm is practicing information resources management?
2. What is the reasoning that underlies the enterprise data modeling approach?
3. What three things does an entity represent?
4. Where does the CIO fit in the top-down project control structure?
5. List the types of organizations that might be included with the firm in an IOS.
6. What effect is the IOS having on the composition of project teams?
7. Why is the information center an example of consolidation?
8. What technology makes downsizing a feasible strategy?
9. Explain the difference between outsourcing and insourcing.
10. Does BPR affect a firm's physical systems, conceptual systems, or both? Explain.
11. Under what conditions would a firm engage in restructuring? In reverse engineering? In reengineering?

GLOSSARY

Accounting package A prewritten program or set of programs designed to perform one or more standard accounting applications.

Accounting system *See* **Data processing system**.

Accounts receivable system The accounting system responsible for collecting money owed to the firm by its customers.

Alphanumeric Data that can take any form—numeric, alphabetic, or special characters.

Analysis phase *See* **Definition effort**.

Analyst workbench Software-based documentation tools intended for use by the systems analyst during analysis and design. Also called **Analyst tool kit**.

Application-development software The name used in this text to describe the new breed of software that does not clearly fit into the system or application categories, such as Lotus 1-2-3 and dBASE III Plus. These are not prewritten packages in the true sense in that the user must tailor them to fit particular applications.

Application software The programs that process a firm's data. Examples are payroll, inventory, mathematical models, and statistical packages. Contrast with **Application-development software** and **System software**.

Arithmetic and logic unit (ALU) The part of the CPU that performs the mathematical and logical functions.

Artificial intelligence (AI) The activity of providing machines such as computers with the ability to display behavior that would be regarded as intelligent if observed in humans. AI includes work in the areas of perception, learning, automatic programming, and expert systems.

Ascending sequence The arrangement of records where the one with the lowest-valued key (000 or AAA) appears first and the one with the highest-valued key (999 or ZZZ) appears last. *See* **Key.**

Assembler The system software that transforms a source program written in assembly language into machine language.

Assembly language A programming language that is machine dependent in that it is developed for use only on specified computers. It is often called **symbolic language**.

Asynchronous exchange The manner in which users of computer conferencing, electronic mail, and voice mail can exchange information without participants being involved at the same time. Contrast with **Synchronous exchange**.

Audio conferencing An office automation application that provides for audio communication only between geographically dispersed sites. It is a form of teleconferencing.

Audit trail A history of some aspect of a firm's activity. The history might be a detail report or a magnetic tape file containing a record for each transaction. The audit trail enables past activity to be reconstructed if necessary. For example, the audit trail would enable the firm to determine whether an invoice was sent to a customer on a certain date or a payroll check was prepared for a certain amount.

Backorder A sales transaction consisting of an order for merchandise that is not available. The order is not rejected or canceled, but is held until the merchandise becomes available. At that point, the order is filled.

Backward chaining *See* **Reverse reasoning**.

BASIC (Beginner's All-Purpose Symbolic Instruction Code) The most popular programming language used to process business data on small computers. The original version has been expanded to provide most of the capabilities of other popular languages. The main disadvantage of BASIC is the lack of standardization between versions supplied by different vendors.

Batch processing One of the two basic ways to process data that is characterized by grouping transactions so that all are handled at one time. It is the most efficient way to use computing equipment, but its main disadvantage is that files are not kept current as transactions occur. Contrast with **Online processing**.

Bill of material The list of parts and subassemblies, along with their quantities, that go into the production of a finished good. It is analogous to a recipe.

Billing system The accounting system that prepares invoices for customers, advising them the amount of money owed to the firm for their purchases.

Bit An electronic storage position that contains either a 1 or a 0. The 1 represents an *on* condition, and the 0 represents an *off* condition. The bit is the basis of the binary coding system used by the computer. Several bits comprise a byte. *See* **Byte.**

Business process redesign (BPR) Activity aimed at improving the efficiency or economy of fundamental processes of the firm.

Byte The position in a computer's storage that represents a character. A byte includes the number of bits necessary to represent a character. The number of bits is usually seven or eight, depending on the computer. *See* **Bit.**

Cash-flow analysis A process that produces a report reflecting the money entering and leaving the firm during a coming time period such as a year. The process can be performed manually or with the aid of an information processor. The report enables the firm to plan its loans and investments.

Cathode ray tube (CRT) The electronic device most frequently used to display input and output on a keyboard terminal or microcomputer. The tube has the appearance of a TV screen, and a terminal using such a screen is called a CRT terminal.

Central processing unit (CPU) The main part of a computer system that houses the arithmetic and logic unit, control unit, and primary storage unit. In the IBM PC the CPU is incorporated into the system unit.

Centralized decision making The policy followed by some firms of restricting all important decisions to only top management at the headquarters site.

Certainty factor A measure of the degree of certainty that is used in an expert system. The certainty can apply to an entire rule or to a variable in a rule condition. The certainty factor is analogous to a probability in a mathematical model.

Channel Used in data communications, this term applies to the pathway that connects the sender and the receiver. The channel can exist in such various forms as air space through which face-to-face communications travel, a telephone line, or a microwave circuit. Multiple channels can exist in a single circuit. *See* **Circuit.**

Character string Alphanumeric data.

Chauffeur A person who assists a user, usually a top-level manager, in entering data and instructions into a DSS, and in receiving output. The chauffeur *drives* the DSS for the user.

Chief executive officer (CEO) The person who is the top-ranking manager of a firm. The CEO is usually the chairperson of the board of directors or the president.

Chief information officer (CIO) The title given to the top-level manager who has overall responsibility for computer use in a firm.

Circuit The transmission facility that provides one or more channels in a data communications network. Commonly used circuits are telephone lines, coaxial cables, fiber-optical cables, and microwave signals. Also called a **line.**

Client/server computing An approach to network use whereby large, organizational applications are processed on the central computer, or server, and the smaller applications of users, or clients, are processed on their networked workstations or desktop computers.

Closed Loop system A system with a feedback loop.

Coach Someone who instructs a user in the operation of a DSS. After the user learns the DSS operation, the coach is no longer needed.

COBOL (COmmon Business Oriented Language) The most popular programming language used on mainframe systems for business applications.

Code generator A software-based productivity tool intended for use by a programmer in creating a program without the need to code each statement. The programmer enters the specifications of what the program is to accomplish, and the code generator produces the required statements. Also called a **programmer workbench.**

Column heading The description above a vertical data column in a report.

Command A high-level order issued to the computer. A command is more powerful than a statement or an instruction. In DOS, you initiate commands by entering such names as Format and Erase. In BASIC, you initiate commands by entering such names as List or Run, or by pressing Function keys. In dBASE III Plus, you initiate commands by selecting such command names as Create or Display from menus, or by keying in the commands at the dot prompt. In 1-2-3, you initiate commands by making menu selections and by typing the diagonal (/). In PrintGraph, you initiate commands by making menu selections. In WordPerfect, you initiate commands with the Function keys.

Command mode The status of a software system when it is prepared to accept commands.

Common carrier A company such as AT&T or GTE that furnishes communications facilities for a fee.

Compact disk (CD) *See* **Laser disk.**

Compiler A system program that translates a source program written in a problem-oriented language into an object program in machine language. The entire program is translated at once. Contrast with **Interpreter.**

Complete information system The term used in this text to describe an information system that gathers data and information from all sources, and uses both formal and informal systems to provide information in all media forms.

Computer aided design (CAD) The use of a computer to design something such as an automobile.

Computer aided manufacturing (CAM) The use of the computer in the manufacturing process. Computer controlled lathes, drill presses, and conveyor belts are examples.

Computer aided software engineering (CASE) The complete set of software based documentation tools, code generators, and prototyping tools that facilitate software development. The term **productivity tools** is also used.

Computer-based information system (CBIS) The term used in this text to describe all of the computer applications in a firm—data processing, MIS, DSS, OA, and expert systems.

Computer conferencing An office automation application that enables conference members to communicate with each other using their computer terminals. The distinguishing feature is that members do not have to be online at the same time—a situation referred to as an asychronous exchange. Computer conferencing is a form of teleconferencing.

Computer literacy The term used to describe knowledge of the computer—generally how it works, its terminology, its capabilities and limitations, and so on.

Computer schematic The diagram showing the basic parts of a computer system—input unit(s), central processing unit, output unit(s), and secondary storage. It applies to any computer system.

Conceptual resource A resource that represents a physical resource. Examples are data and information.

Conceptual system The representation of a physical system. A good example is the MIS, which can represent the physical status of an organization. The representation is accomplished by the storage of data reflecting conditions (such as the level of inventory) and activities (such as the work flow).

Consolidation A strategy of reducing the number of locations where information resources are installed for the purpose of reducing costs.

Constant A value in an arithmetic expression that does not change. Contrast with **Variable.**

Consultation The act of using an expert system.

Contention-based control A way to control LAN use by letting each user contend for the circuit. When the circuit is free the first user to request use is able to transmit.

Context diagram The highest-level data flow diagram. It presents the system in context with its environmental interfaces.

Contingency plan A formal plan that outlines in detail the actions to be taken when the firm's computing resource is destroyed or damaged. The purpose of the plan is to ensure the safety of persons working in the computing facility and to speed the return to normal operations.

Control break The condition in batch processing when the first record of a group is encountered (read). The condition usually signals the need to perform such special processing as printing totals for the previous group.

Control field The data element used to identify all of the records of a particular group. The point where the contents of the control field change is called the control break. *See* **Control break.**

Control unit The part of the CPU that causes the program instructions to be executed in the proper order.

CPU *See* **Central processing unit.**

Critical success factor (CSF) A particular activity recognized as having a strong influence on the success of a firm. Managers can use a few CSFs, rather than a volume of information relating to overall operations, to monitor firm performance.

Current receivable An account receivable that is no more than thirty days old.

Current state The condition of an entity at the present time. The entity, such as the firm or one of its operations, is monitored by comparing the current state with the desired state. *See* **Desired state.**

Cursor The symbol displayed on the screen that specifies to the user where data or instructions are to be entered. The cursor can take different forms, depending on the software system. It often is an underline mark, a square, or a rectangle.

Data Facts and figures that are relatively meaningless to the user. Data is transformed into information by an information processor. Data is the raw material of information.

Data communications The transmission of data from one geographic location to another. Also called **teleprocessing, telecommunications,** and **datacom.**

Data dictionary A description of all of the data elements used by all of the firm's computer programs. The description includes the data element name, the type of data (numeric, alphabetic, alphanumeric), the number of positions, how the element is used, and so on. Some data dictionaries are maintained in secondary storage.

Data element The smallest unit of data in a record. Examples are name, age, sex, and so on. Also called a **data item.**

Data flow diagram (DFD) A top-down, structured analysis and design tool consisting primarily of circles representing processes and arrows representing flows of data between the processes.

Data management All of the activities concerned with keeping the firm's data resource accurate and up-to-date.

Data processing Operations on data that transform it into a more usable form such as sorted data, summarized data, or stored data. The term often is used to describe accounting applications as opposed to those of a decision support nature. Also called **transaction processing.**

Data processing system The group of procedures concerned primarily with processing the firm's accounting data. The term **accounting system** is also used.

Data store The symbol in a data flow diagram that represents a repository of data, such as a file or database.

Database In the broadest sense, all of the data existing within an organization. In a narrower sense, only the data stored in the computer's storage in such a manner that retrieval is facilitated.

Database administrator (DBA) The person in a firm who has overall responsibility for the computer based data resource. There may be several DBAs in a large firm.

Database concept A relatively new way of thinking about an organization's data resource that regards multiple files as comprising a single reservoir. Files continue to exist separately in the computer's storage, but can be logically integrated using a variety of techniques. The logical integration makes it possible to quickly and easily extract the contents from several files for processing.

Database management system (DBMS) The software that handles the storage, maintenance, and retrieval of data in a database. The DBMS establishes the logical integration that facilitates retrieval.

Database structure The manner in which logical relationships are established between records and files in a database. The most popular structures are hierarchical, network, and relational.

Datacom The term used in this text to mean data communications.

Datacom control matrix A matrix used to identify strengths and weaknesses in a datacom network. System parts are listed along one axis and system threats are listed along the other. The means of counteracting the threats are identified in the appropriate cells.

Decentralized decision making The policy followed by some firms whereby managers other than those on the top level at the headquarters site are given authority to make important decisions.

Decision The selection of a course of action. A problem solver makes multiple decisions in the process of solving a single problem.

Decision support system (DSS) A concept originating in the early 1970s that focuses on the decisions necessary to solve single problems, usually of a semistructured nature. Contrast with **Management information system (MIS)**.

Decision variable An input value entered by a user into a mathematical model to gauge its effect on the entity being simulated.

Dedicated word processor A microcomputer designed specifically to perform word processing.

Default What the computer will do unless you instruct otherwise. The most common options are usually established as defaults, saving the user the trouble of specifying them each time they are to be used. This is called the **default mode**.

Definition effort The portion of the systems approach to problem solving that consists of a definition of the problem—where it is located and what is causing it. Also called the analysis phase.

Descending sequence The arrangement of records in a file whereby the one with the highest-valued key (999 or ZZZ) appears first and the one with the lowest-valued key (000 or AAA) appears last. *See* **Key.**

Descriptor A data element that describes, but does not identify, a data entity.

Design phase *See* **Solution effort.**

Desired state The state or condition of the entity when it is meeting its objectives. A problem exists when the desired state is not the same as the current state. *See* **Current state**.

Desktop publishing (DTP) An office automation application that produces high-quality printing such as that found in a book or magazine.

Detail line A line on a report that provides detail information concerning an action or transaction. The report containing such detail lines is called a **detail report.**

Detail record A record used to print a detail line. See **Detail line.**

Detail report A report containing detail, as opposed to summary, information.

Deterministic model A model that does not include probabilities. Contrast with **Probabilistic model.**

Development engine The portion of an expert system used by the expert and the systems analyst in developing the system.

Dial-up circuit The ordinary type of transmission facility that is obtained by dialing the telephone number of the receiver.

Direct access The ability to send the access mechanism of a storage device directly to a certain location where data can be written or read. A device that has this capability is called a **direct access storage device (DASD)**. Magnetic disk storage is a DASD; magnetic tape is not.

Direct access storage device (DASD) *See* **Direct access.**

Disk operating system (DOS) The version of the IBM PC operating system that resides on a diskette.

Disk stack A vertical arrangement of metal disks that share the same rotating shaft. The stack is mounted permanently in a cabinet. This technology is used in the disk units attached to a mainframe or mini computer.

Diskette The small plastic disk that serves as the secondary storage medium for a microcomputer. Also called a **floppy.**

Diskette drive The hardware unit that rotates the diskette and writes data onto it or reads data from it. Either one or two diskette drives are housed in the system unit of the IBM PC.

Distributed processing A datacom network consisting of multiple computers. Also called **distributed data processing (DDP).**

Distribution system The set of data processing subsystems commonly found in distribution firms—manufacturers, wholesalers, and retailers.

Documentation tool A graphic or narrative description of a system that can be produced by hand or with the aid of the computer. Examples are flowcharts, data flow diagrams, and data dictionaries.

DOS *See* **Disk Operating System.**

DOS prompt The prompt displayed on the screen when you are in the DOS mode. The prompt consists of the letter A, followed by the greater than (>) sign.

Dot matrix printer A printer that prints characters as a pattern of dots within a matrix.

Downsizing A strategy of transferring applications to smaller, less expensive computers for the purpose of reducing costs.

Driver module The main module in a structured program. The driver module causes the subsidiary modules to be executed by transferring control to them. Control is transferred back to the driver module when the processing of the subsidiary module is completed.

DSS *See* **Decision support system.**

Dumb terminal A terminal that can be used only to enter and receive information. It has no processing ability.

Dynamic model A mathematical model that includes time as a variable; it simulates activity over time. It is analogous to a motion picture.

Economic manufacturing quantity (EMQ) An optimum quantity to be manufactured that minimizes the total costs of producing too little or too much. Also called an **economic lot size**.

Economic order quantity (EOQ) An optimum quantity of replenishment stock to be ordered from a supplier that minimizes the total costs of ordering too much or too little.

Edit This term has at least three different uses in computing. First, it can mean the correction or change of material that previously has been stored. In many software systems, this is initiated by pressing an Edit key prior to making the change. Second, the term can mean the checking of data for errors. This usually is accomplished by including special subroutines in the program. Third, editing can mean the insertion of such special characters as dollar signs and commas into output data to enhance its appearance.

EDP auditor An internal auditor with a knowledge of computer operations.

Electronic bulletin board A use of electronic mail whereby the same message is sent to all users of the system. It is a way of disseminating information on a wide scale.

Electronic calendaring An office automation application that maintains an appointments calendar for the user. Some systems enable one person to view another person's calendar for the purpose of scheduling appointments.

Electronic data interchange (EDI) The transmission of data from one firm's computer to that of another firm.

Electronic data processing (EDP) The term that was used initially to mean computer processing. It sometimes is used as a synonym for **data processing.**

Electronic funds transfer (EFT) The technique of transferring funds between individuals and organizations using the electronic medium rather than paper documents.

Electronic mail An office automation application that enables users in a computer network to use their terminals or micros to send messages to one another.

Electronic mailbox The area in the computer's storage where electronic mail is stored for a specific user.

Electronic spreadsheet A spreadsheet maintained in computer storage. Electronic spreadsheet packages such as Lotus 1-2-3, Symphony, and Framework facilitate the creation, use, and storage of such spreadsheets.

Encryption The coding of data stored in a computer or transmitted over a datacom channel for the purpose of making the data meaningless to an unauthorized viewer.

End-of-job routine The portion of a program executed after all of the records have been processed. For example, a final total is printed after processing a file of transaction records. Also called an **end-of-file routine** that is triggered when the end of the input file is reached.

End-user computing Use of a computer independent of assistance provided by an information specialist.

Enterprise data model A specification of all the data to be stored in a firm's database.

Enterprise data modeling approach A way to develop computer-based systems by first providing a database for the entire firm and then making that data available for problem solving.

Entity Something that is described with data in an entity-relationship diagram. *See* **Entity-relationship diagram.**

Entity-relationship diagram A drawing that identifies data entities, using rectangles, and their relationships, using diamonds.

Error routine A subroutine executed when an error condition is detected. *See* **Subroutine.**

Evaluation criteria The factors used in measuring each alternate solution to a problem. The criteria are intended to identify the solution that best enables the system to meet its objectives.

Exception report An application of the principle of management by exception to the preparation of reports. A report is prepared that calls the manager's attention to only the exceptional situations—variations above or below the acceptable range.

Executive routine *See* **Supervisor.**

Expert system A computer program that can function as a consultant to a problem solver by not only suggesting a solution, but also by explaining the line of reasoning that leads to the solution. Such a program is an example of artificial intelligence.

Expert system shell An expert system that includes all of the components except the knowledge base. The shell is tailored to a particular problem domain by providing the applicable knowledge base. *See* **Knowledge base.**

Explicit relationship A logical relationship between records and files of a database that is explicitly accomplished by incorporating link fields into the records. Contrast with **Implicit relationship.**

Exploding the bill of material The process of multiplying the quantities of each item listed on the bill of material times the number of units to be produced. This process produces the gross requirements. *See* **Gross requirements.**

Extension (file name) The characters added to the end of a file name to specify the type of file. For example, BASIC program files are identified with a BAS extension. The extension is separated from the file name by a period.

Facsimile transmission (FAX) An office automation application that transmits a copy of a document over a datacom channel.

Feasibility The inherent ability of a possible solution to be implemented and to solve the problem. Different kinds of feasibility are technical, economic, legal, operational, and schedule.

Feedback loop The portion of a system that enables the system to regulate itself. Signals are obtained from the system describing the system's status, and are transmitted to a control mechanism. The control mechanism makes adjustments to the system when necessary. *See* **Closed loop system, Open loop system.**

Field The portion of a record reserved for a single data element. *See* **Data element.**

File A group of records relating to a particular subject.

File maintenance The process of keeping a file up-to-date by adding, deleting, and modifying records.

Final total A total printed at the end of a report that includes all records processed. Sometimes called an **overall total.**

Find and replace The ability of a word processor to scan a document and identify each instance where a word is used, and to replace that word with another supplied by the user. The process is not restricted to whole words; portions of words or multiple words can be used.

Flowchart A schematic diagram of a process, using standardized symbols. When the diagram is that of an entire system, it is called a system flowchart. When it is of only a single program within the system, it is a program flowchart.

Font A type style.

Form-filling technique One of the three ways to enter data and instructions into a computer from an online keydriven device. The screen is designed to resemble a printed form so that you can move the cursor from field to field as the data elements are entered. *See also* **Menu-display technique** and **Questions-and-answers technique.**

Formal system A system that is described by a procedure.

FORTRAN (FORmula TRANslator) The first widely adopted problem-oriented programming language designed for use in solving mathematical and scientific problems.

Forward reasoning One of the two basic approaches to reasoning that an expert system uses whereby each rule in the rule set is examined in sequence. When a rule condition is true, the rule is fired. Multiple passes are made until no more rules can be fired. Also called **forward chaining**. Contrast with **Reverse reasoning.**

Fourth-generation language (4GL) A new breed of software that is intended to facilitate end-user computing. The name **natural language** is also used because of the user-friendly syntax, and the name **nonprocedural language** is used since it is not as necessary that the processes be performed in a particular order as with a programming language.

Front-end processor The component of a datacom network that performs most of the control functions. The front-end processor is often a minicomputer that relieves the larger host computer of much of the datacom responsibility so that the host can concentrate on data processing.

Function key One of the set of ten keys at the left of the IBM PC keyboard labeled F1 through F10. These keys perform special functions depending on the software system in use. For example, in BASIC the F1 key is used to LIST the program, and in 1-2-3 it displays a help screen.

Functional attitude An attitude by members of an organization that the welfare of their particular functional area, such as finance or marketing, is more important than that of the entire organization.

Functional information system A subset of the MIS that is tailored to meet the needs of a particular functional area. Examples are manufacturing information systems and marketing information systems.

Functional organization structure A way of organizing a firm by subdividing it based on the major functions that are performed. The three main functional areas are marketing, manufacturing, and finance.

Functionality The ability of a system to perform certain processes.

General ledger system The accounting system that assembles data from other systems to maintain a composite record of the firm's operations. The data is maintained in a general ledger file used to print such standard accounting reports as the balance sheet and income statement.

Global Applying to everything.

Go/no-go decision A decision on whether to continue with a project or to terminate it.

Goal variable The overall solution sought by an expert system. For example, the goal variable for an expert system designed to produce a sales forecast would be the forecast figure.

Graphic report A report that conveys information primarily using such pictorial techniques as charts, graphs, and diagrams. Contrast with **Tabular report.**

Graphical user interface (GUI) GUI, pronounced "gooey," is a way to interact with the computer by making selections from displayed graphical symbols such as buttons or icons. GUI emphasizes the use of a mouse rather than the keyboard.

Gross requirements The total amount of inventory needed to produce a certain quantity of finished goods.

Group problem solving The situation where more than one person is responsible for solving a problem.

Hard copy A paper document.

Hardware The equipment comprising the computer system.

Help key A designated key that the user can press to display a help message. The particular key depends on the software package, but the F1 key is often used.

Help message A screen display intended to assist the user in overcoming difficulty in using the computer.

Help screen *See* **Help message.**

Hierarchical structure The database structure using explicit relationships, where a child can have only a single parent. *See* **Explicit relationship.**

Highlight bar The rectangle-shaped cursor that is moved to a menu item to be selected.

Horizontal title A spreadsheet title arrayed across one or more rows.

Host computer The computer in a datacom network that performs most of the processing. In a large network the host is usually a mainframe. Control of the network is shared by the host and the front-end processor. *See* **Front-end processor.**

Human resource information system (HRIS) A subset of the MIS providing information concerning the firm's personnel resource.

Identifier A data element that identifies an entity in an entity-relationship diagram. *See* **Entity-relationship diagram.**

Image storage and retrieval An office automation application featuring the storage and retrieval of document images using some type of microform—microfilm or microfiche.

Implicit relationship The linking of records and files in a database without addition of special fields. The relationships are implied using the contents of fields already in the records. This is accomplished through the use of a relational calculus, and is characteristic of the relational database structure.

Industry package A prewritten program or set of programs designed to solve problems unique to a particular industry.

Inference engine The portion of an expert system that performs the logical reasoning.

Informal information Information coming to the manager from an informal system.

Informal system An information system that is not described by a procedure. Examples are telephone calls, letters, memos, and unscheduled meetings.

Information Processed data that is meaningful to the user.

Information center An area in a firm containing computing equipment that can be used by any of the firm's employees.

Information literacy An understanding of how to apply the computer in problem solving.

Information management All of the activities involved with managing the firm's information resource.

Information overload The situation when a problem solver is presented with more information than is needed.

Information processor The unit that transforms data into information. It can be a human, a computer, or some other device.

Information resource management (IRM) A firm's formal program for utilizing its computing resource so that it provides maximum user support.

Information specialist Any person whose primary occupation is concerned with providing computer based systems. Examples are systems analysts, programmers, operators, network managers, and database administrators.

Initialization The process of preparing the computer by setting certain storage locations to zero or other predetermined values. A slang term is **housekeeping.**

Input bottleneck The situation that exists when a system cannot handle its volume of input data.

Insert mode The condition of the computer when a typed character will not replace a character previously stored at that location, but will *bump* the character to the right. Contrast with **Typeover mode.**

Insourcing A strategy of retrieving applications that have previously been farmed out to outsourcers. *See* **Outsourcer.**

Instruction The machine language that tells the computer which operation to perform. The term is also used to describe a line of code in an assembly language program.

Intelligent terminal A terminal that can perform some processing in addition to its ability to handle input and output.

Intermediate sort key When records are sorted using more than two keys, the keys in the hierarchy between the major and minor keys are intermediate keys. For example, to sort by salesperson number within sales region within state, the sales region is the intermediate sort key.

Internal auditor An employee whose main responsibility is to ensure the integrity of the firm's accounting system.

Interorganizational information system (IOS) A system composed of multiple firms that are connected by data flows.

Interpreter A system program that executes each statement as it is translated. Most BASIC translators are interpreters. Contrast with **Compiler.**

Interrupt A temporary halt in the processing of one program so that another can be processed. This is the manner in which the operating system performs multiprogramming. *See* **Multiprogramming.**

Inventory system The accounting system that maintains a record of the firm's inventory of raw materials, work-in-process, or finished goods.

Invoice The document provided to the customer by the billing system as an official notice of the money owed to the firm for a purchase.

Job control language (JCL) The codes provided to an operating system for the purpose of identifying the user and specifying the work to be done.

Job enhancement The strategy of using the computer to make employees more productive rather than to replace them.

Job lot A specific quantity of products to be produced in a single production run.

Justification *See* **Right-justification.**

Key A data element used to sequence records in a file.

Kilobyte (KB) In storage capacity, 1024 bytes, computed by raising 2 (the basis of the computer's binary coding system) to the tenth power.

Knowledge base The portion of an expert system containing rules and other types of knowledge representation that describe a particular problem domain.

Knowledge engineer The name used to describe a person who is capable of working with an expert in developing an expert system.

Knowledge worker An employee whose contribution is primarily intellectual rather than physical. Managers and professionals are knowledge workers.

Laser disk A storage medium that represents data in the form of tiny pits or blemishes made in a disk by a laser beam. Also called **compact disk** and **optical disk.**

Less structured expert system (LSES) A possible next step in the application of expert systems to business problems by addressing those with less structure.

Letter quality Output printed by a computer that is as good as that of an electric typewriter. The technology of the print mechanism is the determining factor. A daisy wheel or ink jet printer can produce letter quality.

License agreement The contract between the vendor and the user of prewritten software that specifies any limitations in how the software can be used, such as the authorization to make backup copies.

Line *See* **Circuit.**

Line item The detail line on an invoice describing a product that the customer has purchased.

List This term can describe an arrangement of data or it can describe a command. In BASIC, a list (also called an array) is a one-dimensional arrangement of data, such as a column or a row. In BASIC, the List command is used to display a program on the screen. In dBASE III Plus, the List command is used to display records on the screen or print them on the printer.

Listing A report that simply lists records without including totals.

Local area network (LAN) A network of computers connected by circuitry owned by the firm. In most cases the network is restricted to a small area such as a building.

Logic error An error made by a programmer whereby the wrong statements are used.

Logical organization The organization of the data in the database as viewed by the user. Contrast with **Physical organization.**

Loop A structure incorporated into a program enabling it to repeat certain processes multiple times.

Machine language The language understood by the computer; it consists of only 0s and 1s. Programs written in a problem-oriented language or a machine-oriented language must be translated into machine language before they can be run.

Machine-oriented language A language intended for use on a particular computer. An assembly language is machine oriented.

Macro A single statement given to a software system that causes multiple machine language instructions to be executed.

Magnetic ink character recognition (MICR) The means of entering data into a computer in the form of characters printed on paper documents using an ink that is easily magnetized.

Mail merge The ability of a word processor to merge the contents of two files, such as a file containing a form letter and a file of names and addresses of persons to receive the form letter.

Main-memory resident Software kept in main memory, or in primary storage, the entire time it is used. The supervisor of an operating system is an example.

Main menu The top-level menu in a hierarchy. In Lotus, there is a main menu of 1-2-3 Graph commands and a main menu of PrintGraph commands. In dBASE III Plus the main menu consists of eight command categories accessible through The Assistant.

Major sort key The most important key involved in a sort. When you sort using two keys, such as salesperson number within sales region, the sales region is the major key.

Management by exception A technique whereby a manager is concerned only with activities falling outside an area of acceptable performance.

Management function The basic tasks that all managers perform—plan, organize, staff, direct, and control.

Management information system (MIS) A system providing the manager with information for decision making. The term was used originally to distinguish such a computer application from the traditional accounting jobs. Over the years, the term has come to mean the firm's overall computer operation.

Management role A category of management activity, as viewed by Henry Mintzberg.

Manager A person who directs the activity of others.

Manufacturing information system A subset of the MIS that provides information concerning the firm's manufacturing activity.

Marketing information system A subset of the MIS providing information concerning the firm's marketing activity.

Master file A file containing data of a fairly permanent nature. Master files typically are maintained for a firm's customers, personnel, inventory, and so on. They form the conceptual resource.

Mathematical model Any formula or set of formulas that represents an object or activity.

Matrix A group of data elements assembled in rows and columns, forming two or more dimensions. The term **table** is also used.

Menu A list of choices displayed on a screen. You can make a selection in a number of ways, depending on the software system. For example, in Lotus, you can type the first letter of the choice, or move the highlight bar to the desired choice and press Enter.

Menu-display technique One of three ways to enter data and instructions into a computer from an online keydriven device. The computer displays a menu, and the user selects the item that instructs the computer what to do next. *See* **Menu.**

Microcomputer The smallest computer—smaller than a minicomputer. Also called a **micro.**

Microprocessor The central processing unit (less primary storage) housed on a single metal-oxide-semiconductor (MOS) chip. It forms a major portion of the circuitry of a microcomputer, and accounts for its small size.

Minicomputer The class of smaller computers that became popular during the early 1970s. Also called a **mini.** A mini is smaller than a mainframe, but larger than a micro. A large mini is called a **super mini.**

Minimally structured DSS (MSDSS) A possible next step in the application of the DSS concept to business problems by addressing those with very little structure.

Minor sort key The least important key involved in a sort. For example, if you are sorting records by salesperson number within sales region, the salesperson number is the minor sort key.

MIS steering committee The group in an organization with responsibility for establishing policy concerning the computing resource, and overseeing the development of computer-based systems.

Model A representation of some phenomenon. Various types of models exist—physical, graphic, narrative, and mathematical.

Modem The device in a datacom network that transforms the digital impulses of computing equipment into the form used by communications equipment, and vice versa. A datacom channel usually includes a modem on each end.

Module A subsidiary part of a larger system. In structured programming, the routines are designed as modules existing in a hierarchy. The module at the top is called the **driver module.** Modules on lower levels are called **subsidiary modules.**

Monitor *See* **Supervisor.**

MS-DOS The version of the disk operating system for the IBM PC and PC compatibles marketed by Microsoft.

Multiprogramming The ability of a computer to process several programs concurrently.

Natural language *See* **Fourth-generation language.**

Navigation The movement up and down a hierarchy of menus.

Near-letter quality Output printed by a computer that is almost as good as that produced by an electric typewriter. A dot matrix printer can produce near-letter quality output by striking each character more than once, making the characters appear darker.

Nested IF statement A combination of multiple IF statements, one inside the other.

Nested parentheses Parentheses within parentheses. Nested parentheses are used in arithmetic statements to control the sequence of the processes. The processes within the inner parentheses are performed first.

Net requirements The amount of new inventory that must be acquired to produce a certain quantity of finished goods, computed by subtracting the on-hand inventory from the gross requirements. *See* **Gross requirements.**

Network An interconnection of computing equipment using data communications circuitry. Networks often consist of small computers linked to a mainframe. This arrangement enables users of the small computers to have access to the database or the processing power of the larger computer.

Network manager The person or persons responsible for the firm's datacom network.

Network structure The database structure using explicit relationships, where a child can have multiple parents. *See* **Explicit relationship.**

Nonprocedural language *See* **Fourth-generation language.**

Object program The machine language program produced by a compiler or an assembler. An interpreter does not normally produce an object program, as such.

Objective What a system is intended to accomplish, usually stated in broad terms. More specific standards are used to guide the system toward its objectives. *See* **Standard.**

Off-the-shelf software *See* **Prewritten software.**

Office automation (OA) All of the technologies used to facilitate the flow of communications within the firm, and between the firm and its environment. Examples are word processing, electronic mail, and teleconferencing.

Offline The term describing the situation when something is not connected directly to the computer. For example, if a key-to-disk unit is used to prepare a disk for processing on a mainframe, the key-to-disk unit is offline. Contrast with **Online.**

Online The term describing the situation when something is connected directly to the computer. For example, if a terminal is used to enter data into a mainframe, the terminal is said to be online to the mainframe. Contrast with **Offline.**

Online processing One of two basic ways to process data. It requires the computer configuration to include some type of keyboard to enter transactions as they occur, plus direct access storage. Its main advantage is that it enables the conceptual system to stay up-to-date with the physical system. Contrast with **Batch processing.**

Open loop system A system without a feedback loop. *See* **Feedback loop.**

Open system A system that interfaces with its environment.

Open Systems Interconnection (OSI) model A set of datacom network standards implemented on an international basis.

Operating system The master program controlling the computer. In most cases, you cannot use the computer without following the instructions from the operating system. Early computers did not have operating systems and many system tasks had to be performed by the operator. The IBM System/360, introduced in 1964, was the first computer to offer an operating system furnished by the vendor.

Operator The information specialist who operates the computer.

Optical character recognition (OCR) The means of entering data into a computer with an input unit that reads printed characters in much the same way as does the human eye.

Optical disk *See* **Laser disk.**

Optimizing model A mathematical model that identifies the best solution in terms of achieving the specified objective. The objective is usually to minimize something, such as costs, or to maximize something, such as profit.

Optimizing solution The best solution to a problem.

Order entry system The accounting system that performs the initial processing on sales orders received from customers.

Order log A record of sales orders received by the order entry system.

Outsourcer A firm that performs computing applications or activity for other firms for a fee.

Outsourcing A strategy of farming out computer applications or activity to another firm, called an outsourcer.

Overlay area The portion of primary storage shared by several programmed routines. The routines are maintained in secondary storage and read into the overlay area when they are needed. When one routine is read into the overlay area, it erases the previously stored routine.

Packaged software *See* **Prewritten software.**

Pascal The programming language developed with the intent of facilitating structured programming. It has been adopted very slowly in business.

Password The unique combination of characters entered by the user of a system in order to gain access to all or part of the system—its programs and data.

Past-due receivable An account receivable that is more than thirty days old.

PC compatible A computer that can run programs written for the IBM PC.

PC-DOS The version of the PC disk operating system marketed by IBM. PC-DOS was developed by Microsoft for IBM, and is almost identical to MS-DOS.

Periodic report A report prepared on a certain schedule, such as monthly. Also called a **repetitive report**.

Personal computer A computer used by an individual rather than an entire organization. The use can occur in the home or in an office.

Physical organization The organization of the data in the database as viewed by the computer. Contrast with **Logical organization.**

Physical resource A resource that physically exists. Personnel, material, machines, and money are examples.

Physical system A system that physically exists. Examples are humans, computers, and firms. Contrast with **Conceptual system.**

Planning horizon The future time period for which a manager has a planning responsibility.

Point of sale (POS) The time and place a sales transaction occurs. POS terminals are used in lieu of cash registers.

Postimplementation review A formal evaluation of a system that is conducted after it is implemented.

Prefix (file name) The addition of a diskette drive identification (such as a: or b:) in front of a file name so that the file operation will not take place on the default drive.

Preparation effort The portion of the systems approach to problem solving that involves taking a systems view of the problem area.

Presentation graphics Pictorial aids that are viewed by groups. Transparencies and color slides are examples.

Prewritten software Software purchased from a vendor, as opposed to software produced by a firm's programmers. The terms **packaged software** and **off-the-shelf software** are also used.

Primary storage The storage contained within the CPU. Often called **main memory.**

Priming the pump A slang expression used to describe the manner in which the first record is made available to a structured program. Thereafter, the user indicates whether another record is to be processed.

Print-screen technique The method used to print the information displayed on the screen by holding down the Shift key and pressing the Print Screen key (labeled Prt Sc).

Print-switch-toggle technique The method used to print information as it is displayed on the screen.

PrintGraph The Lotus subsystem that prints graphs of spreadsheet data.

Probabilistic model A mathematical model that incorporates probabilities.

Probability The chance that something will happen. Probabilities range from 0.00 (no chance) to 1.00 (absolute certainty).

Problem A condition or event that damages or threatens to damage the organization in some negative way, or improves or threatens to improve the organization in some positive way.

Problem avoider A manager who dislikes problems and will not attempt to solve them even when they become evident.

Problem domain The problem area where an expert system is applied.

Problem-oriented approach A way to develop computer-based systems by first identifying the problem to be solved and then, successively, identify the decisions, information, processes, and data that will be involved.

Problem-oriented language A language designed to solve a particular class of problems. FORTRAN, COBOL, and BASIC are examples. Contrast with **Machine-oriented language.**

Problem seeker A manager who enjoys the challenge of solving problems and seeks them out.

Problem signal The notification of a problem or a potential problem.

Problem solver A manager who will not make a special effort to uncover problems, but will not back away when they become evident.

Productivity tool *See* **Computer aided software engineering.**

Professional A nonmanager who provides specialized knowledge and is usually compensated on a salary, rather than hourly, basis. Examples are marketing researchers, buyers, and economists.

Program The list of instructions or statements, written using a programming language, that causes a computer to perform the desired operations. The term **software** is commonly used.

Program flowchart *See* **Flowchart.**

Programmer The person who prepares programs.

Programmer workbench *See* **Code generator.**

Prompt A cue that appears on the screen, telling the user that an action is required. For example, the DOS prompt tells the user that the system is ready to execute a DOS command.

Protocol The standards used in interfacing datacom equipment and circuitry. It is commonly called shaking hands.

Prototype A system developed with the intention of not completely meeting a user's needs, but of providing the user with an idea of how the system ultimately will appear and be used. Over time, the prototype is modified until it either serves as the blueprint of the operational system or becomes the operational system.

Prototyping The act of using a series of prototypes as a means of defining users' needs.

Pull-down menu A submenu displayed on the screen when you select an item from the main menu.

Query A request for a special report. In most cases, the request is entered into a terminal or the keyboard of a microcomputer. A database management system such as dBASE III Plus makes it easy for the user to enter the query, and then rapidly produces the desired output.

Query language A special language enabling the user to make a query. It can exist alone or as a subset of a database management system.

Questions-and-answers technique One of the main ways to enter data and instructions into a computer from an online keydriven device. The computer asks a question and the user enters the answer.

Ragged margin A right-hand margin that does not form a straight line. Contrast with **Right justification.**

Random-access memory (RAM) Primary storage that enables direct access to any location without the need for sequential search. The storage permits writing of data as well as reading. The RAM is used to store programs and data.

Random sequence The arrangement of records in no particular order.

Read-only memory (ROM) Primary storage that enables the user only to read data or instructions that have been recorded there by the manufacturer. The user cannot alter the contents of ROM. In the IBM PC, a limited version of BASIC is stored in ROM.

Realtime system A conceptual system sufficiently responsive to control a physical system as actions and transactions occur. An online credit approval system in a department store is an example.

Record A collection of data elements relating to a certain subject. Multiple records comprise a file.

Reengineering The activity of taking a fresh approach to the redesign of a system for the purpose of improving its efficiency or economy.

Relational operator The name given to the special character used in a statement or command to show the logical relationship between data elements. For example, in the BASIC statement IF SALES.AMT > 10000 THEN GOSUB 500, the > is a relational operator.

Relational structure The database structure using implicit relationships. *See* **Implicit relationship.**

Repetition construct The structured programming construct that causes certain processes to be repeated in a loop.

Restructuring The activity of revising an existing system that exists in a nonstructured format so that it has a structured format.

Reverse engineering The activity of repeating phases of the system life cycle for the purpose of developing missing documentation.

Reverse reasoning One of the two basic approaches to reasoning that an expert system uses whereby the inference engine selects a rule that assigns a value to the goal variable and regards it as a problem to be solved. If other rules must be fired before the problem can be solved, the other rules become subproblems. The inference engine selects one of the subproblem rules and it becomes the problem. In this manner, the inference engine backtracks through the rule set, attempting to fire rules that will produce a value for the goal variable. It is also called **backward chaining.** Contrast with **Forward reasoning.**

Right justification A right-hand margin that forms a straight line. Also called **justification.**

Right to privacy One of an individual's basic rights that has prompted government legislation aimed at preventing harm caused by inaccurate or irrelevant data in a computerized database.

ROM *See* **Read-only memory.**

Root cause The primary cause of a problem.

Rule The most popular knowledge representation technique used by an expert system. A rule consists of a condition and an action, and is fired when the condition is true.

Rule set The group of rules in the knowledge base of an expert system that represents a particular problem domain.

Sales analysis report A report analyzing a firm's sales in various ways—by product, by customer, by salesperson, and so on.

Sales order form The document used to enter sales orders into the order entry system.

Satisficing model *See* **Suboptimizing model.**

Satisficing solution A problem solution that might not be the best, but satisfies the problem solver.

Scenario The specifications entered into a mathematical model to tailor the model to a certain situation.

Schema A description of all data elements in the database.

Scrolling The process of losing a row or column at one edge of the screen as a row or column is added at the opposite edge. It occurs because there are too many rows or columns to display on the screen at one time.

Secondary storage Storage that is online to the computer but is not a part of the CPU. Magnetic disk, magnetic tape, and diskette units are examples.

Sector A section of a disk or diskette surface shaped like a slice of pie. When a diskette is formatted on an IBM PC using a DOS version 2.0 or higher, each diskette surface is divided into nine sectors. When a diskette is formatted with a version lower than 2.0, each surface is divided into eight sectors.

Selection construct The structured programming construct enabling the selection of one of two alternate paths that program execution can follow.

Semistructured problem A problem including some variables that are identifiable and their composition and relationships are understood. This is the type of problem that the DSS is intended to address. Contrast with **Structured problem.**

Sequence construct The structured programming construct consisting of one process following another.

Sequential storage A type of secondary storage in which records are arranged one after the other, and must be processed in the same order.

Simulation The process of using a model to represent some phenomenon.

Simulator The device, usually a computer, used to simulate some phenomenon.

Software Computer programs.

Software engineering The application of scientific principles to the process of developing computer programs.

Solution criteria The level of performance that must be achieved in order to solve a particular problem.

Solution effort The portion of the systems approach to problem solving that includes the identification of the best solution, its implementation, and follow up. Also called the **synthesis phase.**

Sort key The data element used as the basis for sorting the records of a file. For example, if you sort the records into customer number sequence, the customer number is the sort key.

Source data automation The design of a source document so that its data can be entered into a computer without the need for manual keying. Magnetic ink character recognition and optical character recognition are examples.

Source document The document containing input data to a system.

Source program The program the programmer writes, using a problem-oriented language or an assembly language.

Special report A report prepared in response to a special request or event as opposed to one prepared on a regular schedule.

Spelling checker The portion of a word processor used to detect spelling errors in a document.

Standard A measure of the ability of a system to meet an objective.

Statement This term has two meanings. First, a statement is the order given to the computer in a problem-oriented language. Programs written in such languages consist of multiple statements. Second, a statement is a document mailed to a customer as a reminder of a past-due receivable.

Static model A mathematical model that reflects the condition of the entity at a single point in time. It is analogous to a snapshot.

Stored-program concept The technique of storing the program in primary storage along with the data being processed.

Structured design *See* **Top-down design.**

Structured English A relatively disciplined narrative description of a system or procedure. Only the three structured programming constructs are used. Names of conditions such as IF and WHILE and data names such as EMPLOYEE.NO are capitalized. Only data names in the data dictionary are used. Structured English is excellent for supplementing structure charts and data flow diagrams.

Structured problem A problem consisting of variables that are all identifiable and their composition and relationships are understood. The problem of how much of an item to order (the economic order quantity) is an example. Contrast with **Semistructured problem.**

Structured programming The currently popular approach to programming where processing modules are arranged in a hierarchy, and only the three constructs of sequence, selection, and repetition are used.

Submenu *See* **Pull-down menu.**

Suboptimizing model A mathematical model that does not necessarily produce the best solution, but one that satisfies the user. Also called a **satisficing model.**

Subroutine A group of statements that accomplish some particular type of processing, such as compute a square root. The subroutine is a module of the program.

Subsidiary module A module of a structured program on a lower hierarchical level than the driver module. *See* **Driver module**.

Subsystem A system within a system.

Subtotal A total computed for a portion of the records in the overall group. An example would be the total sales for all customers in sales territory 33.

Summary report A report in which each line can represent multiple transactions.

Supercomputer The largest type of computer. It has not been widely adopted in business since its architecture is tailored to solving problems of a scientific nature.

Supervisor When applied to computer software, the supervisor is the portion of the operating system that remains in primary storage so that it can perform the major control functions and retrieve other routines from secondary storage when they are needed. Also called **monitor** and **executive routine.**

Symptom A result of a problem rather than its root cause.

Synchronous exchange The manner in which participants in an audio or video conference are in attendance at the same time. Contrast with **Asynchronous exchange.**

Syntax error An error made by the programmer whereby the proper statements are used, but they are not used as intended.

Synthesis phase *See* **Solution effort.**

System An integration of elements designed to accomplish some objective.

System flowchart *See* **Flowchart.**

System life cycle The phases of implementing and using a computer-based system.

System performance criteria Standards established early in the system life cycle to establish the level of performance the system must achieve in order to be successful.

System software The programs that perform useful functions for all users of a particular computer. Examples are the operating system and the various language translators.

System unit The part of the IBM PC housing the CPU and the diskette drive(s).

Systems analyst The information specialist who interfaces with the user for the purpose of analyzing the existing system and then designing a new or improved system that better meets the user's needs.

Systems approach An approach to problem solving consisting of understanding the problem before a solution is attempted, and evaluating several alternate solutions.

Systems concept A systems view of an organization in its environment.

Systems Network Architecture (SNA) The name given to the standards IBM incorporates in the design of its datacom equipment.

Systems study The name often given to the analysis phase of the system life cycle.

Table *See* **Matrix.**

Tabular report A report presenting information in the form of columns and rows. Contrast with **Graphic report.**

Telecommunications *See* **Data communications.**

Teleconferencing The blanket term used to describe the office automation applications of audio conferencing, computer conferencing, and video conferencing.

Telephone tag The game that you and another person play when you alternately call each other and the other person is unavailable or out.

Teleprocessing *See* **Data communications**.

Timesharing The use of a computer by multiple users.

Toggle key A key that switches the computer between two modes of operation. An example is the Caps Lock key; each time it is depressed the keyboard shifts from lowercase to uppercase or vice versa.

Token-passing control A way to control LAN use by providing a single set of electronic bits, called a token, which enables a user to use the circuit. The token is passed from user to user.

Top-down approach The method followed in problem solution that consists of starting with a broad picture and gradually making it more detailed until the system is understood.

Top-down design The method followed in system design that consists of initially specifying the system in general terms and gradually making the description more detailed. Synonymous with **structured design.**

Track A circular area on a disk or diskette surface on which data is recorded. The diskette used by the IBM PC has forty tracks on each surface.

Transaction A business activity involving the firm and an element in its environment.

Transaction file A file containing descriptions of transactions, such as product sales, used to update a master file.

Transaction processing *See* **Data processing.**

Transient routine A portion of the operating system residing in secondary storage and brought into primary storage when needed.

Translate A Lotus subsystem that converts 1-2-3 spreadsheet data for use by another software system, and vice versa.

Translator Any type of system program that converts a source program into an object, machine-language program. Assemblers, compilers, and interpreters are translators.

Type font A type style.

Typeover mode The condition of the computer when a typed character replaces a character previously stored at the location.

Unstructured problem A problem consisting of variables and their relationships that cannot be identified.

User friendly The term used to describe hardware and software that is easy to learn and use.

User interface The portion of an expert system that accepts inputs from the user and displays the results of the consultation.

Utility program The portion of an operating system performing tasks required by all users of a particular computer. Task examples include printing the contents of a disk, sorting records, and formatting diskettes.

Variable An element in an arithmetic formula that can take on different values. The variable is given a name, and the name rather than the value is used in a computer program. This enables the same program to be used with many different values assigned to the variable.

Video conferencing The office automation application that uses both video and audio signals to link conference participants in geographically dispersed locations.

Videotex The office automation application featuring the retrieval of textual information using a computer terminal.

Voice mail The office automation application enabling a person to send a message by speaking into an ordinary telephone. The message is stored in secondary storage. The other party retrieves the message at his or her convenience, using an ordinary telephone.

Voice mailbox the area in the computer's storage reserved for a certain person's voice messages, stored in a digital form.

WATS circuit *See* **Wide Area Telecommunications Service.**

What-If game A method of trying out alternate decision strategies using a mathematical model. The user asks, in effect: "What if I change this decision? What will the result be?"

Wide Area Telecommunications Service (WATS) A special billing arrangement offered by a common carrier that provides datacom circuits at lower prices as the volume of calls increases.

Window A portion of a screen display that is dedicated to certain material. The user causes a window to appear by taking some action, such as pointing the cursor at a menu selection and clicking on the mouse. It is possible to display several windows at a time, very often in an overlapped pattern. The technique has been popularized by the Macintosh line of computers and the Windows graphical user interface software from Microsoft.

Word processing The office automation application using a combination of computer hardware and software to perform typing operations. The main feature is the computer storage, which enables a document to be revised easily and used many times.

Word wrap The name given to the manner in which a word processor automatically moves to the next line when the line being typed becomes full.

Wraparound A computer feature in which data is not lost when it exceeds the allowed space, but appears at the opposite end of the space. An example is the manner in which variables are printed in zones by a BASIC program. If there are too many variables to print on one line, they will be printed in sequence from left to right on successive lines.

X axis The horizontal axis of a graph.

Y axis The vertical axis of a graph.